Practical Skills in Sport and Exercise Science

PEARSON

We work with leading authors to develop the strongest educational materials in sport science, bringing cutting-edge thinking and best learning practice to a global market.

Under a range of well-known imprints, including Benjamin Cummings, we craft high-quality print and electronic publications which help readers to understand and apply their content, whether studying or at work.

To find out more about the complete range of our publishing, please visit us on the World Wide Web at: www.pearsoned.co.uk

Practical Skills in Sport and Exercise Science

Peter Reaburn
Ben Dascombe
Rob Reed
Allan Jones
Jonathan Weyers

Prentice Hall
is an imprint of

Harlow, England • London • New York • Boston • San Francisco • Toronto • Sydney • Singapore • Hong Kong
Tokyo • Seoul • Taipei • New Delhi • Cape Town • Madrid • Mexico City • Amsterdam • Munich • Paris • Milan

Pearson Education Limited
Edinburgh Gate
Harlow
Essex CM20 2JE
England

and Associated Companies throughout the world

Visit us on the World Wide Web at:
www.pearsoned.co.uk

First published 2011

ISBN: 978-1-4082-0377-4

British Library Cataloguing-in-Publication Data
A catalogue record for this book is available from the British Library

Library of Congress Cataloging-in-Publication Data
Practical skills in sport and exercise science / Peter Reaburn . . . [et al.].
p. cm.
ISBN 978-1-4082-0377-4 (pbk.)
1. Sports sciences 2. Exercise. 3. Sports--Physiological aspects. 4. Exercise--Physiological aspects. I. Dascombe, Ben.
GV558.P73 2011
613.7'1--dc22

2010054124

10 9 8 7 6 5 4 3 2 1
15 14 13 12 11

Typeset in 10/12 pt Times Roman by 73

Printed and bound in Great Britain by Ashford Colour Press Ltd, Gosport, Hampshire

Contents

List of boxes *vii*
Preface *xi*
Guided tour *xii*
Acknowledgements *xiv*

Study and examination skills **1**

1. The importance of transferable skills 3
2. Managing your time 7
3. Working with others 11
4. Taking notes from lectures and texts 17
5. Learning and revising 22
6. Curriculum options, assessment and exams 31
7. Preparing your curriculum vitae or résumé 40

Information technology and library resources **47**

8. Finding and citing published information 49
9. Evaluating information 55
10. Using online resources 63
11. Using spreadsheets 73
12. Word processors, databases and other packages 79

Communicating information **87**

13. Reporting and interpreting test results 89
14. General aspects of scientific writing 94
15. Writing essays and literature reviews 101
16. Organising a poster display 107
17. Giving a spoken presentation 112

The investigative approach **119**

18. The principles of measurement 121
19. Making valid and reliable measurements 125
20. SI units and their use 132
21. Scientific method and design of experiments 139
22. Conducting and writing up project work 145

Fundamental laboratory techniques **151**

23. Your approach to practical work 153
24. Health and safety 157
25. Working with body fluids 165

Pre-exercise screening 173

26. Preparing for fitness tests 175
27. Pre-exercise health screening procedures 179

Basic laboratory procedures 187

28. Blood and urine collection and analysis 189
29. Measuring cardiac function 197
30. Testing pulmonary function 211
31. Measuring endurance exercise intensity 221
32. Measuring hydration status and body temperature 228
33. Measuring flexibility 236
34. Kinanthropometry 242
35. Measuring body composition 253

Measuring physiological capacities 263

36. Measuring maximal aerobic capacity 265
37. Indirect measures of aerobic capacity 274
38. Measuring energy expenditure and physical activity 281
39. Measuring anaerobic power and capacity 294
40. Measuring muscle strength and endurance 304
41. Common field tests 317
42. Specific field tests 328

Calculating physiological measures 335

43. Measuring endurance training thresholds 337
44. Measuring economy of exercise 344
45. Monitoring training load 349

Analysis and presentation of data 357

46. Manipulating and transforming raw data 359
47. Graphs 363
48. Presenting data in tables 374
49. Descriptive statistics 378
50. Choosing and using statistical tests 389
51. Statistics for sport and exercise science 401

Index 405

List of boxes

2.1 Tips for effective planning and working 10
4.1 The SQ3R technique for skimming texts 20
5.1 How to diagnose your learning preferences using the VARK learning styles scheme 23
5.2 How to prepare and use a revision timetable 27
5.3 How to use past exam papers in your revision 28
6.1 Problem-based learning (PBL) 32
6.2 Writing under exam conditions 34
6.3 Reasons for poor exam answers to essay-style questions 35
6.4 Strategies for combating the symptoms of exam anxiety 38
7.1 The structure and components of a typical CV or résumé 43
7.2 Tips on the presentation of your résumé or CV 44
9.1 How to avoid plagiarism and copyright infringement 56
9.2 Evaluating a website 59
10.1 Important guidelines for using PCs and networks 64
10.2 Getting to grips with e-learning 65
10.3 Useful tips for using search engines 68
10.4 Getting the most from Google searches 69
10.5 How to evaluate information on the World Wide Web 70
13.1 Worked example: identifying a real change 92
14.1 How to achieve a clear, readable style 97
14.2 Using appropriate writing styles for different purposes (with examples) 98
14.3 Improve your writing ability by consulting a personal reference library 99
16.1 How to create a poster using PowerPoint 110
17.1 Tips on preparing and using PowerPoint slides in a spoken presentation 113
17.2 Hints on spoken presentations 116
19.1 Example of calculation of TEM (triceps skinfold) 127
19.2 Worked example of ICC calculation 129
21.1 Checklist for designing and performing an experiment 143
22.1 The structure of reports of project work 148
22.2 Steps in producing a scientific paper 150
23.1 Human ethics 154
24.1 Conducting a risk assessment using a risk rating system 159
25.1 Useful safety precautions when working with body fluids 168
27.1 Signs and symptoms questionnaire used to categorise high-risk clients 182
27.2 Risk factors used to stratify clients into low-, moderate- and high-risk categories before starting an exercise programme or aerobic fitness testing 183
28.1 How to take a capillary blood sample 191
28.2 How to take a blood sample into a capillary tube 192
28.3 Urine sampling 194
29.1 Using Einthoven's triangle in electrocardiography 201
29.2 Recognising indicators of cardiac stress – stopping an exercise ECG test 206
30.1 How to correct pulmonary function values for environmental variables 212
31.1 Example of calculating exercise intensity using % $\dot{V}O_2R$ 224
31.2 Using metabolic calculations to determine running speed on a treadmill 224
31.3 Example calculation to estimate target METs 226
32.1 How to measure urine specific gravity using *Multistix* reagent strips 231
32.2 How to measure oral temperature 234
33.1 How to carry out a Thomas test 239
33.2 How to carry out a straight leg raise test 240
33.3 How to carry out a shoulder flexibility test 240
34.1 How to locate the bony landmarks used for finding skinfold, girth and bone breadth sites 244
34.2 How to find location for bone girth and breadth measurements 248

List of boxes

35.1 Equations and methods for determining percentage body fat 253
35.2 Summary of the common body density (BD) prediction equations found in the scientific literature that use the anthropometric measures described in Chapter 34 255
35.3 Summary of common percentage body fat (%BF) prediction equations found in the scientific literature that use the anthropometric measures (skinfolds and girths) described in Chapter 34 255
35.4 Example: estimating ideal (goal) body mass or amount of weight to lose 256
35.5 Steps in determining body density using the underwater weighing technique 257
35.6 Bioelectrical prediction equations for specific Caucasian populations 259
36.1 How to perform a $\dot{V}O_2$ max test 269
36.2 How to communicate during a $\dot{V}O_2$ max test 270
36.3 How to analyse expired gas data from a $\dot{V}O_2$ max test 271
36.4 Identifying $\dot{V}O_2$ max during a test 273
37.1 How to carry out a 1.5 mile (2.4 km) run test 275
37.2 How to carry out a 12-minute (Cooper) walk-run test 276
37.3 How to carry out a Rockport one mile walk test 276
37.4 Example of a $\dot{V}O_2$ calculation 278
37.5 How to carry out a submaximal treadmill test 279
37.6 How to carry out the Queen's College step test 280
38.1 How to measure basal metabolic rate (and resting energy expenditure) 286
38.2 An example of a self-report questionnaire – the International Physical Activity Questionnaire 290
39.1 Analysis from the 10-second alactic cycling test 298
39.2 Analysis from the Wingate cycling test 300
40.1 How to carry out a grip strength test 305
40.2 How to carry out a back strength test 305
40.3 How to carry out a leg strength test 306
40.4 How to carry out a chin-up test 307
40.5 How to carry out a bench press test 308
40.6 How to carry out an incline leg press test 309
40.7 How to carry out a back squat test 311
40.8 How to carry out a multistage abdominal strength test 312
40.9 How to carry out a push-up test 314
40.10 How to carry out a YMCA bench press test 315
41.1 How to carry out a vertical jump test using a *Vertec* device 321
41.2 How to carry out a seated medicine ball throw test 322
41.3 How to carry out a 1RM strength test 322
41.4 How to conduct sprint speed and acceleration tests 323
41.5 How to conduct a 5-0-5 agility test 324
41.6 Procedure for phosphate recovery test 325
41.7 Procedure for multistage fitness test 326
42.1 How to carry out a YOYO IRT test 329
42.2 How to carry out a tennis agility test 331
42.3 How to carry out a 'run-a-three' test 332
42.4 How to carry out a 2000-m rowing ergometer test 333
43.1 How to measure ventilatory threshold (VT) using ventilatory equivalents 338
43.2 How to measure ventilatory threshold (VT) using the V-slope technique 339
43.3 How to determine lactate thresholds LT_1 and LT_2 340
44.1 Protocol for measuring running economy 345
45.1 Example of a TRIMPS calculation 352
45.2 Example of an adjusted TRIMPS calculation 353
45.3 Example of session-RPE loading calculations 355
47.1 Checklist for the stages in drawing a graph 364
47.2 How to create and amend graphs within a Microsoft Excel 2007 spreadsheet for use in reports and dissertations 368
47.3 How graphs can misrepresent and mislead 371
48.1 Checklist for preparing a table 375

48.2 How to use a word processor (Microsoft Word 2007) or a spreadsheet (Microsoft Excel 2007) to create a table for use in coursework reports and dissertations 376
49.1 Descriptive statistics for an illustrative sample of data 380
49.2 Three examples where simple arithmetic means are inappropriate 381
49.3 How to use a spreadsheet (Microsoft Excel 2007) to calculate descriptive statistics 386
50.1 How to carry out a *t*-test 394
50.2 Worked example of a *t*-test 395
50.3 Using a spreadsheet (Microsoft Excel 2007) to calculate hypothesis-testing statistics 399

Preface

Sport and exercise science is a fast-evolving discipline within the sciences. Its foundations began within physical education and evolved through health and physical education and the study of human movement science and kinesiology to become a stand-alone discipline within the sciences. As the discipline has evolved, the number and complexity of the practical skills required of professionals in the field have developed.

While practical work forms the cornerstone of all scientific knowledge, the training required in sport and exercise science is wide, covering the areas of physiology, kinanthropometry, biochemistry, statistics and nutrition, as well as the generic skills of working in teams, critical thinking, information literacy and communication. To be successful in these areas, students must develop a number of specific skills and abilities, ranging from those required to observe, measure, record and calculate accurately, to those associated with operating equipment in both the laboratory and the field. Students must also develop an ability to communicate information effectively in both written and verbal form. This book aims to provide support and guidance that will help students of exercise and sport science to maximise the development of their skills and abilities in all these areas.

The book has been written for students taking undergraduate and postgraduate degree courses in exercise and sport science. However, it will also be relevant to those taking related courses such as clinical dietetics, biomedical science, allied health and medicine. As with the other books in the *Practical Skills* series, we have tried to write in a concise and user-friendly style, giving key points and definitions, real-world illustrations and worked examples, tips and hints, 'how to' boxes and checklists – all designed to assist the student to become a better practitioner.

The book is a labour of love for the authors. The material included in *Practical Skills in Sport and Exercise Science* has been selected on the basis of our extensive teaching background and professional experience in working with both athletes and the general population as sport and exercise scientists. We hope that students will find this book useful in both the laboratory and the field, as well as in clinical and industry placements and during project and research work. The book is not intended to replace conventional laboratory handbooks or study guides, but to provide information that will help students to maximise their learning. The book covers a wide range of general procedures such as preparing graphs, presenting research projects and tackling statistical analyses. We hope that lecturers will find that the text is an effective way to supplement the information given in practical classes, by acting as a highly comprehensive resource that exercise and sport science students can use across their whole degree programme and beyond as a 'must have' reference guide on their shelves.

Practical Skills in Sport and Exercise Science also aims to support the development of a broad range of skills. There are chapters dealing with the evaluation of information, the use of online resources and technologies, revision and examination skills. Given the breadth of material covered, we have tried to focus on the broad principles and key points, rather than providing recipe-like solutions for every potential scenario. However, each chapter is supported by a section giving key sources for further study, including Websites and conventional printed texts or key papers relevant to the topics discussed.

The writing of a comprehensive book such as this is demanding on both time and energy. It is also a team effort for all those involved. We would like to take this opportunity to thank the following colleagues and friends who have provided resources, comments, ideas and constructive feedback at various points during the writing of this book: Aaron Coutts, Greg Rowsell, Aaron Scanlan, Rob Stanton, Bill Aspden, Mitch Duncan, David Kelly and Jonathon Brown. To the Pearson Education team, especially Rufus Curnow and Dawn Phillips, thanks for your guidance and professionalism in working with us from afar. Finally, to our wives, partners and children, especially Claire, Rebecca and Megan Reaburn, Katie Dakin, Polly Reed, Angela Jones and Mary Weyers, a heartfelt thanks. This one's for you.

PETER REABURN

BEN DASCOMBE

ROB REED

ALLAN JONES

JONATHAN WEYERS

Guided tour

Key Points highlight critical features of methodology.

Safety Notes highlight specific hazards and appropriate practical steps to minimise risk.

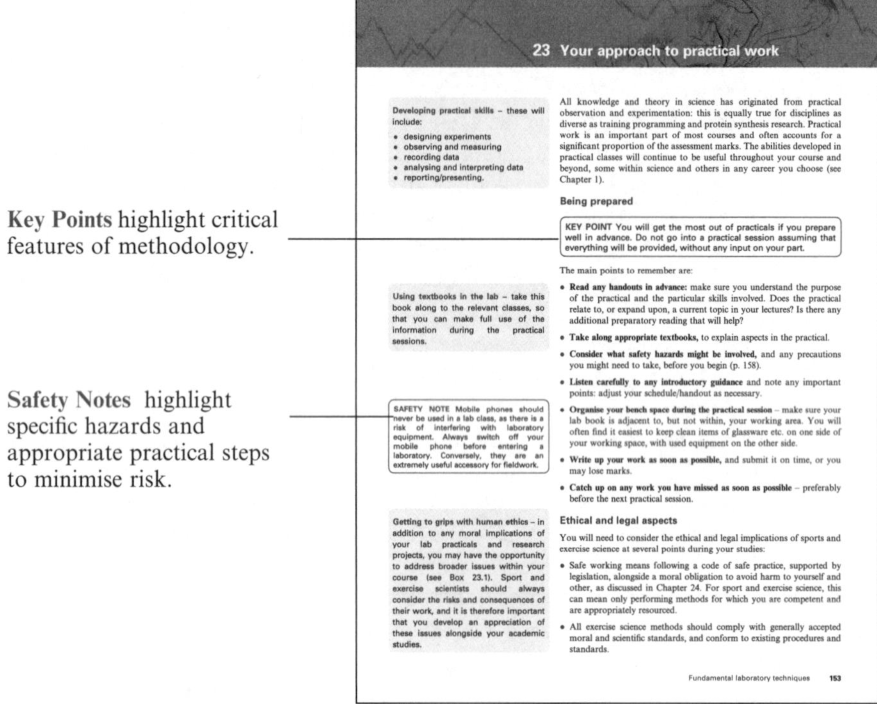

23 Your approach to practical work

Developing practical skills – these will include:

- designing experiments
- observing and measuring
- recording data
- analysing and interpreting data
- reporting/presenting.

All knowledge and theory in science has originated from practical observation and experimentation: this is equally true for disciplines as diverse as training programming and protein synthesis research. Practical work is an important part of most courses and often accounts for a significant proportion of the assessment marks. The abilities developed in practical classes will continue to be useful throughout your course and beyond, some within science and others in any career you choose (see Chapter 1).

Being prepared

KEY POINT You will get the most out of practicals if you prepare well in advance. Do not go into a practical session assuming that everything will be provided, without any input on your part.

Using textbooks in the lab – take this book along to the relevant classes, so that you can make full use of the information during the practical sessions.

The main points to remember are:

- **Read any handouts in advance:** make sure you understand the purpose of the practical and the particular skills involved. Does the practical relate to, or expand upon, a current topic in your lectures? Is there any additional preparatory reading that will help?
- **Take along appropriate textbooks,** to explain aspects in the practical.
- **Consider what safety hazards might be involved,** and any precautions you might need to take, before you begin (p. 158).
- **Listen carefully to any introductory guidance** and note any important points: adjust your schedule/handout as necessary.
- **Organise your bench space during the practical session** – make sure your lab book is adjacent to, but not within, your working area. You will often find it easiest to keep clean items of glassware etc. on one side of your working space, with used equipment on the other side.
- **Write up your work as soon as possible,** and submit it on time, or you may lose marks.
- **Catch up on any work you have missed as soon as possible** – preferably before the next practical session.

SAFETY NOTE Mobile phones should never be used in a lab class, as there is a risk of interfering with laboratory equipment. Always switch off your mobile phone before entering a laboratory. Conversely, they are an extremely useful accessory for fieldwork.

Ethical and legal aspects

Getting to grips with human ethics – in addition to any moral implications of your lab practicals and research projects, you may have the opportunity to address broader issues within your course (see Box 23.1). Sport and exercise scientists should always consider the risks and consequences of their work, and it is therefore important that you develop an appreciation of these issues alongside your academic studies.

You will need to consider the ethical and legal implications of sports and exercise science at several points during your studies:

- Safe working means following a code of safe practice, supported by legislation, alongside a moral obligation to avoid harm to yourself and other, as discussed in Chapter 24. For sport and exercise science, this can mean only performing methods for which you are competent and are appropriately resourced.
- All exercise science methods should comply with generally accepted moral and scientific standards, and conform to existing procedures and standards.

Fundamental laboratory techniques 153

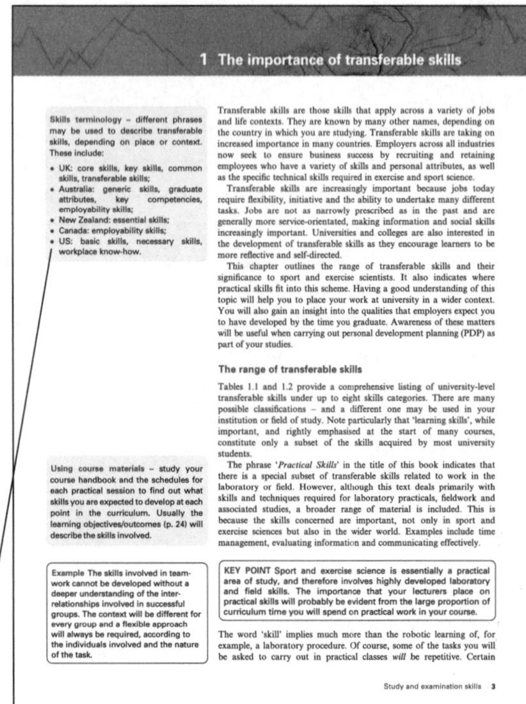

1 The importance of transferable skills

Skills terminology – different phrases may be used to describe transferable skills, depending on place or context. These include:

- UK: core skills, key skills, common skills, transferable skills;
- Australia: generic skills, graduate attributes, key competencies, employability skills;
- New Zealand: essential skills;
- Canada: employability skills;
- US: basic skills, necessary skills, workplace know-how.

Transferable skills are those skills that apply across a variety of jobs and life contexts. They are known by many other names, depending on the country in which you are studying. Transferable skills are taking on increased importance in many countries. Employers across all industries now seek to ensure business success by recruiting and retaining employees who have a variety of skills and personal attributes, as well as the specific technical skills required in exercise and sport science.

Transferable skills are increasingly important because jobs today require flexibility, initiative and the ability to undertake many different tasks. Jobs are not as narrowly prescribed as in the past and are generally more service-orientated, making information and social skills increasingly important. Universities and colleges are also interested in the development of transferable skills as they encourage learners to be more reflective and self-directed.

This chapter outlines the range of transferable skills and their significance to sport and exercise scientists. It also indicates where practical skills fit into this scheme. Having a good understanding of this topic will help you to place your work at university in a wider context. You will also gain an insight into the qualities that employers expect you to have developed by the time you graduate. Awareness of these matters will be useful when carrying out personal development planning (PDP) as part of your studies.

The range of transferable skills

Tables 1.1 and 1.2 provide a comprehensive listing of university-level transferable skills under up to eight skills categories. There are many possible classifications – and a different one may be used in your institution or field of study. Note particularly that 'learning skills', while important, and rightly emphasised at the start of many courses, constitute only a subset of the skills acquired by most university students.

Using course materials – study your course handbook and the schedules for each practical session to find out what skills you are expected to develop at each point in the curriculum. Usually the learning objectives/outcomes (p. 24) will describe the skills involved.

The phrase '*Practical Skills*' in the title of this book indicates that there is a special subset of transferable skills related to work in the laboratory or field. However, although this text deals primarily with skills and techniques required for laboratory practicals, fieldwork and associated studies, a broader range of material is included. This is because the skills concerned are important, not only in sport and exercise sciences but also in the wider world. Examples include time management, evaluating information and communicating effectively.

Example The skills involved in team-work cannot be developed without a deeper understanding of the inter-relationships involved in successful groups. The context will be different for every group and a flexible approach will always be required, according to the individuals involved and the nature of the task.

KEY POINT Sport and exercise science is essentially a practical area of study, and therefore involves highly developed laboratory and field skills. The importance that your lecturers place on practical skills will probably be evident from the large proportion of curriculum time you will spend on practical work in your course.

The word 'skill' implies much more than the robotic learning of, for example, a laboratory procedure. Of course, some of the tasks you will be asked to carry out in practical classes *will* be repetitive. Certain

Study and examination skills 3

Tips and Hints provide useful hints and practical advice, and are highlighted in the text margin.

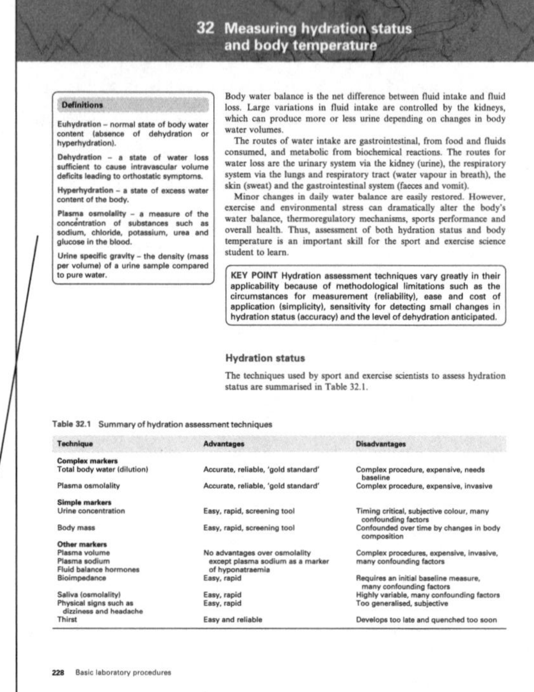

32 Measuring hydration status and body temperature

Definitions

Euhydration – normal state of body water content (absence of dehydration or hyperhydration).

Dehydration – a state of water loss sufficient to cause intravascular volume deficits leading to orthostatic symptoms.

Hyperhydration – a state of excess water content of the body.

Plasma osmolality – a measure of the concentration of substances such as sodium, chloride, potassium, urea and glucose in the blood.

Urine specific gravity – the density (mass per volume) of a urine sample compared to pure water.

Body water balance is the net difference between fluid intake and fluid loss. Large variations in fluid intake are controlled by the kidneys, which can produce more or less urine depending on changes in body water volumes.

The routes of water intake are gastrointestinal, from food and fluids consumed, and metabolic from biochemical reactions. The routes for water loss are the urinary system via the kidney (urine), the respiratory system via the lungs and respiratory tract (water vapour in breath), the skin (sweat) and the gastrointestinal system (faeces and vomit).

Minor changes in daily water balance are easily restored. However, exercise and environmental stress can dramatically alter the body's water balance, thermoregulatory mechanisms, sports performance and overall health. Thus, assessment of both hydration status and body temperature is an important skill for the sport and exercise science student to learn.

KEY POINT Hydration assessment techniques vary greatly in their applicability because of methodological limitations such as the circumstances for measurement (reliability), ease and cost of application (simplicity), sensitivity for detecting small changes in hydration status (accuracy) and the level of dehydration anticipated.

Hydration status

The techniques used by sport and exercise scientists to assess hydration status are summarised in Table 32.1.

Table 32.1 Summary of hydration assessment techniques

Technique	Advantages	Disadvantages
Complex markers		
Total body water (dilution)	Accurate, reliable, 'gold standard'	Complex procedure, expensive, needs baseline
Plasma osmolality	Accurate, reliable, 'gold standard'	Complex procedure, expensive, invasive
Simple markers		
Urine concentration	Easy, rapid, screening tool	Timing critical, subjective colour, many confounding factors
Body mass	Easy, rapid, screening tool	Confounded over time by changes in body composition
Other markers		
Plasma volume Plasma sodium Fluid balance hormones	No advantages over osmolality except plasma sodium as a marker of hyponatraemia	Complex procedures, expensive, invasive, many confounding factors
Bioimpedance	Easy, rapid	Requires an initial baseline measure, many confounding factors
Saliva (osmolality)	Easy, rapid	Highly variable, many confounding factors
Physical signs such as dizziness and headache	Easy, rapid	Too generalised, subjective
Thirst	Easy and reliable	Develops too late and quenched too soon

228 Basic laboratory procedures

Definitions of key terms and concepts are highlighted in the margin.

'How to' boxes and Worked Examples set out the essential procedures in a step-by-step manner.

Figures are used to illustrate key points, techniques and equipment.

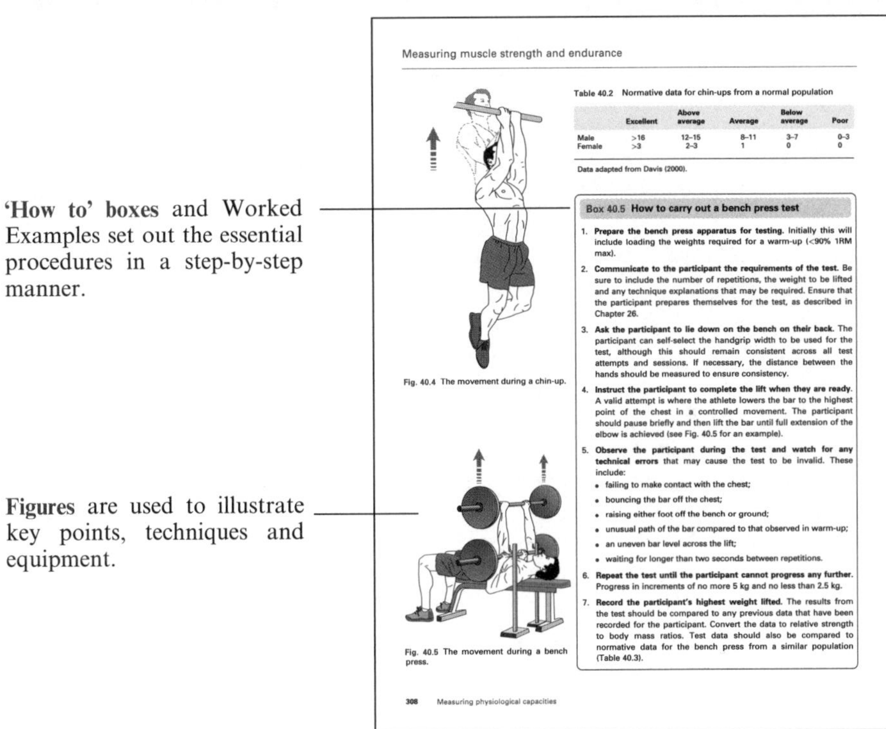

Measuring muscle strength and endurance

Table 40.2 Normative data for chin-ups from a normal population

	Excellent	Above average	Average	Below average	Poor
Male	>16	12–15	8–11	3–7	0–3
Female	>3	2–3	1	0	0

Data adapted from Davis (2000).

Fig. 40.4 The movement during a chin-up.

Box 40.5 How to carry out a bench press test

1. **Prepare the bench press apparatus for testing.** Initially this will include loading the weights required for a warm-up (<90% 1RM max).
2. **Communicate to the participant the requirements of the test.** Be sure to include the number of repetitions, the weight to be lifted and any technique explanations that may be required. Ensure that the participant prepares themselves for the test, as described in Chapter 26.
3. **Ask the participant to lie down on the bench on their back.** The participant can self-select the handgrip width to be used for the test, although this should remain consistent across all test attempts and sessions. If necessary, the distance between the hands should be measured to ensure consistency.
4. **Instruct the participant to complete the lift when they are ready.** A valid attempt is where the athlete lowers the bar to the highest point of the chest in a controlled movement. The participant should pause briefly and then lift the bar until full extension of the elbow is achieved (see Fig. 40.5 for an example).
5. **Observe the participant during the test and watch for any technical errors** that may cause the test to be invalid. These include:
   - failing to make contact with the chest;
   - bouncing the bar off the chest;
   - raising either foot off the bench or ground;
   - unusual path of the bar compared to that observed in warm-up;
   - an uneven bar level across the lift;
   - waiting for longer than two seconds between repetitions.
6. **Repeat the test until the participant cannot progress any further.** Progress in increments of no more 5 kg and no less than 2.5 kg.
7. **Record the participant's highest weight lifted.** The results from the test should be compared to any previous data that have been recorded for the participant. Convert the data to relative strength to body mass ratios. Test data should also be compared to normative data for the bench press from a similar population (Table 40.3).

Fig. 40.5 The movement during a bench press.

308 Measuring physiological capacities

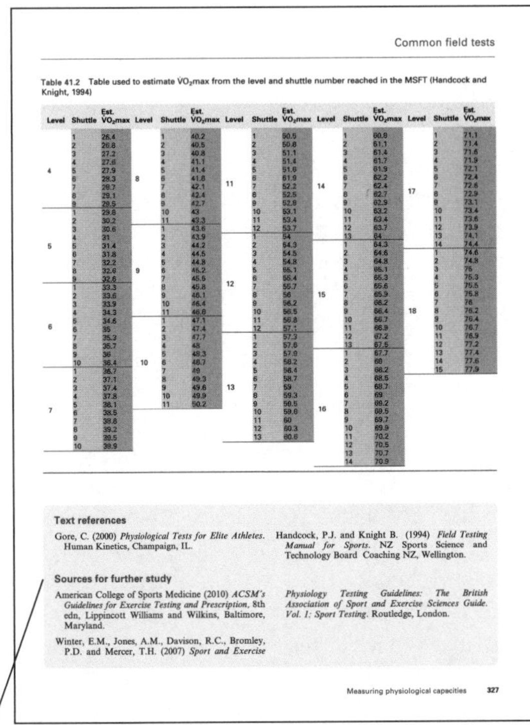

Common field tests

Table 41.2 Table used to estimate $\dot{V}O_2$max from the level and shuttle number reached in the MSFT (Handcock and Knight, 1994)

Level	Shuttle	Est. $\dot{V}O_2$max
4	1	26.4
	2	26.8
	3	27.2
	4	27.6
	5	27.9
	6	28.3
	7	28.7
	8	29.1
	9	29.5
5	1	29.8
	2	30.2
	3	30.6
	4	31
	5	31.4
	6	31.8
	7	32.2
	8	32.6
	9	32.9
6	1	33.3
	2	33.6
	3	33.9
	4	34.3
	5	34.6
	6	35
	7	35.3
	8	35.7
	9	36
	10	36.4
7	1	36.7
	2	37.1
	3	37.4
	4	37.8
	5	38.1
	6	38.5
	7	38.8
	8	39.2
	9	39.5
	10	39.9
8	1	40.2
	2	40.5
	3	40.8
	4	41.1
	5	41.4
	6	41.8
	7	42.1
	8	42.4
	9	42.7
	10	43
	11	43.3
9	1	43.6
	2	43.9
	3	44.2
	4	44.5
	5	44.8
	6	45.2
	7	45.5
	8	45.8
	9	46.1
	10	46.4
	11	46.8
10	1	47.1
	2	47.4
	3	47.7
	4	48
	5	48.3
	6	48.7
	7	49
	8	49.3
	9	49.6
	10	49.9
	11	50.2
11	1	50.5
	2	50.8
	3	51.1
	4	51.4
	5	51.6
	6	51.9
	7	52.2
	8	52.5
	9	52.8
	10	53.1
	11	53.4
	12	53.7
12	1	54
	2	54.3
	3	54.5
	4	54.8
	5	55.1
	6	55.4
	7	55.7
	8	56
	9	56.2
	10	56.5
	11	56.8
	12	57.1
13	1	57.3
	2	57.6
	3	57.9
	4	58.2
	5	58.4
	6	58.7
	7	59
	8	59.3
	9	59.5
	10	59.8
	11	60
	12	60.3
	13	60.6
14	1	60.8
	2	61.1
	3	61.4
	4	61.7
	5	61.9
	6	62.2
	7	62.4
	8	62.7
	9	62.9
	10	63.2
	11	63.4
	12	63.7
	13	64
15	1	64.3
	2	64.6
	3	64.8
	4	65.1
	5	65.3
	6	65.6
	7	65.9
	8	66.2
	9	66.4
	10	66.7
	11	66.9
	12	67.2
	13	67.5
16	1	67.7
	2	68
	3	68.2
	4	68.5
	5	68.7
	6	69
	7	69.2
	8	69.5
	9	69.7
	10	69.9
	11	70.2
	12	70.5
	13	70.7
	14	70.9
17	1	71.1
	2	71.4
	3	71.6
	4	71.9
	5	72.1
	6	72.4
	7	72.6
	8	72.9
	9	73.1
	10	73.4
	11	73.6
	12	73.9
	13	74.1
	14	74.4
18	1	74.6
	2	74.8
	3	75
	4	75.3
	5	75.5
	6	75.8
	7	76
	8	76.2
	9	76.4
	10	76.7
	11	76.9
	12	77.2
	13	77.4
	14	77.6
	15	77.9

Text references

Gore, C. (2000) *Physiological Tests for Elite Athletes*. Human Kinetics, Champaign, IL.

Handcock, P.J. and Knight B. (1994) *Field Testing Manual for Sports*. NZ Sports Science and Technology Board Coaching NZ, Wellington.

Sources for further study

American College of Sports Medicine (2010) *ACSM's Guidelines for Exercise Testing and Prescription*, 8th edn, Lippincott Williams and Wilkins, Baltimore, Maryland.

Winter, E.M., Jones, A.M., Davison, R.C., Bromley, P.D. and Mercer, T.H. (2007) *Sport and Exercise Physiology Testing Guidelines: The British Association of Sport and Exercise Sciences Guide. Vol. 1: Sport Testing*. Routledge, London.

Measuring physiological capacities 327

Sources for further study – every chapter is supported by a section giving printed and electronic sources for further study.

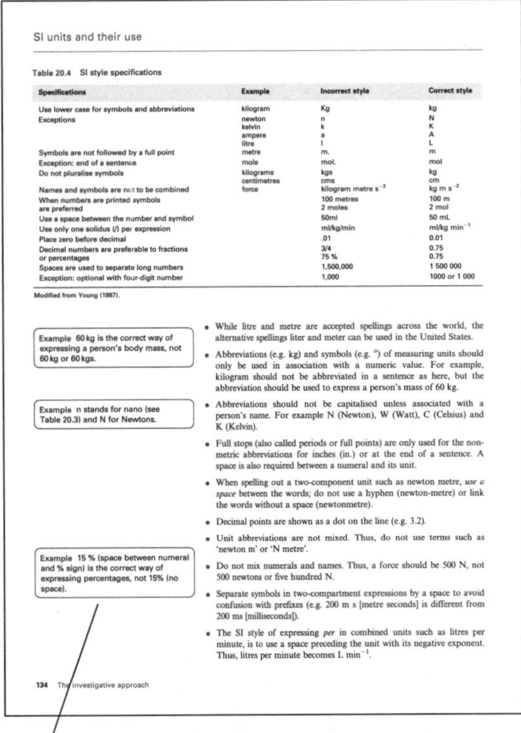

SI units and their use

Table 20.4 SI style specifications

Specifications	Example	Incorrect style	Correct style
Use lower case for symbols and abbreviations	kilogram	Kg	kg
Exceptions	newton	n	N
	kelvin	k	K
	ampere	a	A
	litre	l	L
Symbols are not followed by a full point	metre	m.	m
Exception: end of a sentence	mole	mol.	mol
Do not pluralise symbols	kilograms	kgs	kg
	centimetres	cms	cm
Names and symbols are not to be combined	force	kilogram metre s^{-2}	kg m s^{-2}
When numbers are printed symbols are preferred		100 metres	100 m
		2 moles	2 mol
Use a space between the number and symbol		50ml	50 mL
Use only one solidus (/) per expression		ml/kg/min	ml/kg min^{-1}
Place zero before decimal		.01	0.01
Decimal numbers are preferable to fractions or percentages		3/4	0.75
		75 %	0.75
Spaces are used to separate long numbers		1,500,000	1 500 000
Exception: optional with four-digit number		1,000	1000 or 1 000

Modified from Young (1987).

Example 60 kg is the correct way of expressing a person's body mass, not 60kg or 60 kgs.

Example n stands for nano (see Table 20.3) and N for Newtons.

Example 15 % (space between numeral and % sign) is the correct way of expressing percentages, not 15% (no space).

- While litre and metre are accepted spellings across the world, the alternative spellings liter and meter can be used in the United States.
- Abbreviations (e.g. kg) and symbols (e.g. °) of measuring units should only be used in association with a numeric value. For example, kilogram should not be abbreviated in a sentence as here, but the abbreviation should be used to express a person's mass of 60 kg.
- Abbreviations should not be capitalised unless associated with a person's name. For example N (Newton), W (Watt), C (Celsius) and K (Kelvin).
- Full stops (also called periods or full points) are only used for the non-metric abbreviations for inches (in.) or at the end of a sentence. A space is also required between a numeral and its unit.
- When spelling out a two-component unit such as newton metre, *use a space* between the words; do not use a hyphen (newton-metre) or link the words without a space (newtonmetre).
- Decimal points are shown as a dot on the line (e.g. 3.2).
- Unit abbreviations are not mixed. Thus, do not use terms such as 'newton m' or 'N metre'.
- Do not mix numerals and names. Thus, a force should be 500 N, not 500 newtons or five hundred N.
- Separate symbols in two-compartment expressions by a space to avoid confusion with prefixes (e.g. 200 m s [metre seconds] is different from 200 ms [milliseconds]).
- The SI style of expressing *per* in combined units such as litres per minute, is to use a space preceding the unit with its negative exponent. Thus, litres per minute becomes L min^{-1}.

134 The investigative approach

Examples are included in the margins to illustrate important points without interrupting the flow of the main text.

Acknowledgements

We are grateful to the following for permission to reproduce copyright material:

Figures

Figure 2.1 from *Practical Skills in Biology*, 4th edn, Pearson Education Ltd. (Jones, A., Reed, R. and Weyers, J. 2007) p. 9; Figure 6.1 from *Practical Skills in Biology*, 4th edn, Pearson Education Ltd. (Jones, A., Reed, R. and Weyers, J. 2007) p. 31; Figure 11.3 from *Practical Skills in Biology*, 4th edn, Pearson Education Ltd. (Jones, A., Reed, R. and Weyers, J. 2007) p. 71; Figure 15.1 from *Practical Skills in Biology*, 4th edn, Pearson Education Ltd. (Jones, A., Reed, R. and Weyers, J. 2007) p. 101; Figure 16.1 from *Practical Skills in Biology*, 4th edn, Pearson Education Ltd. (Jones, A., Reed, R. and Weyers, J. 2007) p. 83; Figure 17.1 from *Practical Skills in Biology*, 4th edn, Pearson Education Ltd. (Jones, A., Reed, R. and Weyers, J. 2007) p. 91; Figure 18.1 from *Practical Skills in Biology*, 4th edn, Pearson Education Ltd. (Jones, A., Reed, R. and Weyers, J. 2007) p. 155; Figure 18.2 from *Practical Skills in Biology*, 4th edn, Pearson Education Ltd. (Jones, A., Reed, R. and Weyers, J. 2007) p. 157; Figure 21.1 from *Practical Skills in Biology*, 4th edn, Pearson Education Ltd. (Jones, A., Reed, R. and Weyers, J. 2007) p. 184; Figure 21.2 from *Practical Skills in Biology*, 4th edn, Pearson Education Ltd. (Jones, A., Reed, R. and Weyers, J. 2007) p. 190; Figure 22.1 from *Practical Skills in Biology*, 4th edn, Pearson Education Ltd. (Jones, A., Reed, R. and Weyers, J. 2007) p. 198; Figure 27.1 from *Physical Activity Readiness Questionnaire (PAR-Q) (c) 2002*, used with permission from the Canadian Society for Exercise Physiology, www.csep.ca; Figure 29.9 from http://www.ambulancetechnicianstudy.co.uk/ecgbasics.html, Ambulance Technician Study; Figure 34.6 adapted from ROSSCRAFT Innovations Incorporated; Figure 35.3 from http://www.bodpod.com/products/howBloodWorkBodpod, Life Measurement Inc.; Figure 35.4 reprinted by permission from J.E. Graves et al., 2006, Anthropometry and body composition measurement. In *Physiological assessment of human fitness*, 2nd ed. edited by P.J. Maud and C. Foster (Champaign, IL: Human Kinetics), 2011; Figure 46.2 from *Practical Skills in Biology*, 4th edn, Pearson Education Ltd. (Jones, A., Reed, R. and Weyers, J. 2007) p. 384; Figures 46.3 and 46.4 from *Practical Skills in Biology*, 4th edn, Pearson Education Ltd. (Jones, A., Reed, R. and Weyers, J. 2007) p. 385; Figures 49.1, 49.2 and 49.3 from *Practical Skills in Biology*, 4th edn, Pearson Education Ltd. (Jones, A., Reed, R. and Weyers, J. 2007) p. 415; Figure 49.4 from *Practical Skills in Biology*, 4th edn, Pearson Education Ltd. (Jones, A., Reed, R. and Weyers, J. 2007) p. 416; Figure 49.5 from *Practical Skills in Biology*, 4th edn, Pearson Education Ltd. (Jones, A., Reed, R. and Weyers, J. 2007) p. 418; Figures 49.6 and 49.7 from *Practical Skills in Biology*, 4th edn, Pearson Education Ltd. (Jones, A., Reed, R. and Weyers, J. 2007) p. 419; Figures 49.8 and 49.9 from *Practical Skills in Biology*, 4th edn, Pearson Education Ltd. (Jones, A., Reed, R. and Weyers, J. 2007) p. 421; Figure 49.10 from *Practical Skills in Biology*, 4th edn, Pearson Education Ltd. (Jones, A., Reed, R. and Weyers, J. 2007) p. 422; Figure 50.2 from *Practical Skills in Biology*, 4th edn, Pearson Education Ltd. (Jones, A., Reed, R. and Weyers, J. 2007) p. 428; Figure 50.3 from *Practical Skills in Biology*, 4th edn, Pearson Education Ltd. (Jones, A., Reed, R. and Weyers, J. 2007) p. 429; Figures 50.4 and 50.5 from *Practical Skills in Biology*, 4th edn, Pearson Education Ltd. (Jones, A., Reed, R. and Weyers, J. 2007) p. 430; Figure 50.6 from *Practical Skills in Biology*, 4th edn, Pearson Education Ltd. (Jones, A., Reed, R. and Weyers, J. 2007) p. 433; Figure 50.7 from *Practical Skills in Biology*, 4th edn, Pearson Education Ltd. (Jones, A., Reed, R. and Weyers, J. 2007) p. 434.

Tables

Table 3.2 from *Practical Skills in Biology*, 4th edn, Pearson Education Ltd. (Jones, A., Reed, R. and Weyers, J. 2007) p. 14; Table on pages 23-4 from *Practical Skills in Biology*, 4th edn, Pearson Education Ltd. (Jones, A., Reed, R. and Weyers, J. 2007) pp. 21-2; Table 5.1 adapted from *Practical Skills in Biology*, 4th edn, Pearson Education Ltd. (Jones, A., Reed, R. and Weyers, J. 2007) p. 23; Table 7.1 from *Practical Skills in Biology*, 4th edn, Pearson Education Ltd. (Jones, A., Reed, R. and Weyers, J. 2007) p. 39; Table 9.1 from *Practical Skills in Biology*, 4th edn, Pearson Education Ltd. (Jones, A., Reed, R. and Weyers, K. 2007) p. 54; Table 15.1 from *Practical Skills in Biology*, 4th edn, Pearson Education Ltd. (Jones, A., Reed, R. and Weyers, J. 2007) p. 102; Table 18.1 from *Practical Skills in Biology*, 4th edn, Pearson Education Ltd. (Jones, A., Reed, R. and Weyers, J. 2007) p. 156; Table 46.1 from *Practical Skills in Biology*, 4th edn, Pearson Education Ltd. (Jones, A., Reed, R. and Weyers, J. 2007) p. 384; Table 50.1 from *Practical Skills in Biology*, 4th edn, Pearson Education Ltd. (Jones, A., Reed, R. and Weyers, J. 2007) p. 430; Table 50.2 from *Practical Skills in Biology*, 4th edn, Pearson Education Ltd. (Jones, A., Reed, R. and Weyers, J. 2007) p. 431.

Text

Box 27.1 from Pre-exercise screening system 2005: Sports Medicine Australia (SMA) – Stage 1 Questionnaire, Sports Medicine Australia.

Photographs

(Key: b-bottom; c-centre; l-left; r-right; t-top)

Page 167 Alamy Images: Pete Jenkins; Page 170 First Aid Distributions; Page 171 MidMeds Ltd.; Page 193 Alamy Images: SciMed images; Page 197 Alamy Images: Grant Pritchard; Page 212 Medical International Research: (r). Science Photo Library Ltd: (l); Page 234 Alamy Images: Peter Hudeck (b). Science Photo Library Ltd: GIPHOTOSTOCK (t); Page 246 fitnessASSIST: (t); Page 251 ROSSCRAFT Innovations Incorporated; Page 260 Alamy Images: medicalpicture; Page 261 Science Photo Library Ltd: SUSAN LEAVINES (b); MEDICAL RF.COM (t); Page 277 Monark Exercise.co.uk; Page 288 Alamy Images: ST-images (t). CamNtech: (b). Phillips: (c); Page 297 Lode B.V: (b). Monark Exercise.co.uk: (c). Peter Reaburn PhD (Associate Professor): (t); Page 320 Peter Reaburn PhD (Associate Professor); Page 333 Concept2 Ltd.: Concept2 Model D Indoor Rower.

In some instances we have been unable to trace the owners of copyright material, and we would appreciate any information that would enable us to do so.

Study and examination skills

1. The importance of transferable skills 3
2. Managing your time 7
3. Working with others 11
4. Taking notes from lectures and texts 17
5. Learning and revising 22
6. Curriculum options, assessment and exams 31
7. Preparing your curriculum vitae or résumé 40

1 The importance of transferable skills

Skills terminology – different phrases may be used to describe transferable skills, depending on place or context. These include:

- UK: core skills, key skills, common skills, transferable skills;
- Australia: generic skills, graduate attributes, key competencies, employability skills;
- New Zealand: essential skills;
- Canada: employability skills;
- US: basic skills, necessary skills, workplace know-how.

Transferable skills are those skills that apply across a variety of jobs and life contexts. They are known by many other names, depending on the country in which you are studying. Transferable skills are taking on increased importance in many countries. Employers across all industries now seek to ensure business success by recruiting and retaining employees who have a variety of skills and personal attributes, as well as the specific technical skills required in exercise and sport science.

Transferable skills are increasingly important because jobs today require flexibility, initiative and the ability to undertake many different tasks. Jobs are not as narrowly prescribed as in the past and are generally more service-orientated, making information and social skills increasingly important. Universities and colleges are also interested in the development of transferable skills as they encourage learners to be more reflective and self-directed.

This chapter outlines the range of transferable skills and their significance to sport and exercise scientists. It also indicates where practical skills fit into this scheme. Having a good understanding of this topic will help you to place your work at university in a wider context. You will also gain an insight into the qualities that employers expect you to have developed by the time you graduate. Awareness of these matters will be useful when carrying out personal development planning (PDP) as part of your studies.

The range of transferable skills

Tables 1.1 and 1.2 provide a comprehensive listing of university-level transferable skills under up to eight skills categories. There are many possible classifications – and a different one may be used in your institution or field of study. Note particularly that 'learning skills', while important, and rightly emphasised at the start of many courses, constitute only a subset of the skills acquired by most university students.

Using course materials – study your course handbook and the schedules for each practical session to find out what skills you are expected to develop at each point in the curriculum. Usually the learning objectives/outcomes (p. 24) will describe the skills involved.

The phrase '*Practical Skills*' in the title of this book indicates that there is a special subset of transferable skills related to work in the laboratory or field. However, although this text deals primarily with skills and techniques required for laboratory practicals, fieldwork and associated studies, a broader range of material is included. This is because the skills concerned are important, not only in sport and exercise sciences but also in the wider world. Examples include time management, evaluating information and communicating effectively.

Example The skills involved in team-work cannot be developed without a deeper understanding of the inter-relationships involved in successful groups. The context will be different for every group and a flexible approach will always be required, according to the individuals involved and the nature of the task.

KEY POINT Sport and exercise science is essentially a practical area of study, and therefore involves highly developed laboratory and field skills. The importance that your lecturers place on practical skills will probably be evident from the large proportion of curriculum time you will spend on practical work in your course.

The word 'skill' implies much more than the robotic learning of, for example, a laboratory procedure. Of course, some of the tasks you will be asked to carry out in practical classes *will* be repetitive. Certain

Table 1.1 Summary of Australian Chamber of Commerce and Industry and Business Council of Australia transferable skills (Australian Chamber of Commerce and Industry and Business Council of Australia, 2002)

Transferable skills	Relevant chapters in this textbook
Communication skills that contribute to productive and harmonious relations between employees and customers	4, 7, 10, 11, 12, 13, 14, 15, 16, 17, 22, 47, 48
Teamwork skills that contribute to productive working relationships and outcomes	3, 16, 17, 21, 22
Problem-solving skills that contribute to productive outcomes	8, 9, 10, 11, 12, 16, 17, 18, 21, 22, 52, 53, 54
Initiative and enterprise skills that contribute to innovative outcomes	3, 8, 9, 10, 11, 12, 14, 15, 16, 17, 18, 21, 22, 52, 53, 54
Planning and organising skills that contribute to long-term and short-term strategic planning	2, 10, 11, 12, 13, 15, 16, 17, 19, 21, 22, 26, 46, 47, 48, 50, 54
Self-management skills that contribute to employee satisfaction and growth	2, 3, 4, 5, 7, 8, 9, 14, 15, 16, 17, 22, 47, 48
Learning skills that contribute to ongoing improvement and expansion in employee and company operations and outcomes	4, 5, 6, 7, 8, 9, 10, 11, 12, 14, 15, 16, 17, 18, 19, 21, 22
Technology skills that contribute to effective execution of tasks	8, 9, 10, 11, 12, 13, 14, 15, 16, 17, 18, 20, 21, 22, 46, 47, 48, 49, 50, 51

Table 1.2 Example of a university list of transferable skills (taken from CQUniversity's Management Plan for Teaching and Learning, 2006–2011)

Generic skills	Attributes
Monitor the environment, develop strategies and capitalise on change	Enthusiasm for and commitment to their work
Acquire, evaluate and use information effectively	Self-confidence in managing themselves and others
Solve problems and apply scientific reasoning	Critical, creative and strategic thinking
Use information technology	Ethical behaviour towards others
Apply discipline-related theory to practice in both familiar and unfamiliar situations	Capability in and commitment to upholding professional values and ethics
Function effectively as team members and as team leaders	Commitment to learning throughout life
Communicate effectively	Willingness to challenge current knowledge and thinking
	Frequent reflection on and realistic evaluation of their performance and their plans to achieve personal and professional goals
	Readiness to participate in and ambition to lead regional and global societies, in both professional and personal roles

techniques require a high level of skill and attention to detail if accuracy and precision are to be attained, and the necessary competence often requires practice to make perfect. However, a deeper understanding of the context of a technique is important if the skill is to be appreciated fully and then transferred to a new situation. That is why this text is not simply a 'recipe book' of methods and why it includes background information, tips and worked examples.

Transferability of skills

Transferable skills are those that allow someone with knowledge, understanding or ability gained in one situation to adapt or extend this for application in a different context. In some cases, the transfer of a skill is immediately obvious. Take, for example, the ability to use a spreadsheet to summarise fitness test data and create a graph to illustrate results. Once the key concepts and commands are learned (Chapter 11), they can be applied to many instances outside the sport and exercise sciences where this type of output is used. This is not only true for similar datasets, but also in unrelated situations, such as making a financial balance sheet and creating a pie chart to show sources of expenditure. Similarly, knowing the requirements for good graph drawing and tabulation (Chapters 47 and 48), perhaps practised by hand in earlier work, might help you use spreadsheet commands to make the output suit your needs.

Opportunities to develop and practise skills in your private or social life – you could, for example, practise spreadsheet skills by organising personal or club finances using Microsoft Excel, or teamwork skills within any university clubs or societies you may join (see Chapter 7).

Other cases may be less clear but equally valid. For example, towards the end of your undergraduate studies you may be involved in designing experiments as part of project work. This task will draw on several skills gained at earlier stages in your course, such as fitness testing (Chapters 26–42), deciding about experimental layout (Chapters 18–22) and perhaps carrying out some particular method of observation, measurement or analysis (Chapters 28–45). How and when might you transfer this complex set of skills? In the workplace, it is unlikely that you would be asked to repeat the same process, but in critically evaluating a problem or in planning a complex project for a new employer, you will need to use many of the time management, organisational and analytical skills developed when designing and carrying out projects. The same applies to information retrieval and evaluation and writing essays and dissertations, when transferred to the task of analysing or writing a business report.

Types of PDP portfolio and their benefits – some PDP schemes are centred on academic and learning skills, while others are more focused on career planning. Some are carried out independently and others in tandem with a personal tutor or advisory system. Some PDP schemes involve creating an online portfolio, while others are primarily paper-based. Each method has specific goals and advantages, but whichever way your scheme operates, maximum benefit will be gained from being fully involved with the process.

Personal development planning

Many universities have schemes for PDP, which may go under slightly different names such as progress file or professional development plan. You will usually be expected to create a portfolio of evidence on your progress, then reflect on this, and subsequently set yourself plans for the future, including targets and action points. Analysis of your transferable skills profile will probably form part of your PDP. Other aspects commonly included are:

- your aspirations, goals, interests and motivations;
- your learning style or preference (see p. 22);
- your assessment transcript or academic profile information (e.g. record of grades in your modules);
- your developing CV (see p. 41).

Taking part in PDP can help focus your thoughts about your university studies and future career. This is important in sport and exercise science, because these degrees do not lead only to a specific occupation. The PDP process will introduce you to some new terms and will help you to describe your personality and abilities. This will be useful when constructing your CV and when applying for jobs.

What your future employer will be looking for

At the end of your course, which may seem some time away, you will aim to get a job and start on your chosen career path. You will need to sell yourself to your future employer, firstly in your application form

Definition

Employability – refers to a person's capability of gaining initial employment, maintaining employment and obtaining new employment if required. For individuals, employability depends on the knowledge, skills and attitudes they possess, the way they use those assets and present them to employers, and the context (e.g. personal circumstances and labour market environment) within which they seek work.

and curriculum vitae (Chapter 7), and perhaps later at interview. Companies rarely employ sport and exercise science graduates simply because they know how to carry out a particular test or because they can remember specific facts about their chosen degree subject. Instead, employers tend to look for a range of qualities and transferable skills that together define an attribute known as 'graduateness' or 'employability'. This encompasses, for example, the ability to work in a team, to speak effectively and write clearly about your work, to understand complex data and to manage a project to completion. All of these skills can be developed at different stages during your university studies.

KEY POINT Factual knowledge can be important in degrees with a strong vocational element, but understanding how to find and evaluate information is usually rated more highly by employers than the ability to memorise facts.

Most likely, your future employer(s) will seek someone with an organised yet flexible mind, capable of demonstrating a logical approach to problems – someone who has a range of skills and who can transfer these skills to new situations. Many competing applicants will probably have similar qualifications. If you want the job, you will have to show that your additional skills place you above the other candidates.

Text references

Anon. *CQUniversity Generic Skills and Attributes.* Available: http://www.learning.cqu.edu.au/lt_resources/gen_skills.htm Last accessed: 23/12/10

Australian Chamber of Commerce and Industry & Business Council of Australia (2002). *Employability Skills for the Future.* Department of Education, Science and Training, Canberra.

Sources for further study

Cooper, N., Forrest, K. and Cramp, P. (2006) *Essential Guide to Generic Skills.* Blackwell BMJ Books, London.

Fallows, S. and Steven, C. (2000) *Integrating Key Skills in Higher Education: Employability, Transferable Skills, and Learning for Life.* Stylus Publishing, Sterling VA.

Hager, P., Holland, S. and Beckett, D. (2002) *Enhancing the Learning and Employability of Graduates: The Role of Generic Skills.* The Business/Higher Education Round Table, Melbourne.

Race, P. (2007) *How to Get a Good Degree*, 2nd edn, Open University Press, Maidenhead.

2 Managing your time

> **Definition**
>
> **Time management** – a system for controlling and using time as efficiently and as effectively as possible.

One of the most important activities that you can do is to organise your personal and working time effectively. There is a lot to do at university and a common complaint is that there just isn't enough time to accomplish everything. In fact, research shows that most people use up a lot of their time without realising it through ineffective study or activities such as extended coffee breaks. Developing your time management skills will help you to achieve more in work, rest and play, but it is important to remember that putting time management techniques into practice is an individual matter, requiring a level of self-discipline not unlike that required for dieting. A new system won't always work perfectly straight away, but through time you can evolve a system that is effective for you. An inability to organise your time effectively, of course, results in feelings of failure, frustration, guilt and being out of control in your life.

> **Advantages of time management** – these include:
>
> - a much greater feeling of control over your activities;
> - avoidance of stress;
> - improved productivity – achieve more in a shorter period;
> - improved performance levels – work to higher standards because you are in charge;
> - an increase in time available for non-work matters – work hard, but play hard too;
> - improved incorporation of exercise in daily lifestyle – training time is organised and fits into study schedule.

Setting your goals

The first step is to identify clearly what you want to achieve, both in work and in your personal life. We all have a general idea of what we are aiming for, but to be effective, your goals must be clearly identified and priorities allocated. Clear, concise objectives can provide you with a framework in which to make these choices. Try using the 'SMART' approach, in which objectives should be:

- Specific – clear and unambiguous, including what, when, where, how and why;
- Measurable – having quantified targets and benefits to provide an understanding of progress;
- Achievable – being attainable within your resources;
- Realistic – being within your abilities and expectations;
- Timed – stating the time period for completion.

Having identified your goals, you can now move on to answer four very important questions:

1. Where does your time go?
2. Where should your time go?
3. What are your time-wasting activities?
4. What strategies can help you?

> **Example** The objective 'to spend an extra hour each week on directed study in biochemistry next term' fulfils the SMART criteria, in contrast to a general intention 'to study more'.

Analysing your current activities

The key to successful development of time management is a realistic knowledge of how you currently spend your time. Start by keeping a detailed time log for a typical week (Fig. 2.1); you will need to be truthful in this process. Once you have completed the log, consider the following questions:

- How many hours do I work in total and how many hours do I use for 'relaxation'?
- What range of activities do I do?
- How long do I spend on each activity?

Fig. 2.1 Example of how to lay out a time log. Write activities along the top of the page, and divide the day into 15-minute segments as shown. Think beforehand how you will categorise the different things you do, from the mundane (laundry, having a shower, drinking coffee, etc.) to the well timetabled (tutorial meeting, sports club meeting), and add supplementary notes if required. At the end of each day, place a dot in the relevant column for each activity and sum the dots to give a total at the bottom of the page. You will need to keep a diary like this for at least a week before you see patterns emerging.

Source: Jones, A., Reed, R. and Weyers, J., (2007), p. 9.

Time slots	Activity										Notes
7.00–7.15											
7.15–7.30											
7.30–7.45											
7.45–8.00											
8.00–8.15											
8.15–8.30											
8.30–8.45											
8.45–9.00											
9.00–9.15											

- What do I spend most of my time doing?
- What do I spend the least amount of my time doing?
- Are my allocations of time in proportion to the importance of my activities?
- How much of my time is ineffectively used, e.g. for uncontrolled socialising or interruptions?

If you wish, you could use a spreadsheet (Chapter 11) to produce graphical summaries of time allocations in different categories as an aid to analysis and management. Divide your time into:

- committed time – timetabled activities involving your main objectives/goals;
- maintenance time – time spent supporting your general life activities (shopping, cleaning, laundry, etc.);
- discretionary time – time for you to use as you wish, e.g. recreation, sport, hobbies, socialising.

Quality in time management – avoid spending a lot of time doing unproductive studying, e.g. reading a textbook without specific objectives for that reading.

Avoiding time-wasting activities

Look carefully at those tasks that could be identified as time-wasting activities. They include gossiping, over-long breaks, uninvited interruptions and even ineffective study periods. Try to reduce these to a minimum, but do not count on eliminating them entirely. Remember also that some exercise and relaxation *should* be programmed into your daily schedule.

Being assertive – if friends and colleagues continually interrupt you, find a way of controlling them, before they control you. Indicate clearly on your door that you do not wish to be disturbed and explain why. Otherwise, try to work away from disturbance.

Organising your tasks

Having analysed your time usage, you can now use this information, together with your objectives and prioritised goals, to organise your activities, on both a short-term and a long-term basis. Consider using a diary-based system (such as those produced by Filofax, TMI and Day-timer) that will help you plan ahead and analyse your progress.

	Week beginning:						
	Sunday	Monday	Tuesday	Wednesday	Thursday	Friday	Saturday
DATE							
6–7 am		EXERCISE		EXERCISE		EXERCISE	
7–8		Breakfast	Breakfast	Breakfast	Breakfast	Breakfast	Breakfast
8–9	Breakfast	Preparation	Preparation	Preparation	Preparation	Preparation	Travel
9–10	FREE	PHYS (L)	PE112 (L)	PHYS (T)	PE112 (L)	BIOL (P)	WORK
10–11	STUDY	STUDY	PE112 (L)	STUDY	PE112 (L)	BIOL (P)	WORK
11–12	STUDY	STATS (L)	STUDY	BIOL (L)	STATS (T)	BIOL (P)	WORK
12–1 pm	STUDY	STATS (L)	STUDY	STUDY	STATS (T)	STUDY	WORK
1–2	Lunch	Lunch	Lunch	Lunch	Lunch	Lunch	Lunch
2–3	FREE	STUDY	STUDY	STUDY	PHYS (P)	PE112 (P)	WORK
3–4	FREE	BIOL (L)	STUDY	STUDY	PHYS (P)	PE112 (P)	RUGBY
4–5	EXERCISE	BIOL (L)	STUDY	STUDY	PHYS (P)	PE112 (P)	RUGBY
5–6	EXERCISE	STUDY	EXERCISE	SHOPPING	EXERCISE	FREE	RUGBY
6–7	Tea	STUDY	EXERCISE	SHOPPING	EXERCISE	Tea	Tea
7–8	FREE*	Tea	Tea	Tea	Tea	FREE*	FREE
8–9	FREE*	STUDY	STUDY	FREE*	STUDY	FREE*	FREE
9–10	FREE*	STUDY	STUDY	FREE*	STUDY	FREE*	FREE
Study (h)	3	11	9	7	9	7	0
Other (h)	13	5	7	9	7	9	16
						Total study time = 46 h	

Fig. 2.2 A weekly diary with an example of entries for a first-year exercise science student who plays competitive rugby and has a Saturday job. *Note that 'free time' changes to 'study time' for periods when assessed work is to be produced or during revision for exams. Study time (including attendance at lectures (L), practicals (P) and tutorials (T)) thus represents between 42 and 50% of the total time.

Divide your tasks into several categories, such as:

- urgent – must be done as a top priority and at short notice (e.g. doctor's appointment);
- routine – predictable and regular and therefore easily scheduled (e.g. preparation, lectures or playing sport);
- one-off activities – usually with rather shorter deadlines and which may be of high priority (e.g. a tutorial assignment or seeking advice);
- long-term tasks – sometimes referred to as 'elephant tasks' that are too large to 'eat' in one go (e.g. learning a language). These are best managed by scheduling frequent small 'bites' to achieve the task over a longer timescale.

Matching your work to your body's rhythm – everyone has times of day when they feel more alert and able to work. Decide when these times are for you and programme your work accordingly. Plan relaxation events for periods when you tend to be less alert.

Use checklists as often as possible – post your lists in places where they are easily and frequently visible, such as in front of your desk. Ticking things off as they are completed gives you a feeling of accomplishment and progress, increasing motivation.

You should make a weekly plan (Fig. 2.2) for the routine activities, with gaps for less predictable tasks. This should be supplemented by individual daily checklists, preferably written at the end of the previous working day. Such plans and checklists should be flexible, forming the basis for most of your activities except when exceptional circumstances intervene. The planning must be kept brief, however, and should be scheduled into your activities. Box 2.1 provides tips for effective planning and working.

KEY POINT Review each day's plan at the end of the previous day, making such modifications as are required by circumstances, e.g. adding an uncompleted task from the previous day or a new and urgent task.

Box 2.1 Tips for effective planning and working

- Set guidelines and review expectations regularly.
- Don't procrastinate: don't keep putting off doing things you know are important – they will not go away but they will increase to crisis point.
- Don't be a perfectionist – perfection is paralysing.
- Learn from past experience – review your management system regularly.
- Don't set yourself unrealistic goals and objectives – this will lead to procrastination and feelings of failure.
- Avoid recurring crises – they are telling you something is not working properly and needs to be changed.
- Learn to concentrate effectively and don't let yourself be distracted by casual interruptions.
- Learn to say 'no' firmly but graciously when appropriate.
- Know your own body rhythms: e.g. are you a morning person or an evening person?
- Learn to recognise the benefits of rest and relaxation at appropriate times.
- Take short but complete breaks from your tasks – come back feeling refreshed in mind and body.
- Work in suitable study areas and keep your own workspace organised.
- Avoid clutter (physical and mental).
- Learn to access and use information effectively (Chapter 8).
- Learn to read and write accurately and quickly (Chapters 4 and 5).

Sources for further study

Anon. *Day-Timer*. Available: http://www.daytimer.co.uk Last accessed: 23/12/10.
[Website for products Day-Timers Europe Ltd, Chene Court, Poundwell Street, Modbury, Devon PL21 0QJ.]

Anon. *Filofax*. Available: http://www.filofax.co.uk Last accessed: 23/12/10.
[Website for products of Filofax UK, Unit 3, Victoria Gardens, Burgess Hill, West Sussex RH15 9NB.]

Anon. *TMI Website*. Available: http://www.tmi.co.uk Last accessed: 23/12/10.
[Website for products of TMI (Time Manager International A/S), 50 High Street, Henley-in-Arden, Solihull, West Midlands B95 5AN.]

Mayer, J.L. (1999) *Time Management for Dummies*, 2nd edn, IDG Books Worldwide, Inc., Foster City, CA.

3 Working with others

Definitions

Team – a group of individuals working cooperatively towards a common goal.

Teamwork – joint action by a group to complete a given task.

Team role – a tendency to behave, contribute and interrelate with others in a particular way.

It is highly likely that during your university or college studies you will be expected to work with fellow students during practicals, written or oral projects, and study exercises. This might take the form of sharing tasks or casual collaboration through discussion, or it might be formally directed teamwork such as problem-based learning (Box 6.1) or preparing a poster (Chapter 16). Interacting with others can be extremely rewarding and realistically represents the professional world, where teamworking is common and a highly sought-after transferable skill. The advantages of working with others include:

- Teamworking is usually synergistic in effect – it often results in better ideas, produced by the interchange of views, and better output, owing to the complementary skills of team members.
- Working in teams can provide support for individuals within the team.
- Levels of personal commitment can be enhanced through concern about letting the team down.
- Responsibilities for tasks can be shared.
- Ideas can be shared so that each team member can benefit.
- Being able to tap into a wider pool of experiences, background knowledge and styles of working.
- Stimulating each other's thinking.
- Clarifying your own thinking through talking and answering questions.
- Learning to deal with challenges and criticism.
- Realising that there are more dimensions and answers to a question or problem than you could discover on your own.

However, you can also feel both threatened and exposed if teamwork is not managed properly. Some of the main reasons for negative feelings towards working in groups include:

- reservations about working with strangers – not knowing whether you will be able to form a friendly and productive relationship;
- worries over rejection – a perception of being unpopular or being chosen last by the group;
- levels of personal commitment – these can be enhanced through a desire to perform well, so the team as a whole achieves its target;
- fear of being held back by others – especially for those who have been successful in individual work already;
- lack of previous experience – worries about the kinds of personal interactions likely to occur and the team role likely to suit you best;
- concerns about the outcomes of peer assessment – in particular, whether others will give you a fair mark for your efforts.

Peer assessment – this term applies to marking schemes in which all or a proportion of the marks for a teamwork exercise are allocated by the team members themselves. Read the instructions carefully before embarking on the exercise, so you know which aspects of your work your fellow team members will be assessing. When deciding what marks to allocate yourself, try to be as fair as possible with your marking.

Table 3.1 Offering and receiving constructive criticism

Offering constructive criticism	Receiving constructive criticism
• Phrase the criticism in a positive way • Suggest ways for improvement rather than criticising what is wrong • Offer criticism only if invited to do so • Point out what is good *first*, then what could be improved • Comment on ideas, behaviour and products, not on people • Be realistic – only suggest changes or ideas that can be achieved • Be selective – choose one or two items that will make a difference • Be precise – give clear examples • Be sympathetic – use a voice and manner that help others to accept your criticism	• Listen attentively • Take time to think about what has been said and look for the truth in what was said • Thank others for their constructive comment(s) • Ask questions to clarify anything you do not understand

Gaining confidence through experience – the more you take part in teamwork, the more you know how teams operate and how to make teamwork effective for you.

Studying with others – teaming up with someone else on your course for revision ('study buddying') is a potentially valuable activity and may especially suit some types of learners (Box 5.1). It can help keep your morale high when things get tough. You might consider:

- sharing notes, textbooks and other information;
- going through past papers together, dissecting the questions and planning answers;
- talking to each other about a topic (good for aural learners: see Box 5.1);
- giving tutorials to each other about parts of the course that have not been fully grasped.

Teamwork skills

Some of the key skills you will need to develop to maximise the success of your teamworking activities include:

- **Interpersonal skills.** How do you react to new people? Are you able both to listen and to communicate easily with them? How do you deal with conflicts and disagreements?
- **Delegation/sharing of tasks.** The primary advantage of teamwork is the sharing of effort and responsibility. Are you willing/able to do this? It involves trusting your team members. How will you deal with those group members who don't contribute fully?
- **Effective listening.** Successful listening is a skill that usually needs developing, e.g. during the exchange of ideas within a group.
- **Speaking clearly and concisely.** Effective communication is a vital part of teamwork, both between team members and when presenting team outcomes to others. Try to develop your communication skills through learning and practice (see Chapter 17).
- **Providing constructive criticism (see Table 3.1).** It is all too easy to be negative, but only constructive criticism will have a positive effect in interactions with others.

Collaboration for learning

Much collaboration is informal and consists of pairs or groups of individuals getting together to exchange materials and ideas while studying. It may consist of a 'brainstorming' session for a topic or piece of work, or sharing efforts to research a topic. This has much to commend it and is generally encouraged. However, it is vital that this collaborative learning is distinguished from the collaborative writing of assessed documents: the latter is not usually acceptable and, in its most extreme form, is plagiarism, usually with a heavy potential punishment in university assessment systems. Make sure you know what plagiarism is, what unacceptable collaboration is, and how they are treated within your institution (see p. 56).

KEY POINT Collaboration is inappropriate during the final phase of an assessed piece of work unless you have been directed to produce a group report. Collaboration is encouraged during research and learning activities but the final write-up must normally be your own work. The extreme of producing copycat write-ups is regarded as plagiarism (p. 56) and will be punished accordingly.

Web-based resources and support for brainstorming – websites such as http://www.brainstorming.co.uk give further information and practical advice for teamworking.

The dynamics of teamworking

It is important that team activities are properly structured so that each member knows what is expected of them. Allocation of responsibilities usually requires the clear identification of a leader. Several studies of groups have identified different team roles that derive from differences in personality. You should be aware of such categorisations, both in terms of your own predispositions and those of your fellow team members, as it will help the group to interact more productively. Belbin (2008) identified nine such roles, as shown in Table 3.2.

Table 3.2 A summary of the team roles described by Belbin (2008). No one role should be considered 'better' than any other, and a good team requires members who are able to undertake appropriate roles at different times. Each role provides important strengths to a team, and its compensatory weaknesses should be accepted within the group framework

Team role	Personality characteristics	Typical function in a team	Strengths	Allowable weaknesses
Coordinator	Self-confident, calm and controlled	Leading: causing others to work towards goals	Good at spotting others' talents and delegating activities	Often less creative or intellectual than others in the group
Shaper	Strong need for achievement; outgoing; dynamic; highly strung	Leading: generating action within a team; imposing shape and pattern to work	Providing drive and realism to group activities	Can be headstrong, emotional and less patient than others
Innovator[1]	Individualistic, serious-minded; often unorthodox	Generating new proposals and solving problems	Creative, innovative and knowledgeable	Tendency to work in isolation; ideas may not always be practical
Monitor–evaluator	Sober, unemotional and prudent	Analysing problems and evaluating ideas	Shrewd judgement	May work slowly; not usually a good motivator
Implementer	Well organised and self-disciplined, with practical common sense	Doing what needs to be done	Organising abilities and common sense	Lack of flexibility and tendency to resist new ideas
Teamworker	Sociable, mild and sensitive	Being supportive, perceptive and diplomatic; keeping the team going	Good listener; reliable and flexible; promotes team spirit	Not comfortable when leading; may be indecisive
Resource investigator	Extrovert, enthusiastic, curious and communicative	Exploiting opportunities; finding resources; external relations	Quick thinking; good at developing others' ideas	May lose interest rapidly
Completer–finisher	Introvert and anxious; painstaking, orderly and conscientious	Ensuring completion of activity to high standard	Good focus on fulfilling objectives and goals	Obsessive about details; may wish to do all the work to control quality
Specialist	Professional, self-motivated and dedicated	Providing essential skills	Commitment and technical knowledge	Contributes on a narrow aspect of project; tends to be single-minded

[1] May also be called 'plant' in some texts
Source: Jones, A., Reed, R. and Weyers, J. (2007) p. 14.

In formal team situations, your course organiser should deal with these issues; even if they do not, it is important that you are aware of these roles and their potential impact on the success or failure of teamwork. You should try to identify your own 'natural' role: if asked to form a team, bear the different roles in mind during your selection of colleagues and your interactions with them. The ideal team should contain members capable of adopting most of these roles. However, you should also note the following points:

- People will probably fit one of these roles naturally as a function of their personality and skills.
- Group members may be suited to more than one of these roles.
- In some circumstances, team members may be required to adapt and take a different role from the one that they feel suits them.
- No one role is 'better' than any other. For good teamwork, the group should have a balance of personality types present.
- People may have to adopt multiple roles, especially if the team size is small.

Recording group discussions – make sure you structure meetings (including writing agendas) and note their outcomes (taking minutes and noting action points).

KEY POINT In formal teamwork situations, be clear as to how individual contributions are to be identified and recognised. This might require discussion with the course organiser. Make sure that recognition, including assessment marks, is truly reflective of effort. Failure to ensure that this is the case can lead to disputes and feelings of unfairness.

Making the group work

Before you start the project, use planning to prevent team problems. Firstly, write down your own thoughts under each of the following headings; then openly discuss each heading as a group, ensuring that you contribute your individual points.

1. advantages of working as a group;
2. potential difficulties of working as a group;
3. brainstorm ways the team could solve these difficulties. If you get stuck, speak to a friend, tutor or the lecturer.

There are many advantages to working in groups. However, being part of a group working on an assignment, written or oral project or major event is often not easy. Coping with the challenges of working in a team can develop a range of skills that will benefit you in the long term. The following guidelines may help for team-based work.

1. Create a supportive group atmosphere
   - **Be aware that other people have feelings** and may be anxious about being criticised or found wanting in some areas.
   - **Address anxieties directly.** In your first team meeting, brainstorm (www.brainstorming.co.uk) how every member feels about being in the team, their concerns and how the team can turn these worries into opportunities.

- **Make ground rules** such as when and where to meet, what to do if someone dominates or doesn't pull their weight, and what kinds of behaviour or comments are unacceptable.
- **Investigate group strengths** by brainstorming the range of skills and experiences brought to the group by each member. Who is the best chairperson, verbal presenter, organiser, writer, computer guru, statistics guru, etc. You might even rotate roles. Ensure every member has a role.

2. Create an effective group environment

   - **Set clear agendas and boundaries.** Set an agenda for each meeting and decide how long to spend on each item. Set the meeting times and venues well in advance. Keep any socialising for after the meeting.
   - **Check team progress.** If the group is not working well, address this directly and allow every team member to have a say on their feelings and what they suggest the team does about it, including what they could do better.
   - **Task allocation.** Be clear about who is doing what and by when. Ensure tasks are allocated fairly.
   - **Group roles.** For each meeting decide who will take which role in the meeting. The key roles are: chairperson (forms the agenda, sticks to agenda, ensures members all get a say, sums up main points, keeps focus on agenda item), timekeeper (keeps team to allocated time for each agenda item), record-keeper (keeps notes on who is doing what and by when) and task manager (checks between meetings that team members are doing the agreed tasks).

Being an effective team member

The responsibility for the success of a team lies with each member of the group. If a problem arises, even if it appears the fault of one team member, every person in the group shares the responsibility for sorting out the problem so the group can work effectively to achieve its goal. Below are a number of ways that each team member can help the team to succeed.

- Ensure you have done the tasks agreed to at the team meeting.
- Be open to hearing something new.
- If you don't understand something, ask for more detail.
- Make positive contributions and suggestions to the meetings.
- Contribute openly but don't dominate discussions.
- Check that you know what tasks to do and when.
- Take your fair share of responsibility – don't leave everything to one person.
- Be encouraging (e.g. say things like 'Great idea,' 'I found that interesting,' etc.).

- Ensure everyone has a say and build on other people's ideas.
- If you disagree, explore why (e.g. 'What makes you think that?' 'Have you thought about ...?').
- Indicate when you agree (e.g. 'So do I,' 'Yes, that's true.').
- Admit mistakes.
- Sum things up.

Text reference

Belbin, R.M. (2008) *The Belbin Guide to Succeeding at Work*. Belbin, Suffolk.

Sources for further study

The Belbin Website.
Available: http://www.belbin.com
Last accessed: 23/12/10.

Brainstorming.co.uk.
Available: http://www.brainstorming.co.uk/
Last accessed: 23/12/10.

4 Taking notes from lectures and texts

Choose note-taking methods appropriately – the method you choose to take notes might depend on the subject; the lecturer and their style of delivery; and your own preference.

Note-taking is an essential skill that you will require in many different situations, such as when:

- listening to lectures and seminars;
- attending meetings and tutorials;
- reading texts and research papers;
- attending field and practical sessions;
- finding information on the World Wide Web.

KEY POINT Good performance in assessments and exams is built on effective learning and revision (Chapters 5 and 6). However, both ultimately depend on the quality of your notes.

Compare lecture notes with a colleague – looking at your notes for the same lecture may reveal interesting differences in approach, depth and detail.

Adjusting to the different styles of your lecturers – recognise that different approaches to lecture delivery demand different approaches to note-taking. For example, if a lecturer seems to tell lots of anecdotes or spend much of the time on examples during a lecture, do not switch off – you still need to be listening carefully to recognise the key take-home messages. Similarly, if a lecture includes a section consisting mainly of images, you should still try to take notes – names of organisms, locations, key features, even quick sketches. These will help prompt your memory when revising. Do not be deterred by lecturers' idiosyncrasies; in every case you still need to focus and take useful notes.

Taking notes from lectures

Taking legible and meaningful lecture notes is essential if you are to make sense of them later, but many students find it difficult when starting their university studies. Begin by noting the date, course, topic and lecturer on the first page of each day's notes. Number every page in case they get mixed up later. The most popular way of taking notes is to write in a linear sequence down the page, emphasising the underlying structure via headings, as in Fig. 14.3. However, the 'pattern' and 'mind map' methods (Figs 4.1 and 4.2) have their advocates: experiment, to see which method you prefer.

Whatever technique you use, don't try to take down all the lecturer's words, except when an important definition or example is being given, or when the lecturer has made it clear that he/she is dictating. Listen first, then write. Your goal should be to take down the structure and reasoning behind the lecturer's approach in as few words and phrases as possible. At this stage, follow the lecturer's sequence of delivery. Use headings and leave plenty of space, but don't worry too much about being tidy – it is more important that you get down the appropriate information in a readable form. Use abbreviations to save time. Recognise that you may need to alter your note-taking technique to suit different lecturers' styles.

Make sure you note down references to texts and take special care to ensure accuracy of definitions and numerical examples. If the lecturer repeats or otherwise emphasises a point, highlight (e.g. by underlining) or make a margin note of this – it could come in useful when revising. If there is something you don't understand, ask at the end of the lecture, and make an appointment to discuss the matter if there isn't time to deal with it then. Tutorials may provide an additional forum for discussing course topics.

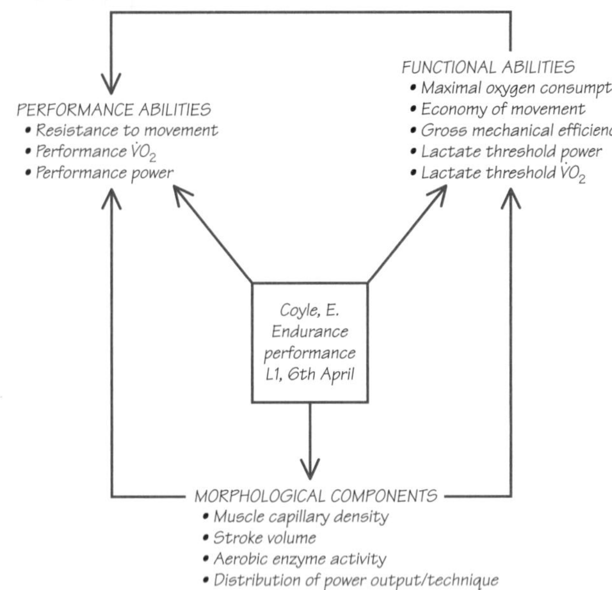

Fig. 4.1 An example of 'pattern' notes, an alternative to the more commonly used 'linear' format. Note the similarity to the 'spider diagram' method of brainstorming ideas (Fig. 14.2).

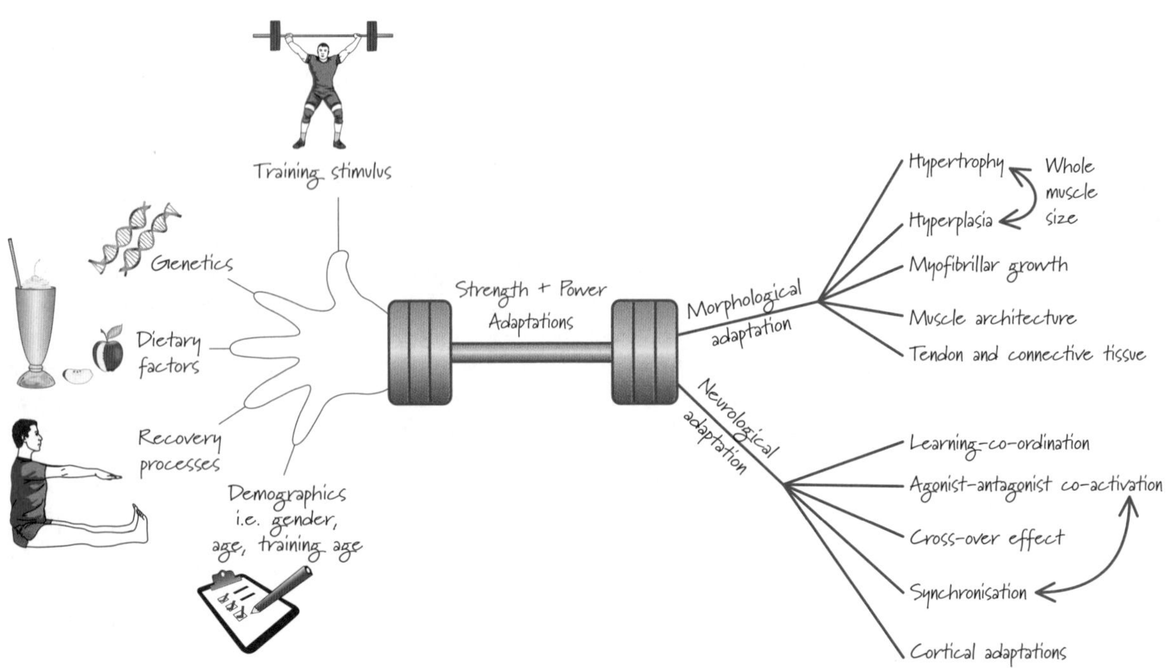

Fig. 4.2 Example of the 'mind map' approach to note-taking and 'brainstorming'. Start at the centre with the overall topic title, adding branches and sub-branches for themes and subsidiary topics. 'Basic' maps consist of a branched hierarchy overwritten with key words (e.g. shaded portion). Connections should be indicated with arrows; numbering and abbreviations are encouraged. To aid recall and creativity, Buzan (2006) recommends use of colour, different fonts, three-dimensional doodles and other forms of emphasis (e.g. non-shaded portion).

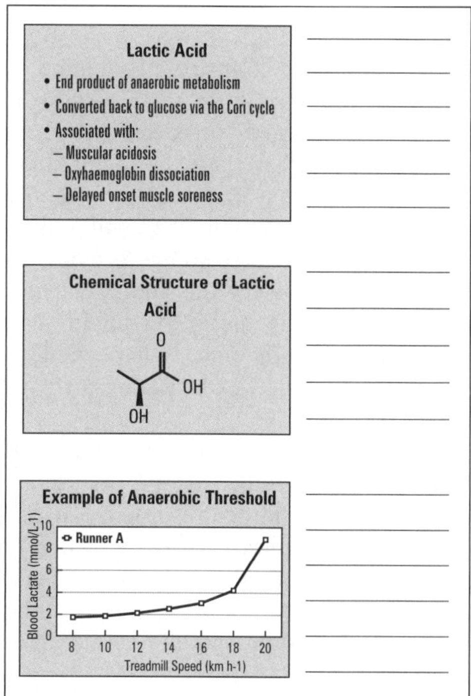

Fig. 4.3 An example of a print-out from PowerPoint in handouts (three slides per page) format.

Lectures delivered by PowerPoint or similar presentation programs

Some students make the mistake of thinking that lectures delivered as computer-based presentations with an accompanying handout or web resource require little or no effort by way of note-taking. While it is true that you may be freed from the need to copy out large diagrams and the basic text may provide structure, you will still need to adapt and add to the lecturer's points. Much of the important detail and crucial emphasis will still be delivered verbally. Furthermore, if you simply listen passively to the lecture, or worse, try to work from the handout alone, it will be far more difficult to understand and remember the content.

If you are not supplied with handouts, you may be able to print out the presentation beforehand, perhaps in the '3 slides per page' format that allows space for notes alongside each slide (Fig. 4.3). Scan through this before the lecture if you can; then, during the presentation, focus on listening to what the lecturer has to say. Note down any extra details, points of emphasis and examples. After lectures, you could also add notes from supplementary reading. The text in presentations can be converted to word processor format if you have access to the electronic file. In PowerPoint, this can be achieved from the *Outline View* option on the *View* menu. You can copy and paste text between programs in the normal fashion, then modify font size and colour as appropriate.

Printing PowerPoint slides – use the 'black and white' option on the print menu to avoid wasting ink on printing coloured backgrounds. If you wish to use colour, remember that slides can be difficult to read if printed in small format. Always print a sample page before printing the whole lecture.

'Making up' your notes

As soon as possible after each lecture, work through your notes, tidying them up and adding detail where necessary. Add emphasis to any headings you have made, so that the structure is clearer. If you feel it would be more logical for your purposes, change the order. Compare your notes with material in a textbook and correct any inconsistencies. Make notes from, or photocopy, any useful material you see in textbooks, ready for revision.

Taking notes from books and journal papers

Scanning and skimming are useful techniques to find sections to read in detail and to make notes from.

Scanning effectively – you need to stay focused on your key words, otherwise you may be distracted by apparently interesting but irrelevant material.

Scanning

This involves searching for relevant content. Useful techniques are to:

- decide on key words relevant to your search;
- check that the book or journal title indicates relevance;
- look through the contents page (either paper titles in a journal volume, or chapter titles in a text);
- look at the index if present.

Spotting sequences – writers often number their points (firstly, secondly, thirdly, etc.) and looking for these words in the text can help you skim it quickly.

Making sure you have all the details – when taking notes from a text or journal paper: (a) always take full details of the source (Chapter 8); (b) if copying word-for-word make sure you indicate this using quotes and take special care to ensure you do not alter the original.

Example Commonly used abbreviations include:

$\exists$	there are, there exist(s)
$\therefore$	therefore
$\because$	because
$\propto$	is proportional to
$\rightarrow$	leads to, into
$\leftarrow$	comes from, from
$\rightarrow\rightarrow$	involves several processes in a sequence
1°, 2°	primary, secondary (etc.)
$\approx$,$\cong$	approximately, roughly equal to
$=$, $\neq$	equals, not equal to
$\equiv$, $\not\equiv$	equivalent, not equivalent to
$<$, $>$	smaller than, bigger than
$\gg$	much bigger than
[X]	concentration of X
$\sum$	sum
Δ	change
f	function
#	number
∞	infinity, infinite

You should also make up your own abbreviations relevant to the context, e.g. if a lecturer is talking about muscle fibres, you could write 'MF' instead.

Skimming

This is a valuable way to gain the maximum amount of information in the minimum amount of time, by reading as little of a text as is required. Essentially, the technique (also termed 'surveying') requires you to look at the structure of the text, rather than the detail. In a sense, you are trying to see the writer's original plan and the purpose behind each part of the text. Look through the whole of the piece first, to gain an overview of its scope and structure. Headings provide an obvious clue to structure, if present. Next, look for the 'topic sentence' in each paragraph (p. 97), which is often the first. You might then decide that the paragraph contains a definition that is important to note, or it may contain examples, so may not be worth reading for your purpose.

When you have found relevant material, note-taking fulfils the vital purpose of helping you to understand and remember the information. If you simply read it, either directly or from a photocopy, you are at risk of accomplishing neither. The act of paraphrasing (using different words to give the same meaning) makes you think about the meaning and express this for yourself. It is an important active learning technique. A popular method of describing skimming and note-taking is called the SQ3R technique (Box 4.1).

KEY POINT Obtaining information and understanding it are distinct parts of the process of learning. As discussed in Chapter 5 (Table 5.1), you must be able to do more than recall facts to succeed.

Methods for finding and evaluating texts and articles are discussed further in Chapters 8 and 9.

Box 4.1 The SQ3R technique for skimming texts

Survey Get a quick overview of the contents of the book or chapter, perhaps by rapidly reading the contents page or headings.

Question Ask yourself what the material covers and how precisely it relates to your study objectives.

Read Now read the text, paying attention to the ways it addresses your key questions.

Recall Recite to yourself what has been stated every few paragraphs. Write notes of this if appropriate, paraphrasing the text rather than copying it.

Review Think about what you have read and/or review your notes as a whole. Consider where it all fits in.

Sources for further study

Anon. *Mind map*. Available: http://en.wikipedia.org/wiki/Mind_mapping. Last accessed: 23/12/10. [An independent review of mind mapping and its history.]

Buzan, T. (2006) *The Ultimate Book of Mind Maps*. Harper Thorsons, New York.

Buzan, T., Morris, S. and Smith, J. (1998) *Understanding Mind Maps . . . in a Week*. Hodder & Stoughton, London.

5 Learning and revising

There are many different ways of learning. At university you have the freedom to choose which approach to study suits you best. You should tackle this responsibility with an open mind, and be prepared to consider new options. Understanding how you learn best and how you are expected to think about your discipline will help you to improve your approach to study and to understand sport and exercise science at a deeper level. Adopting active methods of studying and revision that are suited to your personality can make a significant difference to your performance. Your department will publish material that can help too. Taking account of learning outcomes and marking/assessment criteria, for example, can help you focus your revision.

KEY POINT At university, you are expected to set your own agenda for learning. There will be timetabled activities, assessments and exam deadlines, but it is your responsibility to decide how you will study and learn, how you will manage your time, and, ultimately, what you will gain from the experience. You should be willing to challenge yourself academically to discover your full potential.

Learning styles

Significance of learning styles – no one learning style is 'better' than the others; each has its own strengths and weaknesses. However, since many university exams are conducted using 'reading and writing' modes of communication, you may need to find ways of expressing yourself appropriately using the written word (see Box 5.1).

Learning styles and teaching styles – there may be a mismatch between your preferred learning style and the corresponding teaching style used by your lecturers, in which case you will need to adapt appropriately (see Box 5.1).

We don't all learn in the same way. Your preferred learning style is simply the one that suits you best for receiving, communicating and understanding information. It therefore involves approaches that will help you learn and perform most effectively. There are many different ways of describing learning styles, and you may be introduced to specific schemes during your studies. Although methods and terminology may differ among these approaches, it is important to realise that the important thing is the *process* of analysing your learning style, together with the way that you use the information to modify your approach to studying, rather than the specific type of learner that you may identify yourself to be.

A useful scheme for describing learning styles is the VARK system devised by Fleming (2001). By answering a short online questionnaire, you can 'diagnose' yourself as one of the types shown in Box 5.1, which also summarises important outcomes relating to how information and concepts can be assimilated, learned and expressed. People show different degrees of alignment with these categories, and research indicates that the majority of students are multimodal learners – that is, falling into more than one category – rather than being only in one grouping. By carrying out an analysis like this, you can become more aware of your personal characteristics and think about whether the methods of studying you currently use are those that are best suited to your needs.

KEY POINT Having a particular learning preference or style does not mean that you are automatically skilled in using methods generally suited to that type of learner. You must work at developing your ability to take in information, study and cope with assessment.

Box 5.1 How to diagnose your learning preferences using the VARK learning styles scheme

Visit www.vark-learn.com to carry out the online diagnostic test, reflect on whether it is a fair description of your preferences, and think about whether you might change the way you study to improve your performance. None of the outcomes should be regarded as prescriptive – you should mix techniques as you see fit and only use methods that you feel comfortable adopting. Adapted with permission from material produced by Fleming (2001).

	Outcomes for your learning, studying and exam technique		
Learning style ***Description of learning preferences***	**Advice for taking in information and understanding it**	**Best methods of studying for effective learning**	**Ways to cope with exams so you perform better**
Visual: *You are interested in colour, layout and design. You probably prefer to learn from visual media or books with diagrams and charts. You tend to add doodles and use highlighters on lecture and revision notes and express ideas and concepts as images*	Use media incorporating images, diagrams, flow-charts, etc. When constructing notes, employ underlining, different colours and highlighters. Use symbols as much as you can, rather than words. Leave plenty of white space in your notes. Experiment with the 'mind map' style of note-taking (p. 18)	Use similar methods to those described in column two. Reduce lecture notes to pictures. Try to construct your own images to aid understanding, then test your learning by redrawing these from memory	Plan answers diagrammatically. Recall the images and doodles you used in your notes. Use diagrams in your answers (making sure they are numbered and fully labelled, p. 18). As part of your revision, turn images into words
Aural: *You prefer discussing subjects and probably like to attend tutorials and listen to lecturers, rather than read textbooks. Your lecture notes may be poor because you would rather listen than take notes*	Make sure you attend classes, discussions and tutorials. Note and remember the interesting examples, stories, jokes. Leave spaces in your notes for later recall and 'filling'. Discuss topics with 'study buddy'. Record lectures (with lecturer's permission)	Expand your notes by talking with others and making additional notes from the textbook. Ask others to 'hear' you talk about topics. Read your summarised notes aloud to yourself. Record your vocalised notes and listen to them later	When writing answers, imagine you are talking to an unseen examiner. Speak your answers inside your head. Listen to your voice and write them down. Practise writing answers to old exam questions
Read–write: *You prefer using text in all formats. Your lecture notes are probably good. You tend to like lecturers who use words well and have lots of information in sentences and notes. In note-taking, you may convert diagrams to text and text to bullet points*	Focus on note-taking. You may prefer the 'linear' style of note-taking (p. 18). Use the following in your notes: lists; headings; glossaries and lists of definitions. Expand your notes by adding further information from handouts, textbooks and library reading	Reduce your notes to lists or headings. Write out and read the lists again and again (silently). Turn actions, diagrams, charts and flowcharts into words. Rewrite the ideas and principles into other words. Organise diagrams and graphs into statements, e.g. 'The trend is . . .'	Plan and write out exam answers using remembered lists. Arrange your words into hierarchies and points

(continued)

Box 5.1 Continued

Kinaesthetic: *You tend to recall by remembering real events and lecturers' 'stories'. You probably prefer field excursions and lab work to theory and like lecturers who give real-life examples. Your lecture notes may be weak because the topics did not seem 'concrete' or 'relevant'*	Focus on examples that illustrate principles. Concentrate on applied aspects and hands-on approaches, but try to understand the theoretical principles that underpin them. When taking in information, use all your senses – sight, touch, taste, smell, hearing	Put plenty of examples, pictures and photographs into your notes. Use case studies and applications to help with principles and concepts. Talk through your notes with others. Recall your experience of lectures, tutorials, experiments or field trips	Write practice answers and paragraphs. Recall examples and things you did in the practical sessions or laboratory work. Role-play the exam situation in your own room
Multimodal: *Your preferences fall into two or more of the above categories. You are able to use these different modes as appropriate*	If you are diagnosed as having two dominant preferences or several equally dominant preferences, read the study strategies above that apply to each of these. You may find it necessary to use more than one strategy for learning and communicating, feeling less secure with only one		

Source: Jones, A., Reed, R. and Weyers, J. (2007) pp. 21–2.

Thinking about thinking

The thinking processes that students are expected to carry out can be presented in a sequence, starting with shallower thought processes and ending with deeper processes, each of which builds on the previous level (see Table 5.1). The first two categories in this ladder apply to gaining basic knowledge and understanding, important when you first encounter a topic. Processes three to six are those additionally carried out by high-performing university students, with the latter two being especially relevant to final-year students, researchers and professionals. Naturally, the tutors assessing you will want to reward the deepest thinking appropriate for your level of study. This is often signified by the words they use in assessment tasks and marking criteria (column four, Table 5.1, and p. 102), and, while this is not an exact process, being more aware of this agenda can help you to gain more from your studies and appreciate what is being demanded of you.

Example A set of learning outcomes or objectives taken from an introductory lecture on *The Principles of Test Selection and Administration* might be: After this class, you should be able to:

- Define the following:
  - Test validity
  - Test reliability
  - Test sensitivity.
- Discuss the major factors that a coach, conditioner or sport and exercise scientist needs to consider when selecting a test of an athlete's fitness.
- Design a battery of sequential sport-specific tests for a sporting team of your own choice.
- Justify the selection of each test and the order in which you do the tests.
- Review a battery of tests widely used by elite sporting teams and comment on what modifications may need to be made to ensure their suitability for use at a local team level.

KEY POINT When considering assessment questions, look carefully at words used in the instructions. These cues can help you to identify what depth is expected in your answer. Take special care in multipart questions, because the first part may require lower-level thinking, while in later parts marks may be awarded for evidence of deeper thinking.

The role of assessment and feedback in your learning

Your starting point for assessment should be the learning outcomes or objectives for each module, topic or learning activity. You will usually find them in your subject's handbook. They state in clear terms what your tutors or lecturers expect you to be able to accomplish after participating in each part and reading around the topic. Also of value

Table 5.1 A ladder of thinking processes, moving from shallower thought processes (top of table) to deeper levels of thinking (bottom of table). This table is derived from research by Benjamin Bloom *et al.* (1956) and is still extensively used today by both school and university educators. When considering the cue words in typical question instructions, bear in mind that the precise meaning will always depend on the context. For example, while 'describe' is often associated with relatively simple processes of recall, an instruction like 'describe how the human heart works' demands higher-level understanding. Note also that while a 'cue word' is often given at the start of a question/instruction, this is not universally so.

Thinking processes and description (in approximate order of increasing 'depth')	Example from sport and exercise sciences	Example of typical question structure, with *cue word* highlighted	Other cue words used in question instructions
1. **Knowledge (knowing facts).** If you know information, you can *remember* or *recognise* it. This does not always mean you understand it at a higher level	You might know the major skeletal muscle fibre types but not know the implications of their metabolic characteristics as they apply to athlete conditioning	*Describe* the major skeletal muscle fibre types	• define • list • state • identify
2. **Comprehension.** If you comprehend a fact, you *understand* what it means	You might know the twitch and metabolic characteristics of the major skeletal muscle fibre types	*Explain* the neural, morphological and biochemical characteristics of the major skeletal muscle fibre types	• contrast • compare • distinguish • interpret
3. **Application.** To apply a fact means that you can *put it to use* in a particular context	You might be able to apply the fibre recruitment theory to athlete conditioning	*Suggest* which skeletal muscle fibre types may be used in marathon running and sprint running	• calculate • illustrate • solve • show
4. **Analysis.** To analyse information means that you are able to *break it down into parts* and show how these components *fit together*	You might be able to analyse which skeletal fibre types are most widely used in any position in a football team	Using the fibre recruitment theory, *defend* the use of interval training in elite endurance athletes	• compare • explain • consider • infer
5. **Synthesis.** To synthesise, you need to be able to *extract relevant facts* from a body of knowledge and use these to *address an issue in a novel way* or *create something new*	You might be able to develop a training programme for a sprint runner or marathoner based on the energy system needs and fibre recruitment theory	*Devise* a track training programme for an elite 800 m track runner	• design • integrate • test • create
6. **Evaluation.** If you evaluate information, you *arrive at a judgement* based on its importance relative to the topic being addressed	You might be able to comment on the training programme used by elite sprint cyclists based on their energy system needs and fibre characteristics	*Evaluate* the on-track and resistance training programme of the National Track Cycling team in the lead-up to the London Olympics	• review • assess • consider • justify

Source: Jones, A., Reed, R. and Weyers, J. (2007) p. 23.

will be marking/assessment criteria or grade descriptors, which state in general terms what level of attainment is required for your work to reach specific grades. These are more likely to be defined at faculty/college/school/department level and consequently published in appropriate student handbooks or websites. Reading learning outcomes and grade descriptors will give you a good idea of what to expect and the level of performance required to reach your personal goals. Relate them to both the material covered (e.g. in lectures and practicals, or online) and past exam papers. Doing this as you study and revise will indicate whether further reading and independent studying are required, and of what type. You will also have a much clearer picture of how you are likely to be assessed.

Definitions

Learning outcomes/objectives – statements of the knowledge, understanding or skills that a learner will be able to demonstrate on successful completion of a module, topic or learning activity.

Formative assessments – these may be mid-term or mid-semester tests and are often in the same format as later exams. They are intended to give you feedback on your performance. You should use the results to measure your performance against the work you put in, and to find out, either from grades or tutor's comments, how you could do better in future. If you don't understand the reason for your grade, contact your tutor.

Summative assessments – these include end-of-year or end-of-term or -semester exams. They inform others about the standard of your work. In continuous or 'in-course' assessment, the summative elements are spread out over the course. Sometimes these assessments may involve a formative aspect, if feedback is given.

KEY POINT Use the learning outcomes for your course (normally published in the handbook) as a fundamental part of your revision planning. These indicate what you will be expected to be able to do after taking part in the course, so exam questions are often based on them. Check this by reference to past papers.

There are essentially two types of assessment – formative and summative, although the distinction may not always be clear-cut (see margin). The first way you can learn from formative assessment is to consider the grade you obtained in relation to the work you put in. If this is a disappointment to you, then there must be a mismatch between your understanding of the topic and the marking scheme and that of the marker, or a problem in the writing or presentation of your assignment. This element of feedback is also present in summative assessment.

The second way to learn from formative assessment is through the written feedback and notes on your work. These comments may be cryptic, or scribbled hastily, so if you don't understand or can't read them, ask the tutor who marked the work. Most tutors and lecturers will be pleased to explain how you could have improved your mark. If you find that the same comments appear frequently, it may be a good idea to seek help from your university's academic support unit. Take along examples of your work and feedback comments so they can give you the best possible advice. Another suggestion is to ask to see the work of another student who obtained a good mark, and compare it with your own. This will help you to judge the standard you should be aiming for.

Preparing for revision and examinations

The main purpose of most exams is for lecturers to check that you have understood and know the work covered in the course under controlled conditions where the work is entirely your own.

Before you start revising, find out as much as you can about each exam, including:

- its format and duration;
- the date and location;
- the types of questions;
- whether any questions/sections are compulsory;
- whether you need to take calculators, pencils or erasers into the exam;
- whether the exam is 'open book' and, if so, which texts or notes are allowed.

Time management when revising – this is vital to success and is best achieved by creating a revision timetable (Box 5.2).

Your course tutor or lecturer is likely to give you details of exam structure and timing well beforehand, so that you can plan your revision; the course handbook and past papers (if available) can provide further useful details. Always check that the nature of the exam has not changed before you consult past papers.

Filing lecture notes – make sure your notes are kept neatly and in sequence by using a ring binder system. File the notes in lecture or practical sequence, adding any supplementary notes or photocopies alongside.

Organising and using lecture notes, assignments and practical reports

Given their importance as a source of material for revision, you should have sorted out any deficiencies or omissions in your lecture notes and

Box 5.2 How to prepare and use a revision timetable

1. **Make up a grid showing the number of days until your exams are finished**. Divide each day into several sections. If you like revising in large blocks of time, use am, pm and evening slots, but if you prefer shorter periods, divide each of these in two, or use hourly divisions.
2. **Write in your non-revision commitments**, including any time off you plan to allocate and physical activity at frequent intervals. Try to have about a third or a quarter of the time off in any one day. Plan this in relation to your best times for useful work – for example, some people work best in the mornings, while others prefer evenings. If you wish, use a system where your relaxation time is a bonus to be worked for; this may help you motivate yourself.
3. **Decide on how you wish to subdivide your subjects** for revision purposes. This might be among subjects, according to difficulty (with the hardest getting the most time), or within subjects, according to topics. Make sure there is an adequate balance of time among topics and especially that you do not avoid working on the subject(s) you find least interesting or most difficult.
4. **Allocate the work to the different slots available on your timetable**. You should work backwards from the exams, making sure that you cover every exam topic adequately in the period just before each exam. You may wish to colour-code the subjects.
5. **As you revise, mark off the slots completed** – this has a positive psychological effect and will boost your self-confidence.
6. **After the exams, revisit your timetable** and decide whether you would do anything differently next time.

Using tutors' or lecturers' feedback – it is always worth reading any comments on your work as soon as it is returned. If you don't understand the comments, or are unsure about why you might have lost marks in an assignment, ask for an explanation.

practical reports at an early stage. For example, you may have missed a lecture or practical due to illness, sporting commitments, injury, etc., but the exam is likely to assume attendance throughout the year. Make sure you attend classes whenever possible and keep your notes up to date. Your practical reports and any assignment work will contain specific comments from the teaching staff, indicating where marks were lost, corrections, mistakes, inadequacies, etc. Most lecturers are quite happy to discuss such details with students on a one-to-one basis and this information may provide you with 'clues' to the expectations of individual lecturers that may be useful in exams set by the same members of staff. However, you should never 'fish' for specific information on possible exam questions, as this is likely to be counterproductive.

Revision

Recognise when your concentration powers are dwindling – take a short break when this happens and return to work refreshed and ready to learn. Remember that 20 minutes is often quoted as a typical limit to full concentration effort.

Begin early, to avoid last-minute panic. Start in earnest several weeks beforehand, and plan your work carefully:

- **Prepare a revision timetable** – an 'action plan' that gives details of specific topics to be covered (Box 5.2). Find out at an early stage when (and where) your examinations are to be held, and plan your revision around this. Try to keep to your timetable. Time management during this period is as important as keeping to time during the exam itself.
- **Study the learning outcomes/objectives for each topic** (usually published in the course handbook) to get an idea of what lecturers expect from you.
- **Use past papers as a guide** to the form of exam and the type of question likely to be asked (Box 5.3).

Box 5.3 How to use past exam papers in your revision

Past exam papers are a valuable resource for targeting your revision.

1. **Find out where the past exam papers are kept.** Copies may be lodged in your department or the library; or they may be accessible online.
2. **Locate and copy relevant papers for your module(s).** Check with your tutor, lecturer or course handbook that the style of paper will not change for the next set of examinations.
3. **Analyse the design of the exam paper.** Taking into account the length in weeks of your module, and the different lecturers and/or topics for those weeks, note any patterns that emerge. For example, can you translate weeks of lectures/practicals into numbers of questions or sections of the paper? Consider how this might affect your revision plans and exam tactics, taking into account (a) any choices or restrictions offered in the paper, and (b) the different types of questions asked (i.e. multiple choice, short-answer or essay).
4. **Examine carefully the style of questions.** Can you identify the expectations of your lecturers? Can you relate the questions to the learning objectives? How much extra reading do they seem to expect? Are the questions fact-based? Do they require a synthesis based on other knowledge? Can you identify different styles for different lecturers? Consider how the answers to these questions might affect your revision effort and exam strategy.
5. **Practise answering questions.** Perhaps with friends, set up your own mock exam when you have done a fair amount of revision, but not too close to the exams. Use a relevant past exam paper; don't study it beforehand! You need not attempt all of the paper at one sitting. You'll need a quiet room in a place where you will not be interrupted (e.g. a library). Keep close track of time during the mock exam and try to do each question in the length of time you would normally assign to it (see p. 33) – this gives you a feel for the speed of thought and writing required and the scope of answer possible. Mark each other's papers and discuss how each of you interpreted the question and laid out your answers and your individual marking schemes.
6. **Practise writing answer plans and starting answers.** This can save time compared with the 'mock exam' approach. Practice in starting answers can help you get over stalling at the start and wasting valuable time. Writing essay plans gets you used to organising your thoughts quickly and putting your thoughts into a logical sequence.

- **Remember to have several short (five-minute) breaks** during each hour of revision and a longer break every few hours. In any day, try to work for a maximum of three-quarters of the time.
- **Include recreation within your schedule:** there is little point in tiring yourself with too much revision, as this is unlikely to be profitable.
- **Make your revision as active and interesting as possible** (see below): the least productive approach is simply to read and reread your notes.
- **Ease back on the revision near the exam:** plan your revision to avoid last-minute cramming and overload fatigue.

Active revision

Aiding recall through effective note-taking – the mind map technique (p. 18), when used to organise ideas, is claimed to enhance recall by connecting the material to visual images or linking it to the physical senses.

The following techniques may prove useful in devising an active revision strategy:

- **'Distil' your lecture notes to show the main headings and examples.** Prepare revision sheets with details for a particular topic on a single sheet of paper, arranged as a numbered checklist. Wall posters are another useful revision aid.
- **Confirm that you know about the material by testing yourself** – take a blank sheet of paper and write down all you know. Check your full

notes to see if you missed anything out. If you did, go back immediately to a fresh blank sheet and redo the example. Repeat, as required.

- **Memorise definitions and key phrases:** definitions can be a useful starting point for many exam answers. Make lists of relevant facts or definitions associated with particular topics. Test yourself repeatedly on these, or get a friend to do this. Try to remember *how many* facts or definitions you need to know in each case – this will help you recall them all during the exam.
- **Use mnemonics and acronyms** to commit specific factual information to memory. Sometimes, the dafter they are, the better they seem to work.
- **Use pattern diagrams or mind maps** as a means of testing your powers of recall on a particular topic (pp. 18).
- **Draw diagrams from memory:** make sure you can label them fully.
- **Try recitation as an alternative to written recall.** Talk about your topic to another person, preferably someone in your class. Talk to yourself if necessary. Explaining something out loud is an excellent test of your understanding.
- **Associate facts with images** or journeys if you find this method works.
- **Use a wide variety of approaches** to avoid boredom during revision (e.g. record information on audio tape, use cartoons, or any other method, as long as it's not just reading).
- **Form a revision group** to share ideas and discuss topics with other students.
- **Prepare answers to past papers**, e.g. write essays or, if time is limited, write essay plans (see Box 5.3).
- **Work through representative problems** if your subject involves numerical calculations.
- **Make up your own questions:** the act of putting yourself in the examiner's mindset by inventing questions can help revision. However, you should not rely on 'question-spotting': this is a risky practice!

The evening before your exam should be spent in consolidating your material, and checking through summary lists and plans. Avoid introducing new material at this late stage: your aim should be to boost your confidence, putting yourself in the right frame of mind for the exam itself.

Question-spotting – avoid adopting this risky strategy to reduce the amount of time you spend revising. Lecturers are aware that this approach may be taken and try to ask questions in an unpredictable manner. You may find that you are unable to answer on unexpected topics that you failed to revise. Moreover, if you have a preconceived idea about what will be asked, you may also fail to grasp the nuances of the exact question set, and provide a response lacking in relevance.

Revision checks – it is important to test yourself frequently during revision, to ensure that you have retained the information you are revising.

Final preparations – try to get a good night's sleep before an exam. Last-minute cramming will be counter-productive if you are too tired during the exam.

Text references

Bloom, B., Englehart, M., Furst, E., Hill, W. and Krathwohl, D. (1956) *Taxonomy of Educational Objectives: The Classification of Educational Goals. Handbook I: Cognitive Domain.* Longmans, Green, New York and Toronto.

Fleming, N.D. (2001) *Teaching and Learning Styles: VARK Strategies.* Neil Fleming, Christchurch.

Fleming, N.D. *VARK: A Guide to Learning Styles.* Available: http://www.vark-learn.com/ Last accessed: 23/12/10.

Sources for further study

Hamilton, D. (2003) *Passing Exams: A Guide for Maximum Success and Minimum Stress.* Continuum, London.

Tracey, E. (2002) *The Student's Guide to Exam Success.* Open University Press, Buckingham.

Many universities host study skills websites; these can be found using 'study skills', 'revision' or 'exams' as key words in a search engine.

6 Curriculum options, assessment and exams

Definition

Transcript – this is your record of achievement at university. Normally it will consist of details of each module or course you have taken, and an indication of the grade or mark achieved. It will also show your final (honours) classification – that is: first class, upper second class (2.1), lower second class (2.2), third class or unclassified (some UK universities do not differentiate second class degrees).

Many universities adopt a modular system for their sport and exercise science degree courses. This allows greater flexibility in subject choice and accommodates students studying on different degree paths. Modules also break a subject into discrete, easily assimilated elements. They have the advantage of spreading assessments over the academic year, but they can also tempt you to avoid certain difficult subjects or to feel that you can forget about a topic once the module is finished.

KEY POINT You should select your modules with care, mindful of potential degree options and how your transcript and CV will appear to a prospective employer. If you feel you need advice, consult your personal tutor or study adviser.

Aiming high – your goal should be to perform at your highest possible level and not simply to fulfil the minimum criteria for progression. This will lay sound foundations for your later studies. Remember too that a future employer might ask to see your academic transcript, which will detail all your module grades, including any fails/resits, and will not just state your final degree classification.

As you move between levels of the university system, you will be expected to have passed a certain number of modules, as detailed in the progression criteria. These may be expressed using a credit point system. Students are normally allowed two attempts at each module exam and the resits often take place at the end of the summer vacation. If a student does not pass at the second attempt, they may be asked to 'carry' the subject in a subsequent year, and in severe cases of multiple failure, they may be asked to retake the whole year or even leave the course. Consequently, it is worth finding out about these aspects of your degree. They are usually published in relevant handbooks.

You are unlikely to have reached this stage in your education without being exposed to the examination process. You may not enjoy being assessed, but you probably want to do well in your course. It is therefore important to understand why and how you are being tested. Identifying and improving the skills required for exam success will allow you to perform to the best of your ability.

Assessed coursework

Avoiding plagiarism – this is a key issue for assessed coursework – see p. 56 for a definition and Chapter 8 for appropriate methods of referring to the ideas and results of others using citation.

There is a component of assessed coursework in many modules. This often tests specific skills, and may require you to demonstrate thinking at deeper levels (see Table 5.1). The common types of coursework assessment are covered at various points in this book:

- practical exercises (throughout);
- essays (Chapters 14 and 15);
- numerical problems;
- data analysis (Chapters 49–51);
- poster and spoken presentations (Chapters 16 and 17);
- fieldwork (Chapter 41);
- literature surveys and reviews (Chapter 15);
- project work (Chapter 22);
- problem-based learning (Box 6.1).

At the start of each year or module, read the course handbook or module guide carefully to find out when any assessed work needs to be submitted.

Box 6.1 Problem-based learning (PBL)

In this relatively new teaching method, you are presented with a 'real-world' problem or issue, often working within a team. As you tackle the problem, you will gain factual knowledge, develop skills and exercise critical thinking. Because there is a direct and relevant context for your work, and because you have to employ active learning techniques, the knowledge and skills you gain are likely to be more readily assimilated and remembered. This approach also more closely mimics workplace practices. PBL usually proceeds as follows:

1. **You are presented with a problem** (e.g. a case study, a hypothetical patient, a topical issue).
2. **You consider what issues and topics you need to research**, by discussion with others if necessary. You may need to identify where relevant resources can be found (Chapters 8 and 9).
3. **You then need to rank the issues and topics in importance**, allocating tasks to group members, if appropriate.
4. **Having carried out the necessary research, you should review what information has been obtained.** As a result, new issues may need to be explored and, where appropriate, allocated to group members.
5. **You will be asked to produce an outcome, such as a report, diagnosis, seminar presentation or poster.** An outline structure will be required, and for groups, further allocation of tasks to accomplish this goal.

If asked to carry out PBL as part of your course, it is important to get off to a good start. At first, the problem may seem unfamiliar. However, once you become involved in the work, you will quickly gain confidence. If working as part of a group, make sure that your group meets as early as possible, that you attend all sessions and that you do the necessary background reading. When working in a team, a degree of self-awareness is necessary regarding your 'natural' role in group situations (Table 3.2). Various methods are used for assessing PBL, and the assessment may involve peer marking.

Note relevant dates in your diary, and use this information to plan your work. Take special note if deadlines for different modules clash, or if they coincide with sporting or social commitments.

KEY POINT If, for some valid reason (e.g. illness), you will be late to hand in an assessment, speak to your tutors as soon as possible. They may be able to take extenuating circumstances into account by not applying a marking penalty. They will let you know what paperwork you may require to submit to support your claim.

Summative exams – general points

Summative exams normally involve you answering questions without being able to consult other students or your notes. Invigilators are present to ensure appropriate conduct, but departmental representatives may be present for some of the exam. Their role is to sort out any subject-related problems, so if you think something is wrong, ask at the earliest opportunity. It is not unknown for parts of questions to be omitted in error, or for double meanings to arise, for example.

Planning

When preparing for an exam, make a checklist of the items you'll need (see p. 37). On the day of the exam, give yourself sufficient time to arrive at the correct room, without the risk of being late. Double-check the times and places of your exams, both well before the exam and also on arrival. If you arrive at the exam venue early, you can always rectify a mistake if you find you've gone to the wrong place.

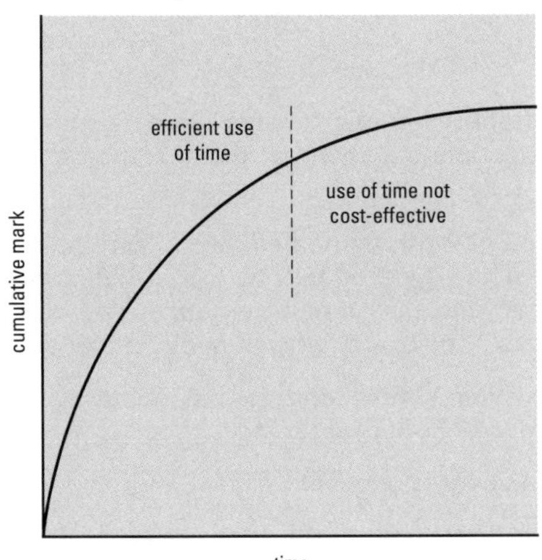

Fig. 6.1 Exam marks as a function of time. The marks awarded in a single answer will follow the law of diminishing returns – it will be far more difficult to achieve the final 25% of the available marks than the initial 25%. Do not spend too long on any one question.

Source: Jones, A., Reed, R. and Weyers, J. (2007) p. 31.

Using the question paper – unless this is specifically forbidden, you should write on the question paper to plan your strategy, keep to time and organise answers.

Tackling the paper

Begin by reading the instructions at the top of the exam paper carefully, so that you do not make any errors based on lack of understanding of the exam structure. Make sure that you know:

- how many questions are set;
- how many must be answered;
- whether the paper is divided into sections;
- whether any parts are compulsory;
- what each question/section is worth, as a proportion of the total mark;
- whether different questions should be answered in different books.

Do not be tempted to spend too long on any one question or section: the return in terms of marks will not justify the loss of time from other questions (see Fig. 6.1). Take the first 10 minutes or so to read the paper and plan your strategy, before you begin writing. Do not be put off by those who begin immediately; it is almost certain that they are producing unplanned work of a poor standard.

Underline the key phrases in the instructions, to reinforce their message. Next, read through the set of questions. If there is a choice, decide on those questions to be answered and decide on the order in which you will tackle them. Prepare a timetable which takes into account the amount of time required to complete each section and which reflects the allocation of marks – there is little point in spending one-quarter of the exam period on a question worth only 5% of the total marks. Use the exam paper to mark the sequence in which the questions will be answered and write the finishing times alongside; refer to this timetable during the exam to keep yourself on course.

Reviewing your answers

At the end of the exam, you should allow at least 10 minutes to read through your script, to check for:

- errors of fact;
- missing information;
- grammatical and spelling errors;
- errors of scale and units;
- errors in calculations.

Make sure your name and/or ID number is on each exam book as required and on all other sheets of paper, including graph paper, even if securely attached to your script, as it is in your interest to ensure that your work does not go astray.

KEY POINT Never leave any exam early. Most exams assess work carried out over several months in a time period of two to three hours and there is always something constructive you can do with the remaining time to improve your script.

Box 6.2 Writing under exam conditions

Always go into an exam with a strategy for managing the available time.

- **Allocate some time (say 5% of the total) to consider which questions to answer and in which order.**
- **Share the rest of the time among the questions, according to the marks available.** Aim to optimise the marks obtained. A potentially good answer should be allocated slightly more time than one you don't feel so happy about. However, don't concentrate on any one answer (see Fig. 6.1).
- **For each question divide the time into planning, writing and revision phases** (see p. 32).

Employ time-saving techniques as much as possible.

- **Use spider diagrams** (Fig. 14.2) **or mind maps** (Fig. 4.2) to organise and plan your answer.
- **Use diagrams and tables** to save time in making difficult and lengthy explanations, but make sure you refer to each one in the text.
- **Use standard abbreviations** to save time repeating text but always explain them at the first point of use.
- **Consider speed of writing and neatness** – especially when selecting the type of pen to use – ballpoint pens are fastest, but they tend to smudge. You can only gain marks if the examiner can read your script.
- **Keep your answer simple and to the point**, with clear explanations of your reasoning.

Make sure your answer is relevant.

- **Don't include irrelevant facts** just because you memorised them during revision, as this may do you more harm than good. You must answer the specific question that has been set.
- **Time taken to write irrelevant material is time lost from another question.**

Special considerations for different types of exam question

Essay questions

Essay questions let examiners test the depth of your comprehension and understanding as well as your recall of facts. Essay questions give you plenty of scope to show what you know. They suit those with a good grasp of principles but who perhaps have less ability to recall details.

Before you tackle a particular question, you must be sure of what is required in your answer. Ask yourself 'What is the examiner looking for in this particular question?' and then set about providing a *relevant* answer. Consider each individual word in the question and highlight, underline or circle the key words. Make sure you know the meaning of the terms given in Table 15.1 (p. 102) so that you can provide the appropriate information, where necessary. Spend some time planning your writing (see Chapter 14). Refer back to the question frequently as you write, to confirm that you are keeping to the subject matter. Box 6.2 gives advice on writing essays under exam conditions.

It is usually a good idea to begin with the question that you are most confident about. This will reassure you before tackling more difficult parts of the paper. If you run out of time, write in note form. Examiners are usually understanding, as long as the main components of the question have been addressed and the intended structure of the answer is clear. Common reasons for poor exam answers in essay-style questions are listed in Box 6.3.

Adopting different tactics according to the exam – you should adjust your exam strategy (and revision methods) to allow for the differences in question types used in each exam paper.

Penalties for guessing – if there is a penalty for incorrect answers in a multiple-choice test, the best strategy is not to answer questions when you know your answer is a complete guess. Depending on the penalty, it may be beneficial to guess if you can narrow the choice down to two options (but beware false or irrelevant alternatives). However, if there are no such penalties, then you should provide an answer to all questions.

Multiple-choice and short-answer questions

Multiple-choice questions (MCQs) and short-answer questions (SAQs) are generally used to test the breadth and detail of your knowledge. The

Box 6.3 Reasons for poor exam answers to essay-style questions

The following are reasons that lecturers cite when they give low marks for essay answers:

- **Not answering the exact question set**. Either failing to recognise the specialist terms used in the question, or failing to demonstrate an understanding of the terms by not providing definitions, or failing to carry out the precise instruction in a question, or failing to address all aspects of the question.
- **Running out of time**. Failing to match the time allocated to the extent of the answer. Frequently, this results in spending too long on one question and not enough on the others, or even failing to complete the paper.
- **Failing to answer all parts** of a multiple-part question, or to recognise that one part (perhaps involving more complex ideas) may carry more marks than another.
- **Failing to provide evidence** to support an answer. Forgetting to state the 'obvious' – either basic facts or definitions.
- **Failing to illustrate an answer appropriately**, either by not including a relevant diagram, or by providing a diagram that does not aid communication, or by not including examples.
- **Incomplete answer(s)**. Failing to answer appropriately owing to lack of knowledge.
- **Providing irrelevant evidence** to support an answer. 'Waffling' to fill space.
- **Illegible handwriting.**
- **Poor English**, such that facts and ideas are not expressed clearly.
- **Lack of logic** or structure to the answer.
- **Factual errors**, indicating poor note-taking or poor revision or poor recall.
- **Failing to correct obvious mistakes** by rereading an answer before submitting the script.

At higher levels, the following aspects are especially important:

- **Not providing enough in-depth information.**
- **Providing a descriptive rather than an analytical answer** – focusing on facts, rather than deeper aspects of a topic.
- **Not setting a problem in context**, or not demonstrating a wider understanding of the topic. (However, make sure you don't overdo this, or you may risk not answering the question set).
- **Not giving enough evidence of reading around the subject**. This can be demonstrated, for example, by quoting relevant papers and reviews and by giving author names and dates of publication.
- **Not considering both sides of a topic/debate, or not arriving at a conclusion if you have done so.**

various styles that can be encompassed within the SAQ format allow for more demanding questions than MCQs, which may emphasise specific factual knowledge.

A good approach for MCQ papers is as follows:

1. **First trawl:** read through the questions fairly rapidly, noting the 'correct' answer in those you can attempt immediately, perhaps in pencil.
2. **Second trawl:** go through the paper again, checking your original answers and this time marking up the answer sheet properly.
3. **Third trawl:** now tackle the difficult questions and those that require longer to answer (e.g. those based on numerical problems).

One reason for adopting this three-phase approach is that you may be prompted to recall facts relevant to questions looked at earlier. You can also spend more time per question on the difficult ones.

When unsure of an answer, the first stage is to rule out options that are clearly absurd or have obviously been placed there to distract you. Next, looking at the remaining options, can you judge between contrasting pairs with alternative answers? Logically, both cannot be correct, so you should see if you can rule one of the pair out. Watch out, however, in

Answer the question as requested – This is true for all questions, but especially important for SAQs. If the question asks for a diagram, make sure you provide one; if it asks for *n* aspects of a topic, try to list this number of points; if there are two or more parts, provide appropriate answers to all aspects. This may seem obvious, but many marks are lost for not following instructions.

Example These are the principal types of question you are likely to encounter in a practical or information-processing exam:

- **Practical skills** Often based on work carried out during your course. Test practical competency and specific techniques (e.g. calibration procedures; blood collection).
- **'Spot' tests** Short questions requiring an identification, comparison or brief descriptive notes on a specific item (e.g. health screening or training programme design). Test knowledge of seen material or ability to transfer this to a new example.
- **Calculations** May include working out of test results from raw data and statistical exercises. Test numeracy.
- **Data analyses** May include the preparation and interpretation of graphs and numerical information, from data either obtained during the exam or provided by the examiner. Test problem-solving skills.
- **Drawing specimens** May include the drawing of anatomical models or systems for which accurate representation and labelling will be important. Tests drawing and interpretation abilities.
- **Practical demonstration** May include the demonstration of practical exercises learnt during courses (e.g. backsquats, plyometric exercises). Tests technical competency and knowledge.

case *both* may be irrelevant to the answer. If the question involves a calculation, try to do this independently from the answers, so you are not influenced by them.

In SAQ papers, there may be a choice of questions. Choose your options carefully – it may be better to gain half marks for a correct answer to half a question, than to provide a largely irrelevant answer that apparently covers the whole question but lacks the necessary detail. For this form of question, few, if any, marks are given for writing style. Think in 'bullet point' mode and list the crucial points only. The time for answering SAQ questions may be tight, so get down to work fast, starting with answers that demand remembered facts. Stick to your timetable by moving on to the next question as soon as possible. Strategically, it is probably better to get part-marks for the full number of questions than good marks for only a few.

Practical and information-processing exams

The prospect of a practical or information-processing exam in exercise science may cause you more concern than a theory exam. This may be because of a limited experience of practical examinations, or due to the fact that practical and observational skills are tests, as well as recall, description and analysis of factual information. Your first thoughts may be that it is not possible to prepare for such exams, but, in fact, you can improve your performance by mastering the various practical techniques described in this book.

The practical exam should only cover the material that was undertaken during any practical or tutorial sessions. Typically in exercise science, a practical exam will be divided between written questions and physical demonstrations of practical skills or techniques owing to the wide range of practical skills required by exercise scientists. You will need to prepare appropriately for both written and physical components. In all aspects, the preparation for a practical exam should be similar to that of other exams. Make sure that you are familiar with all of the practical exercises, including any skills shared within group work during class (as practical exams are assessed on an individual basis). Importantly, check with the teaching staff to see whether you can be given access to the laboratory or equipment to complete any exercises that you have missed, or skills that you wish to revise. If necessary, revise and study important normative values for physical measures, technical cues and common errors that the teaching staff have commented on during class. During the term, try to write down such points during class (see Chapter 4).

During the practical exam, there will typically be stations that you will move around to complete the practical exercises within a specified time limit. During each component, focus on the practical exercise that is required at that station to maximise the use of the allocated time until you are satisfied with your answer and have double-checked it. It is no use worrying about or focusing on the station that you have just moved on from as, normally, you can't go back to repeat and correct your answer. If you are confident that you have finished the required task and have time remaining, it may be beneficial to start to prepare for the next station. This may be in terms of preparing the required equipment, remembering technical cues or normative values. If any calculations are required, make sure that you set them out in full so that partial credit may be given, even if the final answer is incorrect.

Terminology – the oral exams are sometimes known simply as 'orals' or, borrowing Latin, as '*viva voces*' (by or with the living voice) or '*vivas*'.

Allow yourself to relax in oral exams – external examiners are experienced at putting students at ease. They will start by asking 'simple-to-answer' questions, such as what modules you did, how your project research went, and what your career aspirations are. Imagine the external examiner as a friend rather than a foe.

Creating an exam action list – knowing that you have prepared well, checked everything on your list and gathered together all you need for an exam will improve your confidence and reduce anxiety. Your list might include:

- Verify time, date and place of the exam.
- Confirm travel arrangements to exam hall.
- Double-check module handbooks and past papers for exam structure.
- Think through use of time and exam strategy.
- Identify a quiet place near the exam hall to carry out a last-minute check on key knowledge (e.g. formulae, definitions, diagram labels).
- Ensure you have all the items you wish to take to the exam, e.g.
  - pens, pencils (with sharpener and eraser);
  - ruler;
  - correction fluid;
  - calculator (allowable type);
  - sweets and drink, if allowed;
  - tissues;
  - watch or clock;
  - ID card;
  - texts and/or notes, if an open book exam;
  - mascot.
- Lay out clothes (if exam is early in the morning).
- Set alarm and/or ask a friend or family member to check you are awake on time.

Oral exams and interviews

An oral interview is sometimes a part of final degree exams, representing a chance for the external examiner(s) to get to know the students personally and to test their abilities directly and interactively. In some departments, orals are used to validate the exam standard, or to test students on the borderline between exam grades. Sometimes an interview may form part of an assessment, as with project work or posters. This type of exam is often intimidating – many students say they don't know how to revise for an oral – and many candidates worry that they will be so nervous they won't be able to do themselves justice.

Preparation is just as important for orals as it is for written exams:

- **Think about your earlier performances** – if the oral follows written papers, it may be that you will be asked about questions you did not do so well on. These topics should be revised thoroughly. Be prepared to say how you would approach the questions if given a second chance.
- **Read up a little about the examiner** – he or she may focus their questions in their area of expertise.
- **Get used to giving spoken answers** – it is often difficult to transfer between written and spoken modes. Write down a few questions and get a friend to ask you them, possibly with unscripted follow-up queries.
- **Research and think about topical issues in your subject area** – some examiners will feel this reflects how interested you are in your subject.

Your conduct during the oral exam is important, too:

- **Arrive promptly and wear reasonably smart clothing.** Not to do either might be considered disrespectful by the examiner.
- **Take your time before answering questions.** Even if you think you know the answer immediately, take a while to check mentally whether you have considered all angles. A considered, logical approach will be more impressive than a quick but ill-considered response.
- **Start answers with the basics, then develop into deeper aspects.** There may be both surface and deeper aspects to a topic, and more credit will be given to students who mention the latter.
- **When your answer is finished, stop speaking.** A short, crisp answer is better than a rambling one.
- **If you don't know the answer, say so.** To waffle and talk about irrelevant material is more damaging than admitting that you don't know.
- **Make sure your answer is balanced.** Talk about the evidence and opinions on both sides of a contentious issue.
- **Don't disagree strongly with the examiner.** Politely put your point of view, detailing the evidence behind it. Examiners will be impressed by students who know their own mind and subject area. However, they will expect you to support a position at odds with the conventional viewpoint.
- **Finally, be positive and enthusiastic about your topic.**

Box 6.4 Strategies for combating the symptoms of exam anxiety

Sleeplessness – this is commonplace and does little harm in the short term. Get up, have a snack, do some light reading or other activity, then return to bed. Avoid caffeine (e.g. tea, coffee and cola) for several hours before going to bed.

Lack of appetite – again commonplace. Eat what you can, but take sugary sweets into the exam to keep energy levels up in case you become tired.

Fear of the unknown – it can be a good idea to visit the exam room beforehand, so you can become familiar with the location. By working through the points given in the exam action list on p. 37 you will be confident that nothing has been left out.

Worries about timekeeping – get a reliable alarm clock or a new battery for an old one. Arrange for an alarm phone call. Ask a friend or relative to make sure you are awake on time. Make reliable travel arrangements, to arrive on time. If your exam is early in the morning, it may be a good idea to get up early for a few days beforehand.

Blind panic during an exam – explain how you feel to an invigilator. Ask to go for a supervised walk outside. Do some relaxation exercises (see below), then return to your work. If you are having problems with a specific question, it may be appropriate to speak to the departmental representative at the exam.

Feeling tense – shut your eyes, take several slow, deep breaths, do some stretching and relaxing muscle movements. During exams, it may be a good idea to do this between questions, and possibly to have a complete rest for a minute or so. Prior to exams, try some exercise activity or escape temporarily from your worries by watching TV or a movie.

Running out of time – don't panic when the invigilator says 'five minutes left'. It is amazing how much you can write in this time. Write note-style answers or state the areas you would have covered: you may get some credit.

Counteracting anxiety before and during exams

Adverse effects of anxiety need to be overcome by anticipation and preparation well in advance (Box 6.4). Exams, with their tight time limits, are especially stressful for perfectionists. To counteract this tendency, focus on the following points during the exam:

- Don't expect to produce a perfect essay – this won't be possible in the time available.
- Don't spend too long planning your answer – once you have an outline plan, get started.
- Don't spend too much time on the initial parts of an answer, at the expense of the main message.
- Concentrate on getting all of the basic points across – markers are looking for the main points first, before allocating extra marks for the detail.
- Don't be obsessed with neatness, either in handwriting, or in the diagrams you draw, but make sure your answers are legible.
- Don't worry if you forget something. You can't be expected to know everything. Most marking schemes give a first class grade to work that misses out on up to 30% of the marks available.

After the exam – try to avoid becoming involved in prolonged analyses with other students over the 'ideal' answers to the questions; after all, it is too late to change anything at this stage. Go for a walk, watch TV for a while, or do something else that helps you relax, so that you are ready to face the next exam with confidence.

KEY POINT Everyone worries about exams. Anxiety is a perfectly natural feeling. It works to your advantage, as it helps to provide motivation and the adrenaline that can help you 'raise your game' on the day.

There is a lot to be said for treating exams as a game. After all, they are artificial situations contrived to ensure that large numbers of candidates can be assessed together, with little risk of cheating. They have conventions and rules, just like games. If you understand the rationale behind them and follow the rules, this will aid your performance.

Sources for further study

Acres, D. (1998) *How to Pass Exams Without Anxiety: How to get Organised, Be Prepared and Feel Confident of Success.* How To Books, London.

Burns, R. (1997) *The Student's Guide to Passing Exams.* Kogan Page, London.

Hamilton, D. (1999) *Passing Exams: A Guide for Maximum Success and Minimum Stress.* Cassell, London.

Many universities host study skills websites; these can be found using 'study skills', 'revision' or 'exams' as key words in a search engine.

7 Preparing your curriculum vitae or résumé

The terms résumé and curriculum vitae (CV) (Latin for 'the course your life has taken') are sometimes used interchangeably. However, a résumé should be a convincing brief introduction and summary of your skills and experience with respect to a specific field, industry or job vacancy. Conversely, a CV is an in-depth record of your academic performance and credentials, as well as your accomplishments to date. In summary, your CV is your 'master résumé' that you update continuously throughout your career development. Your résumé is a more succinct document that modifies and summarises your CV to emphasise the key elements relative to a position you apply for.

Many students only think about their CV immediately before applying for a job. Reflecting this, chapters on preparing a CV are usually placed near the end of texts of this type. Putting the chapter near the beginning of this book emphasises the importance of focusing your thoughts on your CV at an early stage in your studies. There are four main reasons why this can be valuable:

1. Considering your CV and how it will look to a future employer will help you to think more deeply about the direction and value of your academic studies.
2. Creating a draft CV will prompt you to assess your skills and personal qualities and how these fit into your career aspirations.
3. Your CV can be used as a record of all the relevant things you have done at university and then, later, will help you to communicate these to a potential employer.
4. Your developing CV can be used when you apply for vacation or part-time employment.

KEY POINT Developing your skills and qualities needs to be treated as a long-term project. It makes sense to think early about your career aspirations so that you can make the most of opportunities to build up relevant experience. A good focus for such thoughts is your developing curriculum vitae, so it is useful to work on this from a very early stage.

Skills and personal qualities

Skills (sometimes called competences) are generally what you have learned to do and have improved with practice. Table 1.1 summarises some important skills for sport and exercise scientists. This list might seem quite daunting, but your lecturers and tutors will have designed your courses to give you plenty of opportunities for developing your expertise. Personal qualities, on the other hand, are predominately innate. Examples include honesty, determination and thoroughness (Table 7.1). These qualities need not remain static, however, and can be developed or changed according to your experiences. By consciously deciding to take on new challenges and responsibilities, not only can you develop your personal qualities, but you can also provide supporting evidence for your CV.

Definitions

Curriculum vitae (CV) – is a *complete* history of your education, professional and personal history, job qualifications and skills.

Résumé – a *brief* written document that lists your work experience, skills, qualifications and educational background, often submitted with an employment application.

Table 7.1 Some positive personal qualities

Adaptability
Conscientiousness
Curiosity
Determination
Drive
Energy
Enthusiasm
Fitness and health
Flexible approach
Honesty
Innovation
Integrity
Leadership
Logical approach
Motivation
Patience
Performance under stress
Perseverance
Prudence
Quickness of thought
Seeing others' viewpoints
Self-confidence
Self-discipline
Sense of purpose
Shrewd judgement
Social skills (sociability)
Taking initiative
Team work
Tenacity
Tidiness
Thoroughness
Tolerance
Unemotional approach
Willingness to take on challenges

Source: Jones, A., Reed, R. and Weyers, J. (2007) p. 39.

Personal development planning (PDP) and your CV – many PDP schemes (p. 5) also include an element of career planning that may involve creating a draft or generic CV. The PDP process can help you improve the structure and content of your CV, and the language you use within it.

Understanding skills and qualities – it may be helpful to think about how the skills and qualities in Tables 1.1 and 7.1 apply to particular activities during your studies, since this will give them a greater relevance.

Focusing on evidence – it is important to be able to provide specific concrete information that will back up the claims you make under the 'skills and personal qualities' and other sections of your CV. A potential employer will be interested in your level of competence (what you can actually do) and in situations where you have used a skill or demonstrated a particular quality. These aspects can also be mentioned in your covering letter or at interview.

Personal qualities and skills are interrelated because your personal qualities can influence the skills you gain. For example, you may become highly proficient at working in a team if you are used to playing team sports. Being able to transfer your skills is highly important (Chapter 1) – many employers take a long-term view and look for evidence of the adaptability that will allow you to be a flexible employee and one who will continue to develop skills.

Developing your curriculum vitae

The initial stage involves making an audit of the skills and qualities you already have, and thinking about those you might need to develop. Tables 7.1 and 1.1 could form a basis for this self-appraisal. Assessing your skills may be easier than critically analysing your personal characteristics. In judging your qualities, try to take a positive view and avoid being overly modest. It is important to think of your qualities in a specific context, e.g. 'I have shown that I am trustworthy, by acting as treasurer for the University Football Club', as this evidence will form a vital part of your CV and job applications (see Table 7.2 for other examples).

Table 7.2 Examples of skills and qualities developed from academic and university life

Category	Example	Skills
Academic life	Group projects	Listening skills, research skills, communication skills, time management, meeting skills, prioritising, project management, reliability, public speaking, computer skills (e.g. PowerPoint)
Leisure	Stamp collecting	Research skills, record-keeping, self-discipline, tidiness, personal organisation, curiosity
Volunteer work	Swim coach	Supervisory skills, reliability, compliance with regulations, leadership, self-discipline, energy and enthusiasm, willingness to take on challenges
Travel	Lived and/or worked in other places	Adaptability, change management, enthusiasm, self-confidence, tolerance, social skills, willingness to accept challenges
Family	Planned a wedding	Organisational skills, coordination and planning, enthusiasm, project management, sense of purpose, thoroughness, social skills, willingness to take on challenges
Community work	Rotary club	Mentoring skills, meeting procedures, integrity, social skills, respect
Church work	Hospital volunteer	Liaison skills, interpersonal skills, trust, reliability, integrity, perform under stress, willingness to take on challenges
Sport	Football team	Teamwork, training and discipline, willingness to take on challenges, fitness and health, self-discipline, enthusiasm, drive and determination, time management

If you can identify gaps in your skills, or qualities that you would like to develop, especially in relation to the needs of your intended career, the next step is to think about ways of improving them. This will be reasonably easy in some cases, but may require some creative thinking in others. A relatively simple example would be if you decided to learn a new language or to keep up with one you learned at school. There are likely to be many local college and university courses dealing with foreign languages at many different levels, so it would be a straightforward matter to join one of these. A rather more difficult case might be if you wished to demonstrate 'responsibility', because there are no courses available on this. One route to demonstrate this quality might be to put yourself up for election as an officer in a student society or sporting club; another could be to take a leading role in a relevant activity within your community (e.g. voluntary work such as hospital radio). If you already take part in activities like these, your CV should relate them to this context.

Basic CV structures and their presentation

Box 7.1 illustrates the typical parts of a CV and explains the purpose of each part. Employers are more likely to take notice of a well organised and well presented CV, in contrast to one that is difficult to read and assimilate. They will expect it to be concise, complete and accurate. There are many ways of presenting information in a CV, and you will be assessed partly on your choices.

Apart from the general content, the presentation of the CV or résumé is critical. There will be different forms of résumés for different countries, industries and disciplines, but the look and feel of the document are paramount. Box 7.2 highlights a few simple rules that are consistent across most forms of résumés or CVs.

Seeing yourself as others see you – you may not recognise all of your personal qualities and you may need someone else to give you a frank appraisal. This could be anyone whose opinion you value: a friend, a member of your family, a tutor or a careers adviser.

Apart from the résumé itself, the covering letter will immediately convey to a potential employer your suitability for the position by outlining your unique selling points and your knowledge of the organisation's needs. Effective covering letters will:

- grab the reader's attention;
- focus attention on your accomplishments;
- spell out clearly how you are an excellent match for the position;
- provide succinct information regarding your qualifications, skills and experience;
- highlight your understanding of the organisation and how you would be an asset;
- reflect your career objectives and interest in the position;
- summarise your key attributes in an expressive and original way.

Setting your own agenda – you have the capability to widen your experience and to demonstrate relevant personal qualities through both curricular and extracurricular activities.

The five major components of an effective cover letter are:

1. **Letterhead:** include your contact details, the recipient's name and title (if known) and address plus any job reference number.
2. **Introductory paragraph:** explain who you are and the position for which you are applying.
3. **Main message:** sell yourself, highlighting attributes, strengths, qualifications and experience. Keep this to three or four sentences

Paying attention to the quality of your CV – your potential employer will regard your CV as an example of your very best work and will not be impressed if it is full of mistakes or badly presented, especially if you claim 'good written communication' as a skill!

Box 7.1 The structure and components of a typical CV or résumé

There is no right or wrong way to write a CV or résumé and no one format applies to all people or all jobs applied for. However, you should include the following with appropriate subheadings, generally in the order given below:

1. **Personal details:** you should provide the following information:
   a. Full name
   b. Mailing address (both home and term address)
   c. Contact phone numbers (at each address and mobile)
   d. Email address
   e. Gender (if your name could be male or female).
2. **Career objective:** in 100 words or so. It shows that you are motivated and have goals. Customise it to the job for which the résumé is being used. An ineffective statement might read 'To gain employment with a company where my experience and knowledge can be used effectively'. In contrast, an effective example might be: 'Seeking a strength and conditioning position in a nationally recognised sporting organisation. Ability to communicate with high-performance athletes from a variety of economic and social circumstances.'
3. **Professional summary:** this is where you pull together a high-level summary of your experience, talents and personal strengths from the various positions and experiences you have had. Highlight the talents and experiences relevant to the position you are seeking. For example, you might include a sentence describing yourself as results-focused, persistent and collaborative: 'University qualified person offering three years of fitness testing experience with university athletes. Results-focused and efficient leader with proven talent for productively identifying and resolving problems, resulting in continuous improvement in athlete and team performance. Demonstrated proficiency in fitness test selection, data collection, analysis and presentation, and strong record of communication with coaches and athletes.'
4. **Education:** put your qualifications in reverse chronological order with dates listed on the left hand side. List the qualification you are currently enrolled in and the expected graduation date. You may wish to highlight your average grade or result, three or four key subjects relevant to the position (don't include all subjects), and any prizes, scholarships or awards you have won. List any gap years. You do not need to include your secondary school education if it is over 10 years old, as your recent employment history is now more important. If you feel your university entry score was good, then include this. *Note:* you should be able to fit all of the above on the first page of your CV/résumé. It needs to catch the eye of the employer.
5. **Employment history:** start this on a new page and place it in reverse chronological order using the same format as your education listing. Details need to include dates, employer, job title and major duties involved. Include all temporary, part-time and full-time or voluntary work from the past 5–10 years (list any gap years and explain these, e.g. child-rearing, travel), but include more detail about your most current relevant job. This allows you to give examples of current industry knowledge or newly obtained transferable skills (see Chapter 1). Begin sentences with action verbs (e.g. achieved, developed, coordinated, assisted, designed). Tables 1.1, 7.1 and 7.2 give examples of aspects you might include under this heading. Emphasise your strengths and transferable skills and tailor this section to the specific requirements of the job for which you have applied. Always provide supporting evidence for your statements. This section should be no more than two pages.
6. **Professional associations and licences:** make a list of all associations and clubs or societies with which you have been involved. List any licences you may have (e.g. driver's licence, first aid).
7. **Achievements:** this is a way to market yourself as an achiever. Even the briefest list will help. Include two lists of both personal and academic achievements as far back as the start of secondary school.
8. **Interests and hobbies:** aim to keep this section short as it may suggest your social life is more important than your education or work life. List three or four hobbies or interests and, importantly, detail the positive aspects of your interests (e.g. teamwork, communication). For example: 'Athletics – member of track and field club from 2000 with regular attendance at training at state and district championships. 2008 District 100 m sprint champion.' This conveys the message that you can be disciplined, set goals and strive to achieve.
9. **Referees:** you will need to have at least three and no more than five referees. Academic referees are a plus if possible, but try and keep work-related referees and/or a personal referee from someone in the industry in which you are seeking employment. Inform your referees in advance of the jobs for which you are applying and the requirements of that job. You will need to list the following details for each referee:
   - full name and titles;
   - position;
   - full postal address;
   - contact telephone numbers;
   - email address.

Box 7.2 Tips on the presentation of your résumé or CV

- **Keep the resume brief but full of substance:** employers must be able to see at a glance that you are capable of doing the job. Three to five pages is a good-sized graduate résumé. Only use standard fonts. Times New Roman, Tahoma or Arial in font size 11 or 12 are good as they make it easier to read.
- **Check for spelling, grammatical or typographical errors:** these mistakes indicate poor writing quality or that you do not value the position enough. Have a friend or family member proofread your résumé.
- **Avoid jargon and over-complicated phrases or sentences:** use direct, active words and phrases (see Box 14.1).
- **Write the résumé in the third person** (e.g. Peter or Nicole): this enables you to market yourself without appearing brash or over-using the words 'I' and 'me'.
- **Keep the information relevant and honest:** you don't want to be caught out at interview.
- **Have your name and the page number on each page:** this keeps your name in the mind of the reader (employer) and prevents them from having to turn back to page 1 to remind them of who you are. Use the page numbering style 'page 2 of 5'.
- **Do not use coloured fonts, graphics or pictures unless requested:** if sent by email, graphics can be very large in size and take time to print out. They may not scan or copy well. Coloured fonts printed or copied in black and white may be difficult to read. Quality presentation is paramount – do not compromise it.
- **Do not use CV or résumé templates from websites or on Word or other software programs:** be unique, not like everyone else.
- **Use key words sprinkled throughout your résumé:** key words are used to explain the key aspects of the position (e.g. excellent communication skills, MS Word skills). Recruitment agencies and online employment sites use computer scanning technology to assess applications by repetition of key words. You may want to check with the employer on how the applications might be assessed before you submit yours.
- **Don't clutter your résumé:** use clear headings and subheadings, wide spaces and margins.
- **Tailor your résumé:** a strong résumé is targeted to specific jobs within specific organisations within specific industries. Research the organisation (website, annual report, current employee) and position, ensure that your career objective and professional summary are relevant to the position and industry, and write a directed covering letter.

and relate it to the skills and attributes specified in the position description. State what you have done and what you want to do next in your exercise and/or sport science career.

4. **Concluding paragraph:** a brief statement that you look forward to hearing the outcome of your application.
5. **Sign off correctly:** use 'Yours sincerely' where you know the name of the recipient or 'Yours faithfully' in a letter beginning 'Dear Sir or Madam' where you do not know the recipient's name. End with your signature.

KEY POINT A well constructed and relevant résumé won't necessarily guarantee you a job, but it may well get you on to the short list for interview. A poor-quality résumé is a sure route to failure.

Creating a generic CV – as you may apply for several jobs, it is useful to construct a CV in electronic format (e.g. as a Word file) which includes all information of potential relevance. This can then be modified to fit each post. Having a prepared CV on file will reduce the work each time you apply, while modifying this will help you focus on relevant skills and attributes for the particular job.

Adjusting your CV

You should fine-tune your résumé for each post. Employers frequently use a 'person specification' to define the skills and qualities demanded in a job, often under headings such as 'essential' and 'desirable'. This will help you decide whether to apply for a position and it assists the selection panel to filter the applicants. Highlight relevant qualifications as early in your résumé as possible. Be selective – don't include every detail about yourself. Emphasise relevant parts and leave out irrelevant details, according to the job. Similarly, your cover letter of application is not merely a formal document but is also an opportunity for persuasion (Box 7.1). You can use it to state your ambitions and highlight particular qualifications and experience. However, don't go over the top – always keep the letter to a single page.

Sources for further study

Anon. (2007) *How to Write a Curriculum Vitae*. University of London Careers Service, London. Available: http://thecareersgroup.wordpress.com/2007/02/26/how-to-write-a-cv/
Last accessed: 23/12/10.

Anon. *Proven Resumes*. Available: http://www.provenresumes.com/
Last accessed: 23/12/10.

Anon. *Applications and CVs*. Available: http://targetjobs.co.uk/general-advice/applications-and-cvs.aspx
Last accessed: 23/12/10.

Simons, W. and Curtis, R. (2004) *The Resume.Com Guide to Writing Unbeatable Resumes*. McGraw-Hill, New York.

Information technology and library resources

8. Finding and citing published information 49
9. Evaluating information 55
10. Using online resources 63
11. Using spreadsheets 73
12. Word processors, databases and other packages 79

8 Finding and citing published information

Browsing in a library – this may turn up interesting material, but remember the books on the shelves are those not currently out on loan. Almost by definition, the latter may be more up to date and useful. To find out a library's full holding of books in any subject area, you need to search its catalogue (normally available as an online database).

Example The book *Biochemistry of Exercise & Training* by Ron Maughan, Micheal Gleeson and Paul L. Greenhaff (1997; Oxford University Press) is likely to be classified as follows:

Dewey Decimal system: 612.044

Where	612	refers to human physiology
	612.04	refers to physiology of exercise
	612.044	refers to physiology of exercise and sport

Library of Congress system: QP301

Where	Q	refers to science
	QP	refers to physiology
	QP300	refers to general physiology
	QP301	refers to musculoskeletal system and movements

The ability to find scientific information is a skill required for many exercises in your degree programme. You will need to research facts and published findings as part of writing essays, literature reviews and project introductions, and when amplifying your lecture notes and revising for exams. You must also learn how to follow scientific convention in citing source material as the authority for the statements you have made.

Sources of information

For essays and revision

You are unlikely to delve into the primary literature (p. 50) for these purposes – books and reviews are much more readable. If a lecturer or tutor specifies a particular book, then it should not be difficult to find out where it is shelved in your library, using the computerised index system. Library staff will generally be happy to assist with any queries. If you want to find out which books your library holds on a specified topic, use the system's subject index. You will also be able to search by author or by key words.

There are two main systems used by libraries to classify books: the Dewey Decimal system and the Library of Congress system. Libraries differ in the way they employ these systems, especially by adding further numbers and letters after the standard classification marks to signify, for example, shelving position or edition number. Enquire at your library for a full explanation of local usage.

The World Wide Web is an ever-expanding resource for gathering both general and specific information (see Chapter 10). Websites fall into analogous categories to those in the printed literature: there are sites with original information, sites that review information, and bibliographic sites. One considerable problem is that websites may be frequently updated, so information present when you first looked may be altered or even absent when the site is next consulted. Further, very little of the information on the World Wide Web has been monitored or refereed. Another disadvantage is that the site information may not state the origin of the material, who wrote it or when it was written.

For literature surveys and project work

You will probably need to consult the primary literature. If you are starting a new research project or writing a report from scratch, you can build up a core of relevant papers by using the following methods:

- **Asking around:** supervisors or their postgraduate students will almost certainly be able to supply you with a reference or two that will start you off.
- **Searching an online database:** these cover very wide areas and are a convenient way to start a reference collection, although a charge is often made for access and sending out a listing of the papers selected (your library may or may not pass this on to you).

Web resources – your university library will provide you with access to a range of web-based databases and information systems. The library web pages will list these and provide links, which may be worth bookmarking on your web browser. Resources especially useful to sport and exercise scientists include:

- ISI Web of Knowledge, *including the* Science Citation Index
- IngentaConnect, *including* Ingenta Medline
- PubMed
- ScienceDirect
- SPORTDiscus
- Scopus
- ProQuest
- Ovid, *including* Cinahl *and* Medline.

Most of these electronic resources operate on a subscription basis and may require an 'Athens' username and password – for details of how to obtain these, consult library staff or your library's website.

Definitions

Journal/periodical/serial – any publication issued at regular intervals. In biosciences, usually containing papers (articles) describing original research findings and reviews of literature.

e-journal – a journal published online, consisting of articles structured in the same way as a paper-based journal. A valid username and password may be required for access (arranged via your library, if it subscribes to the e-journal).

The primary literature – this comprises original research papers, published in specialist scientific periodicals. Certain prestigious general journals (e.g. *Nature*) contain important new advances from a wide subject area.

Monograph – a specialised book covering a single topic.

e-book – a book published online in downloadable form.

ebrary – a commercial service offering e-books and other online resources.

HERON (Higher Education Resources ON demand) – a national service for UK higher education offering copyright clearance, digitisation and delivery of book extracts and journal articles.

Review – an article in which recent advances in a specific area are outlined and discussed.

- **Consulting the bibliography of other papers in your collection**: an important way of finding the key papers in your field. In effect, you are taking advantage of the fact that another researcher has already done all the hard work.
- **Referring to 'current awareness' online databases:** these are useful for keeping you up to date with current research; they usually provide a monthly listing of article details (title, authors, source, author address) arranged by subject and cross-referenced by subject and author. Current awareness databases cover a wider range of primary literature than could ever be available in any one library.

  Examples relevant to exercise science include: Current Contents Connect (ISI), SPORTDiscus (Sport Information Resource Centre) and PubMed (US National Library of Medicine). Some online databases also offer a service whereby they will email registered users with updates based on saved search criteria. Consult library staff or your library website to see which of these databases and services are available to you.
- **Using the *Science Citation Index* (SCI):** this is a very valuable source for exploring the published literature in a given field, because it lets you see who has cited a given paper; in effect, SCI allows you to move forward through the literature from an existing reference. The Index is available online via ISI Web of Science.

For specialised information

You may need to consult reference works, such as encyclopedias, maps and books providing specialised information. Much of this is now available online (consult your library's information service or web pages). Three books worth noting are:

- The *Oxford Dictionary of Sports Science and Medicine*, 3rd edn: a useful resource for information for exercise science and anatomy;
- *Gray's Anatomy*, 40th edn: a classic text that contains detailed anatomical diagrams and description;
- *Textbook of Work Physiology: Physiological Bases of Exercise*, 4th edn: a classic modern text on exercise science and physiology.

Obtaining and organising research papers

Obtaining a copy

It is usually more convenient to have personal copies of key research articles for direct consultation when working in a laboratory or writing. The simplest way of obtaining these is to photocopy the originals or download and/or print off copies online (e.g. as .pdf or HTML files). For academic purposes, this is normally acceptable within copyright law. If your library does not subscribe to the journal, it may be possible for them to borrow it from a nearby institute or obtain a copy via a national borrowing centre (an 'inter-library loan'). If the latter, you will have to fill in a form giving full bibliographic details of the paper and where it was cited, as well as signing a copyright clearance statement concerning your use of the copy.

Definitions

Proceedings – volume compiling written versions of papers read at a scientific meeting on a specific topic.

Abstracts – shortened versions of papers, often those read at scientific meetings. These may later appear in the literature as full papers.

Bibliography – a summary of the published work in a defined subject area.

Alternative methods of receiving information – RSS (Really Simple Syndication) feeds and email updates from publishers are increasingly used to provide automated information services to academic clients, for example, by supplying links to relevant contents of new editions of online journals.

Copyright law – in Europe, copyright regulations were harmonised in 1993 (Directive 93/98/EEC) to allow literary copyright for 70 years after the death of an author and typographical copyright for 25 years after publication. This was implemented in the UK in 1996, where, in addition, the Copyright, Designs and Patents Act (1988) allows the Copyright Licensing Agency to license institutions so that lecturers, students and researchers may take copies for teaching and personal research purposes – no more than a single article per journal issue, one chapter of a book, or extracts to a total of 5% of a book.

Storing research papers – these can easily be kept in alphabetical order within filing boxes or drawers, but if your collection is likely to grow large, it will need to be refiled as it outgrows the storage space. You may therefore wish to add an 'accession number' to the record you keep in your database, and file the papers in sequence according to this as they accumulate. New filing space is only required at the 'end' and you can use the accession numbers to form the basis of a simple cross-referencing system.

Your department might be able to supply 'reprint request' postcards to be sent to the designated author of a paper. This is an unreliable method of obtaining a copy because it may take some time (allow at least one to three months) and some requests will not receive a reply. Taking into account the waste involved in postage and printing, it is probably best simply to photocopy or send for a copy via inter-library loan.

Organising papers

Although the number of papers you accumulate may be small to start with, it is worth putting some thought into their storage and indexing before your collection becomes disorganised and unmanageable. Few things are more frustrating than not being able to lay your hands on a vital piece of information, and this can seriously disrupt your flow when writing or revising.

Indexing your references

Whether you have obtained a printed copy, have stored downloaded files electronically, or have simply noted the bibliographic details of a reference, you will need to index each resource. This is valuable for the following reasons:

- You will probably need the bibliographic information for creating a reference list for an assignment or report.
- If the index also has database features, this can be useful, allowing you to search for key words or authors.
- If you include an 'accession number' and if you then file printed material sequentially according to this number, then it will help you to find the hard copy.
- Depending on the indexing system used, you can add comments about the reference that may be useful at a later time, e.g. when writing an introduction or conclusion.

The simplest way to create an index system is to put the details on reference cards, but database software can be more convenient and faster to sort, once the bibliographic information has been entered. If you do not feel that commercial software is appropriate for your needs, consider using a word processor or spreadsheet; their rudimentary database sorting functions (see Chapters 11 and 12) may be all that you require.

If you are likely to store lots of references and other electronic resources digitally, then you should consider carefully how this information is kept, for example by choosing file names that indicate what the file contains and that will facilitate sorting.

Making citations in text

There are two main ways of citing articles and creating a bibliography (also referred to as 'references' or 'literature cited').

The Harvard system

For each citation, the author name(s) and the date of publication are given at the relevant point in the text. The bibliography is organised

Example Incorporating references in text – this sample shows how you might embed citations in text using the Harvard approach:
'... Davis *et al.* (2001) proposed that oxygen delivery to the muscle cell is the limiting factor to aerobic energy production and oxygen consumption at the onset of exercise. However, other researchers (Duncan and Macabe, 2001; Dakin, 2000; 2004) have reported no changes as a result of improved oxygen delivery to the muscle. Interestingly, Waterhouse *et al.* (2001a; 2001b) demonstrated that reducing oxygen delivery to muscles significantly lowers oxygen consumption and aerobic energy production, which other investigations (Baker, 2003; Anderson *et al.*, 2003) have supported...'

alphabetically and by date of publication for papers with the same authors. Formats normally adopted are, for example, 'Smith and Jones (1983) stated that ...' or 'it has been shown that ... (Smith and Jones, 1983)'. Lists of references within parentheses are separated by semi-colons, e.g. '(Smith and Jones, 1983; Jones and Smith, 1985)', normally in order of date of publication. To avoid repetition within the same paragraph, an approach such as 'the investigations of Smith and Jones indicated that' could be used following an initial citation of the paper. Where there are more than two authors it is usual to write '*et al.*'; this stands for the Latin *et alii* meaning 'and others'. If citing more than one paper with the same authors, put, for example, 'Smith and Jones (1987; 1990)' and if papers by a given set of authors appeared in the same year, letter them (e.g. Smith and Jones, 1989a; 1989b).

The numerical or Vancouver system

Papers are cited via a superscript or bracketed reference number inserted at the appropriate point. Normal format would be, for example: 'DNA sequences[4,5] have shown that ...' or 'Jones [55,82] has claimed that ...'. Repeated citations use the number from the first citation. In the true numerical method (e.g. as in *Nature*), numbers are allocated by order of citation in the text, but in the alpha-numerical method (e.g. the *Annual Review* series), the references are first ordered alphabetically in the bibliography, then numbered, and it is this number that is used in the text. Note that with this latter method, adding or removing references is tedious, so the numbering should be done only when the text has been finalised.

KEY POINT The main advantages of the Harvard system are that the reader might recognise the paper being referred to and that it is easily expanded if extra references are added. The main advantages of the Vancouver system are that it aids text flow and reduces length.

Using commercial bibliographic database software to organise your references – for those with large numbers of references in their collection, and who may wish to produce lists of selected references in particular format, e.g. for inclusion in a project report or journal paper, systems like *EndNote, Reference Manager* or *ProCite* can reward the investment of time and money required to create a personal reference catalogue. Appropriate bibliographic data must first be entered into fields within a database (some versions assist you to search online databases and upload data from these). The database can then be searched and used to create customised lists of selected references in appropriate citation styles.

How to list your citations in a bibliography

Whichever citation method is used in the text, comprehensive details are required for the bibliography so that the reader has enough information to find the reference easily. Citations should be listed in alphabetical order with the priority: first author, subsequent author(s), date. Unfortunately, in terms of punctuation and layout, there are almost as many ways of citing papers as there are journals! Your department may specify an exact format for project work; if not, decide on a style and be consistent – if you do not pay attention to the details of citation you may lose marks. Take special care with the following aspects:

- **Authors and editors:** give details of *all* authors and editors in your bibliography, even if given as '*et al.*' in the text.
- **Abbreviations for journals:** while there are standard abbreviations for the titles of journals (consult library staff), it is a good idea to give the whole title, if possible.

Example Incorporating references in text – this sample shows how you might embed citations in text using the Vancouver approach:
'... Davis *et al.*[1] proposed that oxygen delivery to the muscle cell is the limiting factor to aerobic energy production and oxygen consumption at the onset of exercise. However, other researchers[2–4] have reported no changes as a result of improved oxygen delivery to the muscle. Interestingly, Waterhouse *et al.*[5,6] demonstrated that reducing oxygen delivery to muscles significantly lowers oxygen consumption and aerobic energy production, which other investigations[7,8] have supported...'.

Examples

Paper in journal:
Smith, A.B., Jones, C.D. and Professor, A. (1998). Innovative results concerning our research interest. *Journal of New Results*, 11, 234–5.

Book:
Smith, A.B. (1998). *Summary of My Life's Work.* Megadosh Publishing Corp., Bigcity. ISBN 0-123-45678-9.

Chapter in edited book:
Jones, C.D. and Smith, A.B. (1998). Earth-shattering research from our laboratory. In: *Research Compendium 1998* (ed. A. Professor), pp. 123–456. Bigbucks Press, Booktown.

Thesis:
Smith, A.B. (1995). *Investigations on my Favourite Topic.* PhD thesis, University of Life, Fulchester.

Note: if your references are handwritten, you should indicate italics by underlining text or numerals.

Finding dates on websites quickly – when visiting a particular page, you can find occurrences of year dates beginning '200' by pressing *Control* and *F* keys together, entering 200 in the *Find* window that appears, then carrying out a search using the *Find next* command.

Adding web references in other systems – if you are using a different referencing system than Harvard, consult Pears and Shield (2008) or McMillan and Weyers (2006) for further information on how to cite websites in these systems.

- **Books:** the edition should always be specified as contents may change between editions. Add, for example, '5th edn' after the title of the book. You may be asked to give the International Standard Book Number (ISBN), a unique reference number for each book published.
- **Unsigned articles,** e.g. unattributed newspaper articles and instruction manuals – refer to the author(s) in text and bibliography as 'Anon'.
- **Websites:** there is no widely accepted format at present. You should follow departmental guidelines if these are provided, but if these are not available, we suggest providing author name(s) and date in the text when using the Harvard system (e.g. Hacker, 2006), while in the bibliography giving the URL details in the following format: Hacker, A. (2006) *University of Anytown Homepage on Aardvarks.* Available: http://www.myserver.ac.uk/homepage. Last accessed: 23/02/11. In this example, the web page was constructed in 2006, but accessed in February, 2011. If no author is identifiable, cite the sponsoring body (e.g. University of Anytown, 2006), and if there is no author or sponsoring body, write 'Anon.' for 'anonymous', e.g. Anon. (2006), and use Anon. as the 'author' in the bibliography. If the web pages are undated, *either* use the 'Last accessed' date for citation and put no date after the author name(s) in the reference list, *or* cite as 'no date' (e.g. Hacker, no date) and leave out a date after the author name(s) in the reference list – you should be consistent whichever option you choose.
- **Unread articles:** you may be forced to refer to a paper via another without having seen it. If possible, refer to another authority who has cited the paper, e.g. '... Jones (1980), cited in Smith (1990), claimed that ...'. Alternatively, you could denote such references in the bibliography by an asterisk and add a short note to explain at the start of the reference list.
- **Personal communications:** information received in a letter, seminar or conversation can be referred to in the text as, for example, '... (Smith, pers. comm.)'. These citations are not generally listed in the bibliography of papers, though in a thesis you could give a list of personal communicants and their addresses.
- **Online material:** some articles are published solely online and others online ahead of publication in printed form. The article may be given a DOI (digital object identifier), allowing it to be cited and potentially tracked before and after it is allocated to a printed issue (see http://www.doi.org/). DOIs allow for web page redirection by a central agency, and CrossRef (see http://www.crossref.org) is the official DOI registration organisation for scholarly and professional publications. DOIs can be used as 'live' hyperlinks in online articles, or cited in place of (and, when they become available, following) the volume and page numbers for the article, with the remainder of the details cited in the usual fashion; for example:

  'Smith, A. and Jones, B. (2006) Our latest important research in the form of a web-published article. *Online Exersciences* 8/2006 (p. 232). Published Online: 26 March 2006. DOI: 10.1083/mabi.200880021.'

Text references

McMillan, K.M. and Weyers, J.D.B. (2006) *The Smarter Student: Study Skills and Strategies for Success at University*. Pearson Education, Harlow.

Pears, R. and Shields, G. (2008) *Cite Them Right! The Essential Guide to Referencing and Plagiarism*, 2nd edn, Pear Tree Books, Durham.

Sources for further study

Åstrand, P-O., Rodahl, K., Dahl, H.A. and Strømme, S.B. (2003) *Textbook of Work Physiology: Physiological Bases of Exercise,* 4th edn, Human Kinetics, Champaign, IL.

Kent, M. (2006) *The Oxford Dictionary of Sports Science and Medicine*, 3rd edn, Oxford University Press, Oxford.

Standring, S. (2008) *Gray's Anatomy: The Anatomical Basis of Clinical Practice*, 39th edn, Churchill Livingstone, London.

9 Evaluating information

Checking the reliability of information, assessing the relative value of different ideas and thinking critically are skills essential to the scientific approach. You will need to develop your abilities to evaluate information in this way because:

- You will be faced with many sources of information, from which you will need to select the most appropriate material.
- You may come across conflicting sources of evidence and may have to decide which is the more reliable.
- The accuracy and validity of a specific fact may be vital to your work.
- You may doubt the quality of the information from a particular source.
- You may wish to check the original source because you are not sure whether someone else is quoting it correctly.

Example A Google search for the term 'fitness' will reveal this term appears in approximately 430 million websites. Not all of these deal with fitness as defined by sport and exercise scientists. Many of the sites market and promote commercial fitness centres around the world, including Mumbai, or unqualified personal trainers who specialise in working with vegans. As sport and exercise science students, how can you be sure that the information you find out there in the Internet is valid and unbiased or represents what mainstream sport and exercise science research has proven as factual and reliable information based on proven scientific methods? These are some of the issues with which an evaluation of information sources might deal.

KEY POINT Evaluating information and thinking critically are regarded as higher-order academic skills. The ability to think deeply in this way is greatly valued in the sport and exercise sciences, and will consequently be assessed in coursework and exam questions (see Chapters 5 and 6).

The process of evaluating and using information can be broken down into four stages:

1. **Selecting and obtaining material.** How to find sources is covered in Chapter 8. Printed books and journals are important, but if you identify a source of this kind there may be delays in borrowing it or obtaining a photocopy. If the book or journal is available online, then downloading or printing sections or papers will be more convenient and faster. The Internet is often the first port of call if you wish to find something quickly. For many websites, however, it can be difficult to verify the authenticity of the information given (see Box 10.5).
2. **Assessing the content.** You will need to understand fully what has been written, including any technical terms and jargon used. Establish the relevance of the information to your needs and assure yourself that the data or conclusions have been presented in an unbiased way.
3. **Modifying the information.** In order to use the information, you may need to alter it to suit your needs. This may require you to make comparisons, interpret or summarise. Some sources may require translation. Some data may require mathematical transformation before they are useful. There is a chance of error in any of these processes and also a risk of plagiarism.
4. **Analysis.** This may be your own interpretation of the information presented, or an examination of the way the original author has used the information.

Definition

Plagiarism – the unacknowledged use of another's work as if it were one's own. In this definition, the concept of 'work' includes ideas, writing, data or inventions, and not simply words; and the notion of 'use' does not only mean copy 'word for word', but also 'in substance' (i.e. a copy of the ideas involved). Use of another's work is acceptable if you acknowledge the source but you may use your own words, unless it is a quotation, where the text must be within quotation marks ie."..." (see Box 9.1).

Box 9.1 How to avoid plagiarism and copyright infringement

Plagiarism is defined on page 55. Examples of plagiarism include:

- copying the work of a fellow student (past or present) and passing it off as your own;
- using 'essay-writing services', such as those on offer on certain websites;
- copying text or images from a source (book, journal article or website, for instance) and using this within your own work without acknowledgement;
- quoting others' words without indicating who wrote or said them;
- copying ideas and concepts from a source without acknowledgement, even if you paraphrase them.

Most students would accept that some of the above can only be described as cheating. However, many students, especially at the start of their studies, are unaware of the academic rule that they must *always* acknowledge the originators of information, ideas and concepts, and that not doing so is regarded as a form of academic dishonesty. If you adopt the appropriate conventions that avoid such accusations, you will achieve higher marks for your work as it will fulfil the markers' expectations for academic writing.

Universities have a range of mechanisms for identifying plagiarism, from employing experienced and vigilant coursework markers and external examiners to analysing students' work using sophisticated software programs. Plagiarism is always punished severely when detected. Penalties may include awarding a mark of zero to all involved – both the copier(s) and the person whose work has been copied (who is regarded as complicit in the crime). Further disciplinary measures may be taken in some instances. In severe cases, such as copying substantive parts of another's work within a thesis, a student may be dismissed from the university.

If you wish to avoid being accused of plagiarism, the remedies are relatively simple:

1. **Make sure the work you present is always your own.** If you have been studying alongside a colleague, or have been discussing how to tackle a particular problem with your peers, make sure you write on your own when working on your assignments.
2. **Never be tempted to 'cut and paste'** from websites or online sources such as word-processed handouts. Read these carefully, decide what the important points are, express these *in your own words* and *provide literature citations to the original sources* (see Chapter 8). In some cases, further investigations may be required to find out details of the original sources. The lecturer's reading list or a book's references may help you here.
3. **Take care when note-taking.** If you decide to quote word for word, make sure you show this clearly in your notes with quotation marks. If you decide to make your own notes based on a source, make sure these are original and do not copy phrases from the text. In both cases, write down full details of the source at the appropriate point in your notes.
4. **Place appropriate citations throughout your text where required.** If you are unsure about when to do this, study reviews and articles in your subject area (see also Chapter 8).
5. **Show clearly where you are quoting directly from a source.** For short quotes, this may involve using quotation marks and identifying the source afterwards, as in the example '... as Samuel Butler (1877) wrote: "a hen is only an egg's way of making another egg". ' For longer quotes (say 40 words or more), you should create a separate paragraph of quoted text, usually identified by inverted commas, indentation, italicisation or a combination of these. A citation must *always* be included, normally at the end. Your course handbook may specify a layout. Try not to rely too much on quotes in your work. If a large proportion of your work is made up from quotes, this will almost certainly be regarded as lacking in originality, scoring a poor mark.

Copyright issues are often associated with plagiarism, and refer to the right to publish (and hence copy) original material, such as text, images and music. Copyright material is indicated by the symbol © and a date (see, for example, p. iv of this book). Literary copyright is the aspect most relevant to students in their academic studies. For example, UK copyright law protects authors' rights for life and gives their estates rights for a further 70 years. Publishers have 'typographical copyright' that lasts for 25 years. This means that it is illegal to photocopy, scan or print out copyright material unless you have permission, or unless your copying is limited to an extent that could be considered 'fair dealing'. For educational purposes – private study or research – in a scientific context, this generally means:

- no more than 5% in total of a work;
- one chapter of a book;
- one article per volume of an academic journal;
- 20% of a short book;
- one separate illustration or map.

You may only take one copy within the above limits, may not copy for others, and may not exceed these amounts *even if you own a copy of the original.* These rules also apply to web-based materials, but sometimes you will find sites where the copyright is waived. Some copying may be licensed; you should consult your library's website or helpdesk to see whether it has access to licensed material. Up-to-date copyright information is often posted close to library and departmental photocopiers.

KEY POINT Advances in communication and information technology mean that we can now access almost limitless knowledge. Consequently, the ability to evaluate information has become an extremely important skill.

Evaluating sources of information

One way of assessing the reliability of a piece of scientific information is to think about how it was obtained in the first place. Essentially, facts and ideas originate from someone's research or scholarship, whether they are numerical data, descriptions, concepts or interpretations. Sources are divided into three main types:

Distinguishing between primary and secondary sources – try the 'IMRaD test'. Many primary sources contain information in the order: **I**ntroduction, **M**aterials and **M**ethods, **R**esults **a**nd **D**iscussion. If you see this format, and particularly if *data* from an experiment, study or observation are presented, then you are probably reading a primary source.

1. **Primary sources** – those in which ideas and data are first communicated. The primary literature is generally published in the form of 'papers' (articles) in journals, whether printed or online. These are usually refereed by experts in the academic peer group of the author, and they will check the accuracy and originality of the work and report their opinions back to the editors. This peer review system helps to maintain reliability, but it is not perfect. Books and, more rarely, websites and articles in magazines and newspapers, can also be primary sources but this depends on the nature of the information published rather than the medium. These sources are not formally refereed, although they may be read by editors and lawyers to check for errors and unsubstantiated or libellous allegations.
2. **Secondary sources** – those which quote, adapt, interpret, translate, develop or otherwise use information drawn from primary sources. It is the act of quoting or paraphrasing that makes the source secondary, rather than the medium. Reviews are examples of secondary scientific sources, and books and magazine articles are often of this type.
3. **Tertiary sources** – those in which significant knowledge is condensed and summarised. Such sources include encyclopedias, dictionaries and thesauruses as well as journal database indexes such as Scopus, PubMed or SPORTDiscus. No original research data are included, and specific research results from primary or secondary sources are not referred to.

Example If a journalist wrote an article about a new 'performance-enhancing drug' for the *New York Times* that was based on an article in the *British Medical Journal*, the *New York Times* article would be the secondary source, while the *British Medical Journal* article would be the primary source.

When information is modified for use in a secondary source, alterations are likely to occur, whether intentional or unintentional. Most authors do not deliberately set out to change the meaning of the primary source, but they may unwittingly do so, e.g. in changing text to avoid plagiarism or by oversimplification. Others may consciously or unconsciously exert bias in their reporting, for example, by quoting evidence that supports only one side of a debate. Therefore, the closer you can get to the primary source, the more reliable the information is likely to be. On the other hand, modification while creating a secondary source could involve correcting errors, or synthesising ideas and content from multiple sources.

Taking account of the changing nature of websites, blogs and wikis – by their very nature, these sources may change. This means that it is important to quote accurately from them and to give a 'Last accessed' date when citing (see p. 53).

Authorship

Clearly, much depends on who is writing the source and on what basis (e.g. who paid them?). Consequently, an important way of assessing

Finding out about authors – these pieces of information are easy to find in most printed sources and may even be presented just below the title, for convenience. In the case of the Web, it may not be so easy to find what you want. Relevant clues can be obtained from 'home page' links and the header, body and footer information. For example, the domain (e.g. .gov or .edu) may be useful, while the use of the tilde symbol (~) in an address usually indicates a personal, rather than an institutional, website.

Assessing substance over presentation – just because the information is presented well (e.g. in a glossy magazine or particularly well constructed website), this does not necessarily tell you much about its quality. Try to look below the surface, using the methods mentioned in this chapter.

sources is to investigate the ownership of the work (who and where it originated from, and why).

Can you identify who wrote the information? If it is signed or there is a 'byline' showing who wrote it, you might be able to make a judgement on the quality of what you are reading. This may be a simple decision, if you know or can assume that the writer is an authority in the area; otherwise a little research might help (for example, by putting the name into a search engine). Of course, just because Professor X thinks something does not make it true. However, if you know that this opinion is backed up by years of research and experience, then you might take it a little more seriously than the thoughts of a school pupil. If an author is not cited, effectively nobody is taking responsibility for the content. Could there be a reason for this?

Is the author's place of work cited? This might tell you whether the facts or opinions given are based on an academic study. Is there a company with a vested interest behind the content? If the author works for a public body, there may be publication rules to follow and they may even have to submit their work to a publications committee before it is disseminated. They are certainly more likely to get into trouble if they include controversial material.

Evaluating facts and ideas

However reliable the source of a piece of information seems to be, it is probably a good idea to retain a slight degree of scepticism about the facts or ideas involved. Even information from impeccable primary sources may not be perfect – different approaches can give different outcomes, and interpretations can change with time and with further advances in knowledge.

Table 9.1 and Box 9.2 provide checklists to use when evaluating information sources.

Critically examining facts and ideas is a complex task depending on the particular issues involved, and a number of different general approaches can be applied. You will need to decide which of the following general tips are useful in your specific case:

- **Make cross-referencing checks** – look at more than one source and compare what is said in each. The cross-referenced sources should be as independent as possible (for example, do not compare a primary source with a secondary review based on it). If you find that all the sources give a similar picture, then you can be more confident about the reliability of the information.
- **Look at the extent and quality of citations** – if references are quoted, these indicate that a certain amount of research has been carried out beforehand, and that the ideas or results are based on genuine scholarship. If you are doubtful about the quality of the work, these references might be worth looking at. How up to date are they? Do they cite independent work, or is the author exclusively quoting their own work, or solely the work of one person?
- **Consider the age of the source** – the fact that a source is old is not necessarily a barrier to truth, but ideas and facts may have altered since the date of publication, and methods may have improved. Can you

Table 9.1 Checklist for assessing information in science. How reliable is the information you have been reading? The more 'yes' answers you can give below, the more trustworthy you can assume it to be

Assessing sources

- Can you identify the author's name?
- Can you determine what relevant qualifications he/she holds?
- Can you say who employs the author?
- Do you know who paid for the work to be done?
- Is this a primary, secondary or tertiary source?
- Is the content original or derived from another source?

Evaluating information

- Have you checked a range of sources?
- Is the information supported by relevant literature citation?
- Is the age of the source likely to be important regarding the accuracy of the information?
- Have you focused on the substance of the information presented rather than its packaging?
- Is the information fact or opinion?
- Have you checked for any logical fallacies in the arguments?
- Does the language used indicate anything about the status of the information?
- Have the errors associated with any numbers been taken into account?
- Have the data been analysed using appropriate statistics?
- Are any graphs constructed correctly?

Source: Jones, A., Reed, R. and Weyers, J. (2007) p. 54.

Box 9.2 Evaluating a website

With the rapid development of the Internet, an almost overwhelming amount of information is readily available online. A variety of searchable electronic databases (e.g. PubMed, SPORTDiscus, EBSCOhost), as well as many full-text online sport and exercise science journals (e.g. *Sports Medicine, Medicine and Science in Sports and Exercise, British Journal of Sports Medicine*), is accessible from a desktop. Below is a series of questions students should ask when evaluating information on the Internet:

1. **What is the source of the information?** Check the website address (URL), especially the domain of the website. If it ends with *edu* (education), *gov* (government) or *org* (organisation), the information is probably valid. In contrast, domain names ending in *com* (commercial), *net* (telecommunications), or a tilde (~) (personal home page) may need to be evaluated more closely.
2. **Who is the author?** Is the author well known or recognised within sport and exercise science? Is there information about the author such as their qualifications, affiliations with universities or research institutions, previous publications? Is the author biased toward a particular viewpoint or might they have a hidden agenda such as promoting a product or service?
3. **Is the information current?** Does the document have a publication date, date of copyright or a date when the website was last modified? For research purposes, especially in some areas (e.g. supplementation, controversial treatments), it is imperative to have current information.
4. **Are references provided?** In most assessment pieces, lecturers and tutors like to see a list of references used in projects or assignments to support your argument or conclusions. The same holds for the information you find on the Web. Are the sources supporting the information you found on the web supported by valid references or are they just an author's opinions?
5. **Are links to other websites provided?** Most websites have 'additional' or 'related' links that provide related information on the same topic. If provided, are these links credible and do they work? If so, it reflects well on the site you are looking at and evaluating.

In general, information obtained from the Internet should be treated with caution. Articles published in professional journals and reputable textbooks are more credible and trustworthy sources of information. Chapter 10 gives further advice on using and evaluating online resources.

trace changes through time in the sources available to you? What key events or publications have forced any changes in the conclusions?

- **Try to distinguish fact from opinion** – to what extent has the author supported a given viewpoint? Have relevant facts been quoted, via literature citations or the author's own researches? Are numerical data used to substantiate the points used? Are these reliable and can you verify the information, for example, by looking at the sources cited? Might the author have a reason for putting forward biased evidence to support a personal opinion?
- **Analyse the language used** – words and their use can be very revealing. Subjective wording might indicate a personal opinion rather than an objective conclusion. Propaganda and personal bias might be indicated by absolute terms, such as 'everyone knows...', 'It can be guaranteed that ...', or a seemingly one-sided consideration of the evidence. How carefully has the author considered the topic? A less studious approach might be indicated by exaggeration, ambiguity or the use of 'journalese' and slang. Always remember, however, that content should be judged above presentation.
- **Look closely at any numbers** – if the information you are looking at is numerical in form, have statistical errors been taken into consideration, and, where appropriate, quantified? If so, does this help you arrive at a conclusion about how genuine the differences are between important values?
- **Think carefully about any hypothesis-testing statistics used** – are the methods appropriate? Are the underlying hypotheses the right ones? Have the results of any tests been interpreted correctly in arriving at the conclusion? To deal with these matters, you will need at least a basic understanding of the 'statistical approach' and of commonly used techniques (see Chapters 49–51).

Learning from examples – as your lecturers introduce you to case studies, you will see how sport and exercise scientists have applied critical thinking to understand the nature of ageing, gender, the environment, fitness levels and disease on exercise or sports performance. Some of your practical or classroom experiences may mimic the processes involved – observation, hypothesis testing, experimental design, data gathering and analysis or formulating conclusions (see Chapter 22). These skills and approaches can then be applied in your coursework when writing about a topic in sport and exercise science or carrying out a research project or practical session and writing it up.

Critical thinking

Critical thinking involves the application of logic to a problem, issue or case study. It requires a wide range of skills. Key processes involved include: acquiring and processing information; creating appropriate hypotheses and formulating conclusions; and acting on the conclusions towards a specific objective.

KEY POINT Critical thinking needs reliable knowledge, but it requires you to use this appropriately to analyse a problem. It can be contrasted with rote learning – where you might memorise facts without an explicit purpose other than building your knowledge base.

'You can prove anything with statistics' – leaving aside the issue that statistical methods deal with probability, not certainty (Chapters 50, 51), it *is* possible to analyse and present data in such a way that they support one chosen argument or hypothesis rather than another. Detecting a bias of this kind can be difficult, but the critical thinking skills involved are essential for all scientists (see e.g. Box 50.3).

Critical thinking is particularly important in sport and exercise science, because the subject deals with complex and dynamic systems. These can be difficult to understand for several reasons:

- They are often multifaceted, involving many interactions.
- It can be difficult to alter one variable in an experiment without producing confounding variables (see p. 142).

- Many variables may be unmeasured or unmeasurable.
- Heterogeneity (variability) is encountered at all levels, from the molecular to the whole human organism.
- Perturbation of the system can lead to unexpected ('counterintuitive') results.

As a result, conclusions in sport and exercise science research are seldom clear-cut. Critical thinking allows you to arrive at the most probable conclusion from the results at hand; however, it also involves acknowledging that other conclusions might be possible. It allows you to weigh up these possibilities and find a working hypothesis or explanation, but also to understand that your conclusions are essentially dynamic and might alter when new facts are known. Hypothesis testing with statistics (Chapter 50) is an important adjunct to critical thinking because it demands the formulation of simple hypotheses and provides rational reasons for making conclusions.

Recognising fallacies in arguments is an important aspect of critical thinking. Philosophers and logicians recognise different forms of argument and many different fallacies in each form. Damer (2004) provides an overview of this wide-ranging and complex topic.

Analysing a graph – this process can be split into six phases:

1. Considering the context and purpose of the graph.
2. Recognising the type of presentation and examining the axes.
3. Looking closely at the scale on each axis.
4. Examining the data presented (e.g. data points, symbols, curves).
5. Considering errors and statistics associated with the graph.
6. Reaching conclusions based on the above.

These processes are examined in detail in Chapter 47.

Interpreting data

Numerical data

Information presented in public, whether as a written publication or spoken presentation, is rarely in the same form as it was when first obtained. Chapters 13 and 46 deal with processes in which data are recorded, manipulated and transformed, while Chapter 49 describes the standard descriptive statistics used to 'encapsulate' large datasets. Chapters 50 and 51 cover some relevant mathematical techniques. Sampling (essentially, obtaining representative measurements) is at the heart of many observational and experimental approaches in sport and exercise science (see Chapters 18, 19 and 21), and analysis of samples is a key component of hypothesis-testing statistics (Chapter 50). Understanding these topics and carrying out the associated study exercises will help you to improve your ability to interpret numerical data.

Analysing a table – as with analysing a graph, this process can be split into six phases:

1. Considering the context and purpose.
2. Examining the subheadings to see what information is contained in the rows and columns.
3. Considering the units used and checking any footnotes.
4. Comparing the data values across rows and/or down columns, looking for patterns, trends and unusual values.
5. Taking into account any statistics presented.
6. Reaching conclusions based on the above.

Graphs

Frequently, understanding and analysis in science depend on your ability to interpret data presented in graphical form. Sometimes, graphs may mislead. This may be unwitting, as in an unconscious effort to favour a 'pet' hypothesis of the author. Graphs may be used to 'sell' a product, e.g. in advertising, or to favour a viewpoint as, perhaps, in politics. Experience in drawing and interpreting graphs will help you spot these flawed presentations, and understanding how graphs can be erroneously presented (Box 47.3) will help you avoid the same pitfalls.

Tables

Tables, especially large ones, can appear as a mass of numbers and thus be more daunting at first sight than graphs. In essence, however, most tables are simpler than most graphs. The construction of tables is dealt with in Chapter 48.

Text reference

Damer, T.E. (2004) *Attacking Faulty Reasoning: A Practical Guide to Fallacy-Free Arguments*, 5th edn, Wadsworth, Belmont, California.

Sources for further study

Anon. *Evaluating Web Pages: Techniques to Apply & Questions to Ask*.
Available: http://www.lib.berkeley.edu/TeachingLib/Guides/Internet/Evaluate.html
Last accessed: 23/12/10.

Smith, A. *Evaluation of Information Sources*.
Available: http://www.vuw.ac.nz/staff/alastair_smith/evaln/evaln.htm
Last accessed: 23/12/10. Part of the Information Quality www Virtual Library.
[An excellent one-stop shop site for resources related to evaluating primary and secondary information sources ranging from books, through journals to websites. The site is maintained by Alastair Smith who teaches in the Library and Information Management group of the School of Information Management at Victoria University of Wellington in New Zealand.]

Van Gelder, T. *Critical Thinking on the Web*.
Available: http://www.austhink.org/critical/
Last accessed: 23/12/10.
[A useful directory of web-based resources on the topic of critical thinking. The site is linked to *Austhink*, a group based in Australia that specialises in complex reasoning and argument, including critical thinking research, training and consulting.]

10 Using online resources

> **Definitions**
>
> **Browser** – a program to display web pages and other Internet resources.
>
> **FAQ** – Frequently Asked Question; a file or web page giving information on common queries, sometimes used as a file extension (.faq).
>
> **FTP** – File Transfer Protocol; a mechanism of downloading files.
>
> **URL** – Uniform Resource Locator; the 'address' for www resources.

Information and communication technology (ICT) is vital in the modern academic world and 'IT literacy' is a core skill for all sports and exercise scientists. This involves a wide range of computer-based skills, including:

- accessing web pages using a web browser such as Microsoft Internet Explorer, Mozilla Firefox or Opera;
- searching the Web for useful information and resources using a search engine such as Google, or a meta-search engine such as Dogpile;
- finding what you need within online databases, such as library catalogues, or complex websites, such as your university's home page;
- downloading, storing and manipulating files;
- communicating via the Internet;
- using e-learning facilities effectively;
- working with 'office'-type programs and other software (dealt with in detail in Chapters 11 and 12).

You will probably receive an introduction to your university's networked IT systems and will be required to follow rules and regulations that are important for the operation of these systems. Whatever your level of experience with PCs and the Internet, you should also follow the basic guidelines shown in Box 10.1. Reminding yourself of these from time to time will reduce your chances of losing data.

Understanding the technology – you do not need to understand the workings of the Internet to use it – most of it is invisible to the user. To ensure you obtain the right facilities, you may need to know some jargon, such as terms for the speed of data transfer (megabits) and the nature of Internet addresses. Setting up a modem and/or local wireless network can be complex, but instructions are usually provided with the hardware. White and Downs (2005) and Gralla (2003) are useful texts if you wish to learn more about computing and the Internet.

The Internet as a global resource

The Internet is a complex network of computer networks; it is loosely organised and no one group organises it or owns it. Instead, many private organisations, universities and government organisations fund and operate discrete parts of it.

The most popular application of the Internet is the World Wide Web (www or 'the Web'). It allows easy links to information and files which may be located on networked computers across the world. The www enables you to access millions of 'home pages' or 'websites' – the initial point of reference with many individuals, institutions and companies. Besides text and images, these sites may contain 'hypertext links', highlighted words or phrases that take you to another location via a single mouse click.

You can gain access to the Internet either through a local area network (LAN) at your university, at most public libraries, at a commercial 'Internet cafe' or from home via a modem connected to a broadband or dial-up Internet service provider (e.g. Virgin Media, British Telecom or AOL).

> **KEY POINT** Most material on the Internet has not been subject to peer review or vetting. Information obtained from the www or posted on newsgroups may be inaccurate, biased or spoof; do not assume that everything you read is true or even legal.

Box 10.1 Important guidelines for using PCs and networks

Hardware

- Don't drink, eat or smoke around the computer.
- Try not to turn the computer off more than is necessary.
- Never turn off the electricity supply to the machine while in use.
- Switch off the computer and monitor when not in use (saves energy and avoids dangers of 'hijacking').
- Rest your eyes at frequent intervals if working for extended periods at a computer monitor. Consult Health and Safety Executive publications for up-to-date advice on working with display screens (http://www.hse.gov.uk/pubns/).
- Never try to reformat the hard disk without the help of an expert.

CDs and USB drives

- Protect CDs when not in use by keeping them in holders or boxes.
- Label USB (Universal Serial Bus) drives with your name and return details and consider adding these to a file stored on the drive.
- Try not to touch the surface of CDs, and if they need cleaning, do so carefully with a clean cloth, avoiding scratching. If floppy disks are used, keep these away from sources of magnetism (e.g. speakers).
- Keep disks and USB drives away from moisture, excess heat or cold.
- Don't use disks from others, unless you first check them for viruses.
- Don't insert or remove a disk or USB drive when it is operating (drive light on). Close all files before removing a USB drive and use the *Safely Remove Hardware* feature.
- Try not to leave a disk or USB drive in the drive when you switch the computer off.

File management

- Organise your files in an appropriate set of folders.
- Always use virus checking programs on copied or imported files before running them.
- Make back-ups of all important files at frequent intervals (say, every 10 minutes or half hour), e.g. when using a word processor or spreadsheet.
- Periodically clear out redundant files.

Network rules

- Never attempt to 'hack' into other people's files
- Do not give out any of your passwords to others. Change your password from time to time. Make sure it is not a common word, is longer than eight characters, and includes numerical characters and punctuation symbols, as well as upper- and lower-case letters.
- Never use network computers to access or provide financial or other personal information: spyware and Trojan programs may intercept your information.
- Never open email attachments without knowing where they came from; always virus check attachments before opening.
- Remember to log out of the network when finished; others can access your files if you forget to log out.
- Be polite when sending email messages.
- Periodically reorganise your email folder(s). These rapidly become filled with acknowledgements and redundant messages that reduce server efficiency and take up your allocated filespace.
- Do not play games without approval – they can affect the operation of the system.
- If you are setting up your own network, e.g. in your flat, always install up-to-date firewall software, anti-spyware and anti-virus programs.

The Golden Rule – always make back-up copies of important files and store them well away from your working copies. Ensure that the same accident cannot happen to both copies.

Online communication

You will be allocated an email account by your university and should use this routinely for communicating with staff and fellow students, rather than using a personal account. You may be asked to use email to submit work as an attachment, or you may be asked to use a 'digital drop-box'

Box 10.2 Getting to grips with e-learning

Some key aspects of tackling e-learning are outlined below.

1. **Develop your basic IT skills, if required.** e-learning requires only basic IT skills, such as: use of keyboard and mouse; word processing; file management; browsing and searching. If you feel weak on any of these, seek out additional courses offered by the IT administration or your department.
2. **Visit your e-learning modules regularly.** You should try to get into a routine of doing this on a daily basis at a time that suits you. Staff will present up- to-date information (e.g. lecture room changes) via the 'announcements' section, may post information about assessments, or links to the assessments themselves, and you may wish to provide feedback or look at discussion boards and their threads.
3. **Participate.** e-learning requires an active approach.
   - At the start of each new course, spend some time getting to know what's been provided online to support your learning. As well as valuable resources, this may include crucial information such as learning outcomes (p. 26), dates of submission for coursework and weighting of marks for different elements of the course.
   - If you are allowed to download lecture notes (e.g. in the form of PowerPoint presentations), do not think that simply reading through these will be an adequate substitute for attending lectures and making further notes (see p. 17).
   - Do not be tempted to 'lurk' on discussion boards: take part. Ask questions; start new threads; answer points raised by others if you can.
   - Try to gain as much as you can from formative online assessments (p. 26). If these include feedback on your answers, make sure you learn from this and if you do not understand it, consult your tutors.
   - Learn from the critical descriptions that your lecturers provide of linked websites. These pointers may help you to evaluate such resources for yourself in future (p. 59).
   - Don't think that you will automatically assimilate information and concepts, just because you are viewing them online. The same principles apply as with printed media: you must apply active learning methods (Box 5.1).
   - Help your lecturers by providing constructive feedback when they ask for it. You may find this easier to do when using the computer interface, and it may be more convenient than hurriedly filling out a feedback sheet at the end of a session.
4. **Organise files and web links.** Take the time to create a meaningful folder- and file-naming system for downloaded material in tandem with your own coursework files and set up folders on your browser for bookmarked websites (*Favorites* in Internet Explorer).
5. **Take care when submitting coursework.** Make sure you keep a back-up of any file you email or submit online and check the version you are sending carefully. Follow instructions carefully, for example regarding file type, or how to use your system's 'digital drop-box'.

within the university's e-learning system (Box 10.2). When using email at university, follow these conventions, including etiquette, carefully:

- **Check your email account regularly (daily).** Your tutors may wish to send urgent messages to you in this way.
- **Respond promptly to emails.** Even if you are just acknowledging receipt, it is polite to indicate that you have received and understood a message.
- **Be polite.** Email messages can seem to be abrupt and impersonal. Take care to read your messages through before sending and if you are at all in doubt, do not send your message right away: reread at a later time and consider how others might view what you say.
- **Consider content carefully.** Only send what you would be happy to hear being read out loud to classmates or family.

Spam, junk mail and phishing – these should be relatively easy to identify, and should never be responded to or forwarded. Some may look 'official' and request personal or financial details (for example, they may pretend to come from your bank, and ask for account details). Never send these details by email or your identity may be used illegally.

Newsgroups – these can be useful for obtaining answers to a specific problem: just post a query to the appropriate group and wait for someone to reply. Bear in mind that this may be the view of an individual person. A useful list of newsgroups for sport and exercise scientists can be found at: http://www.sportsci.org/links/maillists.html.

- **Take care with language and names** when communicating with tutors. Slang phrases and text message shorthand are unlikely to be understood. Overfamiliarity does not go down well.
- **Use email for academic purposes** – this includes discussing coursework with classmates, but not forwarding off-colour jokes, potentially offensive images, links to offensive websites, etc. In fact, doing so may break regulations and result in disciplinary action.
- **Beware of spam, junk and 'phishing' via email.**

Similar rules apply to discussion boards.

The Usenet Newsgroup service is an electronic discussion facility, and there are thousands of newsgroups representing different interests and topics. Any user can contribute to the discussion within a topic by posting their own message; it is like email, but without privacy, since your message becomes available to all other subscribers. To access a newsgroup, your system must be running, or have access to, a newsgroup server that has subscribed to the newsgroup of interest. Obtain a list of newsgroups available on your system from the IT administration service and search it for those of interest, then join them. Contact your network administrator if you wish to propose the addition of a specific newsgroup, but expect a large amount of information to be produced.

Internet tools

The specific programs you will use for accessing the Internet will depend on what has been installed locally, on the network you are using, and on your Internet service provider. The best way to learn the features of the programs is to try them out, making full use of whatever help services are available.

e-learning systems

Most university departments present their courses through a mixture of face-to-face sessions (e.g. lectures, tutorials, practicals) and online resources (e.g. lecture notes, websites, discussion boards, computerised tests and assessments). This constitutes 'blended learning' on your part, with the online component also being known as e-learning.

The e-learning element is usually delivered through an online module within a virtual learning environment (e.g. Moodle, WebCT, Blackboard). It is important not to neglect the e-learning aspects of your course just because they may not be as rigidly timetabled as your face-to-face sessions. This flexibility is to your advantage, as you can work when it suits you, but it requires discipline on your part. Box 10.2 provides tips for making the most of the e-learning components of your courses.

Internet browsers

These are software programs that interact with remote server computers around the world to carry out the tasks of requesting, retrieving and displaying the information you require. Many different browsers exist, but the most popular are Internet Explorer, Mozilla Firefox and Opera. These three browsers dominate the market and have plug-ins and add-on programs available that allow, for example, video sequences to be seen online. Many browsers incorporate email and newsgroup functions. The standard functions of browsers include:

- accessing web documents;
- following links to other documents;
- printing the current document;
- maintaining a history of visited URLs (including 'bookmarks' for key sites);
- searching for a term in a document;
- viewing images and image maps.

Definition

Bookmark – a feature of browsers that allows you to save details of websites you have visited. This is termed *Add to Favorites* in Internet Explorer. Bookmarks save you the trouble of remembering complex URL names and of typing them into the browser's address window.

Browsers provide access to millions of websites. Certain sites specialise in providing catalogued links to other sites; these are known as portals and can be of enormous help when searching within a particular area of interest. Your university's library website will almost certainly provide a useful portal to catalogues and search services, often arranged by subject area, and this is often the first port of call for electronic resources; get to know your way around this part of the website as early as possible during your course.

When using a web browser program to get to a particular page of information on the web, all you require is the location of that page, i.e. the URL (uniform resource locator). Most web page URLs take the form http:// or https://, followed by the various terms (domains and subdomains) that direct the system to the appropriate site. If you don't have a specific URL in mind but wish to explore appropriate sites, you will need to use a search tool with the browser.

Examples Common domains and subdomains include:

.ac	academic
.com	commercial
.co	commercial
.edu	education (USA mainly)
.gov	government (USA and UK)
.mil	military (USA only)
.net	internet-based companies
.org	organisation
.uk	United Kingdom

www search tools

With the proliferation of information on the Web, one of the main problems is finding the exact information you require. There is a variety of information services that you can use to filter the material on the network. These include:

- search engines (Boxes 10.3 and 10.4);
- meta-search engines;
- subject directories;
- subject gateways (portals).

Search engines such as Google (http://www.google.com/), Altavista (http://uk.altavista.com/) and Lycos (http://www.lycos.com/) are tools designed to search, gather, index and classify web-based information. Searching is usually by key word(s), although specific phrases can be defined. Many search engines offer advanced searching tools such as the use of Boolean operators to specify combinations of key words to filter the sites more precisely. Box 10.3 provides tips for refining key word searches while Box 10.4 provides tips for enhancing searches with Google.

'Dissecting' a web address – if a URL is specified, you can often find out more about a site by progressively deleting sections of the address from the right-hand side. This will often take you to 'higher levels' of the site, or to the home page of the organisation or company involved.

It is important to realise that each search engine will cover at most about 40% of the available sites; if you want to carry out an exhaustive search it is necessary to use several to cover as much of the Web as possible. Meta-search engines make this easier. These operate by combining collections of search engines. Examples include Mamma

Box 10.3 Useful tips for using search engines

- **Key words should be chosen with care.** Try to make them as specific as possible, e.g. search for 'Krebs cycle' rather than 'aerobic metabolism' or 'energy production'.
- **Most search engines are case-insensitive.** Thus 'Muscle Fibre' will return the same amount of hits as 'muscle fibre'. If in doubt, use lower case throughout.
- **Putting key word phrases in double quotes (e.g. "leg ergometry") will result in a search for sites with the phrase as a whole** rather than sites with both (all parts) parts of the phrase as separate words (i.e. 'leg' and 'ergometry' at different places within a site). This feature allows you to include common words normally excluded in the search, such as 'the'.
- **Use multiple words/phrases plus similar words to improve your search** (e.g. *'vastus lateralis "thigh muscle" skeletal muscle'*). If you can, use scientific terms, as you are likely to find more relevant sites, e.g. search for the name of a particular enzyme such as '*phosphofructokinase*'.
- **Adding words preceded with + or – will add or exclude sites with that word present** (e.g. training response –hypertrophy will search for all training responses excluding hypertrophy). This feature can also be used to include common words normally excluded by the search engine.
- **Check that your search terms have the correct spelling**, otherwise you may only find sites with the same mis-spelled word. In some cases, the search engine may prompt you with an alternative (correct) spelling. If a word has an alternative US spelling (e.g. color, hemoglobin), then a search may only find hits from sites that use the spelling you specify.
- **Boolean operators (AND, OR, NOT) can be used with some search engines to specify combinations of key words** to filter the sites identified more precisely (e.g. 'sport NOT physical activity' will avoid sites about physical activity and focus on sport).
- **Some search engines allow 'wildcards' to be introduced with the symbol *.** For example, this will allow you to specify the root of a word and include all possible endings, as with diabet*, which would find diabetes, diabetic, etc. If the search engine does not allow wildcards (e.g. Google), then you will need to be especially careful with the key words used, including all possible words of relevance.
- **Numbers can be surprisingly useful in search engines.** For example, typing in 'Polar s610i' will find you sites concerned with this model heart rate monitor. If you know the phone number for a person, institute or company or the ISBN of a book, this can often help you find relevant pages quickly.
- **If you arrive at a large site and cannot find the point at which your search word or phrase appears, press *Control+F*** together and a 'local' search window will appear, allowing you to find the point(s) where it is mentioned.

Downloading files from the Internet and emails – read-only files are often available as 'pdf' files that can be viewed by Adobe reader software (available free from http://www.adobe.com), while other files may be presented as attachments to emails or as links from web pages that can be opened by suitable software (e.g. Microsoft Word or 'paint' programs like Paint Shop Pro). Take great care in the latter cases as the transfer of files can result in the transfer of associated viruses. Always check new files for viruses (especially .exe files) before running them, and make sure your virus-detecting software is kept up to date.

(http://www.mamma.com/), Dogpile (http://www.dogpile.com/index.gsp/) and Metacrawler (http://www.metacrawler.com/index.html/).

Some useful approaches to searching include the following:

- For a comprehensive search, use a variety of tools including search engines, meta-search engines and portals or directories.
- For a complex, finely specified search, employ Boolean operators and other tools to refine your key words as fully as possible (Box 10.3). Some search engines allow you to include and exclude terms or restrict by date.
- Use 'cascading' searching when available – this is searching within the results of a previous search.
- Use advanced search facilities to limit your search, where possible, to the type of medium you are looking for (e.g. graphics, video), language, sites in a specific country (e.g. UK) or to a subject area (e.g. news only).

Box 10.4 Getting the most from Google searches

Google (http://www.google.com) has become the search engine of choice for millions of people owing to its simplicity and effectiveness. However, you may be able to improve your searches by understanding its default searches and how they can be changed.

- **Download the Google toolbar to your browser.** This is available from the Google home page and will give you quick access to the Google search facility.
- **Understand how standard operators are used.** For combinations of key words Google uses the minus operator '–' instead of NOT (exclude) and '+' instead of AND (include). Since Google usually ignores small words ('stop words' such as *in* or *the*), use '+' to include them in a search. Where no operator is specified, Google assumes that you are looking for both terms (i.e. '+' is default). If you want to search for alternative words, you can use 'OR' (e.g. *fibre* OR *fiber*). Google does not allow brackets and also ignores most punctuation marks.
- **When wildcard truncation of words using '*' is not allowed, you can use '*' to replace a whole word (or number).** For example, if you type the phrase *"a muscle fibre is approximately * in diameter"* your results will give you results for web pages where the wildcard is replaced by a number.
- **Search for exact wording.** By placing text in double inverted commas ("), you can ensure that only websites with this exact phrasing will appear at the head of your search results.
- **Search within your results to improve the outcome.** If your first search has produced a large number of results, use the *Search within results* option near the bottom of each page to type in a further word or phrase.
- **Search for words within the title of a web page.** Use the command *intitle:* to find a web page, for example *intitle: "oxygen consumption"* returns web pages with this phrase in the title (note that phrases must always be in double speech marks, not single quotes).
- **Search within a website.** Use the *site*: command to locate words/phrases on a specific website, for example *site:gssiweb.com electrolytes* returns only those results for 'electrolytes' on the Gatorade Sports Science website (http://www.gssiwbd.com). Pressing *Control+F* when visiting a web page will give you a pop-up search window.
- **Locate definitions, symbols and spellings.** The operator *define:* enables you to find the meaning of a word. If you are unsure as to the spelling of a word, try each possibility: Google will usually return more results for the correct spelling and will often also prompt you with the correct spelling (*Did you mean . . . .* ?).
- **Find similar web pages.** Simply click the Similar pages option at the end of a Google search result to list other sites (note that these sites will not necessarily include the term(s) searched for).
- **If a web link is unavailable, try the cached (stored) page.** Clicking on *Cached* at the end of a particular result should take you to the stored page, with the additional useful feature that the search term(s) will be highlighted.
- **Use the calculator functions.** Simply enter a calculation and press *Enter* to display the result, for example '10+(2*4)' returns 18. The calculator function can also carry out simple interconversion of units, e.g. '*2 feet 6 inches in metres*' returns 0.762 (see Chapter 20 for interconversion factors between SI and non-SI units).
- **Try out the advanced search features.** In addition to the standard operators these include the ability to specify the number of results per page (e.g. 50, to reduce the use of the *next* button), language (e.g. English), file format (e.g. for PDF files), recently updated web pages (e.g. past three months), usage (free to use/share).
- **Find non-text material.** These include images, video and maps – always check that any material you use is not subject to copyright limitations (p. 56).
- **Use Google alerts to keep up to date.** This function (http://www.google.co.uk/alerts) enables you to receive regular updated searches by email.
- **Use Google Scholar to find articles and papers.** Go to http://scholar.google.com/ and type in either the general topic or specific details for a particular article, e.g. author name or words from the title. Results show titles/authors of articles, with links to either the full article, abstract or citation. A very useful feature is the *Cited by . . .* link, taking you to those papers that have cited the article in the bibliography and enabling you to carry out forward citation searching to locate more recent papers. Also try out the advanced scholar search features to limit your search to a particular author, journal, date or subject area. However, you should note that Google Scholar provides only a basic search facility to easily accessible articles and should not be viewed as a replacement for your library's electronic journal holdings and search software. For example, if you find the title of a paper via Google Scholar you may be able to locate the electronic version through your library's databases, or request through interlibrary loan. Another significant limitation is that old (more cited) references are typically listed first.
- **Use Google Earth to explore locations.** This allows you to zoom in on satellite images in find locations.

Box 10.5 How to evaluate information on the World Wide Web

It is often said that 'you can find anything on the Web'. The two main disadvantages of this are, firstly, that you may need to sift through many sources before you find what you are looking for and, secondly, that the sources you find will vary in their quality and validity. *It is important to realise that evaluating sources is a key aspect of using the Internet for academic purposes, and one that you will need to develop during the course of your studies.* The ease with which you can 'point and click' to reach various sources should not make you complacent about evaluating their information content. The following questions can help you to assess the quality of a website – the more times you can answer 'yes', the more credible the source is likely to be, and vice versa.

Authority

- Is the author identified?
- Are the author's qualifications or credentials given?
- Is the owner, publisher or sponsoring organisation identified?
- Is an address given (postal and/or email)?

It is sometimes possible to obtain information on authority from the site's metadata (try the 'View' 'Source' option in Internet Explorer, or look at the URL to see if it gives any clues as to the organisation, e.g. does the domain name end in .ac, .edu, .gov or .org, rather than .co or .com?).

Content

- Is there any evidence that the information has been peer-reviewed (p. 59), edited or otherwise validated, or is it based on such sources?
- Is the information factual or based on personal opinions?
- Are the factual data original (primary) or derived from other sources (secondary)?
- Are the sources of specific factual information detailed in full (p. 52)?
- Is there any indication that the information is up to date, or that the site has been recently updated?
- What is the purpose of the site and who is it aimed at?
- Is the content relevant to the question you are trying to answer?
- Is there any evidence of a potential conflict of interest, or bias? (Is the information comprehensive and balanced, or narrowly focused?)
- Did you find the information via a subject-specific website (e.g. an exercise science database such as SPORTDiscus), or through a more general source, such as a search engine (e.g. Google)?

The above questions are similar to those that you would use in assessing the value of a printed resource (pp. 55–8), and similar criteria should be applied to web-based information. You should be especially wary of sites containing unattributed factual information or data whose primary source is not given.

Presentation

- What is your overall impression of how well the site has been put together?
- Are there many grammatical or spelling mistakes?
- Are there links to other websites to support statements and factual information?

The care with which a site has been constructed can give you an indication of the credibility of the author/organisation. However, while a poorly presented site may cause you to question the credibility of the information, the reverse is not always necessarily true: don't be taken in by a slick, well presented website – authority and content are *always* more important than presentation.

It is important to understand the impermanence of the Web. The temporary nature of much of the material on the Web is a disadvantage for academic purposes because it may change or even disappear after you have cited it. You may also find it difficult or impossible to find out who authored the material (p. 58). A case in point are wikis, such as Wikipedia (www.wikipedia.org). This online encyclopedia has many potential authors and the content may change rapidly as a result of new submissions or edits; nevertheless, it can be a useful resource for up-to-date general information about a wide range of topics, though it is not necessarily regarded as the best approach for researching assignments.

Using traditional sources – remember that using the Internet to find information is not a substitute for visiting your university library. Internet resources complement rather than replace CD-ROM and more traditional printed sources.

Remembering useful websites – create a 'bookmark' (=*Add a Favorite*) for the ones you find of value, to make revisiting easy. This can be done from the menu of your browser program. Make a copy of your bookmark file occasionally, to avoid loss of this information.

Examples Selected websites of interest to sport and exercise scientists:

British Association of Sport and Exercise Science
http://www.bases.org.uk/home.asp

Gatorade Sport Science Institute
http://www.gssiweb.com/

Sportscience http://www.sportsci.org/

National Strength and Conditioning Association http://www.nsca-lift.org/

European Congress of Sports Science
http://www.ecss.de/

American College of Sports Medicine
http://www.acsm.org//AM/Template.cfm?Section=Home_Page

English Institute of Sport http://www.eis2win.co.uk/pages/

Australian Institute of Sport
www.ausport.gov.au/ais/

MAPEI Sports Science Centre
http://www.mapeisport.it/default.asp?LNG=EN

Note that URLs may change – make a key word search using a search engine to find a particular site if the URL information you have does not lead you to an active page.

However well defined your search is, you will still need to evaluate the information obtained. Chapter 9 covers general aspects of this topic, while Box 10.5 provides specific advice on assessing the quality of information provided on websites.

Directories

A directory is a list of web resources organised by subject. It can usually be browsed and may or may not have a search facility. Directories often contain better-quality information than the lists produced by search engines, as they have been evaluated, often by subject specialists or librarians. The BUBL information service directory of links (http://bubl.ac.uk/) is a good example.

Using the Internet as a resource

A common way of finding information on the Web is by browsing or 'surfing'. However, this can be time-consuming; try to restrict yourself to sites known to be relevant to the topic of interest. Some of the most useful sites are those that provide hypertext links to other locations. Some other resources you can use on the www are:

- **Libraries, databases and publishers.** Your university library is likely to subscribe to one or more databases providing access to scientific articles (p. 50). A password is usually required, especially for off-campus use; consult your library staff for further details. Some scientific databases give free access, without subscription or passwords (p. 50). Most libraries have subject guides specific to sport and exercise science that can help guide you to these databases, as well as serving as useful references themselves. Publishers such as Pearson (http://vig.pearsoned.co.uk/) and booksellers such as Amazon.com (http://www.amazon.com) provide online catalogues and resources as well.
- **Online journals and e-books.** The majority of sport and exercise science journals have websites and now publish electronically as well as in print. However, to access these journals you will most likely be required to access using your library's subscription. Some journals offer free access to articles which have been published for longer than 12 months (e.g. *British Journal of Sports Medicine* (http://bjsm.bmj.com/), *Journal of Applied Physiology* (http://jap.physiology.org/), and some publish complete access at no cost, e.g. *Journal of Exercise Physiology Online* (http://faculty.css.edu/tboone2/asep/JEPonline.html) and *Journal of Sports Science and Medicine* (http://www.jssm.org/)).
- **Data and images.** Archives of text material, video clips and photographs are readily available and can be accessed via the Internet. A highly useful search engine for this is Google Images (http://images.google.com.au/imghp?ie=UTF-8&hl=en&tab=wi). When downloading such material, you should (1) check that you are not breaching copyright, and (2) avoid potential plagiarism by giving a full citation of the source, if you use such images in an assignments (p. 56).

- **Exercise science institutions.** Many sporting institutions around the world are online and post useful information on their websites. Such famous institutions include the English Institute of Sport, the Australian Institute of Sport and the MAPEI Sports Science Centre. Some commercial organisations (e.g. British Association of Sport and Exercise Science, American College of Sports Medicine) also provide useful web resources.

Text references

Gralla, P. (2003) *How the Internet Works*, 7th edn, Pearson, Harlow.

White, R. and Downs, T. (2005) *How Computers Work*, 8th edn, Pearson, Harlow.

Sources for further study

Anon. *The Essentials of Google Search*. Available: http://www.google.co.uk/intl/en/help/basics.html
Last accessed: 23/12/10.
[Advice for using the Google search engine.]

Anon. *Using the Internet*. Available: http://www.sofweb. vic.edu.au/internet/research.htm
Last accessed: 23/12/10.
[Provided by the State of Victoria, Department of Education and Training.]

Brandt, D.S. *Why We Need to Evaluate What We Find on the Internet*. Available: http://www.lib.purdue.edu/research/techman/eval.html
Last accessed: 23/12/10.

Dussart, G. (2002) *Biosciences on the Internet*. Wiley, Chichester.

Grassian, E. *Thinking Critically about World Wide Web Resources*. Available:
http://www.library.ucla.edu/libraries/college/help/critical/index.htm
Last accessed: 23/12/10.

Isaacs, T. and Isaacs, M. (2000) *Internet Users Guide to Network Resource Tools*, 2000 edn, Addison-Wesley, Harlow.

Winship, I. and McNab, A. (2000) *Students' Guide to the Internet 2000–2001*. Library Association, London.

11 Using spreadsheets

Definitions

Spreadsheet – a display of a grid of cells into which numbers, text or formulae can be typed to form a worksheet. Each cell is uniquely identifiable by its column and row number combination (i.e. its 2-D coordinates) and can contain a formula that makes it possible for an entry to one cell to alter the contents of one or more other cells.

Template – a predesigned spreadsheet without data but including all formulae necessary for (repeated) data analysis.

Macro – a sequence of user-defined instructions carried out by the spreadsheet, allowing complex repeated tasks to be 'automated'.

Office suite – a package of complementary and integrated programs such as a word processor, a spreadsheet and a database.

The spreadsheet is one of the most powerful and flexible computer applications. It can be described as the electronic equivalent of a paper-based longhand calculation, where the sums are carried out automatically. Spreadsheets provide a dynamic method of storing, manipulating and analysing datasets. Advantages of spreadsheets include:

- Ease and convenience – especially when complex calculations are repeated on different sets of data.
- Accuracy – providing the entry data and cell formulae are correct, the result will be free of calculation errors.
- Improved presentation – data can be produced in graphical or tabular form to a very high quality.
- Integration with other programs – graphs and tables can be exported to other compatible programs, such as a word processor in the same office suite.
- Useful tools – advanced features include hypothesis-testing statistics, database features and macros.

Spreadsheets can be used to:

- manipulate raw data by removing the drudgery of repeated calculations, allowing easy transformation of data and calculation of statistics;
- graph out your data rapidly to get an instant evaluation of results. Printouts can be used in practical and project reports;
- carry out statistical analysis by built-in procedures or by allowing construction of formulae for specific tasks;
- model 'what if' situations where the consequences of changes in data can be seen and evaluated.

The spreadsheet (Fig. 11.1) is divided into rows (identified by numbers) and columns (identified by alphabetic characters). Each individual combination of column and row forms a cell that can contain either a data item, a formula or a piece of text. Formulae can include scientific and/or statistical functions and/or a reference to other cells or groups of cells (often called a range). Complex systems of data input and analysis can be constructed. The analysis, in part or complete, can be printed out. New data can be added at any time and the sheet will recalculate automatically. The power a spreadsheet offers is directly related to your ability to create arrays of formulae (models) that are accurate and templates that are easy to use.

Data output from analytical instruments – many devices provide output in spreadsheet-compatible form (e.g. a 'comma delimited' file). Once you have uploaded the information into a spreadsheet, you can manipulate, analyse and present it according to your needs. Consult instrument manuals and the spreadsheet help function for details.

Data entry

Spreadsheets have built-in commands that allow you to control the layout of data in the cells (see Fig. 11.2). These include number format, the number of decimal places to be shown (the spreadsheet always calculates using eight or more places), the cell width and the location of the entry within the cell (left, right or centre). An auto-entry facility assists greatly in entering large amounts of data by moving the entry cursor either vertically or horizontally as data are entered. Recalculation default is usually

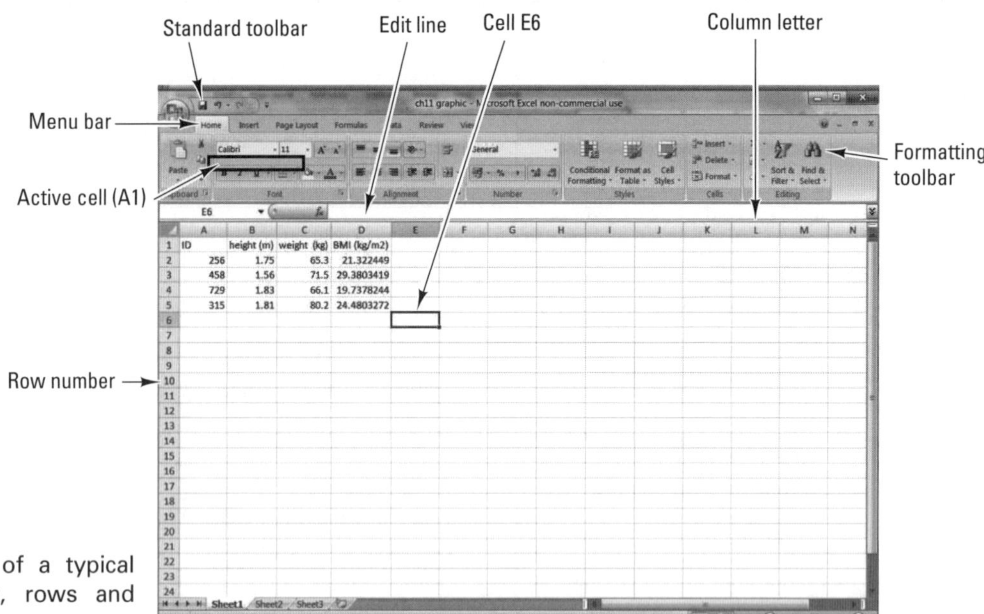

Fig. 11.1 The appearance of a typical spreadsheet, showing cells, rows and columns, toolbars, etc.

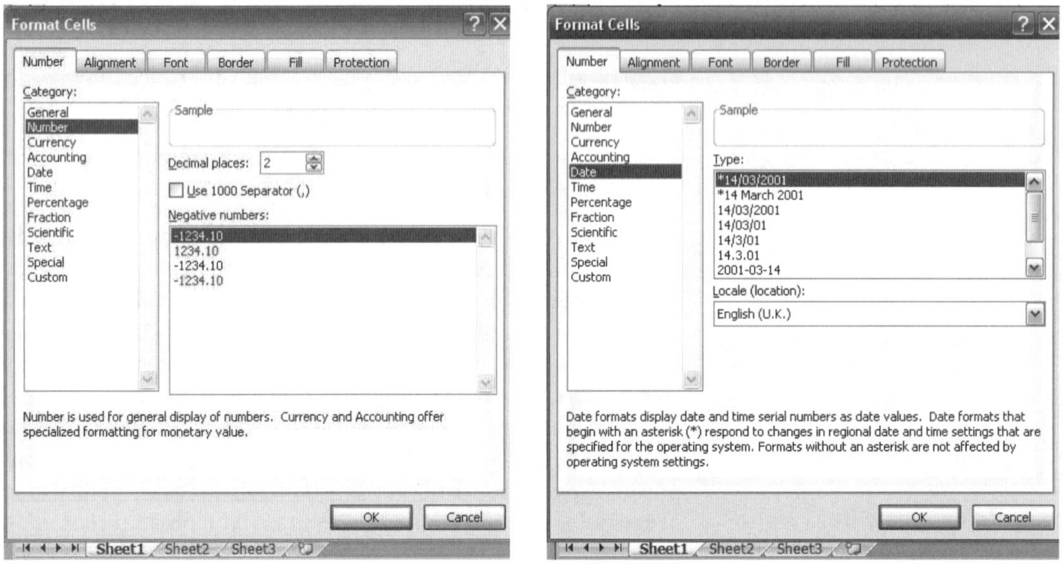

(a)

(b)

Fig 11.2 Example of cell formatting options within the Microsoft Excel spreadsheet. These menus are accessed via the *Format > Cell* option and would apply to all of a range of selected cells. **(a)** Use of the number formatting option to specify that data will be presented to three decimal places (the underlying data will be held to greater accuracy). **(b)** Use of the date formatting option to specify that dates will be presented in day/month/year format. (Spreadsheet dates are stored numerically and converted to appropriate formats. This allows a period between two dates to be calculated more easily.)

Source: Microsoft Excel 2007 screenshots reprinted with permission from Microsoft Corporation.

automatic so that when a new data value is entered the entire sheet is recalculated immediately.

The parts of a spreadsheet

Labels

These should be used to identify parts of the spreadsheet – for example, stating what data are contained in a particular column or indicating that a cell's contents represent the endpoint of a calculation. It may be useful to use the *Format Cells Border* and *Format Cells Fill* function to delimit numerical sections of your spreadsheet. Note that spreadsheet programs have been designed to make assumptions about the nature of data entry being made. If the first character is a number, then the entry is treated as numerical data; if it is a letter, then it is treated as a text entry; and if it is a specific symbol ('=' in Microsoft Excel), then what follows is a formula. If you wish to enter text that starts with a number, then you must type a designated character to show this (a single quote mark in Microsoft Excel).

Using hidden (or zero-width) columns – these are useful for storing intermediate calculations that you do not wish to be displayed on the screen or printout.

Numbers

You can also enter numbers (values) in cells for use in calculations. Many programs let you enter numbers in more than one way and you must decide which method you prefer. The way you enter the number does not affect the way it is displayed on the screen as this is controlled by the cell format at the point of entry. There are usually special ways to enter data for percentages, currency and scientific notation for very large and small numbers.

Operators and brackets in spreadsheets – the standard mathematical operators ÷ and × are usually replaced by / and * respectively, while ^ signifies 'to the power'. In complex formulae, brackets should be used to separate the elements, otherwise the results may not be what you expect. For example, Excel will calculate =A1*B1/C1−D1 differently from (A1*B1)/(C1−D1).

Formulae

These are the 'power tools' of the spreadsheet because they do the calculations. A cell can be referred to by its alphanumeric code, e.g. A5 (column A, row 5) and the value contained in that cell manipulated within a formula, e.g. = (A5 + 10) or (A5 + B22) in another cell. Formulae can include pre-programmed functions that can refer to a cell, so that if the value of that cell is changed, so is the result of the formula calculation. They may also include branching options through the use of logical operators (e.g. IF, TRUE, FALSE, OR, etc.).

Definition

Function – a pre-programmed code for the transformation of values (mathematical or statistical functions) or selection of text characters (string functions).

Functions

A variety of functions is usually offered, but only mathematical and statistical functions will be considered here.

Example – sin(A5) is an example of a function in Excel. If you write this in a cell, the spreadsheet will calculate the sine of the number in cell A5 (assuming it to be an angle in radians) and write it in the cell. Different programs may use a slightly different syntax.

Mathematical functions

Spreadsheets offer a wide range of functions, including trigonometrical functions, angle functions, logarithms and random number functions. Functions are invaluable for transforming sets of data rapidly and can be used in formulae required for more complex analyses. Spreadsheets work with an order of preference of the operators in much the same way as a standard calculator, and this must always be taken into account when operators are used in formulae. They also require a very precise syntax – the program should warn you if you break this.

Empty cells – note that these may be given the value 0 by the spreadsheet for certain functions. This may cause errors, e.g. by rendering a minimum value inappropriate. Also, an 'error return' may result for certain functions if the cell content is zero.

Statistical calculations – make sure you understand whether any functions you employ are for populations or samples (see p. 141).

Using text functions – these allow you to manipulate text within your spreadsheet and include functions such as 'search and replace' and alphabetical or numerical 'sort'.

	Cell	Formula	
Original → cell	A1	=B1+C1	← Original formula
Copied cells ↓	A2	=B2+C2	Copied formulae (relative)
	A3	=B3+C3	
	A4	=B4+C4	

(a)

	Cell	Formula	
Original → cell	A1	=B1/$C$1	← Original formula
Copied cells ↓	A2	=B2/$C$1	Copied formulae (mixed relative and absolute)
	A3	=B3/$C$1	
	A4	=B4/$C$1	

(b)

Fig. 11.3 Illustration of relative (**a**) and absolute (**b**) copying. In Excel, the $ sign before and after the column letter makes the cell reference absolute, as shown in (**b**).

Statistical functions

Modern spreadsheets incorporate many sophisticated statistical functions, and if these are not appropriate, the spreadsheet can be used to facilitate the calculations required for most of the statistical tests found in textbooks. The descriptive statistics normally available include:

- the sum of all data present in a column, row or block;
- the minimum and maximum of a defined range of cells;
- counts of cells – a useful operation if you have an unknown or variable number of data values;
- averages and other statistics describing location;
- standard deviations and other statistics describing dispersion.

A useful function where you have large numbers of data allows you to create frequency distributions using predefined class intervals.

The hypothesis-testing statistical functions are usually reasonably powerful (e.g. *t*-test, ANOVA, regressions) and they often return the *probability* (P) of obtaining the test statistic when the null hypothesis (p. 139) is true (where $0 < P < 1$), so there may be no need to refer to statistical tables. Again, check on the effects of including empty cells.

Database functions

Many spreadsheets can be used as simple databases and offer a range of functions to support this, including filtering and sorting options. The rows and columns of the spreadsheet are used as the fields and records of the database (see Chapter 12). For many purposes in sport and exercise sciences, this form of database is perfectly adequate and should be seriously considered before using a full-feature database product.

Copying

All programs provide a means of copying (replicating) formulae or cell contents when required, and this is a very useful feature. This is usually accomplished by 'dragging' a cell's contents to a new range, using the mouse. When copying, references to cells may be either relative, changing with the row/column as they are copied, or absolute, remaining a fixed cell reference and not changing as the formulae are copied (Fig. 11.3).

KEY POINT The distinction between relative and absolute cell references is very important and must be understood; it provides one of the most common forms of error when copying formulae.

In Excel, copying is normally *relative* and if you wish a cell reference to be *absolute* when copied, this is done by putting a dollar ($) sign before and after the column reference letter, e.g. $C$56.

Naming blocks

When a group of cells (a block) is carrying out a particular function, it is often easier to give the block a name that can then be used in all formulae referring to that block. This powerful feature also allows the spreadsheet to be more readable.

Templates – these should contain:

- a data input section;
- data transformation and/or calculation sections;
- a results section, which can include graphics;
- text in the form of headings and annotations;
- a summary section.

Spreadsheet templates

A template is a preconstructed spreadsheet containing the formulae required for repeated data analysis. Data are added when they become available, and results are available as soon as the last item is entered. To create a template, the sequence of operations is:

1. Determine what information/statistics you want to produce.
2. Identify the variables you will need to use, both for original data that will be entered and for any intermediate calculations that might be required.
3. Set up areas of the spreadsheet for data entry, calculation of intermediate values (statistical values such as sums of squares, etc.), calculation of final parameters/statistics and, if necessary, a summary area.
4. Establish the format of the numeric data if this is different from the default values. This can be done globally (affecting the entire spreadsheet) or locally (affecting only a specified part of the spreadsheet).
5. Establish the column widths required for the various activities.
6. Add text (labels) to identify input, intermediate formulae and output cells. This is valuable in error tracking and when carrying out further development work. Text can be entered in designated cells, or cells can be annotated using the 'comments' feature (*Insert* > *Comment*).
7. Enter a test set of values to use during formula entry: use a fully worked example to check that formulae are working correctly.
8. Enter the formulae required to make all the calculations, both intermediate and final. Check that results are correct using the test data.

Constructing a spreadsheet – start with a simple model and extend it gradually, checking for correct operation as you go.

The spreadsheet is then ready for use. Delete all of the test data values and you have created your template. Save the template to a disk and it is then available for repeated operations.

Graphics display

Most spreadsheets now offer a wide range of graphics facilities that are easy to use, and this represents an ideal way to examine your datasets rapidly and comprehensively. The quality of the final graphics output (to a printer) is variable but is usually perfectly sufficient for data exploration and analysis. Many of the options are business graphics styles but there are usually histogram, bar charts, X–Y plotting, line and area graphics options available. Note that some spreadsheet graphics may not come up to the standards expected for the formal presentation of scientific data, unless you manipulate the initial output appropriately (see Box 47.2).

Printing spreadsheets

This is usually a straightforward menu-controlled procedure, made difficult only by the fact that your spreadsheet may be too big to fit on one piece of paper. Try to develop an area of the sheet that contains only the data that you will be printing, e.g. perhaps a summary area. Remember that columns can usually be hidden for printing purposes and you can control whether the printout is in portrait or landscape mode, and for continuous paper or single sheets (depending on printer capabilities). Use a screen-preview option, if available, to check your layout before printing. A 'print to fit' option is also available in some programs, making the output fit the page dimensions.

Sources for further study

Hart-Davies, G. (2007) *How to Do Everything with Microsoft Office Excel 2007.* McGraw-Hill Education, Berkeley, California.

Harvey, G. (2006) *Excel 2007 for Dummies.* Wiley, New York.

(And similar texts for other release versions.)

12 Word processors, databases and other packages

A well presented assignment, literature review or project write-up will be looked upon very favourably by lecturers and tutors marking your work. Learning how to format documents properly in word processing packages, making them typographically friendly in an easy-to-read layout, and knowing how to embed graphs and tables into the document will enhance your chances of getting higher marks in your assessment piece.

Word processors

Word processing is a transferable skill valuable beyond the immediate requirements of your degree programme. The word processor has facilitated writing because of the ease of revising text. Using a word processor will improve your writing skills and speed because you can create, check and change your text on the screen before printing it as 'hard copy' on paper. Once entered and saved, multiple uses can be made of a piece of text with little effort.

When using a word processor you can:

- refine material many times before submission;
- insert material easily, allowing writing to take place in any sequence;
- use a spellchecker to check your text;
- use a thesaurus when composing your text;
- carry out ongoing checks of the word count;
- produce high-quality final copies;
- reuse part or all of the text in other documents.

The computerised office – many word processors are sold as part of an integrated suite, e.g. Corel WordPerfect Office and Microsoft Office, with the advantage that they share a common interface in the different components (word processor, spreadsheet, database, etc.) and allow ready exchange of information (e.g. text, graphics) between component programs.

The potential disadvantages of using a word processor include:

- lack of ready access to a computer, software and/or a printer;
- time taken to learn the operational details of the program;
- the temptation to make 'trivial' revisions;
- loss of files due to computer breakdown, or disk loss or failure.

There is a variety of word processing programs or 'packages' available. These include Microsoft Word, WordPerfect, Open Office and Star Office (PC and Mac); iWork Pages, Apple Works and TextEdit (Mac).

Word processors come as 'packages' comprising the program and a manual, often with a tutorial program that may be available in full text online (see Sources for further study). Examples are WordPerfect and Microsoft Word. Most word processors have similar general features but differ in operational detail; it is best to pick one and stick to it as far as possible so that you become familiar with it. Learning to use the package is like learning to drive a car – you need only to know how to drive the computer and its program, not to understand how the engine (program) and transmission (data transfer) work, although a little background knowledge is often helpful and will allow you to get the most from the program.

Using textbooks, manuals and tutorials – most programs no longer come with paper-based manuals, and support information is usually provided in one or more of the following ways: as a help facility within the program; as a help file on the program CD; or as an online help support site. It is still often worthwhile investing in one of the commercial textbooks that support specific programs.

In most word processors, the appearance of the screen realistically represents what the printout on paper will look like (WYSIWYG – what you see is what you get). Because of variation in operational details, only general and strategic information is provided in this chapter: you must learn the details of your word processor through use of the appropriate manual and 'help' facilities.

Before starting you will need:

- the program (usually installed on a hard disk or available via a network);
- a medium for storage, retrieval and back-up of your own files when created;
- a draft page layout design: in particular you should have decided on page size, page margins, typeface (font) and size, type of text justification, and format of page numbering;
- an outline of the text content;
- access to a suitable printer: this need not be attached to the computer you are using since your file can be taken or sent to an office where a printer is available, providing that it has the same word processing program.

Using a word processor – take full advantage of the differences between word processing and 'normal' writing (which necessarily follows a linear sequence and requires more planning):

- Simply jot down your initial ideas for a plan, preferably at paragraph topic level. The order can be altered easily and if a paragraph grows too much it can easily be split.
- Start writing wherever you wish and fill in the rest later.
- Just put down your ideas as you think, confident in the knowledge that it is the concepts that are important to note; their order and the way you express them can be adjusted later.
- Don't worry about spelling and use of synonyms – these can (and should) be checked during a separate revision run through your text, using the spellchecker first to correct obvious mistakes, then the thesaurus to change words for style or to find the mot juste.
- Don't forget that a draft printout may be required to check (a) for spacing – difficult to correct for on-screen; and (b) to ensure that words checked for spelling fit the required sense.

Laying out (formatting) your document

Although you can format your text at any time, it is good practice to enter the basic commands at the start of your document: entering them later can lead to considerable problems due to reorganisation of the text layout. If you use a particular set of layout criteria regularly, e.g. an A4 page with space for a letterhead, make a template containing the appropriate settings that can be called up whenever you start a new document. Note that various printers may respond differently to particular settings, resulting in a different spacing and layout.

Typing the text

If new to word processing, think of the screen as a piece of typing paper. The cursor marks the position where your text/data will be entered and can be moved around the screen by use of the cursor-control keys. When you type, don't worry about running out of space on the line because the text will wrap around to the next line automatically. Do not use a carriage return (usually the [ENTER] or [↵] key) unless you wish to force a new line, e.g. when a new paragraph is wanted. If you make a mistake when typing, correction is easy. You can usually delete characters or words or lines and the space is closed automatically. You can also insert new text in the middle of a line or word. You can insert special codes to carry out a variety of tasks, including changing text appearance such as <u>underlining</u>, **emboldening** and *italics*. Paragraph indentations can be automated using [TAB] or [⇆], but you can also indent or bullet whole blocks of text using special menu options. The function keys are usually pre-programmed to assist in many of these operations. Most word processing programs have a 'help' (?) function at the top right of the menu toolbar to guide you through any problems. Most programs allow you to customise your toolbar to meet your own word processing needs.

Deleting and restoring text – because deletion can sometimes be made in error, there is usually an 'undelete' or 'restore' feature that allows the last deletion to be recovered.

Editing features

Word processors usually have an array of features designed to make editing documents easy. In addition to the simple editing procedures described above, the program usually offers facilities to allow blocks of text to be moved ('cut and paste'), copied or deleted.

An extremely valuable editing facility is the 'find' or 'search' procedure: this can rapidly scan through a document looking for a specified word, phrase or punctuation. This is particularly valuable when combined with a 'replace' facility so that, for example, you could replace the word 'test' with 'trial' throughout your document simply and rapidly.

Most word processors have a command that reveals the normally hidden codes controlling the layout and appearance of the printed text. When editing, this can be a very important feature, since some changes to your text will cause difficulties if these hidden codes are not taken into account; in particular, make sure that the cursor is at the correct point before making changes to text containing hidden code, otherwise your text will sometimes change in apparently mystifying ways.

Fonts and line spacing

Most word processors offer a variety of fonts depending upon the printer being used. Fonts come in a wide variety of types and sizes, but they are defined in particular ways as follows:

Presenting your documents – it is good practice not to mix typefaces too much in a formal document; also the font size should not differ greatly for different headings, subheadings and the text.

- **Typeface:** the term for a family of characters of a particular design, each of which is given a particular name. The most commonly used for normal text is Times Roman (as used here for the main text) but many others are widely available, particularly for the better-quality printers. They fall into three broad groups: serif fonts with curves and flourishes at the ends of the characters (e.g. Times Roman); sans serif fonts without such flourishes, providing a clean, modern appearance (e.g. Helvetica, also known as Swiss); and decorative fonts used for special purposes only, such as the production of newsletters and notices.
- **Size:** measured in points. A point is the smallest typographical unit of measurement, there being 72 points to the inch (about 28 points per cm). The standard sizes for text are 10, 11 and 12 point, but typefaces are often available up to 72 point or more.

Preparing draft documents – use double spacing to allow room for your editing comments on the printed page.

- **Appearance:** many typefaces are available in a variety of styles and weights. Many of these are not designed for use in scientific literature but for desktop publishing.
- **Spacing:** can be either fixed, where every character is the same width, or proportional, where the width of every character, including spaces, varies. Line spacing can be 1.0, 1.15, 1.5, 2.0 or greater. For university assignments, 1.5 or 2.0 spacing is usually recommended with wide margins so that comments can be written between lines or in margins.

Preparing final documents – for most work, use a 12-point proportional serif typeface, with spacing dependent upon the specifications for the work.

- **Justification:** this is the term describing the way in which text is aligned vertically. Left justification is normal, but for formal documents, both left and right justification may be used (as here).

You should also consider the vertical spacing of lines in your document. Drafts and manuscripts are frequently double-spaced. If your document has unusual font sizes, this may well affect line spacing, although most word processors will cope with this automatically.

Table construction

Tables can be produced by a variety of methods:

- Using the tab key [⇆] that moves the cursor to predetermined positions on the page, equivalent to the start of each tabular column. You can define the positions of these tabs as required at the start of each table.
- Using special table constructing procedures (see Box 48.2). Here the table construction is largely done for you and it is much easier than using tabs, providing you enter the correct information when you set up the table.
- Using a spreadsheet to construct the table and then copying it to the word processor (see Box 48.2). This procedure requires considerably more manipulation than using the word processor directly and is best reserved for special circumstances, such as the presentation of a very large or complex table of data, especially if the data are already stored as a spreadsheet.

Graphics and special characters

Many word processors can incorporate graphics from other programs into the text of a document. Files must be compatible (see your manual) but when this is the case, it is a relatively straightforward procedure. For example, Microsoft office programs (Word, Excel, PowerPoint) are all compatible. For professional documents this is a valuable facility, but for most undergraduate work it is probably better to produce and use graphics as a separate operation, e.g. using a spreadsheet (see Box 47.2).

You can draw lines and other graphical features directly within most word processors, and special characters (e.g. Greek characters or ±) may be available dependent upon your printer's capabilities.

Inserting special characters – Greek letters and other characters are available using the 'Insert' and 'Symbols' features in Word.

Tools

Many word processors also offer you special tools, the most important of which are:

- **Macros:** special sets of files you can create when you have a frequently repeated set of keystrokes to make. You can record these keystrokes as a 'macro' so that it can provide a shortcut for repeated operations.
- **Thesaurus:** used to look up alternative words of similar or opposite meaning while composing text at the keyboard.
- **Spellcheck:** a very useful facility that will check your spellings against a dictionary provided by the program. This dictionary is often expandable to include specialist words that you use in your work. The danger lies in becoming too dependent upon this facility, as they all have limitations: in particular, they will not pick up incorrect words that happen to be correct in a different context (i.e. 'was' typed as 'saw' or 'see' rather than 'sea'). Be aware of American spellings in programs from the USA, e.g. 'color' instead of 'colour'. The rule, therefore, is to use the spellcheck first and then carefully read the text for errors that have slipped through.

Using a spellcheck facility – do not rely on this to spot all errors. Remember that spellcheck programs do not correct grammatical errors.

- **Grammar check:** many word processing packages automatically check both spelling and grammar as you type your document. For example, Microsoft Word uses wavy red lines under words that may be misspelt and wavy green lines under phrases or sentences with possible grammatical errors.
- **Word count:** useful when you are writing to a prescribed limit.

Printing from your program

If more than one printer is attached to your PC or network, you will need to specify which one to use from the word processor's print menu. Most printers offer choices as to text and graphics quality, so choose draft (low) quality for all but your final copy since this will save both time and materials.

Using the print preview mode – this can reveal errors of several kinds, e.g. spacing between pages, that can prevent you wasting paper and printer ink unnecessarily.

Use a 'print preview' option to show the page layout if it is available. Assuming that you have entered appropriate layout and font commands, printing is a straightforward operation carried out by the word processor at your command. Problems usually arise because of some incompatibility between the criteria you have entered and the printer's own capabilities. Make sure that you know what your printer offers before starting to type: although settings are modifiable at any time, changing the page size, margin size, font size, etc., all cause your text to be rearranged, and this can be frustrating if you have spent hours carefully laying out the pages.

KEY POINT It is vital to save your work frequently to a memory stick, hard drive or network drive. This should be done every 10 minutes or so. If you do not save regularly, you may lose hours or days of work. Many programs can be set to 'autosave' every few minutes.

Databases

A database is an electronic filing system whose structure is similar to a manual record card collection. Its collection of records is termed a file. The individual items of information on each record are termed fields. Once the database is constructed, search criteria can be used to view files through various filters according to your requirements. The computerised catalogues in your library are just such a system; you enter the filter requirements in the form of author or subject key words.

You can use a database to catalogue, search, sort and relate collections of information. The benefits of a computerised database over a manual card file system are:

- The information content is easily amended/updated.
- Printout of relevant items can be obtained.
- It is quick and easy to organise through sorting and searching/selection criteria, to produce subgroups of relevant records.
- Record displays can easily be redesigned, allowing flexible methods of presenting records according to interest.

Choosing between a database and a spreadsheet – use a database only after careful consideration. Can the task be done better within a spreadsheet? A database program can be complex to set up and usually needs to be updated regularly.

- Relational databases can be combined, giving the whole system immense flexibility. The older 'flat-file' databases store information in files that can be searched and sorted, but cannot be linked to other databases.

Relatively simple database files can be constructed within spreadsheets using the columns and rows as fields and records respectively. These are capable of reasonably advanced sorting and searching operations and are probably sufficient for the types of databases you are likely to require as an undergraduate. You may also make use of a bibliographic database (e.g. EndNote) specially constructed for that purpose.

Statistical analysis packages

Statistical packages vary from small programs designed to carry out very specific statistical tasks to large sophisticated packages (SPSS, SYSTAT, SigmaStat, Minitab, etc.) intended to provide statistical assistance, from experimental design to the analysis of results. Consider the following features when selecting a package:

Using spreadsheet statistics functions – before using a specific statistics package, check whether your spreadsheet is capable of carrying out the form of analysis you require (see Boxes 49.3 and 50.3), as this can often be the simpler option.

- The data entry and editing section should be user-friendly, with options for transforming data.
- Data exploration options should include descriptive statistics and exploratory data analysis techniques.
- Hypothesis-testing techniques should include *t*-tests, ANOVA, correlation and regression analysis, multivariate techniques and parametric and non-parametric statistics.
- The program should provide assistance with experimental design and sampling methods.
- Output facilities should be suitable for graphical and tabular formats.

Presentation using computer packages – although many computer programs enhance presentational aspects of your work, there are occasions when they can make your presentation worse. Take care to avoid the following common pitfalls:

- Default or 'chart wizard' settings for graphs may result in output that is non-standard for the sciences (see Box 47.2).
- Fonts in labels and legends may not be consistent with other parts of your presentation.
- Some programs cannot produce Greek symbols (e.g. μ); do not use 'u' as a substitute. The same applies to scientific notation and superscripts: do not use 14C for ^{14}C, and replace, e.g., 1.4E+09 with 1.4×10^9. First try cutting and pasting symbols from Word or, if this fails, draw correct symbols by hand.

Some programs have very complex data entry systems, limiting the ease of using data in different tests. The data entry and storage system should be based on a spreadsheet system, so that subsequent editing and transformation operations are straightforward.

KEY POINT Make sure that you understand the statistical basis for your test and the computational techniques involved *before* using a particular program.

Graphics/presentation packages

Microsoft Office programs can be used to achieve most coursework tasks, e.g. PowerPoint is useful for creating posters (Box 16.1) and slide shows for oral presentations (Box 17.1). Should you need more advanced features, additional software may be available on your network; for example:

- SigmaPlot can produce graphs with floating axes.
- Macromedia Freehand is useful for designing complex graphics.
- Dreamweaver enables you to produce high-quality web pages.
- MindGenius can be used to produce mind maps.

Important points regarding the use of such packages are:

- The learning time required for some of the more complex operations can be considerable.
- The quality of your printer will limit the quality of your output.
- Not all files will readily import into a word processor such as Microsoft Word – you may need to save your work in a particular format. The different types of file are distinguished by the three-character filename extension, e.g. .jpg and .bmp.

KEY POINT Computer graphics are not always satisfactory for scientific presentation. You should not accept the default versions produced – make appropriate changes to suit scientific standards and style. Box 47.1 gives a checklist for graph drawing and Box 47.2 provides guidelines for adapting Microsoft Excel output.

Image storage and manipulation

With the widespread use of digital images, programs that facilitate the storage and manipulation of electronic image files have become increasingly important. These programs create a library of your stored images and provide a variety of methods for organising and selecting images. The industry-standard program, Adobe Photoshop, is one of many programs for image manipulation that vary widely in capability, cost and associated learning time. Many are highly sophisticated programs intended for graphic artists. For most scientific purposes, however, relatively limited functions are required.

Sources for further study

Anon. *Office 2007 Courseware*. Available: http://office2007courseware.com/index.asp?ad=gauc01a&gclid=COOziMK7hZcCFQhJagodaAMq-w Last accessed: 23/12/10.
[Print-on-demand customisable Office 2007 training materials for Word, Excel, PowerPoint, Access, Publisher, Project and many other Microsoft software programs.]

Marshall, J. *Top 6 Word Processing Programs*. Available: http://wordprocessing.about.com/od/choosingsoftware/tp/WPsofttop.htm Last accessed: 23/12/10.
[This 'About.com' site is an excellent site with related links to online or hard copy tutorials for most word processing software packages, tips on organising documents, use of macros and many other tips.]

Communicating information

13. Reporting and interpreting test results 89
14. General aspects of scientific writing 94
15. Writing essays and literature reviews 101
16. Organising a poster display 107
17. Giving a spoken presentation 112

13 Reporting and interpreting test results

Sport and exercise scientists have the important task of reporting data to the test participant as well as to coaches and other interested parties. The reporting of information may cover anything from basic health screenings (Chapter 27) to in-depth physiological laboratory tests (Chapter 36). Therefore, you may be required to use and produce a range of separate reports for different populations. Sport and exercise scientists are required to give immediate and concise verbal feedback on the physical fitness of the participant, as well as in-depth written results and analysis to interested parties. Consequently, it is vital to learn how to report and interpret test data correctly and how to communicate the findings. The ability to present the data generated from a testing session in an effective fashion increases the usefulness of the testing session. The interpretation of data within a report is valuable, typically involving comparison with previous test data and normative data. Being able to determine whether a change in a particular physiological parameter is meaningful is an important skill, as this is extremely useful in determining if 'actual' change has occurred.

Generate a 'skeleton report' – developing a skeleton report as a template that can be easily adapted to new data over time before exercise testing is a great way of saving time. Make sure to save an electronic copy every time you adapt it to a different test.

Reporting information

Generating a report to contain all the information necessary is important for several reasons.

1. The final report should act as a historical record of the testing session. It should present the data generated from the tests and compare the new data against previous test data.
2. The test results should be interpreted in the context of normative data from similar populations.
3. A report allows you to simplify the presentation of the data and to demonstrate changes in the test parameters easily. This helps in communicating the data to the participant and/or coach by allowing visual presentation of the results in addition to verbal explanation.

It is important that the information presented in a report is clear and easy to understand. A coach or fellow scientist should be able to find relevant data and make any comparisons that might be necessary easily. Similarly, the report should be unique, so that there can be no confusion with other testing times. To do this, the report must contain a considerable amount of specific information, as shown below in Figs. 13.1 and 13.2.

Maintain confidentiality – any reports generated from testing must remain confidential and must be released only to the participant and to persons approved by the participant.

Data reports are often specific to an individual or sport, and may take time to develop and complete. You will need to put in some thought and consideration as to the raw data you collect, and then the physiological or performance measurements that are included. If you are unsure, be sure to consult your tutors, other experienced sport and exercise scientists and coaches as to what data should be included. An example of an effective report is shown below in Fig. 13.1.

① Name

② Date of birth

③ Anthropometric data

④ Exercise scientist name

⑤ Contact details

⑥ Testing location

⑦ Environmental conditions

⑧ Testing date

⑨ Protocol details

⑩ Equipment used

⑪ Reliability of equipment

⑫ Basic raw data

⑬ Graphical display

⑭ Performance data

⑮ Previous testing data

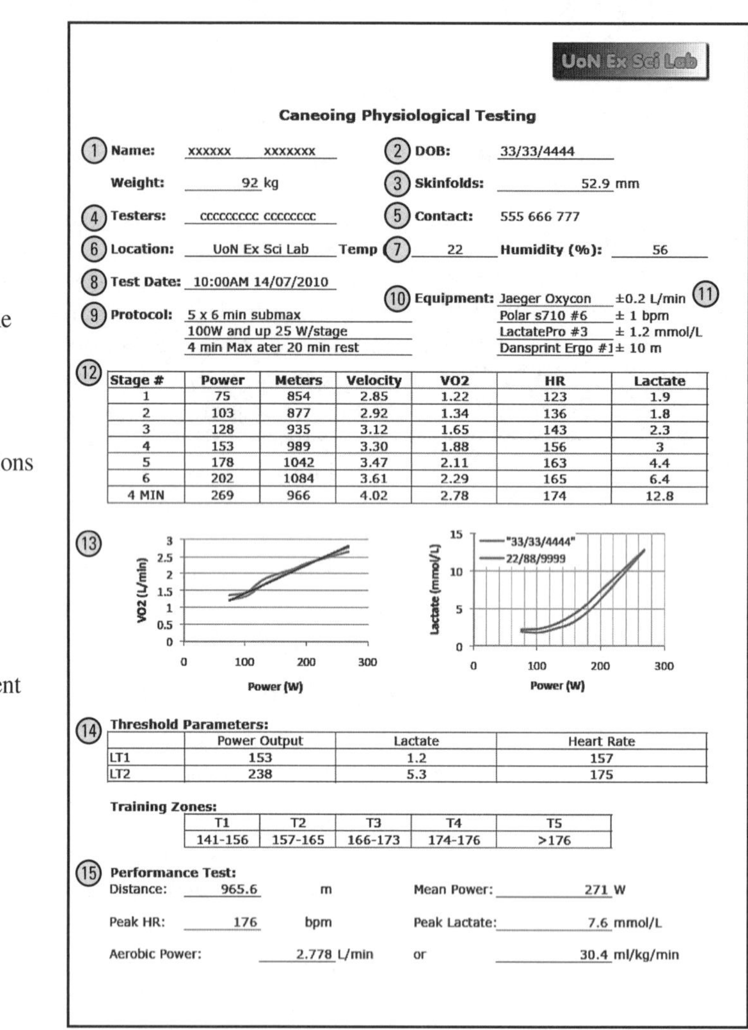

UoN Ex Sci Lab

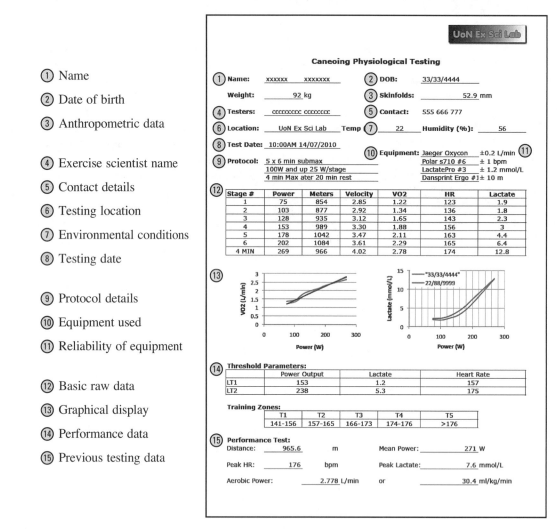

Caneoing Physiological Testing

① **Name:** xxxxxx xxxxxxx ② **DOB:** 33/33/4444

Weight: 92 kg ③ **Skinfolds:** 52.9 mm

④ **Testers:** ccccccccc cccccccc ⑤ **Contact:** 555 666 777

⑥ **Location:** UoN Ex Sci Lab **Temp** ⑦ 22 **Humidity (%):** 56

⑧ **Test Date:** 10:00AM 14/07/2010

⑨ **Protocol:** 5 x 6 min submax
100W and up 25 W/stage
4 min Max ater 20 min rest

⑩ **Equipment:** Jaeger Oxycon ±0.2 L/min ⑪
Polar s710 #6 ± 1 bpm
LactatePro #3 ± 1.2 mmol/L
Dansprint Ergo #1 ± 10 m

⑫

Stage #	Power	Meters	Velocity	VO2	HR	Lactate
1	75	854	2.85	1.22	123	1.9
2	103	877	2.92	1.34	136	1.8
3	128	935	3.12	1.65	143	2.3
4	153	989	3.30	1.88	156	3
5	178	1042	3.47	2.11	163	4.4
6	202	1084	3.61	2.29	165	6.4
4 MIN	269	966	4.02	2.78	174	12.8

⑬

⑭ **Threshold Parameters:**

	Power Output	Lactate	Heart Rate
LT1	153	1.2	157
LT2	238	5.3	175

Training Zones:

T1	T2	T3	T4	T5
141-156	157-165	166-173	174-176	>176

⑮ **Performance Test:**

Distance: 965.6 m Mean Power: 271 W

Peak HR: 176 bpm Peak Lactate: 7.6 mmol/L

Aerobic Power: 2.778 L/min or 30.4 ml/kg/min

Fig. 13.1 An example of a simple descriptive report detailing the testing data from a lab test of a kayaking athlete.

Interpreting test results

Overall, fitness testing is usually carried out to identify health measures, to monitor training progress, to help in team selection or readiness for competition, and to provide training guidelines as well as to predict changes in performance. The interpretation of results should be guided by the purpose of the test session. Correct interpretation of data should identify real changes in physiological and performance capacities rather than small variations owing to biological variation (including biorhythms) and/or technical error. The interpretation of results from exercise testing should clearly address one or more of the following questions:

- Has the participant improved or declined in the selected physiological capacities tested?
- How does the result compare with other previously established normative data?
- Are the observed changes likely to be real or biological variation?

Be sure to address the right question – the emphasis of detail may differ with the nature of the participant. For example, a basic health screening test may simply require comparison to established normative data, whereas for an elite footballer with a five-year testing history a more detailed comparison with previous test data for the participant may help to identify real changes, rather than comparing the test results to other footballers.

Make use of online resources – electronic spreadsheets for basic calculations are available at http://sportsci.org/resource/stats/

Results from exercise testing can be interpreted against either internal or external criteria. An internal comparison is an interpretation of any new test results against previous testing data from the participant. This approach is a within-individual approach and is useful to determine training progression and improvement or decline in physiological capacities, as described below. Consequently, an internal comparison is difficult to perform in young athletes who have little or no testing history. When established, the testing history can be built upon over the series of tests or career.

An external comparison is where test data are compared to previously established normative values or percentile rankings based on population data. This allows between-subjects comparison of data to establish where the subject would fit within that population. Obviously, collecting such large amounts of data would be extremely difficult for most sport and exercise scientists and consequently this is typically performed by large organisations or by collaboration across institutions/teams. A number of texts (Gore, 2000; Hoffman, 2006) that contain tables of normative data for a range of exercise tests and physiological capacities are available, and these span different ethnic and geographical groups. For sports-specific tests, publications from national sport science institutes usually contain a range of normative data for their selected test protocols relevant to their high-level athletes. Typically, normative data use either percentile rankings (1 = lowest; 100 = highest) or qualitative terms (e.g. 'good' or 'below average') relating to a range of scores. If possible, the comparison of the test results to both internal and external scores should be shown on the written report provided. Fig. 13.2 shows an example of a detailed interpretive report.

Caneoing Physiological Testing UoN Ex Sci Lab

Name: XXXXXX XXXXXXX **DOB:** 33/33/4444

Weight: 92 kg **Skinfold** 52.9 mm

Testers: CCCCCCCCC CCCCCCCC **Contact:** 555 666 777

Location: UoN Ex Sci Lab **Temp (C):** 22 **Humidity (%):** 56

Test Date: 10:00AM 14/07/2010

Measure	33/33/4444	22/88/9999	Diff	TEM	95%CI	Change	External Data
Body Mass (kg)	92	92.15	-0.15	2	88 - 96	STABLE	90 ± 2
Sum of 7 Skinfolds (mm)	52.9	56.4	-3.5	1.3	50 - 55	REAL	50.2 ±1.1
LT1 Power Output (W)	153	144	9	8	137 - 169	REAL	154 ± 9
LT1 Heart Rate (bpm)	157	156	1	3	151 - 163	STABLE	150 ±7
LT1 Lactate (mmol/L)	1.2	1.5	-0.3	0.2	1 - 2	REAL	1.3 ± 0.2
LT2 Power Output (W)	238	221	17	15	209 - 267	REAL	229 ± 8
LT2 Heart Rate (bpm)	175	174	1	5	165 - 185	STABLE	178 ± 4
LT2 Lactate (mmol/L)	5.3	4.7	0.6	0.5	4 - 6	STABLE	3.9 ±0.5
Distance (m)	965.6	951.2	14.4	10	946 - 985	REAL	955 ± 12
Mean Power (W)	271	264	7	4	263 - 279	REAL	275 ± 7
VO2max (L/min)	4.556	4.324	0.232	0.25	4.1 - 5.0	STABLE	4.25 ±0.39

INTERPRETATION

The results from the tests demonstrated real improvement in a number of measures. Importantly, the majority of these improvements were observed in power output at LT1, LT2 and across the 4-minute performance test. This suggests that the on-water strength training has benefited your lab test performance, which is supported by the improvement in the total distance covered. A real decrease was also observed in your skinfold measures with no change in body mass.

Fig. 13.2 An example of a suitable report and its interpretation. Note the presence of reliability data (Chapters 19 and 49), a defined answer to whether the change was real or not and readily available external data for comparison.

Defining a real change in performance

To be able to interpret the results from testing correctly, it is important to establish the technical error of measurement (TEM) (Chapter 19, p. 126) and the 95% confidence interval. A worked example is provided in Box 13.1. When performing fitness testing, it is common that only one or a small number of repeat tests are performed. If the test was to be continually repeated, the results would obviously continue to fall across a range of where the 'real' (and unknown) result would lie, so the ability of one number to represent that physical capacity or performance is limited in its accuracy. The range is calculated as below and is termed the 95% confidence interval (CI).

$$95\% \text{ confidence interval} = 1.96 \times \text{TEM of the test} \qquad (13.1)$$

By calculating the 95% CI, we determine the range around the test score in which we are 95% confident that the 'true' value lies. The establishment of this range helps to avoid errors associated with relying on a single test measure to represent the participant's physical capacity.

The ability to determine whether any observed change is the result of physical improvement or biological variation is key when interpreting results from exercise testing. This process is straightforward, and is carried out by comparing the magnitude of change to the TEM of the measure:

- A 'real improvement' is defined as an observed positive change between tests that is greater than the TEM of the test.
- A 'real decline' is defined as an observed negative change between tests that is greater than the TEM.
- A 'stable' measure is defined as an observed change between tests that is less than the TEM.

Using TEM data – collecting reliability data to calculate the TEM of testing protocols, monitoring equipment or performance tests requires a large investment of time and resources. This might make it impractical for you to collect your own TEM data. However, most large sport and exercise science institutions collect these data and, assuming that you are using their listed protocol and specified equipment, then using such data is a more practical approach.

Box 13.1 Worked example: identifying a real change

A hockey athlete completed a vertical jump test (Box 41.1) and recorded a pre-season score of 51 cm. From available data, the TEM (p. 126) of the vertical jump test is 1.5 cm.

Therefore, to determine the range of where the 'real' score lies we calculate the 95% CI as below (see example 13.1 above):

95% CI = 1.96 × 1.5 cm = 2.94 cm

Therefore, from this we are now 95% confident that the real score for the athlete's vertical jump is between 48.1 and 53.9 cm. Following the pre-season test, the athlete repeats the test in the pre-competition phase and records a score of 55 cm (95% CI = 52.1 – 57.9 cm). To determine whether the change is significant we compare it to the TEM of the test.

Observed change = 4 cm (51 → 55 cm)

Vertical jump TEM = 1.5 cm

Observed change > TEM = 'real improvement'

This is further strengthened by the observation that the second test result is greater than the 95% CI range of the pre-season test (55 > 53.9 cm).

Text references

Gore, C. (ed.) (2000) *Physiological Tests for Elite Athletes*. Human Kinetics, Champaign, IL.

Hoffman, J. (2006) *Norms for Fitness, Performance, and Health*. Human Kinetics, Champaign, IL.

Sources for further study

Heyward, V.H. (2006) *Assessing Muscular Fitness in Advanced Fitness Assessment and Exercise Prescription,* 5th edn, Human Kinetics, Champaign, IL.

Sportsci (2010) *A New View of Statistics.* Available: http://sportsci.org/resource/stats/ Last accessed: 23/12/10. [A range of specific statistical spreadsheets specific for sport science.]

14 General aspects of scientific writing

Monday:	morning afternoon evening	Lectures (University) Practical (University) **Initial analysis and brainstorming (Home)**
Tuesday:	morning afternoon evening	Lectures (University) **Locate sources (Library)** **Background reading (Library)**
Wednesday:	morning afternoon evening	**Background reading (Library)** Squash (Sports hall) **Planning (Home)**
Thursday:	morning afternoon evening	Lectures (University) **Additional reading (Library)** **Prepare outline (Library)**
Friday:	morning afternoon evening	Lab class (University) **Write first draft (Home)** **Write first draft (Home)**
Saturday:	morning afternoon evening	Shopping (Town) **Review first draft (Home)** **Revise first draft (Home)**
Sunday:	morning afternoon evening	Free **Produce final copy (Home)** **Proof read and print essay (Home)**
Monday:	morning	**Final read-through and check** **Submit essay** **(deadline mid-day)**

Fig. 14.1 Example timetable for writing a short essay.

Written communication is an essential component of all sciences. Most courses include writing exercises in which you will learn to describe ideas and results accurately, succinctly and in an appropriate style and format. The following features are common to all forms of scientific writing.

Organising your time

Making a timetable at the outset helps ensure that you give each stage adequate attention and complete the work on time (e.g. Fig. 14.1). To create and use a timetable:

1. Break down the task into stages.
2. Decide on the proportion of the total time each stage should take.
3. Set realistic deadlines for completing each stage, allowing some time for slippage.
4. Refer to your timetable frequently as you work: if you fail to meet one of your deadlines, make a serious effort to catch up as soon as possible.

KEY POINT The appropriate allocation of your time to reading, planning, writing and revising will differ according to the task in hand (see Chapters 13 and 15).

Organising your information and ideas

Before you write, you need to gather and/or think about relevant material (Chapters 8 and 9). You must then decide:

- what needs to be included and what doesn't;
- in what order it should appear.

Creating an outline – an informal outline can be made simply by indicating the order of sections on a spider diagram (as in Fig. 14.2).

Start by jotting down headings for everything of potential relevance to the topic (this is sometimes called 'brainstorming'). A spider diagram (Fig. 14.2) or a mind map (Fig. 4.2) will help you organise these ideas. The next stage is to create an outline of your text (Fig. 14.3). Outlines are valuable because they:

- force you to think about and plan the structure;
- provide a checklist so nothing is missed out;
- ensure the material is balanced in content and length;
- help you organise figures and tables by showing where they will be used.

KEY POINT A suitable structure is essential to the narrative of your writing, and should be carefully considered at the outset.

Talking about your work – discussing your topic with a friend or colleague might bring out ideas or reveal deficiencies in your knowledge.

In an essay or review, the structure of your writing should help the reader to assimilate and understand your main points. Subdivisions of the topic could simply be related to the physical nature of the subject matter (e.g. different environments) and should proceed logically (e.g. exercise in hot

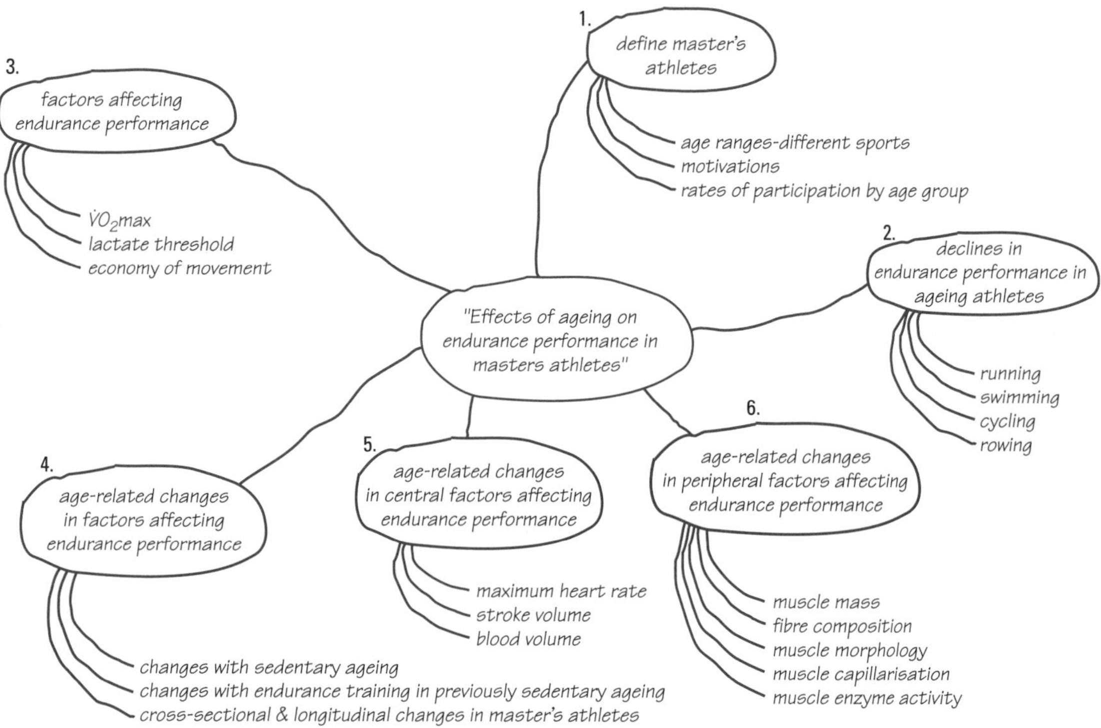

Fig. 14.2 Spider diagram showing how you might 'brainstorm' an essay with the title 'Effects of ageing on endurance performance in master's athletes'. Write out the essay title in full to form the spider's body, and as you think of possible content, place headings around this to form its legs. Decide which headings are relevant and which are not and use arrows to note connections between subjects. This may influence your choice of order and may help to make your writing flow because the links between paragraphs will be natural. You can make an informal outline directly on a spider diagram by adding numbers indicating a sequence of paragraphs (as shown). This method is best when you must work quickly, as with an essay written under exam conditions.

or cold environments or at altitude or deep-sea diving environments). A chronological approach is good for evaluation of past work (e.g. the development of the concept of muscle fibre typing), whereas a step-by-step comparison might be best for certain exam questions (e.g. 'Discuss the differences between type I and type II muscle fibre types'). There is little choice about structure for practical and project reports (see Chapter 22).

Writing

Adopting a scientific style

Your main aim in developing a scientific style should be to get your message across directly and unambiguously. Although you can try to achieve this through a set of 'rules' (see Box 14.1), you may find other requirements driving your writing in a contradictory direction. For instance, the need to be accurate and complete may result in text littered with technical terms, and the flow may be continually interrupted by references to the literature. The need to be succinct also affects style and readability through the use of, for example, stacked noun-adjectives (e.g. 'prolonged high-intensity intermittent exercise') and acronyms (e.g. 'PHIIE'). Finally, style is very much a matter of taste and each tutor, examiner, supervisor or editor will have pet loves and hates that you may have to accommodate. Different assignments will need different styles; Box 14.2 gives further details.

(a)

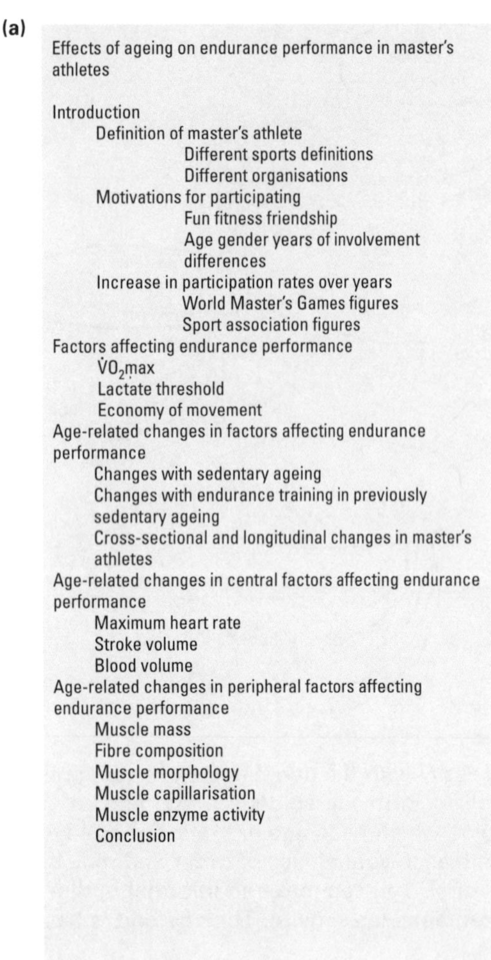

Effects of ageing on endurance performance in master's athletes

- Introduction
  - Definition of master's athlete
    - Different sports definitions
    - Different organisations
  - Motivations for participating
    - Fun fitness friendship
    - Age gender years of involvement differences
  - Increase in participation rates over years
    - World Master's Games figures
    - Sport association figures
- Factors affecting endurance performance
  - $\dot{V}O_2$max
  - Lactate threshold
  - Economy of movement
- Age-related changes in factors affecting endurance performance
  - Changes with sedentary ageing
  - Changes with endurance training in previously sedentary ageing
  - Cross-sectional and longitudinal changes in master's athletes
- Age-related changes in central factors affecting endurance performance
  - Maximum heart rate
  - Stroke volume
  - Blood volume
- Age-related changes in peripheral factors affecting endurance performance
  - Muscle mass
  - Fibre composition
  - Muscle morphology
  - Muscle capillarisation
  - Muscle enzyme activity
  - Conclusion

(b)

Effects of ageing on endurance performance in master's athletes

1. Introduction
    - 1.1 Definition of master's athlete
        - 1.1.1 Different sports definitions
        - 1.1.2 Different organisations
    - 1.2 Motivations for participating
        - 1.2.1 Fun fitness friendship
        - 1.2.2. Age gender years of involvement differences
    - 1.3 Increase in participation rates over years
        - 1.3.1 World Master's Games figures
        - 1.3.2. Sport association figures
2. Age-related declines in endurance performance in master's athletes
    - 2.1 Marathon running
    - 2.2 Track running
    - 2.3 Swimming
    - 2.4 Cycling
    - 2.5 Rowing
3. Factors affecting endurance performance
    - 3.1 $\dot{V}O_2$max
    - 3.2 Lactate threshold
    - 3.3 Economy of movement
4. Age-related changes in factors affecting endurance performance
    - 4.1 Changes with sedentary ageing
    - 4.2 Changes with endurance training in previously sedentary ageing
    - 4.3 Cross-sectional and longitudinal changes in master's athletes
5. Age-related changes in central factors affecting endurance performance in master's athletes
    - 5.1 Maximum heart rate
    - 5.2 Stroke volume
    - 5.3 Blood volume
6. Age-related changes in peripheral factors affecting endurance performance in master's athletes
    - 6.1 Muscle mass
    - 6.2 Fibre composition
    - 6.3 Muscle morphology
    - 6.4 Muscle capillarisation
    - 6.5 Muscle enzyme activity
7. Conclusion

Fig. 14.3 Formal outlines. These are useful for a long piece of work where you or the reader might otherwise lose track of the structure. The headings for sections and paragraphs are simply written in sequence with the type of lettering and level of indentation indicating their hierarchy. Two different forms of formal outline are shown, a minimal form (**a**) and a numbered form (**b**). Note that the headings used in an outline are often repeated within the essay to emphasise its structure. The content of an outline will depend on the time you have available and the nature of the work, but the most detailed hierarchy you should reasonably include is the subject of each paragraph.

Improving your writing skills – you need to take a long-term view if you wish to improve this aspect of your work. An essential preliminary is to invest in and make full use of a personal reference library (see Box 14.3).

Developing technique

Writing is a skill that can be improved, but not instantly. You should analyse your deficiencies with the help of feedback from your lecturers or tutors, be prepared to change work habits (e.g. start planning your work more carefully), and be willing to learn from some of the excellent texts that are available on scientific writing (p. 100).

Getting started

A common problem is 'writer's block' – inactivity or stalling brought on by a variety of causes. If blocked, ask yourself these questions:

- **Are you comfortable with your surroundings?** Make sure you are seated comfortably at a reasonably clear desk and have minimised the possibility of interruptions and distractions.

Box 14.1 How to achieve a clear, readable style

Words and phrases

- Choose short, clear words and phrases rather than long ones: e.g. use 'build' rather than 'fabricate'; 'now' rather than 'at the present time'. At certain times, technical terms must be used for precision, but don't use jargon if you don't have to.
- Don't worry too much about repeating words, especially when to introduce an alternative might subtly alter your meaning.
- Where appropriate, use the first person to describe your actions ('We decided to'; 'I conclude that'), but not if this is specifically discouraged by your supervisor.
- Favour active forms of writing ('the observer completed the survey in 10 minutes') rather than a passive style ('the survey was completed by the observer in 10 minutes').
- Use tenses consistently. Past tense is always used for Materials and Methods ('samples were taken from...') and for reviewing past work ('Smith (1990) concluded that...'). The present tense is used when describing data ('Fig. 1 shows...'), for generalisations ('Most authorities agree that...') and conclusions ('To conclude,...').
- Use statements in parentheses sparingly – they disrupt the reader's attention to your central theme.
- Avoid clichés and colloquialisms – they are usually inappropriate in a scientific context.

Punctuation

- Try to use a variety of types of punctuation, to make the text more interesting to read.
- Decide whether you wish to use 'closed' punctuation (frequent commas at the end of clauses) or 'open' punctuation (less frequent punctuation) – be consistent.
- Don't link two sentences with a comma. Use a full stop, this is an example of what *not* to do.
- Pay special attention to apostrophes, using the following rules:
  - To indicate possession, use an apostrophe before an 's' for a singular word (e.g. the athlete's temperature was...) and after the s for a plural word ending in s (e.g. the athletes' temperatures were = the temperatures of the athletes were). If the word has a special plural (e.g. woman → women) then use the apostrophe before the s (the women's temperatures were...).
  - When contracting words, use an apostrophe (e.g. do not = don't; it is = it's), but remember that contractions are generally *not* used in formal scientific writing.
  - Do *not* use an apostrophe for 'its' as the possessive form of 'it' (e.g. 'the university and its surroundings') Note that 'it's' is reserved for 'it is'. This is an exception to the general rule for possessives and a very common mistake.
  - Never use an apostrophe to indicate plurals of any kind, including abbreviations.

Sentences

- Don't make them overlong or complicated.
- Introduce variety in structure and length.
- If unhappy with the structure of a sentence, try chopping it into a series of shorter sentences.

Paragraphs

- Get the paragraph length right – five sentences or so. Do *not* submit an essay that consists of a single paragraph, nor one that contains many single-sentence paragraphs.
- Make sure each paragraph is logical, dealing with a single topic or theme.
- Take care with the first sentence in a paragraph (the 'topic' sentence); this introduces the theme of the paragraph. Further sentences should then develop this theme, e.g. by providing supporting information, examples or contrasting cases.
- Use 'linking' words or phrases to maintain the flow of the text within a paragraph (e.g. 'for example'; 'in contrast'; 'however'; 'on the other hand').
- Make your text more readable by adopting modern layout style. The first paragraph in any section of text is usually *not* indented, but following paragraphs may be (by the equivalent of three character spaces). In addition, the space between paragraphs should be slightly larger than the space between lines. Follow departmental guidelines if these specify a format.
- Group paragraphs in sections under appropriate headings and subheadings to reinforce the structure underlying your writing.
- Think carefully about the first and last paragraphs in any piece of writing: these are often the most important as they respectively set the aims and report the conclusions.

Note: If you are not sure what is meant by any of the terms used here, consult a guide on writing (see p. 100).

Box 14.2 Using appropriate writing styles for different purposes (with examples)

Note that courses tend to move from assignments that are predominantly descriptive in the early years to a more analytical approach towards the final year (see Chapter 5). Also, different styles may be required in different sections of a write-up, e.g. descriptive for introductory historical aspects, becoming more analytical in later sections.

Descriptive writing

This is the most straightforward style, providing factual information on a particular subject, and is most appropriate:

- in essays where you are asked to 'describe' or 'explain' (Table 15.1);
- when describing the results of a practical exercise, e.g. 'The experiment shown in Figure 1 confirmed that cycling performance was significantly improved by pre-cooling in an air-conditioned room, as the total work done in the 15-minute time trial was 10% greater when the initial core temperature was 36.4°C versus 38.3°C.'

However, in literature reviews and essays where you are asked to 'discuss' (Chapter 15) a particular topic, the descriptive approach is mostly inappropriate, as in the following example, where a large amount of specific information from a single scientific paper has been used without any attempt to highlight the most important points:

> In a study carried out between May and October, 2007, a total of 225 blood samples was taken from patients attending outpatient diabetes clinics in 12 different Queensland and New South Wales public hospitals. Total cholesterol levels were above the recommended National Heart Foundation (NHF) 'desirable' level of less than 5.5 $mmol \cdot L^{-1}$ in 83% of patients and above the NHF 'elevated' level of greater than 6.5 $mmol \cdot L^{-1}$ in 73% of patients (Dark and Gloomy, 2008).

In the most extreme examples, whole paragraphs or pages of essays may be based on descriptive factual detail from a single source, often with a single citation at the end of the material, as above. Such essays often score low marks because evidence of deeper thinking is required (Chapter 5).

Comparative writing

This technique is an important component of academic writing, and it will be important to develop your comparative writing skills as you progress through your course. Its applications include:

- answering essay questions and assignments of the 'compare and contrast' type (Table 15.1);
- comparing your results with previously published work in the Discussion section of a practical report.

To use this style, first decide on those aspects you wish to compare and then consider the material (e.g. different literature sources) from these aspects – in what ways do they agree or disagree with each other? One approach is to compare/contrast a different aspect in each paragraph. At a practical level, you can use 'linking' words and phrases to help orientate your reader as you move between aspects where there is agreement and disagreement. These include, for agreement: 'in both cases'; 'in agreement with'; 'is also shown by the study of'; 'similarly'; 'in the same way'; and for disagreement: 'however'; 'although'; 'in contrast to'; 'on the other hand'; 'which differs from'. The comparative style is fairly straightforward, once you have decided on the aspects to be compared. The following brief example compares two different studies using this style:

> While Dark and Gloomy (2008) reported elevated cholesterol levels in 73% of the 225 diabetes patients tested in Australian public hospitals, Bright and Shiny (2005) had previously shown that 69% of a larger sample of 987 diabetes patients in Australian private hospitals had elevated cholesterol levels.

Comparative text typically makes use of two or more references per paragraph.

Analytical writing

Typically, this is the most appropriate form of writing for:

- a review of scientific literature on a particular topic;
- an essay where you are asked to 'discuss' (Table 15.1) different aspects of a particular topic;
- evaluating a number of different published sources within the Discussion section of a final-year project dissertation.

By considering the significance of the information provided in the various sources you have read, you will be able to take a more critical approach. Your writing should evaluate the importance of the material in the context of your topic (see also Chapter 9). In analytical writing, you need to demonstrate critical thinking and personal input about the topic in a well structured text that provides clear messages, presented in a logical order and demonstrating synthesis from a number of sources by appropriate use of citations (pp. 51–52). Detailed information and relevant examples are used only to explain or develop a particular aspect, and not simply as 'padding' to bulk up the essay, as in the following example:

> Elevated total cholesterol levels are often observed in diabetes patients from Australian hospitals. For example, a recent study examining Australian public hospital outpatients (225 patients) observed elevated total cholesterol levels in 73% of the sample (Dark and Gloomy, 2008) while an earlier and larger study of Australian private hospital outpatients (987 patients) observed a similar high percentage (69%) of diabetes patients with elevated cholesterol levels (Bright and Shiny, 2005).

Analytical writing is based on a broad range of sources, typically with several citations per paragraph.

Box 14.3 Improve your writing ability by consulting a personal reference library

Using dictionaries

We all know that a dictionary helps with spelling and definitions, but how many of us use one effectively? You should:

- keep a dictionary beside you when writing and always use it if in any doubt about spelling or definitions;
- use it to prepare a list of words that you have difficulty in spelling: apart from speeding up the checking process, the act of writing out the words helps commit them to memory;
- use it to write out a personal glossary of terms. This can help you memorise definitions. From time to time, test yourself.

Not all dictionaries are the same! Ask your lecturer or tutor or supervisor whether he/she has a preference and why. Try out the *Oxford Advanced Learner's Dictionary*, which is particularly useful because it gives examples of use of all words and helps with grammar, e.g. by indicating which prepositions to use with verbs. Dictionaries of biology tend to be variable in quality, possibly because the subject is so wide and new terms are continually being coined. *Henderson's Dictionary of Biological Terms* (Addison Wesley Longman) is a useful example. Another useful dictionary for sport and exercise science students is the *Stedmans Medical Dictionary*.

Using a thesaurus

A thesaurus contains lists of words of similar meaning grouped thematically; words of opposite meaning always appear nearby.

- Use a thesaurus to find a more precise and appropriate word to fit your meaning, but check definitions of unfamiliar words with a dictionary.
- Use it to find a word or phrase 'on the tip of your tongue' by looking up a word of similar meaning.
- Use it to increase your vocabulary.

Roget's Thesaurus is the standard. Collins publish a combined dictionary and thesaurus.

Using guides for written English

These provide help with the use of words.

- Use guides to solve grammatical problems such as when to use 'shall' or 'will', 'which' or 'that', 'effect' or 'affect', 'can' or 'may', etc.
- Use them for help with the paragraph concept and the correct use of punctuation.
- Use them to learn how to structure writing for different tasks.

Writing with a word processor – use the dynamic/interactive features of the word processor (Chapter 12) to help you get started: first make notes on structure and content, then expand these to form a first draft and finally revise/improve the text.

- **Are you trying to write too soon?** Have you clarified your thoughts on the subject? Have you done enough preliminary reading?
- **Are you happy with the underlying structure of your work?** If you haven't made an outline, try this. If you are unhappy because you can't think of a particular detail at the planning stage, just start writing – it is more likely to come to you while you are thinking of something else.
- **Are you trying to be too clever?** Your first sentence doesn't have to be earth-shattering in content or particularly smart in style. A short statement of fact or a definition is fine. If there will be time for revision, first get your ideas down on paper and then revise grammar, content and order later.
- **Do you really need to start writing at the beginning?** Try writing the opening remarks after a more straightforward part. For example, with reports of practical work, the Materials and Methods section may be the easiest place to start.
- **Are you too tired to work?** Don't try to 'sweat it out' by writing for long periods at a stretch: stop frequently for a rest.

Learning from others – ask a colleague to read through your draft and comment on its content and overall structure.

Revising your text – to improve clarity and shorten your text, 'distil' each sentence by taking away unnecessary words and 'condense' words or phrases by choosing a shorter alternative.

Revising your text

Wholesale revision of your first draft is strongly advised for all writing, apart from in exams. Using a word processor, this can be a simple process. Where possible, schedule your writing so you can leave the first draft to 'settle' for at least a couple of days. When you return to it fresh, you will see more easily where improvements can be made. Try the following structured revision process, each stage being covered in a separate scan of your text:

1. **Examine content.** Have you included everything you need to? Is all the material relevant?
2. **Check the grammar and spelling,** both manually and using the spellcheck and grammar check functions in your word processing software. Can you spot any 'howlers'?
3. **Focus on clarity.** Is the text clear and unambiguous? Does each sentence really say what you want it to say?
4. **Be succinct.** What could be missed out without spoiling the essence of your work? It might help to imagine an editor has set you the target of reducing the text by 15%.
5. **Improve style.** Could the text read better? Consider the sentence and paragraph structure and the way your text develops to its conclusion.

Common errors

These include (with examples):

- problems over singular and plural words ('the athletes is'; 'the results shows');
- verbose text ('One definition that can be employed in this situation is given in the following sentence');
- misconstructed sentences ('Health and safety regulations should be made aware of');
- misuse of punctuation, especially commas and apostrophes (for examples, see Box 14.1);
- poorly constructed paragraphs (for advice/examples, see Box 14.1).

Sources for further study

Hopkins, W. (1999) *Guidelines for Style on Scientific Writing*. Available: http://www.sportsci.org/jour/9901/wghstyle.html Last accessed: 23/12/10.
[An exercise and sport science-specific site that examines in detail the general comments made on many of the issues discussed within this chapter.]

Kane, T.S. (2000) *The Oxford Essential Guide to Critical Writing*. Oxford University Press, New York.

Lindsay, D. (1995) *A Guide to Scientific Writing*. Longman, Harlow.

Matthews, J.R., Bowen, J.M. and Matthews, R.W. (2000) *Successful Scientific Writing: a Step-by-Step Guide for Biomedical Scientists*. Cambridge University Press, New York.

Tischler, M.E. *Scientific Writing Booklet*. Available: http://www.biochem.arizona.edu/marc/Sci-Writing.pdf Last accessed: 23/12/10.

15 Writing essays and literature reviews

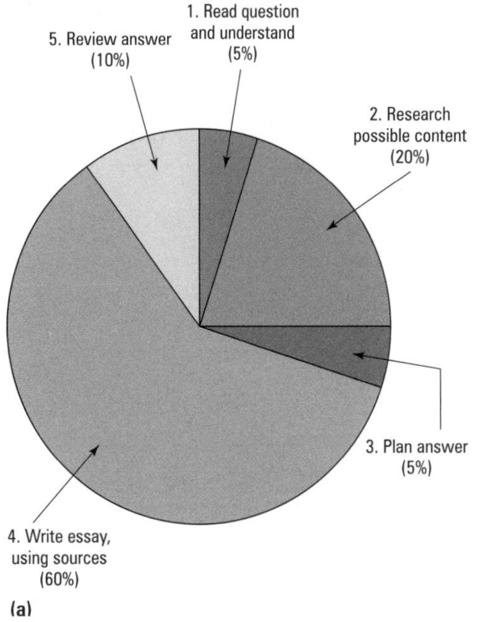

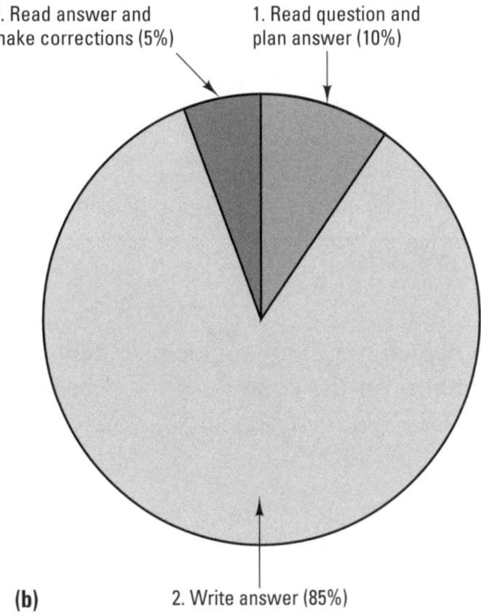

Fig. 15.1 Typical division of time for an essay written as part of in-course assessment (**a**) or under exam conditions (**b**).
Source: Jones, A., Reed, R. and Weyers, J. (2007) p. 101.

Considering essay content – it is rarely enough simply to lay down facts for the reader – you must analyse them and comment on their significance (see Box 14.2).

The function of an essay is to show how much you understand about a topic and how well you can organise and express your knowledge. A literature review is a specialised form of essay that describes and summarises the research literature related to a specific topic.

Essays

Organising your time

The way you should divide your time when producing an essay depends on whether you are writing it for in-course assessment or under exam conditions (Fig. 15.1). Essays written over a long period with access to books and other resources will probably involve a research element, not only before the planning phase but also when writing (Fig. 15.1a). For exams, it is assumed that you have revised appropriately (Chapter 5) and essentially have all the information at your fingertips. To keep things uncomplicated, the time allocated for each essay should be divided into three components – planning, writing and reviewing (Fig. 15.1b), and you should adopt time-saving techniques whenever possible (Box 6.2).

Making a plan for your essay

Dissect the meaning of the essay question or title

Read the title very carefully and think about the topic before starting to write. Consider the definitions of each of the important nouns (this can help in approaching the introductory section). Also think about the meaning of the verb(s) used and try to follow each instruction precisely (see Table 15.1). Do not get sidetracked because you know something about one word or phrase in the title: consider the whole title and all its ramifications. If there are two or more parts to the question, make sure you give adequate attention to each part.

Consider possible content and examples

Research content using the methods described in Chapters 8 and 9. If you have time to read several sources, consider their content in relation to the essay title. Can you spot different approaches to the same subject? Which do you prefer as a means of treating the topic in relation to your title? Which examples are most relevant to your case, and why?

KEY POINT Most marks for essays are lost because the written material is badly organised or is irrelevant. An essay plan, by definition, creates order and, if thought about carefully, should ensure relevance.

Construct an outline

Every essay should have a structure related to its title. Your plan should be written down (but scored through later if written in an exam book). Think about an essay's content in three parts:

Ten Golden Rules for essay writing – these are framed for in-course assessments, though many are also relevant to exams (see also Box 6.2).

1. Read the question carefully, and decide exactly what the assessor wants you to achieve in your answer.
2. Make sure you understand the question by considering all aspects – discuss your approach with colleagues or a tutor.
3. Carry out the necessary research (using books, journals, www), taking appropriate notes. Gain an overview of the topic before getting involved with the details.
4. Always plan your work in outline before you start writing. Check that your plan covers the main points and that it flows logically.
5. Introduce your essay by showing that you understand the topic and stating how you intend to approach it.
6. As you write the main content, ensure it is relevant by continually looking back at the question.
7. Use headings and subheadings to organise and structure your essay.
8. Support your statements with relevant examples, diagrams and references where appropriate.
9. Conclude by summarising the key points of the topic, indicating the present state of knowledge, what we still need to find out and how this might be achieved.
10. Always reread the essay before submitting it. Check grammar and spelling and confirm that you have answered all aspects of the question.

Table 15.1 Instructions often used in essay questions and their meanings. When more than one instruction is given (e.g. compare and contrast; describe and explain), make sure you carry out *both* or you may lose a large proportion of the available marks (see also Table 5.1)

Account for:	give the reasons for
Analyse:	examine in depth and describe the main characteristics of
Assess:	weigh up the elements of and arrive at a conclusion about
Comment:	give an opinion on and provide evidence for your views
Compare:	bring out the similarities between
Contrast:	bring out dissimilarities between
Criticise:	judge the worth of (give both positive and negative aspects)
Define:	explain the exact meaning of
Describe:	use words and diagrams to illustrate
Discuss:	provide evidence or opinions about, arriving at a balanced conclusion
Enumerate:	list in outline form
Evaluate:	weigh up or appraise; find a numerical value for
Explain:	make the meaning of something clear
Illustrate:	use diagrams or examples to make clear
Interpret:	express in simple terms, providing a judgement
Justify:	show that an idea or statement is correct
List:	provide an itemised series of statements about
Outline:	describe the essential parts only, stressing the classification
Prove:	establish the truth of
Relate:	show the connection between
Review:	examine critically, perhaps concentrating on the stages in the development of an idea or method
State:	express clearly
Summarise:	without illustrations, provide a brief account of
Trace:	describe a sequence of events from a defined point of origin

Source: Jones, A., Reed, R. and Weyers, J. (2007) p. 102.

1. **The introductory section,** in which you should include definitions and some background information on the context of the topic being considered. You should also tell your reader how you plan to approach the subject.

2. **The middle** of the essay, where you develop your answer and provide relevant examples. Decide whether a broad analytical approach is appropriate or whether the essay should contain more factual detail.

3. **The conclusion,** which you can make quite short. You should use this part to summarise and draw together the components of the essay, without merely repeating previous phrases. You might mention such things as the broader significance of the topic, its future, its relevance to other important areas of sport and exercise science. Always try to mention both sides of any debate you have touched on, but beware of 'sitting on the fence'.

KEY POINT Use paragraphs to make the essay's structure obvious. Emphasise them with headings and subheadings unless the material beneath the headings would be too short or trivial.

Using diagrams – give a title and legend to each diagram so that it makes sense in isolation and point out in the text when the reader should consult it (e.g. 'as shown in Fig. 1 ...' or 'as can be seen in the accompanying diagram ...').

Start writing

- **Never lose track of the importance of content and its relevance.** Repeatedly ask yourself: 'Am I really answering this question?' Never waffle just to increase the length of an essay. Quality, rather than quantity, is important.
- **Illustrate your answer appropriately.** Use examples to make your points clear, but remember that too many similar examples can stifle the flow of an essay. Use diagrams where a written description would be difficult or take too long. Use tables to condense information.
- **Take care when handwriting essays, especially in examinations.** You can't get marks if your writing is illegible. Try to cultivate an open form of handwriting, making the individual letters large and distinct. If there is time, make out a rough draft from which a tidy version can be copied.
- **Handwritten assignments or coursework essays are not widely accepted by lecturers nowadays.** Word processing packages and the widespread availability of computers on home desktops or on university or college campuses, plus the fact that information technology is a highly valued transferable skill (see Chapter 1), mean that essays prepared using word processing software for assignments are becoming the norm. However, in exams, handwritten essays are standard.

Learning from lecturers' and tutors' comments – ask for further explanations if you don't understand a comment or why an essay was less successful than you thought it should have been.

Reviewing your answer

Make sure that you leave enough time to:

- re-read the question to check that you have answered all points;
- re-read your essay to check for errors in punctuation, spelling and content. Make any corrections obvious. In an exam don't panic if you suddenly realise you've missed a large chunk out as the reader can be redirected to a supplementary paragraph if necessary.

Literature review

The literature survey or review is a specialised form of essay that summarises and reviews the evidence and concepts concerning a particular area of research.

KEY POINT A literature review should *not* be a simple recitation of facts. The best reviews are those that analyse information rather than simply describe it.

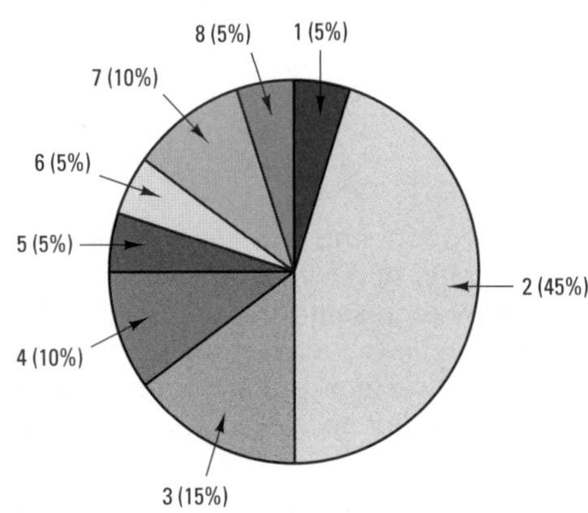

Fig. 15.2 Pie chart showing how you might allocate time for a literature survey:

1. Select a topic
2. Scan the literature
3. Plan the review
4. Write first draft
5. Leave to settle
6. Prepare a structured review of text
7. Write final draft
8. Produce top copy.

Making up a timetable

Fig. 15.2 illustrates how you might divide up your time for writing a literature review. There are many subdivisions in this chart because of the size of the task: in general, for lengthy tasks, it is best to divide up the work into manageable chunks. Note also that proportionately less time is allocated to writing itself than with an essay. In a literature survey, make sure that you spend adequate time on research and revision.

Selecting a topic

You may have no choice in the topic to be covered, but if you do, carry out your selection as a three-stage process:

1. **Identify a broad subject area** that interests you.
2. **Find and read relevant literature in that area.** Try to gain a broad impression of the field from books and general review articles. Discuss your ideas with your supervisor, lecturer or tutor.
3. **Select a relevant and concise title.** The wording should be considered very carefully as it will define the content expected by the reader. A narrow subject area will cut down on the amount of literature you will be expected to review, but will also restrict the scope of the conclusions you can make (and vice versa for a wide subject area).

Creating a glossary – one barrier to developing an understanding of a new topic is the jargon used. To overcome this, create your own glossary. You may wish to cross-reference a range of sources to ensure the definitions are reliable and context-specific. Remember to note your sources in case you wish to use the definition within your review.

Scanning the literature and organising your references

You will need to carry out a thorough investigation of the literature before you start to write. The key problems are as follows:

- **Getting an initial toe-hold in the literature.** Seek help from your supervisor, lecturer or tutor, who may be willing to supply a few key papers to get you started. Hints on expanding your collection of references are given on p. 49. In general, commence reading recent review articles in the area upon which you are focusing.
- **Assessing the relevance and value of each article.** This is the essence of writing a review, but it is difficult unless you already have a good understanding of the field. Try reading earlier reviews in your area and discussing the topic with your supervisor or other academic staff. Table 15.2 lists some of the most widely respected journals and review journals in sport and exercise science.

Using index cards or bibliographic software packages such as EndNote – cards can help you to organise large numbers of references. Write key points and author information on each card – this helps when considering where the reference fits into the literature. Arrange the cards in subject piles, eliminating irrelevant ones. Order the cards in the sequence in which you wish to write. For honours, master's or PhD students, consult your library liaison person to access training in the bibliographic software your university or college uses. It is generally available at no cost to enrolled students.

Table 15.2 A selection of the most widely respected peer-reviewed journals in sport and exercise science. In brackets is the 2007 'Impact Factor' for each journal. This represents the average number of recent citations (previous two years) received in all subsequent journal articles. For example, the figures below represent the citations in 2007 per article published in 2005 and 2006. In general, the higher the impact factor, the greater the respect the journal has in sport and exercise science. The factors are compiled by Thomson Scientific, a highly respected and international publishing company. *While each of the journals below publishes reviews, the journals that specialise in reviews are identified.*

1. *Sports Medicine* (3.6) (review journal)
2. *American Journal of Sports Medicine* (3.4)
3. *Exercise and Sport Sciences Reviews* (3.0) (review journal)
4. *Medicine and Science in Sports and Exercise* (2.9)
5. *British Journal of Sports Medicine* (2.5)
6. *Scandinavian Journal of Medicine & Science in Sports* (2.3)
7. *Clinics in Sports Medicine* (1.7) (review journal)
8. *Journal of Sport and Exercise Psychology* (1.7)
9. *Clinical Journal of Sport Medicine* (1.6)
10. *International Journal of Sport Nutrition & Exercise Metabolism* (1.5)
11. *International Journal of Sports Medicine* (1.5)
12. *Journal of Orthopaedic & Sports Physical Therapy* (1.5)
13. *Exercise and Immunology Reviews* (1.4) (review journal)
14. *Journal of Athletic Training* (1.4)
15. *Journal of Sports Sciences* (1.4)
16. *Journal of Strength and Conditioning Research* (1.4)
17. *Human Movement Science* (1.3)
18. *Journal of Aging and Physical Activity* (1.3)
19. *Journal of Applied Sport Psychology* (1.3)
20. *Psychology of Sport and Exercise* (1.2)
21. *Journal of Science and Medicine in Sport* (1.1)

- **Clarifying your thoughts.** Subdividing the main topic and assigning your references to these smaller subject areas may help you to gain a better overview of the literature.

Deciding on structure and content

The general structure and content of a literature review are described below. The *Annual Review* series (available in most university libraries) provides good examples of the style expected in reviews of biosciences. In sport and exercise science, the journals *Sports Medicine* and *Exercise and Sport Sciences Reviews* give excellent examples of the writing style widely expected. Undergraduate and postgraduate students should also read the Hopkins (1999) paper *How to Write a Literature Review,* which gives excellent tips on writing literature reviews in sport and exercise science.

Introduction

The introduction should give the general background to the research area, concentrating on its development and importance. You should also make a statement about the scope of your review; as well as defining the subject matter to be discussed, you may wish to restrict the period being considered.

Defining terms – the Introduction is a good place to explain the meaning of the key terms used in your literature review.

Main body of text

The review itself should discuss the published work in the selected field and may be subdivided into appropriate sections. Within each portion of a review, the approach is usually chronological, with appropriate linking phrases (e.g. 'Following on from this...'; 'Meanwhile, Bloggs (1980) tackled the problem from a different angle ...'). However, a good review is much more than a chronological list of work done. It should:

- allow the reader to obtain an overall view of the current state of the research area, identifying the key areas where knowledge is advancing.
- show how techniques are developing and discuss the benefits and disadvantages of using particular tests or methods.
- assess the relative worth of different types of evidence – this is the most important aspect (see Chapter 9). Do not be intimidated from taking a critical approach as the conclusions you may read in the primary literature aren't always correct.
- indicate where there is conflict in findings or theories, suggesting, if possible, which side has the stronger case.
- indicate gaps in current knowledge.

Balancing opposing views – even if you favour one side of a disagreement in the literature, your review should provide a balanced and fair description of all the published views of the topic. Having done this, if you do wish to state a preference, give reasons for your opinion.

You do not need to wait until you have read all the sources available to you before starting to write the main body. Word processors allow you to modify and move pieces of text at any point and it will be useful to write paragraphs about key sources, or groups of related papers, as you read them. Try to create a general plan for your review as soon as possible. Place your draft sections of text under an appropriate set of subheadings that reflects your plan (see Fig. 14.2), but be prepared to rearrange these and retitle or reorder sections as you proceed. Not only will working in this way help to clarify your thoughts, but it may help you avoid a last-minute rush of writing near to the submission date.

Conclusions

The conclusions should draw together the threads of the preceding parts and point the way forward, perhaps listing areas of ignorance or where the application of new techniques may lead to advances.

Making citations – a review of literature poses stylistic problems because of the need to cite large numbers of papers; in the *Annual Review* series this is overcome by using numbered references.

References, etc.

The References or Literature Cited section should provide full details of all papers referred to in the text (see pp. 52–53). The regulations for your department, faculty or university may also specify a format and position for the title page, contents page, acknowledgements, etc.

Text reference

Hopkins, W. (1999) *How to Write a Literature Review* and *How to Write a Research Paper*. Available: http://www.sportsci.org/
Last accessed: 23/12/10.
[A sport and exercise science-specific site. From the home page, go to *Research Resources* > *Writing*].

Sources for further study

Anon. (2008) *Writing a Literature Review*. Available: http://www.canberra.edu.au/studyskills/writing/literature
Last accessed: 23/12/10.

Anon. *Writing Tips: Essay Builder*. Available: http://www2.actden.com/Writ_Den/Tips/essay/index.htm
Last accessed: 23/12/10.

Anon. *Free Essay Writing Tips*. Available: http://www.bestessaytips.com/
Last accessed: 23/12/10.

Good, S. and Jensen, B. (1995) *The Student's Only Survival Guide to Essay Writing*. Orca Book Publishers, Victoria, BC, Canada.

Learn from others – look at the various types of posters around your university and elsewhere; the best examples will be visual, not textual, with a clear structure that helps get the key messages across.

A scientific poster is a visual display of the results of an investigation, usually mounted on a rectangular board. Posters are used in undergraduate courses, to display project results or assignment work, and at scientific meetings such as conferences to communicate research findings.

In a written report you can include a reasonable amount of specific detail and the reader can go back and reread difficult passages. However, if a poster is long-winded or contains too much detail, your reader is likely to lose interest.

KEY POINT A poster session is like a competition – you are competing for the attention of people in a room. Because you need to attract and hold the attention of your audience, make your poster as interesting as possible. Think of it as an advertisement for your work and you will not go far wrong.

An effective poster has three major features. Firstly, it is focused on a single message; secondly, it is visual in that it uses graphs and images to tell the story; and thirdly, it is structured in that it keeps the sequence well ordered and obvious.

(a)
Title
1 2 3 4
5 6 7 8

(b)
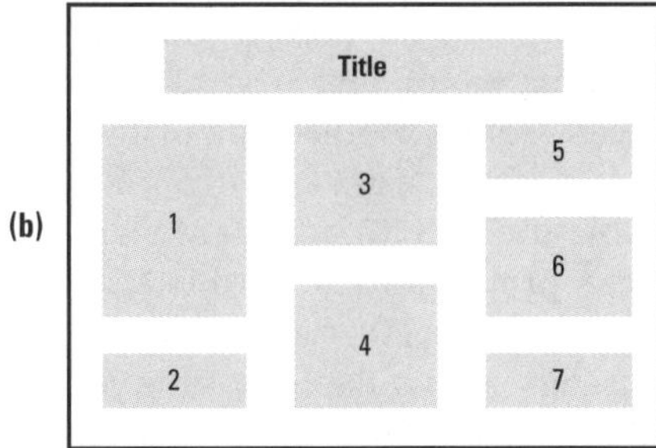

(c)
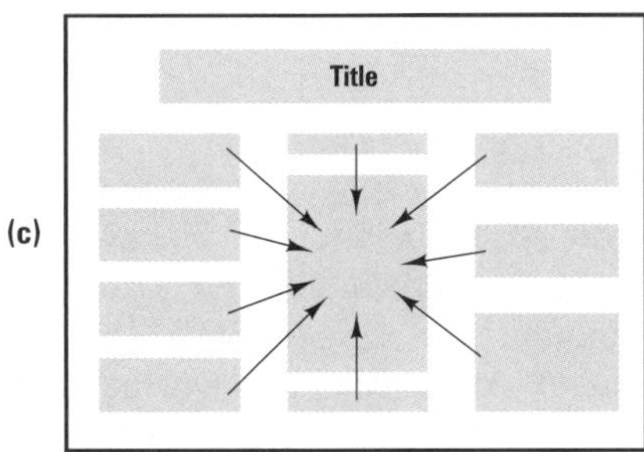

Fig. 16.1 Poster design. (**a**) An uninspiring design: subunits of equal area, reading left to right, are not recommended. (**b**) This design is more interesting and the text will be easier to read (column format). (**c**) An alternative approach, with a central focus and arrows to guide the reader.

Source: Jones, A., Reed, R. and Weyers, J. (2007) p. 83.

Preliminaries

Before considering the content of your poster, you should find out:

- the linear dimensions of your poster area, typically up to 1.5 m wide by 1 m high;
- the composition of the poster board and the method of attachment, whether drawing pins, Velcro tape or some other form of adhesive; and whether these will be provided – in any case, it is safer to bring your own;
- the time(s) when the poster should be set up and when you should attend;
- the room where the poster session will be held.

Design

Plan your poster with your audience in mind, as this will dictate the appropriate level for your presentation. Aim to make your poster accessible to a broad audience. Since a poster is a *visual* display, you must pay particular attention to the presentation of information: work that may have taken hours to prepare can be ruined in a few minutes by the ill-considered arrangement of items (Fig. 16.1). Begin by making a draft sketch of the major elements of your poster. It is worth discussing your intended design with someone else, as constructive advice at the draft stage will save a lot of time and effort when you prepare the final version (or consult Simmonds and Reynolds, 1994).

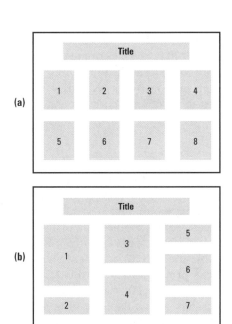

Layout

One approach is to divide the poster into several smaller areas, perhaps six or eight in all, and prepare each as a separate item on a piece of card.

Alternatively, you can produce a single large poster on one sheet of paper or card and store it inside a protective cardboard tube. However, a single large poster may bend and crease, making it difficult to flatten out. In addition, photographs and text attached to the backing sheet may work loose; a large poster with embedded images is an alternative approach.

Arrange the sections so that the order of reading is clear. Be generous with white space, keep lists at two to four items and keep blocks of text to just a few lines.

Subdividing your poster means that each smaller area can be prepared on a separate piece of paper or card, of A4 size or slightly larger, making transport and storage easier. It also breaks the reading matter up into smaller pieces, looking less formidable to a potential reader. By using pieces of card of different colours you can provide emphasis for key aspects, or link text with figures or photographs.

Presenting a poster at a formal conference – it can be useful to include your photograph for identification purposes, e.g. in the top right-hand corner of the poster.

You will need to guide your reader through the poster and headings/subheadings will help with this aspect. It may be appropriate to use either a numbering system, with large, clear numbers at the top of each piece of card, or a system of arrows (or thin tapes), to link sections within the poster (see Fig. 16.1). Make sure that the relationship is clear and that the arrows or tapes do not cross.

Title

Your chosen title should be concise (no more than eight words), specific and interesting, to encourage people to read the poster. Make the title large and bold – it should run across the top of your poster, in letters at least 4 cm high, so that it can be read from the other side of the room. Coloured spirit-based marker and block capitals drawn with a ruler work well, as long as your writing is readable and neat (the colour can be used to add emphasis). Alternatively, you can print out each word in large type, using a word processor. Details of authors, together with their addresses (if appropriate), should be given, usually across the top of the poster in somewhat smaller lettering than the title. Use first names to encourage interactions with readers and avoid middle initials.

Making up your poster – text and graphics printed on good-quality paper can be glued directly onto a contrasting mounting card: use photographic spray mountant or Pritt rather than liquid glue. Trim carefully using a guillotine to give equal margins, parallel with the paper. Photographs should be placed in a window mount to avoid the tendency for their corners to curl. Another approach is to trim pages or photographs to their correct size, then encapsulate in plastic film: this gives a highly professional finish and is easy to transport.

Text

Write in short sentences and avoid verbosity. Keep your poster as visual as possible and make effective use of the spaces between the blocks of text. Your final text should be double-spaced and should have a minimum capital letter height of 8 mm (minimum type size 36 point), preferably greater, so that the poster can be read at a distance of 1 m. One method of obtaining text of the required size is to photo-enlarge standard typescript (using a good-quality photocopier), or use a high-quality (laser) printer. It is best to avoid continuous use of text in capitals, since it slows reading and makes the text less interesting to the reader. Also avoid italic, 'balloon' or decorative styles of lettering. Use Arial font that is thick enough to read and embolden the title, headings and subheadings.

KEY POINT Keep text to a minimum – aim to have a *maximum* of 500 words in your poster.

Subtitles and headings

These should have a capital letter height of 12–20 mm, and should be restricted to two or three words. They can be produced by word processor, photo-enlargement, by stencilling, or by hand, using pencilled guidelines (but make sure that no pencil marks are visible on your finished poster).

Producing composite material for posters – PowerPoint is generally more useful than Word when you wish to include text, graphics and/or images on the same page. It is possible to use PowerPoint to produce a complete poster (Box 16.1), although it can be expensive to have this printed out commercially to A1 or A0 size.

Colour

Consider the overall visual effect of your chosen display, including the relationship between your text, diagrams and the backing board. Colour can be used to highlight key aspects of your poster. However, it is very easy to ruin a poster by the inappropriate choice and application of colour. Careful use of two, or at most three, complementary colours and shades will be easier on the eye and should aid comprehension. Colour can be used to link the text with the visual images (e.g. by picking out a colour in a photograph and using the same colour on the mounting board for the accompanying text). For PowerPoint posters, careful choice of colours for the various elements will enhance the final product (Box 16.1). Use coloured inks or water-based paints to provide colour in diagrams and figures, as felt pens rarely give satisfactory results.

Presenting at a scientific meeting – never be tempted to spend the minimum amount of time converting a piece of scientific writing into poster format – the least interesting posters are those where the author simply displays pages from a written communication (e.g. a journal article) on a poster board.

Content

The typical format is that of a scientific report (see Box 22.1), i.e. with the same headings, but with a considerably reduced content. Keep references within the text to a minimum – interested parties can always ask you for further information. Also note that most posters have a summary/conclusions section at the end, rather than an abstract.

Introduction

This should give the reader background information on the broad field of study and the aims of your own work. It is vital that this section is as interesting as possible, to capture the interest of your audience. It is often worth listing your objectives as a series of numbered points.

Designing the Materials and Methods section – photographs or diagrams of apparatus can help to break up the text of this section and provide visual interest. It is sometimes worth preparing this section in a smaller typeface.

Materials and Methods

Keep this short, and describe only the principal techniques used. You might mention any special techniques, or problems of general interest.

Results

Do not present your raw data: use data reduction wherever possible, i.e. figures and simple statistical comparisons. Graphs, diagrams, histograms and pie charts give clear visual images of trends and relationships and should be used in place of data tables (see Chapter 47). Final copies of all figures should be produced so that the numbers can be read from a distance of 1 m. Each should have a concise title and legend, so that it is self-contained: if appropriate, a series of numbered points can be used to link a diagram with the accompanying text. Where symbols are used, provide a key on each graph (symbol size should be at least 5 mm). Avoid using graphs straight from a written version, e.g. a project report, textbook or a paper, without considering whether they need modification to meet your requirements.

Keeping graphs and diagrams simple – avoid composite graphs with different scales for the same axis, or with several trend lines (use a maximum of three trend lines per graph).

Box 16.1 How to create a poster using PowerPoint

Software such as PowerPoint can be used to produce a high-quality poster, providing you have access to a good colour printer. However, you should avoid the standard templates available on the Web as they encourage unnecessary uniformity and stifle creativity, leading to a less satisfying end result. The following steps give practical advice on creating a poster as a single PowerPoint 2007 slide:

1. **Sketch out your plans.** Decide on the main poster elements (images, graphs, tables and text sections) and their relationship with each other and draw out a one-page 'storyboard' (see Fig 16.1). Think about colours for background, text and graphics (use two or three complementary colours): dark text on a light background is clearer (high contrast), and uses less ink when printing. Also consider how you will link the elements in sequence, to guide readers through your 'story'.
2. **Get your material ready.** Collect together individual files for pictures, figures and tables. Make any required adjustments to images, graphs or tables before you import them into your poster.
3. **Create a new/blank slide.** Open PowerPoint and select the *Design* ribbon (tab), then use the *Slide Orientation* menu to select either *Portrait* or *Landscape* orientation and the *Page Setup* menu to set the correct page size (use *Width* and *Height* commands, or select a standard size, such as A4, A3, A2, etc.). Right-click on the slide and select *Ruler* and *Grid and Guides* and *Display grid on screen* (to help position elements within the slide – the horizontal and vertical guidelines can be dragged to different positions at later stages, as required) and also select an appropriate colour using *Format Background > Fill* options. In general, avoid setting a picture as your background as this tends to detract from the content of the poster. Before going further, save your work. Repeat this frequently and in more than one location (e.g. hard drive and USB memory stick).
4. **Add graphics.** For images, use the *Insert* ribbon (tab) menu, select *Picture,* and browse to *Insert* the correct file. The *Insert, Chart* command performs a similar function for Excel charts (graphs). Alternatively, use the copy-and-paste functions of complementary software. Once inserted, resize using the *sizing handles* in one of the corners (for photographs, take care not to alter one dimension relative to the other, or the image will be distorted – it is best only to resize images and photographs using the sizing handles in each corner, as this will maintain the correct height-to-width ratio of the picture). To reposition, put the mouse pointer over the image, left-click and hold, then drag to new location. While the *Drawing* toolbar offers standard shapes and other useful features, you should avoid clipart (jaded and over-used) and poor-quality images from the Web (always use the highest resolution possible) – if you do not have your final images, use blank text boxes to show their position within the draft poster.
5. **Add text.** Use the *Text box* options on the *Insert* ribbon to select a *Text box* and place this on your slide, then either type in your text (use the *Enter* key to provide line spacing within the box) or copy-and-paste text from a word-processed file. You will need to consider the type size for the final printed poster (e.g. for an A0 poster (size 1189 × 841 mm), a printed type size of 20 point is appropriate for the main text, with larger sizes for headings and titles. If you find things difficult to read on-screen, use the *View* ribbon (tab) >*Zoom* function (either select a larger percentage in the *Zoom* box, or hold down the [Ctrl] key and use the mouse wheel to scroll up (*zoom*) or down (*reduce*). Use a separate text box for each element of your poster and don't be tempted to type too much text into each box – write in succinct phrases, using bullet points and numbered lists to keep text concise (aim for no more than 50 words per text box). Select appropriate font styles and colours using the *Font* menu on the *Home* ribbon (tab). For a background colour or surrounding line, right-click and use the *Format Shapes* menu options. Present supplementary text elements in a smaller type: for example, details of methodology, references cited.
6. **Add boxes, lines and/or arrows** to link elements of the poster and guide the reader (see Fig. 16.1). These features are available from the *Shapes* menu. Note that new inserts are overlaid over older inserts – if this proves to be a problem, select (right-click) the relevant item and use the *Bring to front* or *Send to Back* functions to change the relative positions.
7. **Review your poster.** Get feedback from another student or your tutor, e.g. on a small printed version, or use a projector to view your poster without printing (adjust the distance between projector and screen to give the correct size).
8. **Revise and edit your poster.** Revisit your work and remove as much unnecessary text as possible. Delete any component that is not essential to the message of the poster. Keep graphs simple and clear (Chapter 47 gives further advice). 'White space' is important in providing structure.
9. **Print the final version.** Use a high-resolution colour printer (this may be costly, so you should wait until you are sure that no further changes are needed).

Listing your conclusions – a series of numbered points is a useful approach, if your findings fit this pattern.

Conclusions

This is where many readers will begin, and they may go no further unless you make this section sufficiently interesting. This part needs to be the strongest part of your poster, summarising the main points. Refer to your figures here to draw the reader into the main part of your poster. A slightly larger or bolder typeface may add emphasis, though too many different typefaces can look messy. For references, smaller type can be used.

The poster session

Consider providing a handout – this is a useful way to summarise the main points of your poster, so that your readers have a permanent record of the information you have presented.

Coping with questions in assessed poster sessions – you should expect to be asked questions about your poster, and to explain details of figures, methods, etc.

A poster session may be organised as part of the assessment of your coursework, and this usually mirrors those held at most scientific conferences and meetings. Staff and fellow students (delegates at conferences) will mill around, looking at the posters and chatting to their authors, who are usually expected to be in attendance. If you stand at the side of your poster throughout, you are likely to discourage some readers, who may not wish to become involved in a detailed conversation about the poster. Stand nearby. Find something to do – talk to someone else, or browse among the other posters, but remain aware of people reading your poster and be ready to answer any queries they may raise. Do not be too discouraged if you aren't asked lots of questions: remember, the poster is meant to be a self-contained, visual story, without need for further explanation.

A poster display will never feel like an oral presentation, where the nervousness beforehand is replaced by a combination of satisfaction and relief as you unwind after the event. However, it can be a very satisfying means of communication, particularly if you follow these guidelines.

Text reference

Simmonds, D. and Reynolds, L. (1994) *Data Presentation and Visual Literacy in Medicine and Science*. Butterworth-Heinemann, London.

Sources for further study

Alley, M. (2003) *The Craft of Scientific Presentations: Critical Steps to Succeed and Critical Errors to Avoid*. Springer-Verlag, New York.

Anon. *Creating Better Presentations*. Available: http://www.easternct.edu/smithlibrary/library1/presentations.htm
Last accessed: 23/12/10.
[This website has a vast range of links to other sites that all focus on various aspects of poster and oral presentations, including tips on the use of PowerPoint for both.]

Briscoe, M.H. (2000) *Preparing Scientific Illustrations: a Guide to Better Posters, Presentations and Publications*. Springer-Verlag, New York.

Erren, T.C. and Bourne, P.E. (2007) *Ten Simple Rules for a Good Poster Presentation*. Available: http://www.ploscompbiol.org/article/info%3Adoi%2F10.1371%2Fjournal.pcbi.0030102
Last accessed: 23/12/10.

Gosling, P.J. (1999) *Scientist's Guide to Poster Presentations*. Kluwer, New York.

Hess, G., Tosney, K. and Liegel, L. (2008) *Creating Effective Poster Presentations*. Available: http://www.ncsu.edu/project/posters/NewSite/
Last accessed: 23/12/10.

Hopkins, W. (1997) *How to Give Talks*. Available: http://www.sportsci.org/
Last accessed: 23/12/10.
[The best website for sport and exercise science information, including great resources on presenting posters, oral presentations and the use of PowerPoint for both poster and oral presentations. Look under the *Research Resources* link on the home page.]

17 Giving a spoken presentation

Opportunities for practising speaking skills – these include:

- answering lecturers' questions;
- contributing in tutorials;
- talking to informal groups;
- giving your views at formal (committee) meetings;
- demonstrating or explaining to other students, e.g. during a practical class;
- asking questions in lectures/seminars;
- answering an examiner's questions in an oral exam.

Most students feel very nervous about giving talks. This is natural, since very few people are sufficiently confident and outgoing that they look forward to speaking in public. Additionally, the technical nature of the subject matter may give you cause for concern, especially if you feel that some members of the audience have a greater knowledge than you have. However, this is a fundamental method of scientific communication and an important transferable skill, therefore it forms an important component of many courses.

The comments in this chapter apply equally to informal talks, e.g. those based on assignments and project work, and to more formal conference presentations. It is hoped that the advice and guidance given below will encourage you to make the most of your opportunities for public speaking, but there is no substitute for practice. Do not expect to find all of the answers from this, or any other, book. Rehearse, and learn from your own experience.

KEY POINT The three 'Rs' of successful public speaking are: reflect – give sufficient thought to all aspects of your presentation, particularly at the planning stage; rehearse – to improve your delivery; revise – modify the content and style of your material in response to your own ideas and to the comments of others.

Preparation

Preliminary information

Learning from experience – use your own experience of good and bad lecturers to shape your performance. Some of the more common errors include:

- speaking too quickly;
- reading from notes or from slides and ignoring the audience;
- unexpressive, impersonal or indistinct speech;
- distracting mannerisms;
- poorly structured material with little emphasis on key information;
- factual information too complex and detailed;
- too few or too many visual aids.

Begin by marshalling the details needed to plan your presentation, including:

- the duration of the talk;
- whether time for questions is included;
- the size and location of the room;
- the projection/lighting facilities provided, and whether pointers or similar aids are available.

It is especially important to find out whether the room has the necessary equipment for digital projection (e.g. PC, projector and screen, black-out curtains or blinds, appropriate lighting) or overhead projection before you prepare your audiovisual aids. If you concentrate only on the spoken part of your presentation at this stage, you are inviting trouble later on. Have a look around the room and try out the equipment at the earliest opportunity, so that you are able to use the lights, projector, etc. with confidence. For digital projection systems, check that you can load/present your material. Box 17.1 gives advice on using PowerPoint.

Testing the room – if possible, try to rehearse your talk in the room in which it will be presented. This will help you to make allowance for layout of equipment, lighting, acoustics and sight lines that might affect the way you deliver your talk. It will also put you more at ease on the day, because of the familiarity of the surroundings.

Audience

You should consider your audience at the earliest stage, since they will determine the appropriate level for your presentation. If you are talking to fellow students you may be able to assume a common level of background knowledge. In contrast, a research lecture given to your department or a paper at a meeting of a scientific society will be presented to an audience

Box 17.1 Tips on preparing and using PowerPoint slides in a spoken presentation

Microsoft PowerPoint 2007 can be used to produce high-quality visual aids, assuming a computer and digital projector are available in the room in which you intend to speak. The presentation is produced as a series of electronic 'slides' on to which you can insert images, diagrams and text. When creating your slides, bear the following points in mind:

- **Plan the structure of your presentation.** Decide on the main topic areas and sketch out your ideas on paper. Think about what material you will need (e.g. pictures, graphs) and what colours to use for background and text.
- **Choose slide layouts according to purpose.** Once PowerPoint is running, a default new slide will appear. From the *Home* ribbon (tab) select a *Layout* design from the drop down menu. You can then add material to each new slide to suit your requirements.
- **Select your background with care.** Many of the preset background templates available under the *Design* ribbon (tab) are best avoided, since they are overused and fussy, diverting attention from the content of the slides. Conversely, flat, dull backgrounds may seem uninteresting, while brightly coloured backgrounds can be garish and distracting. Choose whether to present your text as a light-coloured type on a dark background (more restful but perhaps less engaging if the room is dark) or a dark-coloured type on a light background (more lively and easier to read). Be consistent with backgrounds and template design, type styles, capitalisation, transitions and effects.
- **Use visual images throughout.** Remember the Maxim, 'A picture is worth ten thousand words.' A presentation composed entirely of text-based slides will be uninteresting: adding images and diagrams will brighten up your talk consi-derably (use the *Insert* ribbon (tab), *Illustrations* option). Images can be taken with a digital camera, scanned in from a printed version or copied and pasted from the Web, but you should take care not to break copyright regulations. Clipart is copyright-free, but should be used sparingly, as most people will have seen the images before and they are rarely wholly relevant. Diagrams can be made from components created using other options under the *Insert* ribbon (tab) (e.g. *Shapes, SmartArt, Chart, Text boxes*), and graphs and tables can be imported from other programs, e.g. Excel (Box 16.1 gives further specific practical advice on adding graphics, saving files, etc.). Use *Chart* function under the *Insert* ribbon (tab) to import figures. You can then manipulate the styles, colours, fonts and legend.
- **Keep text to a minimum.** Aim for no more than 20 words on a single slide (e.g. four/five lines containing a few words per line). Use headings and subheadings to structure your talk: write only key words or phrases as 'prompts' to remind you to cover a particular point during your talk – never be tempted to type whole sentences as you will then be reduced to reading these from the screen during your presentation, which is boring. Adjust the line spacing (*Home* ribbon (tab) > *Paragraph* menu) to improve readability.
- **Use a large, clear font.** Use the *Slide Master* option within the *View* tab (ribbon) to set the default font to a non-serif style such as Arial, Helvetica or Comic Sans MS. Contrast dark letters on light backgrounds or light letters on dark backgrounds. Avoid too much colour (blue and black are easier to read than red or green). Black lettering on a yellow background is most easily read (e.g. road signage). Black lettering on a white background gives the best contrast. Default fonts for headings and bullet points are intentionally large, for clarity. Do not reduce these to anything less than 28-point type size (preferably larger), to cram in more words: if you have too much material, create a new slide and divide up the information.
- **Animate your material.** The *Animations* ribbon (tab) provides a *Custom Animation* function that enables you to introduce the various elements within a slide, e.g. text can be made to appear one line at a time, to prevent the audience from reading ahead and to help maintain their attention. Use the *Add Effect* button once the text has been highlighted. Avoid complex animations such as *Crawl In, Peek In, Flash Once,* etc.
- **Don't overdo the special effects.** PowerPoint has a wide range of features that allow complex slide transitions and animations, backgrounds additional sounds, etc., but these quickly become irritating to an audience unless they have a specific purpose within your presentation.
- **Always edit your slides before use.** Check through your slides and cut out any unnecessary words, adjust the layout and animation. Remember the maxim 'less is more' – avoid too much text; too many bullet points; too many distracting visual effects or sounds.

(continued)

Box 17.1 Continued

When presenting your talk:

- **Work out the basic procedures beforehand.** Practise, to make sure that you know how to move forwards and backwards, turn the screen on and off, hide the mouse pointer, etc.
- **Don't forget to engage your audience.** Despite the technical gadgetry, *you* need to play an active role in the presentation, as explained elsewhere in this chapter.
- **Don't go too fast.** Sometimes, new users tend to deliver their material too quickly: try to speak at a normal pace, and practise beforehand.
- **Consider whether to provide a handout.** PowerPoint has several options, including some that provide space, for notes (e.g. Fig. 4.3). However, a handout should not be your default option, as there is a cost involved.

Using audiovisual aids – don't let equipment and computer gadgetry distract you from the essential rules of good speaking (Box 17.2). Remember that you are the presenter.

from a broader range of backgrounds. An oral presentation is not the place for a complex discussion of specialised information: build up your talk from a low level. The speed at which this can be done will vary according to your audience. As long as you are not boring or patronising, you can cover basic information without losing the attention of the more knowledgeable members in your audience.

Pitching your talk at the right level – the general rule should be: 'Do not underestimate the background knowledge of your audience.' This sometimes happens in student presentations, where fears about the presence of 'experts' can encourage the speaker to include too much detail, overloading the audience with facts.

Content

Although the specific details in your talk will be for you to decide, most spoken presentations share some common features of structure, as described below.

Introductory remarks

It is vital to capture the attention of your audience at the outset. Consequently, you must make sure your opening comments are strong, otherwise your audience will lose interest before you reach the main message. Remember it takes a sentence or two for an audience to establish a relationship with a new speaker. Your opening sentence should be some form of preamble and should not contain any key information. For a formal lecture, you might begin with 'Thank you for that introduction. My talk today is about . . .' then restate the title and acknowledge other contributors, etc. You might show a transparency or slide with the title printed on it, or an introductory photograph, if appropriate. This should provide the necessary settling-in period.

After these preliminaries, you should introduce your topic. Begin your story on a strong note – avoid timid or apologetic phrases.

Opening remarks are unlikely to occupy more than 10% of the talk. However, because of their significance, you might reasonably spend up to 25% of your preparation time on them.

Getting the introduction right – a good idea is to have an initial slide giving your details and the title of your talk, and a second slide telling the audience how your presentation will be structured. Make eye contact with all sections of the audience during the introduction.

What to cover in your introductory remarks – you should:

- explain the structure of your talk;
- set out your aims and objectives;
- explain your approach to the topic.

KEY POINT Make sure you have practised your opening remarks so that you can deliver the material in a flowing style, with fewer chances of mistakes.

Allowing time for slides – as a rough guide you should allow at least two minutes per illustration, although some diagrams may need longer, depending on content. Make a note of the half-way point to help you check timing/pace.

The main message

This section should include the bulk of your experimental results or literature findings, depending on the type of presentation. Keep details of methods to the minimum needed to explain your data. This is *not* the place for a detailed description of equipment and experimental protocol (unless it is a talk about methodology). Results should be presented in an easily digested format.

KEY POINT Do not expect your audience to cope with large amounts of data; use a maximum of six numbers per slide. Remember that graphs and diagrams are usually better than tables of raw data, since the audience will be able to see the visual trends and relationships in your data (Chapter 47).

Present summary statistics (Chapter 49) rather than individual results. Show the final results of any analyses in terms of the statistics calculated, and their significance (p. 390), rather than dwelling on details of the procedures used. Figures should not be crowded with unnecessary detail. Every diagram should have a concise title and the symbols and trend lines should be clearly labelled, with an explanatory key where necessary. When presenting graphical data (Chapter 47), always 'introduce' each graph by stating the units for each axis and describing the relationship for each trend line or dataset.

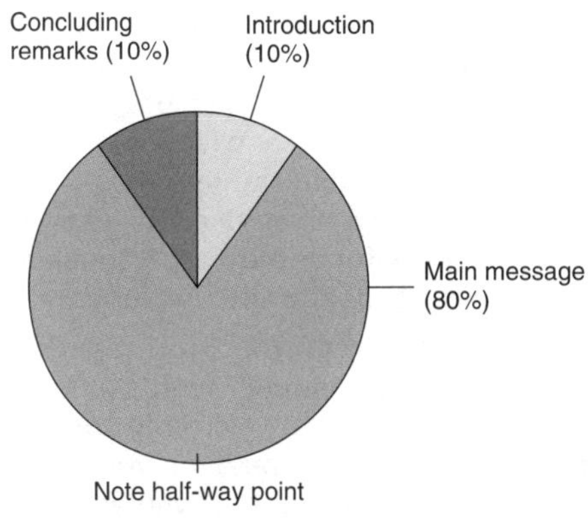

Fig. 17.1 Pie chart showing time allocation for a typical presentation.
Source: Jones, A., Reed, R. and Weyers, J. (2007) p. 91.

KEY POINT Use summary slides at regular intervals, to maintain the flow of the presentation and to emphasise the main points.

Take the audience through your story step by step at a reasonable pace. Try not to rush the delivery of your main message due to nervousness. Avoid complex, convoluted storylines – one of the most distracting things you can do is to fumble backwards through PowerPoint slides. In a presentation of experimental results, you should discuss each point as it is raised, in contrast to written text, where the results and discussion may be in separate sections. The main message typically occupies approximately 80% of the time allocated to an oral presentation (Fig. 17.1).

Concluding remarks

Having captured the interest of your audience in the introduction and given them the details of your story in the middle section, you must now bring your talk to a conclusion. Do not end weakly, e.g. by running out of steam on the last slide. Provide your audience with a clear 'take-home message' by returning to the key points in your presentation. It is often appropriate to prepare a slide or overhead transparency listing your main conclusions as a numbered series.

Signal the end of your talk by saying 'Finally . . .', 'In conclusion . . .', or a similar comment and then finish speaking after that sentence. Your audience will lose interest if you extend your closing remarks beyond this point. You may add a simple end phrase (for example, 'thank you') as you put your notes into your folder, but do not say 'That's all folks!' or make any similar offhand remark. Finish as strongly and as clearly as you started. Box 17.2 gives further advice.

Final remarks – make sure you give the audience sufficient time to assimilate your final slide: some of them may wish to write down the key points. Alternatively, you might provide a handout, with a brief outline of the aims of your study and the major conclusions.

Box 17.2 Hints on spoken presentations

In planning the delivery of your talk, bear the following aspects in mind:

- **Using notes.** Many accomplished speakers use abbreviated notes for guidance, rather than reading word for word from a prepared script. When writing your talk:
  - (i) **Consider preparing your first draft as a full script**: write in spoken English and keep the text simple, to avoid a formal, impersonal style. Your aim should be to *talk* to your audience, not to *read* to them.
  - (ii) **If necessary, use note cards with key words and phrases**: it is best to avoid using a full script in the final presentation. As you rehearse and your confidence improves, a set of note cards may be an appropriate format. Mark the position of slides/key points, etc.: each note card should contain details of structure as well as content. Your notes should be written/printed in text large enough to be read easily during the presentation (also check that the lecture room has a lectern light or you may have problems reading your notes if the lights are dimmed). Each note card or sheet should be clearly numbered, so that you do not lose your place.
  - (iii) **Decide on the layout of your talk**: give each subdivision a heading in your notes, so that your audience is made aware of the structure.
  - (iv) **Memorise your introductory/closing remarks**: you may prefer to rely on a full written version for these sections, in case your memory fails, or if you suffer 'stage fright'.
  - (v) **Using PowerPoint** (Box 17.1): here, you can either use the 'notes' option (*View > Notes Page*), or you may even prefer to dispense with notes entirely, since the slides will help structure your talk, acting as an aide-memoire for your material.
- **Work on your timing.** It is essential that your talk is the right length and the correct pace:
  - (i) **Rehearse your presentation**: ask a friend to listen and to comment constructively on those parts that were difficult to follow, to improve your performance.
  - (ii) **Use 'split times' to pace yourself**: following an initial run-through, add the times at which you should arrive at the key points of your talk to your notes. These timing marks will help you keep to time during the final presentation.
  - (iii) **Avoid looking at your wristwatch when speaking**; this sends a negative signal to the audience. Use a wall clock (where available), or take off your watch and put it beside your notes so that you can glance at it without distracting the audience.
- **Consider your image.** Make sure that the image you project is appropriate for the occasion:
  - (i) **Think about what to wear**: aim to be respectable without 'dressing up', otherwise your message may be diminished.
  - (ii) **Develop a good posture**: it will help your voice projection if you stand upright, rather than slouching, or leaning over a lectern.
  - (iii) **Deliver your material with expression**: project your voice towards the audience at the back of the room and make sure you look round to make eye contact with all sections of the audience. Arm movements and subdued body language will help maintain the interest of your audience. However, you should avoid extreme gestures (it may work for some TV personalities but it is not recommended for the beginner).
  - (iv) **Try to identify and control any repetitive mannerisms**: repeated 'empty' words/phrases, fidgeting with pens, keys, etc. will distract your audience. Note cards held in your hand give you something to focus on, whereas laser pointers will show up any nervous hand tremors. Practising in front of a mirror may help.
- **Think about questions.** Once again, the best approach is to prepare beforehand:
  - (i) **Consider what questions are likely to come up, and prepare brief answers.** However, do not be afraid to say 'I don't know': your audience will appreciate honesty, rather than vacillation, if you don't have an answer for a particular question.
  - (ii) **If no questions are asked, you might pose a question yourself** and then ask for opinions from the audience: if you use this approach, you should be prepared to comment briefly if your audience has no suggestions, to avoid the presentation ending in an embarrassing silence.

Sources for further study

Alley, M. (2003) *The Craft of Scientific Presentations: Critical Steps to Succeed and Critical Errors to Avoid.* Springer-Verlag, New York.

Anon. *Creating Better Presentations.* Available: http://www.easternct.edu/smithlibrary/library1/presentations.htm
Last accessed: 23/12/10.
[This website has a large range of links to other sites that all focus on various aspects of poster and oral presentations, including tips on the use of PowerPoint for both.]

Bourne, P.E. (2007) *Ten Simple Rules for Making Good Oral Presentations.*
Available: http://www.ploscompbiol.org/article/info%3Adoi%2F10.1371%2Fjournal.pcbi.0030077
Last accessed: 23/12/10.

Briscoe, M.H. (2000) *Preparing Scientific Illustrations: a Guide to Better Posters, Presentations and Publications.* Springer-Verlag, New York.

Hopkins, W. (1997) *How to Give Talks.* Available: http://www.sportsci.org/
Last accessed: 23/12/10.
[The best website for sport and exercise science information, including great resources on presenting posters, oral presentations and the use of PowerPoint for both poster and oral presentations. Look under the *Research Resources* link on the home page.]

McCarthy, P. and Hatcher, C. (2002) *Presentation Skills: the Essential Guide for Students.* Sage, London.

Matthews, C. and Marino, J. (1999) *Professional Interaction: Oral Communication Skills in Science, Technology and Medicine.* Pearson, Harlow.

The investigative approach

18.	The principles of measurement	121
19.	Making valid and reliable measurements	125
20.	SI units and their use	132
21.	Scientific method and design of experiments	139
22.	Conducting and writing up project work	145

18 The principles of measurement

> **Definition**
>
> **Variable** – any characteristic or property that can take one of a range of values (contrast this definition with that for a **parameter**, which is a numerical constant in any particular instance).

The term data (singular = datum) refers to items of information. You will use different types of data from a wide range of sources during your practical work. Consequently, it is important to appreciate the underlying features of data collection and measurement.

Variables

Scientific variables (Fig. 18.1) can be classified as follows:

Quantitative variables

These are characteristics whose differing states can be described by means of a number. They are of two basic types:

- **Continuous variables,** such as length; these are usually measured against a numerical scale. Theoretically, they can take any value on the measurement scale. In practice, the number of significant figures of a measurement is directly related to the precision of your measuring system; for example, dimensions measured with Vernier calipers will provide readings of greater precision than a millimetre ruler (p. 123).
- **Discontinuous (discrete) variables,** such as the number of press-ups completed until fatigue; these are always obtained by counting and therefore the data values must be whole numbers (integers). There are no intermediate values – for example, you can never do 56.25 press-ups.

> **Working with discontinuous variables** – note that while the original data values must be integers, derived data and statistical values do not have to be whole numbers. Thus, it is perfectly acceptable to express the mean number of children per family as 2.4.

Ranked variables

These provide data that can be listed in order of magnitude (i.e. ranked). A familiar example is grading the results of any athletic competition, e.g. 1 = first place, 2 = second place, 3 = third place, etc. When such data are given numerical ranks, rather than descriptive terms, they are sometimes called 'semi-quantitative' data. Note that the difference in magnitude between ranks need not be consistent. For example, regardless of whether there was a 1 s or a 5 s difference between first and second in a race, their rank in order of completing the race would be the same.

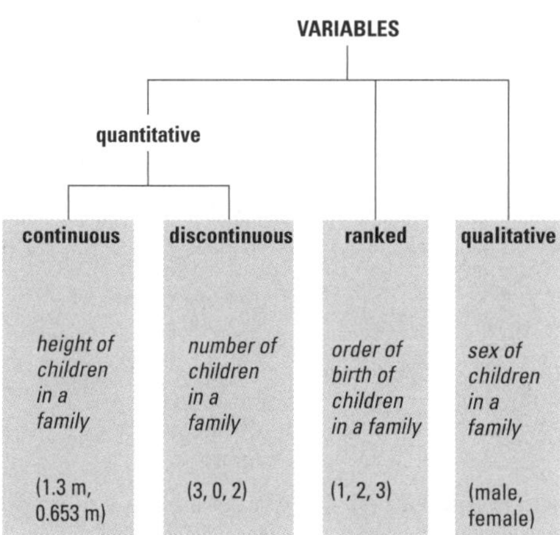

Fig. 18.1 Examples of the different types of variables as used to describe some characteristics of families.
Source: Jones, A., Reed, R. and Weyers, J. (2007) p. 155.

Qualitative variables (attributes)

These are non-numerical and descriptive; they have no order of preference, and therefore are not measured on a numerical scale nor ranked in order of magnitude, but are described in terms of categories. Examples include viability (i.e. dead or alive) and shape (e.g. round, flat, elongated, etc.).

Variables may be independent or dependent. Usually, the variable under the control of the experimenter (e.g. time) is the independent variable, while the variable being measured is the dependent variable (p. 140). Sometimes it is not appropriate to describe variables in this way, and they are then referred to as interdependent variables (e.g. height and weight of an individual).

The majority of data values are recorded as direct measurements, readings or counts, but there is an important group, called derived (or computed), that results from calculations based on two or more data values, e.g. ratios, percentages, indices and rates.

Measurement scales

> **Examples** A **nominal scale** for temperature is not feasible, since the relevant descriptive terms can be ranked in order of magnitude.
> An **ordinal scale** for temperature measurement might use descriptive terms, ranked in ascending order, e.g. cold = 1, cool = 2, warm = 3, hot = 4.
> The **Celsius scale** is an interval scale for temperature measurement, since the arbitrary zero corresponds to the freezing point of water (0 °C).
> The **Kelvin scale** is a ratio scale for temperature measurement since 0 K represents a temperature of absolute zero (for information, the freezing point of water is 273.15 K on this scale).

Variables may be measured on different types of scale:

- **Nominal scale:** this classifies objects into categories based on a descriptive characteristic. It is the only scale suitable for qualitative data.
- **Ordinal scale:** this classifies by rank. There is a logical order in any number scale used.
- **Interval scale:** this is used for quantitative variables. Numbers on an equal-unit scale are related to an arbitrary zero point.
- **Ratio scale:** this is similar to the interval scale, except that the zero point now represents an absence of that character (i.e. it is an absolute zero). In contrast to the interval scale, the ratio of two values is meaningful (e.g. a temperature of 200 K is twice that of 100 K).

The measurement scale is important in determining the mathematical and statistical methods used to analyse your data. Table 18.1 presents a summary of the important properties of these scales. Note that you may be able to measure a characteristic in more than one way, or you may be able to convert data collected in one form to a different form. For instance, you might measure body composition in terms of the body mass (p. 248) to separate individuals using body mass index (ratio scale) or simply as 'healthy' or 'obese' (nominal scale). You could find out the dates of birth of individuals (interval scale) but then use this information to rank them in order of birth (ordinal scale). Where there are no other constraints, you should use a ratio scale to measure a quantitative variable, since this will allow you to use the broadest range of mathematical and statistical procedures (Table 18.1).

Table 18.1 Some important features of scales of measurement

	Measurement scale			
	Nominal	**Ordinal**	**Interval**	**Ratio**
Type of variable	Qualitative (Ranked)* (Quantitative)*	Ranked (Quantitative)*	Quantitative	Quantitative
Examples	Gender Player number Subject code Sport	Competition level Result Test order	Fahrenheit temperature scale Date (BC/AD)	Age Mass Length Most physical measures
Mathematical properties	Identity	Identity Magnitude	Identity Magnitude Equal intervals	Identity Magnitude Equal intervals True zero point
Mathematical operations possible on data	None	Rank	Rank Addition Subtraction	Rank Addition Subtraction Multiplication Division
Typical statistics used	Only those based on frequency of counts made: contingency tables, frequency distributions, etc. Chi-square test	Non-parametric methods, sign tests. Mann–Whitney *U*-test	Almost all types of test, *t*-test, analysis of variance (ANOVA), etc. (check distribution before using, Chapter 50)	Almost all types of test, *t*-test, ANOVA, etc. (check distribution before using, Chapter 50)

*In some instances (see text for examples).
Source: Jones, A., Reed, R. and Weyers, J. (2007) p. 156.

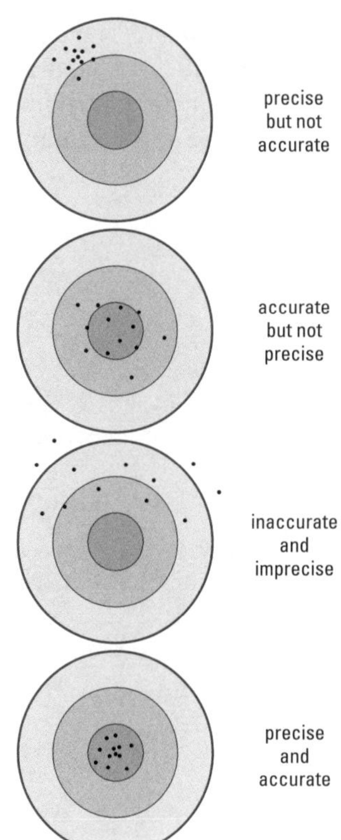

Fig. 18.2 'Target' diagrams illustrating precision and accuracy.

Source: Jones, A., Reed, R. and Weyers, J. (2007) p. 157.

Accuracy and precision

Accuracy is the closeness of a measured or derived data value to its true value, while precision is the closeness of repeated measurements to each other (Fig. 18.2). A balance with a fault in it (i.e. a bias, see below) could give precise (i.e. very repeatable) but inaccurate (i.e. untrue) results. Unless there is bias in a measuring system, precision will lead to accuracy and it is precision that is generally the most important practical consideration, if there is no reason to suspect bias. You can investigate the precision of any measuring system by repeated measurements of individual samples.

Absolute accuracy and precision are impossible to achieve, owing both to the limitations of measuring systems for continuous quantitative data and to the fact that you are usually working with incomplete datasets (samples). It is particularly important to avoid spurious accuracy in the presentation of results; include only those digits that the accuracy of the measuring system implies. This type of error is common when changing units (e.g. inches to metres) and in derived data, especially when calculators give results to a large number of decimal places.

Bias (systematic error) and consistency

Bias is a systematic or non-random distortion and is one of the most troublesome difficulties in using numerical data. Biases may be associated with incorrectly calibrated instruments, e.g. faulty lactate analyser, or with experimental manipulations, e.g. using different ground surfaces to perform field testing. Bias in measurement can also be subjective, or personal, e.g. an experimenter's preconceived ideas about an 'expected' result.

Bias can be minimised by using a carefully standardised procedure, with fully calibrated instruments. You can investigate bias in 'trial runs' by measuring a single variable in several different ways, to see whether the same result is obtained.

If a personal bias is possible, 'blind' measurements should be made where the identity of individual samples is not known to the operator, e.g. using a coding system.

Minimising errors – determine early in your study what the dominant errors are likely to be and concentrate your time and effort on reducing these.

Measurement error

All measurements are subject to error, but the dangers of misinterpretation are reduced by recognising and understanding the likely sources of error and by adopting appropriate protocols and calculation procedures.

A common source of measurement error is carelessness, e.g. reading a scale in the wrong direction or parallax errors. This can be reduced greatly by careful recording and may be detected by repeating the measurement. Other errors arise from faulty or inaccurate equipment, but even a perfectly functioning machine has distinct limits to the accuracy and precision of its measurements. These limits are often quoted in manufacturers' specifications and are applicable when an instrument is new; however, you should allow for some deterioration with age. Further errors are introduced when the subject being studied is open to influences outside your control. Resolving such problems requires appropriate experimental design (Chapter 21) and sampling procedures.

Working with derived data – special effort should be made to reduce measurement errors because their effects can be magnified when differences, ratios, indices or rates are calculated.

One major influence virtually impossible to eliminate is the effect of the investigation itself: even running on a treadmill in a laboratory may change the physiological cost and mechanics compared to running on the ground. The very act of measuring may give rise to a confounding variable (p. 142), as discussed in Chapter 21.

Sources for further study

Anon. *Measurement*. Available: http://wikipedia.org/wiki/Measurement
Last accessed: 23/12/10.

Erikson, B.H. and Nosanchuk, T.A. (1992) *Understanding Data*, 2nd edn, Open University Press, Milton Keynes.
[A text aimed at social science students but with clear explanations of issues that are generic, including information on analysis of data.]

Friedrich, G.W. *Basic Principles of Measurement. Methods of Inquiry*. Available: http://www.scils.rutgers.edu/~gusf/ measurement.html
Last accessed: 23/12/10.
[Course notes covering diverse aspects of enquiry.]

National Instruments *Measurement Encyclopedia*. Available: http://zone.ni.com/devzone/nidzgloss.nsf/glossary/
Last accessed: 23/12/10.

19 Making valid and reliable measurements

Definitions

Validity – the soundness or correctness of a test or measurement in measuring what it is designed to measure.

Reliability – a measure of the consistency of the data when measurements are taken more than once under the same conditions.

Sensitivity – the ability of a test to detect small but important changes.

Performance testing is one of the most common and important procedures used in sport and exercise science. To measure the effect of nutritional, pharmacological or training interventions on performance, or to measure changes in athlete performance over a season, you should try to conduct tests in a controlled and scientific manner.

There are three major factors that must be considered when deciding what performance test or protocol to use.

1. **Validity:** the protocol or test measures the performance as closely as possible.
2. **Reliability:** the protocol or test provides a similar result from day to day.
3. **Sensitivity:** the protocol or test is able to detect small changes in fitness or performance.

Validity

In sport and exercise sciences, there are three major types of validity.

1. **Construct validity.** A test with high construct validity can discriminate well between different groups. For example, a treadmill VO_2max test as a measure of running aerobic capacity has high construct validity. For example, it would easily discriminate between elite marathon runners and recreational swimmers.
2. **Content validity.** A test with high content validity has been developed by experts in the field and replicates closely the responses seen in actual performance. That is, the original 'beep test' (Loughborough Intermittent Shuttle test) was developed to have subjects complete 12.4 km of running with 55–60 turns, similar to that seen in an actual football match. The 'beep test' responses in blood lactate, heart rate and fluid loss were also similar to those of a football match.
3. **Criterion validity.** A test with high criterion validity may have a good correlation (*r*) with a criterion measure (see Chapter 50). There are two types of criterion validity: concurrent and predictive. Concurrent validity means that the performance test or protocol is correlated with a criterion measure. For example, a laboratory cycling time trial performance may correlate very closely with actual road race performance. Predictive validity involves using the actual laboratory performance protocol or test result to predict actual road race performance.

Understanding the different types of validity

Criterion validity – the relationship (correlation) between scores on a test and scores on a criterion measure or standard that is widely known or accepted as a valid test.

Construct validity – a measure of the test's ability to discriminate between different groups.

Content validity – expert opinion and/or past research suggests the test measures what it is claiming to measure.

The validity of a performance test or protocol can be reduced by both instrument and investigator error.

Instrument error refers to incorrect data caused by a faulty reading from a possibly faulty instrument. Laboratory equipment needs to be correctly maintained and calibrated (e.g. oxygen analysers, spirometers, ergometers, force plates, dynamometers, blood analysers) to ensure accuracy in instrument measurement and thus validity of results.

Investigator error can occur if a sport and exercise scientist is not skilled in a procedure or method of data collection. An example might be in taking skinfold or girth measures for body composition analysis

Target technical error of measurement

- Sum of seven or eight skinfolds <2%
- Shuttle run <3%
- Vertical jump <5%
- 20 m sprint <1.5%

VO_2max tests

- VO_2max <3%
- HRmax <2%
- Respiratory exchange ratio (RER) <5%
- Maximum expired ventilation <5%(V_Emax)

Lactate threshold tests

- Lactate <15%
- Power output <3%
- VO_2 <5%
- Heart rate <3%

Example An athlete whose sum of seven skinfolds was initially 48 mm was measured by the same measurer six weeks later at 45 mm.

The TEM for the measurer's sum of seven skinfolds was 2.0 mm.

Was the change in skinfolds due to training and/or diet or did it simply reflect the error in measurement?

Step 1: Calculate the error-free range

Standard error of measurement (SEM) = TEM × $\sqrt{2}$

SEM = 2.0 × $\sqrt{2}$

= 2.8 mm

Error-free range at 68% level of confidence equals (–3 + 2.8) to (–3 – 2.8) = –0.2 to –5.8 mm

Error-free range at 95% level of confidence equals (–3 + [2 × 2.8]) to (–3 – [2 × 2.8]) = 2.6 to –8.6 mm

Step 2: Hypothesis test to accept or reject the change

- The change for the skinfold total was –3 mm
- At a 68% confidence interval, –3 mm lies within the error-free range of –0.2 to –5.8, therefore the change was real and possibly due to either training and/or diet
- At a 95% confidence interval, the error-free interval includes 0 or no change. Therefore the change between trial 1 and 2 is rejected and is not due to training and/or diet, but is measurement error.

(see Chapter 35). Sport and exercise science researchers should always try to reduce instrument and investigator error in a number of ways. In doing so, the reliability and validity of the results increases. Ways to reduce error include:

- **Follow manufacturer's instructions and procedures** in exactly the same way every time.
- **Ensure all equipment is well maintained** and calibrated regularly.
- **Have the same person perform the same measurements** on the same individual each time.
- **Repeat the tests a number of times** (e.g. vertical jumps, skinfolds, girths) and record the median or average score as per the test procedures stipulated.
- **Standardise your procedures,** e.g. test warm-up, order of testing, instructions, verbal encouragement, etc.
- **Standardise nutritional and fluid intake** before and during testing.
- **Familiarise the subject with the test or protocol** before testing.
- **Standardise, reduce or record any factors that may influence the measurement process**. These factors may include:
  - Air temperature (labs should normally be between 18 and 22°C);
  - Humidity (labs should normally be below 60%);
  - Barometric pressure;
  - Wind direction;
  - Time of day;
  - Prior exercise;
  - Life stressors;
- **Determine your own technical error of measurement** (TEM) for the common tests you conduct.

Technical error of measurement

The TEM gives an indication of the precision (or more exactly, the imprecision) associated with a measurement – that is, the error due to investigator and instrument error. TEM can be expressed in two ways – in absolute terms or relative to the mean of the original measures.

Absolute TEM

This is expressed in the same units as the variable measured (e.g. in mm for skinfolds) and indicates that the error of a single measurement will be plus or minus the TEM value around two-thirds of the time.

$$\text{Absolute TEM} = \sqrt{\Sigma d^2/2n} \qquad (19.1)$$

where d = difference between trial 1 and 2
n = number of pairs of trials.

Box 19.1 Example of calculation of TEM (triceps skinfold)

Subject	Test X_1 (mm)	Test X_2 (mm)	Difference $(X_1 - X_2)(d)$	Difference squared (d^2)
1	9.9	9.8	0.1	0.01
2	5.5	5.3	0.2	0.04
3	20.2	19.2	1.0	1.00
4	11.1	11.5	−0.4	0.16
5	29.2	29.2	0.0	0.00
6	20.0	20.3	−0.3	0.09
7	20.2	19.2	1.0	1.00
8	27.2	26.8	0.4	0.16
9	14.1	14.5	−0.4	0.16
10	8.1	7.9	0.2	0.04
11	11.1	11.5	−0.4	0.16
12	13.7	13.1	0.6	0.36
13	31.8	32.7	−0.9	0.81
14	16.6	16.3	0.3	0.09
15	5.2	5.3	−0.1	0.01
16	12.5	12.1	0.4	0.16
17	28.1	27.5	0.6	0.36
18	11.4	12.2	−0.8	0.64
19	8.6	8.4	0.2	0.04
20	5.2	5.2	0.0	0.00

Mean $X_1 = 15.485$
Mean $X_2 = 15.400$

Sum $d^2 = 5.29$
$n = 20$

$$\text{Absolute TEM} = \sqrt{\Sigma d^2/2n} = \sqrt{(5.29)/40} = 0.36 \text{ mm}$$

$$\text{Relative \%TEM} = (\text{TEM}/[\text{M1} + \text{M}_2]/2) \times 100 = 0.36/15.4425 \times 100 = 2.3\%$$

The results show that the error in measuring triceps skinfolds for this measurer will be plus or minus 0.36 mm for two-thirds of the time. The %TEM is less than 5%, which is acceptable for skinfold measures, suggesting that this person is a precise measurer of the triceps skinfold.

Relative TEM

The %TEM expresses the error as a percentage of the mean of the original measurements.

$$\%\text{TEM} = (\text{TEM}/[\text{M}_1 + \text{M}_2]/2) \times 100 \qquad (19.2)$$

where M_1 and M_2 are the means of each of the two trials.
See Box 19.1 for worked examples of absolute and relative (%) TEM.

Interpretation of TEM

You can now use the TEM data from your calculations to decide whether changes in performance are likely to be real (due to training, diet or some other intervention) or whether they are likely to be caused by error associated with investigator or equipment.

To evaluate the significance of any changes in test results, you will need to consider the following:

- Standard error of the difference between two measurements equals the TEM $\times \sqrt{2}$.
- The 68% confidence interval (see Chapter 49) for the error-free range equals the difference ± one standard error.
- The 95% confidence interval for the error-free range equals the difference ± two standard errors.
- In hypothesis testing we either accept or reject the null hypothesis; we cannot interpret any magnitude of the effect from the statistical information (see Chapter 51).

Reliability

A crucial requirement for data to be considered meaningful in sport and exercise science is that they must be reproducible and consistent.

Table 19.1 Statistics commonly used in reliability analysis

Statistic	Definition	Advantages	Disadvantages
Pearson's correlation coefficient (*r*)	The strength of the relationship between two variables	Easily calculated Provides a probability value to determine significance	*r* is a bivariate statistic whereas reliability involves univariate measures Cannot detect changes in the mean influenced by intersubject variation Limited to two trials
Intraclass correlation coefficient (ICC)	Measures the relative homogeneity within groups in ratio to the total variation	Use for more than two sets of trials Measures reliability in terms of order and magnitude (mean differences) of the repeated values Can assess changes in both means and standard deviations from trial to trial Uses the same variable repeated many times	Sensitive to systematic bias Affected by sample heterogeneity
Coefficient of variation (CoV)	Expresses error as percentage of the mean	Easy to compare between methods Dimensionless The standard deviation of data must always be understood in the context of the mean of the data Provides magnitude of day-to-day differences	Only accounts for 68% of the variability When the mean value is near zero, the CoV is sensitive to small changes in the mean

Reliability is thus a measure of the consistency of the data when measurements are taken more than once under the same conditions.

There is considerable debate in the sport and exercise science literature as to which test or metric is the best to assess reliability. The statistics most commonly used in sport and exercise science literature to assess reliability include:

1. Pearson's correlation coefficient (*r*) (p. 397);
2. intraclass correlation coefficient (ICC);
3. coefficient of variation (CoV).

The definition of each of the tests and their advantages and disadvantages are shown in Table 19.1.

Pearson r

According to statistical theory, this procedure, sometimes called an interclass correlation) is a bivariate statistic (measures relationships between two different variables) and should *not* be used to measure the reliability of one variable from one occasion to another. Pearson's correlation coefficient, *r*, compares deviations (fluctuations in subjects' scores) from the means of two measurement trials. If the fluctuations from trial 1 to trial 2 all occur (up or down) in the same systematic manner, then the order and deviations of the scores in the two tests will be the same and the Pearson *r* score high, even though the means of each trial may be very different. Thus, Pearson *r* may erroneously conclude the test is reliable when in fact the scores are changing considerably.

ICC classifications in sport and exercise science

High reliability	>0.90
Moderate reliability	0.80–0.89
Unreliable	<0.80

Intraclass correlation (ICC)

In contrast to the Pearson *r* (interclass correlation), the intraclass correlation can be used over several measurement trials and is sensitive to changes in the means and the standard deviations of each set of data.

Box 19.2 Worked example of ICC calculation

Dataset: Sit and reach scores (cm) for a group of young gymnasts.

Subject	Trial 1	Trial 2	Trial 3	Trial 4	Trial 5
1	10	12	11	9	10
2	14	15	13	15	16
3	6	5	6	7	8
4	12	10	11	13	12
5	8	9	7	8	9
Mean	10.0	10.2	9.6	10.4	11.0

Step 1: Conduct a repeated measures ANOVA (see Chapter 51) (Output table shown below)

Source	Sum of squares (SS)	df	Mean square (MS)	*F*	*P*
Treatment (columns)	5.36	4	1.34	1.18	n.s.
Subjects (rows)	198.96	4	49.74	43.63	0.000
T × S (error)	18.24	16	1.14		
Total	222.56	24			

The high *F* value for rows (43.63, $P < 0.000$) shows that the subjects were significantly different in their sit and reach results across all trials. Thus, as expected, they will all have different levels of flexibility. The non-significant (n.s.) *F* for treatment shows that there are no differences among the means of the five trials. This is not surprising because the test conditions were all the same.

Step 2: Calculate the mean square value that represents the sum of the changes in the mean (column, or treatment effects) and error (MS_{C+E})

$$\begin{aligned} MS_{C+E} &= SS_C + SS_E/df_C + df_E \\ &= 5.36 + 18.24/4 + 16 \\ &= 1.18 \end{aligned}$$

Step 3: Calculate ICC (R)

$$\begin{aligned} R &= (MS_R - MS_{C+E})/MS_R \\ &= (49.74 - 1.18)/49.74 \\ &= 0.976 \end{aligned}$$

Given that an ICC value above 0.90 is accepted within sport and exercise sciences as a high reliability value, and that the mean scores for each trial were not significantly different, these results suggest the sit and reach test is a reliable test in these young gymnasts.

Example 50 m swim times for an elite swimmer across an eight-meet season

Meet	Time
1	24.5
2	24.3
3	24.7
4	23.7
5	23.8
6	23.5
7	24.1
8	23.4
Mean($\bar{Y}$): 24.0	SD(*s*) 0.47

$$CoV = 100s/\bar{Y}\ (\%) = 1.96\% \quad (19.3)$$

In this example, it appears the swimmer is relatively inconsistent in their performances.

It is called intraclass because it is designed to measure repeated measures data on the same variable. The ICC is widely used and reported as a measure of reliability in sport and exercise science. Box 19.2 gives a worked example.

Coefficient of variation

The final method often used to measure reliability is the coefficient of variation (CoV), also known as 'relative variability'. It is calculated as the standard deviation (SD) divided by the mean and can be expressed either as a fraction or a percentage (see eqn 19.3).

When the SD and mean come from repeated measurements of a single subject, the resulting CoV can be used as a measure of reliability. This form of within-subject variation is particularly valuable for sport and exercise scientists interested in the variability of an individual athlete's performance from competition to competition or from field test to field test. The CoV of an individual athlete's performance is typically a few per cent. In the example in the margin note on the left, it appears that the swimmer is relatively inconsistent in his swim performances.

Sensitivity

When choosing a performance test or protocol, it is important that it is able to detect small changes in performance. Sport and exercise scientists call this the 'smallest worthwhile effect'. New Zealand sport and exercise scientists have estimated that the variation in performance in elite male track cyclists is as small as 0.5%, increasing to approximately 1% for time trials of around 1 hour.

In elite sport, it appears that the largest training effects improve performance by as little as 2%, with other interventions (e.g. nutritional supplementation) producing even smaller effects. Although still in its early stages of development, a quantitative measure of sensitivity called the Sensitivity Index is being developed. Currell and Jeukendrup (2008) discuss this concept in more detail.

Validity, reliability and sensitivity are not three separate and unrelated factors. They all interact with each other. A test or protocol can be reliable but not valid. In contrast, a valid performance test may not be reliable.

While a number of valid and reliable tests have been developed over many years in sport and exercise science (Table 19.2), it is vital that sport and exercise scientists control the many factors that can affect test results through measures such as:

- familiarisation;
- standardisation of:
  - instructions;
  - verbal encouragement;
  - environmental factors;
  - warm-up and down;
  - clothing;
  - nutrition and fluid intake;
  - prior exercise, fluid and nutrition;
- use of music;
- measurement methods and timing;
- feedback during testing.

Table 19.2 Fitness components and examples of valid and reliable laboratory and field tests

Fitness component	Laboratory test	Field test
Aerobic fitness	Maximal oxygen uptake	Rockport walking test Cooper walk–run test
Anaerobic fitness	Wingate test	40 m sprint test Vertical jump Standing long jump
Muscular strength and endurance	Peak torque (isokinetic) Peak force (handgrip)	1 repetition max (RM) test Timed repetitions (sit-ups in 30 s)
Flexibility	Range of motion (goniometry)	Flexibility (sit and reach)
Body composition	Underwater weighing Air displacement plethysmography	Skinfold, girths and breadths

Crucially, all sport and exercise scientists should determine their own TEM to increase the validity of the results and the accuracy of what they report back to their subjects.

Text reference

Currell, K. and Jeukendrup, A.E. (2008) Validity, reliability and sensitivity of measures of sporting performance. *Sports Medicine*, **38**, 297–316.

Sources for further study

Hopkins, W. (2009) *A New View of Statistics.* Available: http://www.sportsci.org/resource/stats/index.html Last accessed: 23/12/10. [Without a doubt the best website for sport and exercise science information, including common statistical tests used in sport and exercise science. It has an excellent menu to choose most, if not all, statistical methods and terms used in sport and exercise science.]

Vincent, W.J. (2005) *Statistics in Kinesiology,* 3rd edn, Human Kinetics, Champaign, IL.

20 SI units and their use

The Système International d'Unités' (SI) is a single unified system of units and is the internationally ratified form of measurement essential for efficient communication of data within the whole scientific community. Great Britain, Australia and New Zealand, Europe and Canada have widely adopted the metric and SI systems of measurement within schools, workplaces and in science. However, most Americans are familiar with the non-metric measurement units such as inches, feet and pounds that they use in their everyday lives and have been reluctant to change to SI units, despite the US Congress Metric Conversion Act of 1975. In contrast, American scientists, including sport and exercise scientists, have adopted SI units.

Definitions

SI stands for **'Système International d'Unités'** (French) or **'International System of Units'** (English). SI is the officially approved worldwide measuring system for use by scientists. SI is based on the decimal and metric systems, thus simplifying the conversion of one unit to another.

Another important reason for adopting consistent units is to simplify complex calculations where you may be dealing with several measured quantities, e.g. dealing with work (force × distance) or power (work/time). Although the rules of the SI are complex and the scale of the base units is sometimes inconvenient, to gain the full benefits of the system you should observe its conventions strictly.

The description of measurements in SI involves:

- seven base units and two supplementary units, each having a specified abbreviation and symbol (Table 20.1).

Table 20.1 The base and supplementary SI units

Measured quantity	Name of SI unit	Symbol
Base units		
Length	metre	m
Mass	kilogram	kg
Amount of substance	mole	mol
Time	second	s
Electric current	ampere	A
Temperature	Kelvin	K
Luminous intensity	candela	cd
Supplementary units		
Plane angle	radian	rad
Solid angle	steradian	sr

- derived units, obtained from combinations of base and supplementary units, which may also be special symbols (Table 20.2);
- a set of prefixes to denote multiplication factors of 10^3, used for convenience to express multiples of fractions of units (Table 20.3).

Table 20.2 Some important SI and other units commonly used in sport and exercise science

Measured quantity	Name of unit	Symbol
Length	metre	m
Area	square metre	m^2
Volume of liquid or gas	litre	L
Mass	kilogram	kg
Time	second	s
	minute	min
	hour	h
	week	wk
	month	mo
	year	y
Temperature	degree Celsius	°C
Amount of substance	mole	mol
Density	kilogram per litre	$kg\ L^{-1}$
Molality	mole per kilogram	$mol\ kg^{-1}$
Osmolality	osmole per kilogram	$Osmol\ kg^{-1}$
Force	newton	N
Torque	newton metre	Nm
Work and energy	joule	J
Power	watt	W
Angle	radian	rad
Velocity	metres per second	$m\ s^{-1}$
Angular velocity	radians per second	$rad\ s^{-1}$
Acceleration	metres per second per second	$m\ s^{-1}\ s^{-1}$
Frequency	hertz	Hz

Table 20.3 Prefixes sometimes used in the SI

Decimal	Exponent	Prefix	Length (metre)	Mass (gram)	Volume (litre)
100 000 000	10^9	giga	—	—	—
1 000 000	10^6	mega	—		—
1000	10^3	kilo	kilometre	kilogram	—
100	10^2	hecto	—	—	—
10	10^1	deca	—	—	—
1	10^0	—	metre (m)	gram (g)	litre (L)
0.1	10^{-1}	deci	decimetre (dm)	decigram (dg)	decilitre (dL)
0.01	10^{-2}	centi	centimetre (cm)	centigram (cg)	centilitre (cL)
0.001	10^{-3}	milli	millimetre (mm)	milligram (mg)	millilitre (mL)
0.000 001	10^{-6}	micro	micrometre (μm)	microgram (μg)	microlitre (μL)
0.000 000 001	10^{-9}	nano	nanometre (nm)	nanogram (ng)	nanolitre (nL)

Expressing units named after scientists – the SI system recognises the significance of leading scientists. Thus, capital letters are used for abbreviating some units, such as Newton (N), Kelvin (K), Watt (W).

Recommendations for describing measurements in SI units

Sport and exercise scientists must also be concerned with spelling, punctuation and grammar of the SI conventions. Table 20.4 summarises the major SI style specifications and highlights the correct format and some commonly used incorrect styles.

Apart from those summarised in Table 20.4, there are a number of recommended and correct uses of SI and other conventions in sport and exercise science. These include:

Table 20.4 SI style specifications

Specifications	Example	Incorrect style	Correct style
Use lower case for symbols and abbreviations	kilogram	Kg	kg
Exceptions	newton	n	N
	kelvin	k	K
	ampere	a	A
	litre	l	L
Symbols are not followed by a full point	metre	m.	m
Exception: end of a sentence	mole	mol.	mol
Do not pluralise symbols	kilograms	kgs	kg
	centimetres	cms	cm
Names and symbols are not to be combined	force	kilogram metre s^{-2}	kg m s^{-2}
When numbers are printed symbols are preferred		100 metres	100 m
		2 moles	2 mol
Use a space between the number and symbol		50ml	50 mL
Use only one solidus (/) per expression		ml/kg/min	ml/kg min^{-1}
Place zero before decimal		.01	0.01
Decimal numbers are preferable to fractions or percentages		3/4	0.75
		75 %	0.75
Spaces are used to separate long numbers		1,500,000	1 500 000
Exception: optional with four-digit number		1,000	1000 or 1 000

Modified from Young (1987).

Example 60 kg is the correct way of expressing a person's body mass, not 60 kg or 60 kgs.

Example n stands for nano (see Table 20.3) and N for Newtons.

Example 15 % (space between numeral and % sign) is the correct way of expressing percentages, not 15% (no space).

- While litre and metre are accepted spellings across the world, the alternative spellings liter and meter can be used in the United States.
- Abbreviations (e.g. kg) and symbols (e.g. °) of measuring units should only be used in association with a numeric value. For example, kilogram should not be abbreviated in a sentence as here, but the abbreviation should be used to express a person's mass of 60 kg.
- Abbreviations should not be capitalised unless associated with a person's name. For example N (Newton), W (Watt), C (Celsius) and K (Kelvin).
- Full stops (also called periods or full points) are only used for the non-metric abbreviations for inches (in.) or at the end of a sentence. A space is also required between a numeral and its unit.
- When spelling out a two-component unit such as newton metre, *use a space* between the words; do not use a hyphen (newton-metre) or link the words without a space (newtonmetre).
- Decimal points are shown as a dot on the line (e.g. 3.2).
- Unit abbreviations are not mixed. Thus, do not use terms such as 'newton m' or 'N metre'.
- Do not mix numerals and names. Thus, a force should be 500 N, not 500 newtons or five hundred N.
- Separate symbols in two-compartment expressions by a space to avoid confusion with prefixes (e.g. 200 m s [metre seconds] is different from 200 ms [milliseconds]).
- The SI style of expressing *per* in combined units such as litres per minute, is to use a space preceding the unit with its negative exponent. Thus, litres per minute becomes L min^{-1}.

Table 20.5 Conversion factors between older English and American units and the metric equivalent

Measurement	Unit and abbreviation	Metric equivalent	English-to-metric conversion factor	Metric-to-English conversion factor
Length	kilometre (km)	= 1000 metres	1 mile = 1.61 km	1 km = 0.62 mile
	metre (m)	= 100 centimetres = 1000 millimetres	1 yard = 0.914 m 1 foot = 0.305 m 1 foot = 30.5 cm	1 m = 1.09 yards 1 m = 3.28 feet 1 m = 39.37 inches
	centimetre (cm)	= 0.01 metre	1 inch = 2.54 cm	1 cm = 0.394 inch
	millimetre (mm)	= 0.001 metre		
Mass	kilogram (kg)	= 1000 grams	1 pound = 0.454 kg	1 kg = 2.205 pounds
	gram (g)	= 1000 milligrams	1 ounce = 28.35 g	1 g = 0.035 ounce
	milligram (mg)	= 0.001 gram		
Volume (liquids and gases)	litre (L)	= 1000 millilitres	1 quart = 0.046 L	1 L = 0.264 gallon
	millilitre (mL)	= 0.001 litre	1 quart = 946 ml	1 L = 1.057 quarts
	microlitre (μL)	= 1 cubic centimetre	1 gallon = 3.785 L 1 US pint = 473 ml (1 Imperial pint = 568 ml) 1 fluid ounce = 29.57 ml	1 ml = 0.034 fluid ounce
Area	square metre (m^2)	= 10000 square centimetres	1 square yard = 0.836 m^2	1 m^2 = 1.196 square yards
	square centimetre (cm^2)	= 100 square millimetres	1 square inch = 6.452 cm^2	1 cm^2 = 0.155 square inch
Temperature	Degrees Celsius (°C)		°C = 5/9 (°F − 32)	°F = (9/5 °C) + 32
Force	Newton (N)	= 0.1019 kilopond	1 ft-lb sec^{-1} = 0.138 N	
Linear velocity	m sec^{-1}		mi hr^{-1} = 26 m min^{-1}	
Angular velocity	rad sec^{-1}			1 $radian^{-1}$ = $57.3^{0} \cdot s^{-1}$
Work and energy	Joule (J) kcal kg m	= 1 Nm = 426.85 kgm* = 4.18 kJ = 1 kpm† = 0.00234 kcal		1 J = 0.784 ft lb 1 J = 0.239 cal
Power	watt (W)	1 W = 1 joule per sec (J sec^{-1}) 1 W = 6.12 kgm min^{-1}	1 hp = 745.7 W	1 W = 0.0013 hp
Pressure	Newton per square metre (N m^{-2})		1 mmHg = 133.32 Nm^{-2} 1 atmosphere = 760 mmHg	760 mmHg = 29.02 inches

*kg m = kilogram metre;
†kp m = kilopond metre.

- It is *incorrect* to use more than one solidus (/) per expression (e.g. ml/kg/min). It should appear as either ml/(kg min) or more correctly as ml $kg^{-1} \cdot min^{-1}$.
- Use a set of prefixes to denote multiplication factors of 10^3 so that numbers are kept between 0.1 and 1000 (e.g. 6 000 000 is best expressed 6×10^6) (see Table 20.3).
- Avoid the prefixes deci (d) for 10^{-1}, centi (c) for 10^{-2}, deca (da) for 10 and hecto (h) for 100 as they are not strictly SI.

Converting between units – being able to express work, energy and power in different units is important as this skill is essential in sport and exercise science.

KEY POINT For the foreseeable future, you may need to make conversions from other units to SI units. Much of the older literature and some textbooks and papers you may come across will still use older units or other measurement systems (e.g. imperial). You will need to recognise these units and find the conversion factors required. Some common examples from sport and exercise science are given in Table 20.5.

Some implications of SI units in sport and exercise science

Mass (weight)

Mass is the SI base quantity and is represented by the SI base unit kilogram (kg). The most common use in sport and exercise science is in the measurement of *body mass*. However, in the United States, *body weight* is still commonly used.

Length

Length is an SI base quantity described in terms of the unit metre (m) or kilometre (km). Table 20.3 lists common prefixes and the decimals and exponents they represent. Height or, more correctly, *stature* describes the 'vertical length' of a person.

Force

The recommended SI measuring unit is the newton (N). Technically, the most appropriate unit for force (the product of mass and acceleration) should be $kg\,m\,s^{-2}$. However, the derived SI unit N is used to pay tribute to the nineteenth-century scientist Isaac Newton. Although kilogram (kg) is a unit of mass, some laboratories use it as a measure of force exerted to lift a weight, crank a cycle ergometer (note that Monark cycle ergometers common in submaximal exercise tests to estimate aerobic capacity use the non-SI term *kilopond* (kp) to highlight force applied to a flywheel), or push or pull against a dynamometer.

Work

The SI unit for expressing work is the joule (J) and is the product of force and distance. Larger quantities of work can be expressed in kilojoules (kJ). When work is calculated as the product of the force unit (newton) and the distance unit (metre), another accepted derived unit is the newton metre (N m). Just as force can sometimes be described in kilograms, work can be described in kilogram metres (kg m) or, in the case of *Monark* cycle ergometers, kilopond metres (kp m).

Power

The SI unit for power is the watt (W), a name given in honour of Scottish inventor, James Watt. Just as the joule describes work, the watt describes power. When power is broken down into its components (work/time or [force × distance]/time), the unit Nms^{-1} becomes the derived unit. Thus 1 watt can be defined as 1 Nms^{-1} or as 1 $J\,s^{-1}$ since 1 N m is equal to 1 J. In sport and exercise science there are many ways to describe power. Table 20.6 summarises these relationships and the conversion factors between the units.

Expressing power – although not an SI unit of power, you will often see power described in $kg\,m\,min^{-1}$ or $kp\,m\,min^{-1}$. The unit kilopond (kp) is widely used in cycle ergometry, where kilopond was the unit of force developed by exercise scientist Per Olaf Astrand. Astrand coined the term kilopond to differentiate the force applied to the flywheel of a cycle ergometer from the more common use of kilogram used to measure mass.

Energy

The terms energy and work are interrelated and use the same term of measurement – the joule (J). The joule is the SI unit of measure for metabolic energy release, which is the result of energy used (work) and energy wasted (heat). In the US, energy is commonly expressed in the non-SI term kilocalories (kcal).

Table 20.6 Relationships between the various power units. (The watt is the SI unit for power and is equivalent to 1 J s^{-1})

Unit	watt (W)	kcal min^{-1}	kJ min^{-1}	kg m min^{-1}
watt (W)	1.0	0.014	0.060	6.118
kcal min^{-1}	69.77	1.0	4.186	426.78
kJ min^{-1}	16.667	0.2389	1.0	101.97
kg m min^{-1}	0.1634	0.00234	0.00981	1.0

Energy expenditure at rest and during exercise can be estimated by the measurement of oxygen uptake using indirect calorimetry or gas analysis (see Chapter 36). It can be assumed for that for every 1 litre of oxygen uptake, approximately 5 kcal or 21 kJ of energy are expended.

Speed/velocity

Speed and velocity are derived based on distance divided by time. The most appropriate SI unit is m s^{-1}, derived from the two base units metres and seconds. However, other acceptable units are widely used, including m min^{-1} or km h^{-1}.

Angular velocity

Angular velocity describes velocity at which an object rotates around a fixed point. The preferred SI unit is radians per second (rad s^{-1}). However, in isokinetic dynamometry commonly used in sport and exercise science laboratories to measure isokinetic strength, power and endurance, another unit is frequently used – degrees per second ($^{\circ}$ s^{-1}). See Table 20.5 for interconversions.

Torque

Torque is the product of the length of the moment arm (measured from the centre of rotation to the point where the force is applied) and the force applied at that moment arm length. The SI unit for torque is the newton metre (N m), derived from the base units of force (N) and length (m). Many earlier isokinetic dynamometry studies measured peak torque in foot pounds (ft lb). See Table 20.5 for interconversions.

Volume

The capital L is used so as not to confuse the lower case letter *l* with the number 1. Many large volumes (e.g. lung volumes, pulmonary ventilation, cardiac output and stroke volumes) will be expressed in litres (L). For smaller volumes, millilitres (ml) are commonly used.

Converting between the three temperature scales – use the following formulae:

- °C to K: X K = Y °C + 273
- K to °C: X °C = Y K – 273
- °F to °C: X °C = (Y °F – 32)/1.8
- °C to °F: X °F = (Y °C × 1.8) + 32

Temperature

The base unit for temperature is the kelvin (K), named in honour of William Kelvin who developed the scale based on an absolute zero (0 K), the lowest temperature possible in any system. This absolute zero is equal to −273°C in the metric units of degrees Celsius. In the United States, temperature can also be expressed in degrees Fahrenheit (°F). In the Fahrenheit temperature scale, the zero point is 32°F, the same point as 0°C on the Celsius temperature scale. Because there are 9°F for every 5°C, we add or subtract 32 and multiply or divide by 9/5 (1.8) to convert between the Celsius and Fahrenheit scales.

Converting between units of pressure – as with temperature conversions, it is useful to know how to convert between different units of pressure using the following formulae:

- mm Hg to hPa: X hPa = Y mm Hg × 1.333
- hPa to mm Hg: X mm Hg = Y hPa × 0.75

Relative humidity

Relative humidity (RH) indicates the relative (%) amount of water in the air at any particular air temperature expressed as a percentage relative to the saturation value of 100%. Note that at higher temperatures, air can hold more water than at lower temperatures.

Barometric pressure

The pressure being exerted by the weight of the atmosphere is measured as barometric pressure. The derived unit for pressure is $N{\cdot}m^{-2}$ based on the force (N) exerted per unit area (m^2). In honour of the scientist Blaise Pascal, this unit is named the pascal (Pa). Because this unit is so small, barometric pressure is commonly described in hectopascals (1 hPa = 100 Pa) or kilopascals (1 kPa = 1000 Pa).

In the United States, barometric pressure is commonly described in millimetres of mercury (mmHg), which are not SI units. Standard atmospheric pressure is described as 760 mmHg or 1013 hPa or 1 atmosphere.

The American College of Sports Medicine (ACSM) permits exceptions to the SI units for physiological and gas pressures. Thus, blood pressures and lung pressures are reported in mm Hg in the journal *Medicine and Science in Sports and Exercise*.

Text reference

Young, D.S. (1987) Implementation of SI units for clinical laboratory data. *Annals of Internal Medicine*, **106,** 114–29.

Sources for further study

Knuttgen, H.G. (1986) Quantifying exercise performance in SI units. *The Physician and Sportsmedicine*, **14**(12), 156–61.

Knuttgen, H.G. (1995) Force, work and power in athletic training. *Sports Science Exchange*, **57**(4), 1–6. Available: http://www.gssiweb.org/Article_Detail.aspx?articleid=30
Last accessed: 23/12/10.

National Institute of Science and Technology. *The NIST Reference on Constants, Units and Uncertainty: International System of Units (SI)*. Available: http://physics.nist.gov/cuu/Units/
Last accessed: 23/12/10.

21 Scientific method and design of experiments

Definitions

There are many interpretations of the following terms. For the purposes of this chapter, the following will be used.

Paradigm – theoretical framework so successful and well confirmed that most research is carried out within its context and doesn't challenge it – even significant difficulties can be 'shelved' in favour of its retention.

Theory – a collection of hypotheses that covers a range of natural phenomena – a 'larger-scale' idea than a hypothesis. Note that a theory may be 'hypothetical', in the sense that it is a tentative explanation.

Hypothesis – an explanation tested in a specific experiment or by a set of observations. Tends to involve a 'small-scale' idea.

(Scientific) Law – this concept can be summarised as an equation (law) that provides a succinct encapsulation of a system, often in the form of a mathematical relationship. The term is often used in the physical sciences.

Sport and exercise science is a complex area revolving around observation and experimentation across a range of subdisciplines. Sport and exercise scientists attempt to quantify the effects of exercise or physical activity across a range of physiological, physical or psychological measures. However, the principles that underlie the scientific rigour that ensure the outcomes of sport and exercise science research remain valid and applicable are complex and evolve over time.

Fig. 21.1 models an approach that you are most likely to use; that is, testing small-scale hypotheses. These represent the sorts of explanations that can give rise to predictions that can be tested by an experiment or a series of observations. For example, you might put forward the hypothesis that muscular power is best developed using a combination of strength and plyometric exercises. From this hypothesis, a training programme might be developed with specific exercises, loads and repetitions that would optimise the training benefits. An experiment could be set up to test this hypothesis which would confirm or reject the hypothesis that muscular power is best developed by a combination of strength and plyometric exercise compared to isolated methods.

If the hypothesis is accepted by the research, it is retained with greater confidence. If falsified, it is either rejected outright as false, or modified and retested. Alternatively, it might be decided that the experiment was not a valid test of the hypothesis (perhaps this might have been caused by inappropriate training loads within the programme).

Nearly all scientific research deals with the testing of small-scale hypotheses. These hypotheses operate within a theoretical framework that has proven to be successful (i.e. is confirmed by many experiments and is consistently predictive). This operating model or 'paradigm' is not changed readily, and even if a results appears that seems to challenge the conventional view, it would not be overturned immediately. The conflicting results would be 'shelved' until an explanation was found after further investigation. In the example used above, a relevant paradigm could be that the notion that cardiorespiratory fitness is related to a reduced risk of lifestyle diseases.

Importantly, it is important to ask where these small-scale hypotheses come from. Most commonly they arise from one or more of the thought processes of a scientist. Some examples of thought patterns that may lead to the development of hypotheses include:

- analogy with other systems;
- recognition of a pattern;
- recognition of departure from a pattern;
- invention of a new analytical technique;
- development of a mathematical model;
- intuition;
- imagination.

Recently, it has been recognised that the process of science is not entirely an objective one. The choice of analogy that is used to develop

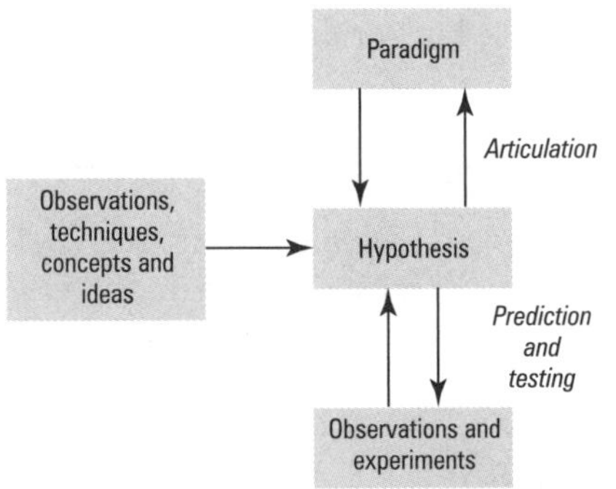

Fig. 21.1 A model of scientific method as used when testing hypotheses on a small scale. Hypotheses can arise as a result of various thought processes on the part of the scientist, and are consistent with the overlying paradigm. Each hypothesis is testable by experiment or observation, leading to its confirmation or rejection. Confirmed hypotheses act to strengthen the status of the paradigm, but rejected ones do not immediately result in the paradigm's replacement.

a new hypothesis might well be subjective, depending on past knowledge or understanding. Interestingly, science is also a social activity where researchers put forward and defend their viewpoints against those who hold opposing views, work together towards a common goal, and where effort may depend on externally dictated financial opportunities and constraints. As with any other human activity, science is bound to involve an element of subjectivity.

Deciding whether to accept or reject a hypothesis – this is sometimes clear-cut, as in some areas of genetics, where experiments can be set up to result in a binary outcome. In many other cases, the existence of 'biological variation' means that statistical techniques need to be employed (Chapters 50 and 51).

Importantly, no hypothesis can ever be rejected with certainty. Statistics allow us to quantify as vanishingly small the probability of an erroneous conclusion, although we can never be left in the position of being 100 % certain of having rejected all other relevant and alternative hypotheses, or that our decision to reject some alternative hypotheses was 100 % correct. However, despite these problems, experimental science has yielded and continues to yield many important findings.

KEY POINT The fallibility of scientific 'facts' is essential to grasp. No explanation can ever be 100 % certain as it is always possible for a new alternative hypothesis to be generated. Our understanding of sport and exercise science changes all the time as new observations and methods force old hypotheses to be retested.

Definition

Mathematical model – an algebraic summary of the relationship between the variables in a system.

Quantitative hypotheses, those involving a mathematical description of the system, have become very important in sport and exercise science. They can be formulated concisely by mathematical models. Formulating models is often useful because it forces deeper thought about mechanisms and encourages simplification of the system. A mathematical model:

- is inherently testable through experiment;
- identifies areas where information is lacking or uncertain;
- encapsulates many observations;
- allows you to predict the behaviour of the system.

Remember, however, that assumptions and simplifications required to create a model may result in it being unrealistic. Further, the results obtained from any model are only as good as the information put into it.

The terminology of experimentation

In many experiments, the aim is to provide evidence for causality. If x causes y, we expect, repeatably, to find that a change in x results in a change in y. Hence, the ideal experiment of this kind involves measurement of y, the dependent (measured) variable, at one or more values of x, the independent variable, and subsequent demonstration of some relationship between them. Experiments therefore involve comparisons of the results of treatments – changes in the independent variable as applied to an experimental subject. The change is engineered by the experimenter under controlled conditions.

The terms listed opposite are used to describe aspects of experimental designs commonly used in sport and exercise science:

- **Participants** – individuals that volunteer or are recruited to engage in a research project.
- **Sample** – a group of participants that form a portion of a population.
- **Population** – a collective group of individuals that share at least one characteristic to allow for comparison and analysis of other data pertaining to the group.
- **Data** – information (numbers or words) that is obtained by measurement or observation of a participant, sample or population.
- **Cross-sectional** – describes a research study that uses a set of data to describe a sample or population at a given time.
- **Longitudinal** – a research study design in which repetitive measures are taken over consistent time periods to observe and assess changes in a sample or population over a given time period.
- **Single-subject** – otherwise known as a 'case study'. Single-subject studies are short experiments or observations on an individual (not a sample or population). They are often used to comprise initial pilot data or to observe unique circumstances (e.g. injury treatment, training responses/progression) that are limited to an individual subject.
- **Randomised** – can describe either the allocation of participants to separate experimental groups or that the order of the trials is randomly determined. Using this strategy helps to decrease any bias of groups (assuming homogenous subjects) or any learning or training effects that may occur with repeat exercise testing sessions. Commonly used randomisation strategies are shown in Box 21.1.
- **Blind** – refers to whether the participants or researcher are aware of who has been allocated into the separate experimental conditions (i.e. intervention or control). Single blind means that either the participants or researchers (more typical) are aware of the allocation of participants to each group. Double blind studies infer that neither participants nor researchers have knowledge of the experimental groups, as the allocation of the experimental conditions is carried out by a neutral third party. This method minimises the likelihood of research bias occuring (see Box 21.1). Using a blind study will require the use of a placebo to ensure that the control group is unaware that they are undertaking no intervention.
- **Control** – refers to a sample that is not subject to any intervention through a research project. A control group is largely used to measure and quantify any biological variation that occurs across a project, by either adaptation to a standardised training programme, maturation or learning effects. The use of a control group allows the real effect of an intervention to be measured, assuming that other confounding factors are standardised.
- **Experimental** – describes the group that is subject to the 'intervention' (i.e. the factor that is being investigated) across a study; hence, the effect of any intervention should be observed in the data collected from this group.

- **Cross-over** – is an experimental design in which each research group undergoes both the control and experimental conditions. A cross-over design allows for each subject to act as their own control, helping to quantify any effect of the experimental condition across the project. Typically, a 'wash-out' period is provided between completing both experimental groups to allow for any changes resulting from either condition to be lost. The order of experimental conditions in a cross-over study should always be randomised.

Why you need to control variables in experiments

Interpretation of experiments is seldom clear-cut because uncontrolled variables always change when treatments are given.

Confounding variables

These increase or decrease systematically as the independent variable increases or decreases. Their effects are known as systematic variation. This form of variation can be disentangled from that caused directly by treatments by incorporating appropriate controls in the experiment. A control is really just another treatment where a potentially confounding variable is adjusted so that its effects, if any, can be taken into account. The results from a control may therefore allow an alternative hypothesis to be rejected. There are often many potential controls for any experiment.

Example Suppose you wish to investigate the effect of protein supplementation on muscular strength. If you used a protein or carbohydrate supplement and measured gains in strength over an eight-week training period, you will have immediately introduced at least two confounding variables, compared to the control of no supplement. Both the protein or carbohydrate may have provided gains separately, or the combination of the two macronutrients may collectively have an impact compared to the control. Both of these effects could be testing using effective controls.

The consequence of systematic variation is that you can never be certain that the treatment, and the treatment alone, has caused an observed result. By careful design, you can, however, 'minimise the uncertainty' involved in your conclusion. Methods available include:

- ensuring, through experimental design, that the independent variable is the only major factor that changes in any treatment;
- incorporating appropriate controls to show that potential confounding variables have little or no effect;
- selecting experimental subjects randomly to cancel out systematic variation arising from biased selection;
- matching or pairing individuals among treatments so that differences in response owing to their initial status are eliminated;
- arranging subjects and treatments randomly so that responses to systematic differences in conditions do not influence the results;
- ensuring that experimental conditions are uniform so that responses to systematic differences in conditions are minimised. Within sport and exercise science, several external factors can have a large influence on several physiological and performance measures that may be of interest.

Evaluating design constraints – a good way to do this is by processing an individual subject through the experimental procedures – a 'preliminary run' can help to identify potential difficulties.

Constraints on experimental design

Box 21.1 outlines the important stages in designing an experiment. At an early stage, you should find out how resources may constrain the design. For example, limits may be set by availability of subjects, cost

Box 21.1 Checklist for designing and performing an experiment

1. **Preliminaries**
   - (a) Read background material and decide on a subject area to investigate.
   - (b) Formulate a simple hypothesis to test. It is preferable to have a clear answer to one question rather than to be uncertain about several questions.
   - (c) Decide which dependent variable you are going to measure and how: is it relevant to the problem? Can you measure it accurately, precisely and without bias?
   - (d) Think about and plan the statistical analysis of your results. Will this affect your design?
2. **Designing**
   - (a) Find out the limitations of your resources.
   - (b) Determine the best study design to minimise any research bias and confounding factors (p. 142).
   - (c) Choose treatments that alter the minimum of confounding variables.
   - (d) Incorporate an appropriate control or placebo to the treatment.
   - (e) Statistically determine the appropriate number of subjects required to complete the experiment (p. 141).
3. **Planning**
   - (a) List all the materials you will need. Order any consumables (i.e. gloves, strips, electrodes) or intervention materials needed for the experiment. Check that the required equipment is available.
   - (b) Organise space and/or time in which to do the experiment (i.e. laboratory or field space).
   - (c) Account for the time taken for interventions to occur or any time that is needed to 'wash out' any intervention in a cross-over design experiment.
4. **Carrying out the experiment**
   - (a) Record the results and make careful notes of everything that you do (Chapter 22). Ensure that all interventions and procedures remain consistent across subjects.
   - (b) Ensure that all methods are repeated in any alternative experiment conditions.
5. **Analysis**
   - (a) Graph data as soon as possible (during the experiment if you can). This will allow you to visualise what has happened and observe trends.
   - (b) Carry out the planned statistical analysis.
   - (c) Jot down conclusions and new hypotheses arising from the experiment.

of treatment, availability of laboratory or field. Logistics may be a factor (e.g. time taken to record or analyse data).

Definition

Interaction – where the effect of treatments given together is greater or less than the sum of their individual effects.

Reporting correctly – it is good practice to report how many times your experiments were repeated (in Materials and Methods); in the Results section, you should add a statement saying that the illustrated experiment is representative.

Multifactorial experiments

The simplest experiments are those in which one treatment (factor) is applied at a time to the subjects. This approach is likely to give clear-cut answers, but it could be criticised for lacking realism. In particular, it cannot take account of interactions among two or more conditions that are likely to occur in real life. A multifactorial experiment (Fig. 21.2) is an attempt to do this; the interactions among treatments can be analysed by specialised statistics.

Multifactorial experiments are economical on resources because of 'hidden replication'. This arises when two or more treatments are given to a subject because the result acts statistically as a replicate for each treatment. Choice of relevant treatments to combine is important in multifactorial experiments; for instance, an interaction may be present at certain concentrations of a chemical but not at others (perhaps because the response is saturated). It is also important that the measurement scale for the response is consistent, otherwise spurious interactions may occur. Beware when planning a multifactorial experiment that the numbers of replicates do not get out of hand: you may have to restrict the treatments to 'plus' or 'minus' the factor of interest (as in Fig. 21.2).

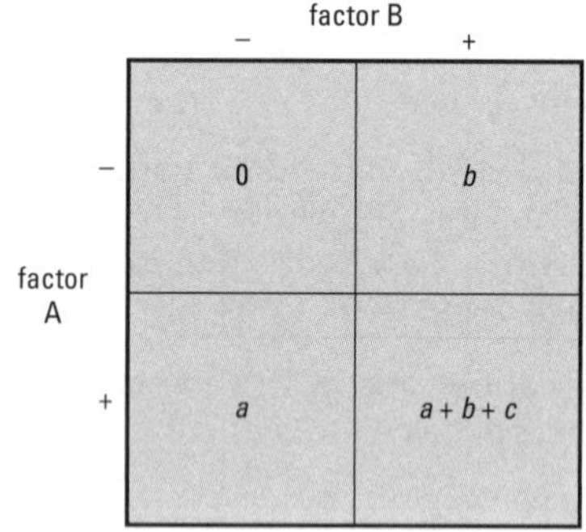

Fig. 21.2 Design of a simple multifactorial experiment. Factors A and B have effects *a* and *b* when applied alone. When both are applied together, the effect is denoted by $a + b + c$.

- If $c = 0$, there is no interaction (e.g. $2 + 2 + c = 4$)
- If *c* is positive, there is a positive interaction (synergism) between A and B (e.g. $2 + 2 + c = 5$)
- If *c* is negative, there is a negative interaction (antagonism) between A and B (e.g. $2 + 2 + c = 3$).

Source: Jones, A., Reed, R. and Weyers, J. (2007) p. 190.

Sources for further study

Peat, J. (2001) *Health Science Research.* Allen and Unwin, Crows Nest, NSW.

Sportsci (2010) *Sportsci–Research Resources.* Available: http://www.sportsci.org Last accessed: 23/12/10. [An excellent resource for research and statistical information for sport and exercise science.]

Thomas, J., Nelson, J. and Silverman, S. (2005) *Research Methods in Physical Activity,* 5th edn, Human Kinetics, Champaign, IL.

22 Conducting and writing up project work

Research projects are an important component of the final-year syllabus for most degree programmes in sport and exercise science, while shorter projects may also be carried out during courses in earlier years. Project work can be extremely rewarding, although it does present a number of challenges. The assessment of your project is likely to contribute significantly to your degree grade, so all aspects of this work should be approached in a thorough manner.

Obtaining ethical approval – if any aspect of your project involves work with human or animal subjects, then you must obtain the necessary ethical clearance before you begin; consult your lecturer, tutor or department's ethical committee for details.

Deciding on a topic to study

Assuming you have a choice, this important decision should be researched carefully. Make appointments to visit your lecturer, tutor or possible supervisors and ask them for advice on topics that you find interesting. Use library texts and research papers to obtain further background information. Perhaps the most important criterion is whether the topic will sustain your interest over the whole period of the project. Other things to look for include:

The Internet as an information source – since many university departments have home pages on the World Wide Web, searches using relevant key words may indicate where research in your area is currently being carried out. Academics usually respond positively to emailed questions about their area of expertise.

- **Opportunities to learn new skills.** Ideally, you should attempt to gain experience and skills that you might be able to 'sell' to a potential employer.
- **Likelihood of obtaining valid results.** An ideal project provides a means to obtain 'guaranteed' data for your report, but also the chance to extend knowledge by doing genuinely novel research.
- **Assistance.** What help will be available to you during the project? A busy lab with many research students might provide a supportive environment should your potential supervisor be too busy to meet you often; on the other hand, a smaller lab may provide the opportunity for more personal interaction with your supervisor.
- **Impact.** Your project may result in publishable data: discuss this with your prospective supervisor.

Asking around – one of the best sources of information about supervisors, laboratories and projects is past students. Some of the postgraduates in your department may be products of your own system and they could provide an alternative source of advice.

Planning your work

As with any lengthy exercise, planning is required to make the best use of the time allocated (p. 143). This is true on a daily basis as well as over the entire period of the project. It is especially important not to underestimate the time it will take to write and produce your thesis (see below). If you wish to benefit from feedback given by your supervisor, you should aim to have drafts in his/her hands in good time. Since a large proportion of marks will be allocated to the report, you should not rush its production.

If your department requires you to write an interim report, look on this as an opportunity to clarify your thoughts and get some of the time-consuming preparatory work out of the way. If not, you should set your own deadlines for producing drafts of the Introduction, Materials and Methods section, etc.

Liaising with your supervisor(s) – this is essential if your work is to proceed efficiently. Specific meetings may be timetabled, e.g. to discuss a term's progress, review your work plan or consider a draft introduction. Most supervisors also have an 'open-door' policy, allowing you to air current problems. Prepare well for all meetings: have a list of questions ready before the meeting; provide results in an easily digestible form (but take your lab notebook along); be clear about your future plans for work.

KEY POINT Project work can be very time-consuming at times. Try not to neglect other aspects of your course – make sure your lecture notes are up to date and collect relevant supporting information as you go along.

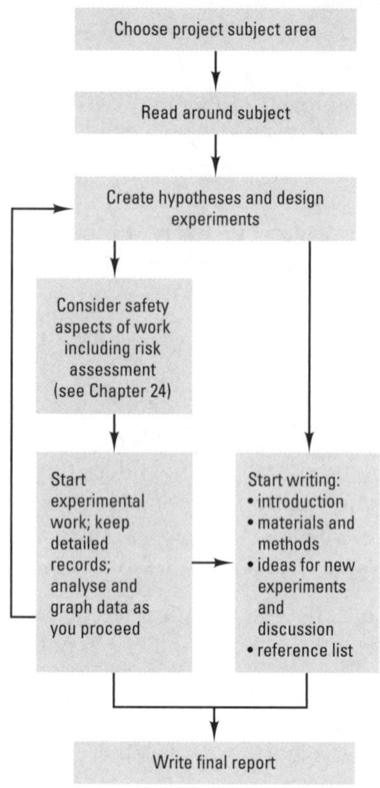

Fig. 22.1 Flowchart showing a recommended sequence of events in carrying out an undergraduate research project.
Source: Jones, J., Reed, R. and Weyers, J. (2007) p. 198.

SAFETY NOTE It is essential that you follow all the safety rules applying to the laboratory or field site. Make sure you know all relevant procedures – normally there will be prominent warnings about these. If in doubt, ask.

Getting started

Fig. 22.1 is a flowchart illustrating how a project might proceed; at the start, don't spend too long reading the literature and working out a lengthy programme of research. Get stuck in and do an experiment. There's no substitute for 'getting your hands dirty' to stimulate new ideas.

- Even a 'failed' experiment will provide some useful information that may allow you to create a new or modified hypothesis.
- Pilot experiments may point out deficiencies in experimental technique that will need to be rectified.
- The experience will help you create a realistic plan of work.

Designing experiments or sampling procedures

Design of experiments and sampling procedures is dealt with in Chapter 21. Avoid being too ambitious at the start of your work. It is generally best to work with a simple hypothesis and design your experiments or sampling around this. A small pilot experiment or test sample will highlight potential stumbling blocks, including resource limitations, whether in materials, or time, or both.

Working in a laboratory environment

During your time as a project student, you are effectively a guest in your supervisor's or department's laboratory.

- **Be considerate** – keep your 'area' tidy and offer to do your share of lab duties such as calibrating the gas analysis system or blood lactate analysers, cleaning and disinfecting the gas analysis mouthpieces and lines or restocking the consumables (gloves, test strips) for blood measures.
- **Use instruments carefully** – they could be worth more than you think. Careless use may invalidate calibration settings and ruin other people's work as well as your own.
- **Do your homework** on techniques you intend to use – there is less chance of making costly mistakes if you have a good background understanding of the methods you will be using.
- **Always seek advice** from the laboratory technician, tutor or lecturer if you are unsure of what you are doing.

Keeping notes and analysing your results

Tidy record-keeping is often associated with good research, and you should follow the advice and hints given below. Sport and exercise science students often forget to collect the details of the equipment used in testing. For example, every piece of equipment that you use in your testing will need to have the make, model, manufacturer and place of manufacture included in the write-up. Try to keep copies of all files relating to your project. As you obtain results, you should always calculate, analyse and graph data as soon as you can (see Fig. 22.1). This can reveal aspects that may not be obvious in numerical or read-out form. Don't be worried by negative results – these can sometimes be as useful as positive results if they allow you to eliminate hypotheses – and do not be too dispirited if things do not work first time. Thomas Edison's maxim 'Genius is one per cent inspiration and ninety-nine per cent perspiration' certainly applies to research work.

Writing your project report

The structure of scientific reports is dealt with in Chapters 13–15. The following advice concerns methods of accumulating relevant information.

Practical reports, project reports, theses and scientific papers will all have the same basic structure (see Box 22.1) that may be altered in format as dictated by your department or university's rules or requirements. Additional parts may be specified. For example, for project reports, theses or dissertations, a title page is often required as well as a list of figures and tables within the contents section. Some universities demand declarations and statements (e.g. that the work is original and has not been published elsewhere) made by the student and/or supervisor. In scientific papers, a list of key words is often added after the abstract to help with cross-referencing within online database systems.

KEY POINT Make sure you are absolutely certain about the deadline for submitting your report and try to submit a few days before it. If you leave things until the last moment, you may find access to printers, photocopiers and binding machines is difficult.

Steps in the production of a practical report or thesis

Choosing between graphs and tables – graphs are generally easier for the reader to assimilate, whereas tables can be used to condense a lot of data into a small space.

Repeating your experiments – remember, if you do an experiment twice, you have repeated it only once.

Choose the experiments you wish to describe and decide how best to present them

Try to start this process before your lab work ends, because at the stage of reviewing your experiments, a gap may become apparent (e.g. a missing control) and you might still have time to rectify the deficiency. Irrelevant material should be ruthlessly eliminated, at the same time bearing in mind that negative results can be extremely important. Use as many different forms of data presentation as are appropriate, but avoid presenting the same data in more than one form. Relegate large tables of primary data to an appendix and summarise the important points within the main text (with a cross-reference to the appendix). Make sure that the experiments you describe are representative: always state the number of times they were repeated and how consistent your findings were.

Make plans or outlines for the component parts

The overall structure of practical and project reports is well defined (see Box 22.1), but individual parts will need to be organised as with any other form of writing (see Chapter 14).

Box 22.1 The structure of reports of project work

Undergraduate practical and project reports are generally modelled on this arrangement or a close variant of it, because this is the structure used for nearly all research papers and theses. The more common variations include Results and Discussion combined into a single section and Conclusions appearing separately as a series of points arising from the work. In scientific papers, a list of key words (for computer cross-referencing systems) may be included after the abstract. Acknowledgements may appear after the contents section, rather than near the end. Department or faculty regulations for producing theses and reports may specify a precise format; they often require a title page to be inserted at the start and a list of figures and tables as part of the contents section, and may specify declarations and statements to be made by the student and supervisor.

Part (in order)	Contents/purpose	Checklist for reviewing content
Title	Explains what the project was about	Does it explain what the text is about succinctly?
Authors plus their institutions	Explains who did the work and where; also where they can be contacted now	Are all the details correct?
Abstract/Summary	Synopsis of methods, results and conclusion of work described. Allows the reader to grasp quickly the essence of the work	Does it explain why the work was done? Does it outline the whole of your work and your findings?
Contents	Shows the organisation of the text (not required for short papers)	Are all the sections covered? Are the page numbers correct?
Abbreviations	Lists all the abbreviations used (but not those of SI, chemical elements, or standard sport and exercise science terms)	Have they all been explained? Are they all in the accepted form? Are they in alphabetical order?
Introduction	Orientates the reader, explains why the work has been done and its context in the literature and why the methods used were chosen. Indicates the central hypothesis behind the experiments	Does it provide enough background information and cite all the relevant references? Is it of the correct depth for the readership? Have all the technical terms been defined? Have you explained why you investigated the problem? Have you outlined your aims and objectives? Have you explained your methodological approach? Have you stated your hypothesis?
Materials and Methods	Explains how the work was done. Should contain sufficient detail to allow another competent worker to repeat the work	Is there sufficient detail to allow repetition of the work? Have you outlined the subject's details (e.g. age, gender, height, mass, type of person – athlete or sedentary, level of athlete)? Have you included the equipment (make, model, manufacturer, place of manufacture) used? Have you included the actual procedures used and in what order? Have you outlined the statistical procedures and level of significance accepted?
Results	Displays and describes the data obtained. Should be presented in a form that is easily assimilated (graphs rather than tables, small tables rather than large ones)	Is the sequence of experiments logical? Are the parts adequately linked? Are the data presented in the clearest possible way? Have SI units been used properly throughout? Has adequate statistical analysis been carried out? Is all the material relevant? Are the figures and tables all numbered in the order of their appearance? Are their titles appropriate? Do the figure and table legends provide all the information necessary to interpret the data without reference to the text? Have you presented the same data more than once?
Discussion/ Conclusions	Discusses the results: their meaning, their importance; compares the results with those of others; suggests what to do next	Have you explained the significance of the results? Have you compared your data with other published work? Are your conclusions justified by the data presented?
Acknowledgements	Gives credit to those who helped carry out the work	Have you listed everyone that helped, including any grant-awarding bodies?
Literature cited (Bibliography)	Lists all references cited in appropriate format: provides enough information to allow the reader to find the reference in a library	Do all the references in the text appear on the list? Do all the listed references appear in the text? Do the years of publications and authors match? Are the journal details complete and in the correct format? Is the list in alphabetical order, or correct numerical order?

Presenting your results – remember that the order of results presented in a report need not correspond with the order in which you carried out the experiments: you are expected to rearrange them to provide a logical sequence of findings.

Using the correct tense – always use the past tense to describe the methodology used in your work, since it is now complete. Use the present tense only for generalisations and conclusions.

Peer review – the process of evaluation and review of a colleague's work. In scientific communication, a paper is reviewed by two or more expert reviewers for comments on quality and significance as a key component of the validation procedure.

Write

The Materials and Methods section is often the easiest to write once you have decided what to report. Remember to use the past tense and do not allow results or discussion to creep in. The Results section is the next easiest as it should only involve description. At this stage, you may benefit from jotting down ideas for the Discussion – this may be the hardest part to compose as you need an overview both of your own work and of the relevant literature. It is also liable to become wordy, so try hard to make it succinct. The Introduction shouldn't be too difficult if you have fully understood the aims of the experiments. Write the Abstract and complete the list of references at the end. To assist with the latter, it is a good idea as you write to jot down the references you use, to pull out their cards from your index system, or from your referencing software (e.g. EndNote).

Revise the text

Once your first draft is complete, try to answer all the questions given in Box 22.1. Show your work to your supervisors and learn from their comments. Let a friend or colleague who is unfamiliar with your subject read your text; they may be able to pinpoint obscure wording and show where information or explanation is missing. If writing a thesis, double-check that you are adhering to your institution's thesis regulations.

Prepare the final version

Markers appreciate neatly produced work, but a well presented document will not disguise poor science! If using a word processor, print the final version with the best printer available. Make sure figures are clear and in the correct size and format.

Submit your work

Your department will specify when to submit a thesis or project report, so plan your work carefully to meet this deadline or you may lose marks. Tell your supervisor early of any circumstances that may cause delay and check to see whether any forms must be completed for late submission, or evidence of extenuating circumstances.

Producing a scientific paper

Scientific papers are the means by which research findings are communicated to others. Peer-reviewed papers are published in journals; each covers a well defined subject area and publishes details of the format they expect.

KEY POINT Peer review is an important component of the process of scientific publication; only those papers whose worth is confirmed by the peer review process will be published.

It would be very unusual for an undergraduate to submit a paper on his or her own – this would normally be done in collaboration with your project supervisor and only then if your research has satisfied appropriate criteria. However, it is important to understand the process whereby a paper comes into being (Box 22.2), as this can help you to understand and interpret the primary literature.

Box 22.2 Steps in producing a scientific paper

Scientific papers are the lifeblood of any science and it is a major landmark in your scientific career to publish your first paper. The main steps in doing this should include the following.

Assessing potential content
The work must be of an appropriate standard to be published and should be 'new, true and meaningful'. Therefore, before starting, the authors need to review their work critically under these headings. The material included in a scientific paper will generally be a subset of the total work done during a project, so it must be carefully selected for relevance to a clear central hypothesis – if the authors won't prune, the referees and editors of the journal certainly will.

Choosing a journal
There are many journals covering sport and exercise science and each covers a specific area (which may change through time). The main factors in deciding on an appropriate journal are the range of subjects it covers, the quality of its content (theoretical versus applied) and the number and geographical distribution of its readers. The choice of journal always dictates the format of a paper since authors must follow to the letter the journal's 'Instructions to Authors'.

Deciding on authorship
In multiauthor papers, a contentious issue is often who should appear as an author and in what order they should be cited. Where authors make an equal contribution, an alphabetical order of names may be used. Otherwise, each author should have made a substantial contribution to the paper and should be prepared to defend it in public. Ideally, the order of appearance will reflect the amount of work done rather than seniority.

Writing
The paper's format will be similar to that shown in Box 22.1, and the process of writing will include outlining, reviewing, etc., as discussed elsewhere in this chapter. Figures must be finished to an appropriate standard and this may involve preparing photographs or digital images.

Submitting
When completed, copies of the paper are submitted to the editor of the chosen journal with a simple covering letter. A delay of one to two months usually follows while the manuscript is sent to two or more anonymous referees who will be asked by the editor to check that the paper is novel, scientifically correct and that its length is justified.

Responding to referees' comments
The editor will send on the referees' comments to the authors who will then have a chance to respond. The editor will decide on the basis of the comments and replies to them whether the paper should be published. Sometimes quite heated correspondence can result if the authors and referees disagree.

Checking proofs and waiting for publication
If a paper is accepted, it will be sent off to the typesetters. The next the authors see of it is the proofs (first printed version in style of journal), which have to be corrected carefully for errors and returned. Eventually, the paper will appear in print, but a delay of six months following acceptance is not unusual. Nowadays, papers are often available electronically, via the Web, in pdf format – see p. 53 for advice on how to cite 'online early' papers.

Sources for further study

Baumgartner, T.A. and Hensley, L.D. (2006) *Conducting and Reading Research in Health and Human Performance*. McGraw-Hill, New York.

Davis, M. (2005) *Scientific Papers and Presentations*. Academic Press, London.

Day, R.A. and Gastel, B. (2006) *How to Write and Publish a Scientific Paper*, 6th edn, Cambridge University Press, Cambridge.

Luck, M. (1999) *Your Student Research Project*. Gower, London.

Thomas, J., Nelson, J. and Silverman, S. (2005) *Research Methods in Physical Activity*. Human Kinetics, Champaign, IL.

Fundamental laboratory techniques

23. Your approach to practical work 153

24. Health and safety 157

25. Working with body fluids 165

23 Your approach to practical work

Developing practical skills – these will include:

- designing experiments
- observing and measuring
- recording data
- analysing and interpreting data
- reporting/presenting.

All knowledge and theory in science has originated from practical observation and experimentation: this is equally true for disciplines as diverse as training programming and protein synthesis research. Practical work is an important part of most courses and often accounts for a significant proportion of the assessment marks. The abilities developed in practical classes will continue to be useful throughout your course and beyond, some within science and others in any career you choose (see Chapter 1).

Being prepared

KEY POINT You will get the most out of practicals if you prepare well in advance. Do not go into a practical session assuming that everything will be provided, without any input on your part.

The main points to remember are:

- **Read any handouts in advance:** make sure you understand the purpose of the practical and the particular skills involved. Does the practical relate to, or expand upon, a current topic in your lectures? Is there any additional preparatory reading that will help?
- **Take along appropriate textbooks,** to explain aspects in the practical.
- **Consider what safety hazards might be involved,** and any precautions you might need to take, before you begin (p. 158).
- **Listen carefully to any introductory guidance** and note any important points: adjust your schedule/handout as necessary.
- **Organise your bench space during the practical session** – make sure your lab book is adjacent to, but not within, your working area. You will often find it easiest to keep clean items of glassware etc. on one side of your working space, with used equipment on the other side.
- **Write up your work as soon as possible,** and submit it on time, or you may lose marks.
- **Catch up on any work you have missed as soon as possible** – preferably before the next practical session.

Using textbooks in the lab – take this book along to the relevant classes, so that you can make full use of the information during the practical sessions.

SAFETY NOTE Mobile phones should never be used in a lab class, as there is a risk of interfering with laboratory equipment. Always switch off your mobile phone before entering a laboratory. Conversely, they are an extremely useful accessory for fieldwork.

Ethical and legal aspects

You will need to consider the ethical and legal implications of sports and exercise science at several points during your studies:

- Safe working means following a code of safe practice, supported by legislation, alongside a moral obligation to avoid harm to yourself and other, as discussed in Chapter 24. For sport and exercise science, this can mean only performing methods for which you are competent and are appropriately resourced.
- All exercise science methods should comply with generally accepted moral and scientific standards, and conform to existing procedures and standards.

Getting to grips with human ethics – in addition to any moral implications of your lab practicals and research projects, you may have the opportunity to address broader issues within your course (see Box 23.1). Sport and exercise scientists should always consider the risks and consequences of their work, and it is therefore important that you develop an appreciation of these issues alongside your academic studies.

Box 23.1 Human ethics

Contemporary exercise science programmes place increasing emphasis on the ethical and social considerations of scientific advances, and on the need for scientists engaged in potentially controversial work to communicate their ideas to the general public. Exercise science research can raise many moral and legal dilemmas, requiring difficult choices to be made (e.g. putting certain populations at a higher level of cardiovascular risk), and students are often asked to reflect on ethical topics and ensure that ethical standards are met prior to engaging in research. Current issues involving humans that are ethically challenging in exercise science research include:

- exercise-specific ethics (e.g. exercising people to exhaustion, elevating cardiac risk, invasive procedures);
- performance ethics (e.g. performance-enhancing procedures such as blood doping, anabolic agents, sporting apparel);
- medical and social ethics (e.g. stem cell research, gene doping).

In discussing such topics (sometimes referred to as ethical, legal and social issues, ELSI), you will find that there is rarely a 'right' or 'wrong' answer. However, it is important to be able to consider these issues in a logical manner within your degree studies, and to provide a reasoned argument in support of a particular viewpoint. Gaining experience in such debates should also help you to understand some of the issues linked to the public understanding of science, and how these can be addressed (see http://www.copus.org.uk/pubs_guides.html). Although a full exposition is beyond the scope of this book, the following provides a framework of principles for considering particular topics:

- **Beneficence** – the obligation to do good (e.g. if it is possible to prevent suffering by a particular course or action, then it should be carried out).
- **Non-maleficence** – the duty to cause no harm (contained within the Hippocratic Oath of medical practitioners).
- **Justice** – the obligation to treat all people fairly and impartially (e.g. lack of discrimination on the grounds of race or sex).
- **Autonomy** – allows an individual to make their own choices, without constraints (this principle underlies the notion of informed consent in medical research).
- **Respect** – the need to show due regard for others (e.g. by taking into account the rights and beliefs of all people equally).
- **Rationality** – the notion that a particular action or choice should be based on reason and logic (many scientists would argue that the scientific method is an example of rationality).
- **Precautionary principle** – the notion that it is better not to carry out an action if there is any risk of harm (e.g. in deciding that the risks of a certain strength testing protocol outweigh the potential benefits).

Understanding the various theories of ethics may also help you to formulate your ideas. These include:

- **Utilitarianism** – the notion that it is ethical to choose the action that produces the greatest good for the greatest number.
- **Deontology** – a theory stating that a particular action is either intrinsically good (right) or bad (wrong). According to deontological theory, decisions should be based on the actions themselves, rather than their consequences.
- **Virtue theory** – the notion that making decisions according to established virtues (e.g. honesty, wisdom, justice) will lead to ethically valid choices.
- **Objectivism** – the theory that what is right or wrong is intrinsic and applies equally to all people, places and times (the alternative is that morality is subjective, being dependent on the views of each individual).

The principles and issues of human ethics are considered on a number of websites, including:

- World Medical Association Declaration of Helsinki, Ethical Principles for Medical Research Involving Human Subjects (http://www.wma.net/e/policy/b3.htm);
- British Philosophy of Sport Association (http://philosophyofsport.glos.ac.uk/ethsport.html);
- Human Research Ethics Handbook (http://www.nhmrc.gov.au/PUBLICATIONS/synopses/e42syn.htm)

In particular the following resources provide further information on the ethical considerations on research projects conducted by health and exercise science students:

- Doyal, L. (2005) The Ethical Governance and Regulation of Student Projects (http://www.dh.gov.uk/en/Researchanddevelopment/A-Z/Researchgovernance/index.htm);
- Maughan, R. Nevill, A., Boreham, C. et al. (2007) Ethical issues when submitting to the *Journal of Sports Sciences. Journal of Sports Sciences,* **25**(6), 617–18.

The following texts give further information and guidance: McNamee (2005), McNamee *et al.* (2006) and Miah (2004).

- The benefits of such work must outweigh the risks and negative outcomes. The trialling of any new exercise science method (e.g. supplementation) should not be undertaken unless appropriate provision has been made for any negative consequences. If it becomes clear that the intervention is harmful, then the experiment must be ceased immediately.
- It is vital that, prior to any practical exercises or research, the subject provides their consent to participate. Typically this should be in writing unless this is not possible. It is important that the subject understands the purpose, procedures, risks and benefits of the research prior to giving their consent and participation. If the subject is under the age of consent or is unable to provide consent (e.g. for any other reason), it is important that the written consent of their guardian is gained.
- When dealing with human subjects it is always important to respect the personality, rights, wishes, beliefs, consent and freedom of the individual subject.
- Any subject involved in exercise science research must be free to withdraw from participation at any time without penalty or negative consequences.
- Subject information and data from all research should remain confidential to the researchers. Steps to maintain subject confidentiality may include coding subject names, password protection of electronic files and filing all written papers and data in a locked cabinet.
- Any tissue or body fluids should be collected and stored appropriately (Chapter 25). Exercise equipment should always be sanitised appropriately to minimise the risk of cross-contamination between subjects.

Basic requirements

Recording practical results

An A4 loose-leaf ring binder offers flexibility, since you can insert laboratory handouts or lined and graph paper at appropriate points. The danger of losing one or more pages from a loose-leaf system is the main drawback. Bound books avoid this problem, although those containing alternating lined/graph or lined/blank pages tend to be wasteful – it is often better to paste sheets of graph paper into a bound book, as required.

A good-quality HB pencil is recommended when recording raw data or drawing diagrams, as mistakes are easily corrected. Always carry a small selection of pens (i.e. ballpoint and felt-tipped, variety of colours) as this is useful for preparing final lab reports and graphs and diagrams for assessment purposes. A black spirit-based (permanent) marker is also handy for any anatomical markings that you may undertake. Similarly, an eye-liner pencil should also be bought and taken to help mark up for anthropometrical measurements. Use a transparent ruler (with an undamaged edge) for graph drawing, so that you can see data points and information below the ruler as you draw.

Presenting results – although you do not need to be a graphic designer to produce work of a satisfactory standard, presentation and layout are important and you will lose marks for poorly presented work. Chapter 22 gives further practical advice.

Using inexpensive calculators – many unsophisticated calculators have a restricted display for exponential numbers and do not show the 'power of 10', e.g. displaying 2.4×10^{-5} as 2.4^{-05}, or even 2.4E−05, or 2.4 − 05.

Calculators

These range from basic machines with no pre-programmed functions and only one memory to sophisticated programmable portable computers with many memories. The following may be helpful when using a calculator:

Using calculators for numerical problems – Chapter 49 gives further advice.

- **Power sources.** Choose a battery-powered machine, rather than a mains-operated or solar-powered type. You will need one with basic mathematical/scientific operations, including powers, logarithms, roots and parentheses (brackets), together with statistical functions such as sample means and standard deviations (Chapter 49).
- **Mode of operation.** The older operating system used by, for example, Hewlett-Packard calculators is known as the reverse Polish notation: to calculate the sum of two numbers, the sequence is 2 [enter] 4 + and the answer 6 is displayed. The more usual method of calculating this equation is as $2 + 4 =$, which is the system used by the majority of modern calculators. Most newcomers find the latter approach to be more straightforward. Spend some time finding out how a calculator operates, e.g. does it have true algebraic logic ($\surd$ then number, rather than number then $\surd$)? How does it deal with (and display) scientific notation and logarithms?
- **Display.** Some calculators will display an entire mathematical operation (e.g. '$2 + 4 = 6$'), while others simply display the last number/operation. The former type may offer advantages in tracing errors.
- **Complexity.** In the early stages, it is usually better to avoid the more complex machines, full of impressive-looking, but often unused, pre-programmed functions – go for more memory, parentheses or statistical functions rather than engineering or mathematical constants. Programmable calculators may be worth considering for more advanced studies. However, it is important to note that such calculators are often unacceptable for exams.

Presenting graphs and diagrams – ensure that these are large enough to be easily read: a common error is to present graphs or diagrams that are too small, with poorly chosen scales (see Box 47.3).

Presenting more advanced practical work

In some practical reports and in project work, you may need to use more sophisticated presentation equipment. Computer-based graphics packages can be useful – choose easily read fonts such as Arial or Helvetica for posters and consider the layout and content carefully (p. 149). Alternatively, you could use fine-line drawing pens and dry-transfer lettering/symbols, although this can be more time-consuming than computer-based systems, e.g. using Microsoft Excel (pp. 368–70).

Printing on acetates – standard overhead transparencies are not suitable for use in laser printers or photocopiers: you need to make sure that you use the correct type.

To prepare overhead transparencies for spoken presentations, you can use spirit-based markers and acetate sheets. An alternative approach is to print directly from a computer-based package, using a laser printer and special acetates, or directly on to 35 mm slides. You can also photocopy on to special acetates. Further advice on content and presentation is given in Chapter 22.

Text references

McNamee, M. (2005) *Philosophy and the Sciences of Exercise, Health and Sport: Critical Perspectives on Research Methods*. Routledge, Oxford.

McNamee, M., Oliver, S. and Wainwright, P. (2006) *Research Ethics in Exercise, Health and Sports Sciences*. Routledge, Oxford.

Miah, A. (2004) *Genetically Modified Athletes: Biomedical Ethics, Gene Doping and Sport*. Routledge, Oxford.

24 Health and safety

> **Definitions**
>
> **Hazard** – something that has the potential to be harmful.
>
> **Risk** – the likelihood that a hazard will cause harm and the consequence of that harm if realised.

Health and safety laws within most countries require institutions and employers to provide a working environment that is safe and without risk to health. Most countries have government legislation in the form of Workplace Health and Safety Acts, which imposes obligations on people at work to ensure workplace health and safety. For example, in Queensland, Australia, the *Workplace Health and Safety Act 1995* helps employers meet health and safety obligations through:

- **workplace health and safety regulations** that describe what must be done to prevent or control certain hazards that cause injury, illness or death;
- **codes of practice,** which are designed to give practical advice about ways of managing exposure to common risks.

In sport and exercise science there is a wide variety of laboratory- and field-based activities that present potential hazards and risks to both the researcher and participants in projects.

Duty of care

Researchers, students doing project work in the laboratory or field, and sport and exercise laboratory staff need to be aware of their responsibility to exercise a *duty of care* to exercisers and athletes taking part in their projects, clients, fellow staff and students, and any other coworkers. This duty of care is made explicit in government legislation in all western countries. For example, in the UK, the *Health and Safety at Work Act 1974* has the following sections:

- **Section 2:** General duties of employers to their employees;
- **Section 3:** General duties of employers and the self-employed to persons other than their employees;
- **Section 4:** General duties of persons concerned with premises to persons other than their employees;
- **Section 7:** General duties of employees at work.

In Australia, each state has its own Act. These Acts have similar sections. Regardless of the country you live in, such legislation is aimed at:

- securing and promoting the health, safety and welfare of people at work;
- protecting people against workplace health and safety risks;
- ensuring that risks are identified, assessed and eliminated or controlled.

> **Distinguishing between hazard and risk** – one of the hazards associated with research based on swimming is drowning. However, the risk of drowning in novice swimmers will be higher than for elite swimmers.

Risk assessment

In sport and exercise science research projects and in laboratory- or field-based practicals, risk assessment is the cornerstone of health and safety management practice. Both government regulations and university rules and regulations require that risk assessments be carried out for all activities and that these findings are documented. Around the world there is typically a

Risk management – to understand the workplace health and safety requirements for risk management and your obligations under the law, you must consider and understand relevant legislation and codes of practice. Consult your university or college Health and Safety Unit or your laboratory technician who should be familiar with these legal requirements.

Conducting a risk assessment – always involve fellow team members in the assessment. Ideally, you should involve cleaners, laboratory technicians and all people with whom you share your workplace or who may be involved in your project and who could be hurt by your activities.

Table 24.1 Typical hazards in sport and exercise science laboratories or field-based projects

Category	Examples
Building and equipment	Electrical cables Rough or slippery surfaces Heavy equipment
Health and fitness of participants	Fitness level of subjects Age of subjects Cardiovascular complications Signs and symptoms of disease Vomiting Musculoskeletal injury
Administration of supplements	Overdose or acute effects Allergic responses
Use of hazardous materials	Chemicals or laboratory reagents Potentially infectious materials (e.g. blood, sweat, saliva or urine)
Environment	Temperature Humidity Altitude Gas mixtures (hypoxia, hyperoxia)

five-step risk assessment process that provides a structured analysis of what can cause harm in any workplace (laboratory, field setting), an assessment of the likelihood and impact of something harmful happening, and a means of identifying measures that can be implemented to mitigate the occurrence of harmful incidents (HSE, 2006). The steps are outlined below.

1. Identify the hazards

Below are some suggestions to help you identify some of the hazards in your projects or practical sessions

- Walk around your workplace (laboratory or field setting) and look at what could reasonably be expected to cause harm.
- Ask other people what they think. They may have noticed things that are not immediately obvious to you.
- Speak to the laboratory technician(s) in your department or laboratory.
- Have a look back at the laboratory accident and ill-health records – these often help to identify the less obvious hazards.
- Remember to think about long-term hazards to health (e.g. high levels of noise or chronic exposure to harmful substances) as well as safety hazards such as water or power lines or cables, slippery floors or surfaces.

In sport and exercise science, the hazards listed in Table 24.1 are likely to exist in laboratories or field settings.

2. Decide who might be harmed and how

For each hazard, look for the ways in which people could be hurt or become ill and at the possible causes of injury or illness. This does not mean listing everyone by name, but rather identifying groups of people (e.g. 'people using the treadmill'). There may be some groups particularly at risk in sport and exercise science. These might include:

- children;
- older people;
- pregnant or breastfeeding women;
- unfit people;
- people with underlying medical conditions;
- people with learning disabilities;
- people with physical disabilities.

In each case, identify how they might be harmed, i.e. what type of injury or ill health might occur. For example, 'Unfit and untrained older people may suffer back injury from repeated lifting of weights.'

3. Evaluate the risks and decide on precautions (controls)

Once you have identified the hazards, you then have to decide what to do about them. The law requires you to do everything 'reasonably practicable' to protect people from harm. A useful approach is to compare what you are

Box 24.1 Conducting a risk assessment using a risk rating system

A risk assessment involves looking for ways in which people could be hurt or become ill, and at the possible causes of injury or illness. For each hazard identified you need to estimate the *likelihood* of an incident occurring at your workplace, bearing in mind existing control measures, and then estimate the *consequences* of an incident occurring at your workplace. The table below outlines one method for rating the risk associated with an identified hazard.

	Consequences (How severely it hurts someone if it happens)			
Likelihood (How likely is it to happen?)	**Minor**	**Moderate**	**Major**	**Catastrophic**
Almost certain	M	S	H	H
Likely (it is possible or has happened)	L	M	S	H
Unlikely	L	M	S	S
Rare (unusual, practically impossible)	L	L	M	M
Legend and statement	*Action and timescale*			
H: HIGH RISK – STOP	Do something about the risk immediately. If it is not possible to reduce the risk, even with unlimited resources, the work should not be started. Contact your supervisor.			
S: SIGNIFICANT RISK – STOP	Do something about the risk immediately. Work should not be started until the risk is reduced. Contact your supervisor.			
M: MODERATE RISK	Effort should be made to reduce the risk but the cost of prevention should be measured and limited. Seek input from supervisor or health and safety advisor before starting.			
L: LOW RISK	No action required. Proceed and manage using normal procedures. Record if any equipment/people/materials/work methods or procedures change.			

proposing to do with good practice. There are many sources of good practice on the HSE website listed in the references.

Risk is an appraisal of the likelihood of a hazard causing harm and the consequence of that harm if realised. Risk can be rated by combining your likelihood and consequence estimates as in Box 24.1. Once calculated, the risks can then be prioritised, managed and controlled.

Table 24.2 gives an example of a risk assessment from a research project that might be undertaken within a master's or PhD project in sport and exercise science.

Managing risk involves reducing the likelihood and consequences of the hazards you identify to an acceptable level through control measures (actions or interventions) that reduce the level of risk. When controlling risks, apply the principles below, in the following order:

- Remove the harm or prevent the risk (e.g. don't use unfit older subjects in the project).
- Try a less risky option (e.g. switch to using a less hazardous dosage of caffeine).

Table 24.2 Sample risk evaluation and control measures study involving a muscle biopsy procedure and blood sampling of elite endurance cyclists while exercising in a climate chamber.

Hazard	Consequence	Likelihood	Risk rating	Control(s)
Heat exhaustion	Moderate	Possible	High	Monitor core temperature Monitor heart rate Constant visual monitoring and communication Constant monitoring of ambient temperature and humidity Ventilation fans used
Dehydration	Moderate	Unlikely	Moderate	Monitor core temperature Monitor heart rate Constant visual monitoring and communication Ready availability of fluids
Nitrogen or dry ice gas during biopsy or blood sampling	Minor	Rare	Low	Minimise time of nitrogen or dry ice in chamber or take blood sample or muscle sample from biopsy needle outside chamber for immersion in liquid nitrogen
Door locking	Moderate	Rare	Moderate	Constant visual monitoring and communication Inside door release mechanism

Definitions

Personal protective equipment (PPE) – clothing, equipment or substances designed to be worn by someone to protect them from risks of injury or illness. PPE should only be considered as a control measure when exposure to a risk cannot be minimised in another way, or when used in conjunction with other control measures as a final barrier between the worker and the hazard. PPE does not control the hazard at the source.

Putting control measures in place – you need to answer the following questions:

- Are there legislated things that must be done in relation to the specific hazard?
- Is there a code of practice relating to the specific hazard?
- What are the existing controls?
- Are controls as high as possible in the hierarchy of priorities?
- Do controls protect everyone exposed to harm?
- What additional controls are required?

- Prevent access to the hazard (e.g. place the ergometer well away from the weights machine).
- Organise work to reduce exposure to the hazard (e.g. do the tests in the afternoon so that athletes are warmer).
- Issue personal protective equipment (e.g. gloves, footwear, goggles, etc.).
- Provide welfare facilities (e.g. first aid and washing facilities for removal of contaminants).

4. Record your findings and put the controls in place

Documenting the results of your risk assessment, and sharing them with your supervisor, tutor, laboratory technician and peers, encourage you to act on them. When writing down your results, keep it simple, for example 'Tripping over power cables: taping provided, all research team instructed, weekly housekeeping checks of the tape', or 'Blood on portable lactate analyser: research team instructed to wipe down analyser regularly with alcowipe, technician to check regularly'. The HSE provides sample risk assessments at: http://www.hse.gov.uk/risk/casestudies/index.htm.

A good risk assessment plan often includes a mixture of different actions such as:

- a few inexpensive or easy improvements that can be done quickly, perhaps as a temporary solution until more reliable controls are in place;
- long-term solutions to those risks most likely to cause accidents or ill-health;
- long-term solutions to those risks with the worst potential consequences;
- arrangements for training others on the main risks that remain and how they are to be controlled;

- regular checks to make sure that the control measures are in place; and clear responsibilities have been identified – who will lead on what action, and by when?

Documenting and retaining the risk assessments are particularly important if any legal liability action is taken as a result of an incident or accident. Outcomes of risk assessments should also be incorporated into laboratory documents such as manuals, codes of practice or standard operating procedures. For example, the British Association of Sport and Exercise Science (BASES) *Code of Conduct* (2000) emphasises the three following principles:

1. All clients have the right to expect the highest standards of professionalism, consideration and respect.
2. The pursuit of scientific knowledge requires that research and testing is carried out with the utmost integrity.
3. The law requires that working practices are safe and that the welfare of the client is paramount.

Moreover, the BASES *Code of Conduct* (Section 7: Professional and personal conduct) highlights the following statements relative to safety:

- Members' paramount concern is the wellbeing of their clients.
- Members must not practise or work when they are not fit to operate effectively and professionally.
- Members must not in any way jeopardise the safety or interests of clients.
- Members must be totally unbiased and objective in their practices and actions.
- Members must ensure, where appropriate, the highest standards of safety and working practices and research both in respect of work undertaken by members themselves or by others under their supervision.

5. Review your assessment and update if necessary

Sport and exercise science equipment and procedures change over time. These changes can mean new hazards. If there is a significant change in procedures or equipment, do not wait: check your risk assessment and, where necessary, amend it. If possible, it is best to think about the risk assessment when you are planning your change. Importantly, ensure the changed documents are version-controlled (e.g. footer at bottom of each page stating version number, date of change and person responsible) and that all individuals who are affected by the changes are informed of the revised risk management procedures.

Personal injury claims and professional indemnity

Neither laboratory-based nor field-based activities in sport and exercise science are ever risk-free. If an incident or accident occurs, it is important that:

- Documentary evidence be provided to demonstrate that a duty of care has been exercised. This may be as an informed consent form supported by ethical clearance from the department or university

Definitions

Professional indemnity – a type of insurance against negligence or misappropriation by a professional adviser.

Public liability – a type of insurance that covers damage that can occur to other people or property.

ethics committee or an incident/accident report form, completed immediately after the event.

- Professional indemnity and public liability insurance is in place to cover any legal costs or awards of damages if a case of negligence is proven. Most universities and colleges have this insurance in place for approved coursework or postgraduate and staff research approved by an ethics committee.

Basic rules for laboratory work

Laboratories can be places of danger, and a lack of experience and knowledge may contribute to a health and safety incident. While it is almost impossible to eliminate the risks of injury totally, you can reduce them by abiding by a number of basic safety rules.

- Ensure that you follow all instructions that your supervisor gives you.
- Wear the correct clothing such as covered shoes and/or laboratory coats. Laboratory coats can provide valuable protection against such things as spills.
- Use appropriate personal protective equipment such as safety glasses, gloves, hearing and respiratory protection when needed.
- Do not eat, drink, smoke, take medication or apply cosmetics.
- Keep loose clothing and long hair away from moving equipment.
- Never undertake potentially hazardous activities while working alone.
- Familiarise yourself with the emergency preparedness procedures. Know the location of the nearest emergency shower, eyewash station, first aid kit, firefighting equipment and emergency exits.
- Know the chemical hazards warning symbols (Fig 24.1).
- If chemical spillages do occur and you are unsure of how to deal with them, *stop* and immediately contact your supervisor or safety officer. You should know how to clean up the chemicals with which you are working.
- Never undertake repairs of electrical equipment. Only qualified persons are permitted to carry out electrical work.
- Ensure that you know how to operate equipment and machinery safely before beginning.
- When planning a new experiment, always consider the hazards that might occur and take the necessary precautions to eliminate or reduce these hazards.
- Always report all known or observed hazards, incidents and injuries to your supervisor and complete and submit the necessary report forms.
- Be aware of posture and ergonomics. Prolonged postures without regular change or rest should be avoided.
- Work in a logical and tidy manner and minimise risks by thinking ahead.

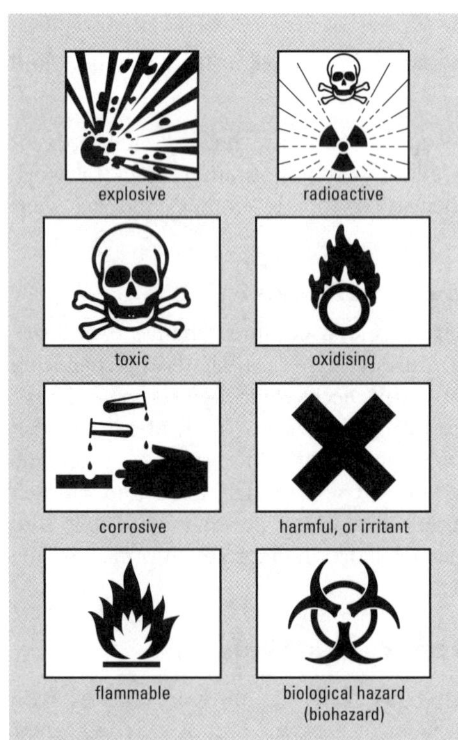

Fig. 24.1 Warning labels for specific chemical hazards. These appear on suppliers containers and on tape used to label working vessels.

'Sharps' – this term refers to any object that can pierce or penetrate the skin easily. Sharps include broken glass, lancets, capillary tubes and needles. Sharps are a major cause of accidents involving potential exposure to biological hazards such as a risk of transmission of hepatitis B and C viruses as well as HIV. Controlling the sharps hazard involves training team members in sharps handling, vaccination if needed, use of protective equipment such as gloves, use of sharps containers, implementation of an incident reporting system and first aid training.

- Always clean up after each laboratory session. Clean and disinfect surfaces and equipment after use. Be sure to come back and put the cleaned equipment away (e.g. do not leave gas analysis or lung function test mouthpieces and hoses in disinfecting solution for more than 60 minutes).
- Clean and disinfect not only the equipment, but also the floor around the equipment you used (to remove blood, sweat or saliva droplets).
- Dispose of waste in appropriate containers. Most sport and exercise science labs will have bags for biological waste (e.g. gloves, alcowipes, cotton wool, test strips) and sharps.

Basic rules for fieldwork

While labs can be intimidating places for athletes or members of the public, conducting research projects or testing at the pool, on the track, on the water or on ice presents different safety issues for the sport and exercise scientist. Again, you can minimise the risks and hazards of fieldwork in a number of ways:

- Ensure that you have permission to use the facility (e.g. pool, running track, skating rink, school classroom, etc.). Work out times and schedules with the managers or local authorities well in advance.
- Check that the equipment is functional under field conditions such as cold, high heat or humidity (e.g. heated swimming pool). Ensure pens and paper work in moist conditions. A water-insoluble grease pen on a plastic slate may be preferred. Alcohol swabs will be needed to clean the slate.
- Plan well ahead as to what equipment or consumables you may need and allow for back-up supplies (e.g. spare batteries, back-up analysers, extension cables).
- Have plenty of dry cloths available if testing in wet and/or humid conditions. Water or sweat can dilute blood, urine, saliva, etc. so dry cloths are very practical.
- Practise the techniques (e.g. fingertip or earlobe blood sampling, pp. 189–190) well before you go into the field.
- Plan how you will dispose of hazardous waste material. Have sharps containers and biological waste bags that can be safely transported back to your home laboratory for proper disposal. If you plan to use a local disposal site such as a hospital, ensure you have permission.
- Identify potential hazards and risks well in advance.
- Take a comprehensive first aid kit and make sure you have up-to-date training in first aid and cardiopulmonary resuscitation.
- Wear appropriate clothing such as layers in winter and hat, sunscreen and long-sleeve shirt in summer.
- Check weather forecast before departing and look out for changes in the weather.
- Inform someone of where you are going, when you are leaving and returning and via which route.
- Carry a mobile phone or two-way radio with you.

Text references

British Association of Sport and Exercise Science (BASES) (2000) *Code of Conduct.*
Available: http://www.bases.org.uk/pdf/Code%20of%20Conduct.pdf.
Last accessed: 23/12/10.

Health and Safety Executive. *Workplace Health Connect.*
Available: http://www.hse.gov.uk/workplacehealth/
Last accessed: 23/12/10.

Health and Safety Executive (HSE) (2006) *Five Steps to Risk Assessment.*
Available: http://www.hse.gov.uk/pubns/indg163.pdf
Last accessed: 23/12/10.

Sources for further study

Furr, A.K. (2000) *CRC Handbook of Laboratory Safety*. CRC Press, Boca Raton.

National Health and Medical Research Council (1996) *Infection Control in the Health Care Setting: Guidelines for the Prevention of Transmission of Infectious Diseases*. Available: http://www.nhmrc.gov.au/publications/synopses/ic6syn.htm
Last accessed: 23/12/10.

Professional Health and Safety Consultants Ltd *(A guide to) The Health and Safety at Work etc. Act 1974*. Available: http://www.healthandsafety.co.uk/haswa.htm
Last accessed: 23/12/10.

25 Working with body fluids

SAFETY NOTE Body fluids can transmit many types of infectious diseases. It is important to adhere to all safety procedures to minimise the risk of exposure and/or infection for both you and the people with whom you are working.

Dealing with body fluids is an inevitable part of sport and exercise science and, as such, it is important to know and understand the correct procedures from both practical and safety aspects. In studying sport and exercise science, you will commonly deal with a variety of body fluids (i.e. blood, saliva, urine and sweat) to measure a wide range of physiological and metabolic variables. Without safe handling of body fluids, it would be dangerous for sport and exercise scientists to acquire information on physiological limits and thresholds (e.g. anaerobic threshold, Chapter 43) and/or appropriately provide specific clinical information that may help to determine an individual's health status. Much useful information can be gained by the simple analysis of blood and urine for particular metabolites. Other body fluids, such as saliva and sweat, can be analysed using more advanced techniques to provide information on specific markers of immune system function and electrolyte balance, respectively. Among other body fluids, blood, urine, saliva and sweat all have the potential to transmit pathogens such as hepatitis B and C virus as well as HIV. Therefore, exposure to any of these body fluids must be treated seriously and appropriate safety precautions used to minimise the risk associated with any exposure.

Definitions

Biohazard – any practice or material that poses a biological threat to an individual's safety.

Bloodborne pathogen – harmful microbes that may be present and spread disease through blood.

Body fluid – any type of liquid that is contained within the body.

Disinfection – the practice of killing disease-causing microbes, typically using chemicals. *Note:* many chemicals are effective only against selected microbes.

Spill containment plan – a plan of action used to enclose and neutralise the threat posed by exposure to a large quantity of body fluid.

Standard precautions – the practice of avoiding contact with body fluids by wearing personal protective equipment (PPE) such as gloves, safety glasses and protective clothing.

Sterilisation – the practice of killing all living organisms and viruses, e.g. by using an autoclave.

KEY POINT You may not feel confident or may feel squeamish when dealing with body fluids in practicals. However, the skills for safely sampling a variety of body fluids can easily be learnt. If you find it hard to deal with body fluids, then take your time and do things in small steps until you feel confident with the procedures. Walk away if need be, and remember, strict safety guidelines are put in place to protect both you and the subject.

It is important to recognise that the circumstances of potential exposure to body fluids are specific to sport and exercise science. While in clinical laboratories, exposure to body fluids occurs within a controlled laboratory environment; when in the field, sport and exercise scientists are presented with unique challenges in sampling and working with body fluids (e.g. on a sports field, pool side or on a motor boat). However, this interesting facet of sport and exercise science places more importance on strict safety precautions and the disinfecting procedures described below to reduce the likelihood of pathogen infection. Given the range of diseases that are communicable in this manner, it is important that all sport and exercise scientists have an appreciation of the health risks associated with exposure to any infectious substance. This chapter highlights the potential hazards of dealing with body fluids and explains the correct procedures that should be used to minimise risk.

Precautions

Personal protective equipment

It is a mandatory health and safety requirement to use personal protective equipment (PPE) to minimise the risks associated with hazardous tasks, such as those where there is exposure to body fluids. The primary purpose of PPE is to create a physical barrier between tester and patient, to block

SAFETY NOTE Some people may suffer an allergic reaction to contact with latex. This will quite often present with redness, itchiness and irritation of the skin. If this is apparent, use nitrile gloves instead.

the transmission of any body fluid and possible pathogens. The PPE required will depend on the laboratory, sampling situation and level of exposure. For tasks involving any potential exposure to body fluids, sterile latex or nitrile gloves are a necessity and should be put on before starting. Gloves should be removed and discarded into a biohazard waste container after each patient dealing or sampling. Other PPE that may be required by sport and exercise scientists includes safety glasses and laboratory coats or gowns. These are typically required when dealing with blood in activities involving pipetting or using venepuncture during exercise.

Handwashing

Although sterile latex gloves should be worn at all times when dealing with body fluids, it is still recommended that you wash your hands before and after all tasks involving body fluids. It is important to use an efficient technique to ensure that hands are properly cleaned, since they are the most common means of transfer of pathogens. The following simple sequence is effective:

SAFETY NOTE Some handwashing soaps may cause skin irritation (e.g. redness, itchiness). Ensuring that your hands are rinsed and dried appropriately should minimise the irritation. If irritation occurs, try a topical cream or consult your doctor.

1. **Remove all rings and other jewellery from your hands.** These can prevent effective handwashing.
2. **Wet your hands with warm water.** Where possible, use forearms and elbows to turn taps on and off if long lever taps are provided.
3. **Place a generous amount of disinfectant soap in the palm of your hand.** Rub hands vigorously for at least 20 seconds. To ensure proper coverage, some techniques are shown in Fig. 25.1. Perform each

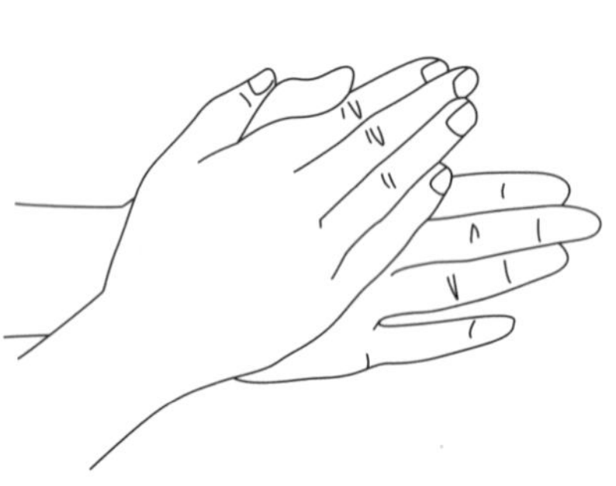

1. Palm to palm

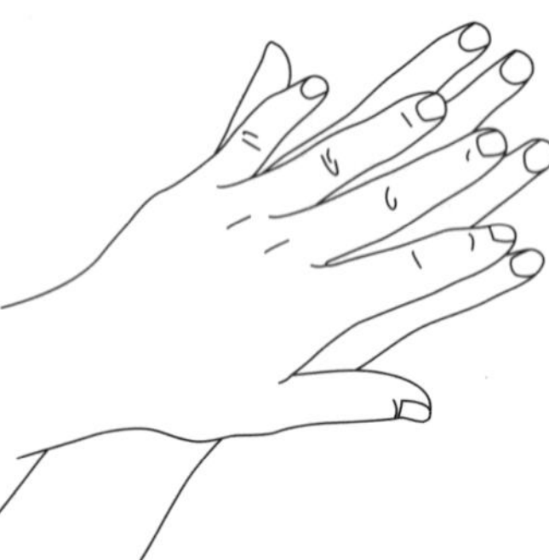

2. Palm over opposing palm

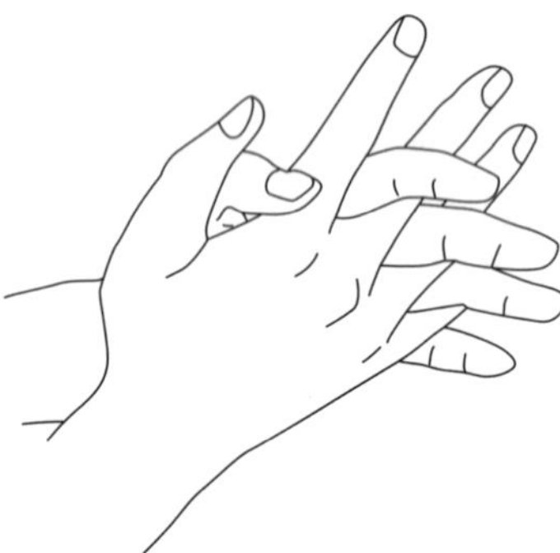

3. Palm to palm with fingers interlocked

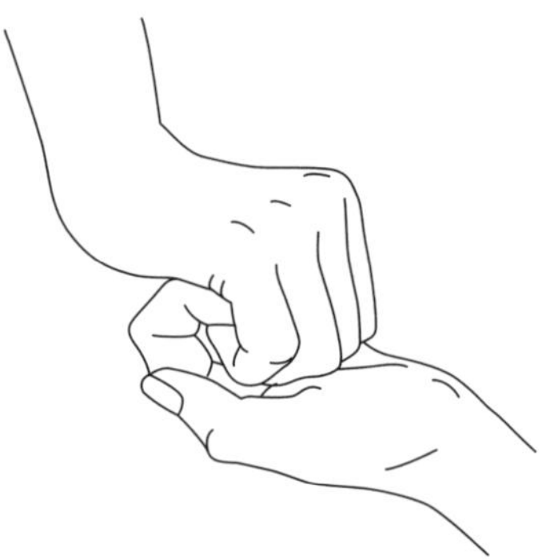

4. Back of fingers into opposing palm with fingers interlocked

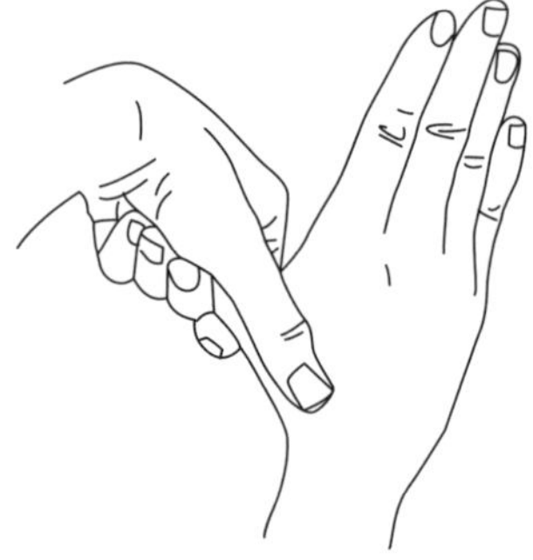

5. Rotate thumb in closed opposing hand

6. Rotate forwards and backwards fingers in palm of opposing hand

Fig. 25.1 Recommended technique for effective handwashing.

movement for a minimum of five strokes on each hand. A soapy lather should appear on your hands – ensure that this lather covers both hands (front and back).

4. **Rinse your hands under warm water,** making sure that all the soap lather is removed.
5. **Dry your hands using a disposable paper towel,** making sure to dry in difficult spots such as in between the fingers. Discard the paper towel into the waste (preferably into a pedal-opening bin).
6. **Put on gloves** once your hands have been washed and dried, and before carrying out the task. Alternatively, you may leave the lab after washing your hands at the end of a procedure.

Fig. 25.2 The universal symbol used to identify a biohazard.

Sampling and handling equipment

It is important to use the correct sampling equipment to minimise the likelihood of infection. For example, all equipment used in the sampling of blood should be sterile and single-use only. Thought should also be put into choosing equipment designed to minimise the likelihood of infection, such as the self-retracting lancets used in capillary puncture. You should not use or come into contact with needles unless you have been appropriately trained and deemed to be competent. Wherever possible, all body fluids should be sampled and handled over a disposable absorbent mat that has a plastic backing; this mat should be discarded after each sampling session as biohazard waste. All other materials (e.g. tissues, alcohol swabs) involved with body fluid sampling should be disposed of as biohazard waste. Any pieces of equipment reused after sampling or exposure to body fluids (e.g. respiratory mouthpieces, large urine containers) must be disinfected or sterilised by an appropriately trained person or waste disposal professional.

Waste disposal

The disposal of contaminated waste products following body fluid sampling or exposure is of great importance to laboratory and personal safety. While each country will have different biohazard disposal guidelines, the general principles are similar. These include:

- All soft materials used when dealing with body fluids (i.e. those that cannot puncture skin) must be immediately placed in a strong plastic and leak-proof biohazard bag after use.
- The waste disposal bag should bear the universal biohazard symbol (Fig. 25.2) to allow fast and simple identification.
- All sharps materials (i.e. those capable of puncturing skin) should be placed in a strong, rigid plastic container that is specifically designed for biohazard material (Fig. 25.3). Most sharps containers are manufactured to allow sharps to be inserted but not removed. These containers should also be marked using the universal biohazard symbol and should not hold more than 20 L. When full, the biohazard storage containers should be sealed (a cable tie is effective for biohazard bags, whereas sharps containers will have their own lid) and given to the appropriate member of staff for disposal. Typically, all biohazard waste is disposed of by specialised personnel.

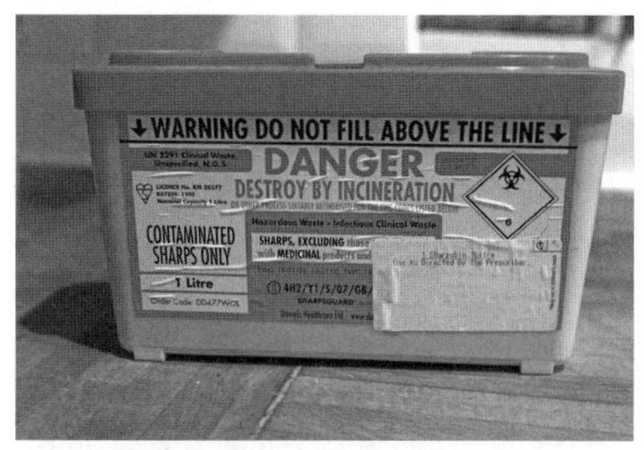

Fig. 25.3 Examples of approved biohazard sharps containers.
Source: Alamy Images: Pete Jenkins.

Disinfecting the work station

While it is recommended that all sampling materials are either single-use and disposed of correctly, or can be autoclaved, the physical environment within a laboratory also needs to be properly cleaned and disinfected. The correct disinfection of equipment helps to lower the risk of accidental cross-infection within a laboratory.

After sampling and waste disposal are complete, the sampling area should be disinfected. This is achieved by using a disinfectant recommended and approved for cleaning body fluids and that will be effective against a wide range of microbes, including viruses. Common recommended disinfectants include dilute sodium hypochlorite ('bleach'), alcohols, iodophors (iodine plus surfactant) and quaternary ammonium compounds (e.g. benzalkonium chloride). They should always be used at the manufacturer's recommended concentration. Disinfectants are often best sprayed onto soiled areas and their surroundings, then wiped up with a disposable absorbent paper towel. This is also essential on ergometers (p. 277) and exercise equipment that is prone to being exposed to sweat or saliva during exercise.

Understanding hepatitis B vaccines – these have been produced by contemporary genetic engineering techniques and include Recombivax-HB® and Enginex-B®.

Vaccination

Exposure to body fluids, in particular blood and saliva, has a risk of transmission of a variety of infectious diseases. During practical work in sport and exercise science, you may be exposed to body fluids that pose a health risk, so it is imperative to take steps to minimise the risk of infection. For several bloodborne pathogens, such as hepatitis C and HIV, no vaccination is currently available, so using standard precautions is the only safeguard. Box 25.1 gives specific safety advice on working with body

Box 25.1 Useful safety precautions when working with body fluids

In procedures where you are handling body fluids, it is always important to carry out sampling in a way that reduces the likelihood of spills, since various communicable diseases, including HIV, hepatitis and influenza, can be transmitted by body fluids. All individuals who routinely deal with body fluids should be vaccinated against hepatitis A and B. To minimise the risk of exposure, apply the following precautions:

- **Treat everyone as potentially infected**, no matter what the circumstances and no matter how many samples you have to take.
- **Always wear disposable sterile gloves before touching a subject or athlete.** These act as a barrier between you and any fluids. Replace gloves (i) if they come into contact with excessive amounts of any body fluid during sampling and (ii) between individuals.
- **Use sterile sampling material for every sample,** even if it is a repeated sample on the same individual. This minimises the risk of cross-contamination and infection of the puncture site.
- **For blood sampling, apply a sterile tissue or gauze to the sampling site until bleeding stops.** Apply tape to hold in place for a prolonged period if necessary.
- **After use, put sampling materials into approved biohazard bags for safe disposal.** Any sharp materials that can puncture the skin (e.g. lancets, capillary tubes) must be placed in designated biohazard sharps containers for correct disposal.
- **Wipe down surfaces** that may have come into contact with body fluids with an approved disinfectant so that the area is clean and safe following sampling.
- **If you are unsure of the nature of any liquids or fluids**, treat them as potentially infectious and decontaminate using a suitable disinfectant.
- **Use appropriate disinfection or sterilisation protocols** to clean any equipment that comes into repeated contact with body fluids (e.g. spirometer mouthpieces).

Steps to safe practice – in any environment where exposure to body fluid is possible it is important to:

1. identify possible biological hazards;
2. ensure that PPE is used by those at risk;
3. provide written details of protection and disinfection protocols;
4. require subjects to follow laboratory safety guidelines at all times.

fluids. However, infection caused by exposure to other bloodborne pathogens (such as hepatitis B) can be prevented by immunisation, although this does not relax the safety guidelines to be followed during practical work. Immunisation for hepatitis B is achieved using a vaccine that typically requires three repeat doses. It is important that you undergo antibody testing after the final vaccination to check your immunity status, as a small percentage of people are unresponsive to the vaccine. At present, there is uncertainty as to the length of immunity that hepatitis B vaccination offers. It is recommended that you undergo immunological testing every three to five years to check your immunity status.

Subject considerations

Ethical aspects

The sampling of body fluids can be associated with pain, anxiety or embarrassment, depending on the procedure to be undertaken. In your training in sport and exercise science, it is always necessary to consider the ethics, safety and value of sampling body fluids. Blood, for example, is not a waste product and therefore taking it from an individual can pose health risks and requires careful attention to process. It is important to consider whether the information gathered from a blood sample is worthwhile, compared to the risks associated with taking it.

Informed consent

Before undertaking any procedures that might involve the sampling and analysis of body fluids, it is important that you receive informed consent from your subject. As discussed elsewhere (Chapter 27), informed consent refers to subjects giving their written (or sometimes verbal) permission to undergo procedures, after they have been informed of the techniques to be used, the possible benefits and the associated risks. While this is not relevant for incidental exposure to some body fluids, it is a necessity prior to blood and urine sampling.

Other aspects

The sampling of body fluids is commonly associated with negative experiences for the subject. To help overcome these, it is important to explain the procedures to be used fully. If dealing with an experienced subject, it may not be necessary to repeat all details, although you should always ensure that they are aware of the overall procedure and its risks. It is also important to be trained and deemed competent, to follow the sampling procedures and to abide by standard precautions to minimise the risk of infection for the subject. Also, you should always monitor the subject during the procedure in case of fainting or other adverse reaction. If required, the sampling procedure may need to be adapted (e.g. a subject may need to sit down during sampling, or a blood sample may need to be taken from the ear so that the subject does not see blood) or completely halted.

Handling body fluids

Transport

Given the nature of the work involved in sport and exercise science, it will be necessary at times to transport body fluid samples. If samples need to be transported over a long distance, by courier or post to a specialist laboratory, it will be important to discuss suitable procedures with the transport organisation to ensure that they are able to transport such biohazardous materials and that all health requirements will be met. More commonly, you may be required to transport samples of body fluid from the field to a laboratory, or between separate laboratories. Transport may increase your risk of exposure to body fluids and may impose additional risks, e.g. in crowded locations. To help minimise these risks, the following are recommended:

Transporting samples by post – body fluids are covered by national and international postal regulations for biological material (e.g. for the UK, see: http://www.postoffice.co.uk/).

- **Appropriate and approved containers should be used for collection and storage.** Ideally, specimen containers should be surrounded by a shock-absorbent material that will help reduce the likelihood of damaging the storage container.
- **All containers used for storage and transport should be labelled appropriately.** The label on the jar should help identify the individual to whom it belongs (either through a name or code), the date and it should also be labelled as biohazard waste (Fig. 25.2).
- **Care should be taken at all times when transporting the containers.** For example, containers should be handled gently and opened carefully.

If a storage or collection container is found to be cracked or broken, it is important that it is cleaned up as detailed in the laboratory's spill containment plan, as described below.

Disposal

It is important to dispose of body fluids correctly to ensure that excess or remaining samples do not pose a risk to other testers or subjects. Disposal methods vary according to the body fluid sampled/present. For example, sweat and saliva are typically not stored and can be dealt with using a disinfectant spray and disposable absorbent paper towels. Blood and urine samples are routinely stored in containers for analysis and pose the biggest risk if they are not disposed of correctly. Excess blood samples can be safely discarded by sealing the sampling containers and placing them in the biohazard waste bag for removal/disposal. Urine samples can be discarded either by pouring the remaining sample into a toilet and flushing into the sewage system or they can be sealed in a collection jar and placed in a biohazard waste bag.

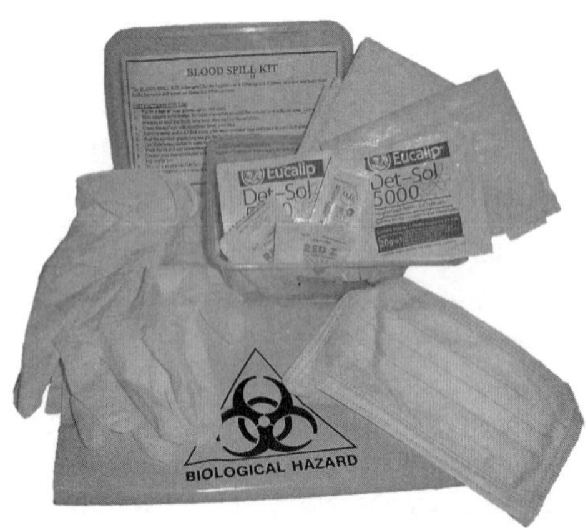

Fig. 25.4 An example of a commercially available body fluid spill kit, showing gloves, apron, disinfectant powder, bags and labels.
Source: First Aid Distributions.

Management of body fluid spills and accidents

It is important that each laboratory has a spill containment plan that can be activated to neutralise the biological risk resulting from accidental spillage of body fluid. A spill containment plan is used to ensure that the area at risk is appropriately disinfected and the incident reported, so that steps can be taken to minimise the likelihood of a repeat spill.

A body fluid spill or accident can result from various activities, such as breakage or leakage of a fluid storage container, excessive bleeding from a skin puncture or an accident that causes a significant laceration. Regardless of the source, the procedure remains consistent. Commercially available body fluid spill kits are available and are extremely useful in cleaning and disinfecting an area after a body fluid spill. Alternatively, you can compile your own spill kit and label appropriately. It can be important to take spill kits into the field or when travelling with samples. If the spill results from injury to a person, the first step is to administer first aid to ensure that the person is treated quickly, with appropriate PPE worn to minimise the risk of infection. Alternatively, if the body fluid spill has occurred from another source, such as a broken storage container, then correctly dispose of it immediately.

After these steps have been completed, it is necessary to clean up the spill. Cleaning any large volume of body fluid should only be carried out while wearing the appropriate PPE. Use disposable absorbent paper towels or disinfectant power (e.g. Cresorb) to soak up as much of the fluid as possible, placing the contaminated waste in a biohazard waste bag. When the majority of the body fluid spill is soaked up, the site should be disinfected, e.g. either by wiping or mopping the site with disposable absorbent towels soaked in an appropriate disinfectant. The contaminated towels are disposed of in a biohazard waste bag. Ensure that you continue to do this until the entire area has been disinfected and then allow it to dry. Once the spill has been disinfected and all contaminated waste has been correctly disposed of, record the incident in a register (each lab should have a log of body fluid spills – check its location with a member of staff).

Understanding how disinfectant powders and granules work – Cresorb combines a hygroscopic polymer that is capable of absorbing many times its own mass of water with a strong disinfectant that will inactivate any pathogens present in the spilled liquid.

KEY POINT Remember to clean and disinfect any laboratory space in which you have been working with body fluids. This helps to minimise the likelihood of cross-infection and makes the workplace safe for anyone working in the laboratory after you have left. Just think, would you want them to do the same before you used the lab?

Another accident often reported when dealing with body fluids is accidental puncture of the skin with a used needle or similar item. This is called a needlestick injury. In the past, this was commonly associated with re-sheathing (putting a used needle back in its original cover) or bending needles after venepuncture sampling. Needlestick injuries pose a significant risk for health professionals and related personnel, particularly those who deal with patients suffering from hepatitis and HIV. In practical work in sport and exercise science, you should be using capillary puncture techniques for all blood sampling (Box 28.1) unless you have received more advanced training. When using capillary puncture techniques, it is always best to use single-use self-retracting lancets (typically spring-loaded) as they significantly reduce the likelihood of needlestick injuries. However, even these lancets pose a risk and therefore it is important that they are safely discarded into a biohazard sharps waste container immediately after puncture. At no point should such lancets be taken apart and the needle/blade exposed. If a needlestick injury occurs, it is important to report it to a member of staff. Encourage bleeding from the puncture site by squeezing while washing under water. Following this, wash and dry the hands as described on p. 166. A needlestick injury will most likely mean testing both parties for hepatitis and HIV, since transmission of both pathogens has been reported for healthcare workers. Full attention should be given to the safe use of sharp instruments for the collection of body fluids and the prescribed procedures should be adhered to at all times, so that risks are minimised.

Fig. 25.5 An example of a safe spring-loaded and self-retracting lancet.
Source: MidMeds Ltd.

Sources for further study

Estridge, B.H. and Reynolds, A.P. (2008) Laboratory safety: biological hazards. In: B.H. Estridge and A.P. Reynolds (eds) *Basic Clinical Laboratory Techniques*. Thomson Delmar Learning, Clifton Park, pp. 61–72.

Maw, G., Locke, S., Cowley, D. and Witt, P. (2000) Blood sampling and handling techniques. In: C.J. Gore (ed.) *Physiological Tests for Elite Athletes*. Human Kinetics, Champaign, IL, pp. 86–97.

Queens University Belfast Nursing and Midwifery Education Centre (2009) *Nursing Education Video – Handwashing*. Available: http://www.qub.ac.uk/schools/SchoolofNursingandMidwifery/clinical/videoshandwashing.htm
Last accessed: 23/12/10.
[An excellent collection of files that show clinical techniques for nurses but can also be used by exercise scientists.]

Wilborn, S.Q. (2004) Needlestick and sharps injury prevention. *Online Journal of Issues in Nursing,* **9**(3). Available:http://www.nursingworld.org/MainMenuCategories/ANAMarketplace/ANAPeriodicals/OJIN/TableofContents/Volume92004/No3Sept04/InjuryPrevention.aspx
Last accessed: 23/12/10.

Pre-exercise screening

26. Preparing for fitness tests 175

27. Pre-exercise health screening procedures 179

26 Preparing for fitness tests

Fitness tests require preparation by both the participant and the tester or test team. Apart from the pre-exercise screening procedures examined in the next chapter, a crucial part of the preparation for fitness testing in either the laboratory or in the field is the planning of the testing session.

Pre-test logistics

In writing and/or verbally, the participant(s) need(s) to know:

- **The purpose and nature of the test(s).** These should be explained in writing or face-to-face.
- **The date, time and exact venue.** Provide a map in hard copy or via a website link.
- **The duration of the test session.** This allows everyone to plan their day.
- **The necessary items to bring to the test session.** For example, should participants bring toiletries for a shower or food and drink to enhance recovery? What clothes and footwear do they need to bring?

Understanding the value of preparation – by providing your subjects with basic information several days before the test session, you are likely to have better compliance and more reliable results.

Pre-test instructions for the subject

Explicit instructions provided to subjects undertaking exercise testing increase test validity and the accuracy of the data. While aspects that should be considered when planning tests for athletes are listed in the margin note, the following points should be included in the pre-test instructions for non-athletes:

- **Participants should refrain from using tobacco products or ingesting food, alcohol or caffeine** (tea, coffee, chocolate, energy drinks) for three hours before testing.
- **Participants should rest on the day of the assessment,** avoiding significant exertion or exercise beforehand.
- **Participants should bring along an accompanying person if the test(s) is/are fatiguing,** to be with them on the journey to and from the assessment.
- **If the test is for diagnostic purposes (e.g. exercise stress test), it may be helpful to discontinue prescribed cardiovascular medication, but only with a doctor's approval.** Currently prescribed anti-anginal agents alter the heart rate response to exercise and significantly alter the sensitivity of electrocardiograph changes for ischaemia. Subjects taking intermediate-level or high-dose β-blocking agents should be asked to taper their medications over a two- to four-day period prior to testing.
- **If the test is for exercise prescription purposes, subjects should continue their normal medication routine** so that their exercise responses will be consistent with those expected during exercise and training.
- **Participants should bring their list of medications, including dosage and frequency of administration, and report the last dose taken.**

Standardising athlete preparation – for athletes, many physiological capacities can be influenced by variables such as diet, fatigue, medication, illness and environmental conditions. Ideally, all of these conditions should be standardised for each testing session. Thus, for athlete testing, the following guidelines might be recommended:

1. No maximal exercise should be carried out 48–72 h before testing.
2. No unaccustomed exercise should be carried out 48–72 h before testing.
3. A consistent diet should be maintained in the period leading into testing.
4. All medication, including that used to manage pain or illness, should be recorded.

Alternatively, subjects can bring their medications with them for the testing staff to record.

- **Subjects should drink ample fluids over the 24-hour period preceding the test** to ensure normal hydration before testing.

What the subject should wear

Clothing for athletes – those undertaking sport-specific tests should wear clothing and footwear appropriate to the tests being undertaken; for example, cyclists should wear cycling shoes and cycling shorts ('knicks').

- **Clothing should allow freedom of movement,** ease of access to body areas, e.g. for skinfold measures, and should include walking or running shoes.
- **Men should wear loose-fitting shorts, light trousers or tracksuit bottoms and a T-shirt or sports shirt.**
- **Women should wear loose-fitting shorts or tracksuit bottoms and a shirt or T-shirt or a loose fitting, short-sleeved blouse that buttons down the front.** They should avoid restrictive underclothes such as leotards or tights because they make skinfold measurement awkward and aerobic capacity tests uncomfortable. Sports bras are recommended.

Tester preparation

Examples of equipment to be calibrated prior to testing:

- skinfold calipers;
- metronome;
- cycle ergometer;
- treadmill;
- gas analysis machine.

The American College of Sports Medicine (2010) recommends that the following should be completed before the subject arrives at the test site:

- **Ensure that all forms, score sheets, tables, graphs and other testing documents are organised** and available for the test session.
- **Calibrate all equipment to ensure accuracy of measurement.**
- **Organise equipment so that tests can follow in sequence** without stressing the same muscle group repeatedly.
- **Provide informed consent form** (Chapter 27).
- **Maintain room temperature at 20°–22°C** and humidity at <60%.

Test planning

A well planned testing schedule should be prepared in advance, especially for athletes. The testing schedule should be outlined in the athlete's annual training plan and reflect the specific objectives for each phase of training. For both professional and recreational athletes, the minimum period for scheduled testing to monitor progress is six weeks. Significant improvements should be greater than the technical error of measurement (Chapter 19).

A number of factors should be taken into account when planning a testing session:

- **Specificity** – the actual tests undertaken can be general or specific in their nature. General tests are widely used in the health and fitness industry to test non-athletes. Such tests include cycle ergometer tests of aerobic capacity (Chapter 37) and the sit and reach test for flexibility (Chapter 33). Specific tests should be used for athletes. That is, rowers should be tested on a rowing ergometer and cyclists on a cycle ergometer so that power output can be measured. For strength and power tests, different results may occur between single-joint and multi-joint testing. Similarly, strength data from one type of muscle contraction may correlate poorly with data from another type of testing. Thus, testing should be as specific as possible to the type of muscle contraction and joint actions as possible.

- **Time of day** – endurance, speed, strength and power have been shown to peak in the early evening, suggesting that testing of these capacities should occur at this time. However, the realities are that both athletes and non-athletes should be tested at the same time of the day in repeat tests to avoid fluctuations in performance owing to individual circadian rhythms. Testing for athletes would normally be carried out at the same time as regular training.
- **Order of testing** – when testing non-athletes using a number of test procedures in the same session, the order of testing becomes important. This order will depend greatly on which aspects of fitness are to be tested. In general, tests should be carried out in the following order:

  1. resting measurements such as heart rate, blood pressure, height, weight and skinfold measures or measures of body composition;
  2. cardiovascular fitness test;
  3. muscular fitness tests of strength and/or power;
  4. flexibility.

  Testing cardiovascular fitness after tests of muscular fitness can produce inaccurate results as a result of the heart rate being elevated from the tests of strength and/or power. Similarly, dehydration from a test of endurance may influence skinfold measurement or the results of bioelectrical impedance analysis measures of body composition.

  For athlete testing, you should aim to carry out strength and power testing at different times from endurance and field testing, because of the effects of such tests on muscle nervous system activity. The timespan between these two groups of tests needs to be greater than one hour to avoid this problem. Moreover, tests of muscle strength and power in athletes should be completed in an order whereby fast and explosive power tests are completed before slower strength tests (Fig. 26.1). Furthermore, multi-joint tests (e.g. vertical jump) should be completed prior to single segment exercises (e.g. biceps curl).

Power tests
Vertical jump
Squat jump
Counter-movement jump
Drop jump

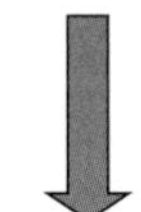

Strength tests
Leg press
Squat
Bench press

Strength endurance tests
Sit-ups in 30 seconds
Push-ups in 60 seconds

Fig. 26.1 A suggested order for strength, power and muscle endurance testing.

- **Warm-up** – when preparing for a test session, you need to have thought through what warm-up should be done by the participant. The warm-up should first be broad/general (e.g. five minutes on an ergometer specific to the test about to be conducted or a cycle ergometer if general fitness tests are being conducted) to raise muscle temperature, followed by specific static and dynamic stretches and finally specific movements that mimic the actual test motions. An example of a warm-up for a maximal strength test is shown in Table 26.1.

Table 26.1 An example of a warm-up for a maximal strength test

Action (duration)
Ergometer (≥5 min)
≤40–60% of 1 RM (≤10 reps)
Recovery (≥2 min)
≤60–80% of 1 RM (≤5 reps)
Recovery (≥2 min)
≤90% of 1 RM (≤3 reps)
Recovery (≥5 min)

RM, repetition maximum.

- **Familiarisation** – many people undertaking physical testing may have little or no experience with the test procedures being used. While most commonly-used tests in sport and exercise science are reliable, novice participants are likely to improve their performance scores on subsequent testing as a result of the increased familiarity and comfort with the test procedures. This is particularly true of tests involving some motor skill such as isotonic testing using free weights (Chapter 40). Thus, novice subjects should be given a familiarisation session. This should take place two to three days before actual testing to allow any residual muscle soreness to disappear.

KEY POINT Suitable safety measures should be in place before starting any test procedure. These include, but are not limited to: inspecting all equipment for broken or frayed components; checking appropriate lighting and temperature of the test environment; and removal of all hazards within and around the testing site.

Emergency procedures should be formalised and all testing personnel should be familiar with these procedures and should be certified in basic life support. Most importantly, all testing should be conducted under the supervision of an accredited sport and exercise scientist.

Text reference

American College of Sports Medicine (2010) *ACSM's Guidelines for Exercise Testing and Prescription,* 8th edn, Lippincott Williams and Wilkins, Baltimore, Maryland.

Sources for further study

Gore, C. (2000) *Physiological Tests for Elite Athletes.* Human Kinetics, Champaign, IL.

Winter, E.M., Jones, A.M., Davison, R.C., Bromley, P.D. and Mercer, T.H. (2007) *Sport and Exercise Physiology Testing Guidelines: The British Association of Sport and Exercise Sciences Guide. Vol. 1: Sport Testing*. Routledge, London.

27 Pre-exercise health screening procedures

> **SAFETY NOTE** All facilities offering exercise equipment or testing services should conduct cardiovascular screening of all new members and/or prospective users.

Health screening is a vital process in identifying individuals at risk of exercise-induced heart problems. They can then be referred to medical professionals for further screening through a graded exercise test with possible electrocardiogram procedures.

Health, fitness and exercise testing centres throughout the world should conduct health screening on all new members and/or prospective users of their equipment, regardless of age. Pre-test screening procedures need to be simple, easy to perform and not so intensive that they discourage participation. The screening questionnaires should also be conducted and interpreted by qualified staff to limit the number of medical referrals and avoid barriers to participation in an exercise programme.

> **SAFETY NOTE** To help protect both the participants and exercise professionals:
>
> 1. Always obtain a medical history and pre-exercise health risk appraisal for each participant.
> 2. Categorise (stratify) each participant according to their disease risk.
> 3. Refer high-risk individuals to a medical professional for medical screening and a graded exercise test.

Sport and exercise science students must develop the skills required to screen both sedentary and active individuals of any age and gender before they start an exercise programme. This chapter will highlight the major screening methods and tools used by peak industry bodies such as the American College of Sports Medicine, British Association of Sport and Exercise Sciences and Australian Association for Exercise and Sport Sciences (now Exercise and Sports Science Australia).

Initial screening for low to moderate intensity programmes

There are a number of questionnaires available for pre-exercise screening. These questionnaires are widely used by sport and exercise science students during coursework and as part of student projects. When testing large numbers in a short period of time or during a practicum in a health and fitness centre, a short and simple yet safe and valid medical/health questionnaire called the *Physical Activity Readiness Questionnaire* (PAR-Q) has been developed and is widely used across the world (Fig. 27.1).

The PAR-Q is widely recognised as a safe pre-exercise screening tool for 15–69-year-olds who plan to engage in low-to-moderate (but not vigorous) exercise training (Table 27.1). If a person answers 'yes' to one or more of the questions in the PAR-Q or is over the age of 69 years, they should be directed to their family doctor for medical clearance before starting an exercise programme. The PAR-Q is handed to the participant/client, who completes the test by himself or herself and hands it back to the lecturer or exercise professional for interpretation.

Comprehensive medical/health screening

If sport or exercise scientists are in any doubt about an individual's involvement in an exercise programme or exercise testing, or the individual wants to embark on a vigorous exercise programme, they should undertake a comprehensive screening procedure.

A comprehensive health screening should include the following:

1. medical diagnoses by a trained professional (doctor or exercise physiologist);
2. previous physical examination findings;

Physical Activity Readiness
Questionnaire - PAR-Q
(revised 2002)

PAR-Q & YOU

(A Questionnaire for People Aged 15 to 69)

Regular physical activity is fun and healthy, and increasingly more people are starting to become more active every day. Being more active is very safe for most people. However, some people should check with their doctor before they start becoming much more physically active.

If you are planning to become much more physically active than you are now, start by answering the seven questions in the box below. If you are between the ages of 15 and 69, the PAR-Q will tell you if you should check with your doctor before you start. If you are over 69 years of age, and you are not used to being very active, check with your doctor.

Common sense is your best guide when you answer these questions. Please read the questions carefully and answer each one honestly: check YES or NO.

YES	NO	
☐	☐	**1. Has your doctor ever said that you have a heart condition and that you should only do physical activity recommended by a doctor?**
☐	☐	**2. Do you feel pain in your chest when you do physical activity?**
☐	☐	**3. In the past month, have you had chest pain when you were not doing physical activity?**
☐	☐	**4. Do you lose your balance because of dizziness or do you ever lose consciousness?**
☐	☐	**5. Do you have a bone or joint problem (for example, back, knee or hip) that could be made worse by a change in your physical activity?**
☐	☐	**6. Is your doctor currently prescribing drugs (for example, water pills) for your blood pressure or heart condition?**
☐	☐	**7. Do you know of any other reason why you should not do physical activity?**

If you answered

YES to one or more questions

Talk with your doctor by phone or in person BEFORE you start becoming much more physically active or BEFORE you have a fitness appraisal. Tell your doctor about the PAR-Q and which questions you answered YES.

- You may be able to do any activity you want — as long as you start slowly and build up gradually. Or, you may need to restrict your activities to those which are safe for you. Talk with your doctor about the kinds of activities you wish to participate in and follow his/her advice.
- Find out which community programs are safe and helpful for you.

NO to all questions

If you answered NO honestly to all PAR-Q questions, you can be reasonably sure that you can:

- start becoming much more physically active – begin slowly and build up gradually. This is the safest and easiest way to go.
- take part in a fitness appraisal – this is an excellent way to determine your basic fitness so that you can plan the best way for you to live actively. It is also highly recommended that you have your blood pressure evaluated. If your reading is over 144/94, talk with your doctor before you start becoming much more physically active.

DELAY BECOMING MUCH MORE ACTIVE:

- if you are not feeling well because of a temporary illness such as a cold or a fever – wait until you feel better; or
- if you are or may be pregnant – talk to your doctor before you start becoming more active.

PLEASE NOTE: If your health changes so that you then answer YES to any of the above questions, tell your fitness or health professional. Ask whether you should change your physical activity plan.

Informed Use of the PAR-Q: The Canadian Society for Exercise Physiology, Health Canada, and their agents assume no liability for persons who undertake physical activity, and if in doubt after completing this questionnaire, consult your doctor prior to physical activity.

No changes permitted. You are encouraged to photocopy the PAR-Q but only if you use the entire form.

NOTE: If the PAR-Q is being given to a person before he or she participates in a physical activity program or a fitness appraisal, this section may be used for legal or administrative purposes.

"I have read, understood and completed this questionnaire. Any questions I had were answered to my full satisfaction."

NAME ______________________

SIGNATURE ______________________ DATE ______________________

SIGNATURE OF PARENT ______________________ WITNESS ______________________
or GUARDIAN (for participants under the age of majority)

Note: This physical activity clearance is valid for a maximum of 12 months from the date it is completed and becomes invalid if your condition changes so that you would answer YES to any of the seven questions.

 Supported by: Health Canada Santé Canada

Fig. 27.1 The physical activity readiness questionnaire (PAR-Q) offers an easy and brief evaluation of an individual's readiness to start an exercise programme.

Source: Physical Activity Readiness Questionnaire (PAR-Q) © 2002, used with permission from Canadian Society for Exercise Physiology.

Table 27.1 Classification of exercise intensities for general population (ACSM, 2010)

Intensity	% VO_2 Reserve or % heart rate reserve	% Maximal heart rate	RPE (6–20 scale)
Low	<40	<63	≤ 11
Moderate	40–59	64–76	12–13
Vigorous	>60	>77	>14

VO_2 Reserve, difference between VO_2max and resting VO_2; heart rate reserve, difference between maximum heart rate and resting heart rate; RPE, rating of perceived exertion (Chapter 31).

3. history of symptoms;
4. recent illness, hospitalisation, new medical diagnoses or surgical procedures;
5. orthopaedic problems;
6. medication use and drug allergies;
7. lifestyle habits (e.g. stress, smoking, drinking, diet);
8. exercise history;
9. work history;
10. family history of disease.

Most comprehensive health and medical screening procedures are based on the American College of Sports Medicine (ACSM) guidelines for pre-exercise screening and testing. These guidelines are recognised worldwide as they are based on many decades of scientific, clinical and epidemiological research. Moreover, the similarities between European, North American and Australasian populations in the areas of physical activity patterns, morbidity and mortality statistics in lifestyle diseases such as cardiovascular disease, diabetes and cancer justify their adaptation for use across these countries.

The health screening procedures outlined below are those adopted by Sports Medicine Australia (SMA) and the Australian Association for Exercise and Sports Science (AAESS). They are based on the ACSM guidelines discussed above and involve two stages – the first to stratify individuals to screen out those who are at *high risk* and the second stage to determine those people who are moderate to low risk.

Purposes of risk stratification according to disease risk

1. To identify individuals in need of a referral to a medical professional for more extensive medical evaluation.
2. To ensure the safety of exercise testing.
3. To ensure the safety of the client's exercise programme.
4. To determine the appropriate exercise intensity for the client.

Stage one

The first stage of the SMA/AAESS screening system is aimed at filtering out those individuals who are at high-risk of exercise-related complications as a result of underlying cardiovascular, cerebrovascular, respiratory or metabolic diseases. These are people with known signs and/or symptoms of disease (Box 27.1).

It is recommended that this relatively small group of high-risk clients seeks medical clearance before beginning an exercise programme of any intensity or undertaking an aerobic fitness test. Box 27.2 contains the stage 1 questionnaire.

Individuals who are not at high risk can begin low or moderate physical activity without the need for formal medical clearance. If these individuals want to exercise at vigorous intensity levels or be tested to maximal levels, they need to proceed to stage 2 of the screening system.

ACSM risk groups (ACSM, 2010)

1. **Low risk** – males <45 years and females <55 years who are asymptomatic and have no more than one risk factor (Box 27.2).
2. **Moderate risk** – males $\geq$ 45 years and females $\geq$ 55 years or those that have two or more risk factors.
3. **High risk** – individuals with one or more signs and symptoms or with known cardiovascular, pulmonary or metabolic diseases, including diabetes mellitus.

Box 27.1 Signs and symptoms questionnaire used to categorise high-risk clients

Pre-exercise screening system 2005
Sports Medicine Australia (SMA) - Stage 1 questionnaire

Name.. Age..................... Gender M F
Address.. Phone................. Date............

1.	Have you ever had a heart attack, coronary revascularisation surgery or a stroke?	No	Yes
2.	Has your doctor ever told you that you have heart trouble or vascular disease?	No	Yes
3.	Has your doctor ever told you that you have a heart murmur?	No	Yes
4.	Do you ever suffer from pains in your chest, especially with exercise?	No	Yes
5.	Do you ever get pains in your calves, buttocks or at the back of your legs during exercise which are not due to soreness or stiffness?	No	Yes
6.	Do you ever feel faint or have spells of severe dizziness, particularly with exercise?	No	Yes
7.	Do you experience swelling or accumulation of fluid about the ankles?	No	Yes
8.	Do you ever get the feeling that your heart is suddenly beating faster, racing or skipping beats, either at rest or during exercise?	No	Yes
9.	Do you have chronic obstructive pulmonary disease, interstitial lung disease or cystic fibrosis?	No	Yes
10.	Have you ever had an attack of shortness of breath that developed when you were not doing anything strenuous, at any time in the last 12 months?	No	Yes
11.	Have you ever had an attack of shortness of breath that developed after you stopped exercising, at any time in the last 12 months?	No	Yes
12.	Have you ever been woken at night by an attack of shortness of breath, at any time in the last 12 months?	No	Yes
13.	Do you have diabetes [IDDM or NIDDM]? If so, do you have trouble controlling your diabetes?	No	Yes
14.	Do you have any ulcerated wounds or cuts on your feet that do not seem to heal?	No	Yes
15.	Do you have any liver, kidney or thyroid disorders?	No	Yes
16.	Do you experience unusual fatigue or shortness of breath with usual activities?	No	Yes
17.	Is there any other physical reason or medical condition, or are you taking any medication(s), which could prevent you from undertaking an exercise programme, or that you are concerned about?*	No	Yes

NOTES:
*Some of these conditions might include a history of blood clotting, osteoporosis bone fractures or serious musculoskeletal disorders, or if they have recently lost a large amount of body mass without trying to. Other types of conditions might include psychiatric disorders, later-stage pregnancy or those with a history of health problems during pregnancy. Those people taking medication(s) for medical conditions listed may also need medical clearance.

Also, if any one or more of the risk factors [in Box 27.2] are extreme, then the health and fitness professional should use professional judgement as to whether medical clearance may be required.

Source: reprinted with permission from Sports Medicine Australia.

Box 27.2 Risk factors used to stratify clients into low-, moderate- and high-risk categories before starting an exercise programme or aerobic fitness testing

- **Age.** Males ≥45 years and females ≥55 years.
- **Smoking.** Cigarettes, pipes, roll-your-own or cannabis regularly, or quit smoking in the last six months.
- **Family history.** Does the client have a first relative (father, mother, son, daughter, sister, brother) who has had a myocardial infarction, coronary revascularisation or died suddenly from a heart attack before age 55 years (male) or 65 years (female)?
- **Hypertension.** Systolic blood pressure of ≥140 mm Hg **or** diastolic blood pressure ≥90 mm Hg on two separate occasions **or** on antihypertensive drugs (see Box 27.1).
- **Impaired blood glucose.** Fasting blood glucose ≥6.1 $mmol.L^{-1}$ (100 $mg\,dL^{-1}$) on two separate occasions.
- **Dyslipidaemia.** Total serum cholesterol of >5.2 $mmol\,L^{-1}$ (200 $mg\,dL^{-1}$) or high density lipoprotein cholesterol of <0.9 $mmol.L^{-1}$ (40 $mg\,dL^{-1}$) **or** on lipid-lowering medication.
- **Obesity.** BMI ≥30 $kg\,m^{-2}$ **or** waist girth >100 cm.
- **Sedentary lifestyle.** An occupation where the client sits for long periods **or** does no regular exercise **or** does not do more than 150 minutes of moderate physical activity per week.

Source: Based on data from Department of Health and Ageing, 2005.

Stage two

The second stage of the SMA/AAESS screening system is aimed at determining those individuals categorised as moderate or low risk for exercise-related complications as a result of underlying cardiovascular, cerebrovascular, respiratory, metabolic diseases or other medical conditions.

It is recommended that those classified as at moderate risk can undertake exercise up to moderate intensity levels without medical clearance from their family doctor. They can also undertake low-to-moderate intensity submaximal aerobic fitness testing. However, those classified as at moderate risk do need a medical clearance before beginning a vigorous exercise programme or undertaking aerobic fitness testing to vigorous intensity levels.

Those who are younger (males <45 years, females <55 years) and have less than two risk factors are considered low risk and can undertake both exercise at vigorous levels and maximal exercise testing without the need for medical clearance. Fig. 27.2 summarises the exercise recommendations, exercise testing and exercise testing supervision recommendations based on the risk stratifications determined above.

Cardiovascular screening of athletes

The death of athletes from heart abnormalities rarely occurs but when it does it receives a lot of media attention. Sport and exercise science students may be exposed to cardiovascular screening in the latter stages of their studies or if undertaking practical work at sports academies or institutes. These screenings combine non-invasive testing such as 12-lead ECG with standard history-taking and physical examinations. The premise of this screening strategy is that the ECG (Chapter 29) is a powerful tool in detecting or raising suspicion of many cardiovascular diseases that cause sudden death in young athletes.

The American Heart Association (AHA) (Maron *et al.*, 2007) developed recommendations (Table 27.2) for the pre-participation

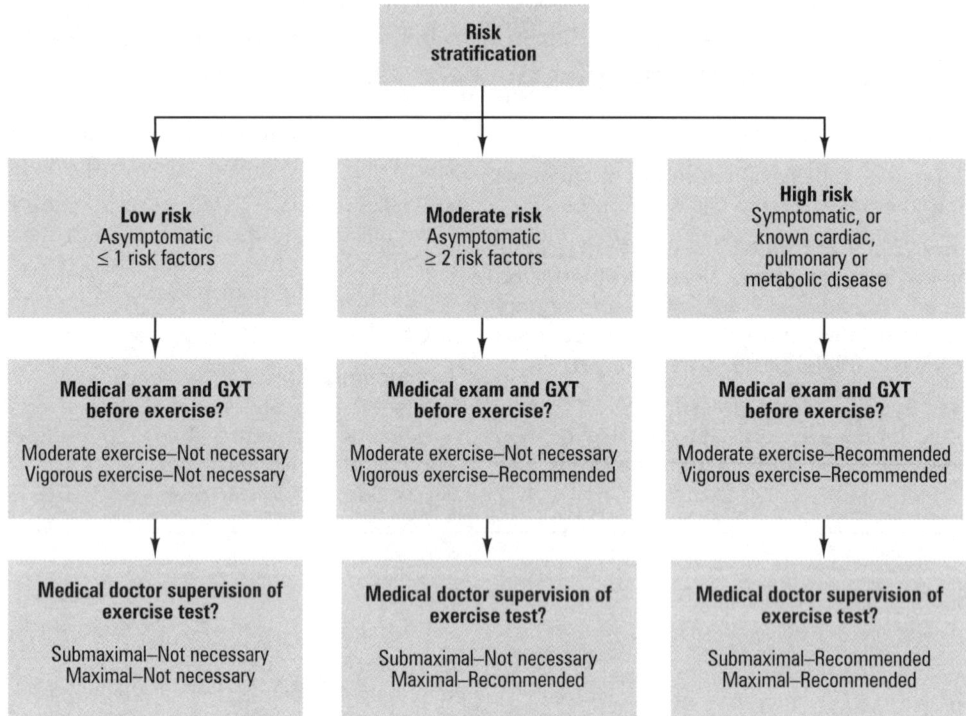

Fig. 27.2 Exercise prescription, aerobic fitness testing and test supervision recommendations based on risk stratifications.

screening of young athletes. The recommendations were developed in response to a number of deaths in young competitive athletes and the growing public policy interest in health and exercise-related initiatives.

As an exercise and/or sport science student, if you have any concerns that an athlete you are working with displays any of the elements in Table 27.2, refer the athlete to your supervisor who should refer the athlete to a medical practitioner or sports physician.

The AHA has also developed recommendations for pre-participation screening and assessment of cardiovascular disease in masters athletes over 40 years of age entering, resuming or continuing in organised sports competition (Maron *et al.*, 2001). If you are working with an older athlete in a project or practicum placement or are involved with coaching or training in the field, you should be aware of these recommendations.

Codes of Conduct – many organisations have developed codes of conduct to guide members in ethical practices. For example, the Australian Association for Exercise and Sports Science (now Exercise and Sports Science Australia) has its own code of ethical conduct and professional practice. http://www.aaess.com.au/aaess/files/image/AAESS%20Code%20of%20Professional%20Conduct%20and% 20Ethical%20Practice(1).pdf

Informed consent

As part of sport and exercise science coursework, students are often encouraged to undertake research projects that may involve health screening, exercise programming or an exercise intervention or test. A crucial component of sport and exercise science research at any level is the need to obtain a person's written voluntary informed consent before any exercise testing or exercise intervention.

'Informed' means that the potential participant (or their legal guardian in the case of children under 18 years of age) knows and understands all the information about the project and the implications

Table 27.2 The 12-element AHA 2007 recommendations for pre-participation cardiovascular screening of competitive athletes (Maron *et al.,* 2007).

Medical history*

Personal history

1. Exertional chest pain/discomfort
2. Unexplained syncope (fainting)/near syncope†
3. Excessive exertional and unexplained dyspnoea (shortness of breath)/fatigue, associated with exercise
4. Prior recognition of a heart murmur
5. Elevated systemic blood pressure

Family history

6. Premature death (sudden and unexpected, or otherwise) before age 50 years owing to heart disease, in one or more relative(s)
7. Disability from heart disease in a close relative <50 years of age
8. Specific knowledge of certain cardiac conditions in family members: hypertrophic or dilated cardiomyopathy, long-QT syndrome or other ion channelopathies, Marfan syndrome or clinically important arrhythmias

Physical examination

9. Heart murmur‡
10. Femoral pulses to exclude aortic coarctation
11. Physical stigmata of Marfan syndrome
12. Brachial artery blood pressure (sitting position)§

*Parental verification is recommended for high school and middle school athletes.
†Judged not to be neurocardiogenic (vasovagal); of particular concern when related to exertion.
‡Auscultation should be performed in both supine and standing positions (or with Valsalva manoeuvre), specifically to identify murmurs of dynamic left ventricular outflow tract obstruction.
§Preferably taken in both arms.

of what their involvement means. 'Consent' implies free, voluntary agreement to participation, without coercion or unfair inducement. Subjects must be fully informed of the risks, procedures and potential benefits, and that they are free to end their participation in the study at any time with no penalty whatsoever.

An informed consent form, normally signed by the participant (and/or guardian if under 18 years of age), should be tailored to the specific project but should include the following features:

1. **an explanation of the purpose** of the project;
2. **a description of the procedures** that will involve the participants, including their required time commitment;
3. **identification and description of any risks and discomforts** and arrangements for treatment in the case of injury;
4. **identification and description of potential benefits** of involvement in the project;
5. **statements** regarding confidentiality, anonymity and privacy;
6. **identification of an appropriate individual involved in the project** and their contact details (phone numbers, email) so that participants can approach them regarding any questions relating to the project;
7. **a statement that participation is voluntary,** that consent has been freely obtained and that participants are free to withdraw at any time for any reason without fear of sanction.

Text references

American College of Sports Medicine (2010) *ACSM's Guidelines for Exercise Testing and Prescription*, 8th edn, Lippincott Williams and Wilkins, Baltimore, Maryland.

Department of Health and Ageing (2005) *Sports Medicine Australia (SMA) Pre-exercise Screening System 2005*. Available: http://sma.org.au/wp-content/uploads/2009/05/new_pre_screening.pdf Last accessed: 23/12/10.

Maron, B.J., Aroujo, C.G., Thompson, P.D. *et al.* (2001) Recommendations for preparticipation screening and the assessment of cardiovascular disease in masters athletes. *Circulation*, **103**, 327–34. Available: http://www.americanheart.org/presenter.jhtml?identifier=3004574 Last accessed: 23/12/10.

Maron, B.J., Thompson, P.D., Ackerman, M.J. *et al.* (2007) American Heart Association Council on Nutrition, Physical Activity, and Metabolism. Recommendations and considerations related to preparticipation screening for cardiovascular abnormalities in competitive athletes: 2007 update. *Circulation*, **115**(12), 1643-55. Available: http://www.americanheart.org/presenter.jhtml?identifier=3004574 Last accessed: 23/12/10.

Basic laboratory procedures

28. Blood and urine collection and analysis 189

29. Measuring cardiac function 197

30. Testing pulmonary function 211

31. Measuring endurance exercise intensity 221

32. Measuring hydration status and body temperature 228

33. Measuring flexibility 236

34. Kinanthropometry 242

35. Measuring body composition 253

28 Blood and urine collection and analysis

Safe working with body fluids – Chapter 25 gives specific advice on how to handle and dispose of blood and other body fluids to minimise risks to yourself and to the test subject.

Definitions

Capillary – the small vessels that link arteries and veins and allow gas exchange.

Capillary action – fluid moves owing to an attraction to a material.

Capillary tube – a small plastic or glass tube used to collect fluid.

Haematocrit – the ratio of blood cells to plasma.

Helix – the large outside rim of the ear.

Lancet – a sterile sharp disposable instrument used to puncture skin.

Lobule – the flexible lobe at the bottom of the ear.

The practice of sport and exercise science involves the routine sampling and analysis of body fluids. Of particular significance is the collection and analysis of blood and urine, given their role in transport of metabolites and waste products that are specific to exercise and health. Their collection and analysis provide a wealth of physiological data that gives insight to a range of health professionals.

A variety of techniques can be used to collect blood and urine samples, although in sport and exercise science it is best to practise the safe and simple methods that are easily performed by individuals with limited training. It is important that appropriate procedures are used to collect and preserve the sample for subsequent analysis. Typically, the routine collection of blood and urine in sport and exercise science only requires small samples (5–100 μL) that are easily analysed using hand-held analysers. This provides versatility in terms of where and how blood is collected and analysed, e.g. capillary blood collection may vary from taking place in a clinical lab to on-water sampling on a rowing boat.

KEY POINT The collection of blood and urine for analysis is an important part of studying sport and exercise science. It is essential that you are competent in the following skills and are confident using them in a variety of situations.

This chapter outlines simple procedures for the collection of blood and urine. These procedures are relatively safe for both subject and tester if the process is followed correctly, minimising the likelihood of injury or infection. Always read and follow manufacturer's instructions for hand-held analysers to ensure accuracy of results.

Blood

This is an important transport medium in the body and can be analysed for several metabolic components that provide data on aspects of health and exercise. In exercise science, blood provides a great deal of specific information on an individual, and sampling methods have evolved to allow small volume samples to be taken in convenient locations as non-invasively as possible. The simplest sampling method is through capillary puncture (also called dermal puncture). Capillary puncture refers to making a small needle puncture in the skin of a finger or earlobe and sampling the blood flowing from the underlying capillaries. For larger blood samples, venepuncture should be carried out by specially trained staff (phlebotomists). Capillary puncture is a minimally invasive and relatively safe way to obtain small amounts of blood, especially since the development of analysers that accept capillary blood samples. Capillary puncture is simple to perform with minimal training. The main drawback of capillary puncture from the fingertip is that this is a sensitive location owing to the large number of nerve endings.

Blood sampling – earlobe sampling is particularly useful in activities where the hands may become cold or undergo long isometric contractions (e.g. rowing). Either condition may slow flow of blood to the fingertips and may provide invalid data.

> **SAFETY NOTE** Some subjects may suffer adverse reactions to either the initial puncture or the sight of blood. This may range from vomiting to dizziness and/or loss of consciousness. It is important that you always ask the subject how they are feeling and that you are aware of how to respond to an adverse reaction. Have the subject seated if possible, or have a chair ready as sitting or lying down for a few minutes is normally an effective remedy.

Using an appropriate analyser, a capillary blood sample of between 5 and 100 μL can provide accurate measurement of the following variables:

- glucose;
- cholesterol (total as well as high and low density lipoproteins);
- triglycerides;
- lactate;
- pH;
- bicarbonate;
- gases (PO_2, PCO_2);
- sodium;
- creatine kinase;
- urea;
- uric acid;
- haemoglobin;
- haematocrit.

Capillary blood sampling

This method is quick and simple, thus allowing collection and analysis of blood during exercise, or immediately afterwards. Box 28.1 gives step-by-step instructions to describe the process of capillary puncture.

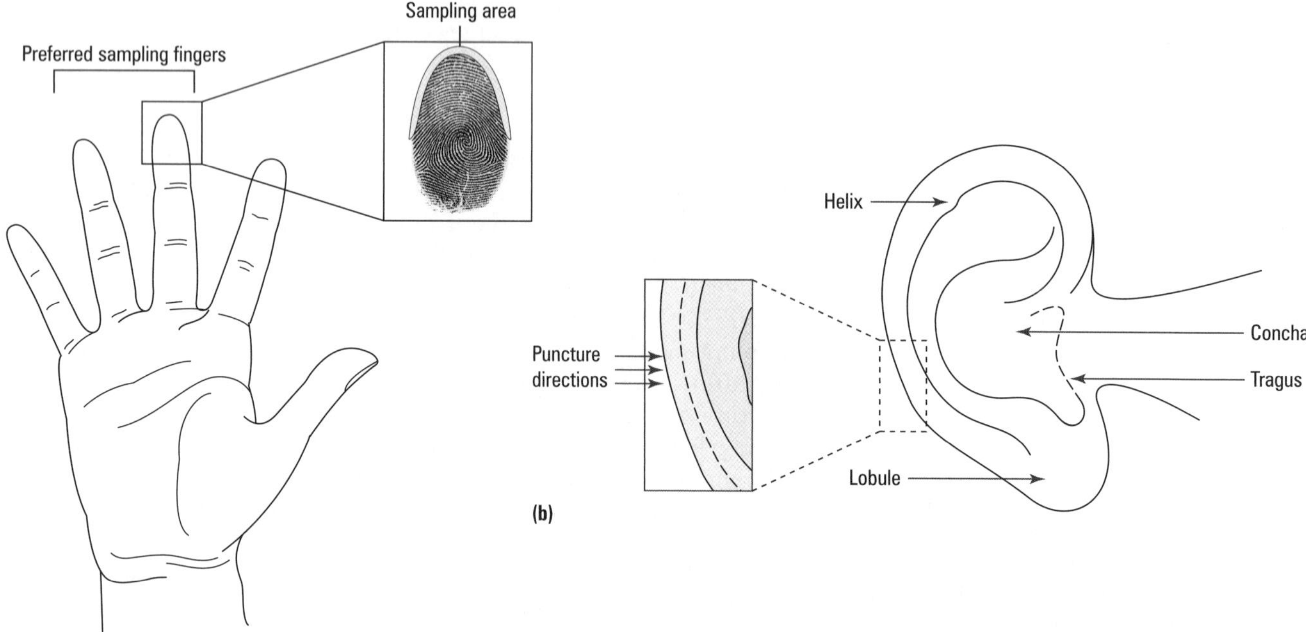

Fig. 28.1 Correct and incorrect puncture sites for (**a**) fingertip and (**b**) earlobe sampling. For fingertip sampling, aim for the lateral region of the fingertip so as not to puncture the pad of the finger. For earlobes, select the low and outside aspect of the helix just above the lobule.

Box 28.1 How to take a capillary blood sample

1. **Set up your work area.** When setting up your work area, make sure that you can access all required consumables easily (e.g. gloves, tissues, lancets, disposal bags) without repeated handling.
2. **Follow all pre-test safety guidelines** (Chapter 25). This minimises the risk of infection from exposure to body fluids.
3. **Carefully select the puncture site** on either the earlobe or fingertip (Fig. 28.1). Try not to puncture the thick pad of the finger as this may reduce the sample volume that can be drawn as a result of a shallower puncture. Further, puncturing the pad of the finger may cause more post-sampling discomfort, so it is better to sample to one side of the pad. If necessary, ask the subject either to swing their arms gently around to force the blood into the outer extremities or to heat their hands passively with hot water. If using hot water, make sure that the hands are fully dry before sampling. For earlobe sampling, you can apply a topical agent such as Finalgon™ around 10 minutes before sampling to the puncture site. Wipe off with a tissue three to four minutes before sampling.
4. **Wipe the selected puncture site** – typically, with an alcohol swab and allow to dry. This ensures that the site is free of water as well as clean of dirt and sweat before puncture.
5. **Prepare the lancet** by either loading a new tip on to the device or removing it from its plastic wrapping, depending on the type used. When using a typical self-retracting automatic lancet (Fig. 25.5), grip the lancet between the index and middle finger and place your thumb on top of the button at the top. Gently press the lancet onto the puncture site, apply a small amount of pressure and press the button with your thumb.
6. **Allow the first drop of blood to form** on the surface of the skin. After it has formed, wipe it away using a tissue or gauze. Wiping this first drop away is important as it may be contaminated by tissue fluid as it initially passes through and onto the skin surface.
7. **Allow a further droplet to form** – if necessary, gently squeeze the skin towards the puncture site. For a fingertip, apply gentle pressure at the second knuckle and slide towards the fingertip. For an earlobe, grip the helix of the ear with one hand and then gently squeeze the medial lobule with the other, working up and towards the puncture site.
8. **Draw the sample into a capillary tube** (Fig. 28.2) or onto a test strip as per the manufacturer's instructions. Typically this will involve placing a set amount on a strip or into a machine for analysis. It is important to know what you are required to do before the blood is available on the skin - if you take too much time, it will clot and be of no use.
9. **Wipe the puncture site** to remove excess blood and apply pressure using a tissue or gauze to prevent any bleeding into the subcutaneous tissue. Ask the patient to hold the pressure on the site until bleeding has stopped. If necessary, apply a small piece of tape or finger cot to the puncture site.
10. **Dispose of all waste materials** into appropriate biohazard safety containers (Chapter 25). Ensure that the work area is cleaned with an appropriate disinfectant (Chapter 25) when sampling is complete.
11. **Remove your gloves** when the work area is clean and disinfected.
12. **Wash your hands** before leaving the sampling area.

Collecting blood into a capillary tube

For certain measurements that require standardised volumes of blood, it may be necessary to draw a blood sample into a capillary tube. This allows an accurate volume of blood to be drawn, or for the sample to be separated in a centrifuge after collection. A capillary tube is a small fine glass tube that draws blood into it by capillary action. Capillary action is where the adhesion of the fluid to the glass pulls the liquid into the tube. Fluid may be collected into a capillary tube after fingertip or earlobe sampling. Once the skin has been punctured and a drop of blood is available on the skin, then the steps outlined in Box 28.2 can be used to fill the capillary tube.

Box 28.2 How to take a blood sample into a capillary tube

1. **Insert one end of the capillary tube into a pipette.** Using a pipette (Fig. 28.2) reduces your chances of breaking the tube and allows you to expel the blood rapidly if required following collection. If a pipette is not available, then gently hold the capillary tube in the middle when collecting the sample.
2. **Touch the end of the capillary tube into the drop of blood** on the skin surface and allow the blood to be drawn up into the tube. It is important to make sure that the end of the tube is not touching the skin as this will block the flow of blood into the tube and may cause discomfort for the patient.
3. **When collecting blood, hold the capillary tube at an angle of around 140°** to the skin surface, as shown in Fig. 28.2. When blood starts to enter the capillary tube, flow can be accelerated by tilting the tube slightly downwards. Be careful if the tube is tilted past the horizontal, as this will increase the risk of air bubbles entering the tube, which will affect the size and quality of the sample.
4. **If a large sample is required, continue to encourage blood flow,** e.g. 'milk' the finger from the second knuckle towards the fingertip to expel more blood through the skin puncture.
5. **Once the capillary tube is filled, process the sample as quickly as possible.** This is important, otherwise the blood may clot and you will have to take another sample. It is important to note that for some tests (e.g. haematocrit measurement in a centrifuge), heparin-lined tubes may be required to ensure that the blood does not coagulate after being drawn.
6. **Once the sample has been drawn, follow the appropriate protocol for puncture treatment and waste disposal** (p. 167).

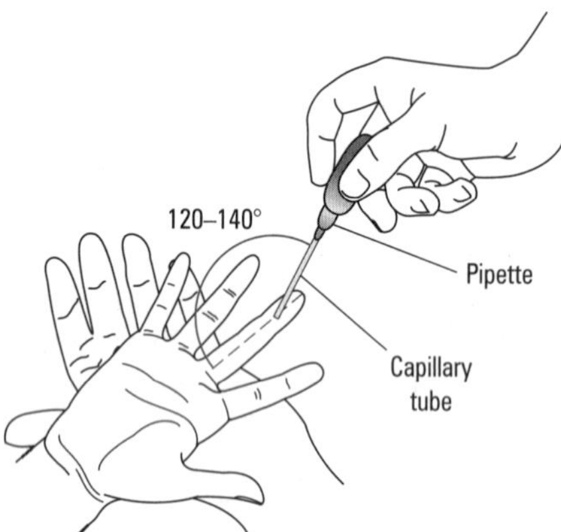

Fig. 28.2 Positioning a capillary tube using a pipette following a capillary puncture.

Table 28.1 Normal ranges for typical blood analytes

Analyte	Acceptable range
Bicarbonate	22–28 mmol L^{-1}
Creatine kinase	60–220 U L^{-1} (male) 30–180 U L^{-1} (female)
Creatinine	62–125 μmol L^{-1}
Ferritin	0.06–0.12 mmol L^{-1} (male) 0.05–0.11 mmol L^{-1} (female
Glucose	3.0–5.4 mmol L^{-1} (fasting) 3.0–7.7 mmol L^{-1} (>2 h after eating)
Haematocrit	0.40–0.54 (male) 0.37–0.47 (female)
Haemoglobin	130–180 g L^{-1} (male) 115–165 g L^{-1} (female)
High density lipoproteins (HDL)	0.9–2.0 mmol L^{-1} (male) (fasting) 1.0–2.2 mmol L^{-1} (female) (fasting)
Iron	10–30 μmol L^{-1}
Lactate	0.3–0.8 mmol L^{-1} (resting) 10–24 mmol L^{-1} (max exercise)
Low density lipoproteins (LDL)	2.0–3.4 mmol L^{-1} (fasting)
PH	7.36–7.44
PCO_2	35–45 mmHg (4.6–6.0 kPa)
PO_2	80–100 mmHg (11.0–13.5 kPa)
Potassium	3.8–4.9 mmol L^{-1}
Sodium	135–145 mmol L^{-1}
Total cholesterol	3.6–6.5 mmol L^{-1} (fasting) (<5.5 mmol L^{-1} is regarded as 'healthy')
Total protein	62–80 g L^{-1}
Transferrin	1.7–3.0 g L^{-1}
Triglycerides	0.1–2.2 mmol L^{-1} (fasting)
Urea	3.0–8.0 mmol L^{-1}
Uric acid	0.21–0.44 mmol L^{-1}

Reference values have been taken from McPherson (1997).

Definitions

Specimen – sample of urine.

Glycosuria – the presence of glucose in urine.

Proteinuria – the presence of protein in urine.

Reagent strips – disposable strips that measure analyte concentration.

Refractometers – optical instruments that are used to measure aqueous concentrations.

Specific gravity – the ratio of density of a liquid in comparison to water.

Ketone bodies – specific metabolites produced during the breakdown of fatty acids to generate energy.

Blood reference values

It is often necessary to compare results from individual tests with those of the general population. This is achieved using tabulated values for normal ranges (Table 28.1). Note that these ranges are for healthy adults – you may need to use more specific reference ranges, e.g. when testing elite athletes.

Urine

This is another body fluid that provides many useful measures in sport and exercise science. Normally the simplest analysis of urine (urinalysis) is performed using reagent strips that react with various analytes. This allows people with minimal training to analyse urine for the presence or concentration of a range of metabolites in a short time period. Measurement and analysis of urine are normally performed to help detail fluid losses and hydration or to help monitor kidney function. Most commonly in sport and exercise science, urinalysis involves testing for total urine volume, specific gravity, proteinuria, glycosuria, as well as pH and ketone bodies. While many routine measurements can be performed using reagent test strips, accurate measurement of the specific gravity of urine can be performed using a refractometer as described below. However, urine can also be used for more detailed biochemical analysis, e.g. to provide information on hormone levels. Although urine is normally free of pathogenic microbes, (unless the person has a genitourinary infection), standard safety precautions should be used (pp. 168–169) such as using latex gloves and appropriate disinfection protocols.

Depending on the metabolite to be analysed, urine sample timing may be crucial. Typically, samples are described as:

Producing a urine sample – sometimes this can be difficult for a subject, but the temptation to drink excessive water must be resisted, as this can dilute the urine sample and provide incorrect data. Be patient and wait until the subject needs to urinate.

- **First-morning specimen:** provided immediately on waking. This is the most concentrated sample as it has had a long time in the bladder – this may change the levels of several metabolites.
- **Second-voided specimen:** provided some time after the initial morning urination. This provides a fresh and concentrated urine sample.
- **Postprandial specimen:** provided following a meal. Typically taken for glucose monitoring.
- **Random specimen:** taken at no particular time period. Typically used for initial consultations and gross abnormalities.
- **Controlled specimen:** taken at specified times, depending upon fluid ingestion and exercise protocols. This is typically used as a control in research studies.

Both the quantity and composition of urine are of interest to sport and exercise scientists. Box 28.3 gives details on taking and processing a urine sample.

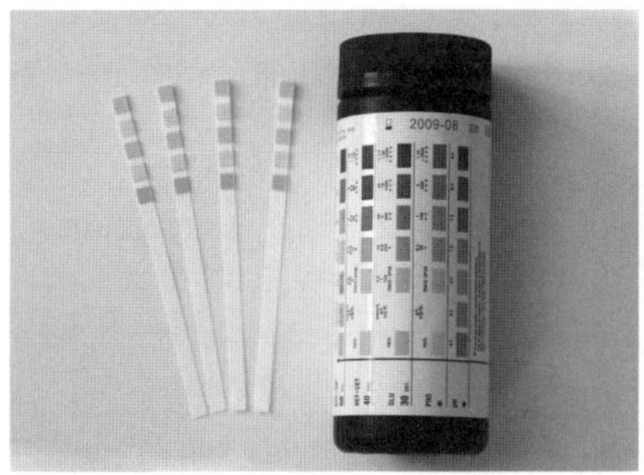

Fig. 28.3 Typical urinalysis reagent strips.
Source: Alamy Images: SciMed Images.

Testing using reagent strips

Using simple reagent strips (Fig 28.3), a wide range of analytes can be measured, including pH, glucose, protein, specific gravity, blood, ketones, nitrite, leukocytes, urobilinogen and bilirubin. Use as follows:

1. **Remove a reagent strip from the container** and replace cap.
2. **Submerge all of the test areas of the strip in the fresh urine sample and remove immediately** (Fig. 28.4a). Excess urine can be removed by running the edge of the reagent strip against the rim of the specimen container.

Box 28.3 Urine sampling

1. **Inform the subject** of the procedures and location of the urine sampling. It is important to have an appropriate collection room available.
2. **Ensure that the appropriate safety precautions are in place** to deal with the fluid exposure before sampling begins.
3. **Consider your subject.** Urine collection can be a sensitive topic and is embarrassing to many people. When asking for a urine sample, it is important to provide a private room (a toilet cubicle works well) so that the subject can more easily produce a sample. It is also necessary to explain the sampling procedures before the subject takes the container for sample collection.
4. **Use a sterile collection container** that can be sealed to maintain sample integrity. If total urine volume is to be measured, the container should hold at least 3 L of fluid, whereas 50 mL is adequate for metabolite analysis. When using a specimen jar to collect urine for analysis, ensure that:
   - It is sterile and has not been used before
   - It has a secure lid and is leak-resistant
   - It is made of robust plastic, rather than glass
   - It has an opening at least 4 cm in diameter, to provide an adequate 'target' for the subject
   - It is appropriately labelled to identify subject, time and date of collection.
5. **Request that the subject initiates and completes urination into the specified container.** Typically, total urine volume collection occurs over 24 hours, and each urine sample is weighed and its mass recorded. Spills of urine should be minimised, although they should be reported by the subject. It is important that the subject captures all urine into the container, particularly at the end of the stream. The container should be kept refrigerated between sampling. Urine should be collected 'mid-stream' for any metabolite or specific gravity analysis. When collecting a 'mid-stream' urine specimen, the subject should discard the initial portion of the stream and then place the container in the stream for collection. Once an adequate sample volume is reached, the subject should interrupt urination, remove the container from the stream and continue if needed. Use of mid-stream urine samples helps to remove bacteria or abnormal concentrations of metabolites that may be present in the initial urine stream.
6. **Gently mix the filled specimen jar and place on a disposable absorbent mat** on the bench or table.

3. **Wait for the appropriate time period.** Each reagent has a reading time which is crucial for optimal results. This may vary between immediately and two minutes after dipping.
4. **Compare each reagent area to the corresponding colour chart** – this is typically located on the side of the reagent strip container or is supplied as a chart (Fig. 28.4b). Hold the strip next to the chart/bottle but do *not* allow the reagent strip to touch the colour chart as urine will contaminate the chart and may affect its colour.

Using a refractometer

A refractometer measures the specific gravity of a liquid via its effect on the refractive index of the liquid. Use a portable refractometer as follows:

1. **Ensure that a mid-stream sample is taken** if specific gravity is to be measured. Initial evacuation of urine may be abnormally concentrated with metabolites and may not provide a valid measurement.
2. **Remove the refractometer from its case.** Be careful not to handle it roughly or drop it, as it is a sensitive piece of equipment.
3. **Open the lens cover and gently clean with a wet cloth,** and then dry it with a separate dry cloth. Do not apply too much pressure on the lens as it is relatively soft and may distort.

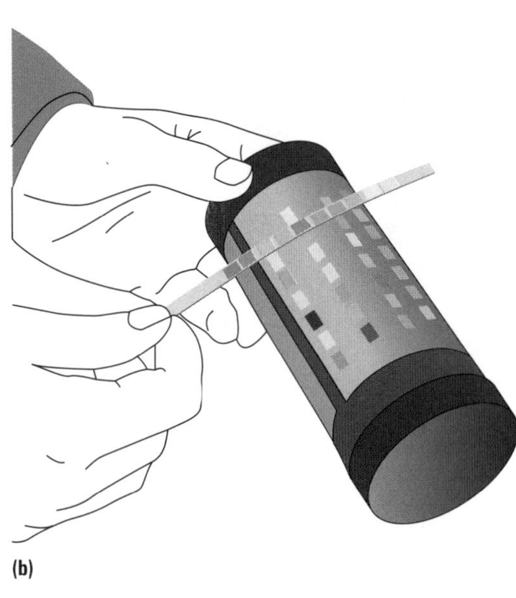

Fig. 28.4 Demonstrating (**a**) how to submerge a urinalysis reagent strip correctly in a urine collection jar; and (**b**) how to interpret changes in the reagent strips after submersion.

Using a portable refractometer – make sure that it is held at the right angle during measurement. The flat surface of the lens should be parallel to the ground, meaning that you will be looking up into the refractometer (Fig. 28.5a).

4. **Pick up the refractometer** between the left thumb and forefinger (right-handed people) rather than grasping it in the hand. The right hand can then be used to change the focus of the refractometer to provide a clear axis for measurement. Make sure that you have checked the focus prior to measurement.
5. **Test a control sample of water.** With the lens cover open, pipette a small amount of water onto the lens: 5–10 mL of water at room temperature is sufficient to act as a control. Close the lens cover and ensure that the liquid has spread evenly over the lens. Hold up the refractometer (Fig. 28.5a), look into the eyepiece and record where the white and dark regions meet on the vertical axis (Fig 28.5b). The water should have a specific gravity of 1.000 $g\,mL^{-3}$. The water used for the control should be at room temperature (let it stand for a sustained period of time beforehand). The test should be repeated around every 20 minutes or after every 10 or 80 samples. Open the lens cover again and wipe the control water off gently using a non-abrasive cloth.
6. **Assay the urine sample.** Pipette a similar amount of urine out of the specimen container and expel it carefully onto the refractometer lens and repeat the procedure from step 5. If the urine sample is highly coloured, it may be necessary to use bright light (e.g. direct sunlight) to measure the sample.
7. **Clean the instrument.** When the assay is complete, open the lens cover and pipette clean water onto the lens to wash off the urine sample into a suitable container. Gently wipe dry with a dry cloth and move onto the next sample, or replace the refractometer in its box.

(a)

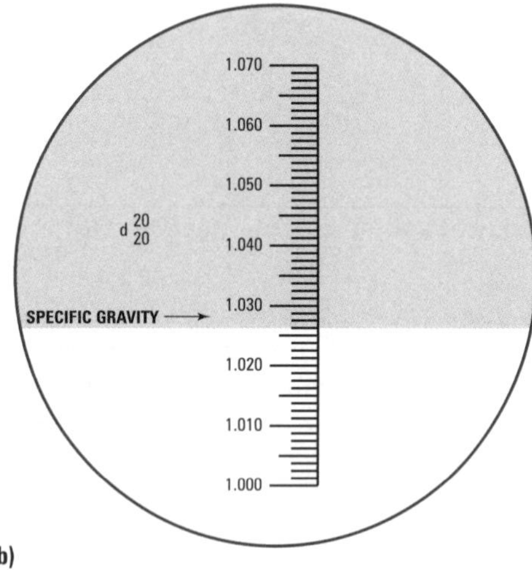

(b)

Fig. 28.5 Using a refractometer. (**a**) How to hold the refractometer and (**b**) inside view.

Table 28.2 Description and ranges for typical urine analytes

Parameter/analyte	Acceptable range
Colour	Pale yellow to amber
Specific gravity	1.005–1.030 g mL^{-3}
pH	4.5–8.0
Protein	Negative–Trace
Glucose	Negative
Ketone	Negative
Bilirubin	Negative
Blood	Negative
Urobilinogen	0.1–1.0 mg dL^{-1}
Bacteria	Negative
Leukocytes	Negative
Adolescent 24-h urine output	750–1500 mL
Adult 24-h urine output	750–2000 mL

Reference values have been taken from McPherson (1997).

Cleaning up

When complete, all urine should be discarded into a toilet or an alternative approved disposal area. Some larger collection containers can be cleaned and reused. Smaller sample cups are typically discarded in a biological waste bag. Make sure that you remove gloves and place them together with any soft materials that have been used into the biohazard waste bags. Finally, wash your hands before leaving.

Urine reference values

As with blood analysis, it is often necessary to compare test results with those of the general population. Table 28.2 provides typical reference ranges (from normal healthy adults) for comparison.

The data provided from blood analysis and urinalysis are essential in several testing procedures used in sport and exercise science (Chapters 31, 32 and 43). By developing your sampling skills, you will be able to maximise subject comfort while obtaining accurate physiological information in a safe and controlled manner.

Text reference

McPherson, J. (1997) *Manual of Use and Interpretation of Pathology Tests.* Royal College of Pathologists of Australia, Sydney.

Sources for further study

Estridge, B.H. and Reynolds, A.P. (2008) *Basic Clinical Laboratory Techniques.* Thomson Delmar Learning, Clifton Park.

King Strasinger, S. and Lorenzo, M.S.D. (2008) *Urinalysis and Body Fluids,* 5th edn, F.A. Davis Company, Philadelphia.

Maw, G., Locke, S., Cowley, D. and Witt, P. (2000) Blood sampling and handling techniques. In: C. Gore (ed.) *Physiological Tests for Elite Athletes.* Human Kinetics, Champaign, IL.

29 Measuring cardiac function

Definitions

Arrhythmia – irregularity of cardiac rhythm.

Depolarisation – the process where electrical potential is changed from the normal resting level.

Einthoven's triangle – a theoretical triangle formed around the heart using three limb leads.

Electrocardiogram – physical trace of the electrical activity that occurs in the heart.

Heart rate monitor – a chest strap and watch system used to measure heart rate during exercise.

Intercostal space – space between ribs filled by costal cartilage.

Ischaemia – reduced blood flow to the heart muscle that can cause pain.

Lead – the electrical trace of the electrical cardiac activity from the perspective of an electrode(s).

Noise – interference in the electrical activity from an electrode.

Palpate – physical examination using hands and fingers.

Repolarisation – the process where the electrical potential in the cell is returned to a normal resting level.

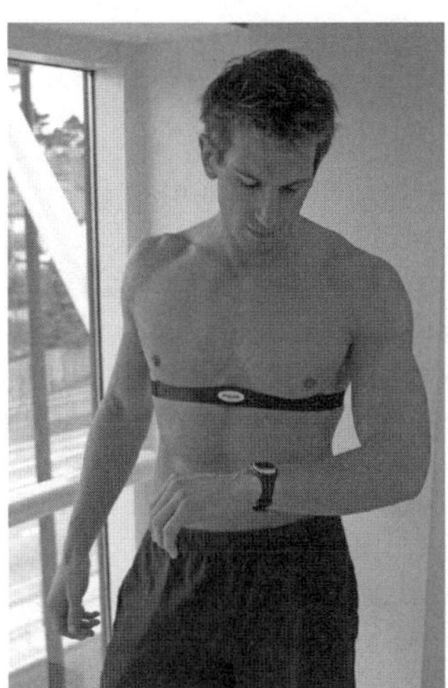

Fig. 29.1 An example of a heart rate monitor.
Source: Alamy Images: Grant Pritchard.

Monitoring a subject's heart rate is particularly useful in sport and exercise science to assess exercise intensity, set safe work rate limits and control training load. During your training you will learn how to monitor heart rate during exercise simply and easily. The equipment used includes heart rate monitors and electrocardiograms (ECG).

Heart rate monitors are simple-to-use devices, designed to provide a rapid and accurate measure of heart rate. While they provide important information during exercise, this becomes limited when assessing whether the heart is working correctly. To provide this more detailed information, an ECG can be performed. An ECG provides substantially more information about the operation of the heart, since it monitors the electrical activity that is required to make the heart beat. ECG monitors can be very simple and use three electrodes to monitor general function of this electrical activity through six leads of activity. Alternatively, ECG monitors can be more complex, using 10 electrodes and 12 leads. The 12-lead ECG provides much more information on the conduction of the electrical signal across the heart as it requires six electrodes to be placed around the heart.

This chapter provides an outline to help you to learn how to use a heart rate monitor and how briefly to perform an ECG test. However, you should read more widely (see Sources for further study, p. 210) to extend your understanding of the role of ECG tests and the skills required for in-depth analysis.

Heart rate monitors

The ability to monitor heart rate quickly and simply is a vital skill for a sport and exercise scientist given its important measure of exercise intensity. A heart rate monitor is a vital piece of technology for any sport and exercise science student to understand and use. It provides accurate measurements of heart rate during exercise. This is extremely useful in monitoring exercise intensity (Chapter 43), which would otherwise be very difficult. For this reason, heart rate monitors have become a basic piece of exercise monitoring equipment. Simply, heart rate monitors consist of a chest band, elastic strap and watch band (Fig. 29.1). Heart rate monitors vary greatly, with some being capable of displaying only heart rate where other, more expensive, heart rate monitors can display heart rate data as well as record it for download to computers for later analysis. The instructions below will guide you to fit a heart rate monitor appropriately.

How to fit a heart rate monitor

1. **Remove all components from heart rate container.**
2. **Attach one end of elastic strap to the chest band**, normally by clipping one of the plastic clips located on the elastic strap to the holes at either end of the chest strap.
3. **Moisten the two electrode surface areas located on the back of the chest band.** These areas are normally visible on the back of the chest strap and should be spaced evenly from the centre of the band. Water will act as a

conductor to help the electrical signals cross between the skin and chest band.

4. **Place the chest band on the chest of the subject.** The chest band should sit slightly below the large chest muscles (pectoralis major).
5. **Pass the elastic band around the back of the subject and insert the free end into the chest band.** Use the adjuster on the elastic strap to tighten or loosen to fit. The heart rate monitor should be fairly tight so that it does not move during exercise. Problems with transmitting the heart rate signal may occur if the strap is too loose.
6. **Place the heart rate monitor watch band on the preferred wrist of the subject.** Most heart rate monitors require you to hold the watch up to the middle of the chest strap for around three to five seconds so that it can detect the signal from the chest strap. Other heart rate monitors may need you to press the start button for them to search for the signal as you do this.
7. **Watch the heart rate monitor until a heart rate appears.** Most heart rate monitors have a small picture of a heart that flashes when a good signal is being received. If no heart rate is detected in 30 seconds, then it may be necessary to troubleshoot the monitor by tightening the strap, re-wetting the electrodes or attempting to search for a signal again. If, during exercise, no heart rate is visible on the watch, check the location of the chest band and tighten the chest band if appropriate.
8. **Use the heart rate monitor as required.** Some heart rate monitors will allow you to time the session and to insert 'intervals' or other features, as detailed in the instruction manual.
9. **Disinfect the heart rate monitor after use.** During exercise the heart rate monitor will be exposed to body fluids that carry the risk of communicable diseases (Chapter 25, pp. 168–170). Ensure that you clean the equipment appropriately to minimise this risk. To do this, thoroughly clean the chest strap with an approved disinfectant (see Chapter 25, p. 168).

Electrocardiography

The purpose of an ECG is to monitor and record the sequence of electrical activity across an individual heartbeat. Similar to wearing a heart rate monitor, it can provide information on heart rate responses at rest and during exercise. In addition, however, it provides extensive diagnostic information on the internal functioning of the heart. Both problems with nerve signals (arrhythmias) and reduced circulation (ischaemia) can be identified simply during an ECG test. They can be performed at rest and during exercise to maximise the detection of any health risks. To gain an appreciation of the use of ECG tests, it is important that you learn the electrical pathways and responses of the heart (Figs. 29.2 and 29.3). It is the consistency of this complex system of electrical signals across the heart that enables ECG tests to be most useful in determining when the heart is not functioning correctly.

Locating the chest strap during heart rate monitoring – Normally there is a logo on the front of the chest strap directly in the middle. This helps you to orientate the chest strap so that the logo is in the middle of the chest.

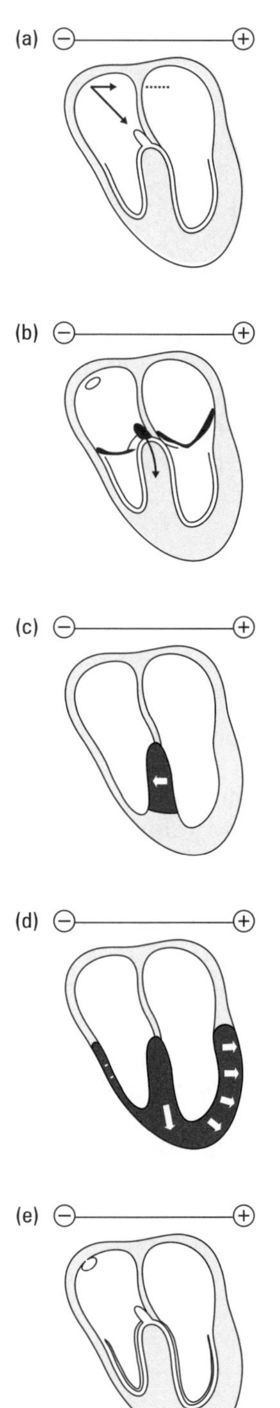

Fig. 29.2 The events as the electrical signal passes across the heart during a contraction. See adjacent text and p. 200 for a written description.

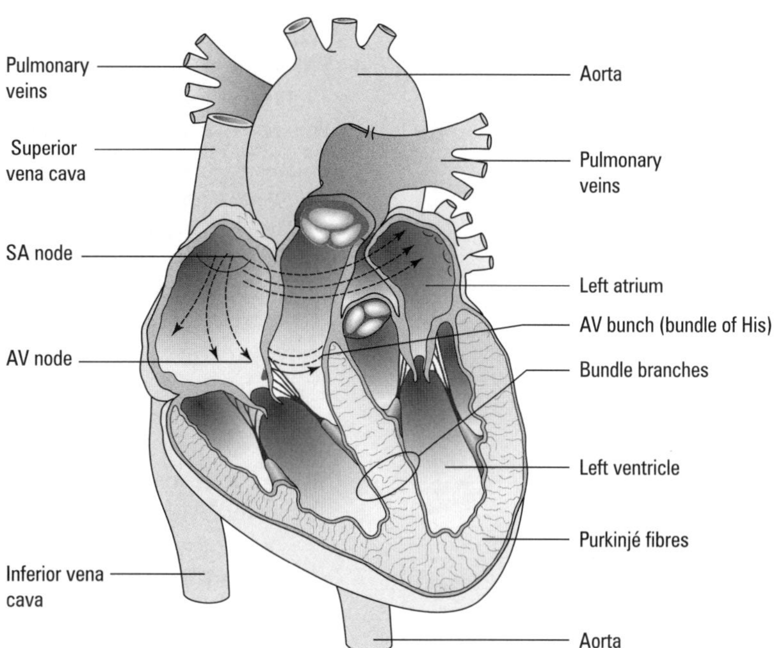

Fig. 29.3 Electrical pathway across the heart.

KEY POINT Subjects are sometimes confused as to the role of ECG. It should always be explained before performing an ECG that it is simply a way of monitoring the electrical activity of the heart, and not a means of controlling it.

Electrical activity of the heart

An ECG recording replicates the depolarisation–repolarisation activity at different locations across the heart. The nervous signal required for a heartbeat is autonomous from the brain and originates in a small group of cells at the top of the right atrium called the sinoatrial, or SA, node (Fig. 29.3). Once the signal is developed in the SA node it is carried through the atrium (causing a depolarisation effect and muscle contraction) until it reaches another group of cells in the floor of the atrium called the atrioventricular, or AV, node (Fig. 29.2a). The peak of the P wave represents the activation of the AV node. This is represented on an ECG signal as the first half of the P wave at the very start of a heartbeat (Fig. 29.4a).

The electrical signal then continues on to the AV node. Once the AV node has been activated, the signal is delayed from passing through to the ventricles. This delay is to allow maximal filling time of the ventricles from the atria, given the transport time of blood. When ready, the signal is passed through the AV node and into the bundle of His which leads down towards the ventricle (Fig. 29.2b). This action is represented as the P–R interval (Fig. 29.4b).

The bundle of His leads to the Purkinjé fibres, which are designed to transfer the electrical signal over the ventricular muscle. The first shift in the signal is through the intraventricular septum towards the right ventricle (Fig. 29.2c). This is demonstrated as the Q phase of the larger

(a)

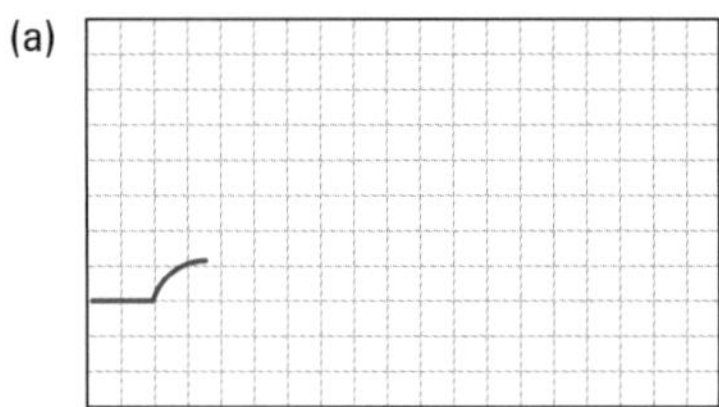

(b)

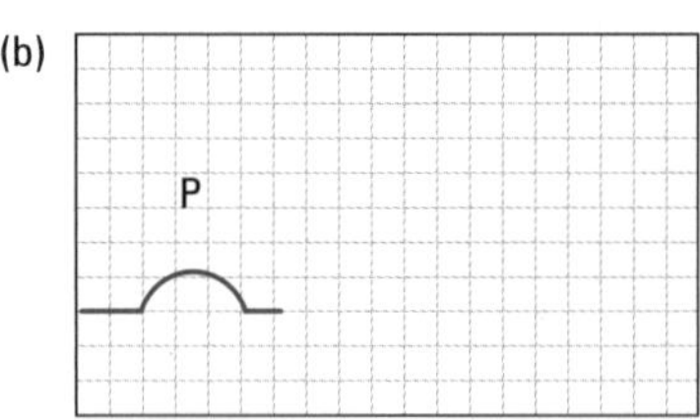

(c)

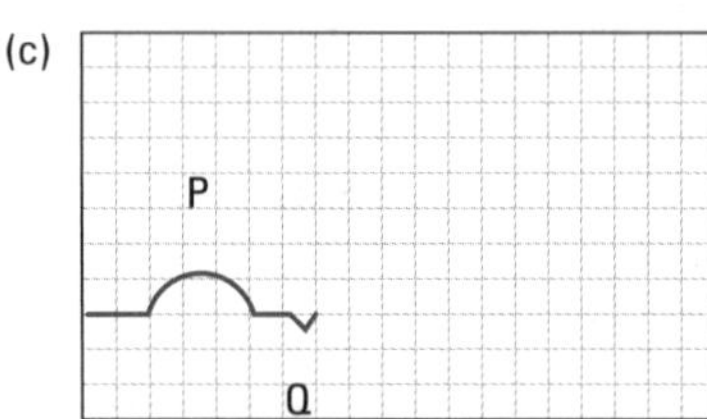

(d)

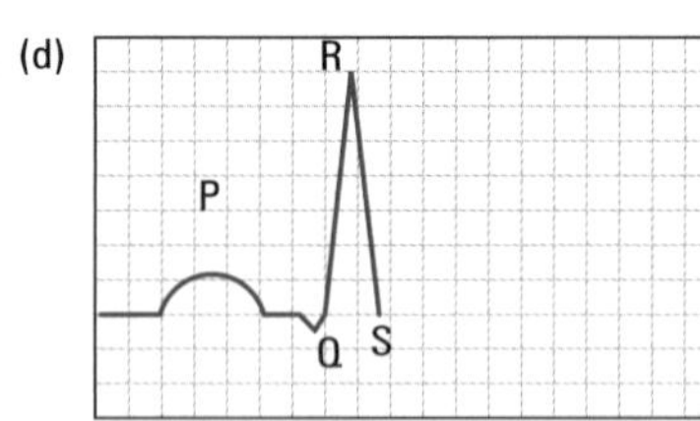

(e)

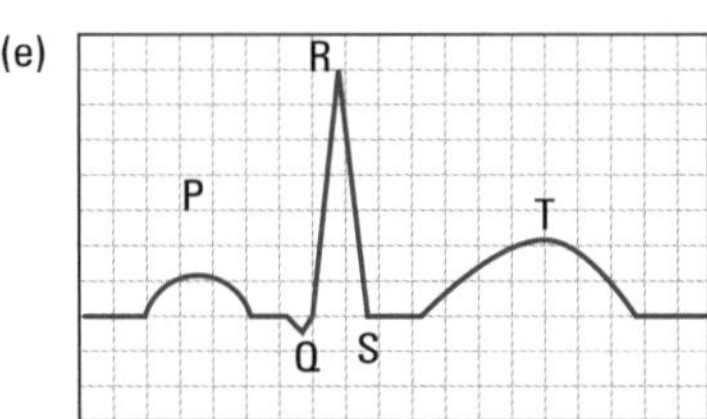

Fig. 29.4 The trace of the electrical signal across the heart during a contraction. See text for description.

QRS complex. The P–Q interval is also used as a measure of AV conduction (Fig. 29.4c).

Once this initial shift is complete, the electrical signal is very quickly passed over the ventricular muscle, causing it to depolarise and contract (Fig. 29.2d). This activation of the ventricles is represented as a tall positive spike (R phase of the QRS complex and a sharp decline in the amplitude of the signal (S phase) (Fig. 29.4d). The duration of the QRS complex is an indicator of ventricular depolarisation and function.

Once the ventricles have depolarised, it is important that they repolarise to prepare for the next beat (Fig. 29.2e). The repolarisation wave follows the depolarisation signal. The repolarisation of the ventricles is represented within the ST segment and T wave (Fig. 29.4e). The ST segment refers to the initial slow repolarisation of the ventricles, whereas the T wave represents the rapid portion. Large elevations or depressions of the slope of the ST segment can represent localised ischaemia within the heart.

Site preparation and positioning of electrodes

It is important that positioning is standardised to maintain the integrity and validity of the ECG signal. A 12-lead ECG consists of 10 leads being placed on the body; there are six chest leads and four limb leads. The 12-lead name is given as the cardiac activity is also assessed through a combination of electrodes to provide further information about cardiac function. You may, however, only be required to set up and use a 3-lead ECG. If so, ignore the instructions on the chest leads and focus on those that detail the placement of the limb leads.

The six chest leads are placed around the heart in standardised positions to follow the cardiac signal across the heart from the SA node to the ventricles. Fig. 29.6b demonstrates the position of the chest leads used in a 12-lead ECG. Simply, the V_1 lead monitors the activity of the right ventricle, whereas leads V_2 and V_3 span the small muscle that separates the two ventricles. Lead V_4 is positioned over the apex of the heart and leads V_5 and V_6 record the activity of the left lateral wall of the heart.

The remaining four limb leads provide a wider view of the cardiac signal across the body. The limb leads are located on the right (R) and left (L) shoulders and the right (N) and left (F) legs. In addition to the six chest leads and three limb leads that provide ECG signals, the three other leads (I, II and III) are formed by the theoretical location of Einthoven's triangle (Box 29.1), and are taken from different axes positioned around the centre of the heart.

The sequence of events is:

1. **Ensure that your work station is appropriately set up** and that you have easy access to sterile latex gloves, disposable razors, tissues, alcohol swabs and ECG electrodes.

2. **Politely ask the subject to remove their shirt** and other clothes so that you can place electrodes on the chest. Females should continue to wear bras and if it is necessary for them to be removed for electrode placement they should be provided with a gown to wear. Participants should also remove all foreign objects (e.g. mobile phones, wallets) so that you can easily access the electrode placement sites.

Box 29.1 Using Einthoven's triangle in electrocardiography

The purpose of the four limb leads is to form Einthoven's triangle, which is an equilateral triangle between three of the leads (right arm, left arm and left leg). The heart is located within the centre of the triangle (Fig. 29.5). Although the placement of the left leg electrode seems to obscure the triangle, it remains equilateral given that all electrodes are an equal distance from the electrical field of the heart. The fourth limb lead (N), placed on the right leg, does not contribute to these signals; rather it is a neutral lead required to complete the circuit.

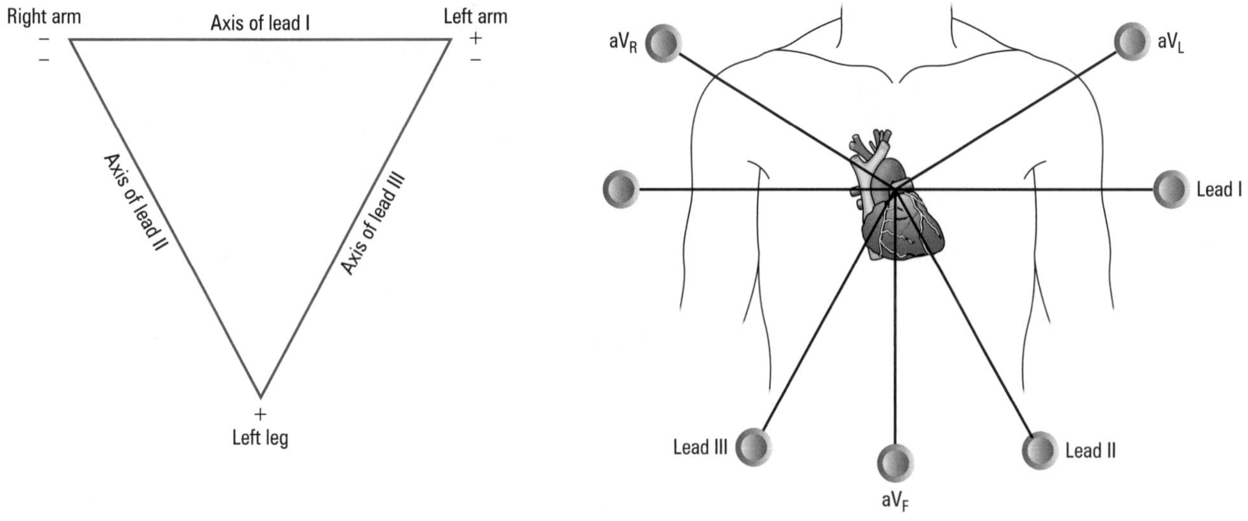

Fig. 29.5 The theoretical Einthoven's triangle and the origin of leads I, II and III with respect to the four limb leads.

Dealing with female patients – this can be difficult and potentially embarrassing when preparing for a 12-lead ECG. It is important to know that electrodes are never placed on top of the breast tissue, unless necessary. If you are required to lift or move the breast to place an electrode, ensure that you use the back of your hand to do so. Record if the electrode is placed on top of the breast.

3. **Palpate and mark electrode sites** and ensure that they are over soft tissue or close to bone, rather than over bony prominences, thick muscles or folds of skin. Placing an electrode over these surfaces may interfere with the passing of the electrical signal. When palpating the location of the electrodes, it is important to be consistent during all tests.
4. **Prepare the skin** by shaving off all excess hair located on and around the electrode site. Briskly rub each site with light sandpaper or abrasive tape until the skin slightly reddens, and then wipe with alcohol swabs to remove traces of sweat, oil and loosened skin.
5. **Apply an electrode to the prepared site** by removing the protective coating from the bottom side of the electrode to expose a sticky surface. Press one side of the electrode against the client's skin, pull gently and then press the opposite side of the electrode against the skin. Avoid excess pressure in the middle of the electrode as this may damage the conductive gel that will help pass the signal. Also, do not place electrodes on top of one another as this may disrupt the contact between the gel and skin.

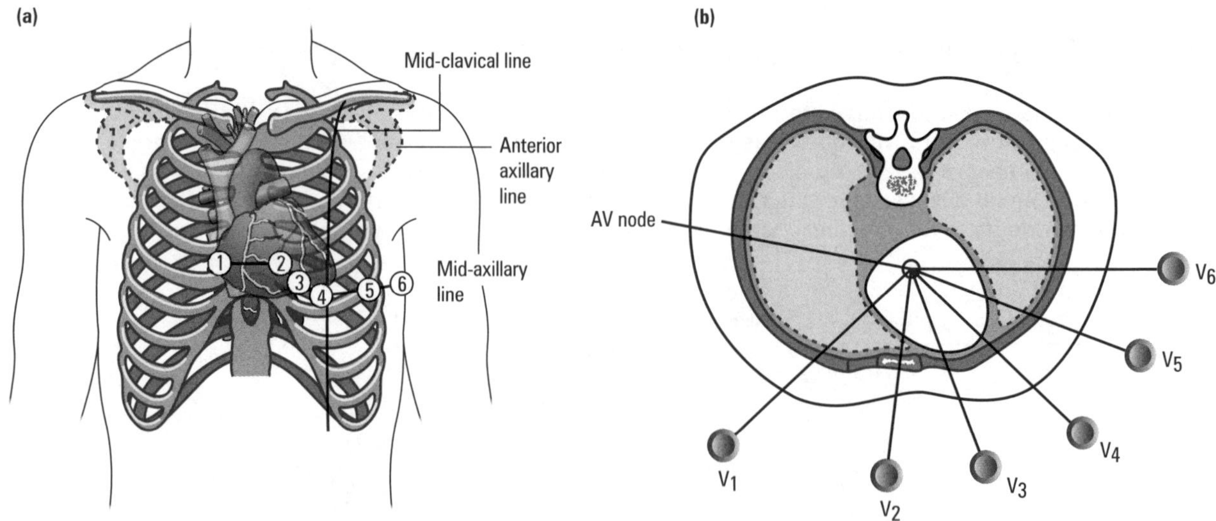

Fig. 29.6 (**a**) Positioning the chest and limb leads on a torso. (**b**) The chest leads in position to the heart's electrical field.

Detailed placement of ECG electrodes

The standard six chest leads are placed in the positions described below (See Fig. 29.6a above for an anatomical view):

- **V_1: palpate the right side of the sternum until you feel the space between the fourth and fifth ribs.** The electrode is placed in the 'intercostal space', as close to the sternum as possible without touching it.

- **V_2: repeat the procedure used to place the V_1 electrode on the left side of the body to position V_2.**

- **V_3: wait until you have placed the V_2 and V_4 electrodes before marking the site for V_3.** The location of the V_3 electrode cannot be determined until the sites for the V_2 and V_4 electrodes are round. Once these sites are located, the site for V_3 is simply midway between them. (*NOTE:* this may place the electrode on a rib.)

Important note – the process of electrode placement carries a risk of exposure to body fluids, so it is important to ensure that standard precautions (Chapter 25) are followed to prevent transmission of infection from any body fluids.

- **V_4: identify the medial and lateral ends of the clavicle** on the left side of the body. Measure the distance and mark the location of the middle (this is called the mid-clavicular line). Then locate the fifth intercostal space (between ribs 5 and 6) on the left side of the body close to the sternum. When located, palpate the space outwards until you are aligned with the mid-clavicular line. The electrode is placed at the intersection of these two lines in the intercostal space.

- **V_5: identify the small fold of skin that is located at the front of the left armpit** (known as the anterior axilla). Palpate the fifth intercostal space again and work outwards until you are underneath the anterior axilla landmark. The V_5 electrode is placed at the intersection of these two lines in the intercostal space.

- **V_6: ask the subject to raise their left arm to the horizontal** and vertically mark the middle of the armpit (known as the mid-axilla). Palpate the sixth intercostal space on the left side of the sternum and continue to palpate laterally until you are underneath the mid-axillary line. The V_6 electrode is placed at the intersection of the two lines.

When the locations of the six chest leads have been marked, you will need to mark where the four limb lead electrodes are placed. The position of the electrodes for the limb leads changes depending whether the ECG test is resting or exercising. For a resting ECG the following electrode placement sites apply (See Fig. 29.7a for an anatomical view):

- **Right arm** (R) – mark the front (same side as the palm of the hand) of the right forearm at the position where a wristwatch would be worn.
- **Left arm** (L) – mark the front (same side as the palm of the hand) of the left forearm at the position where a wristwatch would be worn.
- **Right leg** (N) – identify the small bony lump (malleolus) on the inside of the right ankle. Palpate up the leg (3–4 cm) so that you cannot feel the malleolus and mark the spot.
- **Left leg** (F) – identify the malleolus on the inside of the left ankle. Palpate up the leg (3–4 cm) so that you cannot feel the malleolus and mark the spot.

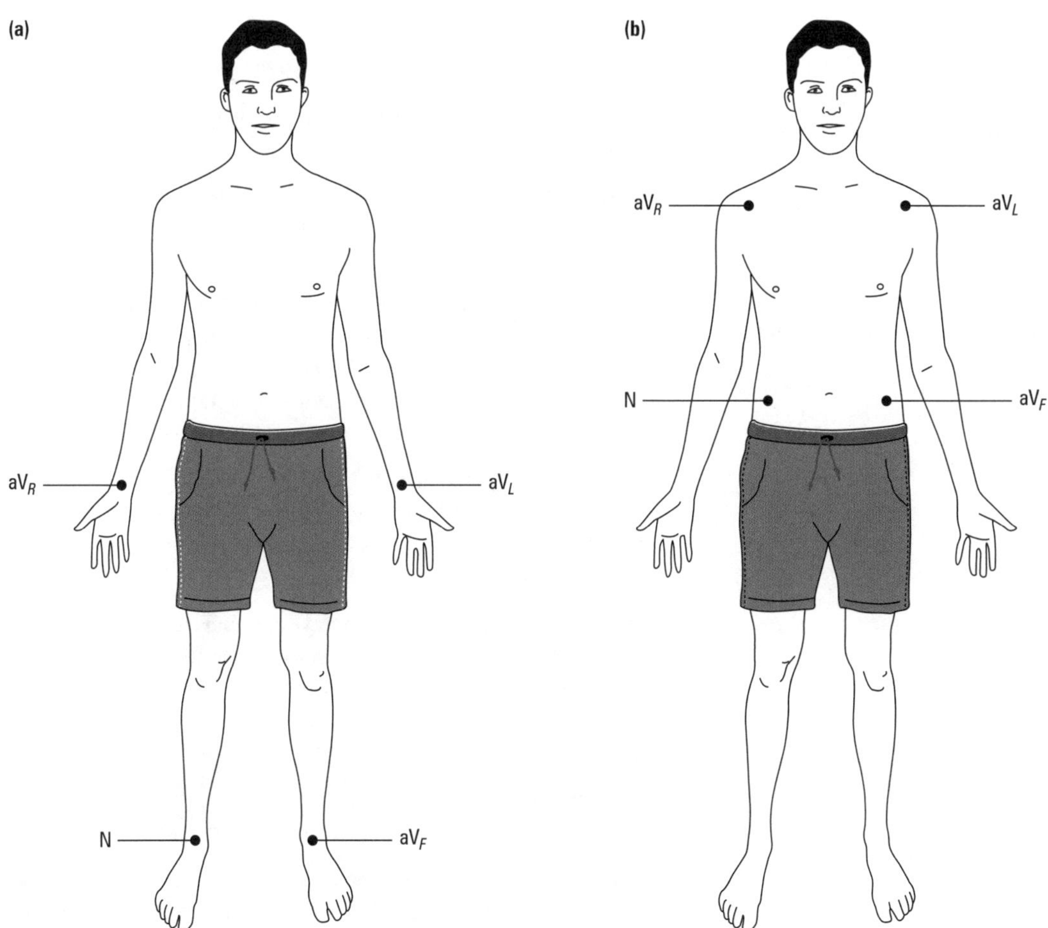

Fig. 29.7 Placement of limb leads for resting (**a**) and exercise ECG (**b**) tests.

For an exercise ECG the following electrode placement sites apply (Fig. 29.7b for an anatomical view).

- **Right arm** (R) – identify the mid-clavicular line of the right clavicle (similar to locating V_4). Palpate slightly downwards (2–3 cm) so that you cannot feel the clavicle and mark the spot. *NOTE:* do not go too low as placement on the pectoral muscle can lead to excessive noise.
- **Left arm** (L) – identify the mid-clavicular line of the left clavicle. Palpate slightly downwards (2–3 cm) so that you cannot feel the clavicle and mark the spot.
- **Right leg** (N) – identify the rectus abdominis and external oblique muscles. Palpate the small area between the two muscle groups on the right side of the body. Mark the spot between the two muscle groups at the level of the belly button.
- **Left leg** (F) – identify the rectus abdominis and external oblique muscles. Palpate the small area between the two muscle groups on the left side of the body. Mark the spot between the two muscle groups at the level of the belly button.

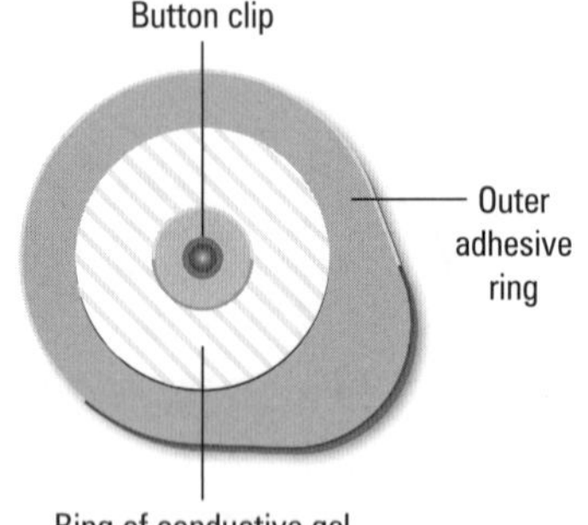

Fig. 29.8 The anatomy of a commonly used ECG electrode.

Performing a resting ECG test

Once all the electrodes have been properly fitted to the subject you can then complete the test using the following steps.

1. **Ensure that the electrodes are correctly placed and securely attached to the subject.**
2. **Instruct the subject to lie still on their back on a bed.** Ensure that the subject is as flat as possible, although there may be a pillow under the head for comfort.
3. **Clip the correct ECG leads to the small button clips in the centre of each electrode** (shown in Fig. 29.8). All ECG leads have their symbol imprinted on the back of the clip at the end of the lead. If you are preparing to complete an exercise ECG, some adhesive tape should be placed on top of the electrode to minimise movement and any risk of falling off.
4. **Enter the subject's details into the ECG system if required** (more sophisticated systems require a range of patient details). Once these are entered, choose to perform a resting ECG from the menu. If not, then just start the ECG monitor recording.
5. **Instruct the subject simply to lay flat and relax** for several minutes to ensure that the resting ECG is stable. Use this time to assess each of the leads to ensure that they demonstrate a clean and strong signal. If there is excessive disturbance or the lead signal is extremely messy, remove the electrode, repeat skin preparation and reapply the electrode.
6. **Check the speed of the ECG trace** is at 25 $mm\,s^{-1}$ and that it has an amplitude scale of 10 $mm\,mV^{-1}$ as this is consistent with standard ECG paper.
7. **Ensure that the ECG signal and heart rate are clean and stable. Record a trace that is 6–10 seconds long.** The trace should be printed out on standardised ECG paper to allow easy and consistent interpretation (Fig. 29.9).

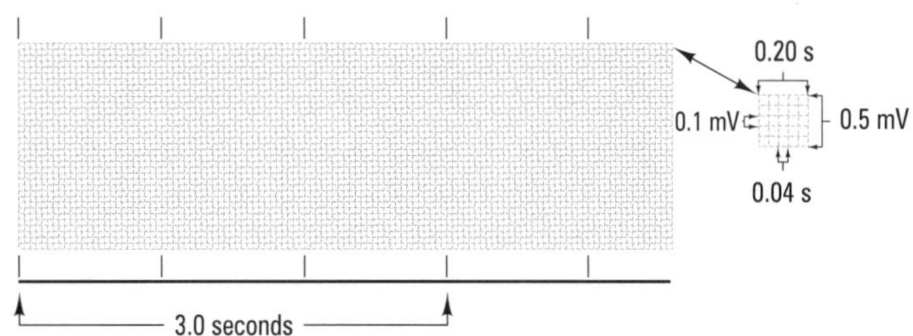

Fig. 29.9 An example of ECG paper and the typical time and amplitude axes used.
Source: http://www.ambulancetechnicianstudy.co.uk/ecgbasics.html, Ambulance Technician Study.

Important note – there is a large difference between a submaximal and maximal exercise test. Submaximal exercise tests are stopped when the subject's heart rate reaches 75% of their age-predicted maximum heart rate. Maximal exercise tests are only stopped when the subject indicates they wish to stop or medical issues arise.

Performing an exercise ECG test

While a resting ECG test is useful to identify cardiac abnormalities, not all will appear in such a test and some will only be observable when the heart is under physical stress. Therefore, increasing the load on the heart by making it work harder can often exacerbate any underlying conditions and fully test the function. To do this, typically a submaximal or maximal exercise test is completed while the subject wears a 12-lead ECG to monitor the electrical activity of the heart. Such tests should be performed after extensive screening and where a diagnostic need has been identified (Chapter 27). The test should be conducted in the presence of a medical practitioner if the patient is deemed to be at high risk of cardiac complications (Chapter 27). As discussed above, an exercise ECG test requires similar electrode placement as a resting ECG, with the exception that all limb leads are truncated (p. 203).

Constant monitoring of the ECG from the exercise test should be performed for three reasons:

1. to assure the safety of the subject during the test;
2. to measure the subject's heart rate accurately;
3. to observe/diagnose cardiovascular disease or cardiac abnormalities when they are present.

The first two objectives can be fulfilled by a sport and exercise scientist and should be a core practical skill within your course. The last responsibility is largely that of the supervising physician. Normally an exercise ECG requires a range of exercise and medical staff to be present to reduce the risks of any health problems that may arise as a result of the test. All parties should be aware of the dangers of performing an exercise ECG and the indications of when a test should be terminated (Box 29.2).

Signal noise – a clean signal is a trace that displays a consistent line without wavering (Fig. 29.10a). A noisy signal demonstrates excessive 'noise' and the true cardiac patterns cannot be so readily observed (Fig. 29.10b).

The following procedures provide useful instructions when performing an exercise ECG test in a laboratory.

1. **Assess (and present to the medical practitioner) the results of the patient's resting ECG.** An exercise ECG test should only be performed if no abnormalities are observed in the resting ECG trace and the person is perceived as being healthy enough for the exercise intensity.

Box 29.2 Recognising indicators of cardiac stress – stopping an exercise ECG test

Owing to the high-intensity nature of exercise ECG testing, participants with undiagnosed cardiovascular disease can be at great risk of adverse effects across a test. Therefore, it is important to ensure that the test is carried out under constant supervision, and that it is stopped immediately if it is observed that the subject is at an increased health risk. Records indicate that, for every 50 000 exercise ECG tests performed, one coronary patient may die, whilst one patient in 3000 will experience cardiac complications as a result of a test. The American College of Sports Medicine has listed some absolute and relative indications for terminating exercise testing, and these are listed below.

Absolute indications

1. Decrease in systolic blood pressure of ≥10 mmHg from baseline blood pressure despite increase in work rate, when accompanied by evidence of restricted cardiac blood flow.
2. Subject reporting moderate to severe chest pain (angina).
3. Observed decrease in sensory feedback and movement coordination.
4. Reports or symptoms (i.e. tingling, pain) of poor circulation and blood flow to the peripheral segments of the body.
5. Technical difficulties that interfere with physiological measures.
6. Subject wishes to stop the exercise ECG test.
7. Continued ventricular heart rate without any apparent atrial heart rate.
8. Elevation of the ST (≥1 mV) (p. 210) in leads that do not possess a Q segment.

Relative indications

1. Decrease in systolic blood pressure of ≥10 mmHg from baseline blood pressure despite increase in work rate, **without** evidence of restricted cardiac blood flow.
2. Large changes in the ST segment or QRS complex (p. 210).
3. Apparent disruption of the ECG trace that is likely to be an arrhythmia other than sustained ventricular tachycardia.
4. Fatigue, shortness of breath, wheezing, leg cramps or muscle pain (claudication).
5. Increasing chest pain during the test.
6. Hypertensive response (systolic >250 mmHg, diastolic >115 mmHg).

Adapted from Thompson *et al.* (2010).

2. **Select the ergometer of choice for the test.** Most commonly exercise ECG tests are completed on a treadmill, similar to VO_2max tests (Chapter 36), although this may need to be modified depending on the physical capabilities of the subject. Before testing, ensure that the subject is given time to familiarise himself or herself with the ergometer. When familiarising yourself with the ergometer, it is best to start from a standstill and gradually increase the intensity until at least the starting intensity of the selected protocol (see below).
3. **Select the required protocol for the exercise ECG test.** A wide variety of exercise protocols exists for use in cardiac exercise testing (Thompson *et al.*, 2010). The protocol used will need to take into account the speed, gradient or workload that the subject is capable of managing across the test and will also be selected to help identify specific cardiac abnormalities. The protocol should be explained to the subject before the test begins.
4. **Calculate the heart rate at which the test will be stopped** if no cardiac abnormalities are observed. Typically this value is set at between 75 and 90% of maximum heart rate. In more sophisticated systems, you will be able to enter this value and an alarm will sound when this has been reached.
5. **Check the speed of the ECG trace** is set to 25 mm s^{-1} and that the amplitude scale is 10 mm mV^{-1} as this is consistent with standard ECG paper.

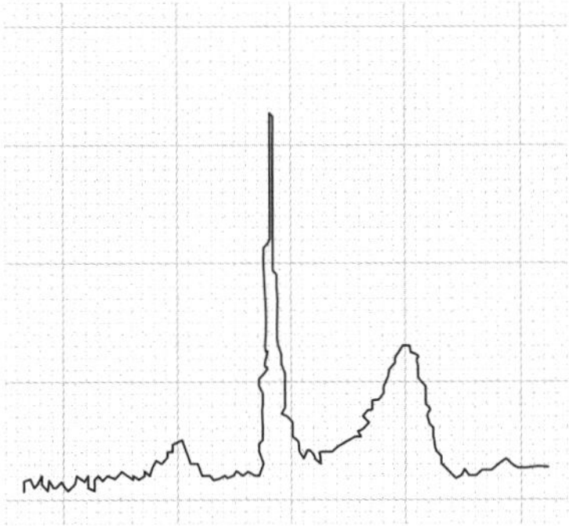

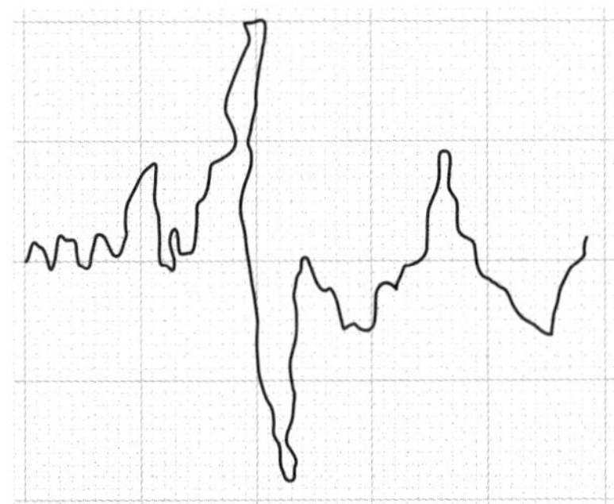

Fig. 29.10 An example of a clean ECG trace (**a**) and one that demonstrates considerable 'noise' in the signal (**b**).

Skin irritation – instruct the subject that some slight irritation may occur from the skin treatment (i.e. shaving and exfoliation). If moderate-to-severe irritation occurs, then recommend that the subject either uses a topical cream or seeks medical advice.

6. **Truncate the limb leads.** As explained earlier (p. 203), all limb leads should be shifted from the limbs to the torso to restrict excess noise and allow movement for exercise. It is recommended that the electrodes and leads are taped to the skin using safe adhesive tape such as Micropore.
7. **Ensure that the ECG signal and heart rate are clean and stable.** In more sophisticated systems you may be able to use digital filters to block electrical noise from the muscles that may be detected and interfere with the ECG signal.
8. **Start the exercise ECG test on the ergometer and follow the selected protocol.** Ensure that the subject is ready to complete the test and is aware of the procedure. Communicate with them across the test (use non-verbal cues if necessary – Box 36.2) to inform them of changes in work rate and to assess their exertion levels.
9. **Continue the exercise test as described by the selected protocol unless any of the listed criteria to terminate the test** (Box 29.2) is observed by you or the medical practitioner. Ensure that you closely monitor changes in the ECG trace and subject during the test. Some newer ECG systems allow you to take 'snapshots' of the ECG trace at different intervals during a test. If this is allowed, take a recording for at least six seconds at the end of each stage. If you cannot record the signal, then it is recommended that you continue to print off the ECG trace. If this is not possible, then try to print a 6–10-second ECG strip at the end of each stage across the protocol.
10. **Perform any other physiological measurements, as required.** Most tests require that other measurements, such as blood pressure, expired gas analysis (Chapter 36) and subjective intensity ratings (Chapter 31), are monitored. Make sure that each measure is recorded during the test.
11. **Make sure that you observe and check all leads during the exercise ECG test.** Each lead provides a unique view of the electrical activity of the heart and may also provide information about cardiac function during the test. In particular, leads II and V_5 should usually be closely monitored as they tend to be sensitive to cardiac abnormalities.
12. **Stop the test as soon as you identify any indicator of cardiac stress.** Make sure that you are aware of the absolute and relative indications of stopping a cardiac stress test (Box 29.2). If completing the test on a treadmill, it is safe to instruct the patient to grab the hand rail in front of them and to keep walking while you slow down the treadmill. If required, help the subject off the ergometer, ensuring that they do not fall over owing to changes in the floor level.
13. **Ensure that the subject is appropriately monitored after the testing,** and continue to check them for any unusual post-test distress.

Removing ECG electrodes

Once either a resting or exercise ECG is complete, you will need to remove all of the electrodes from the subject. While this may not cause a problem in most cases, the adhesive nature of the electrodes may cause skin trauma in elderly people and those with less supple skin. Therefore, it is important that you remember to remove the electrodes with great care to avoid this. When removing ECG electrodes, you should:

1. **Wear sterile latex gloves** to minimise contact with any body fluids.
2. **Unclip the ECG lead from the button clip at the back of the electrode** (see Fig. 29.8).
3. **Gently lift up one side of the electrode and peel back the outer adhesive ring slightly.** Once a sufficient amount is raised up, apply gentle pressure under the electrode with one hand while continuing to peel the remainder off with the other.
4. **Gently wipe the electrode site with an alcohol swab** to remove excess conductive gel that may be left on the skin.

Manual interpretation of an ECG trace

Signal direction – when assessing an ECG recording, the positive and negative amplitudes of the ECG trace indicate the direction of travel of the lead (Fig. 29.11). A positive signal demonstrates that the signal is moving right to left, whereas a negative symbol indicates that the signal is moving rightward.

While some more sophisticated systems can provide automated analysis and interpretation, knowing how to complete this manually is useful if you are using a simpler or older system. To perform a manual in-depth analysis of the output from a 12-lead ECG is a detailed and time-consuming task. Each different component of the rhythm must be analysed across a number of leads to identify the presence of cardiac abnormalities or arrhythmias. Regardless, all ECG tests should be manually reviewed by a trained technician or medical doctor to assess cardiac function, as the automated protocols may miss irregularities. Interpretation of an ECG recording uses a range of amplitudes (signal strengths) or intervals (time between cardiac events) to assess function.

The following text provides a series of simple steps to help you analyse an ECG trace.

Rhythm

The overall nature of the ECG trace can provide information about cardiac function in a variety of ways. Much information can be learned from a general inspection of the ECG signal, including the regularity of the SA node and determining the entirety of the signal. Some easy steps for to initial assessment of an ECG signal include:

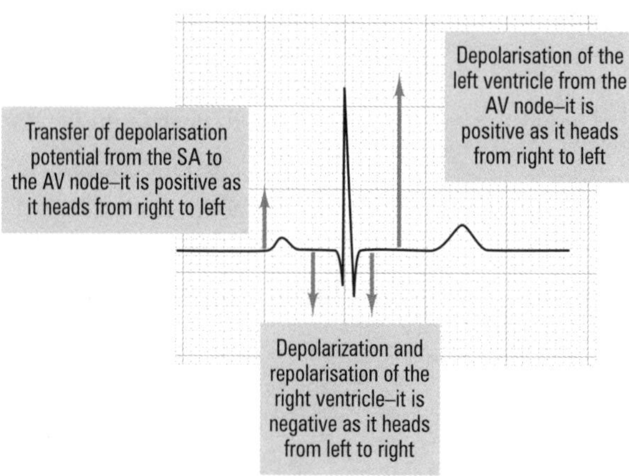

Fig. 29.11 How to identify in which direction the cardiac electrical signal is travelling.

- **Measure the R–R (spike-to-spike) interval** across the entire 6-second strip and determine if it is regular. If all R–R intervals are equal, then the heart rate is regular.

- **Observe whether there are any half beats or double beats that differ from a typical heartbeat.** These may be false beats or the start of a signal outside the cardiac conduction system. These are called ectopic beats.

- **Calculate the heart rate.** Heart rate can simply be calculated from an ECG signal print-out by measuring the number of QRS complexes that occur over time (6 s or 10 s strip) and multiplying this out to determine the number of beats across 60 seconds (see Fig. 29.9 above for an explanation of the timescale of ECG paper).

Conduction of the signal through the atrium

The conduction of the signal through the atrium is very important in the cardiac cycle as it details the path of the signal from the SA node to the AV node. Irregularities in atrium conduction may interfere with the contraction of the atria and reduce the filling of the ventricles. Some steps for simple assessment of atrial conduction are:

- **Determine whether a P wave is present** for each QRS complex. Are there more P waves than QRS complexes?

- **Assess the P waves from lead II** to ensure that they are upright, rounded and last less than 0.12 seconds in duration.

- **Report whether any ectopic beats are present.** Or are there any strange-shaped P waves preceding them?

- **Describe what the area before the QRS complex looks like if there are no P waves.**

Important note – new ECG technology has integrated diagnostic software that allows automatic detection of cardiac abnormalities and arrhythmias that is fast and accurate. However, manual inspection and detection should still be performed on the ECG trace.

Assessing the function of the AV node

The AV node is very important in providing a time delay between the top and bottom chambers in the heart to compensate for the slower filling time of the ventricles. If there are abnormalities in the AV function, these may lead to reduced filling of the ventricles or loss of the electrical signal altogether. AV node function is observed by:

- **Measuring the PR interval.** Is the PR interval between 0.12 and 0.20 seconds?
- **Inspecting the PR interval over several heartbeats.** Measure to see if the PR interval is consistent over a period of time.
- **Determining whether there is a pattern in any changes in the PR interval and any visual ectopic beats.**

Conduction of signal across the ventricles

The most significant part of a heartbeat is the transmission of the electrical signal across the ventricles. The ventricles contain significant cardiac muscle mass and possess specialised nervous system cells to speed the signal from the AV node. The function of the cardiac system is largely determined by the function of the ventricles, given that they are responsible for the transport of blood into the circulatory system. Ventricle conduction and function can be assessed from an ECG trace using the following steps:

- **Measure the duration of the QRS complex.** Is the duration between 0.06 and 0.10 seconds? Long durations may indicate specific forms of arrhythmias and require medical consultation.
- **Inspect the PR interval over several heartbeats.** Measure to see if the PR interval is consistent over a period of time.
- **Assess whether all QRS complexes are similar in shape and amplitude.**
- **Determine whether there are any QRS complexes that are irregular in duration or configuration.**
- **Assess whether there is any ST elevation or depression.** To determine the nature of the ST segment, look at the slope of the ECG signal between the S and T waves. If the signal is lower at the S than at the T, this displays ST segment elevation. If the amplitude of the signal at the T wave is lower, then this is known as ST segment depression (>1.0 mV suggests ischaemia of cardiac muscle). If so, describe the nature of it across the test and determine whether further medical consultation is required (>2 mV). Check all leads because, if a few demonstrate similar ST characteristics, there is strong evidence about the severity of the ischaemia.
- **Inspect the T waves for shape and regularity** following the QRS complex.
- **Measure the QT interval** and report if it is outside its normal range (0.36–0.44 s).

Text reference

Thompson, W.R., Gordon, N.F. and Pescatello, L.S. (2010) *ACSM's Guidelines for Exercise Testing and Prescription.* Lippincott Williams Wilkins, Philadelphia.

Sources for further study

Crimando, J. (1999) *EKG Quizzer 1.* Available: http://www.gwc.maricopa.edu/class/bio202/cyberheart/ekgqzr.htm.
Last accessed: 23/12/10.
[A resource that helps test your ECG knowledge.]

Hampton, J.R. (2008) *The ECG Made Easy.* Churchill, Livingstone, Elsevier, Edinburgh.

30 Testing pulmonary function

Definitions

Exhalation – reduction of chest cavity to force air out of the lungs.

Inhalation – expansion of chest cavity to draw air into the lungs.

Obstructive – type of disease that reduces the ability to exhale air from the lungs.

Pulmonary – relating to the lungs.

Restrictive – type of disease that reduces the ability to inhale air into the lungs.

Spirometry – monitoring of respiratory movements and pulmonary function.

Tidal breath – one movement of air through an inspiration and expiration cycle.

Total lung capacity (TLC) – the maximum volume of air that can be displaced into the lungs.

Ventilation – movement of air into and out of the lung.

Maximal voluntary ventilation (MVV) – the volume of air that is able to be passed through the lungs during one minute of maximal intensity ventilation.

Vital capacity (VC) – the volume of air that is displaced in the lungs as a result of a maximal inhalation followed by a maximal exhalation.

Forced vital capacity (FVC) – the volume of air that is displaced in the lungs as a result of a *maximal* inhalation followed by a *maximal* exhalation that is expelled as hard as possible.

Slow vital capacity (SVC) – the volume of air that is displaced in the lungs as a result of a *maximal* inhalation followed by a *maximal* exhalation that is expelled very slowly.

Residual volume (RV) – the volume of air that remains in the lungs after a maximal exhalation. This volume helps to prevent the lungs from collapsing.

Expiratory reserve volume (ERV) – the volume of gas that is expelled between the end of a tidal breath and the residual volume.

Tidal volume (TV) – the volume of air that is displaced during an inhalation and exhalation cycle at rest.

(continued)

The practice of assessing pulmonary function by spirometry testing is an important skill for a sport and exercise science student to learn because of its importance in pre-exercise screening and health management. In particular, spirometry testing is useful to identify people that have decreased lung function, which may limit their ability to be active. Spirometry testing is strongly recommended for people that report having difficulty breathing (dyspnoea), a continued cough or wheeze, and/or report excessive production of mucus. Also, all smokers should undertake spirometry testing to assess the damage to their lungs. Lung function is related to an increased risk of lung cancer, heart attack, stroke and circulatory problems.

Pulmonary diseases typically affect the physical structure of the respiratory system, and reduce the ability of an individual either to inhale or exhale during exercise. Restrictive diseases are not common and they substantially limit pulmonary function by reducing the elasticity of the lung tissue. Restrictive diseases include cystic fibrosis and pulmonary fibrosis. On the other hand, obstructive diseases reduce the ability to void air from the lungs completely or quickly, typically by blocking pulmonary air tubes. Obstructive diseases are more common and many well known diseases fit into this category, including bronchitis, emphysema and asthma. Testing pulmonary function before exercise sessions may help to guide the preventative steps that minimise any episode of pulmonary dysfunction.

KEY POINT Spirometry testing should form part of the initial health screening of an individual (see Chapter 27). While spirometry alone may not assess whether a subject has a pulmonary disease, it can identify issues and the likelihood of a disease. You should refer any individual suspected of having pulmonary disease to a medical practitioner.

This chapter outlines the practices of initial pulmonary testing and analysis that form part of the practical training in health screening for exercise within a degree course. An ability to perform and interpret basic pulmonary tests is important when dealing with persons that may display pulmonary abnormalities. Such tests may also need to be performed before exercise in pulmonary patients, to assess their readiness to exercise or to gauge medication dosage.

Spirometry testing equipment

Various types of equipment are used to perform spirometry testing in the field or laboratory. The development of new technology has seen spirometers become smaller, digital and more accurate than traditional mechanical spirometers.

There are two main types of spirometers (Fig. 30.1):

1. **Volume-displacement spirometers** – these directly measure the volume of air displaced during ventilation. While these provide information on pulmonary volumes, they provide limited data on the speed of air movement.

Definitions (*continued*)

Inspiratory reserve volume (IRV) – the volume of gas that is inhaled in addition to a tidal breath until total lung capacity is reached.

FEV_1 – the volume of air that can be exhaled from the lungs in the first second of a maximal exhalation.

$FEV_1\%$ – the relative volume of FEV_1 when compared to FVC volume.

Functional residual capacity (FRC) – volume of air within the lungs at the end of a tidal breath.

2. **Flow-sensing spirometers** – these measure the rate of air flow through a tube that has a consistent resistance to air flow. This second type of spirometer provides more useful and in-depth diagnostic information.

Regardless of which spirometer is used, the interpretation of spirometry testing follows a consistent procedure. Spirometers may either simply produce a peak expiratory flow rate (PEFR) or plot a graphical representation of ventilation, either as a volume–time or a flow rate–volume trace (Fig. 30.4). It is also important that the test values taken from spirometry equipment are corrected for changes in gas volume due to temperature and humidity influences (Box 30.1).

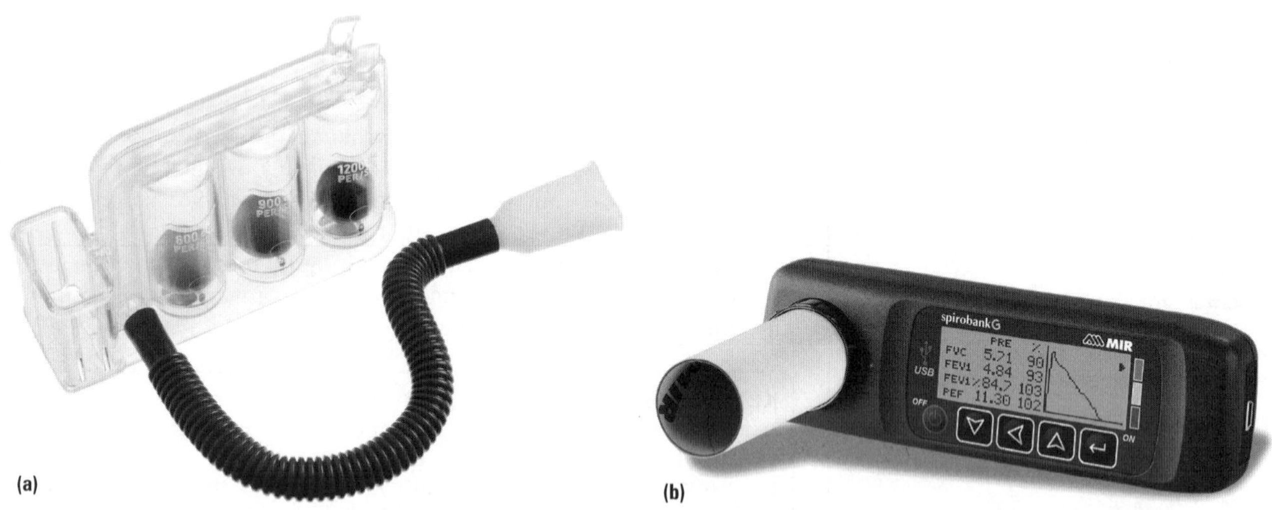

Fig. 30.1 An example of a dry volume-displacement (**a**) and a turbine flow-sensing (**b**) spirometer.
Source: **(a)** Science Photo Library Ltd. **(b)** Medical International Research.

Box 30.1 How to correct pulmonary function values for environmental variables

Tests of pulmonary function are based upon gas volumes that are either inspired into or expired from the lungs. However, gas volumes are open to influence from several environmental factors, such as temperature, humidity and pressure. Therefore, any results from spirometry tests need to be corrected for these variables to allow comparison of consistent volumes of gas under standardised conditions.

For pulmonary tests, the volume of interest is that within the lungs, therefore the figures need to be corrected to standard conditions within the lungs. When air is breathed out of the mouth it is open to external environmental influences and is characterised as 'ambient temperature and pressure, and saturated with water vapour' (ATPS), meaning that the volume of gas has been influenced by the outside temperature and the presence of moisture in the air. For pulmonary measures, it is converted to 'body temperature and pressure, saturated with water vapour' (BTPS).

The formula below details how to convert the gas volume from ATPS to BTPS.

$$V_{BTPS} = V_{ATPS}\frac{(273 + T_B)}{(273 + T_A)} \times \frac{(P_B - P_{H_2O_A})}{(P_B - 47)} \quad (30.1)$$

where

T_B = body temperature (°C);
T_A = ambient room temperature (°C);
P_B = laboratory barometric pressure (mm Hg);
$P_{H_2O_A}$ = partial pressure of water vapour at ambient room temperature (mm Hg).

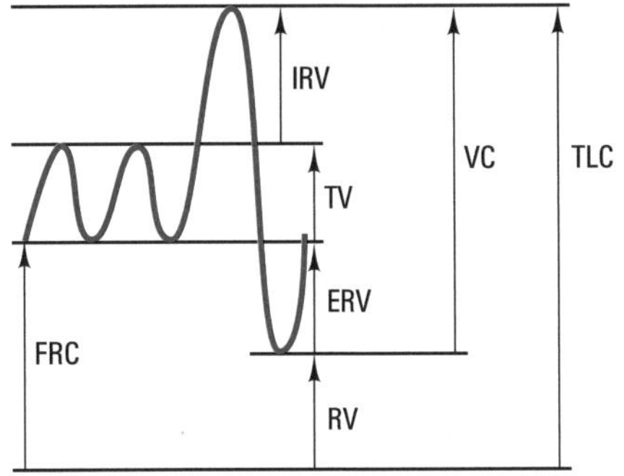

Fig. 30.2 The wide array of pulmonary terms used to monitor pulmonary function (see Definitions on pp. 211–2 for explanation).

Measuring pulmonary function

A wide range of measures is used to assess pulmonary function and describe the changes that occur in lung volume while breathing. A normal tidal breath operates at a considerably smaller volume than that capable by the pulmonary system. Therefore, while breathing at rest the body has considerable reserve volumes in the lungs for inspiration and expiration. To demonstrate this, Fig. 30.2 displays a spiromety trace for an individual that has completed two tidal breaths, which are then followed by a maximal inhalation and exhalation. Normative data for typical measures of pulmonary function are provided in Tables 30.1 and 30.2.

Table 30.1 Predicted peak expiratory flow rate (PEFR) values for females

Height (cm)	Female age (years)															
	8	10	15	20	25	30	35	40	45	50	55	60	65	70	75	80
91	103	139	195	207	214	218	219	216	211	202	191	176	158	137	113	86
99	119	155	211	224	231	234	235	233	227	218	207	192	174	153	129	102
107	136	173	228	241	248	252	252	250	245	236	224	210	192	171	147	119
114	155	192	247	260	267	271	271	269	263	255	243	228	210	189	165	138
122	175	212	267	280	287	291	291	289	284	275	263	248	231	210	186	158
130	197	233	289	302	308	312	313	310	305	296	285	270	252	231	207	180
137	220	256	312	324	331	335	336	333	328	319	307	293	275	254	230	203
145	244	280	336	348	355	359	360	357	352	343	331	317	299	278	254	227
152	269	305	361	374	380	384	385	382	377	368	357	342	324	303	279	252
160	295	332	387	400	407	411	411	409	404	395	383	368	351	330	306	278
168	323	360	415	428	435	439	439	437	431	423	411	396	378	358	333	306
175	353	389	445	457	464	468	469	466	461	452	440	426	408	387	363	336
183	383	419	475	488	495	498	499	497	491	483	471	456	438	417	393	366
191	415	451	507	520	526	530	531	528	523	514	503	488	470	449	425	398
198	448	484	540	553	559	563	564	562	556	547	536	521	503	482	458	431
206	482	519	574	587	594	598	598	596	590	582	570	555	537	516	492	465
213	518	554	610	623	630	633	634	632	626	617	606	591	573	552	528	501

Normative data taken from Hankinson *et al.* (1999).

Table 30.2 Predicted peak expiratory flow rate (PEFR) values for males

Height (cm)	Male age (years)															
	8	10	15	20	25	30	35	40	45	50	55	60	65	70	75	80
91	81	94	156	256	264	267	266	262	254	241	225	205	181	153	122	86
99	102	116	177	278	285	289	288	284	275	263	247	227	203	175	143	108
107	126	139	201	302	309	312	312	307	299	287	270	250	226	199	167	131
114	151	165	226	327	334	337	337	332	324	312	296	276	252	224	192	156
122	178	192	253	354	361	364	364	359	351	339	323	303	279	251	219	183
130	207	220	282	383	390	393	393	388	380	367	351	331	307	279	248	212
137	237	251	312	413	420	424	423	419	410	398	382	362	338	310	278	242
145	269	283	344	445	452	456	455	451	442	430	414	394	370	342	310	275
152	303	317	378	479	486	490	489	485	476	464	448	428	404	376	344	308
160	339	352	414	515	522	525	525	520	512	500	483	463	439	412	380	344
168	376	390	451	552	559	563	562	558	549	537	521	501	477	449	417	382
175	415	429	490	591	598	602	601	597	588	576	560	540	516	488	456	421
183	456	470	531	632	639	643	642	638	629	617	601	581	557	529	497	462
191	499	512	574	675	682	685	685	680	672	660	644	623	599	572	540	504
198	543	557	618	719	726	730	729	725	716	704	688	668	644	616	584	548
206	589	603	664	765	772	776	775	771	762	750	734	714	690	662	630	595
213	637	651	712	813	820	824	823	819	810	798	782	762	738	710	678	642

Normative data taken from Hankinson *et al.* (1999).

Mathematical estimation of pulmonary function

> **SAFETY NOTE** – during some pulmonary tests, subjects may suffer from dizziness owing to large changes in blood gases. You should always monitor the health of subjects while they are performing such tests and be aware of the appropriate treatment if required.

It is important to be able to calculate an individual's expected pulmonary function results. This quickly allows you to compare an individual's test results to a healthy individual of the same age, gender and height. When comparing results from pulmonary testing, three main factors influence the results, namely gender, height and age. More advanced and computerised spirometers are capable of providing calculated normative values. However, when using the simpler, more robust devices you will be required to calculate these yourself. The equations below allow an estimate of an individual's expected pulmonary function.

Women

$$\text{FVC (L)} = (0.0414 \times \text{height in cm}) - (0.0232 \times \text{age in years}) - 2.20 \quad (30.2)$$

$$\text{FEV}_1\ \text{(L)} = (0.0268 \times \text{height in cm}) - (0.0251 \times \text{age in years}) - 0.38 \quad (30.3)$$

$$\text{FEV}_1\% = (-0.2145 \times \text{height in cm}) - (0.1523 \times \text{age in years}) + 124.5 \quad (30.4)$$

$$\text{Maximal voluntary ventilation (MVV) (L min}^{-1}) = \text{FEV}_1 \times 35 \quad (30.5)$$

Men

$$\text{FVC (L)} = (0.0774 \times \text{height in cm}) - (0.0212 \times \text{age in years}) - 7.75 \quad (30.6)$$

$$\text{FEV}_1\text{(L)} = (0.0566 \times \text{height in cm}) - (0.0233 \times \text{age in years}) - 4.91 \quad (30.7)$$

$$\text{FEV}_1\% = (-0.1314 \times \text{height in cm}) - (0.1490 \times \text{age in years}) + 110.2 \quad (30.8)$$

$$\text{(MVV) (L min}^{-1}) = \text{FEV}_1 \times 35 \quad (30.9)$$

Methods of spirometry testing

Testing peak expiratory flow rate

A simple and commonly used field test of pulmonary function is the assessment of PEFR. PEFR meters are small plastic tubes that allow portable measures of pulmonary function. They can be used to assess readiness to exercise providing a measure of an individual's ability to expel air from the lungs. The results can be especially useful to help gauge the correct dose of medication. An example of a PEFR meter is shown in Fig. 30.3. PEFR meters are easy to use and provide a measure of the fastest rate of flow during a short, sharp exhalation. An individual may reuse the provided mouthpiece or disposable mouthpieces are available if there is more than one individual to assess.

To use the PEFR meter correctly, follow the instructions below.

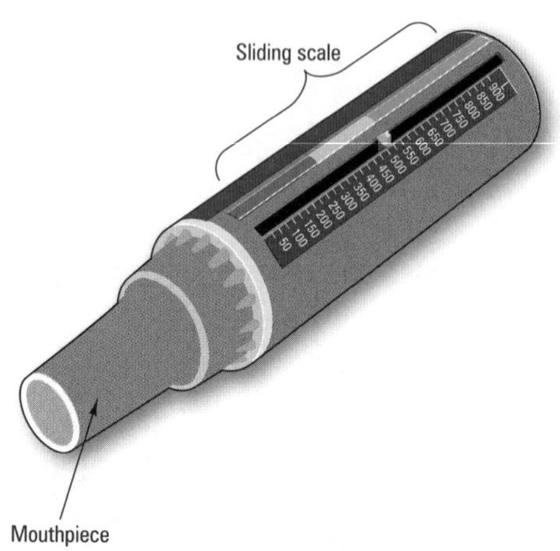

Fig. 30.3 An example of a typical peak expiratory flow rate (PEFR) meter.

1. **Record all the required subject information,** including age, height, mass and details of the last dose of medication.
2. **Insert a mouthpiece** in the hole located in the top of the PEFR meter.

SAFETY NOTE in spirometry testing the use of a mouthpiece by the subject causes a risk of cross-contamination of potentially biohazardous body fluids. All mouthpieces should be sterile before use and either disposed of or appropriately cleaned and resterilised (Chapter 25). Testers should wear gloves to minimise the risk of exposure to saliva. Following testing, all equipment should also be inspected and cleaned appropriately.

3. **Slide the needle back down to the bottom of the numbered scale**. This ensures that each test provides its own score rather than that of previous tests.
4. **Ensure that the subject is standing or sitting up straight.** This is to ensure that the lungs are completely filled. Rounding of the back or slumping can reduce lung volume, which will influence PEFR measures.
5. **Instruct the subject to hold the PEFR meter between two hands with the sliding scale on top.** They can then place the PEFR mouthpiece in their mouth, between their teeth while closing their lips around it. Make sure that they do not put their tongue inside the hole and ensure there are no obstructions at the opposite end of the device. Also ensure that they do not obstruct the movement of the scale pointer.
6. **Instruct the subject on the testing procedure.** The subject is to inhale as much air as possible, so as to fill their lungs completely. When full, the subject is to exhale as rapidly as they can, using a short, sharp breath.
7. **Record the value at which the needle stops** in the sliding scale. This will correspond to the subject's PEFR.
8. **Repeat steps 1–7 at least after a short break**, recording the maximal value. If there is a large difference between the two tests, perform a third test.
9. **Following this, compare the results with the normative values** provided in Tables 30.1 and 30.2. Be sure to use the norms of age and height variances correctly.

Testing forced vital capacity

Comparing the subject's data to a similar population for age and gender – when comparing to the normative values it is most likely that the data will not exactly match that of the participant. Try to select the closest category to the participant when selecting the comparative data.

The FVC test is a simple and commonly performed procedure to help measure exhalation speed and capacity. It consists of an individual completing a maximal inhalation following by a forceful and maximal exhalation of the lungs (until they are completely empty). Follow the simple instructions below to complete an FVC test.

1. **Instruct the subject to either stand or sit down.**
2. **Place the mouthpiece in the subject's mouth.** Make sure that the subject can seal the outside of the mouthpiece with their lips. Place a nose clip on the subject if possible.
3. **Ask the subject to breathe normally before the test.**
4. **Detail the instructions of the test to the subject.** On your command, they are to inhale as much air as they can and then, upon full inhalation, the subject should forcefully and rapidly exhale the air as quickly as possible until their lungs are completely empty.
5. **When ready, ask the subject to complete the test.**
6. **Make sure that the subject starts to breathe normally again after the test.**
7. **Remove the mouthpiece (and nose clip)** from the subject and, if necessary, clean appropriately.
8. **Interpret the spirometry trace** from an FVC test shown in Fig. 30.4.

Correct posture during the FVC test – ensure that the subject does not slouch while performing the pulmonary testing. Such changes in posture may change the values provided from the spirometry testing.

Testing slow vital capacity

The slow vital capacity (SVC) is used to measure the pulmonary volumes of an individual (such as the vital capacity (VC), inspiratory reserve volume (IRV), expiratory reserve volume (ERV) and tidal volume (TV), rather than flow rates (speed of exhalation). In contrast to an FVC test, which involves rapid breathing, an SVC test requires the subject to complete a slow and controlled maximal inhalation followed by a maximal exhalation. An SVC test is performed following the steps outlined below.

Monitor the balance of your subjects during spirometry testing – performing some spirometer tests may make some subjects feel dizzy or light-headed owing to the large changes in blood gases. Ensure that you or another person is in position to help the person during or after the test. Place a chair or bed close to the person so that they can quickly sit or lie down.

1. **Instruct the subject either to stand or sit down.**
2. **Place the mouthpiece in the subject's mouth.** Make sure that the subject can seal the outside of the mouthpiece with their lips. Place a nose clip on the subject if possible.
3. **Ask the subject to breathe normally before the test.**
4. **Detail the instructions of the test to the subject.** On your command, they are to complete at least two normal tidal breaths, before inhaling as much air as possible at a slow and consistent speed. Once the TLC is reached, the subject should then slowly exhale until the lungs are maximally emptied.
5. **When ready, ask the subject to complete the test.**
6. **Make sure that the subject starts to breathe normally again after the test.**
7. **Remove the mouthpiece (and nose clip)** from the subject and, if necessary, clean appropriately.
8. **Interpret the spirometry trace** from an FVC test shown in Fig. 30.5.

Testing maximal voluntary ventilation

Performing a maximal voluntary ventilation (MVV) test provides a dynamic assessment of pulmonary function, whereas the FVC and SVC tests provide only static information on flow rates or volumes. The MVV test aims to determine the maximum amount of air that can be breathed in one minute, which can help to identify respiratory muscle weaknesses. While it is quite an easy test to perform, subjects find it difficult to give maximal effort owing to the potential adverse health effects and high-intensity nature. The instructions for performing an MVV test are detailed below.

Obstructive diseases are identified by changes in expired ventilation speed.

Restrictive diseases are easily identified by reduced pulmonary volumes.

1. **Instruct the subject to stand up straight.**
2. **Place the mouthpiece in the subject's mouth.** Make sure that the subject can seal the outside of the mouthpiece with their lips. Place a nose clip on the subject if possible.
3. **Ask the subject to breathe normally before the test.**
4. **Detail the instructions of the test to the subject.** On your command, they are to breathe as fast as possible using rapid and deep breaths. They should continue this maximally for 15 seconds. The aim for the subject is to breathe in and out as much as possible during this time. Make sure that you tell the subject when the test is complete.

5. **When ready, ask the subject to complete the test.**
6. **Make sure that the subject starts to breathe normally again after the test.**
7. **Remove the mouthpiece (and nose clip)** from the subject and, if necessary, clean appropriately.
8. **Calculate the result of the test from the measured volume.** Multiply the measured volume of air by four to determine the volume of air that would have been inhaled and exhaled in one minute.

Evaluation and interpretation of pulmonary tests

Obstructive diseases and limitations are the most common pulmonary issues reported. As a result, it is important that you learn how to analyse the appropriate pulmonary test and report the appropriate measurements to determine exhalation ability. The interpretation of pulmonary tests is largely being able to identify standard flow and time measures that quantify pulmonary function. Tests used to determine maximal exhalation ability range from the use of a simple PEFR meter, which is a cheap and portable yet robust measure, through to the use of expensive and sensitive ventilometers. Detailed below are steps that will help you to interpret manually a range of flow and time measures from the spirometer tests mentioned above. More sophisticated equipment and software will automatically determine these measures for you.

Forced vital capacity (FVC) test

Completing FVC testing provides several diagnostic parameters.

Forced vital capacity (FVC)

- This is a measure of functional lung volume and helps to identify any diseases/disorders that may cause the effective lung volume to be smaller than normal.
- A reduced FVC may be present despite a 'normal' TLC, which does reduce its use as an accurate measure.
- FVC is measured as the total volume of air that is exhaled following a maximal inhalation (Fig. 30.4).
- Normative values are presented in Tables 30.1 and 30.2 for women and men.

Table 30.3 Normative values for spirometry parameters in healthy adult men and women

Spirometry measure	Men (20–30 years)	Women (20–30 years)
Total lung capacity (mL)	6000	4200
Vital capacity (mL)	4800	3200
Residual volume (mL)	1200	1000
Expiratory reserve volume (mL)	1200	800
Tidal volume (mL)	600	500
Inspiratory reserve volume (mL)	3000	1900
Functional residual capacity (mL)	2400	1800
Ratio of RV to TLC (%)	20	24

Normative data adapted from Miller *et al.* in McArdle *et al.* (2001).

Interpreting a spirometry trace – it is important that the first step in interpreting a spirometry trace is to recognise whether you have a flow–volume or a volume–time trace. To determine which trace you have, simply look at the variables on the *x* and *y* axes.

Forced expiratory volume in one second (FEV_1)

- This is a measure of the volume of air that can be rapidly exhaled during the first second of exhalation.
- FEV_1 identifies any obstructions in medium to large airways.
- FEV_1 is measured as the volume of air displaced after one second during an FVC test (Fig. 30.4).
- The relative percentage of the FEV_1 with respect to the FVC (FEV/FVC or FEV_1%) is between 75 and 85% in a normal population. Individuals suffering from obstructive diseases report a much lower FEV_1%.

Mid-maximal expiratory flow rate (MMEF)

- This is used to provide a sensitive measure of air flow during the middle half of the forced exhalation.
- MMEF identifies and is suggestive of smaller airway obstruction.
- It is calculated as the average flow rate between the middle 50% of the FVC volume.
- To perform this simply, identify the middle 50% of the FVC (25–75% FVC). Identify the time taken to exhale this 50% of the FVC. Then divide 50% of the FVC by the time taken to exhale this portion (Fig. 30.4).

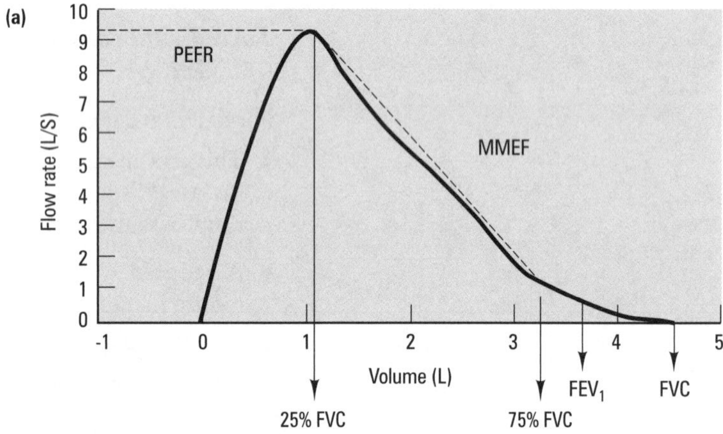

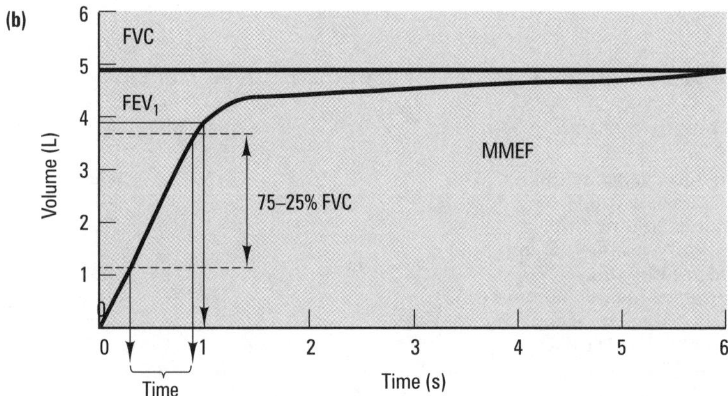

Fig. 30.4 An example of how to interpret the data from an FVC test, demonstrated on flow–volume (**a**) and volume–time (**b**) curves.

Slow vital capacity (SVC) test

Performing an SVC test provides useful information on pulmonary volumes rather than the speed of ventilation. From an SVC test, tidal volume, respiratory reserves and vital capacity measures can be gained. This helps to provide information that is not provided from an FVC test.

Slow vital capacity

- This is a measure of the functional volume of the lungs.
- SVC helps to identify if the subject has a reduced lung volume owing to either a reduced inspiratory or expiratory capacity.
- It is measured as the difference in volume between the point of maximal inhalation and maximal exhalation (Fig. 30.5).

Tidal volume

- This is the volume that is inhaled and exhaled at rest.
- Before completing the SVC test the subject performs two or three normal breaths that should be recorded by the spirometer.
- The tidal volume can simply be measured by determining the difference in volume between the resting exhalation (peak) and inhalation (trough) (Fig. 30.5).

Inspiratory reserve volume

- This is the volume of air that can be inspired after a tidal breath until maximal inspiratory volume is reached.
- IRV can be used to identify restrictive diseases and reduced TLC.
- It is measured as the difference between inspiration on a tidal breath (identified as a trough) and the lowest point on the graph (Fig. 30.5).

Expiratory reserve volume

- This is the volume of air that can be expired after a tidal breath until maximal expiration is reached.
- ERV can be used to identify obstructive diseases and reduced TLC.
- It is measured as the difference between the expiration on a tidal breath (identified as a peak) and the highest point on the graph (Fig 30.5).

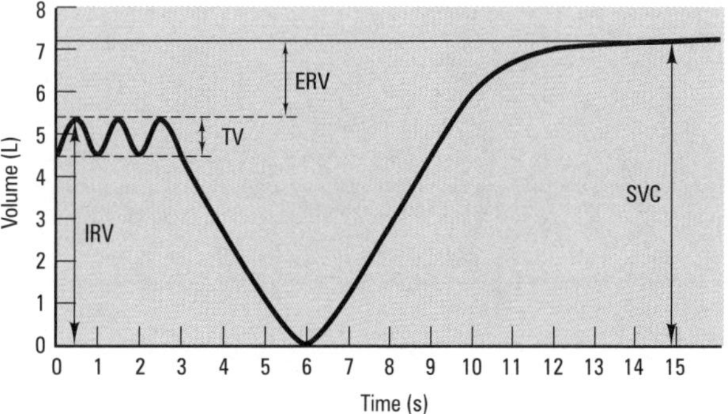

Fig. 30.5 An example of how to interpret the data from an SVC test from a volume–time curve (see definitions on pp. 211–2 for explanation).

Text references

Hankinson, J.L., Odencrantz, J.R., Fedan, K.B. (1999) Spirometric reference values from a sample of the general US population. *American Journal of Respiratory and Critical Care Medicine*, **159**, 179–87.

McArdle, W.D., McArdle, F.I. and Katch, V.L. (2009) *Exercise Physiology: Energy, Nutrition and Human Performance*. Lippincott, Williams and Wilkins, Baltimore, MD.

Spirxpert (2009) *Becoming an Expert in Spirometry*. Available: http://www.spirxpert.com/index.html Last accessed: 23/12/10.

Sources for further study

Franklin, B. A. (ed.) (2000) Clinical exercise testing. In: *ACSM's Guidelines for Exercise Testing and Prescription*, 6th edn, Lippincott, Williams and Wilkins, Baltimore, MD, Chapter 5.

Hyatt, R.R., Scanlan, P. and Nakamura, M. (2007) *Interpretation of Pulmonary Function Testing: A Practical Guide*, 3rd edn, Lippincott, Williams and Wilkins, Philadelphia.

Johns, D.P. and Pierce, R. (2007) *Pocket Guide to Spirometry*, 2nd edn, McGraw-Hill, Sydney.

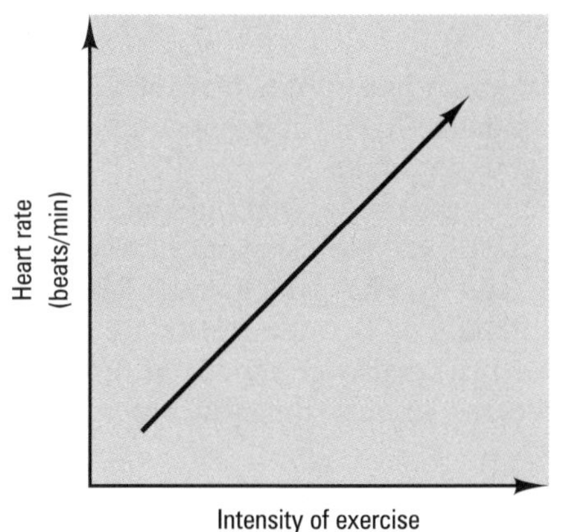

Fig. 31.1 Linear relationship between exercise intensity (e.g. speed) and heart rate.

The key components of any exercise programme for athletes or the general population include frequency, intensity and duration. Frequency (sessions per week) and duration (minutes per session) are easily measured. However, the quantification and regulation of intensity present the most challenging aspect of training programme design for the sport and exercise scientist. The American College of Sports Medicine (ACSM) suggests that the 'art' of exercise prescription is challenging because the variables reflecting exercise intensity are highly variable within individuals and are dependent on external factors such as level of fitness, overtraining, prior exercise, nutritional and hydration status, time of day, and the environmental temperature and conditions.

This chapter presents the more common methods of prescribing and regulating endurance exercise intensity in both the general population and athletes.

Percentage of maximum heart rate

Heart rate (beats min^{-1}) is the most accessible and easily measured method of measuring exercise intensity. The ability to use heart rate (HR) as a measure of endurance exercise intensity is based on the well known linear relationship between heart rate and endurance exercise intensity (Fig. 31.1).

Target heart rate training zones can be established in relation to either maximal heart rate (MHR) or HR reserve (HRR) (MHR – HRrest). MHR can be estimated using well stablished formulae such as those below or measured directly. For medical and practical reasons, estimation of MHR in the general population uses the classic prediction equation:

$$\text{MHR} = 220 - \text{age (years)} \qquad (31.1)$$

Various attempts have been made to improve the accuracy of this equation. Equations have been developed for men and women of various ages.

Resting heart rate (RHR) measurement should be:

- Taken first thing in the morning upon waking.
- Taken after being seated for five minutes.
- Based on the mean of three consecutive morning measures.

For males:

$$\text{MHR} = 203.9 - (0.812 \times \text{age}) + (0.276 \times \text{RHR}) - (0.084 \times \text{kg}) - (4.5 \times \text{SC}) \qquad (31.2)$$

For females:

$$\text{MHR} = 204.8 - (0.718 \times \text{age}) + (0.162 \times \text{RHR}) - (0.105 \times \text{kg}) - (6.2 \times \text{SC}) \qquad (31.3)$$

where MHR = maximal heart rate; RHR = resting heart rate; kg = body weight; SC = smoking code: 1 = smoker, 0 = non-smoker.

These equations allow for the fact that people with higher RHRs tend to have higher MHRs. Moreover, the same equations suggest that smokers and heavier people tend to have lower MHRs. For obese people with body fat greater than 30%, another equation has been developed:

$$\text{MHR} = 200 - (0.5 \times \text{age}) \qquad (31.4)$$

Table 31.1 Classification of endurance training intensities using % MHR

Classification	%MHR
Light aerobic	<75
Moderate aerobic	75–85
Heavy aerobic	85–90
Anaerobic threshold	90–92*
Maximal aerobic	>92*

*These training intensities are recommended for athletes, *not* the general population.

Table 31.2 Common medications and their effect on heart rate, ↓ = decrease, ↑ = increase, ↔ = no change

Beta-blockers	↓
Nitrates	↑ or ↔
Calcium channel blockers	↓ or ↔
Digitalis	↓ or ↔
Diuretics	↔
Vasodilators	
Non-adrenergic	↑ or ↔
ACE inhibitors	↔
Alpha-adrenergic blockers	↔
Antiarrhythmic agents	↑ or ↓ or ↔
Bronchodilators	↑ or ↓
Antilipaemic agents	↔
Psychotropic medications	
Antidepressants	↑ or ↔
Lithium	↔
Minor tranquillisers	↓
Major tranquillisers	↑ or ↔
Nicotine	↑ or ↔
Antihistamines	↔
Cold medications	↑ or ↔
Thyroid medications	↑
Alcohol	↔
Insulin and hypoglycaemic agents	↔
Anticoagulants and antiplatelets	↔
Antigout medications	↔
Anorexiants and diet pills	↑ or ↔

Source: ACSM (2010b).

Furthermore, another equation has been developed that has been shown to be more accurate than the 220 − age formula in estimating MHR:

$$\text{MHR} = 207 - (0.7 \times \text{age}) \pm 10 \qquad (31.5)$$

This equation was developed as research had shown that the 220 − age formula has been shown to underestimate MHR in people over 40 years of age and overestimate MHR in younger adults.

Even allowing for different types of exercise, ageing rates and different levels of health and fitness status, MHR has been shown to carry a large standard deviation of ±10 beats min^{-1}. The palpation of RHRs has shown a mean error of seven beats min^{-1}. Because RHRs are lowered with increased endurance fitness or increased over periods of detraining, target zones for using heart rates as exercise intensities need to be changed periodically.

MHR can also be directly measured in a laboratory or in the field. The laboratory is the most accurate method to measure MHR directly using ECG or telemetry during a maximal graded exercise test to exhaustion. In the field, a number of researchers have shown that performing two consecutive three-to-four-minute repeat maximal efforts (e.g. 800 m runs, 200–300 m swims) with a one-minute recovery in between will elicit MHR. Direct measurements should be made wearing a heart rate monitor as palpation has been shown to be highly inaccurate during high intensity exercise. Importantly, this type of field test should only be undertaken with well trained athletes. In triathletes, it should be noted that MHR while swimming is usually 12 beats min^{-1} lower than treadmill running, with cycling MHR 5–10 beats lower.

Once MHR is known, training heart rate zones can be developed as a percentage of maximal heart rate (Table 31.1). Importantly, particularly in non-athletes, there are many factors that affect training heart rates. These include apprehension, prior exercise, environmental temperature, stimulants, hydration status, overtraining, fitness level and use of medications (Table 31.2).

Percentage of maximum heart rate reserve

Another method of determining exercise training intensity is to use the heart rate reserve (HRR) method, sometimes known as the Karvonen method. The HRR is the most accurate method of establishing target heart rates for two reasons. First, research has shown that HRR accurately reflects the same person's $\dot{V}O_2$ reserve ($\dot{V}O_2R$). The direct linear relationship between % $\dot{V}O_2R$ and % HRR has been confirmed in a wide range of competitive athletes as well as clinical populations, including cardiac patients taking beta-blocker medication. The second advantage of using % HRR is that it takes into account RHR of different clients, which can vary over a wide range.

HRR is defined as the difference between MHR and RHR (Fig. 31.2). The ACSM recommends 60–90% of HRR as the appropriate exercise intensities for endurance exercise benefits. Thus:

$$\text{HRR} = \text{MHR} - \text{RHR} \qquad (31.6)$$

The Karvonen equation shows that:

$$\text{Target HR} = (\text{fractional intensity}) \times (\text{MHR} - \text{RHR}) + \text{RHR} \qquad (31.7)$$

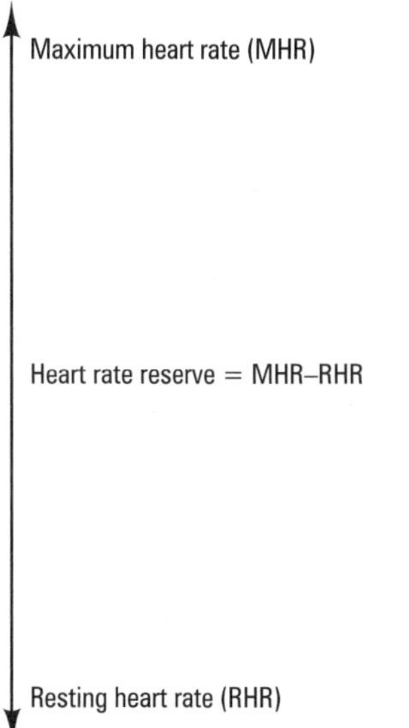

Fig. 31.2 Heart rate reserve shown as the difference between maximal heart rate (MHR) and resting heart rate (RHR).

Thus

$$\text{Lower training HR} = (0.6 \times \text{HRR}) + \text{RHR} \quad (31.8)$$

$$\text{Upper training HR} = (0.9 \times \text{HRR}) + \text{RHR} \quad (31.9)$$

Percentage of $\dot{V}O_2max$

Before 1998, the primary basis of accurately establishing exercise intensity was % $\dot{V}O_2max$. However, recent research has shown that the % $\dot{V}O_2max$ method has several disadvantages. Firstly, $\dot{V}O_2max$ has to be either directly measured or estimated. Secondly, it does not directly translate into % HRR units. This produces a discrepancy between % HRR and % $\dot{V}O_2max$ units that is most noticeable in unfit subjects exercising at low intensities. The final disadvantage is that it does not provide equivalent relative exercise intensities for people with different aerobic fitness levels. More recently, the measure % $\dot{V}O_2max$ reserve has been developed to overcome a number of these disadvantages.

Percentage of $\dot{V}O_2max$ reserve

This method is very useful for people whose HR is affected by medication or who have trouble monitoring HR. It has also been shown to be more related to other intensity measures such as HRR and rating of perceived exertion (RPE). There are three steps in establishing the target exercise intensity using this method:

1. Select the desired intensity in % $\dot{V}O_2R$ units.
2. Calculate the target $\dot{V}O_2$.
3. Convert the target $\dot{V}O_2$ to an exercise intensity (e.g. running speed) using the ACSM equations.

> **Definition**
>
> **$\dot{V}O_2$ reserve ($\dot{V}O_2R$)** is the range of oxygen consumption from rest to maximum; a percentage of this range is used to establish endurance exercise intensity.

Box 31.1 shows an example calculation to calculate a target $\dot{V}O_2$. Box 31. 2 shows a worked example of calculating the actual exercise intensity (e.g. running speed) based on the target $\dot{V}O_2$.

Ratings of perceived exertion

> **Using the 'talk test' can establish 'moderate' exercise intensity** – as a subject exercises, ask them 'Can you speak comfortably?' If they answer 'yes' then they are most likely below the anaerobic threshold. If they say 'no', they may be above the anaerobic threshold.

One of the more popular and easily used methods of prescribing and regulating exercise intensity is based on how hard the exercise feels. Well trained and experienced athletes can easily establish a pace that is easy, moderate or hard. Novice exercisers can also be taught over time to regulate or monitor their exercise intensity subjectively by using scales for rating their own perceived level of exertion.

While the 'talk test' can be used as a tool to measure intensity in beginner exercisers, the more popular and commonly used method of using perceived exertion to monitor exercise intensity is the use of the ratings of perceived exertion (RPE). Table 31.3 shows both the original 15-category, linear Borg scale (6–20) that is most widely used, as well as the newer "category-ratio" Borg scale (0–10).

The Borg scale (6–20) and the newer 'category-ratio' Borg scale (0–10) are most widely used. In the original scale, descriptors are associated with every second number. The original scale (6–20) was designed to

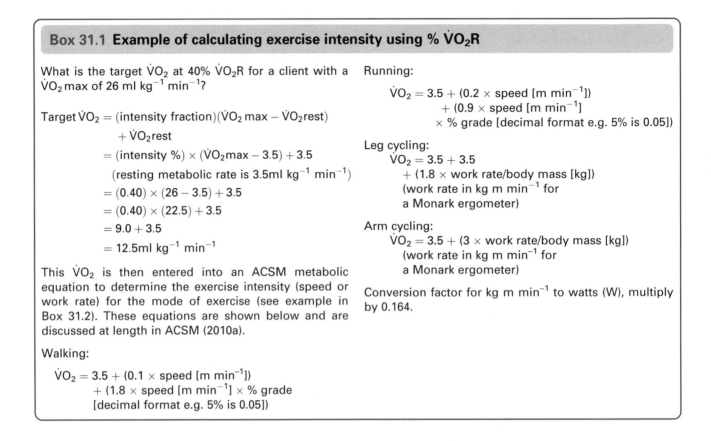

Box 31.1 Example of calculating exercise intensity using % $\dot{V}O_2R$

What is the target $\dot{V}O_2$ at 40% $\dot{V}O_2R$ for a client with a $\dot{V}O_2max$ of 26 ml kg^{-1} min^{-1}?

$$\text{Target } \dot{V}O_2 = (\text{intensity fraction})(\dot{V}O_2max - \dot{V}O_2rest) + \dot{V}O_2rest$$
$$= (\text{intensity } \%) \times (\dot{V}O_2max - 3.5) + 3.5$$
(resting metabolic rate is 3.5ml kg^{-1} min^{-1})
$$= (0.40) \times (26 - 3.5) + 3.5$$
$$= (0.40) \times (22.5) + 3.5$$
$$= 9.0 + 3.5$$
$$= 12.5\text{ml kg}^{-1}\text{ min}^{-1}$$

This $\dot{V}O_2$ is then entered into an ACSM metabolic equation to determine the exercise intensity (speed or work rate) for the mode of exercise (see example in Box 31.2). These equations are shown below and are discussed at length in ACSM (2010a).

Walking:

$\dot{V}O_2 = 3.5 + (0.1 \times \text{speed [m min}^{-1}])$
$+ (1.8 \times \text{speed [m min}^{-1}] \times \%\text{ grade}$
[decimal format e.g. 5% is 0.05])

Running:

$\dot{V}O_2 = 3.5 + (0.2 \times \text{speed [m min}^{-1}])$
$+ (0.9 \times \text{speed [m min}^{-1}]$
$\times$ % grade [decimal format e.g. 5% is 0.05])

Leg cycling:

$\dot{V}O_2 = 3.5 + 3.5$
$+ (1.8 \times \text{work rate/body mass [kg]})$
(work rate in kg m min^{-1} for
a Monark ergometer)

Arm cycling:

$\dot{V}O_2 = 3.5 + (3 \times \text{work rate/body mass [kg]})$
(work rate in kg m min^{-1} for
a Monark ergometer)

Conversion factor for kg m min^{-1} to watts (W), multiply by 0.164.

Box 31.2 Using metabolic calculations to determine running speed on a treadmill

Available data:

- Gender: Male
- Age: 32 years
- Weight: 59 kg
- $\dot{V}O_2max$: 54 ml kg^{-1} min^{-1}

Desired treadmill grade: 2.5%
Desired exercise intensity: 80%

1. Determine target $\dot{V}O_2$

$$\text{Target } \dot{V}O_2 = \text{desired } \% \times \dot{V}O_2max$$
$$= 0.80 \times 54 \text{ ml kg}^{-1}\text{ min}^{-1}$$
$$= 43.2 \text{ ml kg}^{-1}\text{ min}^{-1}$$

2. Determine treadmill speed

$$\dot{V}O_2 = 3.5 + (0.2 \times \text{speed}) + (0.9 \times \text{speed} \times \%\text{ grade})$$
$$43.2 \text{ ml kg}^{-1}\text{ min}^{-1} = 3.5 + (0.2 \times \text{speed}) + (0.9 \times \text{speed} \times 0.025)$$
$$39.7 = (0.2 \times \text{speed}) + (0.9 \times \text{speed} \times 0.025)$$
$$39.7 = (0.2 \times \text{speed}) + (0.0225 \times \text{speed})$$
$$39.7 = 0.2225 \times \text{speed}$$
$$178.4 \text{ m min}^{-1} = \text{speed}$$
$$178.4 \text{ m min}^{-1} = 10.7 \text{ km h}^{-1}$$

correspond to heart rates of 60–200 beats min^{-1} in young adults. However, the scale may be used by individuals of any age to rate their level of effort subjectively.

The RPE scale is very easy to use. After some basic instructions on what the numbers mean and the importance of being honest, the exerciser is asked 'How hard do you feel the exercise to be?' They then give a number from the RPE scale to indicate how the exercise feels to them at that moment.

Table 31.3 Perceived exertion category scales

15-Category RPE scale (Borg scale)		10-Category-ratio Borg scale	
Light intensity			
6	No exertion scale	0	Nothing at all
7	Extremely light	0.5	Very, very weak (just noticeable)
8			
9	Very light	1	Very weak
10		2	Weak (light)
11	Light	3	Moderate
Moderate intensity			
12		4	
13	Somewhat hard	5	Strong (heavy)
14		6	
15	Hard (heavy)	7	Very strong
16		8	
17	Very hard	9	
18		10	Very, very strong (almost maximal)
19	Extremely hard		
20	Maximal exertion		

The two Borg scales have been validated against a number of physiological measures, including $\dot{V}O_2R$, HRR and HR during incremental exercise (Table. 31.4). However, the ability of a client to exercise at the desired intensity subjectively is less certain. Thus, clients should be familiarised with the scales during an incremental test and the levels corresponding to the required exercise intensities should be pointed out and highlighted. In general, exercise between 'very light' and 'light' on the original RPE scale is suitable for warm-up, and exercise between 'somewhat hard' and 'heavy' has an effective endurance training effect.

The advantages of using RPE are:

- It is simple to use, takes minimal time and costs nothing.
- It has good correlations with other physiological measures of exercise intensity ($\dot{V}O_2$, HR and blood lactate).
- For people on medication, such as the elderly or those with chronic disease, it is better than using HR (Table 31.1) as a measure of exercise intensity.
- It teaches people to 'listen to their body' during exercise.

However, there are a number of problems in using RPE scales:

- It may not be accurate in children, the obese or the elderly. In children, a recent OMNI scale (1–10) that uses visual descriptors has been developed for use in cycling and walking/running (ACSM, 2010a).

Table 31.4 Classification of endurance training intensities for a general population

Intensity	% $\dot{V}O_2R$ or % heart rate reserve	% Maximal heart rate	RPE (6–20 scale)
Very light	<20	<50	<10
Light	20–39	60–63	10–11
Moderate	40–59	64–76	12–13
Hard (vigorous)	60–84	77–93	14–16
Very hard	≥85	≥94	17–19
Maximal	100	100	20

- Psychological factors and mood states can affect RPE responses. For example, extroverts tend to give low numbers while people with depression, neuroses or anxiety tend to give high numbers.
- RPE is less reliable at low versus high exercise intensities.
- Different exercise modes (e.g. cycling versus running) might give different RPE responses despite similar % $\dot{V}O_2max$ levels.
- RPEs tend to be higher in hot and humid conditions.
- RPE values in the laboratory tend to be different from those at the same intensity in the field.
- During longer duration exercise, the RPEs tend to be higher despite no change in % $\dot{V}O_2max$.

METs (metabolic equivalents)

In clinical settings, exercise intensity is often defined in METs, with one MET = 3.5 ml kg^{-1} min^{-1}. For example, an elderly participant might have had their exercise capacity measured on a treadmill in a laboratory and have a $\dot{V}O_2max$ of 28 ml kg^{-1} min^{-1}. This represents 8 METs.

METs are a useful and convenient way to describe intensity of a range of activities. Indeed, the ACSM and Centers for Disease Control and Prevention have recently released a joint update defining light physical activity as <3 METs, moderate activities as 3–6 METs, and vigorous activities as >6 METs. Table 31.5 gives some specific examples of activities from each of these 'training' zones. A more comprehensive list can be found within the *ACSM's Resource Manual for Guidelines for Exercise Testing and Prescription* (ACSM, 2010a).

Because MHR and $\dot{V}O_2max$ decline with age, sport and exercise scientists should understand that when older individuals exercise at the same MET level as a younger person, the older individual is exercising at

Table 31.5 MET values of common physical activities

Classification	METs
Light (<3 METs)	
Slow walking	2.0
Working at desk/bench	1.5
Ironing/food preparation	2.0–2.5
Fishing	2.5
Playing instruments	2.0–2.5
Moderate (3–6 METs)	
Brisk walking	5.0
Cleaning	3.0–3.5
Mowing	5.5
Dancing	4.5
Golf	4.3
Swimming (easy)	6.0
Vigorous (>6 METs)	
Hiking	6.0–8.0
Jogging	8.0–10.0
Running	11.5
Shovelling	8.5
Cross-country skiing	7.0–9.0
Swimming (hard)	8.0–11.0

Box 31.3 Example calculation to estimate target METs

What is the target MET level at 60% $\dot{V}O_2R$ for a subject with a $\dot{V}O_2max$ of 22 ml kg^{-1} min^{-1}?

1. $\dot{V}O_2max$ to METs = 22 ml kg^{-1} min^{-1}/3.5 ml kg^{-1} min^{-1} = 6.3 METs
2. Target METs = (Intensity fraction) × [($\dot{V}O_2$ max in METs) – 1 MET] + 1 MET

$$= (0.60) \times (6.3 - 1) + 1$$
$$= (0.60) \times (5.3) + 1$$
$$= 4.2 \text{ METs}$$

3. Consult Table 31.5 to identify activities with the appropriate MET intensity range.

Table 31.6 Classification of physical activity intensity using % MHR and METs

	Relative intensity	Absolute intensity across fitness levels			
Intensity	**% MHR**	**12 MET $\dot{V}O_2$max**	**10 MET $\dot{V}O_2$max**	**8 MET $\dot{V}O_2$max**	**6 MET $\dot{V}O_2$max**
Very light	<50	<3.2	<2.8	<2.4	<2.0
Light	50–63	3.2–5.3	2.8–4.5	2.4–3.7	2.0–3.0
Moderate	64–76	5.4–7.5	4.6–6.3	3.8–5.1	3.1–4.0
Hard	77–93	7.6–10.2	6.4–8.6	5.2–6.9	4.1–5.2
Very hard	≥94	≥10.3	≥8.7	≥7.0	≥5.3
Maximal	100	12	10	8	6

a higher percentage of their $\dot{V}O_2$max. Table 31.6 shows the approximate relationship between the relative and absolute intensities and various aerobic activities (6–12 METs).

Blood lactate concentration

Blood lactate is one of the most widely studied metabolites in sport and exercise science. However, it is also very difficult to interpret, as many factors affect its concentration, including previous exercise, timing of sampling, nutritional status, sampling errors and environmental temperature. Thus, its sensitivity as a measure of exercise intensity might be questioned, especially in the field where variables are hard to control. Its measurement is also relatively costly, requires technical expertise and equipment, and requires multiple assays to be made to increase accuracy of measurement. Moreover, an additional constraint is related to hygiene. Blood samples taken from fingertips or earlobes (Chapter 28) require tissue (skin) damage and collection of body fluids, which increases the chance of transmission of bloodborne disease. While hygiene standards are in place for blood collection, the inconvenience of keeping items such as gloves and eyewear on hand, as well as chemicals for blood spills, increases the constraints of regularly using blood lactate measures, especially in the field.

While the precision offered by direct measures of blood lactate are appealing, the above obstacles may question the feasibility of using such measures.

Chapter 43 outlines many of the commonly used blood lactate thresholds used in the prescribing and monitoring of endurance training thresholds of elite athletes.

Text references

American College of Sports Medicine (2010a) *ACSM's Resource Manual for Guidelines for Exercise Testing and Prescription*, 6th edn, Lippincott Williams and Wilkins, Baltimore, MD.

American College of Sports Medicine (2010b) *ACSM's Guidelines for Exercise Testing and Prescription*, 8th edn. Lippincott Williams and Wilkins, Baltimore, MD.

Source for further study

Robertson, R. (2004) *Perceived Exertion for Practitioners*. Human Kinetics, Champaign, IL.

32 Measuring hydration status and body temperature

Definitions

Euhydration – normal state of body water content (absence of dehydration or hyperhydration).

Dehydration – a state of water loss sufficient to cause intravascular volume deficits leading to orthostatic symptoms.

Hyperhydration – a state of excess water content of the body.

Plasma osmolality – a measure of the concentration of substances such as sodium, chloride, potassium, urea and glucose in the blood.

Urine specific gravity – the density (mass per volume) of a urine sample compared to pure water.

Body water balance is the net difference between fluid intake and fluid loss. Large variations in fluid intake are controlled by the kidneys, which can produce more or less urine depending on changes in body water volumes.

The routes of water intake are gastrointestinal, from food and fluids consumed, and metabolic from biochemical reactions. The routes for water loss are the urinary system via the kidney (urine), the respiratory system via the lungs and respiratory tract (water vapour in breath), the skin (sweat) and the gastrointestinal system (faeces and vomit).

Minor changes in daily water balance are easily restored. However, exercise and environmental stress can dramatically alter the body's water balance, thermoregulatory mechanisms, sports performance and overall health. Thus, assessment of both hydration status and body temperature is an important skill for the sport and exercise science student to learn.

KEY POINT Hydration assessment techniques vary greatly in their applicability because of methodological limitations such as the circumstances for measurement (reliability), ease and cost of application (simplicity), sensitivity for detecting small changes in hydration status (accuracy) and the level of dehydration anticipated.

Hydration status

The techniques used by sport and exercise scientists to assess hydration status are summarised in Table 32.1.

Table 32.1 Summary of hydration assessment techniques

Technique	Advantages	Disadvantages
Complex markers		
Total body water (dilution)	Accurate, reliable, 'gold standard'	Complex procedure, expensive, needs baseline
Plasma osmolality	Accurate, reliable, 'gold standard'	Complex procedure, expensive, invasive
Simple markers		
Urine concentration	Easy, rapid, screening tool	Timing critical, subjective colour, many confounding factors
Body mass	Easy, rapid, screening tool	Confounded over time by changes in body composition
Other markers		
Plasma volume Plasma sodium Fluid balance hormones	No advantages over osmolality except plasma sodium as a marker of hyponatraemia	Complex procedures, expensive, invasive, many confounding factors
Bioimpedance	Easy, rapid	Requires an initial baseline measure, many confounding factors
Saliva (osmolality)	Easy, rapid	Highly variable, many confounding factors
Physical signs such as dizziness and headache	Easy, rapid	Too generalised, subjective
Thirst	Easy and reliable	Develops too late and quenched too soon

Total body water

Water balance can be measured by collecting fluid input and output data by measuring the dilution of trace amounts of an isotope (usually deuterium oxide, ^2H_2O). This method is thus seen as the 'gold standard' in the measurement of hydration status but is very complex, and requires expensive equipment and high levels of technical expertise.

In brief, a known volume and concentration of isotope is taken into the body and the concentration of the isotope is then determined in a sample of body fluid (blood or saliva) after the isotope has been equally distributed throughout the body fluids over a period of three to four hours. The unknown volume (total body water) is then calculated, based on the dilution factor between the concentration of the isotope in the starting liquid and the body fluid. That is:

$$[C_1]V_1 = [C_2]V_2 \tag{32.1}$$

where $[C_1]$ and $[C_2]$ are the initial and final concentrations of the isotope and V_1 and V_2 are their respective volumes.

The error of measuring total body water is as low as 1%, thus allowing measurement of very small changes in fluid status.

Plasma osmolality

Measuring plasma osmolality – this is typically carried out using an osmometer and must be measured directly after blood has been collected and centrifuged because plasma osmolality decreases with storage time (0.1–6.0 h) in cool laboratories, owing to changes in pH, dissolved CO_2, lactic acid concentration, and/or binding of electrolytes to proteins.

A second gold standard of hydration status involves the measurement of plasma osmolality. Plasma osmolality is usually controlled at a set point of ~285 mOsm·kg^{-1} and only varies by 1–2% in healthy, well hydrated individuals. Dehydration, especially when caused by large sweat losses due to exercise, removes relatively more water from body fluids than solutes. These solutes, e.g. sodium and chloride, therefore build up in the blood plasma. Plasma osmolality has been shown to increase by ~5 mOsm kg^{-1} for every ~2% loss of body mass due to sweating.

The gold standards of measuring hydration status discussed above are rarely used except in well controlled and costly research projects. They require methodological control, specialised equipment and analytical expertise. They are thus not practical for regular use in monitoring fluid status in normal subjects or in athletes.

Urine concentration

Intercultural differences in urine osmolality – these may exist because of genetic or dietary factors. For example, mean 24-h values from Germany are 860 mOsm·kg^{-1} but in Poland are 392 mOsm·kg^{-1}.

Urinary markers for dehydration include a reduced urine volume, a high urine specific gravity (USG), a high urine osmolality U_{Osm}, and a dark urinary colour (U_{Col}) (Fig. 32.1). As a screening tool to differentiate euhydration and dehydration, urine concentration as indicated by USG, U_{Osm} or U_{Col} is reliable and has definable thresholds (Table 32.2).

There are a number of confounding factors that affect urine concentration:

- Delayed changes in concentration with acute changes in body water content such as with heavy sweat losses or large intakes of fluid.
- Drink (e.g. sports drinks) concentrations can alter the above response.
- Dietary factors such as taking vitamin supplements or eating foods such as water melon that contain high volumes of water.

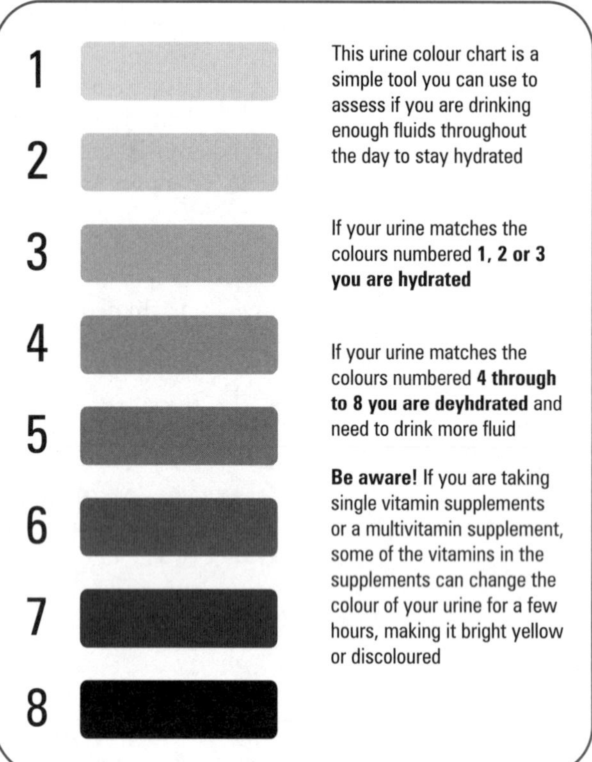

1
2
3
4
5
6
7
8
This urine colour chart is a simple tool you can use to assess if you are drinking enough fluids throughout the day to stay hydrated
If your urine matches the colours numbered **1, 2 or 3 you are hydrated**
If your urine matches the colours numbered **4 through to 8 you are deyhdrated** and need to drink more fluid
Be aware! If you are taking single vitamin supplements or a multivitamin supplement, some of the vitamins in the supplements can change the colour of your urine for a few hours, making it bright yellow or discoloured

Fig. 32.1 Urine colour chart for measuring hydration status. (Note that actual chart colour would be shades of yellow).

Table 32.2 Indices of hydration status

Hydration status	% Body weight change*	Urine colour#	Urine specific gravity†
Well hydrated	+1 to −1	1 or 2	<1.010
Minimal dehydration	−1 to −3	3 or 4	1.010–1.020
Significant dehydration	−4 to −5	5 or 6	1.020–1.030
Serious dehydration	>−5	>6	>1.030

*Body weight change = [(baseline body weight − assessed body weight) / baseline weight] × 100; #see Fig. 32.1; †see Fig. 32.3.

These factors can be controlled by using the first void (urination) of the morning after an overnight fast.

USG is commonly measured using *Multistix* reagent strips. These are plastic strips to which are fixed several separate reagents in different areas. The strips provide tests for glucose, bilirubin, ketone (acetoacetic acid), USG, blood, pH, protein, urobilinogen, nitrite and leukocytes in urine. The procedure for measuring urine specific gravity using *Multistix* reagent strips is shown in Box 32.1.

KEY POINT Analysis of urine specific gravity, osmolality and colour can reliably be used to distinguish euhydration from dehydration as long as the first void in the morning is used for measurement.

Box 32.1 How to measure urine specific gravity using *Multistix* reagent strips

1. **Wash hands and put on gloves and protective eyewear.**
2. **Check the expiry date on the *Multistix* reagent strip container.**
3. **Collect mid-stream urine sample.** The urine must be collected in a clean dry container and should be labelled with the patient's name, and date and time of collection. The sample should be tested within 45 seconds of collection. If not, the specimen should be refrigerated at 2–8°C immediately and returned to room temperature before testing.
4. **Open the reagent strip bottle** – *Multistix* reagent strips should be stored under 30°C. *Multistix* reagent strips are stable in the original capped vial until the listed expiration date on the vial. To avoid exposure to moisture, the vial must be closed immediately after removal of a strip.
5. **Remove a test strip from the bottle and replace the cap** (Fig. 32.2a).
6. **Mix urine specimen well immediately before testing.**
7. **Completely immerse the reagent areas** of the strip in the urine and remove immediately to avoid dissolving out reagents. While removing, run the edge of the strip against the rim of the urine container to remove the excess urine. Hold the strip in a horizontal position to prevent possible mixing of chemicals from adjacent reagent areas (Fig. 32.2b–c).
8. **Compare the reagent areas to the corresponding colour chart** on the bottle label at 45 seconds after immersion. Hold the strip close to the colour blocks and match carefully. Avoid laying the strip directly on the colour chart as this will result in the urine soiling the chart (e.g. Fig. 32.2d).
9. **Compare the colour of the USG test strip** with Fig. 32.3 to obtain a semi-quantitative measure of USG. (The grey shades in Figs. 32.2 and 32.3 represent the colours on the actual *Multitsix* text pack.)

Note: exposing the *Multistix* test strips to heat, light or moisture may cause deterioration of the strips and yield inaccurate results. Do not remove the strip from the bottle until immediately before it is to be used for testing. Do not touch areas of the reagent strip. Replace cap immediately and tightly after removing the reagent strip.

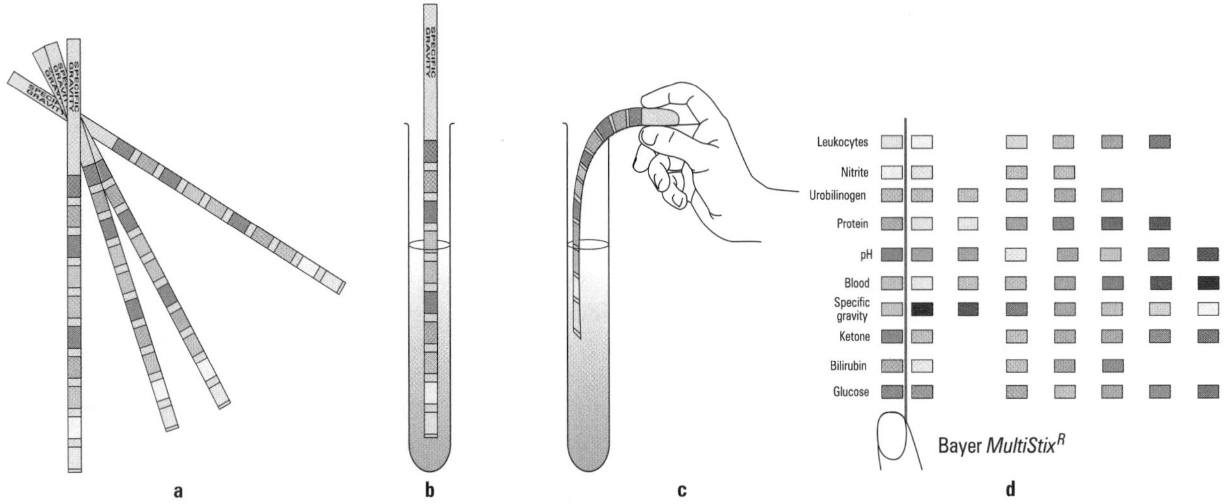

Fig. 32.2 *Multistix* procedures for semi-quantitatively measuring urine specific gravity (as described in Box 32.1).

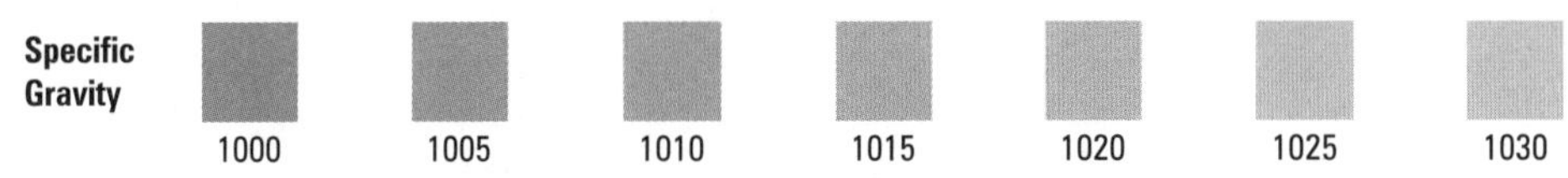

Fig. 32.3 *Multistix* colour chart for semi-quantitatively measuring urine specific gravity.

SAFETY NOTE Gloves and other personal protective equipment should be worn when handling urine for testing. Urine samples should be disposed of in appropriate biohazard containers.

Changes in body mass – this can vary in active people by up to 1% per day. This means that three consecutive measurements provide an accurate assessment of daily body mass variability.

Changes in posture – this can change plasma volume. Standing leads to a significant drop in plasma volume while lying increases plasma volume. Thus, standardising the posture is critical in measuring plasma volume changes.

Body mass (weight)

This is the most common method used in assessing rapid changes in hydration in both the laboratory and the field. Acute changes in hydration are calculated as the difference between pre- and post-exercise body mass. The level of dehydration is expressed as a percentage of starting body mass rather than as a percentage of total body water because the latter can vary widely.

This method assumes that 1 kg of body mass loss equals 1 L of fluid lost. As long as nude body weight (to account for sweat absorbed by clothing) is measured before and after exercise and fluid and food intake and loss (urine and faecal loss) is measured during exercise, the measurement of body mass is a valid and reliable measure of fluid changes in the body.

Other markers of hydration

Plasma volume, plasma sodium concentration and levels of the fluid regulatory hormones arginine-vasopressin and aldosterone can be used reliably as markers of changes in hydration status, providing that conditions such as exercise, temperature and posture are controlled. However, while plasma volume decreases proportionally with levels of dehydration, the change is lessened in heat-acclimatised athletes. Plasma volume changes (ΔPV) before and after exercise can be measured using the equation below:

$$\%\Delta PV = ([(Hb_{pre}/Hb_{post}) \times (100 - Hct_{post})/(100 - Hct_{pre})] - 1) \times 100 \quad (32.2)$$

where PV = plasma volume, Hb = haemoglobin, Hct = haematocrit.

Accurate measurement of haemoglobin and haematocrit requires control of posture, arm position, skin temperature and other factors to ensure that plasma volumes are not altered.

Plasma sodium concentration provides an alternative to measuring plasma osmolality because sodium is the main osmolyte in plasma. However, the relationship between hydration and plasma sodium concentration is more variable than the relationship between hydration and osmolality.

Measuring the fluid regulating hormones arginine-vasopressin and aldosterone is confounded by changes in these hormones with exercise and heat acclimatisation. Measurement also requires expensive and complicated analysis techniques as well as the need to sample blood. Thus, while blood markers all require blood sampling and some degree of complex analysis, plasma osmolality is the simplest, most accurate and reliable marker for monitoring changes in hydration status.

Bioelectrical impedance analysis is a non-invasive technique used to estimate total body water and body fat (Chapter 35). Briefly, it uses a low amperage current passed between skin electrodes and assumes that resistance to the current (impedance) varies inversely with tissue water and electrolyte content. It shows a strong positive correlation with total body water measures using the gold standard isotope dilution method under highly controlled conditions in euhydrated subjects. However, exercise, sweating, hydration strategies, spitting and heavy breathing, that all alter fluid status in athletes, significantly confound its accuracy, thus making it unacceptable for monitoring changes in hydration status in exercisers.

Table 32.3 Recommended hydration assessment index thresholds

Technique	Athlete practicality	Acceptable euhydration cut-off
Change in total body water (L)	Low	<2%
Plasma osmolality (mOsm kg^{-1})	Medium	<290
Urine specific gravity (g mL^{-1})	High	<1.020
Urine osmolality (mOsm kg^{-1})	High	<700
Urine colour (number)	High	<4
Change in body mass (kg)	High	<1%

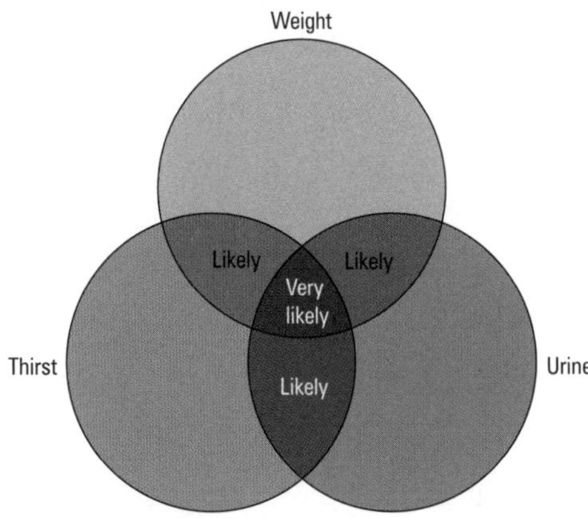

Fig. 32.4 When two or more simple markers (weight loss, thirst or dark urine) of dehydration are present, it is likely that you are dehydrated. If all three markers are present, dehydration is very likely.

Saliva osmolality and signs and symptoms of thirst and dehydration are only rarely used to monitor hydration. While salivary osmolality appears to track changes in hydration caused by sweating, there are wide inter individual responses of saliva osmolality to levels of hydration compared to urine or plasma osmolality. Moreover, food and fluid intakes and individual oral hygiene practices can alter saliva indices and thus affect results.

Clinical signs and symptoms of dehydration, including dizziness, headache and tachycardia (elevated heart rate), are too generalised to be of direct use in monitoring hydration status. Thirst develops only after dehydration is present and is alleviated before euhydration is reached.

Self-monitoring of hydration status

Fig. 32.4 combines three of the simple markers of hydration status (weight, urine and thirst) to identify whether dehydration is likely or very likely. By itself, no one marker provides evidence of dehydration, but the combination of two markers makes dehydration likely. The presence of three markers makes dehydration very likely.

Body temperature variations

1. Normal body temperature ranges from 36 to 37.5°C.
2. Body temperature is often 1°C lower in younger people.
3. Women usually have a higher body temperature then men owing to progesterone changes during ovulation, plus greater insulating body fat levels.
4. Exercise, emotional stress and cold morning temperatures can alter the normal range to 35–39.5°C.

Body temperature

Measuring body temperature is one of the oldest known diagnostic methods and can be an important sign of health or illness. In sport and exercise science, monitoring core body temperature (T_c) is widely used in student projects and in clinical settings to diagnose heat or cold injuries, including hypothermia, hyperthermia and heat stroke.

Oral temperature

Oral temperature (T_{oral}) is the most popular, least invasive and easily accessible method of measuring body temperature. However, T_{oral} is subject to changes in the environmental temperature, making the head and face cooler than the rest of the body. This may result in T_{oral} being lower than core body temperature (T_c). Box 32.2 explains how to measure oral temperature using either liquid (mercury- or alcohol-based) or digital thermometers.

SAFETY NOTE Glass oral thermometers are used less frequently and are being phased out because of their dangerous properties (glass breaking, toxicity of mercury). Plastic thermometers containing alcohol-based liquids are recommended.

Axilla temperature

When measuring underarm temperature (3–4 cm into the armpit), it takes longer for the thermometer to reach equilibrium than is the case with oral temperature. It is also less accurate compared to the rectum, mouth or tympanic membrane measures. It is generally much lower

Box 32.2 How to measure oral temperature

1. **Put on gloves** to prevent saliva contamination.
2. **If using a liquid-based thermometer, check that the level of the liquid column is below 35°C.** Hold the non-bulb end of the thermometer (Fig. 32.5) between the thumb and forefinger and shake it downwards by flicking the wrist.
3. **Explain the procedure to the subject.** Also ask them if they have been smoking or had hot foods or beverages recently. These factors increase oral cavity temperature. The subject needs to wait 30 minutes before another measure is taken.
4. **Insert the bulb end of the thermometer into the mouth** under the tongue. The subject closes their lips to prevent cooling by the ambient temperature.
5. **Remove the thermometer** after two to three minutes for a glass thermometer and 20 seconds for an electronic digital thermometer. Electronic digital thermometers will usually signal (beep or flash) completion.
6. **Wipe the thermometer with a tissue** to remove saliva and mucus. Discard the tissue to prevent contamination.
7. **Read the thermometer** at eye level by reading to the nearest 0.1°C.

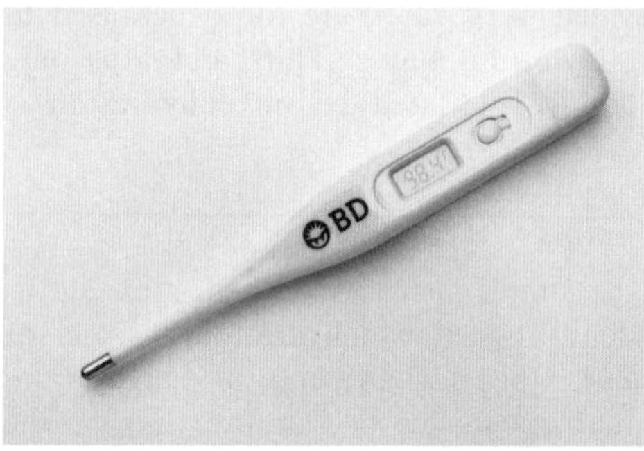

Fig. 32.5 Plastic digital oral thermometer.
Source: Science Photo Library Ltd. GIPHOTOSTOCK.

than core body temperature, particularly in athletes. It is thus not recommended.

Tympanic membrane temperature

The ear is easily accessible for measuring temperature. Probe (Fig. 32.6) placement and lack of skill on the part of the measurer are common issues. Ensure that the probe is placed deeply into the ear canal and held still until the device beeps to acquire reliable and valid results.

Skin temperature

While not a valid measure of core body temperature, skin temperature is widely measured in undergraduate practical classes and sport and exercise science research projects using skin thermistors at four sites:

1. chest – on pectoralis major;
2. arm – medial deltoid;
3. thigh – rectus femoris midway/midline;
4. shin – midway tibialis anterior.

Mean skin temperature (T_s) is calculated using the following formula:

$$\text{Mean } T_s = 0.3\,(\text{chest} + \text{arm}) + 0.2\,(\text{thigh} + \text{shin}) \qquad (32.3)$$

Rectal temperature

This location is considered the most practical and accurate measure of core body temperature. However, the method is highly invasive (3–4 cm into the rectum) and has a slow response time during rapid changes in core temperature compared to other measurement techniques such as oesophageal temperature. It is also very unhygienic and invasive, especially during exercise.

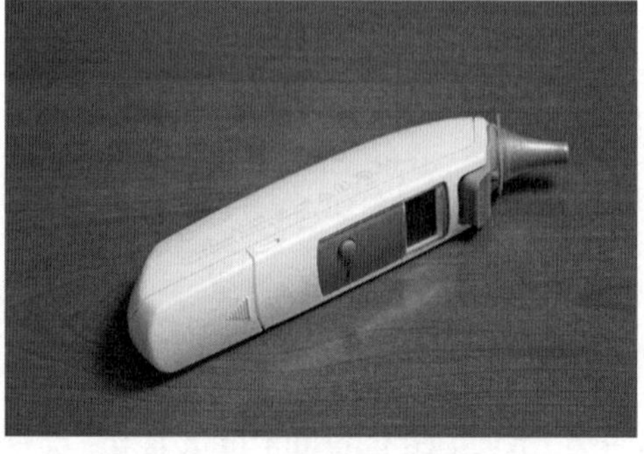

Fig. 32.6 Tympanic thermometer.
Source: Alamy Images: Peter Hudeck.

Oesophageal temperature

This method is preferred in sport and exercise science owing to its deep body location close to the aorta and rapid response time. However, it is highly invasive, with generalised discomfort caused by the insertion and placement of the sensors down the nasal passages. It requires expensive equipment and well trained personnel to operate and is rarely used by sport and exercise science students.

KEY POINT Temperature readings should be interpreted on an individual basis, with the same site and measurement device used consistently by the same tester.

Temperature pill telemetry system

This method is becoming more widely used in sport and exercise science research projects. The ingestible pill has been shown to give valid measures of core body temperature during rest, exercise and in different environmental conditions. The pill contains a sensor that transmits a continuous low frequency signal that varies with body temperature. The data values are collected by a data logger and downloaded to a computer for later analysis. However, the pills are passed through the system in a relatively short period of time, making long duration studies difficult. Moreover, the pills are expensive and collecting them after voiding is problematic.

Sources for further study

Armstrong, L.E. (2007) Assessing hydration status: the elusive gold standard. *Journal of the American College of Nutrition*, **26**, 575S–84S.

Cheuvront, S.N. and Sawka, M.N. (2005) Hydration assessment of athletes. *Sports Science Exchange*, **18**, 97.

King, R.F.G.J., Cooke, C., Carroll, S. and O'Hara, J. (2008) Estimating changes in hydration status from changes in body mass: considerations regarding metabolic water and glycogen storage. *Journal of Sports Sciences*, **26**, 1361–3.

Moran, D.S. and Mendal, L. (2002) Core temperature measurement: methods and current insights. *Sports Medicine*, **32**, 879–85.

Sund-Levander, M., Grodzinsky, E., Loyd, D. and Wahren, L.K. (2004) Errors in body temperature assessment related to individual variation, measuring technique and equipment. *International Journal of Nursing Practice*, **10**, 216–23.

33 Measuring flexibility

Definition

Flexibility – this refers to the range of motion around a joint and directly relates to the capacity of muscles to increase in length (the range of muscle length).

The ability to be flexible is an important physical attribute for any athlete, as it appears to be of particular importance in injury prevention and improved performance. The inability to move a joint freely through a wide range of motion can reduce efficiency through biomechanical changes, inhibit correct technique or increase the chance of injury, in particular by repetitive movement in sporting activities. Therefore, measures of flexibility should form a routine part of any initial athlete screening and should also be monitored across a season.

The assessment of flexibility can be extremely difficult to measure consistently for the range of motion across a joint in a consistent plane. Typically, goniometers (Fig. 33.1) are used to measure the degree of movement around a joint. Other tests of flexibility provide a broader indication of the range of motion around several joints and muscles, therefore not isolating any single joint. However, these gross tests are useful in assessing global measures of flexibility and possibly indicating the need for more specific assessment.

Measures of flexibility

Measurement equipment

Working without equipment – if a goniometer is unavailable, then simply take a photograph of the subject in the test position from an exact side-on view. To make things easy, place an adhesive marker on the anatomical landmarks that you are measuring between. The angle of the range of motion can then be simply measured from the photograph using a manual or electronic protractor.

The range of motion around a joint can simply be assessed using a number of methods, although it is most commonly performed using a goniometer or flexometer (Fig. 33.1).

A goniometer consists of two circular discs joined at the centre. Each disc has a straight arm attached to one side. The discs are marked for angular degrees and slide over each other to provide angular measures. The goniometer can simply be placed on the rotational axis of a joint with the arms aligned with skeletal landmarks (Box 33.1) on the surrounding limbs. This allows the tester to assess the range of motion around a joint in the degrees of movement that can be performed.

A flexometer consists of a 360° dial that is strapped to the body segment to be tested. A weighted pointer is located in the middle of the dial and is controlled by gravity. Other methods to assess flexibility can range from measuring the distance between landmarks with a measuring tape to using custom-built sit and reach boxes.

These pieces of equipment are easy to use and their accuracy relies on your ability to identify landmarks and standardise techniques. Some of the more simple tests that a sport and exercise science student should be aware of are included below.

Sit and reach test

The flexibility of the hamstrings and lower back is most commonly assessed using a sit and reach test. Despite its widespread use, the test is open to several limitations and may not provide a direct method to assess flexibility of these structures. The basis of the sit and reach test is to measure how far past their toes an individual can reach. However, this may be influenced by several other factors, including neural tension, anthropometric measures (e.g. upper body limb length) and flexibility of other body parts (e.g. calf). Despite these factors, the sit and reach test remains a commonly used test in exercise science and

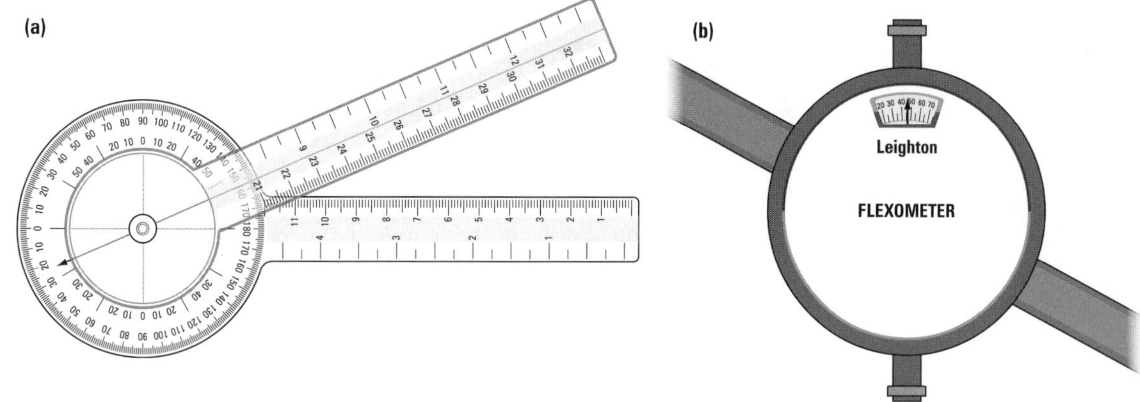

Fig. 33.1 Example of (**a**) goniometer and (**b**) flexometer.

should form part of the flexibility assessment taught in a sport and exercise science course.

To perform a sit and reach test to assess lower back and hamstring flexibility correctly, follow the steps below.

SAFETY NOTE Individuals who suffer from lower back pain or have suffered from serious back injuries during health screening (Chapter 27) should not take part in the sit and reach test owing to the strain that is placed on their lower back.

1. **Communicate to the athlete the requirements of the test.** Be sure to include any technique explanations that may be required.
2. **Ensure that the subject completes a suitable warm-up before completing the test**. This should incorporate a general warm-up on an ergometer and a range of selected static and dynamic stretches for the lower back and hamstrings.
3. **Request that, when ready, the subject sits on the floor in front of the sit and reach apparatus** (Fig. 33.2). The subject should then fully extend their legs and position themselves so that the soles of their bare feet are flat on the vertical surface of the vertical jump apparatus. They should sit up straight with their hips flexed at 90° (Fig. 33.2).

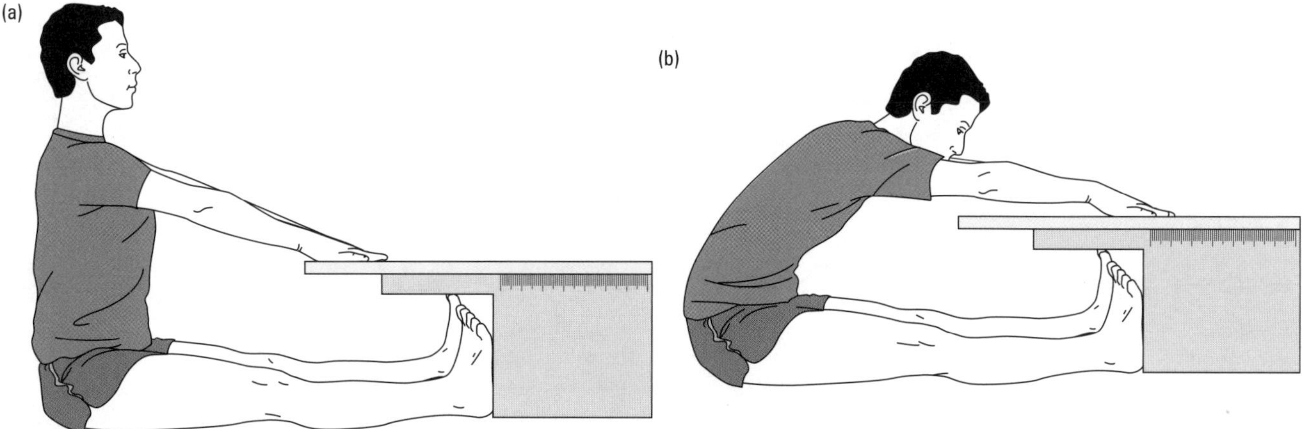

Fig. 33.2 Demonstration of the starting (**a**) and finishing (**b**) positions for the sit and reach test.

4. **Instruct the subject to perform submaximal practice stretches to reduce the risk of injury.** To complete a sit and reach stretch, one hand should be placed over the top of the other with the palms facing down, fingertips overlapping and fingers outstretched and the elbows straight as shown. The subject then leans forward as far as possible, sliding their hands along the slide ruler of the sit and reach box (Fig. 33.2). The subject should complete three incremental stretches, starting at 80% of maximum and increasing 5% at each stretch.
5. **Inform the subject that they need to complete at least three maximal attempts** at the sit and reach test. During the maximal attempts, it may be necessary for you to apply gentle pressure above the knees to ensure maximal leg extension is maintained. Full stretch should be held for at least two seconds to avoid the effect of bouncing. Ensure that the subject does not push the slide ruler during the test and that the movement is slow and controlled.
6. **Record the distance at which the fingers are located with respect to the toes at maximal extension.** If the fingers slide past the toes it is recorded as a positive score. If the fingers fall short of the toes or zero line, the score is recorded as a negative score. The best of three trials is recorded to the nearest 0.5 cm.
7. Compare the best value to the table of comparative data presented Table 33.1.

Thomas test

The Thomas test is an easy-to-perform assessment of hip flexor flexibility. The hip flexor group is made up of several muscles (psoas major, iliacus, pectineus, adductors longus and brevis, rectus femoris, tensor fasciae latae and sartorius). The Thomas test provides a passive measure of the range of motion of the hip joint as well as information on the range of muscle length, as detailed in Box 33.1.

Table 33.1 Comparative data for the sit and reach test distance (cm) for a normal population (where 0 equals fingers in line with feet. −3 : 7 represents a range of −3 cm to 7 cm)

	Age (yrs)					
Men	**15–19**	**20–29**	**30–39**	**40–49**	**50–59**	**60–69**
Excellent	≥13	≥14	≥12	≥9	≥9	≥7
Very good	8:12	8:13	7:11	3:8	2:8	−1:−6
Good	3:7	4:7	2:6	−2:2	−2:1	−6:−2
Fair	−2:−2	−1:−4	−3:1	−8:−3	−10:−3	−11:−5
Needs improvement	≤−3	≤−2	≤−4	≤−9	≤−11	≤−12
Women	**15–19**	**20–29**	**30–39**	**40–49**	**50–59**	**60–69**
Excellent	≥17	≥15	≥15	≥12	≥13	≥9
Very good	12:16	11:14	10:14	8:11	7:12	5:8
Good	8:16	7: 10	6:9	4:7	4:6	1:4
Fair	3:7	2:6	1:5	−1:3	−1:3	−3:0
Needs improvement	≤2	≤1	≤0	≤−2	≤−2	≤−4

The Canadian Physical Activity, Fitness & Lifestyle Approach (adapted from Heyward, 2006, p. 255).

Box 33.1 How to carry out a Thomas test

1. **Ask the subject to sit at the end of an examination bench.** The subject should sit so that their thighs are half off and half on the bench.
2. **Place one hand behind the subject's back and the other under their knee.** Flex the knee to draw the thigh towards the chest and instruct the subject to lie down. The thighs should move so that the knee is now at the end of the bench.
3. **Instruct the subject to grasp the thigh and gently pull towards the chest.** The subject should only provide enough tension so that the lower back flattens on the table. Check that the subject's lower back is flat by visually inspecting it and, if necessary, try to slide your hand underneath where the arch would normally form.
4. **Ask the subject to relax the leg that is hanging over the examination bench** (Fig. 33.3).
5. **Place the goniometer over the axis of rotation in the knee** and align one arm with the femur and the other with the tibial shaft. Measure and record the angle of passive knee flexion.
6. **Place the goniometer over the axis of rotation at the hip** and align one arm with the femur of the thigh and the other horizontal to the ground. Take note of whether the thigh lifts off the examination bench as this indicates whether hip extension is adequate. Measure and record the angle of passive hip extension.
7. **Compare the angles to those typical for a normal population for the test.** An angle of passive knee flexion of 80–90° is an indication that the length of the rectus femoris and tensor fascia lata is normal. The hip joint extension is around 10° in normal subjects.

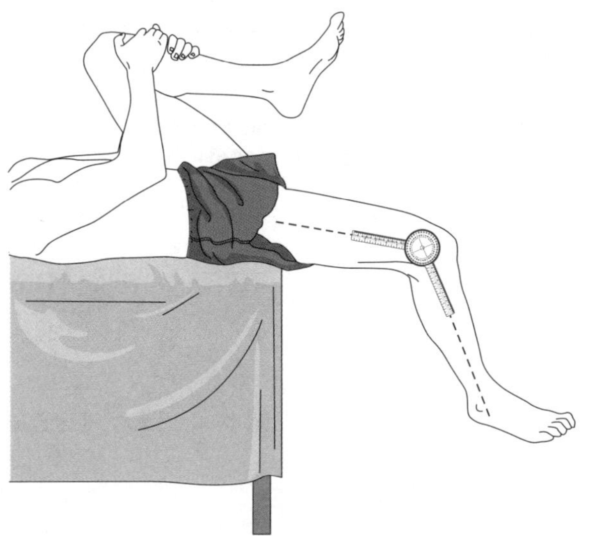

Fig. 33.3 An example of the position of the thigh when performing the Thomas test.

Straight leg raise

This test measures the range of muscle length in the hamstrings. It aims to control for the compounding variables that influence the range of motion assessed using other flexibility tests. The test also aims to control the position of the surrounding joints such as the hips and knees to isolate the change that can occur in the muscle length. The position of these joints needs to be standardised between tests. The procedure is described in Box 33.2.

Shoulder flexibility

Several methods are used to assess shoulder flexibility given the various dimensions in which the head of the arm can be moved. Therefore a range of tests has been developed to assess shoulder flexibility. The method presented in Box 33.3 is a simple method to determine gross movement within the shoulder and to identify any possible impingements.

Box 33.2 How to carry out a straight leg raise test

1. **Ask the subject to lie down on an examination bench or a floor mat.**
2. **Place the subject in the test position.** The subject should be lying supine with legs extended and lower back and sacrum flattened on the bench or floor beneath them. If the subject has tight hip flexors, then the lower back will be hyperextended and the range of the hip will be changed considerably, which will affect the hamstring range. This tightness can be overcome by placing a rolled up towel underneath the subject's lower back to stabilise the pelvis and manipulate it into a neutral position.
3. **Hold one thigh firmly on the ground** before asking the subject to raise the opposing leg in a fully extended position. The foot should be kept relaxed to avoid dorsiflexion (i.e. pulling of the foot upwards) and calf muscle activity, which influences the range of the hamstrings. Ensure that the hip remains in the neutral position.
4. **Place the goniometer over the axis of rotation at the hip** and align one arm with the femur of the thigh and the other horizontal to the torso. Measure and record the angle of hip flexion.
5. **Compare the angles to those typical for a normal population for the test.** An angle of hip flexion of around 80° is considered normal for the majority of subjects.

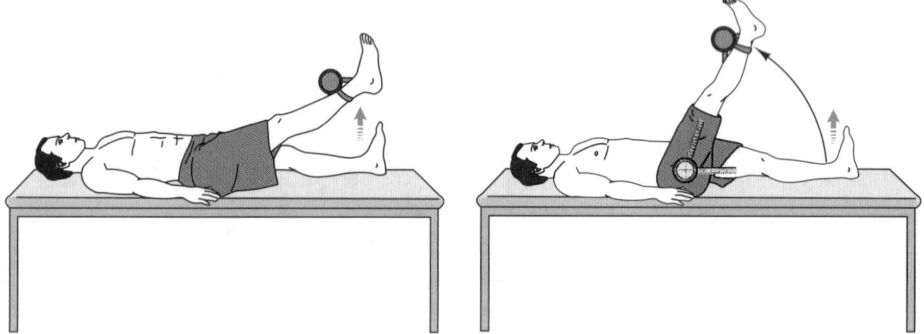

Fig. 33.4 An example of the start (**a**) and finish (**b**) positions of the straight leg raise test.

Box 33.3 How to carry out a shoulder flexibility test

1. **Ask the subject to stand clear of any objects.** To test the flexibility of their left shoulder, instruct them to raise the right arm in a straightened position (with no bending of the elbow).
2. **Instruct the subject to bend the right arm at the elbow** so that their hand falls down behind the head and rests between the shoulder blades. The upper arm should remain stationary for the rest of the test.
3. **Ask the subject to reach behind them with the left hand** so that their palm is facing out. Then instruct them to try to reach upwards so that the left hand is close to the fingers of the right hand.
4. **Measure the distance between the fingertips of the left and right hands.** Repeat the procedure three times on each side (Fig. 33.5).
5. **Rate shoulder flexibility using the scale in Table 33.2.**

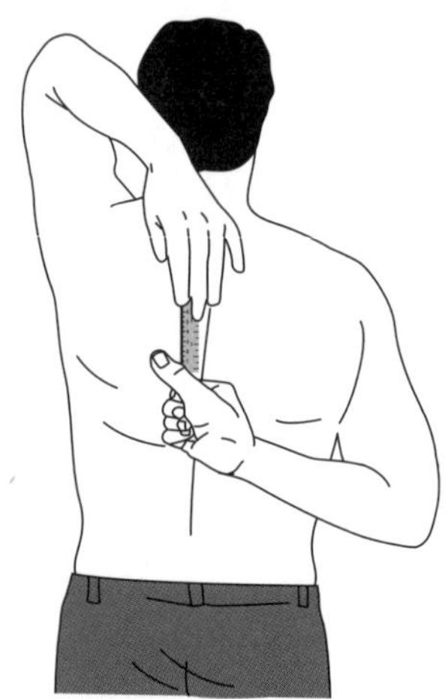

Fig. 33.5 An example of the measurement position for the shoulder flexibility test.

Table 33.2 Rating of shoulder flexibility

Rating	Description
Good	Fingertips of right and left hands touch
Fair	Fingertips are closer than 5 cm apart
Poor	Fingertips are further than 5 cm apart

Text reference

Heyward, V.H. (2006) *Assessing Muscular Fitness in Advanced Fitness Assessment and Exercise Prescription,* 5th edn, Human Kinetics, Champaign, IL.

Sources for further study

Kendall, F. P., McGreary, E.K., Provance, P.G., McIntyre Rogers, M. and Romani, W. A. (2000) *Muscles: Testing and Function, with Posture and Pair,* 5th edn, Lippincott, Williams and Wilkins, Baltimore, ML.

Top End Sports (2010) Flexibility Tests. Available: http://www.topendsports.com/testing/flex.htm. Last accessed: 23/12/10. [An excellent resource for a range of simple flexibility tests.]

34 Kinanthropometry

Restricted profile measures

- Body mass
- Height
- Skinfolds (8)
  1. Triceps
  2. Subscapular
  3. Biceps
  4. Iliac crest
  5. Supraspinale
  6. Abdominal
  7. Front thigh
  8. Medial calf
- Girths (5)
  1. Arm relaxed
  2. Arm flexed and tensed
  3. Waist (minimum)
  4. Gluteal (hips)
  5. Calf (maximum)
- Bone breadths (2)
  1. Humerus
  2. Femur

Full profile measures

- All restricted profile measures plus:
- Sitting height
- Extra girths (8)
  1. Head
  2. Neck
  3. Forearm (maximum)
  4. Wrist (distal styloids)
  5. Chest (mesosternale)
  6. Thigh (1 cm gluteal)
  7. Thigh (middle)
  8. Ankle (minimum)
- Bone breadths (5)
  1. Biacromial
  2. Bi-iliocristal
  3. Foot length
  4. Transverse chest
  5. Ant – post chest depth
- Lengths (8)
  1. Acromiale – radiale
  2. Radiale – stylion
  3. Midstylion-dactylion
  4. Iliospinale height
  5. Trochanterion height
  6. Trochanterion – tibiale laterale
  7. Tibiale laterale height
  8. Tibiale mediale–sphyrion tibiale

Kinanthropometry is the area of science concerned with the measurement of human body composition. The International Society for the Advancement of Kinanthropometry (ISAK) has developed international standards for body composition assessment and an international kinanthropometry accreditation scheme. The accreditation scheme is based on four levels:

- **Level 1:** designed for the majority of ISAK-accredited kinanthropometrists who have little requirement for more than the measurement of height, weight and skinfolds;
- **Level 2:** designed for those kinanthropometrists who wish to undertake a more comprehensive range of measures;
- **Level 3:** designed for those anthropometrists who wish to engage in the training and accreditation of levels 1 and 2 kinanthropometrists;
- **Level 4:** carries with it the responsibility to train and examine level 3 anthropometrists, as well as the right to train and examine the other two levels.

A key element is the objective maintenance of quality assurance by requiring that all levels have to meet an initial technical error of measurement (TEM), discussed in Chapter 19. This chapter presents an outline of the methods and procedures used and promoted by ISAK. Developing the skills and techniques in this chapter is critical for enabling the estimations of body composition used in Chapter 35.

The anthropometric profile

There are two ISAK 'profiles' for kinanthropometric assessment. The first is the restricted profile of 17 measurements (mass, height, eight skinfolds, five girths and two bone breadths) and the second is the full profile of 39 measurements (mass, height, sitting height, eight skinfolds, 13 girths, eight lengths and seven breadths).

The restricted profile measures allow the computation of somatotype (body type – ectomorphy, mesomorphy or endomorphy), relative body fat (using a small number of prediction equations), body surface area, body mass index, fat patterning and waist-to-hip ratio. Somatotyping will not be discussed in this text as the authors feel it is a branch of sport and exercise science rarely used in modern times. If students wish to read more on somatotyping, please refer to Norton and Olds (1996).

The full profile enables additional computations to be made, such as relative body fat (using a larger number of prediction equations) and calculations of bone, muscle adipose and residual masses as well as calculations of skeletal mass and skeletal muscle mass using various methods. In this chapter, the methods used to establish the restricted profile will be presented. For the full profile, refer to Marfell-Jones *et al.* (2007).

Landmarks

Landmarks are identifiable skeletal points which generally lie close to the body's surface and are the 'markers' that identify the exact location of a

Definitions

Ectomorphy – is the relative linearity or slenderness of a physique.

Mesomorphy – is the relative musculo-skeletal robustness of a physique.

Endomorphy – is the relative fatness of a physique.

measurement site, or from which a site is located. Landmarks are found by manual palpation or direct measurement. The measurer's fingernails should be kept trimmed.

- Locate the landmark with the thumb or index finger.
- Release the site to remove any skin distortion and then mark the skin with a fine-tipped felt or dermographic (e.g. eye-liner) pen with a small cross (+).
- Check the mark again to ensure there has been no skin displacement relative to the underlying bone.
- When landmarks are made using a measuring tape (e.g. abdominal landmark), the mark should be made at the top edge of the tape while the tape is held at right angles to the axis of the limb.

The landmarks used in the ISAK restricted profile are shown in Fig. 34.1.

KEY POINT All landmarks and measurements are taken on the right-hand side of the body unless the subject is an amputee or has a plaster cast. In such cases, a note is made on the data sheet that the measure was taken on the left-hand side of the body.

Skinfold measurement

Owing largely to the convenience with which skinfold calipers can be transported and the comparative ease in measuring subcutaneous fat, the use of skinfold data to estimate total body fat has become popular both in the field and laboratory. However, the apparent simplicity of skinfold measures is deceptive. Care in calibration of the calipers, location of sites and overall consistency in measurement are each essential for reliable measurements. The general technique for measuring skinfolds is:

1. **Before measuring, ensure that the caliper is calibrated** for distance between the blades and jaw tension. Ensure the indicator is on zero when the calipers are closed.
2. **Take all skinfold measurements on the right side of the body,** unless the subject is an amputee or has a plaster cast or medical problem. If so, note the problem.
3. **Ensure the skinfold site is located accurately** using the correct landmarks. Check that the near edge of the thumb and finger are in line with the marked site. The back of the hand should be facing the measurer.
4. **Ensure that the fold is under neither tension nor compression** at the point where it is to be measured. If in doubt about the presence of muscle tissue (unlikely) roll the fold slightly between the finger and thumb and/or have the subject make a voluntary contraction of the muscle involved and then relax the muscle.
5. **Apply the calipers.** The near edge of the constant tension calipers should be 1 cm from the fingers and at a point where the edges of the skinfold are parallel (a depth about equal to the thickness of the fold).

Box 34.1 How to locate the bony landmarks used for finding skinfold, girth and bone breadth sites

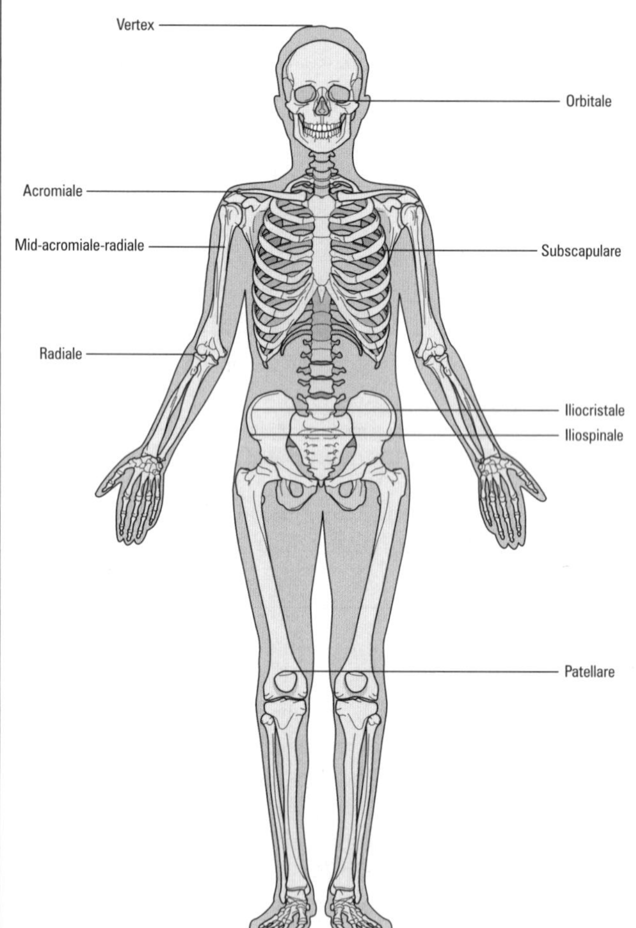

Fig. 34.1 Bony anatomical landmarks.

Vertex: the most superior point of the skull when the head is in the Frankfort plane (see Fig. 34.6).

Orbitale: the lower bony margin of the eye socket.

Acromiale: the point on the superior aspect of the most lateral part of the acromion border. Apply the straight edge of a pencil to the lateral and superior margin of the acromion. Palpate superiorly to the top margin of the acromion.

Mid-acromiale-radiale: midpoint of the straight line between the acromiale and radiale.

Radiale: the point at the proximal and lateral border of the head of the radius. Palpate downwards into the lateral dimple (space between the capitulum of the humerus and the head of the radius). The correct location can be checked by rotating the forearm, causing the head of the radius to rotate.

Iliocristale: the point on the iliac crest where a line drawn from the mid-axilla (middle of the armpit), on the longitudinal axis of the body, meets the ilium. Find the edge of the crest of the hip (ilium) by horizontal palpation with the fingertips. Draw a horizontal line at the level of the crest and a vertical line from the mid-axilla down the midline of the body. The landmark is the intersection of the two lines.

Iliospinale: the most inferior or undermost tip of the anterior superior iliac spine. Palpate the superior aspect of the ilium and follow it anteriorly until the anterior superior iliac spine is reached. On females the landmark might be lower on the trunk because of the flatter and broader shape of the female pelvis.

Patellare: the midpoint of the posterior superior border of the patella.

Subscapulare: the undermost tip of the inferior angle of the scapula (see Fig. 34.2).

6. **Hold the caliper at 90° to the skinfold site at all times** and grasp the skinfold the whole time the caliper is in contact with the skin.

7. **Record the measurement two seconds after the full pressure of the caliper is applied,** that is, the caliper trigger is fully released. With large skinfolds (e.g. thigh) the caliper needle may still be moving at the two-second point as adipose tissue is compressible. Regardless, the recording is still taken at two seconds.

8. **Repeat the measurement sequence twice after all skinfold measurements have been taken,** and take the median of the three readings. Readings that are the same after the first two readings need not be repeated a third time.

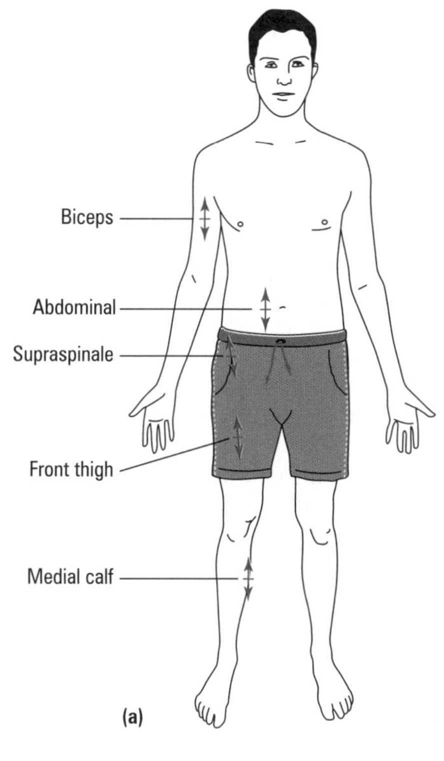

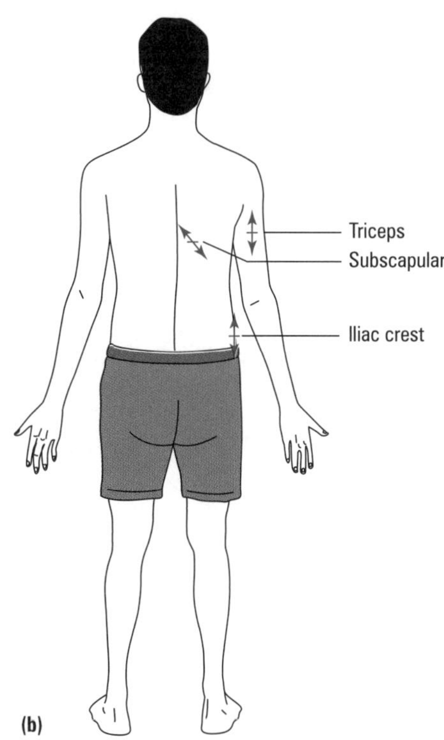

Fig. 34.2 How to locate anterior and posterior skinfold sites. Anterior view (a) and posterior view (b).

Triceps: this point (+) is located by projecting the mid-acromiale-radiale site perpendicularly to the long axis of the arm around to the back of the arm, and intersecting the projected line with a vertical line in the middle of the arm when viewed from behind.

Biceps: this point (+) is located by projecting the mid-acromiale-radiale site perpendicularly to the long axis of the arm around to the front of the arm, and intersecting the projected line with a vertical line in the middle of the arm when viewed from the front.

Subscapular: use a tape measure to locate the point 2 cm from the subscapulare in a line 45° laterally downward.

Abdominal: the point 5 cm horizontally to the right-hand side of the omphalion (midpoint of the navel). The skinfold is taken as a vertical fold.

Iliac crest: with the subject's right arm across their chest, the skinfold is raised superior to the iliocristale landmark. Place the left thumb on the iliocristale landmark and raise the skinfold between the thumb and index finger of the left hand. Once the skinfold has been raised, mark the centre with a cross (+). The fold runs downwards anteriorly as determined by the natural fold of the skin.

Supraspinale: the point at the intersection of (1) the line from the iliospinale landmark to the anterior axillary border (front of armpit) and (2) the horizontal line at the level of the iliocristale. The subject's arm can be abducted after the anterior axillary border has been identified. Use a tape measure.

Front thigh: the midpoint of the linear distance between the inguinal fold (natural fold in skin when the hip flexed) and the patellare. With the subject seated and right leg bent at a right angle, measure the distance along the midline of the thigh between the top of the patella (patellare) and the inguinal point (intersection of the natural crease nine inguinal fold) of the hip and the midline of the anterior thigh) and place a horizontal mark at that midpoint. Now draw a perpendicular line to intersect that line in the midline of the thigh.

Medial calf: the point on the most medial aspect of the calf at the level of the maximal girth with the subject in a standing position.

The skinfolds used in the ISAK restricted profile are described and shown in Fig. 34.2.

There are a number of factors which may reduce the accuracy of skinfold measures:

1. **Condition of subject** – skinfolds may vary with level of hydration. Exercise, showering, swimming or sauna will affect readings as heat leads to increased blood flow to skin and therefore increased thickness. Dehydration may also cause an increase in skinfold thickness owing to changes in skin turgidity (tenseness).
2. **Measurement sites** – these must be carefully described and accurately located for each measurement (Figs. 34.1 and 34.2). The positions in which the site is located and in which the measurement is made may differ. Check and follow the instructions carefully.
3. **Type of instrument** – constant pressure must be applied no matter what the thickness of the skinfold. Standard skinfold calipers are designed to exert a pressure of 10 g mm^{-2}. The instruments

recommended by ISAK are either the *Harpenden* or John Bull calipers (expensive but very sensitive and most accurate) or the *Slimguide* calipers (cheaper but not as sensitive) (Fig. 34.3).

4. **Taking the skinfold** – the skinfold should be pulled well clear of the underlying muscle using the flat pads of the index finger and thumb. If there is doubt about whether muscle is included, ask the subject to contract the underlying muscle.

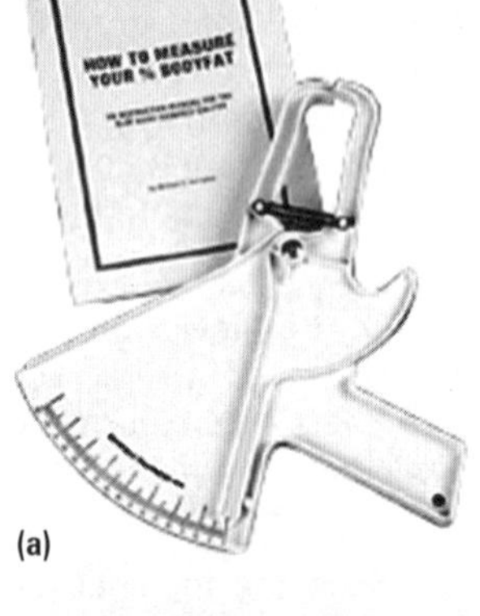

(a)

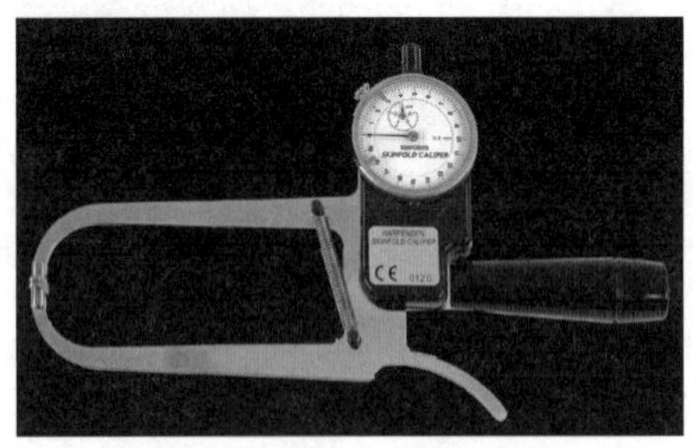

(b)

Fig. 34.3 ISAK recommended skinfold calipers. **(a)** *Slimguide* calipers; **(b)** *Harpenden* calipers.
Source: Fitness ASSIST.

Sum of skinfolds

It is now common practice to monitor body mass and sums of skinfolds of an athlete through the various training phases. While a number of skinfolds can be obtained (Fig. 34.2), the sites selected will depend on the needs of the sport scientist, coach and athlete. In Australian sporting academies and institutes of sport, the following seven skinfolds are taken on all athletes and are known as the 'sum of seven skinfolds':

- triceps
- subscapular
- biceps
- supraspinale
- abdominal
- front thigh
- medial calf

Normal values for elite Australian athletes' sum of seven skinfolds are shown in Table 34.1.

Historically, some athletes have also been profiled using skinfold totals of eight (sum of seven + iliac crest or axilla), nine (sum of seven + iliac crest + axilla) or ten (sum of seven + iliac crest + axilla + pectoral) sites. The sum of eight and nine skinfolds is suitable for both males and females, while the sum of ten is suitable for males only. For more detail on these profiles, see Norton *et al.* (2000).

Table 34.1 Sum of seven skinfolds (mm) for elite Australian male and female athletes (Norton *et al.*, 2000).

Sport	Discipline type	Female	Male
Athletics	Jumps	61.1 ± 12.7	37.3 ± 4.8
	Throws	95.3 ± 49.4	62.8 ± 1.9
	Sprint	60.3 ± 11.9	46.8 ± 5.4
	Middle distance	59.2 ± 19.6	42.0 ± 11.5
	Long distance	51.3 ± 8.8	50.1 ± 11.8
Basketball		70.5 ± 21.8	62.8 ± 19.2
Cricket		90.8 ± 19.7	69.1 ± 21.3
Cycling	Road	61.9 ± 12.0	51.2 ± 9.8
Hockey		87.4 ± 18.5	52.6 ± 15.5
Kayaking		83.1 ± 15.6	51.6 ± 12.4
Netball		83.4 ± 17.3	
Rowing	Lightweight	73.4 ± 13.4	41.6 ± 7.1
	Heavyweight	87.5 ± 17.8	59.7 ± 17.6
Swimming		80.4 ± 18.6	51.9 ± 10.9
Triathlon		73.1 ± 11.9	45.5 ± 7.8
Volleyball		90.5 ± 25.1	49.3 ± 12.0

Girth measurement

A girth measure is simply a circumference measure that results in a linear dimension (e.g. cm). Various equations, tables and nomograms are available to predict body fat using girth and/or skinfold measures and measures of height or weight (Chapter 35). Waist-to-hip girth ratios indicate fat distribution and high values been shown to be related to increased risk of cardiovascular disease, stroke, hypertension, diabetes, gallbladder disease and death. Indeed, waist circumference alone, because it is positively correlated with abdominal fat content, is now being used as a predictor of risk factors and morbidity.

KEY POINT All girth measures are taken perpendicular to the long axis of the limb or body segment.

The general technique for measuring girth is:

1. **Before measuring, ensure the girth tape is ISAK-recommended** (Fig. 34.4) and ideally has the zero point located 3–5 cm from the end of the tape to allow the measurer's fingers to grasp the end of the tape and not obscure the zero point.
2. **Hold the tape correctly.** It should be at right angles to the limb or body segment being measured. Keep the tension of the tape constant. This is achieved by ensuring there is no skin indentation but that the tape holds its place on the designated landmark.
3. **Locate the tape on the subject.** Hold the tape case in the right hand and the stub end of the tape in the left hand. Facing the body part being measured, pass the stub end around the back of the limb or trunk and take hold of the stub in the right hand that is holding both the casing and stub. The left hand is now free to adjust the tape to the correct level. Apply sufficient tension to the tape with the right hand to hold that position while the left hand reaches underneath the casing to hold the stub again. The tape is now round the part to be measured.
4. **Locate the tape at the landmark** using the middle fingers of both hands to orientate the tape and to ensure the zero point is easily read. Ensure the tape measure is perpendicular to the segment or limb axis.
5. **Make the measurement.** When reading the tape, keep your eyes at the same level as the tape to avoid parallax.

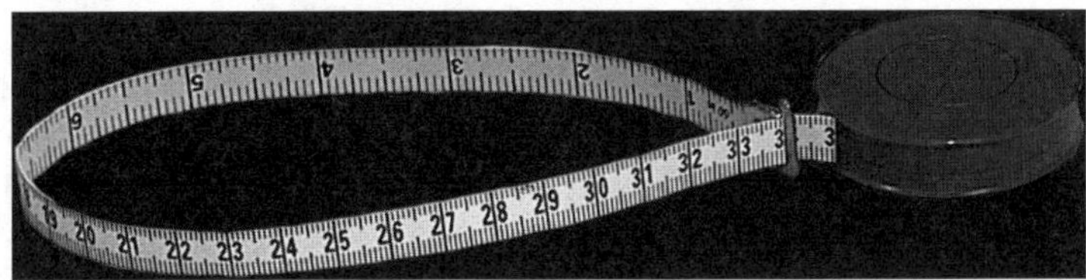

Fig. 34.4 ISAK, recommended girth tape.

Box 34.2 How to find location for bone girth and breadth measurements

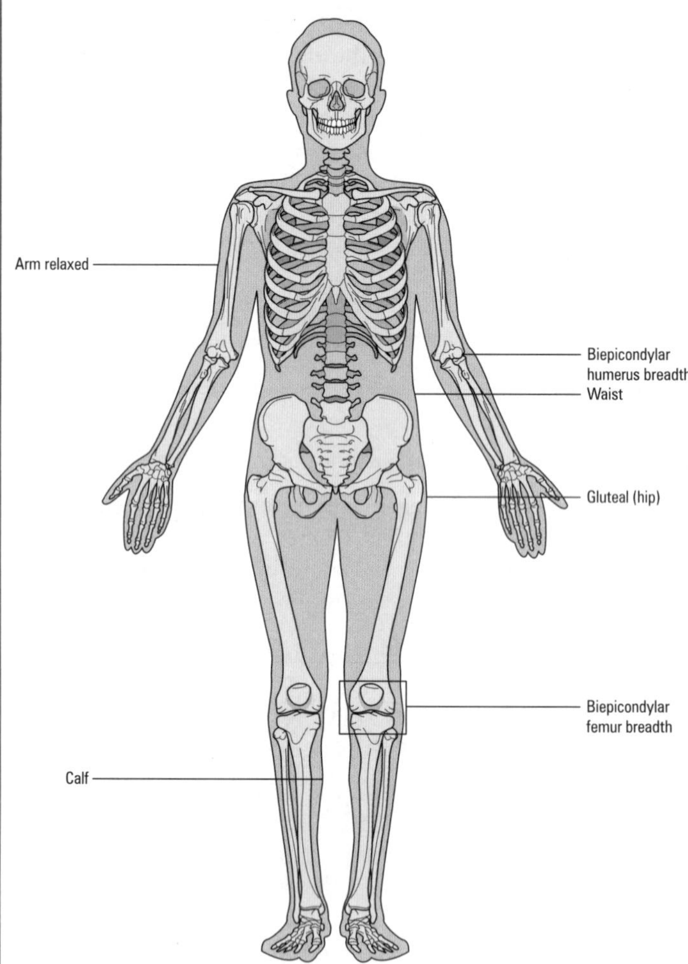

Fig. 34.5 Location of girth and breadth measurements.

Arm relaxed: the circumference of the arm at the level of the mid-acromiale-radiale site, perpendicular to the long axis of the arm with the subject's right arm relaxed but slightly abducted by the side.

Arm flexed (not shown): the circumference of the arm perpendicular to the long axis of the arm at the peak of the contracted biceps when the arm is raised anteriorly to the horizontal and the forearm flexed at about 45° to the humerus. The peak may not be at the mid-acromiale-radiale landmark.

Biepicondylar humerus breadth: the distance between the most lateral aspect of the lateral humeral epicondyle and the most medial aspect of the medial humeral epicondyle. The subject is standing or seated with the right arm raised anteriorly to the horizontal and the forearm flexed at 90°. Because the medial epicondyle is normally lower than the lateral one, the measured distance may be somewhat oblique (see p. 251).

Waist: the circumference of the abdomen at its narrowest point between the lower costal (tenth rib) border and the top of the iliac crest, perpendicular to the long axis of the trunk. The subject's arms are folded across the thorax. The measurement is taken at the end of a normal breath. If there is no obvious narrowing, the measurement is taken at the mid-point between the lower costal (tenth rib) and the iliac crest.

Gluteal (hip): the circumference of the buttocks at the level of the greatest posterior protruberance, perpendicular to the long axis of the trunk. The subject's feet *must* be together.

Biepicondylar femur breadth: the distance between the most lateral aspect of the lateral femoral epicondyle and the most medial aspect of the medial femoral epicondyle. The subject is seated with the right leg flexed at the knee at 90° (see p. 251).

Calf: the circumference of the lower leg at the level of the medial calf skinfold site and perpendicular to its long axis. The subject's feet are separated and the weight is evenly distributed.

Body mass

Body mass is the quantity of matter in the body. It is measured through the measurement of weight, i.e. the force the matter exerts due to gravity.

Nude mass is the ideal recorded measure. If necessary, this can be calculated by first weighing the minimal clothing (underwear) that will be worn during measurement and subtracting this from the measured mass of the person wearing the clothing. However, the mass in minimal clothing is usually accurate enough. Check that the scale is reading zero and have the subject stand in the centre of the scales without support and with their weight evenly distributed on both feet. Read to the nearest 0.1 kg.

Body mass has a diurnal (daily) variation of about 1 kg in children and 2 kg in adults. The most reliable values are obtained in the morning 12 hours after food and after voiding. It is also important to record the time of day that the measurement is made.

Stature (height)

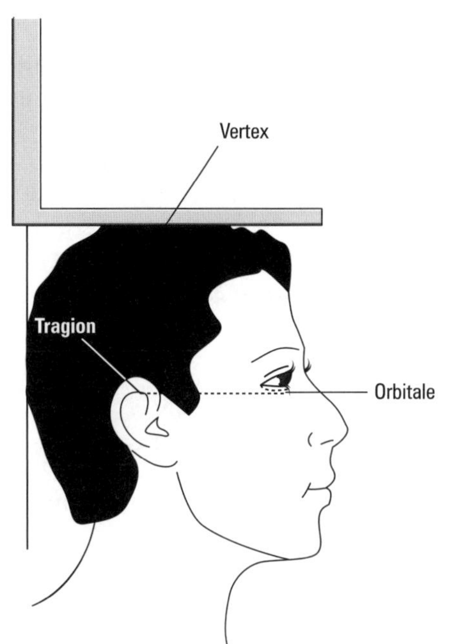

Fig. 34.6 The head in the Frankfort plane.
Source: adapted from ROSSCRAFT Innovations Incorporated.

Height is measured as the distance between the transverse plane of the vertex (Fig. 34.6) and the inferior aspects of the feet. A 1% change in height is common, with subjects being taller in the morning and shorter in the evening. This variation can be reduced by using the stretch stature (height) method below:

1. **Position the subject.** The person should stand with heels together and the heels, buttocks and upper part of the back touching the measuring scale.
2. **Place the subject's head in the Frankfort plane** (Fig. 34.6). This is achieved when the orbitale (lower edge of the eye socket) is in the same horizontal plane as the tragion (the notch superior to the tragus of the ear). When aligned, the vertex is the highest point on the skull. Positioning the head in the Frankfort plane is achieved by placing the tips of the thumbs on each orbitale and the index fingers on each tragion, then horizontally aligning the two points.

   Relocate the thumbs posteriorly towards the subject's ears with the head in the Frankfort plane, and the fingers far enough along the jaw line to be able to exert mild upward pressure on the jaw.
3. **Instruct the subject to take and hold a deep breath** while keeping the head in the Frankfort plane.
4. **Place the measuring board firmly down on the vertex to compress the hair.** An assistant can do this while the measurer holds the head in the Frankfort plane.
5. **Take the measurement** while the breath is held. Read the subject's height to the nearest 0.1 cm.

Body mass index

Being overweight, and in particular carrying too much weight around the waist, increases the risk of cardiovascular disease and diabetes. Body mass index (BMI) is a statistical measure of body weight relative to height. BMI is based on the mean body make-up and is not a valid measure of body fat for people with unusual body types such as body builders, high-performance athletes, pregnant women, the elderly and people with muscle-wasting diseases. BMI does not differentiate between body fat and muscle mass.

It is calculated using the following formula:

$$\text{BMI} = \text{weight (kg)}/\text{height (m)}^2 \tag{34.1}$$

Table 34.2 BMI weight range scale for different population groups*

	BMI (kg/m²)				
Weight range	**European descent**	**Indigenous Australians**	**Asian descent**	**Maori and Pacific islander people**	**Athletes**‡
Underweight	<18.5	N/A†	N/A†	N/A†	N/A†
Normal	>20 but <25	>17 but <22	N/A†	N/A†	N/A†
Overweight	>25 but <30	>22	>23 but <25	>26 but <32	Males >27.9 Females >27.7
Obese	>30	N/A†	>25	>32	N/A†

*Based on World Health Organization and National Health and Medical Research Council (Australia) data. †Validated cut-offs currently unavailable; ‡Ode *et al.* (2007); N/A, not available.

The BMI cut-off points have historically been derived from Caucasian populations. Only recently have normal values been determined for other population groups (Table 34.2).

Being underweight (BMI less than 20) increases the risk of malnourishment, compromises immune function, and increases the risk of developing respiratory disease, tuberculosis, cancer and osteoporosis. Being overweight (BMI greater than 25) increases the risk of developing type 2 diabetes, ischaemic heart disease, stroke, hypertension, osteoarthritis and cancers (colon, kidney, endometrial and postmenopausal breast cancer).

Waist circumference

Waist circumference is considered to be a good predictor of cardiovascular risk and is relatively easy to monitor. Men and women increase their relative risk of morbidity when their waist circumferences exceed 102 cm and 88 cm, respectively.

Owing to racial differences in physique, waist circumference values vary slightly in different populations, with the recommended waist circumferences for European men and women being less than 94 cm and 80 cm, respectively. For South Asian, Chinese and Japanese men and women, the recommended waist circumferences are less than 90 cm and 80 cm, respectively.

A combination of both BMI and waist circumference can be used to determine morbidity risk (Table 34.3).

Table 34.3 Classification of overweight and obesity by BMI, waist circumference and associated disease risks for Caucasian populations*

			Disease risk† relative to normal weight and waist circumference‡	
Classification	**BMI**	**Obesity class**	**Male ≤102 cm Female ≤88 cm**	**Male >102 cm Female >88 cm**
Underweight	<18.5		–	–
Normal	18.5–24.9		–	–
Overweight	25.0–29.9		Increased	High
Obese	30.0–34.9	I	High	Very high
	35.0–39.9	II	Very high	Very high
Extreme obesity	>40.0	III	Extremely high	Extremely high

**Source:* National Heart Lung and Blood Institute (2009). †Disease risk for type 2 diabetes, hypertension and cardiovascular disease; ‡increased waist circumference can also be a marker for increased risk even in persons of normal weight.

Table 34.4 Category for waist-to-hip ratio by gender and age group for Caucasian populations*

	20–29 years		30–39 years		40–49 years	
Category	**Male**	**Female**	**Male**	**Female**	**Male**	**Female**
Well above average	<0.85	<0.78	<0.87	<0.78	<0.91	<0.79
Above average	0.85–0.87	0.78–0.79	0.87–0.92	0.78–0.80	0.91–0.95	0.79–0.82
Average	0.88–0.92	0.80–0.84	0.93–0.96	0.81–0.87	0.96–0.99	0.83–0.90
Below average	0.93–0.98	0.85–0.89	0.97–0.99	0.88–0.91	1.00–1.03	0.91 – 0.92
Well below average	≥0.99	≥0.90	≥1.00	≥0.92	≥1.04	≥0.93
Mean	0.90	0.82	0.94	0.84	0.97	0.86

**Source:* National Center for Health Statistics (2005).

Waist-to-hip ratio

The waist-to-hip (W:H) ratio is a general measure of fat distribution. The waist is measured at its narrowest point and the hips measured at the widest point, with feet placed together.

$$W : H = \text{waist girth (cm)}/\text{hip girth (cm)} \quad (34.2)$$

Greater waist girths and greater waist-to-hip ratios are both indicators of increased abdominal fat deposits and thus increased risk of cardiovascular disease. Normal values for waist-to-hip ratios are shown in Table 34.4.

Bone breadths

For the ISAK-restricted profile, two bone breadths are taken using a set of small sliding calipers such as those shown in Fig. 34.7. These two breadths are the biepicondylar femur and the biepicondylar humerus, and are described in detail in Fig. 34.5.

The general technique for measuring breadths is:

1. **Hold the caliper body correctly,** as shown in Fig. 34.7. That is, the caliper body lies on the backs of the hands while the thumbs rest against the inside edge of the caliper branches, and the extended index fingers lie along the outside edges of the branches.
2. **Use the free middle fingers to locate the bony landmarks** on which the caliper faces are to be placed.
3. **Use the index fingers to exert pressure** to reduce the thickness of any underlying soft tissue.
4. **Take the measurement** when the caliper is in place, with firm pressure maintained along the index fingers.

Fig. 34.7 ISAK-recommended bone breadth calipers.
Source: ROSSCRAFT Innovations Incorporated.

KEY POINT The methods of measurement described in this chapter are widely used in sport and exercise science. They can be used to estimate percentage body fat and body composition, as described in Chapter 35.

Text references

Marfell-Jones, M., Olds, T., Stewart, A. and Carter, L. (2007) *International Standards for Anthropometric Assessment (2007)*. International Society for the Advancement of Kinathropometry, Potchefstroom, South Africa.

National Center for Health Statistics. (2005) *Anthropometric Reference Data, United States, 1988–1994*. Available: http://www.cdc.gov/nchs/ Last accessed: 23/12/10.

National Heart Lung and Blood Institute (2009) *Classification of Overweight and Obesity by BMI, Waist Circumference, and Associated Disease Risks*. Available: http://www.nhlbi.nih.gov/health/public/heart/obesity/lose_wt/bmi_dis.htm Last accessed: 23/12/10.

Norton, K. and Olds, T. (eds) (1996) *Anthropometrica*. University of New South Wales Press, Sydney.

Norton, K., Marfell-Jones, M., Whittingham, N. *et al.* (2000) Anthropometric assessment protocols. In: C. Gore (ed.) *Physiological Tests for Elite Athletes*. Human Kinetics, Champaign, IL, pp. 66–85.

Ode, J.J., Pivarnick, J.M., Reeves, M.J. and Knous, J.L. (2007) Body mass index as a predictor of percent body fat in college athletes and non-athletes. *Medicine and Science in Sports and Exercise,* **39,** 403–9.

Source for further study

Heymsfield, S., Lohman, T., Zi-Mian Wang, Z. and Going, S. (2005) *Human Body Composition*, 2nd edn, Human Kinetics, Champaign, IL.

35 Measuring body composition

Using kinanthropometric measurements – skinfold, height, weight, girths and breadth measures can be used to estimate both body density and percentage body fat. Numerous equations for estimating both of these measures have been developed to enable sport and exercise scientists to monitor changes in body composition, especially body fat and fat-free body mass.

The measurement of body composition is widely practised among sport and exercise scientists, sports trainers and coaches, allied health professionals such as dietitians, and fitness industry professionals.

Being overweight (having excess body fat) in sport lowers power-to-weight ratio, increases the risk of musculoskeletal injuries, increases body surface area and reduces sports performance. In terms of health, excess body fat is associated with numerous health problems, including hypertension, diabetes, depression, hyperlipidaemia, coronary heart disease and death.

This chapter examines the methods of determining body composition using the measures described in Chapter 34 and briefly discusses a number of approaches used within the sport and exercise science literature.

Body composition models

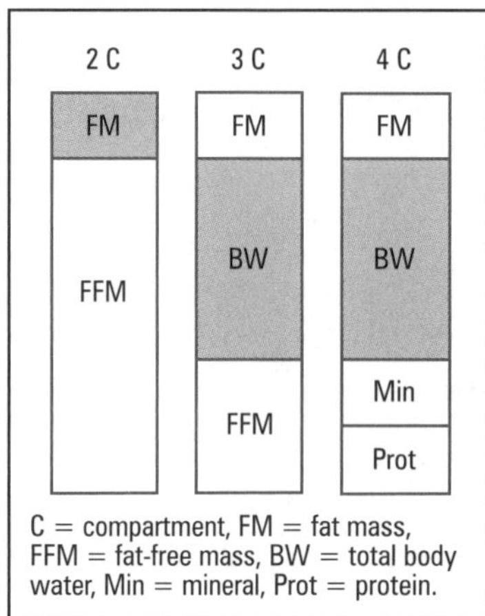

Fig. 35.1 Body composition models.

The most widely used techniques for estimating body composition use a two-compartment model – fat mass (FM) and fat-free mass (FFM). However, when more advanced measurement techniques are employed, three (FM, FFM and body water) and four (FM, body water, mineral and protein/other) compartment models can be used (Fig. 35.1).

The limitation of using the three- and four-compartment models is that measuring each compartment requires large and expensive equipment, needs highly trained expertise to operate and is time-consuming. In contrast, measuring anthropometric sites such as skinfold thicknesses, body segment girths and bone breadths requires far less equipment, expense and time, and can be used to monitor the effect of an exercise and/or dietary intervention regularly. Thus, most sport and exercise scientists use the two-compartment model to estimate relative body fat.

There are numerous equations and methods that can be used to estimate percentage body fat (Box 35.1). These methods will be briefly described later in this chapter.

Box 35.1 Equations and methods for determining percentage body fat

Two-compartment model (D_b from hydrostatic weighing, air displacement plethysmography or anthropometric equations)

$$\% \text{ fat} = (4.95/D_b - 4.50) \times 100 \text{ (Siri, 1956)} \quad (35.1)$$

$$\% \text{ fat} = (4.57/D_b - 4.142) \times 100 \text{ (Brozek } et\ al.\text{, 1963)} \quad (35.2)$$

Three-compartment model (D_b from hydrostatic weighing, air displacement plethysmography and isotopic dilution)

$$\% \text{ fat} = (2.11/D_b - 0.78W - 1.354) \times 100 \text{ (Siri, 1961)} \quad (35.3)$$

Four-compartment model (D from hydrostatic weighing, air displacement plethysmography, isotopic dilution and dual-energy X-ray absorptiometry (DEXA)

$$\% \text{ fat} = [(2.748/D(P + F) - 2.051] [BW - (A + M)]/BW \times 100 \text{ (Heymsfield } et\ al.\text{, 1990)} \quad (35.4)$$

D_b = body density; $D(P + F)$ = density of protein plus fat component mixtures; BW = body weight (kg); A = aqueous mass (kg); M = mineral mass (kg); W = total body water as a fraction of body weight.

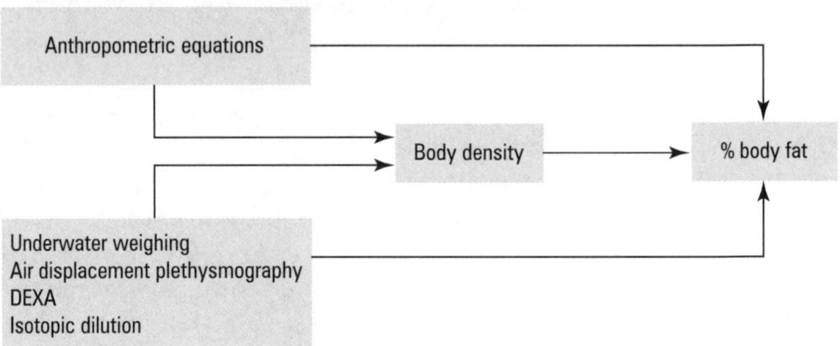

Fig. 35.2 General procedures for estimating % body fat from anthropometric-based equations directly or by the anthropometric estimation of body density or by more direct methods using advanced technical procedures.

The two-compartment model can be used to express the percentage of total body mass (BM) that is body fat (fat mass FM):

$$\% \text{ body fat} = (\text{FM}/\text{BM}) \times 100 \qquad (35.5)$$

Accurate measurement of body fat is important. A wide variety of assessment methods have been developed, ranging from the measurement of skinfold thicknesses (Chapter 34, p. 245) through to the use of dual-energy X-ray absorptiometry (DEXA).

The two-compartment model makes assumptions about the various compartments when body density is used to estimate relative body fat. These assumptions include:

- The densities of FM (0.900 g cm^{-3}) and FFM (1.100 g cm^{-3}) are constant.
- The individual components of FM and FFM have constant densities.
- The proportional contributions of FFM components do not vary.

Moreover, many methods for determining body density use anthropometric equations that also make many assumptions, including:

- Skin and subcutaneous fat compressibility is constant.
- Skin thickness at any one site is constant.
- The relative distribution of fat is constant.
- There is a fixed proportion of internal and external body fat.

Taken together, these assumptions lead to prediction equation errors and biological error. Indeed, research has shown that the variability between different methods of estimating body fat from the same individual using a variety of different prediction equations can vary as much as 10–15%.

Prediction equations

Body fat prediction equations – these have been developed using sophisticated regression techniques from large population studies or cadaver studies.

A wide variety of equations is used to estimate body density and percentage body fat. Each equation is based on the anthropometric measurements taken, the participant's gender and other demographic data, such as age, ethnicity and level of physical activity. Box 35.2 highlights many of the commonly used prediction equations for estimating body density from the anthropometric sites used in Chapter 34. In general, the more measures that are used to predict body density, the greater the accuracy of the prediction.

Box 35.2 Summary of the common body density (BD) prediction equations found in the scientific literature that use the anthropometric measures described in Chapter 34

Males

For normal males 17–72 years

1. BD = 1.1765 – 0.0744 ($\log_{10} X_1$) where X_1 = Σ four skinfolds (triceps, biceps, subscapular and iliac crest) (mm) (35.6)

For young normal males 17–21 years

2. BD = 1.09665 – 0.00103 (X_1) – 0.00056 (X_2) – 0.00054 (X_3) where X_1 = triceps skinfold, X_2 = subscapular skinfold and X_3 = abdominal skinfold (mm) (35.7)

For male athletes 15–39 years

3. BD = 1.0988 – 0.0004 (X_1) where X_1 = Σ seven skinfolds (triceps, biceps, subscapular, supraspinale, abdominal, front thigh and medial calf) (mm) (35.8)

Females

For normal females 16–68 years.

1. BD = 1.1567 – 0.0717 ($\log_{10} X_1$) where X_1 = Σ four skinfolds (triceps, biceps, subscapular and suprailiac) (mm) (35.9)

For college females 19–23 years

2. BD = 1.12569 – 0.001835 (X_1) – 0.002779 (X_2) + 0.005419 (X_3) – 0.0007167 (X_4) where X_1 = triceps skinfold (mm), X_2 = hip girth (inches), X_3 = upper arm flexed girth (inches), X_4 = subscapular skinfold (mm) (35.10)

For female athletes 11–41 years

3. BD = 1.17484 – 0.07229 ($\log_{10} X_1$) where X_1 = Σ four skinfolds (triceps, subscapular, supraspinale and medial calf) (mm) (35.11)

Once BD has been determined, percentage body fat can be estimated by using either of the commonly used prediction equations below:

% fat = ([4.95 / BD] – 4.50) × 100 (Siri, 1956)
% fat = ([4.57 / BD] – 4.142) × 100 (Brozek *et al.*, 1963)

Source: Equations are taken from Norton and Olds, 1996.

Box 35.3 Summary of common percentage body fat (%BF) prediction equations found in the scientific literature that use the anthropometric measures (skinfolds and girths) described in Chapter 34

Males

%BF = 0.29288 (X_1) – 0.0005 $(X_1)^2$ + 0.15845 (age) – 5.76377 where X_1 = Σ four skinfolds (triceps, abdomen, suprailiac and thigh) (mm) (35.12)

Females

%BF = 0.29669 (X_1) – 0.00043 $(X_1)^2$ + 0.02963 (age) – 1.4072 where X_1 = Σ four skinfolds (triceps, thigh, abdominal and suprailiac) (mm) (35.13)

Skinfold measures should be used to estimate %BF in non-obese adults, athletes and children, not obese males and females. Girth measurements should be used to estimate %BF in obese males and females.

Source: Equations are taken from Jackson and Pollock, 1985.

There are also many prediction equations that estimate percentage body fat directly from anthropometric measurements such as skinfold and girth measures. These are highlighted in Box 35.3. Again, the more measures used to predict body density, the greater the accuracy of the prediction.

Box 35.4 Example: estimating ideal (goal) body mass or amount of weight to lose

A male athlete currently weighs 100 kg and has a current estimated body fat of 20%. He wants to get down to 10% body fat and asks you how much mass he needs to lose.

Calculate fat mass

Fat mass = 100 × 20/100
= 20 kg

Calculate fat-free mass (FFM)

Fat-free mass = 100 kg – 20 kg
= 80 kg

Calculate ideal (goal) body mass

Goal body mass (kg) = FFM/(1.0 – desired % body fat)
= 80/(1.0 – 0.10) (0.10 being 10%)
= 80/0.9
= 88.9

Calculate weight loss required

Weight loss required = Current weight – goal body weight
= 100 – 88.9 kg
= 11.1 kg (35.14)

Once percentage body fat has been estimated either from kinanthropometric measurement equations or body density prediction equations, you can estimate ideal body weight and/or the amount of weight a subject needs to lose to attain a goal weight. Box 35.4 gives an example.

Different methods have been used to measure body density directly or as the 'gold standard' when developing predictive equations from anthropometric measures. These include underwater weighing and air displacement plethysmography.

Underwater weighing (hydrodensitometry)

Archimedes's principle states that when a body is immersed in water it is buoyed up by a force equivalent to the weight of the volume of water displaced. The density of a body is defined as its mass per unit volume ($g cm^{-3}$). Thus, if we determine a person's mass both in air and when completely immersed in water, then the density of the body can be calculated from:

$$\begin{aligned} \text{BD (g cm}^{-3}) &= \text{Mass (g)/volume (cm}^3) \\ &= \text{Mass in air (g)/(mass in air (g)} - \text{mass in water (g))} \end{aligned} \quad (35.15)$$

Adjustments need to be made for water density (which is temperature-dependent) and the lung residual volume. Thus, the following formula is used to calculate body density:

$$\text{BD} = \text{MB}_{air}/([\text{MB}_{air} - \text{MB}_{water}]/\text{WD}) - (\text{RV} + 100 \text{ mL}) \quad (35.16)$$

where BD = body density ($g cm^{-3}$ or $g mL^{-1}$), MB_{air} = mass of body in air (g), MB_{water} = mass of body immersed in water (g), WD = water density ($g cm^{-3}$ or $g mL^{-1}$) and RV = ventilated residual lung volume (mL).

Once determined, the BD is normally converted to percentage body fat using the equation of Brozek *et al.* (1963):

$$\% \text{ BF} = (497.1/\text{BD}) - 451.9 \quad (35.17)$$

Box 35.5 summarises the steps in determining body density using underwater weighing.

Table 35.1 Density of water at different temperatures

Temperature (°C)	Density (g mL^{-1})
23.0	0.9975412
24.0	0.9972994
25.0	0.9970480
26.0	0.9967870
27.0	0.9965166
28.0	0.9962371
29.0	0.9959486
30.0	0.9956511
31.0	0.9953450
32.0	0.9950302
33.0	0.9947340
34.0	0.9947071
35.0	0.9940359

Box 35.5 Steps in determining body density using the underwater weighing technique

1. **Obtain basic data for the subject** (name, age, gender, height).
2. **Weigh subject in air –** the subject should wear a swimsuit. No food should be eaten two to three hours before the test and foods that can cause intestinal gas should be avoided.
3. **Weight the subject in water –** place the subject in the dunking chair in the water. Ask them to remove all the air in the swimsuit. Then ask them to make a full exhalation of air from the lungs and slowly lean forward until the head is under water. When all the air is out, ask them to count for five to seven seconds while remaining as still as possible. The measurement should be repeated between four and ten times until a consistent reading is obtained. Try to avoid movement of the weighing scale needle by holding the weighing scale and asking the subject to keep the water as calm as possible by moving slowly in the water.
4. **Record the consistent underwater weight –** record the gross (total) underwater weight then the tare (chair apparatus) to determine the actual subject's body weight in water.
5. **Determine the water density** from Table 35.1.
6. **Determine the residual volume** (air left in the lungs after a full expiration). This can be done using methods called nitrogen washout, helium dilution or oxygen dilution and should be done while immersed in the water. More commonly, estimation formulae can be used as below.

   Males: $RV = (0.017 \times \text{age}) + (0.06858 \times \text{height [inches]}) - 3.447$ (35.18)

   Females: $RV = (0.009 \times \text{age}) + (0.08128 \times \text{height [inches]}) - 3.9$ (35.19)
   (1 inch = 2.5 cm)
7. **Calculate the body density**

   $BD = MB_{air}/([MB_{air} - MB_{water}]/WD) - (RV + 100\text{ mL})$ (100 mL is the assumed volume of air in gut) (35.20)
8. **Calculate the percentage body fat**

   $\%\ BF = (497.1/BD) - 451.9$

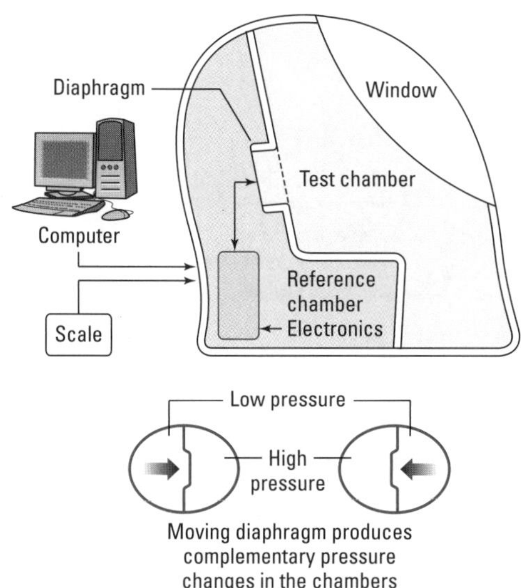

Fig. 35.3 The air displacement plethysmography BOD POD

Source: reprinted with permission of Life Measurement Inc.

Air displacement plethysmography

This relatively new technique is based on the two-compartment model and allows for the estimation of body fat from body density without the need for submerging a subject into water.

The five-minute test consists of first measuring the subject's mass (weight) using a highly accurate electronic scale, and secondly the subject's volume, which is determined by sitting inside the test chamber (Fig. 35.3). From these two measurements, the subject's body composition is calculated.

The surface area of clothing and hair can also have a significant impact on volume measurements. It is extremely important that subjects tested using air displacement plethysmography wear minimal, form-fitting clothing (lycra swimsuits) and a cap to compress the hair on the head.

The BOD POD (Fig. 35.3) consists of two chambers. The front, or test chamber, is where the subject sits and comprises a seat that forms a common wall separating it from the rear reference chamber. During the brief data collection period of the volume measurement, the chamber door is secured by a series of electromagnets and a gasket. A diaphragm is mounted on the common wall, which oscillates during testing. This causes small changes in volume inside the chamber, of which the pressure response to these small volume changes is measured. This is done by measuring the interior volume of the empty chamber, then measuring it again when the subject is seated inside. By subtraction, the subject's body volume is obtained. For example, if the interior air volume of the empty chamber is 400 L, and the volume of the chamber is reduced to 350 L with the subject inside, the body volume of the subject would be 50 L.

Once the subject's mass and volume are determined, body density is calculated and the relative proportions of fat and fat-free mass are determined using equations similar to those used in underwater weighing.

Bioelectrical impedance

Bioelectrical impedance analysis (BIA) is considered a field method for determining fat-free mass and fat mass. This technique is based on the concept that the lean tissue of the body is more conductive than fat tissue owing to its higher water content. Testing involves placement of electrodes on the skin (Fig. 35.4), while a low dose electrical current is passed through the body. The resistance to this current is determined and converted to percentage body fat using a number of population-specific predictive equations.

A harmless 50-kHz current (800 μA maximum) is generated and passed through the person being measured via electrodes attached to one wrist and one ankle on the right-hand side of the body (Fig. 35.4).

The measurement of electrical impedance is detected as the resistance (R, in ohms) to the electrical current passing between the electrodes. Impedance is greatest in fat tissue because the electricity is more conductive in fat-free tissue (~70% water) than in fat tissue (14–22% water). Total body water (TBW) can be estimated using the equation:

$$\text{TBW (kg)} = ([0.593 \times \text{Height (cm)}^2]/\text{Resistance (ohms)}) + (0.065 \times \text{BW (kg)}) \quad (35.21)$$

Where BW = body weight (mass).

Fat-free mass and thus fat mass can be calculated using the population-specific formulae in Box 35.6.

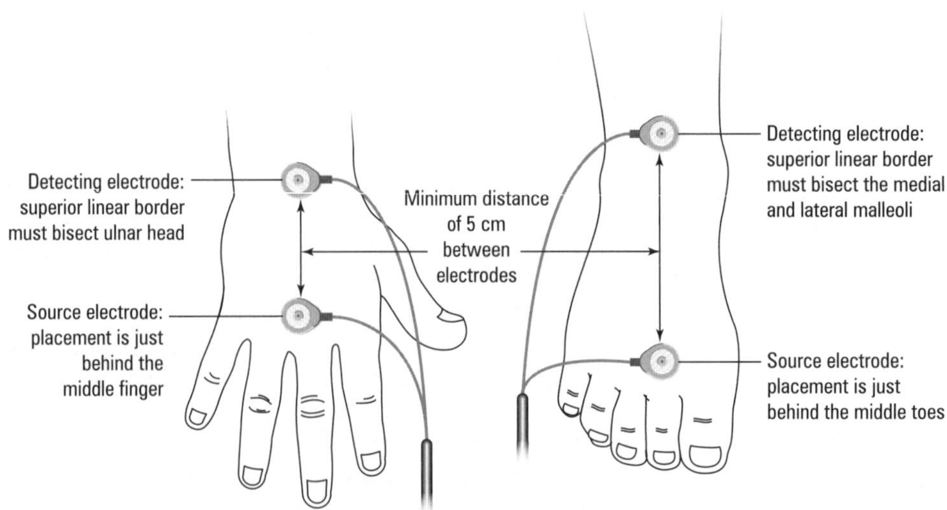

Fig. 35.4 Placement of source and detecting (reference) electrodes for bioelectrical impedance analysis.
Source: Reprinted by permission, from J.E. Graves et al., 2006, Anthropometry and body composition measurement. In *Physiological assessment of human fitness*, 2nd ed., edited by P. J. Maud and C. Foster (Champaign, IL: Human Kinetics), 211.

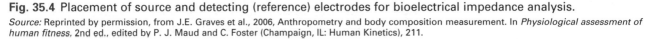

Box 35.6 Bioelectrical prediction equations for specific Caucasian populations

Males 18–29 years: FFM (kg) $= 0.485\ (Ht^2) + 0.338\ (BW) + 5.32$ (35.22)

Males 17–62 years (<20% BF): FFM (kg) $= 0.00066360\ (Ht^2/R) + 0.02117\ (R) + 0.62854\ (BW) - 0.12380\ (age) + 9.33285$ (35.23)

Males 17–62 years ($\geq$20%BF): FFM (kg) $= 0.00088580\ (Ht^2) + 0.2999\ (R) + 0.42688\ (BW) - 0.07002\ (age) + 14.52435$ (35.24)

Females 18–29 years: FFM (kg) $= 0.4764\ (Ht^2/R) + 0.295\ (BW) + 5.49$ (35.25)

Females 30–49 years: FFM (kg) $= 0.493\ (Ht^2/R) + 0.141\ (BW) + 11.59$ (35.26)

Females 50–74 years: FFM (kg) $= 0.474\ (Ht^2/R) + 0.180\ (BW) + 7.3$ (35.27)

FFM = fat-free mass; BW = body weight (kg); Ht = height (cm); R = resistance (ohms); BF = body fat.

There are a number of sources of measurement error that must be controlled with BIA to improve accuracy and reliability. These include:

- **Instrumentation** – the same instrument should be used when measuring changes over time in the same subject.
- **Enviromental factors** – a controlled laboratory setting with constant ambient temperature is needed. Cool ambient temperatures reduce skin temperature and can lead to underestimates of fat-free mass.
- **Subject hydration** – the subject's hydration status is crucial. Thus, the following guidelines are recommended:
  1. No eating or drinking in the four hours before the test.
  2. No exercise during the 12 hours before the test.
  3. Urinate 30 minutes before the test.
  4. No alcohol 48 hours before the test.
  5. No diuretic medications seven days before the test.
  6. No testing of female clients during the water retention phase of the menstrual cycle.
- **Technical skill** – there are numerous BIA devices available on the market. Most are simple to operate. However, the manufacturer's instructions must be strictly followed to obtain accurate results. For example, some devices require a supine position while others require a standing or seated position.

A number of other sophisticated methods are used to determine body composition. These include:

- Isotopic dilution;
- Dual-energy X-ray absorptiometry (DEXA);
- Computerised tomography (CT);
- Magnetic resonance imaging (MRI).

These methods will be outlined only briefly as they are rarely available to sport and exercise scientists and they have a number of additional limitations, including cost and level of expertise required to operate the equipment. For detailed descriptions, see Heymsfield *et al.* (2005).

Example A common isotopic dilution protocol might be a 10 mL saliva sample, followed by the ingestion of 10 g of deuterium oxide (D_2O) mixed with 300 mL of deionised water, a three-hour equilibration period, then a second 10 mL saliva sample.

Isotopic dilution

Water makes up 40–60% of body weight and is associated mainly with fat-free mass. According to the dilution principle, the concentration of a compound in a solvent depends on the volume of the solvent and the amount of the compound within the solvent. Thus, if the amount and concentration of the compound (in this case an isotope) are known, the total body water can be calculated.

Several non-toxic and non-metabolisable isotopes that only distribute evenly through body water can be used. These include tritium, deuterium and oxygen isotopes. After ingestion of a known amount and concentration of the isotope, an equilibration period of two to four hours is allowed.

Two body fluid samples of either blood or saliva are taken – one pre-dose and one after the equilibration period. Analysis of the isotope concentration is then undertaken using radioactive β-counting for tritium, mass spectroscopy for ^{18}O and gas chromatography or mass spectroscopy for deuterium.

The calculation of TBW volume is based upon the simplified relationship:

$$C_1V_1 = C_2V_2 \quad (35.28)$$

where C_1V_1 is the concentration and volume of tracer given, C_2 is the final concentration of tracer in the blood or saliva, and V_2 is volume of TBW. It is important that corrections be made for urinary loss of the tracer.

Research has shown that the accuracy of isotopic dilution for measuring TBW is good but caution should be used when estimating body fat percentage from TBW using the equation:

$$\%\ BF = 100 - \%\ TBW/0.732 \quad (35.29)$$

The caution is based on the large interindividual variation in the proportion of water in the fat-free mass. In addition, the method is laborious and costly.

Dual-energy X-ray absorptiometry

Dual-energy X-ray absorptiometry (DEXA; Fig. 35.5) is widely used to measure bone density but is increasingly being used for body composition research. It is taking over from underwater weighing as the gold standard against which other indirect methods (e.g. predictive equations) are being judged.

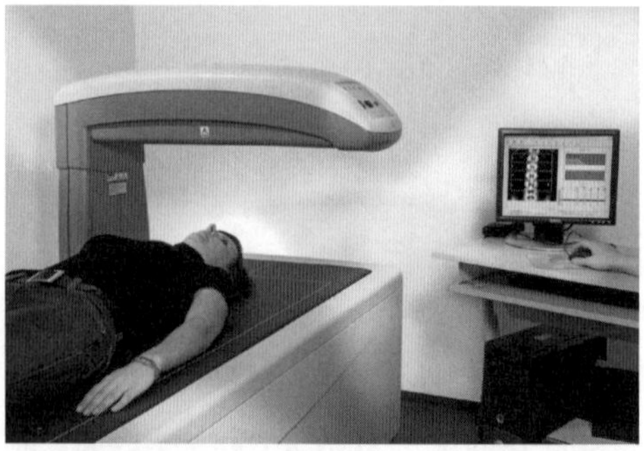

DEXA is a non-invasive radiological projection technique that uses high resolution X-rays. The method is based on a three-compartment model that divides the body into total-body mineral, mineral-free lean and fat tissue masses. Tissue densities are measured directly and are differentiated, thus reducing the errors seen with many other body composition methods that assume constant densities in compartments.

The precision of DEXA in measuring % BF is estimated to be ±1.2% BF. The method is highly reliable, and there is good agreement between % BF estimates obtained by hydrodensitometry and DEXA. In addition to obtaining estimates of relative body fat and lean tissue mass, DEXA provides segmental and regional measures of body composition.

Fig. 35.5 Subject undertaking a DEXA measurement.
Source: Alamy Images: Medicalpicture.

Fig. 35.6 A computerised tomography (CT) machine showing circular gantry and platform.
Source: MEDICAL RF.COM.

One of the limitations of this method is that hydration status must be controlled. Accuracy may also be compromised in people with high anterior–posterior thickness (abdominal thickness), with exogenous fat mass underestimated in subjects with high fat content in the abdomen and thigh.

Computerised tomography

Computerised tomography (CT) is a modern radiographic method to determine regional body composition. This approach relates small differences in X-ray attenuation to differences in the physical density of tissues to construct a two-dimensional image of the underlying anatomy in the scan area.

The CT system consists of an X-ray source and detectors aligned at opposite poles of a circular gantry. Lying on a movable platform, the subject is advanced through the middle of the gantry. As the X-ray beam is rotated around the subject, information about the intensity of the attenuated X-ray beams is recorded and stored in body 'slices' about 10 mm thick. The scanner computer then applies complex algorithms to the stored series of profiles to reconstruct cross-sectional images. The lower density tissues appear black and higher densities are whiter, with air and bone at the low and high ends of absorption, respectively. Thus, high image contrast is observed between bone, adipose and fat-free tissues.

Because slice thickness is known, the system can calculate the relative surface area or volume occupied by each organ or tissue in the reconstructed picture. These methods have been used to assess changes in muscle and adipose tissue in malnutrition and to describe cross-sectional differences in abdominal fat distribution during ageing.

Although the potential of CT scanners for body composition analysis is considerable, a number of constraints limit its use. Because of the exposure to ionising radiation, routine whole-body scans, multiple scans in the same individual and scans of pregnant women or children are not encouraged. Also, the cost and limited availability of modern CT scanners prohibit their routine use for body composition assessment.

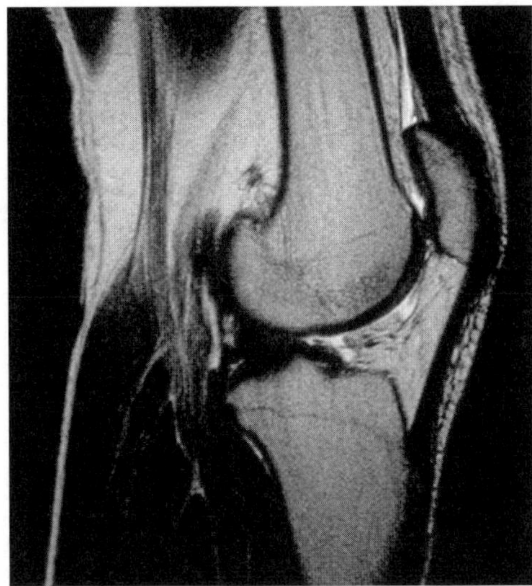

Fig. 35.7 MRI image of a knee joint showing the high resolution that enables analysts to quantify body compartments.
Source: Science Photo Library Ltd.: Susan Leavines.

Magnetic resonance imaging

Magnetic resonance imaging (MRI) is primarily a medical imaging technique most commonly used to visualise the internal structure and function of the body. MRI provides much greater resolution between the different soft tissues of the body than CT. MRI uses a powerful magnetic field to align the hydrogen atoms in water in the body. Radio frequency fields are used to systematically alter the alignment of this magnetisation, causing the hydrogen nuclei to produce a rotating magnetic field detectable by the scanner. This signal can be manipulated by additional magnetic fields to build up enough information to construct an image of the body and its various structures.

Typically, and as with CT, tissue area within an MR image is calculated by segmentation techniques. By selecting regions of interest (e.g. abdomen), fat and lean tissue can be quantified. The region of interest, for example, visceral fat, is traced by a mouse pointer and the area calculated. The area of each region is determined by multiplying the number of pixels in the highlighted region by their known area. If a single image is used, the area values are computed. If multiple images are used, the volume is derived. Thus, the most accurate MRI method for measuring total body fat uses images (slices) covering the subject's whole body. This takes a lot of scanning and thus a lot of time.

Text references

Brozek, J., Grande, F., Anderson, J. and Keys, A. (1963) Densitometric analysis of body composition: revision of some quantitative assumptions. *Annals of the New York Academy of Sciences*, **110**, 113–40.

Heymsfield, S., Lichtman, S., Baumgartner, R. *et al.* (1990) Body composition in humans: comparison of two improved four-compartment models that differ in expense, technical complexity, and radiation exposure. *American Journal of Clinical Nutrition*, **52,** 52–8.

Heymsfield, S., Lohman, T., Zi-Mian, Wang, Z. and Going, S. (2005) *Human Body Composition*, 2nd edn, Human Kinetics, Champaign, IL.

Jackson, A. and Pollock, M. (1985) Practical assessment of body composition. *Physician and Sports Medicine*, **13**, 76–90.

Norton, K. and Olds, T. (eds) (1996) *Anthropometrica.* University of New South Wales Press, Sydney.

Siri, W. (1956) The gross composition of the body. In: J.H. Lawrence and C.A. Tobias (eds) *Advances in Biological and Medical Physics*. Academic Press Inc., New York, pp. 239–80.

Siri, W. (1961) Body volume measurement by gas dilution. In: J. Brozek and A. Henschal (eds) *Techniques for Measuring Body Composition.* National Academy of Science, National Research Council, Washington DC, pp. 108–17.

Measuring physiological capacities

36. Measuring maximal aerobic capacity 265

37. Indirect measures of aerobic capacity 274

38. Measuring energy expenditure and physical activity 281

39. Measuring anaerobic power and capacity 294

40. Measuring muscle strength and endurance 304

41. Common field tests 317

42. Specific field tests 328

36 Measuring maximal aerobic capacity

Definitions

Maximal aerobic capacity ($\dot{V}O_2$max) – the highest amount of oxygen that can be consumed by an individual over a time period (usually 30 seconds).

Peak aerobic capacity ($\dot{V}O_2$peak) – the highest amount of oxygen that is consumed within one measurement.

Indirect open circuit calorimetry – technology used to measure expired ventilation and gas volume to measure $\dot{V}O_2$ max. Also known as a metabolic cart.

Volitional exhaustion – stopping the test as the athlete cannot continue.

Step test – protocol to determine $\dot{V}O_2$ max using longer stages with larger increments.

Ramp test – protocol to determine $\dot{V}O_2$ max using shorter stages with smaller increments.

Maximal oxygen consumption ($\dot{V}O_2$max) is widely used as the 'gold standard' measure of cardiorespiratory fitness or aerobic capacity. The assessment of $\dot{V}O_2$ max is regularly employed to establish physiological limits to endurance performance and is particularly useful when the influence of aerobic training is evaluated. Assessment of $\dot{V}O_2$ max is a core duty of a sport and exercise scientist and has wide applications in a variety of settings outside of sport, including medical and health vocations. While $\dot{V}O_2$ max can be assessed using submaximal tests (see Chapter 37), these can be affected by compounding influences and do not provide an accurate $\dot{V}O_2$ max measurement, particularly in either clinical patients or elite athletes.

However, the accurate assessment of $\dot{V}O_2$ max is only routinely performed within a small number of settings as it requires expensive and sensitive equipment. Typically, $\dot{V}O_2$ max is quantified using expensive and sensitive equipment that is found mainly in exercise science laboratories and a small number of related domains. Developing protocols and utilising this equipment to best determine an individual's $\dot{V}O_2$ max is important in a number of different disciplines outside of exercise science, including medical, physical activity and dietetics. However, this is often the primary responsibility of an exercise scientist. This chapter demonstrates how to calculate $\dot{V}O_2$ max from first principles and describe some simple procedures to assess and determine the measure.

Understanding oxygen consumption – is commonly abbreviated to $\dot{V}O_2$ in sport and exercise science. The dot over the V indicates that the parameter is a rate; this gives a time unit to the volume of oxygen consumed. However, in sport and exercise science, it is also acceptable to use VO_2 to denote oxygen consumption. It is important to note that these two terms are used interchangeably at times.

$\dot{V}O_2$ max remains unaffected by several factors – It is reduced by only 2–3% by a variety of physical stresses, including:

- Blood loss (> 500 mL)
- Moderate to severe dehydration
- High ambient temperature
- Excessive fever
- Acute starvation (24–48 hours).

Theory and importance of $\dot{V}O_2$ max

$\dot{V}O_2$ max is the product of cardiac output (Q) and the highest arterial–venous oxygen difference (a–vO_2diff) that can be elicited during maximal intensity exercise. The Fick equation (shown below) demonstrates how these factors interact to calculate $\dot{V}O_2$ max:

$$\dot{V}O_2\,\text{max} = Q \times (a\text{–}vO_2\text{diff}) \quad (36.1)$$

As cardiac output is the product of both stroke volume (SV) and heart rate (HR), the Fick equation can be expanded to read:

$$\dot{V}O_2\,\text{max} = SV \times HR \times (a\text{–}vO_2\text{diff}) \quad (36.2)$$

Therefore, when an individual is working at $\dot{V}O_2$ max they are working at their maximal cardiac output and arterial–venous oxygen difference. $\dot{V}O_2$ max is a stable and highly reproducible characteristic of an individual.

$\dot{V}O_2$ max decreases with age and physical inactivity, and males generally have higher $\dot{V}O_2$ max values than females. The high $\dot{V}O_2$ max values of elite, middle and long distance athletes are due to a combination of genetic factors and training. Around 40% of the variation in $\dot{V}O_2$ max can be linked to genetic factors, whereas physical training can increase $\dot{V}O_2$ max by between 5 and 30% in athletes. Greater improvements have been observed in cardiac patients, persons of very low initial fitness and those who achieve substantial weight loss. However, with highly trained athletes their $\dot{V}O_2$ max is a relatively weak predictor of endurance performance because of the importance of other factors such as mechanical efficiency, lactate threshold, anaerobic capacity and motivation.

In terms of units, $\dot{V}O_2$ max can be expressed in absolute terms (L min^{-1}) or in relative terms compared to body mass (ml kg^{-1} min^{-1}). Absolute units are useful in comparing data when looking at total power output or work and can help to emphasise the difference between physical performance and physiological function. Relative units are more useful to determine differences in activities where an individual is unsupported and body mass is likely to have a direct influence on performance.

Equipment required to measure $\dot{V}O_2$ max

The laboratory equipment used to measure $\dot{V}O_2$ max is highly specialised, technical and expensive to purchase and maintain. Indirect calorimetry equipment analyses expired gases to estimate energy expenditure during exercise. The equipment allows the subject to breathe in normal atmospheric air and analyses the composition and volume of the expired gas. While this type of equipment was developed for energy estimation (Chapter 38), it is also useful for providing an assessment of $\dot{V}O_2$ max by quantifying the highest amount of O_2 that can be consumed by a subject. Such systems usually monitor expired ventilation and do so through a range of methods (e.g. turbines, pneumotachometers). Similarly, this equipment requires the ability to determine the concentration of O_2 and CO_2 in expired air. The apparatus used to measure $\dot{V}O_2$ max is very sensitive and requires specialised training for operators. The equipment is also very expensive to purchase and maintain within the laboratory, so extreme care needs to be taken with it at all times.

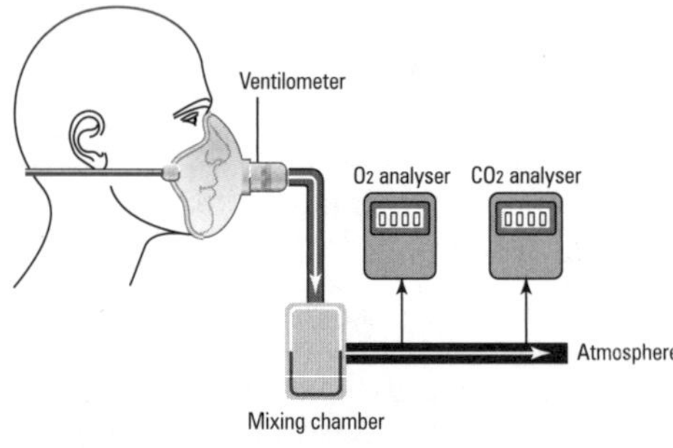

Fig. 36.1 An example of a metabolic cart used to measure $\dot{V}O_2$ max.

Before using an indirect open circuit calorimetry system (otherwise known as a metabolic cart) it must be calibrated against known values before testing. This helps to ensure that the system is working properly and provides an accurate measure of $\dot{V}O_2$ max. All systems will have their own individual calibration routine and requirements, so it is important that the manufacturer's instructions are consulted prior to use. Typically, the ventilometer (or equivalent) must be calibrated at several levels over the range 10–200 L min^{-1}. Also, the O_2 and CO_2 analysers need to be calibrated using gases of known composition. This should be completed before each testing session and at least after every *second* test. Different systems analyse expired gases differently. Some systems (known as breath-by-breath) analyse each individual breath for ventilation volume and gas concentration, whereas others provide an average for these values over a time period. All systems have data published on their reliability and accuracy, and these are important in helping to determine changes between tests (Chapter 19). All systems, however, rely on the same mathematical principles to calculate $\dot{V}O_2$ max from the measured parameters, and it is important that all sport and exercise scientists are aware of these.

Important note – in the mathematical equations described, the percentage concentration of a gas is given as a decimal fraction (represented by a capital F). This means that a concentration of 19.25% is written as 0.1925 when inserted into the equation. Following from this, the measure is identified as either inspired or expired air, using either an I or an E after the F. The name of the gas is included after this information. For example; if the O_2 concentration of inspired air is 20.93% than it is labelled as F_IO_2.

Important note – the inspired concentrations of several gases are assumed to remain constant at all times. These are shown below:

- O_2 20.93%
- CO_2 0.03%
- N_2 79.04%

First principles of $\dot{V}O_2$ max calculations

To understand the concept of $\dot{V}O_2$ max it is important that the mathematical first principles are understood. This relies upon the measurement of both changes in ventilation and gas concentrations between inspired and expired air. During a $\dot{V}O_2$ max test, only three variables are measured using the sophisticated equipment. These are ventilation, either inspired (V_I) or expired (V_E), and the fraction of expired air that is oxygen (F_EO_2) and carbon dioxide (F_ECO_2). However, these variables, as well as the constant concentrations of inspired air (F_IO_2, F_ICO_2, F_IN_2), allow changes in O_2 consumption and CO_2 production to be calculated.

The first step is to correct the measured ventilation values for the effects of the atmospheric environment. Expired ventilation is collected as what is termed *A*mbient (surrounding air) *T*emperature and *P*ressure *S*aturated (with water) (ATPS) conditions. However, each of these factors directly affects the volume of air that is measured (e.g. increased temperature causes gas to expand, creating a larger volume). So that tests from different labs throughout the world or the same lab in different conditions can be accurately compared, the volumes are corrected to be *S*tandard *T*emperature and *P*ressure *D*ry (STPD). Standard temperature is 273K (0°C), with standard pressure being 760 mmHg without moisture in the air. The pressure of water in the atmosphere (P_{H_2O}) varies with temperature; Table 36.1 provides this value for a range of temperatures. Inspired volumes are not saturated and therefore must only be corrected for relative humidity.

The transfer of a volume from ATPS to STPD is as follows:

$$V_{STPD} = V_{ATPS} \times [273/(273 + T^{\circ}C)] \times [(P_B - P_{H_2O})/760] \quad (36.3)$$

The calculation of metabolic changes requires that both V_I and V_E are known. As mentioned above, typically during metabolic testing only one is recorded (typically V_E). However, using the *Haldane transformation,* the other variable can be calculated. The Haldane transformation calculates the missing ventilation value using the calculated changes in N_2 concentration. Nitrogen is an inert gas (so is neither consumed nor produced) and any changes in N_2 concentration are caused by changes in gas volume. The Haldane transformation is:

$$V_I\ (STPD) \times F_IN_2 = V_E\ (STPD) \times F_EN_2 \quad (36.4)$$

Table 36.1 Vapour pressure (P_{H_2O}) of wet gas at temperatures normally encountered in the laboratory

Temperature (°C)	P_{H_2O}(mmHg)	Temperature (°C)	P_{H_2O}(mmHg)
20	17.5	30	31.8
21	18.7	31	33.7
22	19.8	32	35.7
23	21.1	33	37.7
24	22.4	34	39.9
25	23.8	35	42.2
26	25.2	36	44.6
27	26.7	37	47.1
28	28.4	38	49.7
29	30.0	39	52.4

These values assume wet gas (saturated). Inspired volumes are not saturated and therefore must be corrected for relative humidity.

To complete the Haldane transformation, the expired concentration of N_2 must also be calculated. As the other two gases in expired air (F_EO_2 and F_ECO_2) are measured during gas monitoring, the F_EN_2 is the remaining concentration. Quite simply, F_EN_2 is calculated as:

$$F_EN_2 = 1.0 - (F_EO_2 + F_ECO_2) \quad (36.5)$$

Important note – $\dot{V}O_2$ max is most accurately measured in an environmentally controlled laboratory. Testing should be postponed until such conditions can be met to minimise the influence of thermoregulatory responses.

Once these variables have been corrected for relative humidity, then several metabolic parameters can be calculated, including $\dot{V}O_2$, $\dot{V}CO_2$ and respiratory exchange ratio (RER). Oxygen consumption is simply achieved by calculating the volume of O_2 inspired and subtracting the voume of CO_2 that is expired.

$$\dot{V}O_2 = (V_I \times F_IO_2) - (V_E \times F_EO_2) \quad (36.6)$$

The rate of CO_2 production ($\dot{V}CO_2$) is calculated in the opposite manner, with the expired volume of CO_2 calculated and then the inspired volume subtracted.

$$\dot{V}CO_2 = (V_E \times F_ECO_2) - (V_I \times F_ICO_2) \quad (36.7)$$

RER is the ratio of CO_2 produced in relation to the O_2 consumed by the body. Importantly, it varies depending on exercise intensity and the energy substrate that is metabolised.

$$RER = \dot{V}CO_2/\dot{V}O_2 \quad (36.8)$$

Completing an exercise test for $\dot{V}O_2$ max

SAFETY NOTE A laboratory assistant is vital to ensure a safe testing environment. While the risk of major cardiovascular accidents or death is small (~1 in 10 000 tests) during such testing, the assistant is useful in fulfilling the best practice safety procedures for the lab. All testing parties should be aware of the laboratory's safety procedures and the regional first aid practices.

The design of an exercise protocol to best determine $\dot{V}O_2$ max should be carefully considered as it may vary with each athlete's chosen modality as well as the information that is required from the test. As discussed in Chapter 43, information regarding training thresholds can also be gathered across the maximal test. Before completing a $\dot{V}O_2$ max test, the protocol should be decided and explained to the subject. If required, small changes can be made to the protocol during the test. The test protocol should provide the parameters of interest to the sport and exercise scientist, coach or athlete.

There are two main types of exercise tests to determine $\dot{V}O_2$ max: the ramp and step tests. A ramp test is best described as a test during which intensity is increased by small and frequent increases in work intensity; it is the beter option if only a $\dot{V}O_2$ max result is required. On the other hand, a step test consists of larger and less frequent increases and helps to provide information on training thresholds. It is suggested that a ramp test should last between 8 and 15 minutes to elicit $\dot{V}O_2$ max from an athlete, as this seems to pace an athlete best, allowing them to warm up adequately across the test but not exhausting them owing to excessive high intensity exercise. A step test, on the other hand, usually lasts considerably longer owing to each stage being longer, and can last between 20 and 30 minutes.

Protocols for $\dot{V}O_2$ max tests

There are many different protocols that are used within an exercise science laboratory to determine $\dot{V}O_2$ max. These may differ according to the level of the athlete, exercise mode, available ergometers and required

Box 36.1 How to perform a $\dot{V}O_2$ max test

Below are some important steps to complete a $\dot{V}O_2$ max test successfully.

1. **Decide on the testing mode and protocol before the test.** Factors to consider include starting workload, work increment, stage duration, warm-up procedure and desired information from the test. If the subject has previously been tested, it is best to change as little as possible between tests to allow comparison of test data.
2. **Ensure that all testing equipment and recording sheets are available and ready for the test.** During the test you are unable to leave the immediate space around the ergometer as this may cause a significant safety risk to the subject. If other physiological measures are to be taken during the test (e.g. capillary bloods, temperature), then this equipment should also be set up on a bench or table close to the ergometer.
3. **Have at least one laboratory assistant present at all times during testing.** This allows you to perform additional physiological measures and still observe the subject. Ensure, before the test, that you have explained to the assistant what is required of them. Also, in case of a medical emergency this allows first aid to be administered while medical assistance is sought.
4. **Calibrate the metabolic cart before each testing session** or with any changes in equipment (i.e. ventilometers). This ensures that the expired gas data will be as accurate as possible and limit the likelihood of faulty equipment influencing results.
5. **Check that the ergometer is working appropriately before the test.** This should be done before the warm-up as delays should be avoided when the subject is in the laboratory. All ergometers must be calibrated at least once a year and laboratory technicians should be aware of their maintenance schedule. This also includes matching the physical settings of the ergometer to the subjects to maximise comfort and performance for the subject.
6. **Thoroughly explain the testing procedures before the warm-up and test.** This should include details of the warm-up procedure, stage duration and work increments, other physiological tests to be administered and communication strategies (Box 36.2).
7. **Start the warm-up as per the testing guidelines.** Warming up before the test is important to maximise performance, help familiarise the subject with the testing equipment and make any last minute changes to the exercise ergometers. Normally, warm-ups are standardised across all subjects; however, each subject should be given a chance to do any additional work before the test and should not start the test unless they are 'ready' themselves.
8. **Have a small break between the warm-up and the test.** This allows you to double-check that all equipment is ready and also allows the subject to have any last minute preparations like a drink of water or mental preparation. The break should not be any longer than 2–3 minutes.
9. **Make sure to monitor the subject, data and equipment during the test.** Monitoring and communicating with the subject is essential during any test. You can assess the subject by observing changes in their technique that may be caused by fatigue or technical faults. Most metabolic carts will display the data on a computer screen and store them as well. It is important that you monitor all physiological data across the test. It is also important that at least one data point from each stage (towards the end of the stage – see Box 36.3) is recorded on hard copy during the test in case of computer malfunction.
10. **Start the test as per the testing protocol.** Make sure to count the subject into the test and start a stopwatch so that there is a second timer (the metabolic cart will have a clock as well). If required, the laboratory assistant should synchronise any other physiological devices (e.g. heart rate monitors) at the start of the test.
11. **Continue with the test as per the protocol** until it appears that $\dot{V}O_2$ max is reached or the subject indicates that they wish to stop. It is important that you are familiar with the criteria that define the attainment of $\dot{V}O_2$ max (Box 36.4). If the subject wishes to stop, then the test is to be stopped. However, it is important to talk to the subject during the test to encourage them to continue for as long as possible and stop at the end of a stage.
12. **Remove all physiological equipment and check that the participant is fine after the test.** After undergoing additional physiological tests, the subject should perform a cool-down on the ergometer. Care is required when the subject exits the ergometer as they may have a case of ''jelly-legs' or be unsure on firm ground.

(continued)

Box 36.1 Continued

13. **Make sure to save all data as soon as the participant is comfortable.** All data should be saved electronically (if possible) and printed as hard copy as soon as possible for later analysis.
14. **All equipment is to be disinfected appropriately following the test.** After the test, there may be several different body fluids (i.e. saliva, sweat and blood) on testing equipment and the ergometer. It is important that all equipment is disinfected before the next test or after the last test to minimise the likelihood of cross-infection of communicable diseases (Chapter 25).

Box 36.2 How to communicate during a $\dot{V}O_2$ max test

During a $\dot{V}O_2$ max test, the subject is required to wear either a mouthpiece or face mask. This means that verbal communication is difficult and can be near impossible during high intensity exercise. However, communication across the test is important to make sure that the test is successful, and that the subject reaches their $\dot{V}O_2$ max and is safe. As such, a sequence of hand signals has been developed, of which the subject should be informed before the test. It has been demonstrated that verbal communication and encouragement can improve performance during a $\dot{V}O_2$ max test by up to 7%. The level of communication and encouragement should always be standardised between subjects. These are demonstrated below and can be used in addition to a series of verbal commands from the tester.

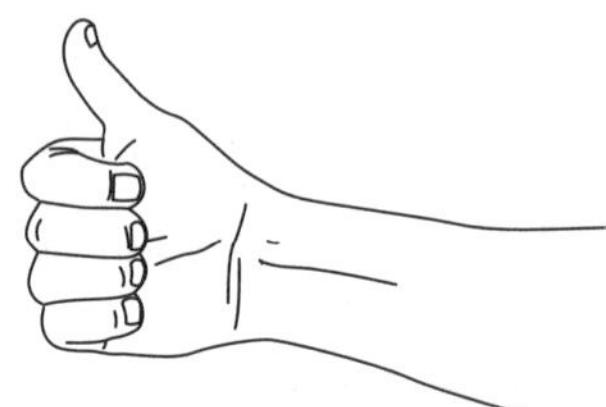

Everything is good

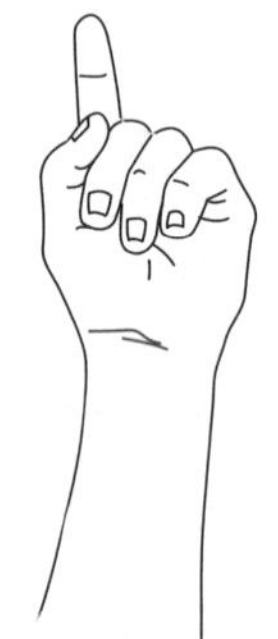

One more minute/stage

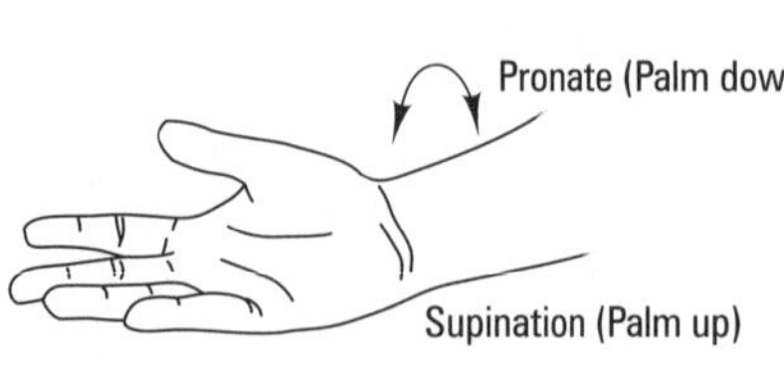

I'm getting tired

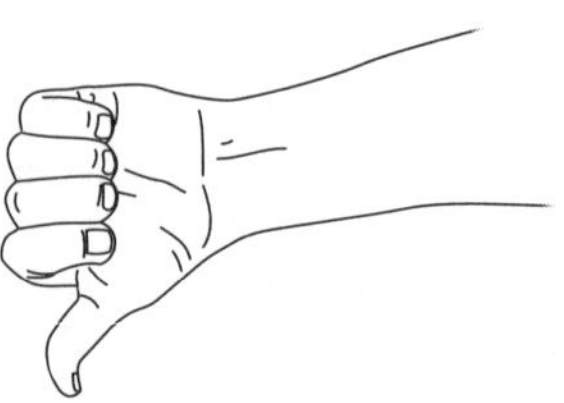

I want to stop

Fig. 36.2 Examples of hand signals that can be used for communication during a $\dot{V}O_2$ max test.

information. While there does appear to be considerable variety in protocols, the standardisation of test protocols is vital for valid and meaningful comparisons. Table 36.2 shows some examples of both ramp and step test protocols for a variety of different exercise modes.

Table 36.2 Examples of common exercise protocols used to safely determine $\dot{V}O_2$ max

TREADMILL					
Ramp test			**Step test**		
Time (min)	**Speed (kmh^{-1})**	**Duration (min)**	**Time (min)**	**Speed (kmh^{-1})**	**Duration (min)**
1	8	1	1	8	3 (+1 min rest)
2	9	1	4	9.5	3 (+1 min rest)
3	10	1	8	11	3 (+1 min rest)
4	11	1	12	13.5	3 (+1 min rest)
5	12	1	16	15	3 (+1 min rest)
6	13	1	20	16.5	3 (+1 min rest)
7	14	1	24	18	3 (+1 min rest)
8	15	1	28	20.5	3 (+1 min rest)
9	16	1			
10	17	1			
CYCLING					
Ramp test			**Step test**		
Time (min)	**Power (W)**	**Duration (min)**	**Time (min)**	**Power (W)**	**Duration (min)**
1	100	1	1	100	3
2	125	1	4	150	3
3	150	1	8	200	3
4	175	1	12	250	3
5	200	1	16	300	3
6	225	1	20	350	3
7	250	1	24	400	3
8	275	1	28	450	3
9	300	1			
10	325	1			
ROWING					
Ramp test			**Step test**		
Time (min)	**Power**	**Duration (min)**	**Time (min)**	**Power**	**Duration (min)**
1	100	1	1	100	3
2	125	1	4	150	3
3	150	1	8	200	3
4	175	1	12	250	3
5	200	1	16	300	3
6	225	1	20	350	3
7	250	1	24	400	3
8	275	1	28	450	3
9	300	1			
10	325	1			

Box 36.3 How to analyse expired gas data from a $\dot{V}O_2$ max test

While setting up and performing a $\dot{V}O_2$ max test in a lab is an important skill for a sport and exercise scientist, it is equally important to be able to analyse the data. Different metabolic carts will provide data differently with regard to the parameters recorded or the sampling strategy. Some systems will provide a measure for each expired breath or will analyse the data over a time period (anywhere between one and 60 seconds) and provide an average measure. Regardless, there are some basic rules that can be applied to both the sampling and interpretation of $\dot{V}O_2$ max.

1. **When manually recording data, always take more than one measurement per stage.** This helps to provide an average metabolic intensity for each stage and reduces the ability for outliers or changes in efficiency to influence test data.

2. **A 30-second average is commonly used in sport and exercise science.** Research has demonstrated that most sport and exercise scientists rely upon a 30-second average for expired gas measurements as it proves to be the most sensitive yet stable time period.

(continued)

Box 36.3 Continued

3. **Record both $\dot{V}O_2$ max and $\dot{V}O_2$peak.** While $\dot{V}O_2$ max is the measure of most interest to a sport and exercise scientist, it may differ significantly from $\dot{V}O_2$peak, which is simply the highest $\dot{V}O_2$ value recorded across the test.
4. **Ensure that $\dot{V}O_2$ max is expressed in both absolute and relative terms.** Providing results in absolute and relative terms allows further interpretation and comparison of the results.
5. **Plot the $\dot{V}O_2$–work rate relationship and observe the relationship.** Most electronic metabolic carts will automatically plot this relationship and, if not, it can easily be performed in a spreadsheet software package or manually. Observing this relationship can help to provide valuable information on metabolic efficiency, and can be compared to previous tests to identify changes and quickly determine whether a plateau was reached in $\dot{V}O_2$ at the end of the test.
6. **Compare to normative data.** A range of typical $\dot{V}O_2$ max values for women and men is provided in Table 36.3. In most instances, comparison of relative $\dot{V}O_2$ max values is preferred to ensure that the results are not influenced by height and size.
7. **Make graphical plots of other important relationships measured across the test** to gather further information (some examples are provided in Fig. 36.3 for step (a) and ramp (b) test protocols. Such relationships include:
   i. $\dot{V}O_2$ against power output/speed;
   ii. $\dot{V}O_2$ against heart rate;
   iii. Heart rate against power output/speed;
   iv. $\dot{V}O_2$ against RER.

Table 36.3 Normative data for $\dot{V}O_2$ max ml kg^{-1} min^{-1} from a normal and healthy population

		WOMEN			
Age (years)	**Poor**	**Fair**	**Good**	**Excellent**	**Superior**
20–29	≤35	36–39	40–43	44–49	≥50
30–39	≤33	34–36	37–40	41–45	≥46
40–49	≤31	32–34	35–38	39–44	≥45
50–59	≤24	25–28	29–30	31–34	≥35
60–69	≤25	26–28	29–31	32–35	≥36
70–79	≤23	24–26	27–29	30–35	≥36
		MEN			
Age (years)	**Poor**	**Fair**	**Good**	**Excellent**	**Superior**
20–29	≤41	42–45	46–50	51–55	≥56
30–39	≤40	41–43	44–47	48–53	≥54
40–49	≤37	38–41	42–45	46–52	≥53
50–59	≤34	35–37	38–42	43–49	≥50
60–69	≤30	31–34	35–38	39–45	≥46
70–79	≤27	28–30	31–35	36–41	≥42

Normative values have been taken from Coopers Institute of Aerobics Research (2005) *The Physical Fitness Specialist Manual.* See Heyward, 2006.

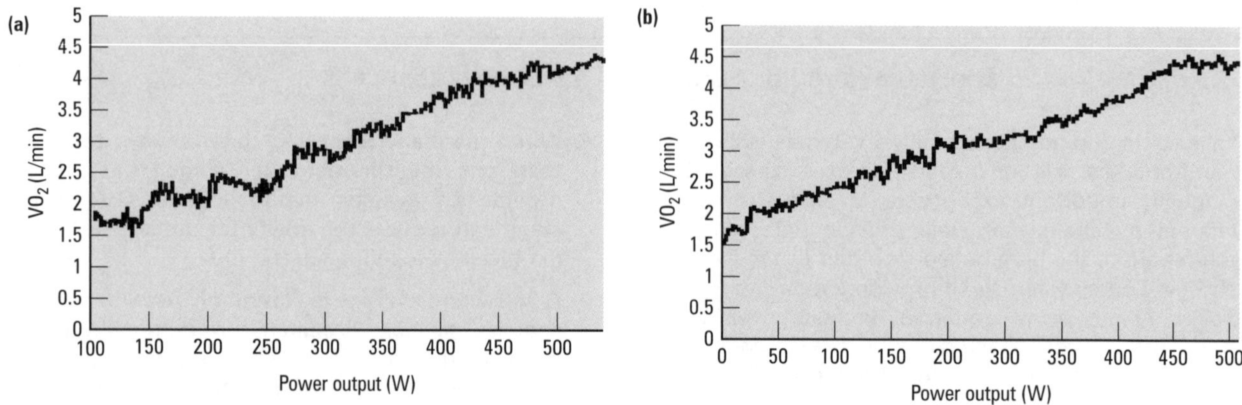

Fig. 36.3 Examples of the $\dot{V}O_2$ against power output response for step (**a**) and ramp (**b**) exercise testing protocols.

Box 36.4 Identifying $\dot{V}O_2$ max during a test

It is important that $\dot{V}O_2$ max is reached during the test. This means that the subject can end the test quickly, which minimises their discomfort and risk of harm. However, it is also important that the subject performs to their maximal level to provide a valid measure of their maximal aerobic capacity. The criteria provided below show when $\dot{V}O_2$ max is reached.

The primary measure of $\dot{V}O_2$ max is where workload is increased but no (or a very small) increase in VO_2 is recorded – less than 2 ml kg^{-1} min^{-1}. This is supported by the linear relationship between VO_2 and work rate, where a change in workload should be met by a proportional change in VO_2 and energy expenditure. Other secondary measures (which would need two to be observed at once) include:

- An RER value of >1.15;
- Attainment of age-predicted maximum heart rate;
- 5-min post-exercise blood lactate level of >8 mmol L^{-1};
- Volitional exhaustion (although this may not necessarily indicate that $\dot{V}O_2$ max was reached, just fatigue).

Text reference

Heyward, V. (2006) *Assessing Musculer Fitness in Advanced Fitness Assessment and Exercise Prescription*, 5th edn, Human Kinetics, Champaign, IL.

Sources for further study

BrianMax SportsCoach (2010) VO_2max. Available: http://www.brianmac.co.uk/vo2max.htm
Last accessed: 23/12/10. [An excellent resource for the lay person to help them understand the basics of VO_2max.]

McArdle, W.D., Katch, F.I. and Katch, V.L. (2009) *Exercise Physiology: Energy, Nutrition and Human Performance*, 7th edn, Lippincott, Williams and Wilkins, Baltimore, MD.

Withers, R., Gore, C., Gass, G. and Hahn, A. (2000) Determining maximal oxygen consumption (VO_2 max) or maximal aerobic power. In: C. Gore (ed.) *Physiological Tests for Elite Athletes*. Human Kinetics, Champaign, IL.

37 Indirect measures of aerobic capacity

Definitions

Maximal oxygen uptake ($\dot{V}O_2$max) – the maximum volume of oxygen that can be transported to and consumed by the working tissues of the body. $\dot{V}O_2$max is defined as the point at which oxygen consumption reaches a peak and plateaus despite an increase in workload.

Recovery heart rate is measured at a fixed (or reference) period after ceasing physical activity.

Indirect measurements of maximum oxygen consumption ($\dot{V}O_2$max) are used to provide rapid and reliable estimates under field conditions and in situations where there is no access to the complex equipment and trained personnel required for direct measurements (Chapter 36). Many valid and reliable field and submaximal tests that indirectly measure $\dot{V}O_2$max have been developed. In general, they are easy to conduct, cost-effective and safe.

These indirect tests are widely used in combination with other health-related fitness tests of body composition (Chapter 35), flexibility (Chapter 33), muscular strength and endurance (Chapter 40). They have a number of applications, including:

1. educating participants about their current level of fitness;
2. preparing individual exercise programmes;
3. evaluating the effectiveness of an exercise programme;
4. improving a participant's risk stratification status (Chapter 27).

Although not as accurate as direct measurement of $\dot{V}O_2$max, these tests provide valid and reliable estimates of $\dot{V}O_2$max by examining:

1. the physiological response to submaximal exercise (e.g. heart rate response to specific power outputs) that correlate with directly measured $\dot{V}O_2$max;
2. a client's test performance (e.g. distance completed in a specified time or time to complete a specified distance) that correlates with directly measured $\dot{V}O_2$max.

Choosing an indirect test – this will depend on:

1. ease of administering the test;
2. cost of test, equipment and personnel;
3. length of the test;
4. willingness of the subject;
5. experience and qualifications of the tester;
6. need for medical supervision;
7. safety concerns;
8. availability of normative data for comparison of results;
9. validity and reliability of test results;
10. subject needs, preferences, current fitness level and risk stratification.

Common health-related tests of aerobic fitness include field tests, cycle ergometer and treadmill tests, and step tests. Medical supervision may be required for moderate or high risk individuals (Chapter 27) for each of the tests described below.

Field tests

These tests are often used to measure aerobic fitness in large groups of healthy, low risk people. The advantages of these tests include:

- ease of administration;
- cheap to conduct;
- ability to test large numbers in a short time frame;
- minimal equipment (e.g. stopwatch, distance measuring device);
- they can be done wherever a measured distance is known (e.g. 400 m oval);
- they can be done using a variety of modes of exercise, including walking, walk-running, running and swimming.

Disadvantages of field tests that indirectly measure aerobic capacity include:

- They can become maximal or near maximal tests in unfit or highly motivated individuals.
- Heart rate and blood pressure cannot be monitored.
- They are affected by an individual's motivation or pacing ability. Thus, field tests are not recommended for moderate or high risk individuals (Chapter 27).

Criteria to determine which test to undertake to measure aerobic capacity indirectly include:

- **Specificity** (especially when working with athletes) – the test chosen should be as close as possible to what the person is planning to do or is currently involved in. For example, a cyclist should do a cycle ergometer test, a runner the 2.4 km run test.
- **Availability of equipment or open spaces** – if a 400-m oval is not available, it makes it hard to do a 2.4 km run test or 12-minute walk-run test. Alternatively, a cycle ergometer is relatively more expensive than a stopwatch and tape measure.
- **Safety considerations** such as elderly people doing a step test and not having the strength, balance or coordination to step-up on benches.
- **Expertise of the tester** – some expertise is required to conduct a cycle ergometer test compared to a 12-minute walk-run test.

1.5 mile (2.4 km) run test

Participants need to be able to jog-run for approximately 15 minutes to complete the test. Box 37.1 shows the procedure. This test is not recommended for unconditioned individuals or those classified as moderate to high risk (symptoms and signs of heart disease).

12 minute walk-run test

A variation of the 1.5-mile run test is to see how much distance is covered in 12 minutes. Box 37.2 shows the procedure.

Box 37.1 How to carry out a 1.5 mile (2.4 km) run test

1. **Ensure** a stopwatch and recording sheets are available.
2. **Ensure** the area for doing the test measures 1.5 miles (2.4 km) – six laps of a 440-yard (400-m) running track.
3. **Warm up** the participant(s) with some slow jogging and static stretching.
4. **Inform** the participant(s) of the purpose of the test and the need to pace themselves over the distance.
5. **Start the test** on a line and start the stopwatch.
6. **Give feedback** on the time taken for each lap and the laps left to complete the test.
7. **Record the total time** to complete the test distance.
8. **Use equation 37.1** to estimate $\dot{V}O_2$max then consult a normal values table (ACSM, 2008).

$$\dot{V}O_2\text{max}(\text{ml kg}^{-1}\ \text{min}^{-1}) = 3.5 + 483/\text{Time} \quad (37.1)$$

(in minutes to nearest hundredth of a minute)

Box 37.2 How to carry out a 12-minute (Cooper) walk-run test

1. **Ensure** a tape measure, stopwatch and recording sheets are available.
2. **Ensure** the area for doing the test is measured in metres (e.g. 400 m running track).
3. **Warm up** the participant(s) with some slow jogging and static stretching.
4. **Inform** the participant(s) of the purpose of the test, the need to pace themselves over the distance while walking or jogging or running continuously for 12 minutes, and the need to stop when they hear the tester call 'Time'.
5. **Start the test** on a line and start the stopwatch.
6. **Give feedback** on the time left to complete the test.
7. **Record the total distance** in metres completed in the 12 minutes.
8. **Use equation 37.2** to estimate $\dot{V}O_2max$, then consult a normal values table (ACSM, 2008).

$$\dot{V}O_2max(\text{mL kg}^{-1}\ \text{min}^{-1}) = (\text{distance in metres} - 504.9)/44.73 \quad (37.2)$$

Box 37.3 How to carry out a Rockport one mile walk test

1. **Ensure** a tape measure, stopwatch and recording sheets are available.
2. **Ensure** the area for doing the test measures one mile (1600 m) – four laps of a 440 yd (400 m) running track.
3. **Warm up** the participant(s) with some brisk walking and static stretching.
4. **Inform** the participant(s) of the purpose of the test, the need to pace themselves over the distance while walking as fast as they can for one mile (four laps of the oval). They must not break into a run.
5. **Start the test** on a line and start the stopwatch.
6. **Give feedback** on the distance left to complete the test.
7. **Record the time** to complete the mile.
8. **Count the recovery heart rate** for 15 seconds immediately after completing the mile and multiply the result by four to determine a 1-minute recovery heart rate (HR) (bpm).
9. **Use equation 37.3** to estimate $\dot{V}O_2max$ then consult normal value tables (ACSM, 2008). The formula is gender-specific with the constant 6.315 added for males only (no constant is used for females).

$$\dot{V}O_2max(\text{mL kg}^{-1}\ \text{min}^{-1}) = 132.853 - (0.1692 \times \text{Wt}) - (0.3877 \times \text{AGE}) + (6.315, \text{males}) - (3.2649 \times \text{TIME}) - (0.1565 \times \text{HR}) \quad (37.3)$$

where Wt = weight in kilograms; age = in years; time = time to nearest hundredth of a minute; HR = recovery HR in bpm

Definitions

Maximal tests – test is conducted to exhaustion with heart rates at or near maximum.

Submaximal tests – test is conducted to a point below maximum heart rate so that participant is not exhausted.

Factors affecting heart rates during exercise – these include:

- emotional state;
- environmental noise;
- stress;
- age;
- previous meal or beverage intake;
- some medications.

Rockport one mile walk test

This test is used for people with low levels of fitness, who are unable to run or have an injury. The participants should be able to walk briskly for one mile (1600 m). The test was developed for healthy individuals across the age range 30–69 years. Box 37.3 shows the procedure.

Submaximal tests to estimate $\dot{V}O_2max$

Many submaximal tests are widely used in sport and exercise science to estimate $\dot{V}O_2max$ without having to take the participant to exhaustion. These tests are based on the linear relationships between heart rate (HR) and work rate, and work rate and oxygen consumption.

When estimating $\dot{V}O_2max$ from submaximal HR responses, the following assumptions are made:

1. A steady-state HR is achieved at each work rate.
2. There is a linear relationship between HR and work rate.

Fig. 37.1 *Monark* cycle ergometer commonly used to conduct sub-maximal tests of aerobic capacity.
Source: Monark Exercise.co.uk.

3. $\dot{V}O_2max$ is achieved at maximal work rate.
4. Maximal HR is uniform for a given age (assumed 220–age).
5. Mechanical efficiency (i.e. $\dot{V}O_2$ at a given work rate) is the same for everyone.
6. The client is not on medication(s) that alter HR.

Cycle ergometer tests

Cycle ergometers are relatively inexpensive, easily transportable, and allow both HR (including ECG) and blood pressure to be measured easily compared to treadmill walking where the arms are moving. Clients are usually more relaxed and comfortable cycling rather than walking or running on a treadmill. Importantly, because of the linear relationship between work rate and heart rate, well calibrated cycle ergometers allow for small and precise alterations in work rates. However, clients must maintain the required pedal rate to ensure work rates are maintained, and local muscle fatigue in the quadriceps is common at higher work rates because of the relative unfamiliarity of cycling compared to walking or running.

The general procedures for laboratory-based submaximal cycle ergometer tests are:

1. **Establish seat height** – approximately 5° bend in the knee at full knee extension with hands holding the handlebars.
2. **Attach the heart rate monitor** (and blood pressure cuff if required).
3. **Warm up** for two to three minutes to accustom the participant with the required cadence (usually 50–60 rpm depending on the protocol), the position and the first workload.
4. **Advise the participant of the protocol** – usually three-minute stages with appropriate increments in workload (see Table 37.1 for the widely used YMCA Protocol).
5. **Monitor and record HR** at least twice per stage, near the end of the second and third minutes of each stage. If HR is >110 bpm, a steady-state HR (i.e. two heart rates within 6 bpm) should be reached before workload is increased.
6. **Monitor blood pressure** in the latter stages of each workload and repeat in the event of a hypotensive or hypertensive response.
7. **Monitor rating of perceived exertion (RPE)** near the end of each stage using either the 6–20 or 0–10 scale (Chapter 31).

Table 37.1 YMCA protocol for submaximal cycle ergometer test

	25 W(150 kpm min^{-1})			
First Stage	**HR <80 bpm**	**HR 80–89 bpm**	**HR 90–100 bpm**	**HR > 00 bpm**
Second Stage	125 W(750 kpm min^{-1})	100 W(600 kpm min^{-1})	75 W(450 kpm min^{-1})	50 W(300 kpm min^{-1})
Third Stage	150 W(900 kpm min^{-1})	125 W(750 kpm min^{-1})	100 W(600 kpm min^{-1})	75 W(450 kpm min^{-1})
Fourth Stage	175 W(1050 kpm min^{-1})	150 W(900 kpm min^{-1})	125 W(750 kpm min^{-1})	100 W(600 kpm min^{-1})

8. **Monitor participant's appearance and symptoms** throughout the test.
9. **Terminate the test by lowering the workload to warm up intensity** when the subject reaches 85% of the age-predicted maximal HR (220 – age), fails to conform to the test protocol, experiences shortness of breath, dizziness or asks to stop.
10. **Request that the participant cools down** by pedalling at the same intensity as warm-up for at least 4 minutes and monitor HR, blood pressure and signs and symptoms.
11. **Plot the HR–workload graph** (Fig. 37.2) and extrapolate to HR_{max} to estimate $\dot{V}O_2max$.

Box 37.4 Example of a $\dot{V}O_2$ calculation

Fig. 37.2 shows an example of the results of a YMCA submaximal cycle ergometer test for an 18-year-old female (HR_{max} = 202) with a body weight of 62 kg. The data collected are shown below:

Stage	Workload (W)	Heart rate (bpm)
1	25	79
2	125	124
3	150	140
4	175	158

Step 1 Plot a HR–Workload graph, as shown on Fig. 37.2.

Step 2 Extrapolate the linear curve to the subject's age-predicted maximal heart rate.

Step 3 Determine the maximal workload (225 W) at maximal heart rate (202 bpm) and the associated $\dot{V}O_2max$ in $L \cdot min^{-1}$.

Step 4 Convert $\dot{V}O_2max$ in $L\,min^{-1}$ (3.15 $L\,min^{-1}$) to $ml\,kg^{-1}min^{-1}$ by multiplying $L\,min^{-1}$ by 1000 (to get to $ml\,min^{-1}$) (3150 $ml\,min^{-1}$), then dividing by body weight (62 kg) to get to $ml\,kg^{-1}\,min^{-1}$ (50.8 $ml\,kg^{-1}\,min^{-1}$).

Step 5 Consult the table of normal values for $\dot{V}O_2max$ (Table 37.2) for age and gender. The subject has an excellent (approximatly 90th percentile) level of aerobic fitness.

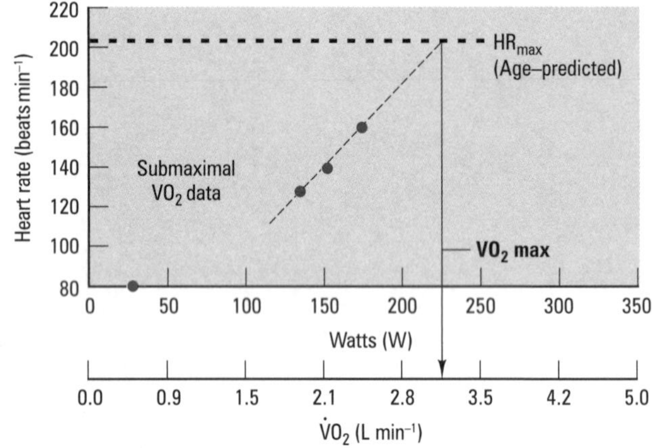

Fig. 37.2 HR–workload plot showing how to calculate $\dot{V}O_2max$ from sub-maximal heart rate and workload data.

Two of the most commonly used submaximal cycle ergometer tests are the YMCA test (multistage) described earlier and the Astrand–Rhyming test (single stage). Both are explained in detail, along with many other submaximal tests of aerobic capacity, in the books in the reference list at the end of this chapter (ACSM, 2008; 2010).

Motor-driven treadmill tests

Treadmills can be used for both maximal and submaximal testing. The advantages of using them are that they provide a common form of exercise (walking through to running), can accommodate unfit through to fit individuals, and allow for on-the-spot monitoring of heart rate

Table 37.2 Estimated $\dot{V}O_2max$ (ml kg^{-1} min^{-1}) percentiles for an Australian population (Gore and Edwards, 1992)

	Age				
Percentiles	**18–29**	**30–39**	**40–49**	**50–59**	**60–69**
Males					
5	30.7	30.7	25.6	23.1	17.3
25	38.8	36.9	32.6	30.1	26.4
50	44.3	40.9	37.2	33.6	30.5
75	50.5	46.3	43.1	37.6	34.3
95	66.5	53.6	53.6	42.4	45.5
Females					
5	26.4	21.0	19.5	17.9	16.9
25	31.1	25.9	23.5	22.2	21.8
50	36.3	31.5	29.0	25.3	25.4
75	40.8	38.5	36.1	29.4	31.4
95	53.0	47.7	44.3	38.4	34.0

and/or blood pressure responses to exercise. However, they are not easily transportable, require familiarisation, are expensive, only allow one person at a time to be tested and require calibration to ensure accuracy of test results.

An example of a submaximal treadmill test is shown in Box 37.5.

Step tests

These tests measure the HR response to stepping at a fixed rate and/or a fixed height or the recovery HR from the same exercise. Advantages of step tests include being able to measure many people at the same time, little or no equipment being required, stepping requires minimal skill or practice, and the test does not last long. However, in people with balance problems and/or those who are unconditioned (e.g. sedentary elderly persons), fatigue of the lead stepping limb may prevent completion of the test. Moreover, step tests require an energy cost of approximately 24.5–31.5 ml kg^{-1} min^{-1}, which may exceed the capacity of unconditioned subjects. Finally, the ability to monitor both HR and blood pressure is difficult with step tests.

Box 37.6 shows the procedure for one of the most commonly used step tests, the Queen's College step test.

Box 37.5 How to carry out a submaximal treadmill test

1. **Attach the heart rate (HR) monitor** and blood pressure cuff.
2. **Familiarise** the participant with the treadmill.
3. **Gradually increase the pace** to establish the first stage of walking at the treadmill at a brisk pace (normally 2.0–4.5 mph (3.2–7.2 kph) and 0% grade.
4. **Maintain the pace and grade** for 4 minutes to elicit a HR of between 50 and 70% of age-predicted maximal heart rate (220–age).
5. **Elevate the treadmill grade** by 5% for the second 4-minute stage, but maintain the same speed.
6. **Measure the HR** at the end of the second stage.
7. **Use equation 37.4** to estimate $\dot{V}O_2max$.
8. **Consult a normal values** table.

$$\dot{V}O_2max\ (\text{ml kg}^{-1}\cdot\text{min}^{-1}) = 15.1 + (21.8 \times \text{speed in mph}) + (0.327 \times \text{end HR}) + (0.00504 \times \text{end HR} \times \text{age}) + (5.98 \times \text{gender}) \quad (37.4)$$

Gender = 0 for females; 1 for males.

Box 37.6 How to carry out the Queen's College step test

1. **Ensure that a 16.25 inch (41.25 cm) step**, metronome, stopwatch and recording sheets are available.
2. **Ensure the participants** know how to take their radial pulse.
3. **Arrange the group** into two smaller groups – one male, one female.
4. **Inform the participant(s)** of the purpose of the test, the length of the test (three minutes), the need to stay in time with the metronome that is set at 96 (24-step cadence) beats per minute for males and 88 (22-step cadence) beats per minute for females.
5. **Have the group(s) practise the action of stepping** up onto the step in time with the metronome. A cadence of 24 steps per minute means stepping up with one leg, step up with the other leg, step down with the first leg, and down with the second leg 24 times in a minute.
6. **Start the test** with a countdown to 'go' and in time with the metronome.
7. **The participant(s) stops** at the end of the three minutes and palpates the pulse or has the pulse found by a partner (preferably at the radial site), while standing within the first five seconds of recovery.
8. **Take a 15-second pulse count** and multiply that figure by four to determine recovery HR in beats per minute.
9. **Use the gender-specific equations 37.5 and 37.6** to estimate $\dot{V}O_2max$, then consult a normal values table (ACSM, 2008).

$$\text{Males: } \dot{V}O_2max\ (\text{ml kg}^{-1}\ \text{min}^{-1}) = 111.33 - (0.42 \times \text{HR}) \quad (37.5)$$

$$\text{Females: } \dot{V}O_2max\ (\text{ml kg}^{-1}\ \text{min}^{-1}) = 65.81 - (0.1847 \times \text{HR}) \quad (37.6)$$

HR = recovery HR (bpm)

Text references

American College of Sports Medicine (2008) *Health-Related Physical Fitness Assessment Manual*, 2nd edn, Lippincott Williams and Wilkins, Philadelphia.

American College of Sports Medicine (2010) *ACSM's Guidelines for Exercise Testing and Prescription*, 8th edn, Lippincott Williams and Wilkins, Baltimore, Maryland.

Gore, C. J. and Edwards, D.A. (1992) *Australian Fitness Norms: A Manual for Fitness Assessors*. The Health Development Foundation, North Adelaide, South Australia.

Sources for further study

Hoffman, J. (2006) *Norms for Fitness, Performance, and Health*. Human Kinetics, Champaign, IL.

Nieman, D.C. (2010) *Exercise Testing and Prescription: A Health-Related Approach*, 7th edn, McGraw-Hill, New York.

38 Measuring energy expenditure and physical activity

Definitions

Physical activity – any bodily movement produced by contraction of skeletal muscle that substantially increases energy expenditure.

Energy expenditure – the amount of energy, measured in kilojoules, that a person uses during a particular activity.

Basal metabolic rate – energy expended when an individual is lying at complete rest, in the morning after sleep in the post-absorptive state.

Thermic effect of food – the increase in energy expenditure associated with digestion, absorption and storage of food.

Energy expenditure of activity – the energy expended above basal metabolic rate that accompanies physical activity and therefore exercise and spontaneous physical activity.

Definitions

Calorimetry – the science of measuring the heat of chemical reactions or physical changes.

Calorimeter – measuring instrument that determines quantities of heat.

Measurement of daily energy expenditure and physical activity levels requires sensitive, reliable and valid instruments. Over the years a wide variety of instruments and measurement methods have been developed to assist sport and exercise scientists in measuring both energy expenditure and, more recently, physical activity.

Sport and exercise science students will be exposed to many of these measurement devices and methods during their undergraduate studies, as well as during possible postgraduate studies and future clinical settings or placements.

Measuring energy expenditure

There are three main components of daily total energy expenditure (TEE):

1. basal metabolic rate;
2. thermic effect of food;
3. energy expenditure of activity.

Each of these can be measured using any of three methods: (i) direct calorimetry, (ii) indirect calorimetry or (iii) non-calorimetric methods. The accuracy, reliability and validity of these methods vary greatly, as does the complexity and cost of these techniques. Table 38.1 summarises these techniques, which are further explained below.

Direct calorimetry

In direct calorimetry, the rate of heat loss from the participant to the calorimeter is directly measured. The instruments (Fig. 38.1) are extremely expensive to build and operate, requiring a full-time technician to operate and maintain them.

The human calorimeter consists of an airtight container where a person can live, work and/or exercise for an extended period. A known volume of water at a specified temperature circulates through a series of coils at the top of the highly insulated chamber. The water absorbs the heat produced and radiated by the participant. For ventilation, the participant's expired air is passed from the room through chemicals that remove moisture and absorb CO_2. Oxygen added to the air recirculates through the chamber. The highly sensitive apparatus directly measures the radiative, convective and evaporative heat lost from the body. However, while direct calorimetry gives the most valid and reliable measure of TEE and its three components, its cost and size means that the method is rarely used by sport and exercise scientists.

Indirect calorimetry

Most energy-releasing reactions in the body depend on O_2 utilisation. Thus, by measuring O_2 uptake during rest, after food intake or during physical activity, scientists can obtain an indirect yet accurate estimate of energy expenditure.

Oxygen consumption and/or CO_2 production is measured and converted to energy expenditure using formulae. In this method, a

Table 38.1 Summary of techniques used to measure energy expenditure in humans

Method	Type of calorimeter	Basal metabolic rate	Resting energy expenditure	Thermic effect of food	Energy expenditure of specific activities	Total daily energy expenditure
Direct calorimeter		Yes	Yes	Yes	Yes	Yes†
Indirect calorimeter	• Closed circuit spirometry	Yes	Yes	Yes	No	No
	• Open circuit spirometry (canopy hood, portable, Douglas bag, computerised systems)	Yes*	Yes*	Yes*	Yes	Yes*
Non-calorimetric methods	• Equations	No	No	No	No	Estimated
	• Doubly labelled water	No	No	No	No	Yes (gold standard)

*Can be imprecise. †Participant is confined in a closed chamber for an extended period (Fig. 38.1).

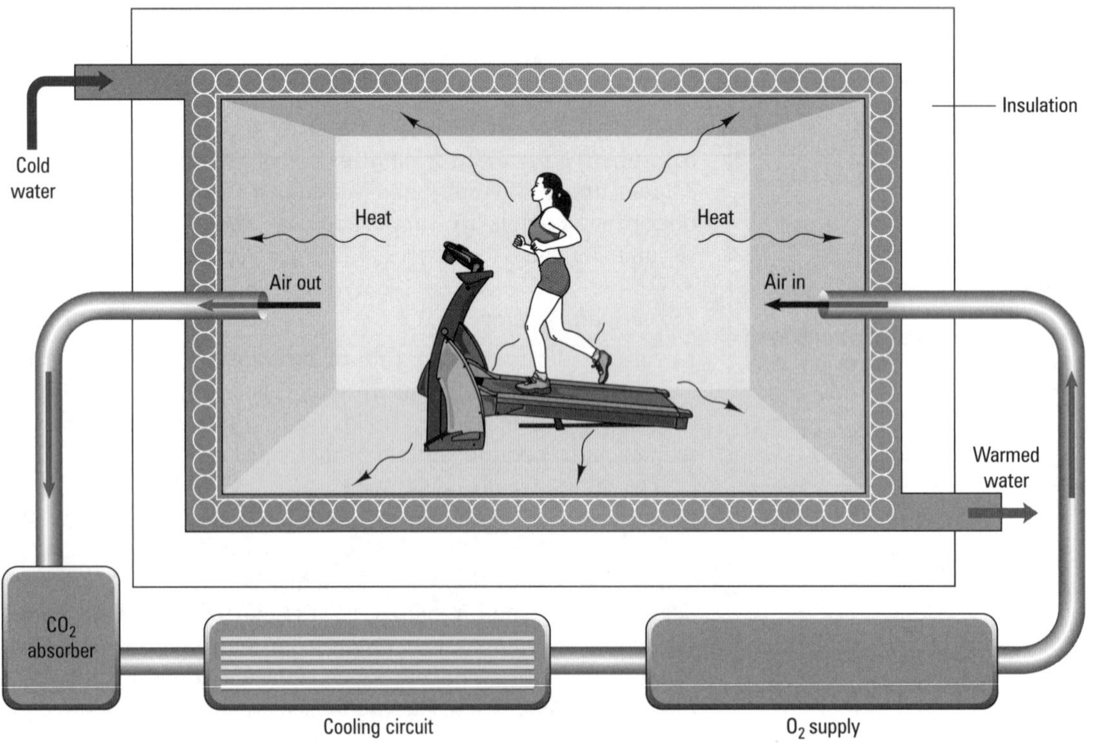

Fig. 38.1 A human calorimeter used for direct calorimetry.

person on a mixed diet of carbohydrate, fat and protein releases approximately 20.1 kJ of energy for every 1 L of oxygen consumed. Thus, if O_2 uptake can be measured during different intensities and types of exercise, scientists can estimate energy expenditure in most physical activities.

Both closed and open circuit spirometry methods (Chapter 36) are used to assess energy expenditure indirectly. Historically, closed circuit spirometry was used to measure basal metabolic rate, resting energy

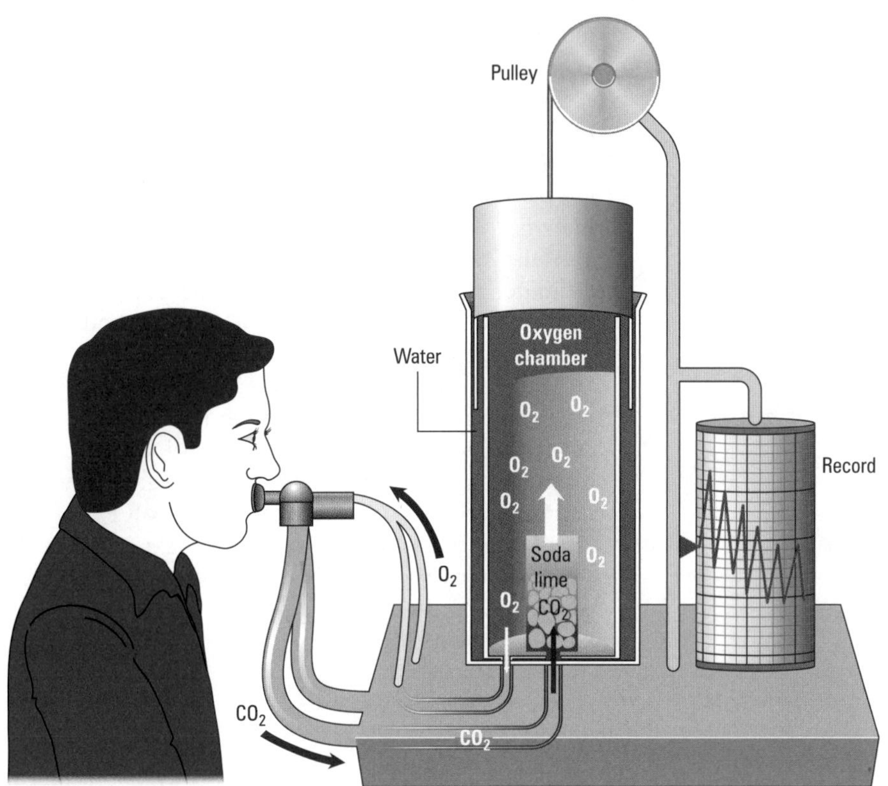

Fig. 38.2 Closed circuit spirometry.

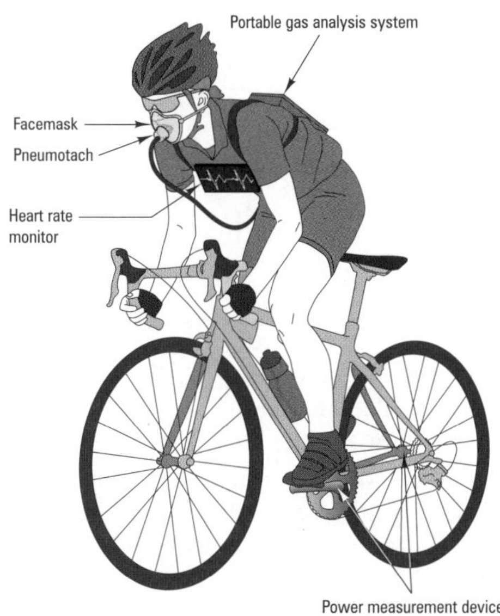

Fig. 38.3 Cyclist wearing a portable gas analysis (open circuit spirometry) to measure oxygen uptake and energy expenditure.

expenditure and the thermic effect of food. The participant breathes 100% O_2 from a pre-filled container within the spirometer. However, the system is closed because the participant re-breathes only the gas in the spirometer (Fig. 38.2). A canister of soda lime placed in the circuit absorbs the expired CO_2 and a recording device attached to the spirometer records O_2 uptake from the changes in the system's volume.

During exercise, the closed circuit system becomes impractical. The participant must remain close to the bulky equipment, the narrow breathing tubes create resistance to airflow, and the ability of the soda lime to remove CO_2 is compromised during vigorous exercise. Thus, open circuit spirometry has become the most widely used system for measurement of energy expenditure.

Open circuit spirometry involves methods discussed at length in Chapter 36. In brief, if we can calculate the oxygen uptake in litres per minute for any bout of exercise, we can estimate the energy expenditure in kilojoules since 20.1 kJ of energy is released when 1 L of O_2 is consumed.

Open circuit systems can be of three types:

1. portable spirometry;
2. Douglas bag;
3. computerised gas analysis systems.

Portable gas analysis systems such as that shown in Fig. 38.3 allow considerable freedom of movement during most activities but can become cumbersome during vigorous exercise. The systems tend to underestimate ventilation volumes during the high flow rates experienced during such exercise.

Douglas bag methods involve wearing headgear similar to Fig. 38.3, but a high velocity, low resistance two-way breathing valve allows ambient air to be breathed through one side of the valve while expired air passes through the other valve into a 150–200-L Douglas bag. A known volume of gas is then analysed for O_2 and CO_2 concentration, and the remaining volume of air is passed through a gas meter to estimate expired volume in the measured time of the task. Oxygen uptake is then calculated using the methods in Chapter 36 and the energy expenditure estimated.

The final and most commonly used type of open circuit spirometry uses computerised instrumentation attached to gas analysis systems to enable an accurate and rapid calculation of O_2 uptake and thus energy expenditure. This type of system measures expired or inspired volumes and the O_2 and CO_2 concentration of expired gases to enable the calculation of O_2 uptake and energy expenditure (Chapter 36). Each of these systems is relatively expensive to purchase and relies greatly on correct calibration using reference standards of O_2 and CO_2 as well as known air volumes.

Non-calorimetric methods

A number of techniques have been developed to predict energy expenditure by extrapolation from physiological measurements and observations. These include the doubly labelled water technique and prediction equations. These methods are often standardised against calorimetric methods.

Doubly labelled water technique

^{18}O and ^{2}H – are found in trace amounts in the human body.

This is sometimes called the isotope dilution method, and is used in controlled studies where only total daily energy expenditure is the required measure. It is often seen as the gold standard to validate other methods, but drawbacks are the cost of the water enriched with non-radioactive isotopes (usually ^{2}H and ^{18}O), as well as the cost of mass spectrometric analysis of the two isotopes in pre-test and post-test samples of urine, saliva or blood.

The principle of the method is based on the fact that in body water, the O_2 of expired CO_2 is in equilibrium with H_2O:

$$CO_2 + H_2O \leftrightarrow H_2CO_3 \quad (38.1)$$

Thus, if O_2 in body water is tagged with the tracer ^{18}O, the label will distribute not only in body water but also the circulating H_2CO_3 and expired CO_2. Over time the concentration of the O_2 label in the body water will decrease as CO_2 is expired and body water is lost in urine, sweat and through respiration. If the H_2 in water is also tagged with the tracer ^{2}H, the label will distribute solely in the circulating H_2O and H_2CO_3. Again, the concentration of ^{2}H label will decrease as body water is lost. Thus, if both oxygen and hydrogen in body water are tagged with known amounts of tracers at the same time, the differences in elimination rates of ^{18}O and ^{2}H tracers (determined by an isotope ratio mass spectrometer) will represent the elimination rate of CO_2.

Oxygen consumption is easily estimated based on CO_2 production and an assumed RQ value of 0.85.

In brief, the method involves:

a. Baseline control values are determined by analysing the participant's urine, blood or saliva.

b. A known dose of doubly labelled water is ingested based on the body mass of the participant. Traditionally, 0.25 g of ^2H and 0.12 g of ^{18}O per kg of estimated body water is given.

c. Five hours are allowed for the doubly labelled water to distribute through the body water.

d. The enriched urine, blood or saliva samples are taken every day or week for between seven and 21 days. The accuracy of measurement is increased with more regular measurement. Samples should be frozen for later analysis.

e. The samples are measured for concentrations of ^{18}O and ^2H over time.

f. The rate of CO_2 production is then calculated using equation 38.2:

$$rCO_2\ (\text{mol day}^{-1}) = TBW/2\ [(1.041 \times k^2H) - (1.007 \times k^{18}O)] \quad (38.2)$$

where TBW is the total body water (L); k is the rate of loss over the measurement period; 1.041 and 1.007 are the hydrogen and oxygen dilution spaces, respectively.

g. The total daily energy expenditure is then determined using equation 38.3:

$$\text{Total daily energy expenditure (kcal day}^{-1}) = (3.94/RQ + 1.10) \times 22.41 \times rCO_2 \quad (38.3)$$

rCO_2 is converted to L day^{-1} by multiplying by 22.41 (1 L = 22.41 moles); RQ is typically assumed to be 0.85.

Definitions

Respiratory quotient (RQ) – the ratio between carbon dioxide produced and oxygen uptake.

$$RQ = CO_2 \text{ produced}/O_2 \text{ uptake}$$

The RQ provides a convenient guide for approximating the nutrient mixture that is catabolised during rest and aerobic exercise.

General rule of thumb – the measurement period should last two to three half-lives of each isotope. This corresponds to roughly 8–10 days for a very active person and 14–18 days for a very sedentary older person.

Prediction equations

Prediction equations for energy expenditure are also available. For example, a number of equations have been developed for estimating resting metabolic rate (RMR) for a variety of age groups and for both genders (Table 38.2):

Table 38.2 Common prediction equations used to measure energy expenditure in humans

Group	Age	Equation	No.
Males:		RMR (kcal day^{-1}) = 66.47 + (13.75 × weight in kg) + (5 × height in cm) – (6.76 × age in years)	(38.4)
Females:		RMR (kcal day^{-1}) = 655.1 + (9.56 × weight in kg) + (1.85 × height in cm) – (4.68 × age in years)	(38.5)
Males	18–30 years	RMR (kcal day^{-1}) = (15.3 × weight in kg) + 679	(38.6)
	30–60 years	RMR (kcal day^{-1}) = (11.6 × weight in kg) + 879	(38.7)
	>60 years	RMR (kcal day^{-1}) = (13.5 × weight in kg) + 487	(38.8)
Females	18–30 years	RMR (kcal day^{-1}) = (14.7 × weight in kg) + 496	(38.9)
	30–60 years	RMR (kcal day^{-1}) = (8.7 × weight in kg) + 829	(38.10)
	>60 years	RMR (kcal day^{-1}) = (10.5 × weight in kg) + 596	(38.11)

1 kcal (Calorie) = 4.2 kJ

Table 38.3 Metabolic calculations for estimating energy expenditure ($\dot{V}O_2$ ml kg^{-1} min^{-1}) during common physical activities

	Sum these components			
Activity	**Resting component**	**Horizontal component**	**Vertical component/ resistance component**	**Limitations**
Walking	3.5	0.1 × speed*	1.8 × speed* × grade#	Most accurate at speeds of 50–100 m min^{-1} (1.9–3.7 mph)
Running	3.5	0.2 × speed*	0.9 × speed* × grade#	Most accurate at speeds of >134 m min^{-1} (>5 mph)
Leg cycling	3.5	3.5	1.8 × work rate† × body mass§	Most accurate at work rates of 300–1200 kg m min^{-1} (50–200 W)

*Speed in m min^{-1} (1 mph = 1.6 km h^{-1} = 28.2 m min^{-1}); #grade is % grade expressed in decimal format (e.g. 10% = 0.10); †Work rate in kg m min^{-1}; §body mass in kg.

Other equations for estimating the energy expenditure of common physical activities such as walking, running and cycling have also been developed and are shown in Table 38.3.

Below are the more common methods used to estimate the three components of daily energy expenditure.

Measuring basal metabolic rate (BMR) and resting metabolic rate (RMR)

While in most clinical settings the prediction equations above are widely used to estimate BMR or RMR, Box 38.1 describes the method more commonly used in laboratory or research settings.

Measuring the thermic effect of food

Ideally, a BMR measure should be undertaken first, after which participants are given a meal of food for which the energy content is known precisely and which is greater than 1680 kJ. Energy expenditure should be measured using gas analysis (Chapter 36) for 400 minutes or

Box 38.1 How to measure basal metabolic rate (and resting energy expenditure)

1. **Calibrate the gas analysis system** according to the manufacturer's instructions.
2. **Perform the measurement between 6 and 9 am** with the participant ideally having slept overnight in the laboratory and not having eaten any food or energy-containing fluids (water is acceptable) for 9 hours before measurement.
3. **Ensure the participant is supine** with a single pillow supporting the head or with the head of the bench at 10° tilt.
4. **Ensure the room is thermally comfortable (22–25°C),** quiet and dimly lit.
5. **Instruct the participant to lie motionless and quiet** during measurement.
6. **Quietly connect the nose clip and mouthpiece** of the gas analysis machine to the participant (Chapter 36).
7. **Measure oxygen consumption** for 20–40 minutes.
8. **Calculate the mean oxygen uptake per minute in L min^{-1}** as well as the mean respiratory quotient for the measurement period.
9. **Consult a table of thermal equivalents** for kcal per litre of O_2 for the mean respiratory quotient measured.
10. **Multiply the mean oxygen uptake (L min^{-1})** by the kcal equivalent to derive the BMR or RMR.

NOTE: Measurement of RMR is as described for BMR except that it can be done at any time of the day but with no energy consumed (food or fluids) or at least 6 hours before the test and no vigorous activity undertaken with in the same time period. The participant should lie supine for 60 minutes before the test.

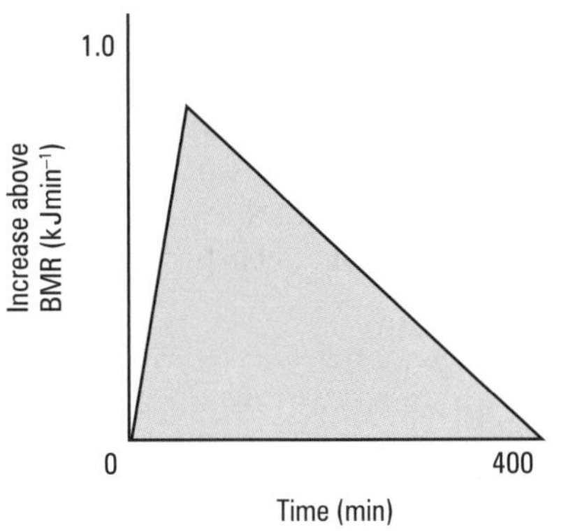

Fig. 38.4 Calculating the thermic effect of a meal. Shaded area under the curve represents thermic effect of a meal.

Table 38.4 Energy expenditure (kcal min^{-1}) of various common physical activities

Activity	Males	Females
Sleeping or bed rest	1.08	0.90
Sitting quietly	1.40	1.15
Standing quietly	1.75	1.37
Normal walking	4.0	3.4
Cooking	2.0	1.7
Cleaning	4.3	3.5
Moderate exercise	7.5	6.0
Vigorous exercise	>7.5	>6.0

Table 38.5 Approximate energy expenditure (expressed as multiples of BMR) of various common physical activities

Activity	Energy cost (range)
Sleeping	1.0 (0.9–1.1)
Sitting quietly	1.2 (1.1–1.3)
Standing busy	1.5 (1.3–1.7)
Slow walking	2.0 (1.5–2.5)
Fast walking	4.0 (3.0–5.0)
Fast walking uphill or with load	6.0 (5.0–7.0)
Light exercise	3.0 (2.0–4.0)
Moderate exercise	4.0 (3.0–5.0)
Vigorous exercise	7.0 (5.0–9.0)
Strenuous exercise	10.0 (7.0–13.0)

until energy expenditure falls within 5% of the previously measured BMR. Because of the long response time of some gas analysis systems, and to avoid participant agitation over a very long test, measurement can be carried out for 15 out of every 30 minutes.

The thermic effect of food is calculated from the area under the energy-expenditure-above-BMR-versus-time curve (Fig. 38.4).

Energy expenditure of physical activity

Table 38.4 enables the energy cost of an activity to be estimated based on the wide variety of physical activities and intensities that people undertake. These values have been previously determined based on gas analysis methods (open circuit spirometry), discussed above.

Resting energy expenditure should be measured first, ideally in the same body position, using open circuit spirometry methods. For example, the energy cost of typing should have the resting metabolic rate measured sitting. Measurement of the activity of interest should be performed for 10–20 minutes to allow a steady-state of energy expenditure. The energy expenditure for the activity is determined by subtracting the resting energy expenditure of the posture from the steady-state expenditure.

Approximate energy costs of common activities can also be estimated as multiples of BMR. Some examples are shown in Table 38.5.

It must be appreciated that these estimates do not take into account the many variables that can affect energy expenditure, including the wide range of intensities of exercise; ambient conditions such as temperature, humidity and wind or altitude; emotional stressors, and food or fluid intake.

Measuring physical activity

The objective measurement of physical activity in large populations and smaller groups has developed rapidly over the past two decades. A number of devices are used to measure physical activity and indirectly estimate energy expenditure objectively.

Pedometers

A pedometer measures the number of steps the wearer takes in a period of time. When a person strides or makes movements, a balance inside the pedometer is disturbed enough to make sensors count a step. Thus, one disadvantage of the pedometer is that, if for example you tap your feet while sitting at a desk, it could include that movement in the total step count. However, it is inexpensive and easy to mount and wear (typically on the hip). While they are suitable for large campaigns and other intervention-based studies because of their low cost and ease of use, they grossly underestimate physical activity when expressed as energy expenditure.

Heart rate monitoring

Heart rate monitoring is based on the linear relationship between heart rate and oxygen consumption in moderate-to-vigorous exercise intensities. Thus, a major limitation, particularly in sedentary or obese persons, is that this relationship is not linear and is confounded by stress, temperature and dietary factors. Moreover, heart rate also depends on the aerobic fitness of the participants and a valid estimation

Fig. 38.5 An example of an electronic pedometer.
Source: Alamy Images: ST-Images.

Piezoelectricity – is the ability of some materials (notably crystals) to generate an electric field or electric potential in response to applied mechanical stress.

Fig. 38.6 An example of an accelerometer – the Tracmor®.
Source: Phillips.

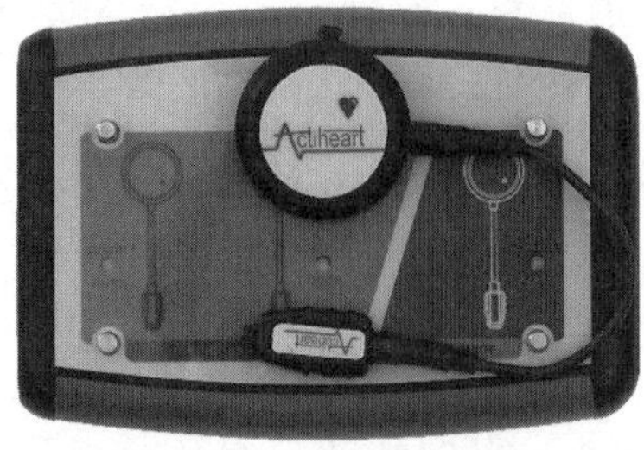

Fig. 38.7 An Actiheart® device and associated reader that combines heart rate monitoring and accelerometry.
Source: CamNtech.

of energy expenditure depends on an individual calibration based on an individual's maximum and resting heart rate or, even better, against a direct measurement of oxygen uptake against heart rate.

Modern heart rate monitors are easy to use and can store data for many days. They are best used in small scale studies owing to the need for individual calibration of resting and maximum heart rates.

Accelerometers

Accelerometers measure movement in one, two or three planes by piezoelectric transducers and microprocessors. The devices are small and easy to carry with the units of measurement (counts per minute) quantifying the magnitude and direction of accelerations. The newer models can store data for several months and can store data for each 10-second period within this time, thus allowing for measurement of short bursts of activity.

There are a number of problems with accelerometers in measuring physical activity and energy expenditure. These include:

- Output is frequency-dependent, making it difficult to compare activity levels of different age groups who may have different step frequencies because of size differences.
- Output plateaus out when speed increases to more than 10 km h^{-1} making studies in very active participants difficult.
- Accelerometers do not measure physical activity where no acceleration occurs, such as in rowing, cycling, skating or hill climbing when the movement might be at a constant speed or velocity.
- Isometric energy expenditure is not recorded, so weight lifting, carrying and pushing activities are not accurately measured.

The challenge of relating counts of accelerations per minute to energy expenditure remains to be solved in accelerometry. However, in walking and running, there appears good agreement that walking at 4 km h^{-1} equates to approximately 2000 accelerometer counts per minute.

Other instruments

Recently, a device that combines heart rate monitoring and accelerometry has been developed. The Actiheart® is being seen as the new gold standard for measuring energy expenditure. It uses both heart rate and activity data to calculate energy expenditure accurately and has been validated against doubly labelled water, the gold standard for measuring daily energy expenditure in humans. The Actiheart® comes with a reader and software that enables downloading of data to estimate energy expenditure. The accelerometer measures changes in body position. It might be unsuitable for large scale projects as, ideally, the instrument should be set up by the same person.

Self-reporting of physical activity levels

Self-report tools include activity records (diaries), logs that are self-administered and questionnaires that can be self- or interviewer-administered.

Behavioural observation

This method involves classifying free-living behaviours into distinct categories (walking, standing, running, sitting, etc.) and contexts (when, where and with whom) that can later be quantified and analysed. It is widely used when assessing the physical activity levels of children who struggle to recall or record physical activity behaviours. Common software tools include BEACHES, SOFIT and SOPLAY that are considered in detail in Welk (2002).

Activity records and logs

Diaries provide a detailed account of all physical activity performed in a given time period. However, they are demanding for respondents and very time-consuming for researchers to process and quantify. Physical activity logs are typically structured as checklists of specific activities based on population-specific physical activity focus groups. However, if the activity is not on the checklist, then the method becomes invalid as a measure of physical activity.

Self-report questionnaires

These have been the method of choice in large scale epidemiological studies examining the relationships between levels of physical activity and health outcomes. Pereira *et al.* (1997) have collected 28 of these into one source together with information on the validity and reliability of each questionnaire.

As an example of a self-report questionnaire, the Karolinska Institute in Sweden has developed an International Physical Activity Questionnaire, which is available in many languages and in short or long versions online at: www.ipaq.kj.se/downloads.htm with the short version (time spent in moderate and vigorous activity) reproduced in Box 38.2 on p. 290.

The longer version examines time spent sitting and time spent in occupational, transport, household and leisure time physical activity, with the intensity of each assessed as well. While the reliability of the IPAQ has been shown to be low to good in test–re-test analysis, it appears to lead to higher estimates of physical activity than other questionnaires. Moreover, typical of most self-report tools, validation against measured criteria is lacking. Furthermore, self-report tools are subject to bias and misclassification.

Choosing a measurement tool

Given the wide array of methods and equipment available, sport and exercise scientists are often faced with the dilemma of which measurement instrument or method to use. Table 38.6 summarises the outputs that the methods discussed above can provide. Students need to be able to ensure the right method is chosen to answer the research question posed in their projects.

More importantly, there are factors such as the imposition on the participants being measured, the time involved and the cost of each of the methods that need to be considered. Table 38.7 and Fig. 38.8 may help in deciding which method to use.

Box 38.2 An example of a self-report questionnaire – the International Physical Activity Questionnaire

INTERNATIONAL PHYSICAL ACTIVITY QUESTIONNAIRE

We are interested in finding out about the kinds of physical activities that people do as part of their everyday lives. The questions will ask you about the time you spent being physically active in the **last 7 days**. Please answer each question even if you do not consider yourself to be an active person. Please think about the activities you do at work, as part of your house and yard work, to get from place to place, and in your spare time for recreation, exercise or sport.

Think about all the **vigorous** activities that you did in the last **7 days. Vigorous** physical activities refer to activities that take hard physical effort and make your breathe much harder than normal. Think only about those physical activities that you did for at least 10 minutes a time.

1. During the **last 7 days**, on how many days did you do **vigorous** physical activities like heavy lifting, digging, aerobics or fast bicycling?

   _____ **days per week**

   ❐ No vigorous physical activities ⟶ ***Skip to question 3***

2. How much time did you usually spend doing **vigorous** physical activities on one of those days?

   ______ **hours per day**

   ______ **minutes per day**

   ❐ Don't know/Not sure

Think about all the **moderate** activities that you did in the **last 7 days. Moderate** activities refer to activities that take moderate physical effort and make you breathe somewhat harder than normal. Think only about those physical activities that you did for at least 10 minutes at a time.

3. During the **last 7 days**, on how many days did you do **moderate** physical activities like carrying light loads, bicycling at a regular pace, or doubles tennis? Do not include walking.

   _______ **days per week**

   ❐ No moderate physical activites ⟶ ***Skip to question 5***

4. How much time did you usually spend doing **moderate** physical activities on one of those days?

   ________ **hours per day**

   _______ **minutes per day**

   ❐ Don't know/Not sure

Think about the time you spent **walking** in the **last 7 days**. This includes at work and at home, walking to travel from place to place, and any other walking that you might do solely for recreation, sport, exercise or leisure.

5. During the **last 7 days**, on how many days did you **walk** for at least 10 minutes at a time?

   _______ **days per week**

   ❐ No walking ⟶ ***Skip to question 7***

6. How much time did you usually spend **walking** on one of those days?

   ________ **hours per day**

   _______ **minutes per day**

   ❐ Don't know/Not sure

The last question is about the time you spent **sitting** on weekdays during the **last 7 days**. Include time spent at work, at home, while doing course work and during leisure time. This may include time spent sitting at a desk, visiting friends, reading, or sitting or lying down to watch television.

7. During the **last 7 days**, how much time did you spend **sitting** on a **week day**?

   ________ **hours per day**

   _______ **minutes per day**

   ❐ Don't know/Not sure

Table 38.6 Methods of measuring physical activity and variables/outputs measured

Method	Units of measurement	Variables	Output measure
Self-report	Bouts of physical activity	Frequency Intensity Duration Energy expenditure	Number of bouts > criterion level Number or % of bouts Number of min > criterion level Estimates based on METs
Activity monitors or motion sensors	Movement counts	Frequency Intensity Duration Energy expenditure	Number of bouts > criterion level Average counts per day or interval Number of min > criterion level Estimates from a calibration equation
Heart rate	Beats (per minute)	Frequency Intensity Duration Energy expenditure	Number of bouts > criterion level Average HR per day or interval Number of min > criterion level Estimates from a calibration equation
Pedometers	Step counts	Frequency Intensity Duration Energy expenditure	Not available Not available Number of steps taken Estimates from a calibration equation
Direct observation	Activity rating	Frequency Intensity Duration Energy expenditure	Number of bouts > criterion level Number or % of bouts Number of min > criterion level Estimates based on METs
Indirect calorimetry	O_2 consumption	Frequency Intensity Duration Energy expenditure	Number of bouts > criterion level Average VO_2 level Monitored time > threshold Total energy expenditure
Doubly labelled water	CO_2 production	Frequency Intensity Duration Energy expenditure	Not available Not available Not available Total energy expenditure

Table 38.7 Ranking of physical activity assessment methods on six different parameters (1 = highest rank; 5 = lowest rank)

Method	Participant interference	Participant effort	Contextual information	Activity structure	Objective data	Observer time/cost
Behavioural observation	5	1	1	2	4	5
Questionnaires/diaries/interviews	4	5	2	4	5	2
Heart rate monitoring	3	4	4	3	3	3
Pedometers and accelerometers	2	3	3	1	2	1
Doubly labelled water	1	2	5	5	1	4

Recently, a number of papers (Jorgensen *et al.*, 2009; Salmon and Okely, 2009; Westerterp, 2009) have been written to help practitioners decide which method(s) to use when measuring physical activity. Students interested in this area are strongly encouraged to consult these. These papers suggest that combining methods might increase the validity of physical activity measurement. Table 38.8 summarises the suggested combinations of methods to use.

In spite of the large number of methods for measuring physical activity, no one 'perfect' method has emerged to date as no one method enables the measurement of frequency, intensity and duration of

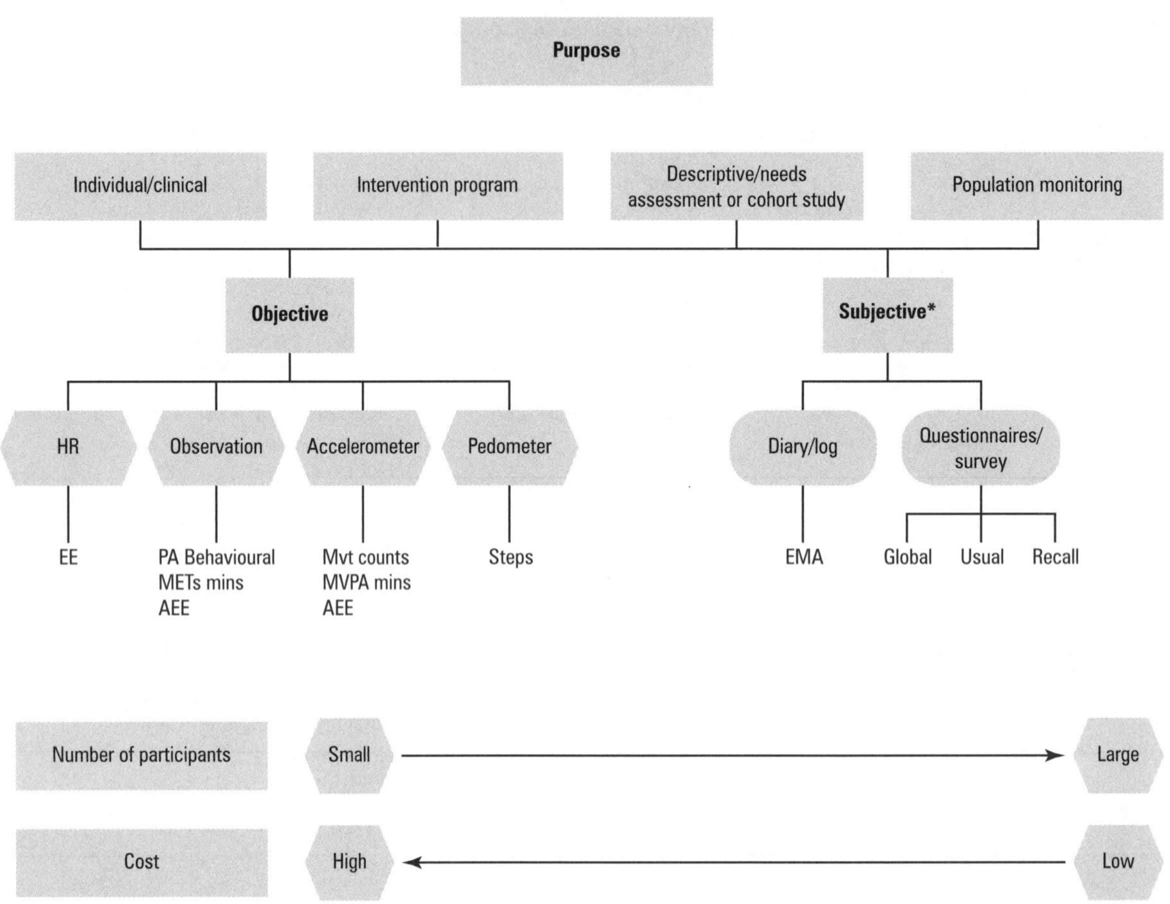

Fig. 38.8 Decision flow chart to select physical activity measurement methods for use with young people. HR, heart rate; EE, energy expenditure; AEE, active energy expenditure; Mvt counts, movement counts; MVPA, moderate-to-vigorous-intensity physical activity; EMA, ecological momentary assessment.

Table 38.8 Recommended ways to combine physical activity assessment methods

Number of participants	Method 1	Method 2
10–20	Doubly labelled water	Heart rate monitoring
	24-hour indirect calorimetry	Heart rate monitoring
	24-hour indirect calorimetry	Accelerometer
	Observation	Heart rate monitoring
	Indirect calorimetry	Motion sensor
	Heart rate monitoring	Pedometer
	Heart rate monitoring	Accelerometer
100–200	Self-report questionnaire	Pedometer
	Self-report questionnaire	Accelerometer
>200	Self-report questionnaire	Heart rate monitoring

physical activity. Thus, the choice of measurement instrument depends on the outcome desired balanced with the cost, time required by the participants and researchers, and the size of the cohort being examined.

Text references and sources for further study

Jorgensen, T., Andersen, L.B., Froberg, K. *et al.* (2009) Position statement: testing physical condition in a population – how good are the methods? *European Journal of Sport Science,* **9**, 257–67.

Levine, J.A. (2005) Measurement of energy expenditure. *Public Health Nutrition*, **8**, 1123–32.

Pereira, M.A., Fitzgerald, S.J., Gregg, E.W. *et al.* (1997) A collection of physical activity questionnaires for health-related research. *Medicine and Science in Sports and Exercise*, **29**, S1–S205.

Salmon, J. and Okely, T. (2009) Physical activity in young people: assessment and methodological issues. *Journal of Science and Medicine in Sport,* **12**, 513–91.

Welk, G.J. (ed.) (2002) *Physical Activity Assessments in Health Related Research*. Human Kinetics, Champaign, IL.

Westerterp, K.R. (2009) Assessment of physical activity: a critical appraisal. *European Journal of Applied Physiology*, **105**, 823–8.

39 Measuring anaerobic power and capacity

Definitions

Alactic – anaerobic energy production that does not result in the production of lactic acid.

Anaerobic – energy production that does not require oxygen.

Anaerobic capacity – the maximum amount of energy that can be produced using anaerobic energy metabolism over a short period of time.

Anaerobic power – the amount of force that can be produced with respect to speed through anaerobic energy production.

Maximal accumulated oxygen deficit (MAOD) – the difference between the measured oxygen cost and predicted oxygen cost during a maximal intensity bout of exercise.

Vertec – device used to measure vertical jump.

Wingate – a type of ergometer commonly used to perform peak power assessment during cycling.

The testing of anaerobic power and capacity is a common requirement when assessing the physiological capacities of an athlete. In the sport and exercise science course you will learn a variety of basic tests that can be used to assess anaerobic performance. Anaerobic power and capacity are important physiological attributes required for performance in a variety of sports. More specifically, the importance of anaerobic power or anaerobic capacity may be a specific performance factor. Sport or exercise that benefit greatly from short, explosive movements are best assessed using tests of anaerobic power. On the other hand, activities that require a short-term bout of sustained high intensity activity are better suited to tests of anaerobic capacity.

Importantly, while the majority of sports performance and testing appears to revolve around the measurement and improvement of aerobic fitness, the importance of anaerobic power and capacity should not be overlooked. These tests can be limited by specificity of the tests; although with new and improved ergometry and measurement systems becoming available, the assessment of anaerobic performance has become more accurate and easy than previously. This chapter details some of the more common tests used to assess both anaerobic power and capacity by sport and exercise scientists.

Tests of anaerobic power

This physiological capacity refers to the ability of an individual to produce explosive power using anaerobic energy production. Tests of anaerobic power quite often focus on short-term and explosive movements or bouts to assess the maximal amount of force that the muscles are capable of producing. Listed below are methods that are typically used to measure anaerobic power simply: the vertical jump and the alactic cycling test.

Vertical jump

The vertical jump test is an easy-to-perform field measure of anaerobic power. An important skill that you will learn across the course is how to measure an individual's vertical jump accurately. The ability to be able to quantify power from such a simple movement is a positive feature of the test, as many other tests do not allow this and therefore are not comparable across time. The vertical jump test is applicable across a wide range of sports to provide a measure of explosive power; a physical quantity that is related to performance in a range of sports. The vertical jump can be performed using a variety of methods, although the development of the *Vertec* or *Yardstick* apparatus (Fig. 39.1) has provided a reliable and accurate system that is easily transportable and user-friendly. The sequence of steps below provide information on how to measure an individual's vertical jump correctly.

1. **Weigh the subject using electronic scales.** Politely ask the subject to remove all clothing that they will not be wearing during the test (i.e. jackets, tracksuit pants). Record their body mass to the nearest 0.1 kg.

Fig. 39.1 A demonstration of the *Vertec* vertical jump measurement device in use.

2. **Assemble the *Vertec* (or other vertical jump apparatus) on a flat, non-slip surface away from any walls or other objects.** If a Vertec is not available, the procedure can be applied to other systems such as a ruler taped to a wall or chalk in the hands.
3. **Align the vanes of the *Vertec* so that they are on the opposite side to the ground supports.** Ensure that all the vanes of the *Vertec* are vertically aligned using the reach stick supplied.
4. **Adjust the height of the *Vertec* to ensure that the subject can touch the bottom vanes (<20 cm)**, but will not jump over the *Vertec* upon performing a maximal jump. (*NOTE:* This may occur in individuals who possess a vertical jump >1 m).
5. **Ask the subject(s) to complete a warm-up.** Try to keep this standardised between individuals and repeat tests. Ensure that the warm-up consists of running and practice jumps before testing.
6. **When ready, place the subject underneath and slightly to the side of the *Vertec* where the vanes are located.** Instruct them to raise their dominant arm above their head to touch the vanes to check their alignment underneath the vanes.
7. **Ask the subject to reach up and touch the highest vane possible** while keeping their feet flat on the ground. Ensure that their knees and elbows are not bent. The number of the highest vane that can be reached is recorded as the standing height. The subject can then lower their arm. Using the reach stick, move the 20 vanes above this mark to decrease interference in the vertical jump.
8. **Inform the subject of the vertical jump protocol that is to be used** as several sports have specific and discrete differences in their protocol. The most common (and for a non-sporting population) is a countermovement jump with arm swing and no step in. This allows the subject to jump from a standing two-legged stance by bending at their knees and swinging their arms to gain momentum as they jump.
9. **Instruct the subject to touch the highest vane possible at the height of their jump.** Record the number of the highest vane touched, as this is the subject's peak jump height. The subject should complete the test at least three times and continue until no improvement in jump height is seen in two consecutive jumps.
10. **Calculate the vertical jump height and explosive power using equations 39.1 and 39.2.** Tables 39.1 and 39.2 provide normative data for comparison from both normal and athletic populations.

Vertical jump height (VJH)

$$\text{VJH (cm)} = \text{peak jump height} - \text{standing height} \quad (39.1)$$

where peak jump height = the number of the highest vane/measure recorded from any jump and standing height = the number of the highest vane or measurement taken from the subject's standing arm extension.

Vertical jump explosive power

$$\text{Power (W)} = \text{body mass} \times (4.9 \times \text{vertical jump height})^{1/2} \times 9.807 \quad (39.2)$$

where body mass (kg) = body mass of subject and vertical jump height (m) = height of a maximal vertical jump.

Table 39.1 Percentile rankings for vertical jump for a non-sporting population

Percentile	Children 9–11 years	Boys 12–14 years	Girls 12–14 years	Boys 15–17 years	Girls 15–17 years	Men 18–34 years	Women 18–34 years
90	38	46	38	61	41	64	33
80	36	43	36	58	38	61	31
70	31	41	33	53	36	58	30
60	28	36	31	48	33	48	25
50	25	33	28	41	28	41	20
40	23	28	25	30	20	33	15
30	18	23	20	20	15	23	10
20	10	13	10	13	8	20	5
10	5	5	5	5	5	5	3

Normative data adapted from Schell and Leelarthaepin (1994). Values given are in centimetres.

Table 39.2 Percentile rankings for vertical jump for various sporting populations

Sport	Gender	Average (±SD)
Basketball	Female	46.6 ± 5.6
	Male	69.5 ± 4.8
Cricket	Female	41.3 ± 5.1
	Male	52.6 ± 9.5
Hockey	Female	46.0 ± 4.0
	Male	56.0 ± 5.0
Netball	Female	53.4 ± 4.6
Soccer	Female	42.0 ± 3.0
Softball	Female	47.0 ± 6.0
Tennis	Female	40.3 ± 5.2
	Male	53.2 ± 4.8

Normative data adapted from Finn *et al.* (2000). Values given are in centimetres.

Alactic power cycling test

Another measure of anaerobic power is a 10-second cycling test, otherwise known as the alactic cycling test, given that it places maximal stress on that energy system. The alactic cycling test is a laboratory-based test to measure short-term maximal power output, which is somewhat of a different quality to what the vertical jump test measures. The alactic cycling test can be adapted to be performed on a variety of cycling ergometers within the laboratory. The steps below give some basic instructions in how to complete an alactic cycling test in your laboratory.

1. **Set up the cycling ergometer to be used for anaerobic power testing.** Ergometers may differ across laboratories, from wind-braked, mechanically braked or electromagnetically braked (Fig. 39.2). Ensure that the equipment is working before the test and that connections to data recording systems are working.
2. **Weigh the subject using electronic scales.** Politely ask the subject to remove all unnecessary clothing and their shoes. Record their body mass to the nearest 0.1 kg.
3. **Ask the subject to sit on the cycle ergometer and adjust the seat height** so that the subject has close to full extension (~170°) when the pedal is at the very bottom of the cycle.
4. **Place their feet into the pedals and tighten the foot straps** or alternatively secure the feet to the pedals so that they cannot become separated during the test.

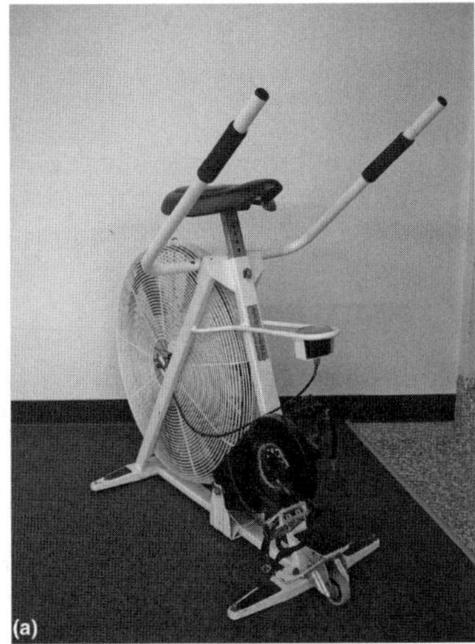

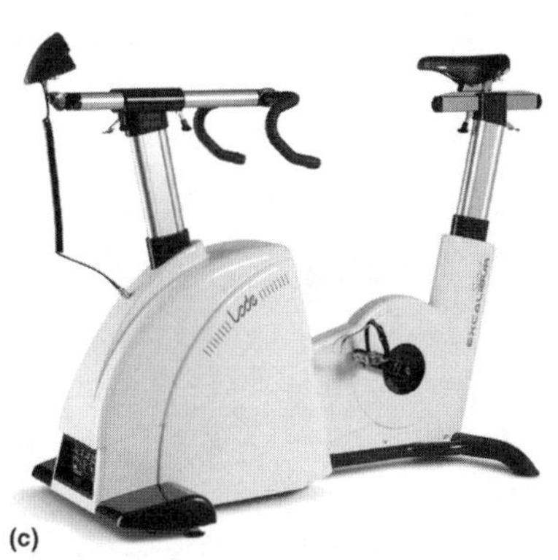

Fig. 39.2 Various cycle ergometers: (**a**) front-accessed wind-braked; (**b**) mechanically braked Monark, and; (**c**) electromagnetically braked Lode ergometer.

Source: (**a**) Peter Reaburn; (**b**) Monark Exercise.co.uk; (**c**) Lode B. V.

5. **Instruct the subject(s) to complete a warm-up.** Try to keep this standardised between individuals and repeat tests. The warm-up should consist of at least five minutes pedalling at a comfortable intensity with brief periods of intense cycling. Following the warm-up, the subject should rest for three to five minutes.
6. **Instruct the subject to take their starting position.** This is normally with the dominant leg slightly forward of the top of the cycle, with the opposing leg near the bottom; however, the subject can self-select where to start.
7. **Communicate with the subject that the test requires maximal effort** to provide their true maximal anaerobic power.
8. **Count the subject down into the test from five seconds.** Give a loud 'go' command as you press the start button on the ergometer or computer. The subject should start to pedal as fast as they can after your 'go' command for the full 10 seconds of the test.
9. **Provide loud and continued verbal encouragement to the subject** across the test as this will help them provide maximal effort. To ensure that the subject continues for the entire time period, count the end of the test down for the last three seconds. Stop recording the test if required.
10. **Allow the subject to recover following the test actively** by remaining on the cycle and slowly pedalling. During this time, ask how the subject is feeling. Ensure that the cool-down continues for at least five minutes at a comfortable intensity. When ready, release the subject's feet and assist them off the cycle ergometer.
11. **Record the available data from the data collection across the test.** In particular, the following measures should be recorded:

    a. Peak power (W): the highest power recorded across the 10-second test.
    b. Mean power (W): the average power recorded across the 10-second test.
    c. Time to peak power (s): time taken from the start to record the maximal peak power.
    d. Final power (W): the final power recorded at 10 seconds.

12. **Calculate the relative (per kilogram of body mass) peak power from the alactic cycling test using the subject's body mass** (see Box 39.1 for an example).
    Table 39.3 provides normative data for comparison against the test results.

Tests of anaerobic capacity

This refers to the capacity of the anaerobic energy systems to produce energy during maximal intensity exercise. Tests of anaerobic capacity place great stress on the anaerobic energy systems and, as such, are physically and psychologically demanding of a subject. There are two main tests used to determine anaerobic capacity: the Wingate test and the assessment of modified accumulated oxygen deficit (MAOD). As part of the sport and exercise science course, you should be able to differentiate anaerobic power and capacity and be able to perform these laboratory tests.

Box 39.1 Analysis from the 10-second alactic cycling test

Fig. 39.3 is an example of a power output trace from a 15-year-old female sprinter. She weighed 52 kg at the time of testing. Following the figure are step-by-step instructions to help identify and calculate important absolute and relative (per kilogram body mass) measures from the test.

- **Peak power (W):** identify the highest power output recorded across the test from either the dataset or graph. On fig. 39.3, the highest power output recorded was 820 W.
- **Time to peak power (s):** identify the time at which the highest power output was recorded. The time to peak power was 1.6 s.
- **Final power (W):** identify the final power output recorded at the end of the test. The final power output in Fig. 39.3 was 580 W.
- **Relative peak power ($W\,kg^{-1}$):** to calculate the relative peak power, divide the recorded peak power by the subject's body mass. For example; the relative peak power for the above figure is calculated as:

$$820\ W \div 52\ kg = 15.8\ W\,kg^{-1}$$

- **Fatigue index ($W\,s^{-1}$):** this is a measure of the rate of fatigue after peak power. To measure, subtract the difference between the peak and final power outputs. Also, calculate how much time was left in the test until it finished. Then, divide the decline in power output by the measured time (x). In the example above, the difference between power outputs was 240 W. As peak power was reached after 1.6 seconds and x was 8.4 s. Therefore:

$$240\ W \div 8.4\ s = 28.6\ W\,s^{-1}$$

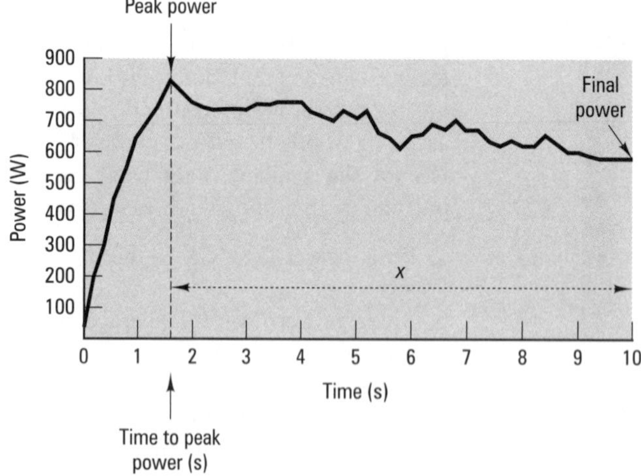

Fig. 39.3 An example of the power output from a 10-second alactic test from a 15-year-old female sprinter.

Table 39.3 Reference norms for relative power output ($W\,kg^{-1}$) for men and women from the alactic cycling test

Age (years)	Poor	Fair	Satisfactory	Good	Excellent	Elite
Male						
14–34	<9.2	9.2–11.7	11.8–14.3	14.4–16.9	17.0–19.5	19.6+
35–44	<8.8	8.8–11.3	11.4–13.8	13.9–16.4	16.5–18.5	18.1+
45–54	<7.8	7.8–10.0	10.1–12.2	12.3–14.5	14.6–15.9	16.0+
54+	<6.8	6.8–8.7	8.8–10.7	10.8–12.7	12.8–14.9	15.0+
Female						
14–34	<7.1	7.1–9.4	9.5–11.8	11.9–14.2	14.3–16.6	16.7+
35–44	<6.4	6.4–8.4	8.5–10.6	10.7–12.8	12.9–14.9	15.0+
45–54	<5.1	5.1–6.6	6.7–8.4	8.5–10.1	10.2–12.6	12.7+
54+	<4.1	4.1–5.2	5.3–6.8	6.9–8.9	9.0–11.0	11.1+

Normative data adapted from Schell and Leelarthaepin (1994).

Wingate cycling test

The Wingate cycling test is the most commonly used method to assess anaerobic capacity. The Wingate test provides a measure of anaerobic capacity as it places maximal stress on the anaerobic energy system. The Wingate test has been repeatedly validated and is the cornerstone measure of anaerobic capacity, and should form part of the laboratory skills gained on a sport and exercise science course. Instructions are given below on how to guide a subject through a Wingate test.

1. **Set up the cycling ergometer to be used for anaerobic power testing.** Ergometers may differ across laboratories, from wind-braked, mechanically braked or electromagnetically braked. Ensure that the equipment is working before the test and that connections to data recording systems are working.
2. **Weigh the subject using electronic scales.** Politely ask the subject to remove all clothing that they will not be wearing during the test (i.e. jackets, tracksuit pants). Record their body mass to the nearest 0.1 kg.
3. **Ask the subject to sit on the cycle ergometer and adjust the seat height** so that the subject has close to full extension (~170°) when the pedal is at the very bottom of the cycle.
4. **Place their feet into the pedals and tighten the foot straps** or alternatively secure the feet to the pedals so that they cannot become separated during the test.
5. **Instruct the subject(s) to complete a warm-up.** Try to keep this standardised between individuals and repeat tests. The warm-up should consist of at least 5 minutes pedalling at a comfortable intensity with brief periods of intense cycling. After the warm-up, the subject should rest for three to five minutes.
6. **Instruct the subject to take their starting position.** This is normally with the dominant leg slightly forward of the top of the cycle, with the opposing leg near the bottom; however, the subject can self-select where to start.
7. **Communicate with the subject that the test requires maximal effort** to provide their true maximal anaerobic power.
8. **Count the subject down into the test from five seconds.** Give a loud 'go' command as you press the start button on the ergometer or computer. The subject should start to pedal as fast as they can after your 'go' command for the full 30 seconds of the test.
9. **Provide loud and continued verbal encouragement to the subject** across the test as this will help them to provide maximal effort. To ensure that the subject continues for the entire time period, count the end of the test down for the last three seconds. Stop recording the test if required.
10. **Allow the subject to recover following the test actively** by remaining on the cycle and slowly pedalling. During this time, ask how the subject is feeling. Ensure that the cool-down continues for at least five minutes at a comfortable intensity. When ready, release the subject's feet and assist them off the cycle ergometer.
11. **Record the available data from the data collection across the Wingate test.** In particular, the following measures should be recorded:
    a. Peak power (W): the highest power recorded across the 30-second test.
    b. Mean power (W): the average power recorded across the 30-second test.

Carrying out a Wingate test – many subjects can find performing the Wingate test very physically draining and may be unwell after the test. Always place an empty bucket within reach before the test as vomiting can be a common occurrence. Make sure to take care of the subject after the test.

Box 39.2 Analysis from the Wingate cycling test

Fig. 39.4 is an example of the power output trace from a Wingate test performed by an elite cyclist. The cyclist was a 27-year-old male weighing 82 kg. Following are step-by-step instructions to help you to identify and calculate important absolute and relative (per kilogram body mass) measures from the test.

- **Peak power (W):** identify the highest power output recorded across the test from either the dataset or graph. On this figure, the highest power output recorded was 1375 W.
- **Mean power (W):** is the average power maintained over the complete Wingate test. Data output from the cycle ergometer is useful in measuring mean power output. The mean power sustained over the Wingate test in Fig. 39.4 was 796 W.
- **Time to peak power (s):** identify the time at which the highest power output was recorded. The time to peak power was 2 s.
- **Final power (W):** identify the final power output recorded at the end of the test. The final power output in Fig 39.4 was 700 W.
- **Relative peak power ($W\,kg^{-1}$):** to calculate the relative peak power, divide the recorded peak power by the subject's body mass. For example, the relative peak power for this athlete is calculated as:

  $1375\ W \div 82\ kg = 16.8\ W\,kg^{-1}$

- **Relative mean power ($W\,kg^{-1}$):** to calculate the relative mean power, divide the recorded mean power by the subject's body mass. For example, the relative mean power for the above figure is calculated as:

  $796\ W \div 82\ kg = 9.7\ W\,kg^{-1}$

- **Fatigue index ($W\,s^{-1}$):** this is a measure of the rate of fatigue following peak power. To measure, subtract the difference between the peak and final power outputs. Also, calculate how much time was left in the test until it finished. Then, divide the decline in power output by the measured time (x). In the example above, the difference between power outputs was 675 W. As peak power was reached after 2 seconds, x was 28 s. Therefore:

  $675\ W \div 28\ s = 24.1\ W\,s^{-1}$

- **Work capacity (J):** is a measure of the total work capacity that can be sustained over the Wingate test. A simple measure of work capacity is simply to multiply the mean power by the duration of the test. To demonstrate how this can be done:

  $796\ W \times 30\ s = 23\,880\ J$

- **Relative work capacity ($J\,kg^{-1}$):** allows the total work capacity to be calculated relative to body mass to allow valid comparisons between individuals of different size. To calculate the relative work capacity, divide the calculated total work by the subject's body mass:

  $23\,880\ J \div 82\ kg = 291.2\ J\,kg^{-1}$

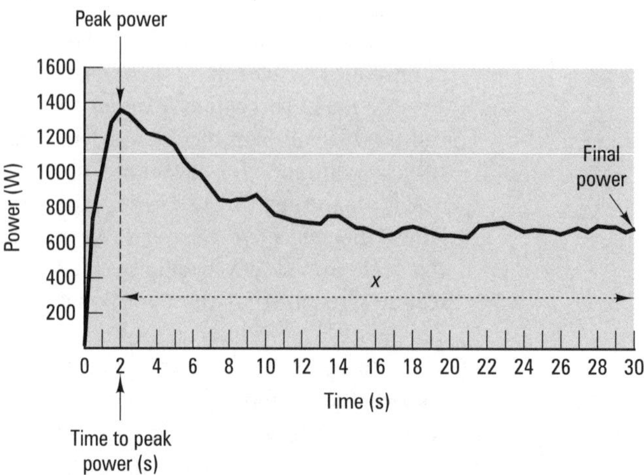

Fig. 39.4 An example of the power output from a Wingate test from a 27-year-old male cyclist.

Table 39.4 Reference norms for relative anaerobic capacity work output ($J kg^{-1}$) for men and women from the Wingate cycling test

Age (years)	Poor	Fair	Satisfactory	Good	Excellent	Elite
Male						
14–34	<204	204–243	244–283	284–323	324–366	367+
35–44	<184	184–218	219–254	255–288	289–325	326+
45–54	<166	166–197	198–228	229–259	260–291	292+
55+	<141	141–168	169–199	200–228	229–257	258+
Female						
14–34	<179	179–213	214–243	244–277	278–325	325+
35–44	<157	157–192	193–226	227–252	253–295	295+
45–54	<132	132–167	168–203	204–235	236–264	265+
54+	<108	108–130	131–161	162–196	197–236	236+

Normative data adapted from Schell and Leelarthaepin (1994).

c. Time to peak power (s): time taken from the start to record the maximal peak power.
d. Final power (W): the final power recorded at 30 seconds.

12. **Calculate the anaerobic work capacity of the subject across the Wingate test.** As 1 W = 1 joule s^{-1}, the work completed across the test is simply calculated as the mean power (W) multiplied by the duration in seconds (see Box 39.2 for an example). Similarly, the relative (per kilogram) peak power and work capacity from the Wingate test can be calculated using the subject's body mass. Normative data for the Wingate test is provided in Table 39.4.

Modified MAOD protocol

SAFETY NOTE there are several methods to assess MAOD that may differ greatly. The protocol provided is useful to allow the quantification of MAOD in a single session. The protocol can be simply adapted on any laboratory ergometer.

The modified MAOD protocol provides a measure of metabolic anaerobic capacity, or the amount of energy that can be produced during high intensity exercise by anaerobic energy systems. While there are several protocols to measure MAOD, they all work along the same principles. There are at least two separate parts to an MAOD test. The first is a series of exercise bouts of sequential submaximal intensities, which are completed to provide a mathematical equation for the $\dot{V}O_2$–work relationship. The second is a short (<2 minutes) bout of maximal intensity exercise where the subject aims to complete as much work as possible. From this, the volume of oxygen required to complete the 'maximal bout of exercise purely aerobically can be estimated. The difference between the measured and predicted $\dot{V}O_2$ values is termed the maximal accumulated oxygen deficit'. This is a direct physiological measure of anaerobic capacity and is performed within the exercise science laboratory. A series of instructions is provided below to explain how to complete an MAOD test.

1. **Set up the required laboratory equipment** to allow analysis of expired gases using open circuit indirect calorimetry. Also set up the selected ergometer, although an electromagnetically braked cycle ergometer is the most commonly used.
2. **Prepare the subject as if they were completing a $\dot{V}O_2$max test** (see Chapter 36, p. 269).
3. **Develop a $\dot{V}O_2$–work rate relationship by making the subject complete five 3-minute bouts of submaximal exercise** at 100 W, 125 W, 150 W, 175 W

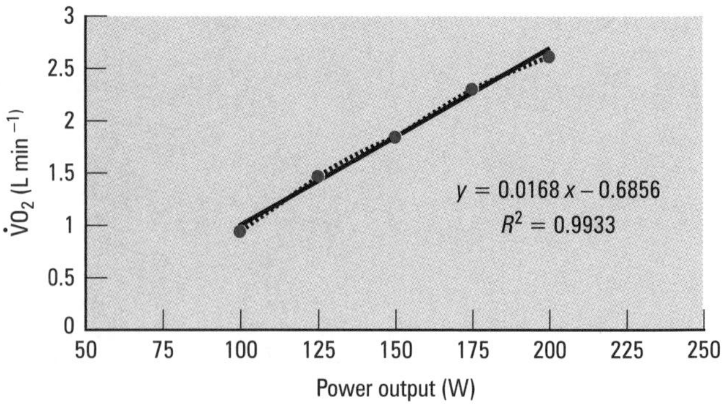

Fig. 39.5 An X–Y scattergram of the linear $\dot{V}O_2$–work rate relationship across the five 3-minute submaximal stages. (R^2 is the regression coefficient between the two variables.)

and 200 W at a cadence of 100 rpm. Ensure that all expired gases are analysed and other physiological data such as heart rate are collected.

4. **Allow the subject to rest for 2 minutes after the protocol.** You may need to change the settings on the electromagnetically braked cycle ergometer to be cadence-limited at 110 rpm. This allows the ergometer to change the resistance automatically to maximise the power that the subject can produce at a cadence of 110 W.
5. **When ready, ask the subject to complete a two-minute test** in which they produce as much power as possible on the cycle ergometer. Make sure that the subject starts from a standing start and use verbal encouragement to produce the best results. Ensure that all expired gases are analysed and other physiological data such as heart rate are collected.
6. **Calculate the linear $\dot{V}O_2$-work rate relationship** from the five three-minute bouts of submaximal exercise using an X–Y scattergram (see Fig. 39.5 for an example). Then, use the equation produced from this to continue.
7. **Estimate the rate of $\dot{V}O_2$** that would have been required to produce the energy required aerobically across the two-minute all-out test using the linear equation produced from the scattergram (Table 39.5 – Estimated $\dot{V}O_2$ ($L\,min^{-1}$)). Then, using the sampling duration, calculate the volume of oxygen that would have been consumed over the time period (Table 39.5 – Estimated $\dot{V}O_2$ consumed (L)). For the example below, the cycle ergometer recorded every five seconds to match the metabolic cart. Data collection rates may vary across systems.
8. **Match the measured $\dot{V}O_2$ from across the two-minute all-out test to time** (Table 39.5 – Measured $\dot{V}O_2$ ($L\ min^{-1}$)). Then calculate the volume of oxygen that would have been consumed over the time period (Table 39.5 – Measured $\dot{V}O_2$ consumed (L)).
9. **Calculate the difference in the estimated and measured $\dot{V}O_2$ consumed in each sampling period (Table 39.5 – Deficit (L)).** Sum the deficit values for the entire two-minute all-out test to determine your MAOD capacity in litres. The larger the MAOD capacity the greater anaerobic contribution provided to the effort.
10. The MAOD can be visualised by graphing the estimated and measured $\dot{V}O_2$ values taken across the two-minute all-out test (see Fig. 39.6). In Figure 39.6 the darker grey area represents the measured $\dot{V}O_2$ and the lighter grey above that is the predicted $\dot{V}O_2$ volume. The difference between the two volumes (what is visible) is the MAOD volume.

Table 39.5 Example of the data from an MAOD test required to determine anaerobic capacity

Time (s)	Power output (W)	Estimated $\dot{V}O_2$ ($Lmin^{-1}$)	Estimated $\dot{V}O_2$ consumed (L)	Measured $\dot{V}O_2$ ($Lmin^{-1}$)	Measured $\dot{V}O_2$ consumed (L)	Deficit (L)
5	346	5.1272	0.43	1.856	0.15	0.27
10	292	4.22	0.35	2.485	0.21	0.14
15	301	4.3712	0.36	3.158	0.26	0.10
20	274	3.9176	0.33	3.571	0.30	0.03
25	297	4.304	0.36	3.567	0.30	0.06
30	310	4.5224	0.38	3.691	0.31	0.07
35	314	4.5896	0.38	3.657	0.30	0.08
40	278	3.9848	0.33	3.62	0.30	0.03
45	325	4.7744	0.40	3.57	0.30	0.10
50	332	4.892	0.41	3.578	0.30	0.11
55	344	5.0936	0.42	3.693	0.31	0.12
60	367	5.48	0.46	3.735	0.31	0.15
65	326	4.7912	0.40	3.668	0.31	0.09
70	310	4.5224	0.38	3.663	0.31	0.07
75	305	4.4384	0.37	3.601	0.30	0.07
80	328	4.8248	0.40	3.564	0.30	0.11
85	329	4.8416	0.40	3.643	0.30	0.10
90	355	5.2784	0.44	3.643	0.30	0.14
95	359	5.3456	0.45	3.663	0.31	0.14
100	360	5.3624	0.45	3.656	0.30	0.14
105	257	3.632	0.30	3.597	0.30	0.00
110	265	3.7664	0.31	3.65	0.30	0.01
115	295	4.2704	0.36	3.685	0.31	0.05
120	300	4.3544	0.36	3.673	0.31	0.06

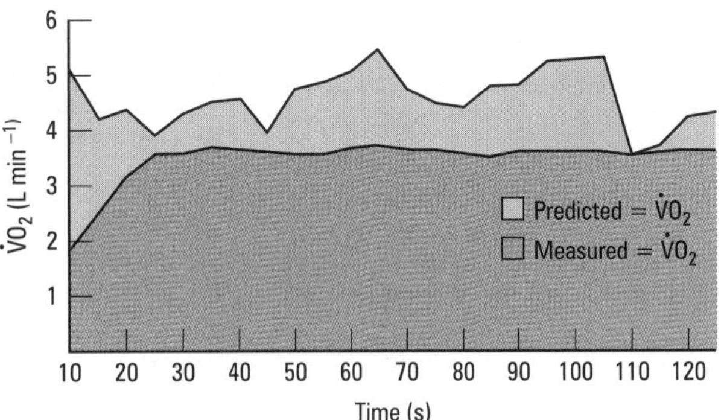

Fig. 39.6 Graphical representation of the difference between predicted and measured $\dot{V}O_2$ values across an MAOD test.

Text references

Finn, J., Gastin, P., Withers, R., Green, S. and Woolford, S. (2000) Estimating peak power and anaerobic capacity of athletes. In: C. Gore (ed.) *Physiological Tests for Elite Athletes*. Human Kinetics, Champaign, IL.

Schell, J. and Leelarthaepin, B. (1994) Tests of anaerobic capacity and power. In: *Physical Fitness Assessment*, 2nd edn, Leelar Biomediscience Services, Matraville, NSW.

Sources for further study

Inbar, O., Bar-Or, O. and Skinner, J. (1994) *The Wingate Anaerobic Test*. Human Kinetics, Leeds.

40 Measuring muscle strength and endurance

Definitions

Absolute strength (kg) – the total force or weight lifted that can be applied during a movement.

Dynamic – smooth, controlled action where movement of the limb is required.

Dynamometer – an instrument that measures total force produced during a movement.

Isokinetic – muscle contraction where speed of movement does not change.

Isometric – muscle contraction where muscle length does not change.

Muscular strength – the ability to produce force by muscle contraction.

Muscular endurance – the ability to resist fatigue during repeated contractions.

Relative strength (unit per kg BM^{-1}) – the total force or weight lifted that can be applied during a movement per kilogram of participants body mass (BM).

Repetition – completion of a single cycle of lifting and lowering the weight in a controlled manner.

Repetition maximum – the maximum load that can be lifted for a predetermined number of repetitions.

Muscle strength and endurance assessments are critical components of health assessments and training programme monitoring. Therefore, learning how to become competent in measuring these variables is an important practical aspect of a sport and exercise science course. The tests are used in health screening protocols for a number of professional vocations (e.g. armed forces, emergency services, etc.) and sport and exercise scientists are typically employed to perform such tests. Similarly, these tests can easily be used to monitor progress in muscular strength and endurance in athletes and sporting teams. Strength tests can be performed in a range of settings, from a field to a gymnasium or a laboratory. In more advanced work and rehabilitation settings, muscular strength can be assessed using an isokinetic dynamometer across a range of movements. However, these systems are rarely found outside exercise science laboratories and require more advanced training.

This chapter aims to provide you with details of some of the basic methods of testing muscular strength, both isometric and dynamic, as well as muscular endurance. The tests focus on easy-to-complete exercises that can easily be performed with minimal equipment and costs.

Tests of muscular strength

Measures of isometric strength

It is common for the assessment of muscle strength to be performed using isometric dynamometers. These provide a measure of the maximal force that the participant can produce in the exercise without any actual shortening of the muscle. Isometric dynamometers provide a very useful method of testing muscle strength, in particular during health screenings and appraisals in participants not accustomed to complex resistance training exercises. In addition, their use is ideal in exercise settings where it is not practical to use large resistance training equipment or where testing time is limited. A variety of isometric dynamometers have been developed to assess different movement strengths: these include grip strength, chest and back strength as well as leg strength. Guidelines for the testing of strength using these devices are provided in Boxes 40.1, 40.2 and 40.3.

Measures of dynamic strength

Assessing isometric strength is limited in several aspects with regard to peak force at muscle length and its application to athletic tasks. The measurement of dynamic strength, or maximal force produced during changes in the muscle length is a more valid approach to measuring muscular strength. This assesses muscular strength over the full range of movement of the exercise rather than purely isometric strength. However, assessing dynamic strength usually requires comprehensive strength testing equipment and long periods of time, given the incremental nature of the tests.

When using the tests detailed below to assess dynamic muscular strength, you should be aware of the following general principles:

- Each participant/athlete should complete an appropriate warm-up before the test (Chapter 41). At minimum, each participant should

Fig. 40.1 How to perform a handgrip strength test.

Fig. 40.2 Measuring back strength using the back dynamometer.

Box 40.1 How to carry out a grip strength test

1. **Ensure that the grip dynamometer is set at zero** before starting the test.
2. **Fit the participant's hand to the dynamometer** by adjusting the base and handle of dynamometer. The handle should rest on the middle finger while the base should rest on the base of the hand.
3. **Communicate to the participant the requirements of the test.** Be sure to include any explanations of technique that may be required. Ensure that the participant is prepared for the test (as described in Chapter 26).
4. **Ask the participant to assume the starting position for the test.** The starting position sees the participant standing with their heels, buttocks and back resting against a wall. The arm is raised vertically above the head with the palms facing inwards, as shown in Fig. 40.1.
5. **Instruct the participant to complete the test when ready.** The participant should grip the dynamometer as hard as possible while lowering their arm through a 180° arc over 3 seconds. The arm must remain straight (that is, fully extended at the elbow) throughout the movement.
6. **Record the score to the nearest 0.5 kg and reset the needle to zero.** Repeat the procedure for the opposite hand. Repeat the test twice more for each hand and record the best score.
7. **Calculate the result.** Add the scores together to calculate the combined grip strength scores. Compare the participant's performance to the normative data in Table 40.1.

Box 40.2 How to carry out a back strength test

1. **Ensure that the chest/back dynamometer is set at zero** before starting the test (see Fig. 40.2 for an example of a chest/back dynamometer).
2. **Communicate to the participant the requirements of the test.** Be sure to include any explanations of technique that may be required. Ensure that the participant prepares themselves for the test as described in Chapter 26.
3. **Ask the participant to assume the starting position for the test.** The starting position sees the feet shoulder-width apart, gripping the handles of the dynamometer and placing it in front of their chest with forearms parallel to the ground.
4. **Instruct the participant to complete the test when ready.** The participant should grip the dynamometer and **pull** the handles apart as hard as possible. Ensure that elbows remain parallel to the ground and that they do not lean forwards or backwards. The participant can stop when they have exerted their maximal force.
5. **Record the score to the nearest 0.5 kg and reset the needle to zero.** Allow the participant to rest for a minimum of 1 minute. Repeat the above protocol twice more (or until the highest score is recorded).
6. **Determine the result.** Record the highest reading of the two trials. Compare the participant's data to the normative data in Table 40.1 and rate their performance.

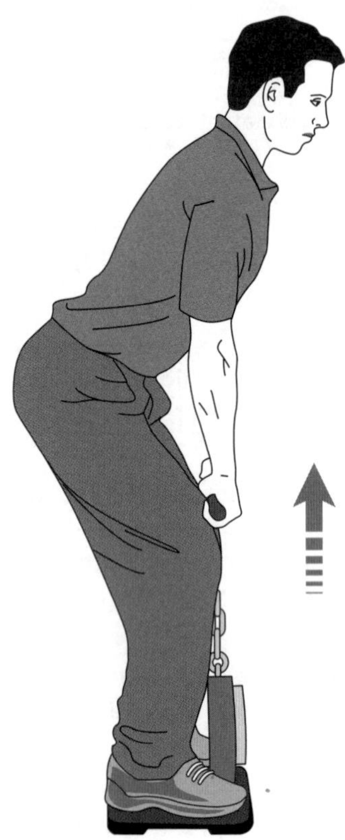

Fig. 40.3 Measuring leg strength using the leg dynamometer.

Box 40.3 How to carry out a leg strength test

1. **Ensure that the leg strength dynamometer is set at zero** before starting the test (see Fig. 40.3 for an example of a leg strength dynamometer).
2. **Communicate to the participant the requirements of the test.** Be sure to include any explanations of technique that may be required. Ensure that the participant prepares themselves for the test as described in Chapter 26.
3. **Ask the participant to assume the starting position for the test.** The starting position requires the participant to stand on the platform of the dynamometer with their feet on either side of the cable/chain attachment. Ask the participant to grip the handle and gently pull so that there is no tension on the chain. The bar should be at a height level with the pubis with knees flexed between 115 and 125° and trunk slightly bent forward (10 and 15°) (see Fig. 40.3). Adjust the length of the chain until the participant is able to be in this position.
4. **Instruct the participant to complete the test when ready.** The participant should grip the dynamometer and stand up as hard as possible. Ensure that their trunk remains slightly flexed and that the participant does not lean back on their heels. The participant's arms must also be not bent during the lift. The participant can stop when they have exerted their maximal force.
5. **Record the score to the nearest 0.5 kg and reset the needle to zero.** Allow the participant to rest for a minimum of one minute. Repeat the above protocol twice more (or until the highest score is recorded).
6. **Determine the result.** Record the highest reading of the two trials. Compare and rate the participant's data to the normative data in Table 40.1.

Table 40.1 Normative data for several dynamometer strength measures for men and women.

Rating	Left grip (kg)	Right grip (kg)	Combined strength (kg)	Back strength (kg)	Leg strength (kg)	Relative strength (kg·BM^{-1})
Excellent	≥68	≥70	≥115	≥209	≥241	≥7.50
Good	56–67	62–69	104–114	177–208	214–240	7.10–7.49
Average	43–55	48–61	95–103	126–176	160–213	5.21–7.09
Below average	39–42	41–47	84–94	91–125	137–159	4.81–5.20
Poor	≤39	≤41	≤83	≤91	≤137	≤4.80
Excellent	≥68	≥70	≥70	≥69	≥61	≥54
Good	60–67	63–69	63–69	61–68	54–60	48–53
Average	53–59	58–62	58–62	54–60	49–53	45–47
Below average	48–52	52–57	52–57	49–53	45–48	41–44
Poor	≤47	≤51	≤51	≤48	≤44	≤40

Data adapted from Corbin *et al.* (1978) in Heyward (2006).

perform at least one trial at ~90% of their previously recorded repetition maximum (RM).

- Strength tests should determine the three-lift RM (3RM) rather than a single-lift RM (1RM). This reduces the risk of injury during the test and places less loading on joint structures. A 1RM should be considered if specific to the sport (e.g. power lifting) or where specific emphasis is placed on *absolute* muscle strength.
- The motion of each lift (the lowering and raising) should be consistent and continuous. No more than two seconds of rest should be taken between repetitions.
- No more than five minutes of recovery should be taken between efforts.
- The weight lifted should be increased by at least 2.5 kg between trials. The participant may request larger increments in weight depending on their exertion for the previous lift.
- The RM should be identified within four trials, separate to the warm-up.
- Data should be compared with respect to relative strength, determined as the weight lifted per kilogram of body mass of the participant. This allows direct comparison between individuals of different body sizes.

Details of common dynamic strength tests are given in Boxes 40.4–40.8.

Box 40.4 How to carry out a chin-up test

1. **Communicate to the participant the requirements of the test.** Be sure to include the number of repetitions, the weight to be lifted and any technique explanations that may be required. Ensure that the participant is prepared for the test, as described in Chapter 26.
2. **Ask the participant to step up on a box and grip the chin bar using** a medium width (no wider than one hand width greater than shoulder width) and pronated (hands facing down), as in Fig. 40.4. Athletes can self-select their handgrip position within these limits.
3. **Place any external mass on the participant.** For more experienced lifters, the difficulty of the lift may need to be increased by the addition of extra weight. To do this safely, secure a weight belt with weight-plate holding attachment around the participant.
4. **Instruct the participant to complete the lift when they are ready.** A valid chin-up starts from a fully extended elbow position without the participant touching the ground. From here, the participant should pull their body up in a continued action until their chin touches the top of the bar (see Fig. 40.4 for the required movement). The head should remain in a neutral position at all times. Leg position can be self-selected but they must remain still and not be swung to help generate momentum.
5. **Observe the participant during the test and watch for any technical errors that may cause the test to be invalid.** These include:
   - failure to raise chin over the bar with head in a neutral position;
   - change in position of hips and knees during the lift;
   - swinging of body during the lift;
   - failure to reach full elbow extension between repetitions;
   - waiting for longer than two seconds between repetitions.
6. **Repeat the test until the participant cannot progress any further.**
7. **Record the number of chin-ups completed by the participant along with details of any external mass carried.** The results from the test should be compared to any previous data that have been recorded for the participant. Test data should also be compared to normative data for chin-ups from a similar population (Table 40.2).

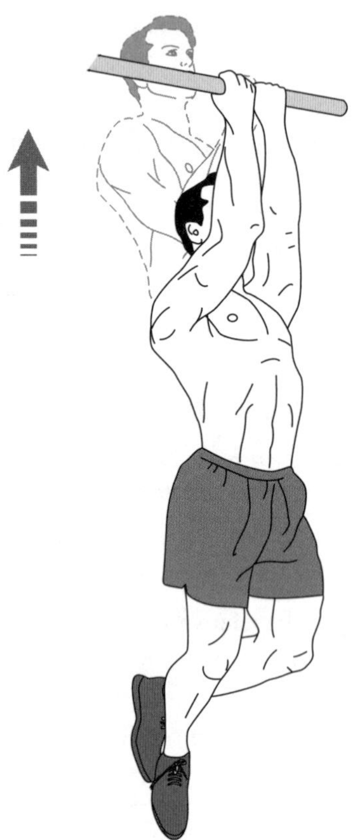

Fig. 40.4 The movement during a chin-up.

Fig. 40.5 The movement during a bench press.

Table 40.2 Normative data for chin-ups from a normal population

	Excellent	Above average	Average	Below average	Poor
Male	>16	12–15	8–11	3–7	0–3
Female	>3	2–3	1	0	0

Data adapted from Davis (2000).

Box 40.5 How to carry out a bench press test

1. **Prepare the bench press apparatus for testing.** Initially this will include loading the weights required for a warm-up (<90% 1RM max).
2. **Communicate to the participant the requirements of the test.** Be sure to include the number of repetitions, the weight to be lifted and any technique explanations that may be required. Ensure that the participant prepares themselves for the test, as described in Chapter 26.
3. **Ask the participant to lie down on the bench on their back.** The participant can self-select the handgrip width to be used for the test, although this should remain consistent across all test attempts and sessions. If necessary, the distance between the hands should be measured to ensure consistency.
4. **Instruct the participant to complete the lift when they are ready.** A valid attempt is where the athlete lowers the bar to the highest point of the chest in a controlled movement. The participant should pause briefly and then lift the bar until full extension of the elbow is achieved (see Fig. 40.5 for an example).
5. **Observe the participant during the test and watch for any technical errors** that may cause the test to be invalid. These include:
   - failing to make contact with the chest;
   - bouncing the bar off the chest;
   - raising either foot off the bench or ground;
   - unusual path of the bar compared to that observed in warm-up;
   - an uneven bar level across the lift;
   - waiting for longer than two seconds between repetitions.
6. **Repeat the test until the participant cannot progress any further.** Progress in increments of no more 5 kg and no less than 2.5 kg.
7. **Record the participant's highest weight lifted.** The results from the test should be compared to any previous data that have been recorded for the participant. Convert the data to relative strength to body mass ratios. Test data should also be compared to normative data for the bench press from a similar population (Table 40.3).

Table 40.3 Normative relative strength data for a 1RM and 3RM bench press for a normal population.

Male	Age (years)									
	20–29		30–39		40–49		50–59		60+	
Percentile	1RM	3RM	1RM	3RM	1RM	3RM	1RM	3RM	1RM	3RM
90	1.48	1.35	1.24	1.13	1.1	1.00	0.97	0.88	0.89	0.81
80	1.32	1.20	1.12	1.02	1.00	0.91	0.90	0.82	0.82	0.75
70	1.22	1.11	1.04	0.95	0.93	0.85	0.84	0.76	0.77	0.70
60	1.14	1.04	0.98	0.89	0.88	0.80	0.79	0.72	0.72	0.66
50	1.06	0.96	0.93	0.85	0.84	0.76	0.75	0.68	0.68	0.62
40	0.99	0.90	0.88	0.80	0.80	0.73	0.71	0.65	0.66	0.60
30	0.93	0.85	0.83	0.76	0.76	0.69	0.68	0.62	0.63	0.57
20	0.88	0.80	0.78	0.71	0.72	0.66	0.63	0.57	0.57	0.52
10	0.8	0.73	0.71	0.65	0.65	0.59	0.57	0.52	0.53	0.48

Female	Age (years)											
	20–29		30–39		40–49		50–59		60–69		70+	
Percentile	1RM	3RM	1RM	3RM	1RM	3RM	1RM	3RM	1RM	3RM	1RM	3RM
90	0.54	0.49	0.49	0.45	0.46	0.42	0.4	0.36	0.41	0.37	0.44	0.40
80	0.49	0.45	0.45	0.41	0.4	0.36	0.37	0.34	0.38	0.35	0.39	0.35
70	0.42	0.38	0.42	0.38	0.38	0.35	0.35	0.32	0.36	0.33	0.33	0.30
60	0.41	0.37	0.41	0.37	0.37	0.34	0.33	0.30	0.32	0.29	0.31	0.28
50	0.4	0.36	0.38	0.35	0.34	0.31	0.31	0.28	0.3	0.27	0.27	0.25
40	0.37	0.34	0.37	0.34	0.32	0.29	0.28	0.25	0.29	0.26	0.25	0.23
30	0.35	0.32	0.34	0.31	0.3	0.27	0.26	0.24	0.28	0.25	0.24	0.22
20	0.33	0.30	0.32	0.29	0.27	0.25	0.23	0.21	0.26	0.24	0.21	0.19
10	0.3	0.27	0.27	0.25	0.23	0.21	0.19	0.17	0.25	0.23	0.2	0.18

Data adapted from Heyward (2006) and assumes that 3RM is 91 % of 1RM.

Box 40.6 How to carry out an incline leg press test

1. **Prepare the leg press apparatus for testing.** For this, set the seat angle at 90° to the slide and, if possible, the foot plate to 110°. Initially this will also include loading the weights required for a warm-up (<90% 1RM max).
2. **Communicate to the participant the requirements of the test.** Be sure to include the number of repetitions, the weight to be lifted and any technique explanations that may be required. Ensure that the participant is prepared for the test, as described in Chapter 26.
3. **Ask the participant to sit down in the seat and place their feet on the foot plate.** Feet should be placed at a height that ensures that the hips are flexed to 90° (Fig. 40.6). Foot width can be self-selected and should remain consistent across tests.
4. **Instruct the participant to complete the lift when they are ready.** A valid attempt is where the athlete lowers the foot plate until 90° of knee flexion, pauses and then fully extends their legs. If necessary, depth marks can be set during the warm-up or initial set-up. Participants should hold the available handles at the side across the test.
5. **Observe the participant during the test and watch for any technical errors** that may cause the test to be invalid. These include:
   - not lowering to the desired depth;
   - changing the position of either the feet or hips from the start position during the test;
   - using hands to assist the lift by placing them on the thighs;
   - waiting for longer than two seconds between repetitions.
6. **Repeat the test until the participant cannot progress any further.** Progress in increments of no more 5 kg and no less than 2.5 kg.
7. **Record the participant's highest weight lifted.** The results from the test should be compared to any previous data that have been recorded for the participant. Convert the data to relative strength to body mass ratios. Test data should also be compared to normative data for the incline leg press from a similar population (Table 40.4).

Table 40.4 Normative relative strength data for a 1RM and 3RM leg press for a normal population.

Male	Age (years)									
	20–29		30–39		40–49		50–59		60+	
Percentile	1RM	3RM	1RM	3RM	1RM	3RM	1RM	3RM	1RM	3RM
90	2.27	2.07	2.07	1.88	1.92	1.75	1.80	1.64	1.73	1.57
80	2.13	1.94	1.93	1.76	1.82	1.66	1.71	1.56	1.62	1.47
70	2.05	1.87	1.85	1.68	1.74	1.58	1.64	1.49	1.56	1.42
60	1.97	1.79	1.77	1.61	1.68	1.53	1.58	1.44	1.49	1.36
50	1.91	1.74	1.71	1.56	1.62	1.47	1.52	1.38	1.43	1.30
40	1.83	1.67	1.65	1.50	1.57	1.43	1.46	1.33	1.38	1.26
30	1.74	1.58	1.59	1.45	1.51	1.37	1.39	1.26	1.30	1.18
20	1.63	1.48	1.52	1.38	1.44	1.31	1.32	1.20	1.25	1.14
10	1.51	1.37	1.43	1.30	1.35	1.23	1.22	1.11	1.16	1.06

Female	Age (years)											
	20–29		30–39		40–49		50–59		60–69		70+	
Percentile	1RM	3RM	1RM	3RM	1RM	3RM	1RM	3RM	1RM	3RM	1RM	3RM
90	2.05	1.87	1.73	1.57	1.63	1.48	1.51	1.37	1.40	1.27	1.27	1.16
80	1.66	1.51	1.50	1.37	1.46	1.33	1.30	1.18	1.25	1.14	1.12	1.02
70	1.42	1.29	1.47	1.34	1.35	1.23	1.24	1.13	1.18	1.07	1.10	1.00
60	1.36	1.24	1.32	1.20	1.26	1.15	1.18	1.07	1.15	1.05	0.95	0.86
50	1.32	1.20	1.26	1.15	1.19	1.08	1.09	0.99	1.08	0.98	0.89	0.81
40	1.25	1.14	1.21	1.10	1.12	1.02	1.03	0.94	1.04	0.95	0.83	0.76
30	1.23	1.12	1.16	1.06	1.03	0.94	0.95	0.86	0.98	0.89	0.82	0.75
20	1.13	1.03	1.09	0.99	0.94	0.86	0.86	0.78	0.94	0.86	0.79	0.72
10	1.02	0.93	0.94	0.86	0.76	0.69	0.75	0.68	0.84	0.76	0.75	0.68

Data adapted from Heyward (2006), and assumes that 3RM is 91% of 1RM.

Fig. 40.6 The start and finish position (**a**) and the midway point (**b**) during an incline leg press repetition.

Fig. 40.7 The movement during a back squat repetition.

Box 40.7 How to carry out a back squat test

1. **Prepare the squat rack for testing.** This may require shifting the safety bars to a height that allows the participant to complete a full range of motion during the squat. Safety blocks should always be used to protect the participant if they fall or are unable to lift the weight. This will also include loading the weights required for a warm-up (<90% 1RM max).
2. **Communicate to the participant the requirements of the test.** Be sure to include the number of repetitions, the weight to be lifted and any technique explanations that may be required. Ensure that the participant prepares for the test, as described in Chapter 26.
3. **Ask the participant to complete the lift.** To complete a squat, they should place the bar high across their back (on the trapezius muscle). The participant should grip the bar with their hands as close to the shoulders as possible. Once the bar is in position, the participant can lift up slightly to remove the weight from the squat rack and take a small step backwards. The participant should assume a shoulder-width stance and, when in position, lower themselves by bending at the hips then knees until their thighs are parallel to the floor. The participant should pause briefly and then extend their legs and stand up with the weight on their back (Fig. 40.7). At all times, knees should move directly over feet to ensure knee stability.
4. **Observe the participant during the test and watch for any technical errors** that may cause the test to be invalid. These include:
   - excessive movement or loss of control during the test;
   - lifting heels of feet off the floor;
   - not lowering to the desired depth;
   - raising hips before shoulder elevation;
   - waiting for longer than two seconds between repetitions.
5. **Repeat the test until the participant cannot progress any further.** Progress in increments of no more than 5 kg and no less than 2.5 kg.
6. **Record the participant's highest weight lifted.** The results from the test should be compared to any previous data that have been recorded for the participant. Convert the data to relative strength to body mass ratios. Test data should also be compared to normative data for the back squat from a similar population (Table 40.5).

Table 40.5 Normative relative strength data for a 1RM and 3RM back squat for a normal population

	Age (years)									
Male	**20–29**		**30–39**		**40–49**		**50–59**		**60+**	
Rating	**1RM**	**3RM**	**1RM**	**3RM**	**1RM**	**3RM**	**1RM**	**3RM**	**1RM**	**3RM**
Excellent	>2.07	>1.88	>1.87	>1.70	>1.75	>1.59	>1.65	>1.50	>1.55	>1.41
Good	2.00	1.82	1.80	1.64	1.70	1.55	1.60	1.46	1.50	1.37
Average	1.83	1.67	1.63	1.48	1.56	1.42	1.46	1.33	1.37	1.25
Fair	1.65	1.50	1.55	1.41	1.50	1.37	1.40	1.27	1.31	1.19
Poor	<1.65	<1.50	<1.55	<1.41	<1.5	<1.37	<1.4	<1.27	<1.31	<1.19

	Age (years)									
Female	**20–29**		**30–39**		**40–49**		**50–59**		**60+**	
Rating	**1RM**	**3RM**	**1RM**	**3RM**	**1RM**	**3RM**	**1RM**	**3RM**	**1RM**	**3RM**
Excellent	>1.62	>1.47	>1.41	>1.28	>1.31	>1.19	>1.25	>1.13	>1.14	>1.04
Good	1.54	1.40	1.35	1.23	1.26	1.15	1.13	1.03	1.08	0.98
Average	1.35	1.23	1.20	1.09	1.12	1.02	0.99	0.90	0.92	0.84
Fair	1.26	1.15	1.13	1.03	1.06	0.96	1.86	1.69	0.85	0.77
Poor	<1.26	<1.15	<1.13	<1.03	<1.06	<0.96	<0.86	<0.78	<0.85	<0.77

Data adapted from Gettman (1993) in Hoffman 2006, and assumes that 3RM is 91% of 1RM.

Box 40.8 How to carry out a multistage abdominal strength test

1. **Communicate to the participant the requirements of the test.** Be sure to include the number of repetitions, the weight to be lifted and any technique explanations that may be required.
2. **Ask the participant to lie down on their back and to raise their knees until they are bent at 90°.** Their feet may rest on the floor at a comfortable distance apart. This is the 'start position' from which all stages are attempted.
3. **Progress the participant through the seven stages of the abdominal strength test detailed below.** See the sequence in Fig. 40.8 for an illustration of the position required for each stage.
   - *Stage 1* – from the start position the participant should rest the palms of the hands on the thighs. When ready, the participant lifts the upper body so that their hands slide along the thighs until fingers touch the kneecap.
   - *Stage 2* – from the start position the participant should rest the palms of the hands on the thighs. When ready, the participant lifts the upper body so that their hands slide along the thighs until elbows touch the kneecap.
   - *Stage 3* – from the start position the participant should cross the arms and rest them on the abdomen. When ready, the participant lifts the upper body off the ground until forearms touch the thighs.

(continued)

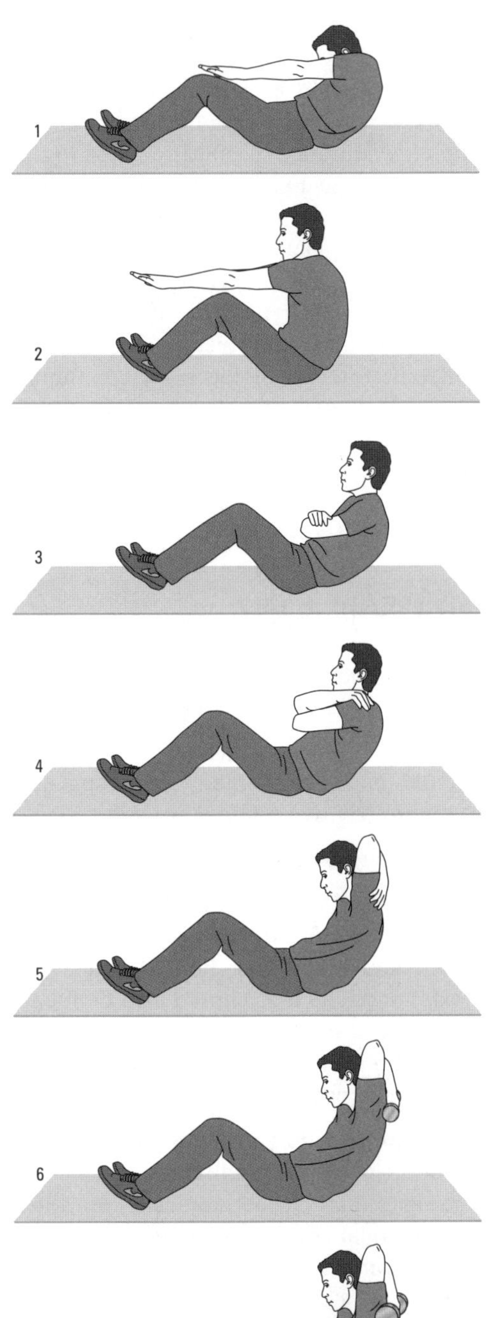

Fig. 40.8 Positions required for each stage of the abdominal strength test.

Box 40.8 Continued

- *Stage 4* – from the start position the participant should cross the arms and place the hands on the opposite shoulder. Forearms should remain in contact with the chest. When ready, the participant lifts the upper body off the ground until forearms touch the thighs.
- *Stage 5* – from the start position the participant should raise the arms above the head and place the hands on the opposite shoulder. Forearms should remain in contact with the chest. When ready, the participant lifts the upper body off the ground until the chest touches the thighs.
- *Stage 6* – from the start position the participant should raise the arms above the head and place the hands on the opposite shoulder while securing a 2.5 kg weight. Forearms should remain in contact with the chest. When ready, the participant lifts the upper body off the ground until the chest touches the thighs.
- *Stage 7* – from the start position the participant should raise the arms above the head and place the hands on the opposite shoulder while securing a 5 kg weight. Forearms should remain in contact with the chest. When ready, the participant lifts the upper body off the ground until the chest touches the thighs.
- Further difficulty can be added by continuing to increase the mass of the weight lifted by 2.5 kg for each step. If this is required, you should record the last additional weight lifted before failure.

4. **Observe the participant during the test and watch for any technical errors** that may cause the test to be invalid. These include:
   - lifting heels of feet or hips off the floor;
   - moving of arms from required position;
   - jerky or powerful movement of the head or arms;
   - change in feet position or angle of knee flexion;
   - failure of the nominated stage;
   - raising hips before shoulder elevation;
   - waiting for longer than two seconds between repetitions.
5. **Record the last stage at which participant was successful.** The results from the test should be compared to any previous data that have been recorded for the participant. Rate the participant's performance for the test (Table 40.6).

Table 40.6 Normative data for the multistage abdominal strength test from a normal population

Level attained	Rating
1	Poor
2	Fair
3	Average
4	Good
5	Very good
6	Excellent
7	Elite

Tests of muscular endurance

While endurance capacity is generally thought to be measured in terms $\dot{V}O_2max$ (Chapter 36), you should also be familiar with the assessment of local muscle endurance. Local muscle endurance specifically refers to the muscle's resistance to fatigue during a repeated low intensity exercise. Typically such tests are used to assess this ability aspect of the performance of large muscle groups during gross movements. Assessing muscle endurance is completed using standard resistance training exercises at a standardised load, and the number of repetitions performed until fatigue or within a specified time period is recorded. Boxes 40. 9 and 40.10 provide details for two of the most commonly performed tests of muscular endurance.

Fig. 40.9 The start/finish (**a**) and middle (**b**) positions of a push-up.

Box 40.9 How to carry out a push-up test

1. **Communicate to the participant the requirements of the test.** There are several variations of the push-up test of muscular endurance. The two most common are:
   a. Timed – participants should perform as many push-ups as possible within a set time; normally two minutes is used.
   b. Maximal – participants continue to perform push-ups until they cannot continue to complete a full push-up.
2. **Instruct the participant to assume the starting position for a push-up.** Men should lie face down and place their hands shoulder-width apart with arms fully extended. The legs should also be fully extended with feet at a neutral distance apart. Women should assume the same position with the exception that their knees are in contact with the floor with ankles crossed.
3. **Instruct the participant to start the test on your command.** A full push-up for men is when the body is lowered so that the chest can make contact with the recorder's fist placed vertically on the ground. For women, a foam roller or rolled towel can be substituted for a fist. Both genders are required to demonstrate full extension of their arms at the top of the push-up, with their torso remaining straight across the test (see Fig. 40.9 for the top and bottom positions of a push-up). Repetitions that do not meet these positions should not be counted in the total.
4. **Count the number of push-ups completed across the test.** You may count out loud to the participant and provide verbal encouragement during the test. Compare to and rate the performance from the data presented in Table 40.7.

Table 40.7 Normative data for a normal population for the maximal number of push-ups before fatigue

	Age (years)					
Men	**15–19**	**20–29**	**30–39**	**40–49**	**50–59**	**60–69**
Excellent	≥39	≥36	≥30	≥25	≥21	≥18
Very good	29–38	29–35	22–29	17–24	13–20	11–17
Good	23–38	22–28	17–21	13–16	10–12	8–10
Fair	18–22	17–21	12–16	10–12	7–9	5–7
Needs improvement	≤17	≤16	≤11	≤9	≤6	≤4

	Age (years)					
Women	**15–19**	**20–29**	**30–39**	**40–49**	**50–59**	**60–69**
Excellent	≥33	≥30	≥27	≥24	≥20	≥17
Very good	25–32	21–29	20–26	15–23	11–20	12–16
Good	18–24	15–20	13–19	11–14	7–10	5–11
Fair	12–17	10–14	8–12	5–10	2–6	2–4
Needs improvement	≤11	≤9	≤7	≤4	≤1	≤1

Data adapted from The Canadian Physical Activity, Fitness & Lifestyle Approach (2003) in Heyward (2006).

Box 40.10 How to carry out a YMCA bench press test

1. **Prepare the bench press apparatus for testing (Fig. 40.5).** The YMCA bench press test includes loading the bar with 36 kg for men and 16 kg for women. A metronome must also be set up at a rate of 60 beats per minute. This relates to 30 repetitions per minute (one beat up, one beat down).
2. **Communicate to the participant the requirements of the test.** The aim of the test is to complete as many repetitions as possible of the weight at the speed set by the metronome.
3. **Review and follow the instructions for the bench press detailed in Box 40.5** with the participant. This should involve the movement patterns and technical faults they may demonstrate. Instruct the participant to assume the starting position for the test and tell them to wait for your cue.
4. **When ready, start the test on your command.** Participants should start to complete the bench press movement in time with the beat of the metronome until they can no longer complete a correct bench press.
5. **Count the number of repetitions completed across the test.** You may count out loud to the participant and provide verbal encouragement during the test. Compare results to the data presented in Table 40.8 and rate the performance.

Table 40.8 Normative data for YMCA bench press test from a normal population

	Age (years)					
Men	**18–25**	**26–35**	**36–45**	**46–55**	**56–65**	**>65**
95	49	48	41	33	28	22
75	34	30	26	21	17	12
50	26	22	20	13	10	8
25	17	16	12	8	4	3
5	5	4	2	1	0	0

	Age (years)					
Women	**18–25**	**26–35**	**36–45**	**46–55**	**56–65**	**>65**
95	49	46	41	33	29	22
75	30	29	26	20	17	12
50	21	21	17	12	9	6
25	13	13	10	6	4	2
5	2	2	1	0	0	0

Data adapted from The YMCA Fitness Manual (2000) in Heyward (2006).

Sources for further study

Abernathy, P. and Wilson, G. (2000) Introduction to assessing strength and power. In: C. Gore (ed.) *Physiological Tests for Elite Athletes.* Human Kinetics, Champaign, IL.

Anonymous (2004) *National Protocols for the Assessment of Strength and Power.* Laboratory Standards Assistance Scheme, Australian Institute of Sport, Canberra.

Schell, J. and Leelarthaepin, B. (1994) *Measurement of Muscular Strength and Endurance in Physical Fitness Assessment,* 2nd edn, Leelar Biomediscience Services, Matraville.

Text references

Davis, B. (2000) *Physical Education and the Study of Sport,* 5th edn, Mosby, Edinburgh.

Heyward, V.H. (2006) *Assessing Muscular Fitness in Advanced Fitness Assessment and Exercise Prescription,* 5th edn, Human Kinetics, Champaign, IL.

Hoffman, J. (2006) *Norms for Fitness, Performance and Health.* Human Kinetics, Champaign, IL.

41 Common field tests

Understanding field testing – these tests are done in the actual context or environment in which the participants exercise, as opposed to controlled laboratory conditions.

In sport and exercise science, a field test usually involves measurement of a physiological capacity while an athlete is performing in a simulated competitive situation.

Usually field tests are not as reliable as laboratory tests, but often have greater validity because of their greater specificity.

For sport and exercise scientists used to working in controlled laboratories, testing in the field can be as much of a challenge for them as it is for athletes to be tested in a laboratory.

Field testing has the advantages of being less complex, in general using less expensive equipment, and it is cheaper and easier to set up than laboratory testing. Field testing also has the advantage of allowing more than one athlete to be tested at once and is thus more time-effective for coaches, athletes and testers. Finally, field tests are, in general, more sports-specific and valid than laboratory tests.

In contrast, field tests sometimes lack the sensitivity to detect small changes in fitness and are not as controlled as laboratory conditions, with results often influenced by wind, heat, rain or changes in surface quality. Finally, many field tests do not have normative data available, making interpretation of results more difficult.

This chapter presents the more common field tests used in sport and exercise science. Most popular sports have their own well developed field tests that are beyond the scope of this chapter. For resources to help with sport-specific tests, see the end of the chapter.

General principles

The following principles are relevant to the conduct of field tests.

Time management of field testing – always allow more time than expected when conducting field tests. Equipment malfunctions, unforeseen athlete problems and recording issues invariably occur.

Practise

If possible, set up in the actual location or a similar environment (e.g. sporting ground, pool) to that used for the testing and practise your protocols to ensure that your ideas translate to the field. Ideally, do the tests yourself before you test others so you know how it feels to be the person being tested.

Time allocation

Field testing usually takes longer than expected. Allow for this and ensure you have plenty of assistants to help that (e.g. setting up and dismantling equipment, data recording). Remember the adage 'many hands make light work'.

Working with athletes

Athletes are social people. They often arrive for testing in groups, are often unprepared mentally or physically for the demands of testing, and are rarely as quiet and cooperative as you would like. Be prepared to give a little on the level of control you might have compared to that in the laboratory.

Scheduling

Work closely with the coach and/or athlete(s) in planning when and where you will conduct the test sessions. The coach will want to schedule the testing for a day and time that suits the weekly training schedules and seasonal plans. For outdoor testing, early morning or late afternoon may be more predictable in terms of lighter winds and cloud cover. In winter, these times of the day may be too cold and the light very poor.

The 'Five Ps' principle of field testing – Perfect Preparation Prevents Poor Performance.

Preparation and planning

Prepare a detailed list of:

- **equipment required** (numbers, availability, spares, recording sheets, clipboards, extension cords, laptops, power sources, etc.);
- **assistants required** (numbers, roles, time needed to arrive and depart, contact details);
- **subject requirements** (e.g. shoes, warm-up protocol, water bottle, warm clothes, food). Advise, verbally and in writing, both the coach and athlete as to their needs before arriving at testing. This may include dietary and training requirements (e.g. no hard training 24 hours before the test).

Preparing and transporting equipment

You should always ensure that:

- **equipment is booked** well in advance;
- **equipment is in working order and calibrated** if needed (e.g. skinfold calipers, weighing scales, metronome);
- **you know how to 'troubleshoot'** the more common equipment problems;
- **venue is booked** well in advance and checked out well beforehand for power points, hazards, toilet and shower availability, shelter, conditions, parking, etc.;
- **spares are available** if experience tells you or others that spare equipment may be required due to malfunction or breakdown;
- **power sources are available** (e.g. batteries, generator, extension cords, power boards);
- **equipment is stored securely** and safely for transporting to venue;
- **rubbish bags** and/or biohazard bags and/or sharps bins are available;
- **recording sheets** are prepared in hard copy or on laptops;
- **vehicles are booked** or arranged that can safely and securely carry the equipment;
- **you allow enough time** to travel, set up, test and dismantle the equipment.

Example (order of testing) – For a basketball player, the following order of tests is suggested:

1. body weight;
2. height;
3. skinfold measures;
4. warm-up;
5. vertical jump;
6. 10-m sprint;
7. agility test;
8. multistage fitness test.

Order of testing

There are a number of general principles that apply when determining the order of tests. These include:

- **Move from the least stressful to the most stressful** (e.g. height, weight, skinfolds before multistage fitness test).
- **Conduct tests that are affected by exercise before exercise testing** (e.g. measure resting blood pressure and skinfolds beforehand).

- **Always allow athletes to warm up before every exercise test.**
- **Rotate between upper and lower body tests** (e.g. vertical jump test followed by seated medicine ball throw followed by 40 m sprint test).
- **Allow adequate recovery between tests** (e.g. between each sprint trial allow two to three minutes).

Waste disposal

Plan how you will dispose of hazardous materials such as sharps, blood-stained gauze, alcohol wipes, etc. It is always advisable to take all biohazard and sharps wastes plus any general rubbish (e.g. water bottles, food wrappers, scrap paper, tape) back to your own laboratory or facility for disposal (see Chapters 24 and 25).

Testing on or in water

Optimal operating temperatures of testing equipment – electrical equipment will always have an optimal operating temperature and humidity range. Ensure that you check the manufacturer's handbook to know what these conditions are if you are testing in cold, wet and/or hot conditions. Take steps to counter these extremes if needed.

When testing around pools, rivers or lakes or in areas with high humidity, it is crucial to consider the effective functioning of equipment and recording sheets. Some tips for working in these areas are:

- **Secure duct tape** before the surface or tape becomes wet.
- **Use clipboards with heavy-grade paper and plastic** sheets that cover the sheets.
- **Use ballpoint pens** as they work better than felt pens or pencils on damp paper.
- **Use a non-water-soluble grease pen on a large white plastic slate in very wet places** such as besides pools or in a boat in the rain. Alcohol swabs help wipe off the data if needed.
- **Dry the earlobes or fingertips** well before blood sampling, as water from sweat or the environment can dilute blood samples. Using small hand cloths or a large towel that remains covered and dry can help.
- **Use pacing devices** if exact pacing is required in a pool, lake or river. Using pacing lights, verbal cues every 20–30 s, marker buoys or domes can help.

Testing in cold conditions

In very cold conditions (e.g. snowfields) blood samples can freeze in capillary tubes while being taken from a fingertip or earlobe. Equipment is designed to operate in a range of temperatures that usually does not include the temperatures seen in snow or icy conditions. Thus, testers need to do the following:

Taking blood samples in the field – the lactate concentration of sweat is usually higher than blood. Thus ensure sweat does not contaminate blood sampling sites by drying earlobes and/or fingertips and ensuring hair is dried for earlobe samples or the fingers are held away from the hair and head when taking blood samples.

- **Protect equipment** from the cold by keeping it insulated and out of the wind just before use.
- **Keep capillary tubes warm and insulated** before sampling.
- **Encourage athletes** to wear mittens, gloves, hoods or ear warmers to keep fingertips or earlobes warm.
- **Dry the earlobes and fingertips** before blood sampling to prevent sweat diluting blood samples.

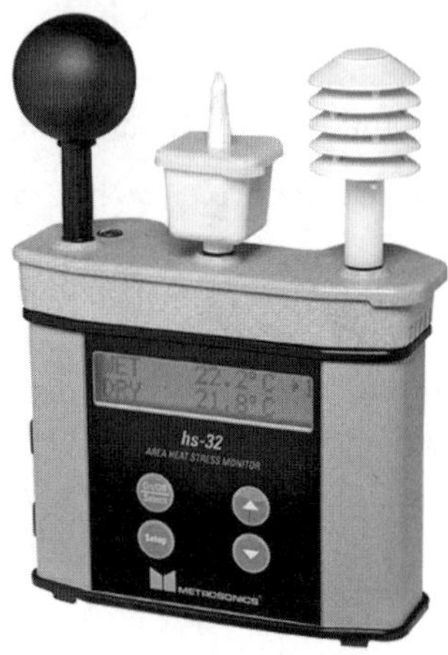

Fig. 41.1 A wet bulb globe temperature monitoring device.
Source: Peter Reaburn.

- **Provide warm conditions for the athletes** (e.g. shelter from the wind, extra clothing, rugs or thermal blankets.
- **Request athletes to bring their own warm clothing** – preferably many layers of clothing that can be removed or added as the conditions change.
- **Encourage testing personnel** to wear mittens, gloves, hoods and hats, scarves to keep the head, neck and hands warm.
- **Have warm drinks available** for athletes and testers.

Testing in hot conditions

Equipment, athletes and testers are all affected when testing in the heat. Tips for working in the heat include the following:

- **Test in the early morning or evening** whenever possible to avoid the extremes of midday temperatures.
- **Ensure the skin surfaces and hair are dry** before sampling. Sweat can contaminate blood, urine or saliva samples.
- **Provide shade** by using an umbrella or portable shelter, or work in a naturally shaded area to keep equipment, athletes and testers cool.
- **Carefully monitor and record temperature and humidity** during testing. Use of a wet bulb globe temperature device (Fig. 41.1) is strongly recommended.

KEY POINT Because of the variability in temperature, humidity, cloud cover and wind conditions in field testing, a portable wet bulb globe temperature device is essential to ensure field conditions are recorded as these may explain variability in tests from one test session to another.

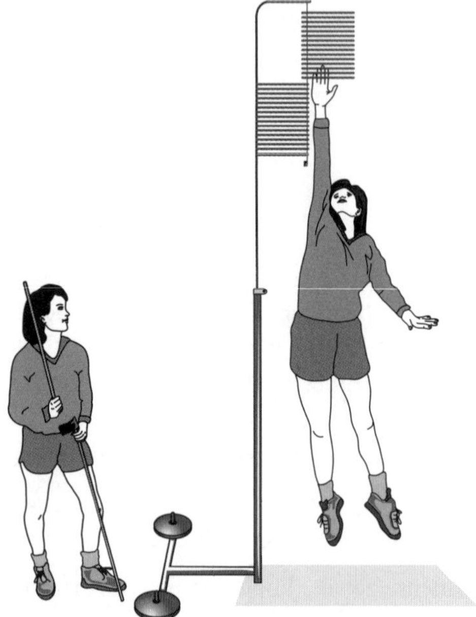

Fig. 41.2 *Vertec* vertical jump device used to measure lower body power.

Testing at altitude

Changes in barometric pressure can alter gas volumes and thus affect gas analysis results when measuring $\dot{V}O_2$ at altitude. For safety reasons, being aware of static electricity in dry winters at altitude is essential. You should also ensure that testers and athletes are acclimatised to altitude before testing at altitudes greater than 3000 m. Thus:

- **Use a portable calibrated barometer** to record changes in gas volumes that can then be used to adjust the volumes to standardised values when measuring lung volumes, such as when measuring $\dot{V}O_2$.
- **Ensure testers and athletes remain well hydrated** before and during testing as moisture is lost with the increased breathing rates at altitude.

Common field tests

Vertical jump

Overall jumping ability incorporating arm swing, trunk extension and leg extension can be measured using a standing vertical jump test (Fig. 41.2). This test provides a measure of leg power, which is an important aspect

Box 41.1 How to carry out a vertical jump test using a *Vertec* device

1. **Assemble the *Vertec*** on a flat, non-slip surface away from any walls or other objects.
2. **Align the vanes of the *Vertec*** so that they are on the opposite side to the ground supports. Ensure that all the vanes of the *Vertec* are vertically aligned using the reach stick supplied.
3. **Adjust the height of the *Vertec*** to ensure that the subject can touch the bottom vanes (<20 cm), but will not jump over the *Vertec* upon performing a maximal jump (*Note:* This may occur in individuals who possess a vertical jump >1 m).
4. **Do a standardised warm-up** that should include hip, knee and ankle stretches as well as light jumping on the spot.
5. **Ask the subject to stand underneath the vanes of the *Vertec*** and extend their dominant arm above their head, touching the highest vane of the *Vertec* possible whilst standing. Testers should ensure that feet are flat on the ground, and that the subject's knees and arms are not bent. The highest number vane shifted is to be recorded as reach height.
6. **Ask the subject to perform a maximal standing vertical jump** using countermovement and arm swing. No step-in or shuffling is allowed unless specified within the specific protocol. The subject should touch the highest vane at the peak of the vertical jump. The number of this vane is to be recorded as peak jump height.
7. **Calculate maximum vertical jump** by subtracting reach height from the subject's peak jump height. The difference is the subject's vertical jump and is measured in centimetres.
8. **Request the subject** to perform the jump three times and record the best result in centimetres.
9. **Consult the table** of normative values (Table 41.1).
10. **Advise the athlete and/or coach** on how to improve the lower leg power through a training programme.

Table 41.1 Vertical jump scores for Australian athletes (cm) (Gore, 2000)

Sport	Squad	Mean	SD*	Range	Count
Basketball	State/national female	46.6	5.6	35–60	132
	State male	69.5	4.8	60–82	28
Cricket	Test female	41.3	5.1	31–53	62
	Test male	52.6	9.5	22–78	27
Hockey	Senior female	46	4	33–56	491
	Senior male	56	5	40–77	363
Netball	National female	53.4	4.6	45–61	16
Soccer	National female	42	3	36–47	19
	Olympic male	57	—	50–68	22
Softball	State female	47	6	39–56	12
Tennis	AIS female	40.3	5.2	32–48	6
	AIS male	53.2	4.8	47–59	6

*SD = Standard deviation.

of a variety of sports requiring lower body power, including netball, basketball, rugby and cycling. The vertical jump test is a simple test that can be performed on a large number of people quickly, with minimal equipment and at minimal cost. Box 41.1 gives details of the procedure.

Seated medicine ball throw

While the vertical jump measures lower body power, the seated medicine ball throw measures upper body power. Differing weights of medicine balls are used depending on gender and age, but commonly used weights for adult athletes are 4–4.5 kg. The test can be conducted in a gym setting or on a grassed area with a wall for the subject to sit against. Box 41.2 gives details of the procedure.

Box 41.2 How to carry out a seated medicine ball throw test

1. **Ask the subject** to sit on the ground with their back against the wall for support and knees bent at 90° to allow the feet to apply pressure backward to hold the subject in place.
2. **Ask the subject** to grasp the medicine ball firmly using both hands and to push from the chest like a netball chest pass.
3. **Request the subject** to do two or three practice throws.
4. **Observe and mark the landing** of three maximum-effort throws for distance with the tester retrieving the ball for the subject.
5. **Measure the best throw** from the centre of the chest to the point of landing to an accuracy of 0.1 m.
6. **Advise the athlete and/or coach** on how to improve the upper body power through a training programme.

Box 41.3 How to carry out a 1RM strength test

1. **Ask the subject to perform 5–10 repetitions** (reps) of the exercise using a light weight and then rest for 1 min.
2. **The tester adds 10–20% of the warm-up** weight and another 5–10 reps are performed.
3. **Request that the subject rest for two to three minutes,** then ask them to perform 2–3 reps of a heavier weight.
4. **Ask the subject to rest** for another three to four minutes, then add more weight and try a 1RM lift with the additional weights.
5. **If successful, ask the subject to have another four-minute rest** before more weight is added and another attempt made for a 1RM.
6. **Divide the 1RM weight by body weight** to determine relative RM.
7. **Advise the athlete and/or coach** on how to improve the strength through a training programme.

SAFETY NOTE A Smith machine or a machine weights system is recommended when determining 1RM, especially in non-athletes unfamiliar with weight training. Such machines reduce the skill demand of the test.

1RM strength test

The one-repetition maximum (1RM) test is the maximum load that can be lifted only once. It is widely used to measure the muscular strength of athletes as well as for prescribing resistance training programmes using the percentage of 1RM as the measure of intensity or load to lift in training. For example, a subject might do 8–10 repetitions at 70% of 1RM to develop strength.

The 1RM squat is commonly used to measure lower body strength and the 1RM bench press is used as a standard test of upper body strength. Box 41.3 gives details of the procedure.

Speed tests

The importance of speed is well known for success in a number of land-based sports involving running. For example, analysis of rugby league match play has shown that the average distance that players sprint ranges from 10 to 20 m. Acceleration is therefore far more important than 'maximal' speed when 'quickness' is both measured and trained. Investigating the speed of players over this distance may be of more use than investigating speed over 40–100 m as very rarely are these distances covered in sports outside athletics.

The introduction of portable timing lights has meant that stopwatches have mostly disappeared from field testing sessions.

Box 41.4 How to conduct sprint speed and acceleration tests

1. **Prepare the test area.** Extend a measuring tape to 20 m, marking intervals at the 5 and 10 m marks. If possible, ensure that any wind is a crosswind.
2. **Prepare the timing system.** Place sets of electronic timing gates or markers at the 0 m, 5 m, 10 m and 20 m intervals. Link the four sets of timing lights together using cables provided or place testers with stopwatches at these markers. Link the timing lights to the operating computer and switch them all on.
3. **Warm up the participants.** Allow the participants to warm up by running and stretching.
4. **Demonstrate the correct starting position.** Sprints must start from a standing, stationary position 30 cm behind the start line timing light. This allows for the participant's feet to be as close as possible to the start line, but far enough behind to prevent them from breaking the light beam.
5. **Begin the test.** Count down to the start with 3–2–1–Go and encourage the participant to continue to run through the timing lights until they are past the last timing light.
6. **Record the times** from the timing lights monitor or stopwatches.
7. **Repeat the test.** Perform three times and take the best (fastest) result.
8. **Advise the athlete and/or coach** on how to improve the sprint time through a training programme.

However, stopwatches are a cheap alternative to portable timing lights and therefore may still be used by a number of amateur sporting clubs or in student-based projects at university or college. Despite the simplicity of recording sprint times, a strict testing protocol is required to maintain accuracy and reproducibility of testing results. Box 41.4 gives details of the procedure.

Agility

Agility is another attribute which is potentially a key determinant of success in a number of land-based team sports such as netball, basketball, rugby league and union, and soccer. A number of drills have been designed specifically to improve an individual's agility, and therefore a test of agility is required to measure any improvements in agility.

The 5-0-5 test is a relatively simple test which measures the time for a single, rapid change of direction over a short 'up and back' course with a running start (Box 41.5). The test is designed to minimise the influence of velocity while accentuating the effect of acceleration immediately before, during and after the change of direction. Therefore, unlike many other agility tests, the results are not adversely affected by individual differences in running speeds before and after the directional changes.

Other common field tests – Chapters 33 and 42 also contain field tests that are often considered 'common'. These include:

1. Sit and reach flexibility test (Chapter 33).
2. YOYO intermittent recovery test (Chapter 42).

Phosphate recovery test

This test is a modified version of a protocol originally called the phosphate decrement test. A player is timed over a 35 m sprint on eight consecutive occasions; each sprint is separated by a recovery period of approximately 24 s. The phosphate recovery test has been modelled on time motion analysis data from Australian Rules football matches, and is indicative of the work-to-rest ratios sustained in that game, and has been successfully applied to similar sports such as rugby union.

Box 41.5 How to conduct a 5-0-5 agility test

1. **Prepare the test area.** Extend a measuring tape to 20 m, marking intervals at the 0 (start), 5, 10 and 20 m (finish) marks. If possible, ensure that any wind is a crosswind.
2. **Prepare the timing system.** Place sets of electronic timing gates or markers at the 0, 5, 10 and 20 m intervals. Link the four sets of timing lights together using the cables provided or place testers with stopwatches at these markers. Link the timing lights to the operating computer and switch them all on.
3. **Allow the participants to warm-up** by running and stretching for a few minutes before testing.
4. **Carry out the test.** After the signal that the light gates are set, the subject should start when ready. The participant should sprint the 10 m from the starting line, through the timing gates to the zero line, where they are required to turn on either the left or right foot, and accelerate off the line back through the timing light gate as fast as possible. The subject may slow down only after passing through the light gate for the second time.
5. **Begin the test.** Count down to the start with 3–2–1–Go and encourage the participant to continue to sprint as fast as possible through each of the timing lights until they are past the last (20 m) timing light.
6. **Record the times** from the timing lights monitor or stopwatches for the distances required (5, 10, 20 m).
7. **Record the outcome of the test** as the fastest time recorded for the preferred foot or for each turn foot.
8. **Advise the athlete and/or coach** on how to improve the agility through a training programme.

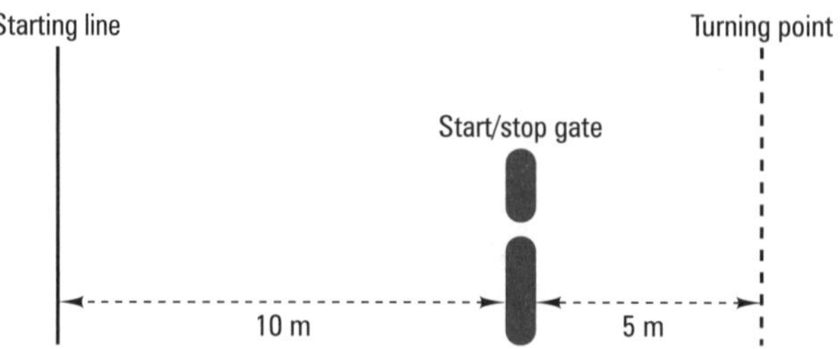

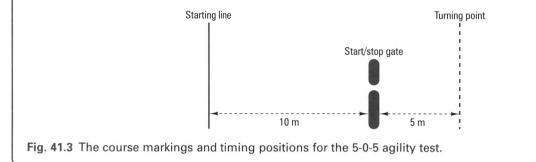

Fig. 41.3 The course markings and timing positions for the 5-0-5 agility test.

The ability to recover quickly following short bouts of high intensity exercise is needed in a number of prolonged high intensity intermittent activities such as football/soccer, rugby and netball. The phosphate recovery test is ideal for evaluating a player's ability to resist fatigue while enduring similar demands (times and distances) as those experienced in a game. Box 41.6 gives details of the procedure.

Multistage fitness test

Multistage fitness test – this is often simply called the 'beep test' because of its use of 'beep' signals to tell the athlete when it is time to start the next run interval.

The multistage fitness test (MSFT) indirectly measures aerobic or endurance capacity. Aerobic fitness is a known predictor of performance in a number of sports and activities that are sustained for a prolonged time. Additionally, endurance capacity has also been shown to be influential in regulating an athlete's ability in a number of other physiological capacities such as repeated sprint ability. Because it is speed-progressive in nature, it has been criticised for lacking specificity to many sports. However, it remains one of the most commonly used field tests in sport. Box 41.7 gives details of the procedure.

Box 41.6 Procedure for phosphate recovery test

1. **Prepare the course.** Mark out a 70 m distance, and place markers at the 35 m mark. Place timing lights at the 0 m, 35 m and 70 m marks in a straight line, as shown in Fig. 41.4. Ensure that any wind is a crosswind.
2. **Brief the participants on the test procedures,** stressing the importance of a maximum effort in each sprint.
3. **Allow the participants to warm up** by running at increasing speeds through the test area and stretching.
4. **Carry out the test.** When ready, the player sprints the 35 m from start line 1 to cross the timing line, and travels to start line 2. The player has 30 s to travel from start line 1 to start line 2. The player can walk or jog the remaining 35 m to start line 2. Upon arrival at start line 2, the player turns and prepares to sprint in the opposite direction (towards start line 1). For the second sprint, the player sprints the 35 m to the timing line, and slows down and travels to start line 1.
5. **Repeat the test.** Repeat the procedure until eight 35-m sprints have been completed. The time between the start of each 35 m sprint should be exactly 30 s. A five-second countdown should be given before each sprint.
6. **Record the results of the test.** Each of the eight sprint times should be recorded to 0.01 of a second.
7. **Calculate the fatigue index (%)** by calculating the mean of sprints 3 and 4, 5 and 6 and 7 and 8 and comparing them to the mean of sprints 1 and 2. These differences are then summed and expressed as a percentage relative to the mean speed of sprints 1 and 2. See sample calculation below.

Sprint	Time (s)	Mean sprint times	Difference from mean if sprints 1 and 2
1	5.25		
2	5.26	5.25 (mean of 1 and 2)	
3	5.32		
4	5.48	5.40 (mean of 3 and 4)	0.15 (mean of 1 and 2 – mean of 3 and 4)
5	5.62		
6	5.78	5.70 (mean of 5 and 6)	0.45 (mean of 1 and 2 – mean of 5 and 6)
7	5.81		
8	5.81	5.81 (mean of 7 and 8)	0.56 (mean of 1 and 2 – mean of 7 and 8)
		Total fatigue	1.16 s (sum of the above)

Fatigue = 1.16 (total fatigue)/5.25 (mean of sprints 1 and 2) = 22.1%.
Note: The lower the value the better in terms of being able to repeat speed during a game.

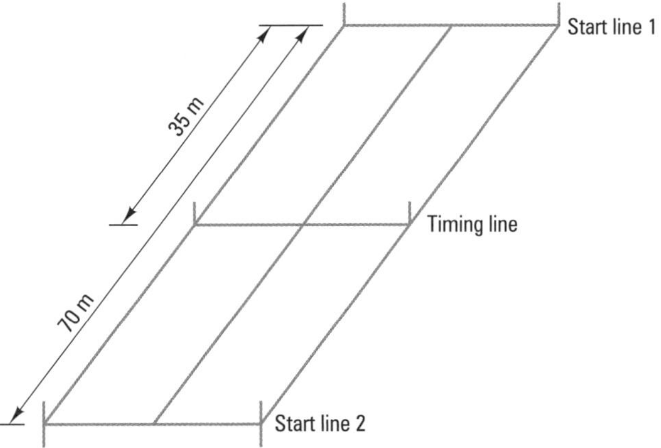

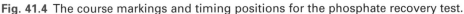

Fig. 41.4 The course markings and timing positions for the phosphate recovery test.

Box 41.7 Procedure for multistage fitness test

1. **Calibrate the speed of the CD/cassette drive** according to the instructions at the beginning of the tape or CD. [A 60 s standard time period is provided on the *Multistage Fitness Test* cassette tape/CD.] Run the cassette on your cassette player and, with a stopwatch (accurate to 0.01 s), check that the duration of the standard time period is actually 60 s long. If it is shorter or longer than 60 s, correct the 20 m running distance as:

$$s = 20 \times \frac{t}{60}$$

   where *s* is the corrected distance (m), *t* is the time (s) measured by stopwatch.
2. **Set out the course.** Measure the '20 m' distance and mark it clearly and frequently with cones.
3. **Allow the participants to warm up** by running and stretching. Discuss the need for the athletes to stick with the timed beeps and to give a maximal effort towards the end of the test.
4. **Start recording** and ensure that the subjects listen carefully to the verbal instructions. Begin the test at Level 1. The tape/CD emits a single 'beep' at various intervals. Participants must be at the opposite end of the 20 m track by the time the following beep sounds. At approximately one-minute intervals, the time interval between beeps decreases and running speed has to increase correspondingly to continue and sustain successful completion of the test.
5. **Check the participant's position during testing.** They need always to place one foot on or over the 20 m mark at the sound of each 'beep'. If they fail to reach the line at the sound of the 'beep' the player ***MUST*** receive a warning that they will be eliminated if they are not at the opposite end of the 20 m track at the sound of the next 'beep'.
6. **Complete the test.** When near exhaustion, a player falling short of the 20 m line twice in succession has their test terminated and their score recorded. Their score is the level and number of shuttles immediately before the 'beep' on which they were eliminated. These can be determined by the numbers read out from the cassette/CD throughout the test.
7. **Estimated $\dot{V}O_2$max.** This can be found by looking up each participant's MSFT score in Table 41.2.
8. **Allow the player(s) to cool down** after completing the test by walking, followed by stretching. Ensure fluid intake is adequate to replace fluid lost throughout the test.

Table 41.2 Table used to estimate $\dot{V}O_2max$ from the level and shuttle number reached in the MSFT (Handcock and Knight, 1994)

Level	Shuttle	Est. $\dot{V}O_2max$
4	1	26.4
	2	26.8
	3	27.2
	4	27.6
	5	27.9
	6	28.3
	7	28.7
	8	29.1
	9	29.5
5	1	29.8
	2	30.2
	3	30.6
	4	31
	5	31.4
	6	31.8
	7	32.2
	8	32.6
	9	32.6
6	1	33.3
	2	33.6
	3	33.9
	4	34.3
	5	34.6
	6	35
	7	35.3
	8	35.7
	9	36
	10	36.4
7	1	36.7
	2	37.1
	3	37.4
	4	37.8
	5	38.1
	6	38.5
	7	38.8
	8	39.2
	9	39.5
	10	39.9
8	1	40.2
	2	40.5
	3	40.8
	4	41.1
	5	41.4
	6	41.8
	7	42.1
	8	42.4
	9	42.7
	10	43
	11	43.3
9	1	43.6
	2	43.9
	3	44.2
	4	44.5
	5	44.8
	6	45.2
	7	45.5
	8	45.8
	9	46.1
	10	46.4
	11	46.8
10	1	47.1
	2	47.4
	3	47.7
	4	48
	5	48.3
	6	48.7
	7	49
	8	49.3
	9	49.6
	10	49.9
	11	50.2
11	1	50.5
	2	50.8
	3	51.1
	4	51.4
	5	51.6
	6	61.9
	7	52.2
	8	52.5
	9	52.8
	10	53.1
	11	53.4
	12	53.7
12	1	54
	2	54.3
	3	54.5
	4	54.8
	5	55.1
	6	55.4
	7	55.7
	8	56
	9	56.2
	10	56.5
	11	56.8
	12	57.1
13	1	57.3
	2	57.6
	3	57.9
	4	58.2
	5	58.4
	6	58.7
	7	59
	8	59.3
	9	59.5
	10	59.8
	11	60
	12	60.3
	13	60.6
14	1	60.8
	2	61.1
	3	61.4
	4	61.7
	5	61.9
	6	62.2
	7	62.4
	8	62.7
	9	62.9
	10	63.2
	11	63.4
	12	63.7
	13	64
15	1	64.3
	2	64.6
	3	64.8
	4	65.1
	5	65.3
	6	65.6
	7	65.9
	8	66.2
	9	66.4
	10	66.7
	11	66.9
	12	67.2
	13	67.5
16	1	67.7
	2	68
	3	68.2
	4	68.5
	5	68.7
	6	69
	7	69.2
	8	69.5
	9	69.7
	10	69.9
	11	70.2
	12	70.5
	13	70.7
	14	70.9
17	1	71.1
	2	71.4
	3	71.6
	4	71.9
	5	72.1
	6	72.4
	7	72.6
	8	72.9
	9	73.1
	10	73.4
	11	73.6
	12	73.9
	13	74.1
	14	74.4
18	1	74.6
	2	74.8
	3	75
	4	75.3
	5	75.5
	6	75.8
	7	76
	8	76.2
	9	76.4
	10	76.7
	11	76.9
	12	77.2
	13	77.4
	14	77.6
	15	77.9

Text references

Gore, C. (2000) *Physiological Tests for Elite Athletes.* Human Kinetics, Champaign, IL.

Handcock, P.J. and Knight B. (1994) *Field Testing Manual for Sports.* NZ Sports Science and Technology Board Coaching NZ, Wellington.

Sources for further study

American College of Sports Medicine (2010) *ACSM's Guidelines for Exercise Testing and Prescription,* 8th edn, Lippincott Williams and Wilkins, Baltimore, Maryland.

Winter, E.M., Jones, A.M., Davison, R.C., Bromley, P.D. and Mercer, T.H. (2007) *Sport and Exercise Physiology Testing Guidelines: The British Association of Sport and Exercise Sciences Guide. Vol. 1: Sport Testing*. Routledge, London.

42 Specific field tests

Understanding the nature of specific field tests – the texts listed at the end of this chapter provide sports-specific field testing guidelines for a range of sports, including:

- badminton
- basketball
- biathlon
- boxing
- cricket
- cross-country skiers
- cycling
- figure skating
- golfing
- gymnastics
- hockey
- judo
- long distance running
- middle distance running
- mountain cyclists
- netball
- pentathlon
- rowing
- rugby league
- rugby union
- sailing
- soccer
- softball
- squash
- swimming
- table tennis
- tennis
- triathlon
- water polo
- winter sports.

The overall physical profile of an athlete can be assessed in the field using a range of common tests that assess certain physiological capacities. However, these generic field tests are limited in their applicability for some sports. Upon completion of your course, you should be competent to carry out all generic field tests and have knowledge of a range of specific field tests. The more specific field tests can provide direct measurements that relate to performance (e.g. simulated racing performance) or help to provide specific information on important physiological variables that may be related to sports performance (e.g. physiological capacities in the context of a particular game).

This chapter provides information on a small number of field tests that are more directly related to sports performance than those presented in Chapter 41. Some of the tests presented below can be applied to a wide range of athletes (e.g. the YOYO intermittent recovery test can be applied to team sport athletes despite being developed for soccer players), whereas others are only applicable to particular sports (e.g. the run-a-three agility test is specific for cricket batsmen). However, the tests presented provide a useful introduction to the principles of specific field testing.

YOYO intermittent recovery test (IRT) – estimation of $\dot{V}O_2$max for team sports

This field test is useful for determining intermittent endurance performance in athletes. The test was originally developed as a more valid test of aerobic capacity for soccer players, as it mimics the intermittent physical activity of the game rather than the repetitive nature of the multistage fitness test, MSFT (Box 41.7). The YOYO IRT requires participants to run a 20 m shuttle (similar to the MSFT) and then have a 10 second recovery period before completing a further shuttle. It is now the preferred test for VO_2 max for a range of team sports with intermittent activity. The YOYO IRT lasts for 2–15 minutes, and has two different levels, to cater for recreational and elite athletes. The YOYO IRT may be performed at two levels (1 and 2) with differing speed profiles. Typically level 1 is used unless the subject has previously completed the full YOYO IRT at level 1. Level 1 of the YOYO IRT consists of four running bouts at 10–13 km h^{-1} (0–160 m) and another seven runs at 13.5–14 km h^{-1} (160–440 m). Following this, the test increases at 0.5 km h^{-1} increments after the completion of every eight running bouts (i.e. after 760 m, 1080 m, 1400 m, 1720 m). The test is ended when the participant fails to reach the 20 m cone for two consecutive shuttles. After completion, the distance covered during the test is used to provide an estimate of the participant's $\dot{V}O_2$ max. The procedure is explained in Box 42.1.

Box 42.1 How to carry out a YOYO IRT test

Try to have a suitable number of participants for the number of testers. If not, it is easy to miss failed attempts and to lose track of shuttles. A good ratio of testers to participants is between 1:6–18. That is, for two testers, you should have 12–16 athletes.

1. **Set up the course on a non-slip surface.** Place a marker on the 0 m mark (preferably a line), measure a 20 m distance and place another marker. For each athlete, create a lane by placing markers 2 m parallel to the 0 m and 20 m marks.
2. **Measure a further 5 m behind the 0 m mark** and place a marker in the middle of the lane (Fig. 42.1).

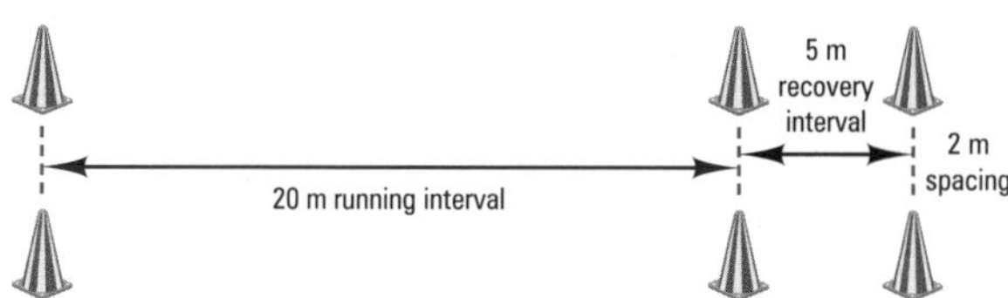

Fig. 42.1 The running course for each participant in the YOYO recovery test.

3. **Ask the participants to warm up before the test.** The test is incremental, but progresses reasonably quickly and therefore subjects will not warm up adequately during the test.
4. **Explain the test to the participants** so that they are familiar with the test procedures. The main aspects are as follows:
   a. On the first audible 'beep' the participants should run from the 0 m mark down to the 20 m mark.
   b. At the sound of the second audible beep, the participant should arrive at the far 20 m mark and turn to run back towards the 0 m mark.
   c. On the third audible beep, the participant should reach the 0 m mark. Once they have reached the 0 m mark, they slow and jog around the 5 m cone and then return to the cone at the 0 m mark. Participants have 10 seconds to complete this recovery.
   d. Participants are then required to wait at the start line for the next audible beep, when this procedure is repeated.
5. **Begin the test.** Instruct participants to stand at the start line. Commence the YOYO IRT by pressing 'play' on the CD player.
6. **Record all successful shuttles completed by the participants.** A successful shuttle requires at least one foot to be placed on or over the line at 0 and 20 m.
7. **Encourage the participants during the test.** Subjects are required to keep running for as long as possible during the test and to use the audible 'beeps' to guide their speed. If the participant fails to complete a successful shuttle, then give them a verbal warning that they will be 'out' if they miss the next step.
8. **Stop the participants when they have failed to complete two shuttles in succession.**
9. **Record the number and speed of the shuttles that each participant completed during the test.** Include the last shuttle that was attempted, even if not successful.
10. **Encourage all participants to cool down following the test.**
11. **Calculate the distance covered** during the test using Table 42.1.
12. **Estimate the VO_2 max using the following** estimation equations:

Level 1

$$VO_2max = \text{IRT1 distance (m)} \times 0.0084 + 36.4 \quad (42.1)$$

Level 2

$$VO_2max = \text{IRT2 distance (m)} \times 0.0136 + 45.3 \quad (42.2)$$

Tennis agility test

The ability to change movement in a variety of directions rapidly is an integral part of being a successful tennis player. Generic tests of agility do not assess a subject's ability to change direction outside of a single plane of running. Furthermore, tennis players typically use a variety of running styles to move around the court to better position themselves for further play. Therefore, an agility test specific for tennis has been developed that provides information relevant to the specific movement patterns and running styles of tennis (Box 42.2).

Table 42.1 The cumulative distance (m) covered during the YOYO IRT for each completed shuttle

	Number of Shuttles							
Stage	1	2	3	4	5	6	7	8
5	40							
9	80							
11	120	160						
12	200	240	280					
13	320	360	400	440				
14	480	520	560	600	640	680	720	760
15	800	840	880	920	960	100	1040	1080
16	1120	1160	1200	1240	1280	1320	1360	1400
17	1440	1480	1520	1560	1600	1640	1680	1720
18	1760	1800	1840	1880	1920	1960	2000	2040
19	2080	2120	2160	2200	2240	2280	2320	2360
20	2400	2440	2480	2520	2560	2600	2640	2680
21	2720	2760	2800	2840	2880	2920	2960	3000
22	3040	3080	3120	3160	3200	3240	3280	3320
23	3360	3400	3440	3480	3520	3560	3600	3640

Cricket-specific agility test

The physical capacities that are related to cricket can largely be assessed using generic field tests (Chapter 41). Typical field assessment of cricket players can include field tests such as vertical jump, sprint, sit and reach, abdominal strength test and the multi stage fitness test. However, these tests do not specifically assess a cricket player's ability to run and turn between wickets. Therefore, to assess this capacity specifically, the 'run-a-three' agility test has been developed. In simple terms, the 'run-a-three' test is an adaptation of the 5-0-5 test described elsewhere (Box 41.5). Box 42.3 gives details of the procedure.

Simulated rowing performance test

The ability to measure the physiological capacities of a rowing athlete are described elsewhere in this book (Chapters 36 and 43). However, these physiological capacities do not provide a valid measure of the ability of the athlete to race. On the other hand, waiting for racing opportunities may not provide useful measurements of physiological condition, as performance will be affected by tactical and environmental considerations. Furthermore, seasonal conditions may also limit the ability to race during times of the year. Given these points, the 2000 m rowing ergometer test has developed as an easy-to-perform and reliable test to determine the racing ability of a rower specifically. The nature of the test described in Box 42.4 can be easily modified to other 'racing' sports such as kayaking (distance: 500 m or 1000 m) and cycling (distance: 1000–4000 m).

Box 42.2 How to carry out a tennis agility test

The following steps explain the main aspects of the tennis agility test.

1. **Set up the course** as shown in Fig. 42.2 from the baseline of a standard tennis court. Be sure to set up the electronic timing gates where shown and set them for one lap.

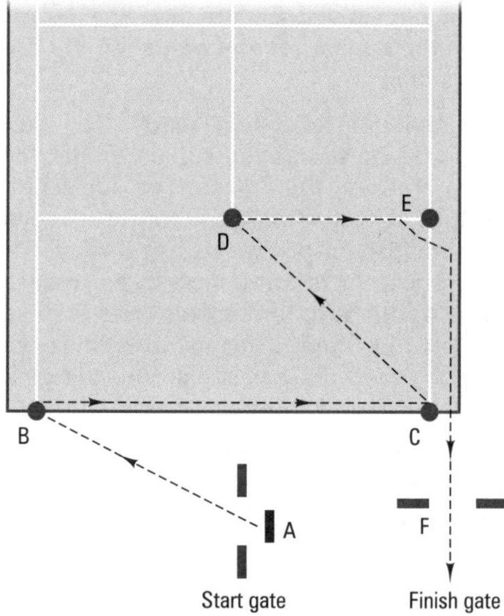

Fig. 42.2 An illustration of the set-up for tennis agility course.

2. **Describe the pattern of the test to the subject** (see below). The subject should complete a number of runs to familiarise themselves with the course, since the procedure is quite complex. Provide feedback on movements and tasks across the test if necessary.
3. **Ask the subject to take the starting position** at the back of the court behind the start gate. Their tennis racquet should be held in their dominant hand and their front foot should be placed at the starting line.
4. **Instruct the subject that they can start the test when ready.** The electronic timing gates will start recording automatically when the subject runs through them. From the start gate, the participant should follow the sequence in Fig. 42.2.
   a. **Participant is to sprint to point B and touch the racquet to the ground beside the cone.** They should then place their feet so that, if right-handed they are playing a backhand and if they are left-handed they are playing a forehand.
   b. **The participant then turns and sprints to point C and touches the racquet to the ground beside the cone.** The subject should place their feet so that if right-handed they are playing a forehand and if they are left-handed they are playing a backhand.
   c. **Following this, the participant sprints to point D before slowing and performing a split-jump to land on the service line** with one foot on opposite sides of the centre line. The subject is not required to touch their racquet to the ground.
   d. **On landing, the participant is to use side steps/cross over steps to point E** and then touch the racquet at the intersection of the service line and singles line (inside tram line).
   e. **After point E, the participant uses side steps/cross over steps between the singles and doubles line** back to the baseline as if moving back to complete an 'overhead smash' shot. The subject should remain 'side on' during this leg of the test and continue to run through the finish gate placed behind the base line.
5. **Record the time taken to complete the circuit** from the electronic timing gates. Reset the gates so that the subject can repeat the test.
6. **Repeat the test.** Each subject should complete five trials of the agility test on a 30 second cycle. A stopwatch should be used to measure the time between test laps. Ensure that the subject has adequate time to prepare before each test repetition.
7. **Calculate the average time taken to complete the test.** Record this as the subject's time for the test. If an 'outlier' (p. 379) result is identified, this should be removed from the analysis.
8. **Compare the test result to normative data** and rate the performance of the test participant. For example, Table 42.2 gives representative normative data for this test in elite athletes.

Box 42.3 How to carry out a 'run-a-three' test

The steps below outline the main components of this agility test.

1. **Measure out a 17.7 m straight line** (this is the length of a cricket pitch from crease to crease). Place a cone at 0 m, 12.7 m and 17.7 m (Fig. 42.3).

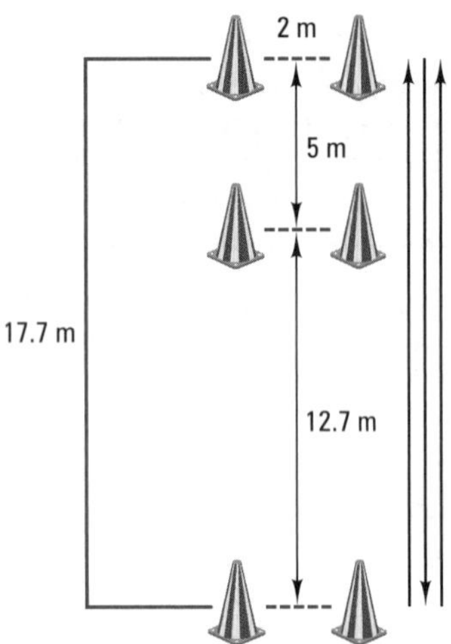

Fig. 42.3 The set-up for a 'run-a-three' agility test.

2. **Set up the timing gate at the 12.7 m line.** The timing gate will need to be set up to have two timing splits. You will also require at least two stopwatches for you and an assistant to 'hand-time' the total run time.
3. **Explain the requirements of the test to the subject.** The test should be consistently performed in typical cricket clothing and equipment (i.e. pads). The subject is required to perform three lengths of the 17.7 m line as fast as possible. The subject should perform each turn as fast as they can and use a typical bat 'slide'. Ensure that the subject clearly understands the requirements of the test before they begin.
4. **Start the subject when ready.** The stopwatches should be started as the subject's back foot lifts up before crossing the crease. The subject should run and turn as fast as possible for three repeat sprints. The timing gate at the 12.7 m line will record the 'turn time' which is the time taken to pass through the gate, run 5 m, turn around and then sprint back through the gate. The stopwatches should be stopped when the bat is slid into the crease at the end of the third repetition.
5. **Record the total run time.** This is the average time of the two stopwatches. The time taken from the timing gates should be recorded as the turn time.
6. **Compare the results to the normative data** in Table 42.3 and rate the performance of the participant.

Table 42.2 Normative values (mean $\pm$ SD) for the tennis agility test for a high performance group of athletes

Trial Number	Males	Females
Trial 1	7.40 ± 0.01	8.08 ± 0.35
Trial 2	7.52 ± 0.21	8.04 ± 0.46
Trial 3	7.29 ± 0.15	8.11 ± 0.40
Trial 4	7.33 ± 0.22	8.06 ± 0.40
Trial 5	7.16 ± 0.05	8.25 ± 0.49
Mean	7.34 ± 0.11	8.11 ± 0.39
Range	7.17–7.66	7.56–8.79

Adapted from Gore (2000).

Box 42.4 How to carry out a 2000-m rowing ergometer test

The steps below outline the details of the test.

1. **Prepare the rowing ergometer** (e.g. Concept II, Fig. 42.4) for the subject.
   a. Ensure that the chain attached to the handle is well oiled and that the seat slide is clean and easily movable.
   b. Check that the screen display of the ergometer is working and readable.
   c. Adjust the foot plates of the ergometer for the subject, if required.

Fig. 42.4 The Concept II rowing ergometer.

2. **Change the resistance settings of the ergometer to suit the participant.** The sliding level on the front wheel of the ergometer changes the resistance of the ergometer by manipulating the volume of air taken in. The slider is read against a numerical scale (Fig. 42.5). For a Concept II rowing ergometer the resistance settings are:
   a. lightweight (<59 kg) female: 2
   b. heavyweight (>59 kg) female: 3
   c. lightweight (<75 kg) male: 3
   d. heavyweight (>75 kg) male: 4

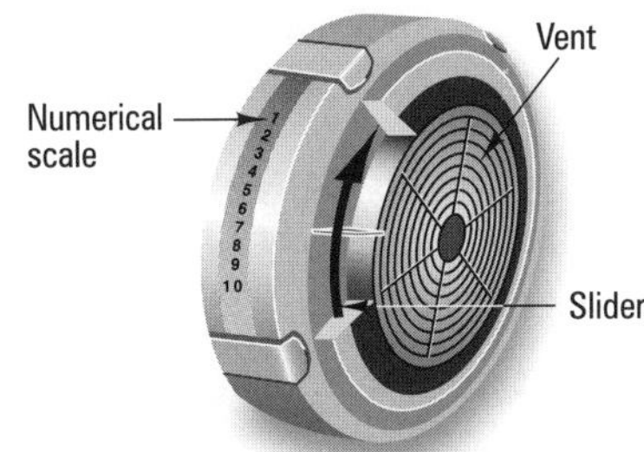

Fig. 42.5 The sliding resistance scale on the Concept II rowing ergometer.

3. **Instruct the subject to warm up on the ergometer.** Given the maximal effort required in the 2000 m ergometer test, a full warm-up (e.g. 5–10 min slow-to-moderate intensity with two to three short high-intensity efforts) is recommended to ensure best performance during the test.
4. **Adjust the screen to display target (maximum) distance in metres and adjust the number to 2000 using the arrows.** Use the manual or consult a tutor to establish how to carry out this step, if necessary.
5. **Instruct the subject to get ready for the test on the ergometer.** Before starting the test, check that the feet of the subject are correctly located in the foot plate, and are held securely by the restraining straps. If you are taking any physiological measures during the test, e.g. expired gas analysis (Chapter 36) or heart rate (Chapter 29), then place the necessary equipment on the participant and check that it is working before the test.
6. **When ready, ask the subject to start the 2000 m test.** Start a stopwatch at the initial movement of their first stroke. The ergometer screen will automatically begin to count down and the test commences when the screen displays zero.
7. **Record the distance covered** and any physiological data. Physiological measurements are often recorded at 30 second intervals across the test. Stroke rates should be recorded from the ergometer display screen after every 250 m interval. Be sure to provide verbal encouragement to the subject during the test.
8. **Stop the stopwatch when the ergometer display reads zero.** Ensure that the subject holds onto the handle after completing the test or it may fly forward and damage the screen. Following completion of the test, take the handle from the subject and gently place it back to its resting position. Remove any other physiological monitoring equipment that may be uncomfortable for the subject (i.e. gas masks or mouthpieces).
9. **If required, collect a capillary sample of blood to be analysed for lactate concentration** (Chapter 28) after two, four and six minutes of passive recovery following the test. Be sure to analyse the blood as quickly as possible and record the values.
10. **Analyse the data and compare to past individual data.** Normative values are shown in Table 42.4 for national-level Australian rowers.

Source: Fig. 42.4: Concept2 Ltd.: Concept2 Model D Indoor Rower.

Table 42.3 Normative values for the 'run-a-three' agility tests for cricket players

		Run-a-three (s)*			Turn speed (s)†		
Level/position	***n***	**Average**	**SD**	**Range**	**Average**	**SD**	**Range**
Elite batsman	62	9.29	0.4	8.60–10.15	2.05	0.1	1.84–2.60
Elite pace bowler	45	9.36	0.4	8.68–10.85	2.08	0.1	1.87–2.43
Elite keeper	13	9.36	0.6	8.67–10.80	2.06	0.2	1.86–2.34
Elite spin bowler	18	9.53	0.3	8.82–10.37	2.12	0.1	1.85–2.36
State/county based	59	9.32	0.4	8.68–9.99	2.16	0.1	1.86–2.39
International test (male)	27	9.65	0.5	8.61–11.20	2.12	0.1	1.79–2.48
International test (female)	62	10.62	0.5	9.80–11.90	2.33	0.1	2.06–2.78

Normative data adapted from Gore (2000). *Timing completed by hand; †timing completed electronically. SD = Standard deviation.

Table 42.4 Normative values for national level Australian rowers for the 2000 m ergometer test

		Test time (minutes)	
Rowing classification	**Sample**	**Mean ± SD**	**Range**
Lightweight females	36	7:27 ± 0:04	7:19–7:53
Heavyweight females	78	7:03 ± 0:20	6:40–7:35
Lightweight males	82	6:27 ± 0:04	6.11–6:56
Heavyweight males	123	6:06 ± 0:26	5:54–6:24

Normative data adapted from Gore (2000). SD = Standard deviation.

Text reference

Gore, C. (ed.) (2000) *Physiological Tests for Elite Athletes*. Human Kinetics, Champaign, IL.

Sources for further study

Bangsbo, J., Marcello J.I. and Krustrup, P. (2008) The yo-yo intermittent recovery test: a useful tool for evaluation of physical performance in intermittent sports. *Sports Medicine*, **38**(1), 37–51.

Top End Sports (2010). Available: http://www.topendsports.com/testing/sportspecific.htm. Last accessed: 11/10/10.
[An excellent resource for a range of sports-specific tests.]

Winter, E.M., Jones, A.M., Davidson, R.C.R., Bromley, P.D. and Mercer, T.H. (2006) *Sport and Exercise Physiology Testing Guidelines. Vol. I: Sports Testing*. Routledge, Oxford.

Calculating physiological measures

43. Measuring endurance training thresholds 337

44. Measuring economy of exercise 344

45. Monitoring training load 349

43 Measuring endurance training thresholds

Definitions

Ventilation – the rate at which gas enters or leaves the lungs.

Ventilatory threshold (VT) – work intensity at which there is a sudden rise in the rate of ventilation to clear CO_2 from the body.

Lactic acid – a metabolic product that arises from anaerobic glycolysis. Simply a combination of lactate and a proton.

Lactate – the ionic form ('salt') of lactic acid.

Ventilatory equivalent – ratio of the volume of ventilation to $\dot{V}O_2$ or $\dot{V}CO_2$.

Blood lactate curve – the line formed by the blood lactate concentrations across an incremental test.

The ability to profile the physiological limits of an athlete is vital to monitoring their ability to perform and the effectiveness of their training. While other tests, such as $\dot{V}O_2$max, provide information on the endurance *potential* of an individual, they do not provide a valid measure of endurance *performance*. Performance in such events relies on the ability to work at the highest intensity possible for a sustained period of time. This requires a mixture of aerobic and anaerobic energy production. The capacity to maintain the highest anaerobic energy yield is determined by an ability to balance the production and clearance of waste products that interfere with muscular function, especially lactic acid and carbon dioxide. As such, sport and exercise scientists have produced a variety of 'thresholds' that help to quantify the important physiological events in the aerobic–anaerobic transition during increasingly intense exercise. These include the ventilatory threshold (VT), the lactate threshold 1 (LT_1) and the lactate threshold 2 (LT_2). These provide indices of important transitions in the body with respect to the production and clearance of waste products.

This chapter provides information on the practical procedures used to determine these thresholds using data taken from incremental testing. These can then be used to monitor training and performance in athletes.

Measuring ventilatory threshold (VT)

An important measure of an athlete's physiological profile is the work intensity at which their ventilation increases to increase the clearance of CO_2 from within the body. This point is called the 'ventilatory threshold' (also known as the 'anaerobic threshold'). During exercise of increasing intensity, there is a shift in the source of fuel and biochemical pathway used to produce energy. At the VT, there is a large increase in CO_2 in the blood that needs to be removed, or it would cause acidification. This CO_2 is the result of an increase in the production of lactic acid from the muscle during anaerobic metabolism. The drop in pH caused by the increase in lactic acid is largely buffered by bicarbonate (HCO_3^-) ions to transport the extra protons ([H^+]) to the lungs as carbonic acid (H_2CO_3) where it is reduced to CO_2 and H_2O. The result is an increased pressure of CO_2 in the blood. The change in CO_2 pressure is detected by chemoreceptors in major arteries, which relay the decrease in pH and increase in the partial pressure of CO_2 (PCO_2) to the brain's inspiratory centre to increase the rate of ventilation. As such, identifying this threshold provides a work intensity that is related to a shift in the biochemical pathways that are responsible for the provision of energy.

Understanding the V-slope technique – the threshold highlighted by the V-slope technique is often termed the anaerobic threshold. The technique uses the sudden change in ventilation to identify the increase in the removal of CO_2 rather than changes in the actual concentration of CO_2 expelled.

To determine the VT, the collection and analysis of the expired gases over an incremental test to exhaustion is required (Fig. 43.1; see also Chapter 36). The analysis of VT is completed after the test by the sport and exercise scientist. For more information on completing an incremental test and expired gas analysis, see Box 36.1.

The determination of VT can be performed using two different methods, using either (1) ventilatory equivalents or (2) the 'V-slope' technique. Ventilatory equivalents refer to the rate of ventilation (V_E)

relative to the VO_2 (V_E/VO_2) or VCO_2 (V_E/VCO_2). The V-slope technique refers to identifying the intensity at which there is a sharp increase in ventilation. Examples of the output of VT determination using the ventilatory equivalent method (Fig. 43.2) and V-slope technique (Fig. 43.3) are shown.

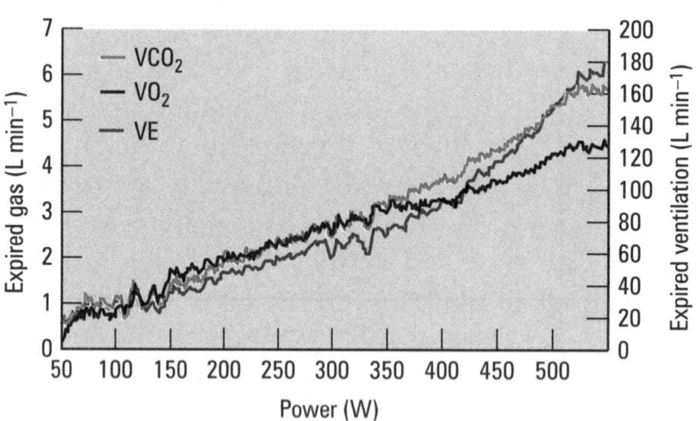

Fig. 43.1 An example of expired gas data from a cyclist during a 'ramp' exercise test.

Box 43.1 How to measure ventilatory threshold (VT) using ventilatory equivalents

1. **Export the expired gas analysis data to a spreadsheet,** for example, Microsoft Excel (Chapter 11). Label the data for each measured variable.
2. **Calculate the ventilatory equivalent for VO_2 and VCO_2.** To do this, divide the ventilation rate (V_E) by the VO_2 and VCO_2. All measures should be in L min^{-1}. Depending on the sampling rate, you may need to calculate average ventilatory equivalents for incremental periods at particular work intensities (e.g. 20–25 W).
3. **Plot ventilatory equivalents (vertical axis) against work intensity (horizontal axis) on a line graph** (Chapter 47, p. 364), as shown in Fig. 43.2.
4. **Analyse the graph to identify VT from the changes in V_E/VO_2 and V_E/VCO_2 against the increase in power output.** During the initial stages of the incremental test, both V_E/VO_2 and V_E/VCO_2 decrease. During the later stages of the test, an intensity will be reached where V_E/VO_2 will begin to increase at a much faster rate than the V_E/VCO_2 (Fig. 43.2). This work intensity corresponds to the ventilatory threshold.

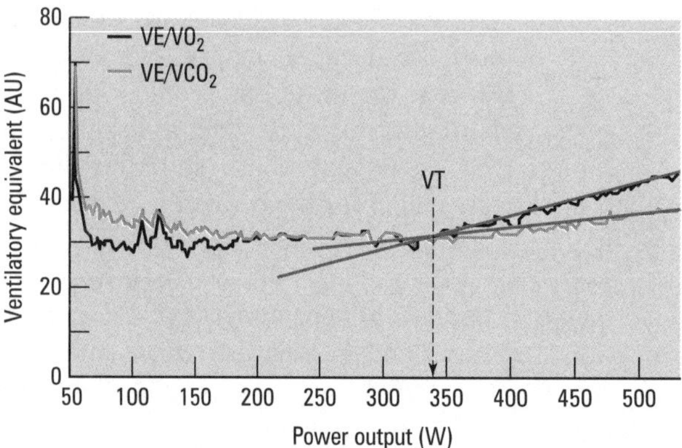

Fig. 43.2 An example of determining ventilatory threshold using the ventilatory equivalent method.

Box 43.1 gives details of the approach using ventilatory equivalents while Box 43.2 explains the main steps in the process using the V-slope technique.

Box 43.2 How to measure ventilatory threshold (VT) using the V-slope technique

1. **Export the expired gas analysis data to a spreadsheet** for example, Microsoft Excel (Chapter 11). Label the data for each measured variable.
2. **Plot the $\dot{V}O_2$ and $\dot{V}CO_2$ responses across work intensity on the same line graph** (Chapter 47, p. 364). Be sure to use the same units of measurement (L min^{-1}).
3. **Plot the $\dot{V}O_2$ and $\dot{V}CO_2$ responses on an X–Y scattergram** (Chapter 47, p. 365).
4. **Draw a line at a slope of 1.0 on the scattergram.** This is most easily done by joining points with the same value on the Y and X axes.
5. **Analyse the graph to identify the $\dot{V}O_2$ and $\dot{V}CO_2$ responses over the test.** Identify the point at which $\dot{V}CO_2$ increases at a faster rate than $\dot{V}O_2$ (Fig. 43.3).
6. **Identify VT.** Note that the gradient of the $\dot{V}O_2$:$\dot{V}CO_2$ plot *below* the VT is always $\leq$1.0 (more O_2 consumed than CO_2 produced). At a particular work intensity, the $\dot{V}CO_2$ will increase dramatically, giving a gradient >1.0 (Fig. 43.3). The work intensity at which this increase is first observed is the VT.

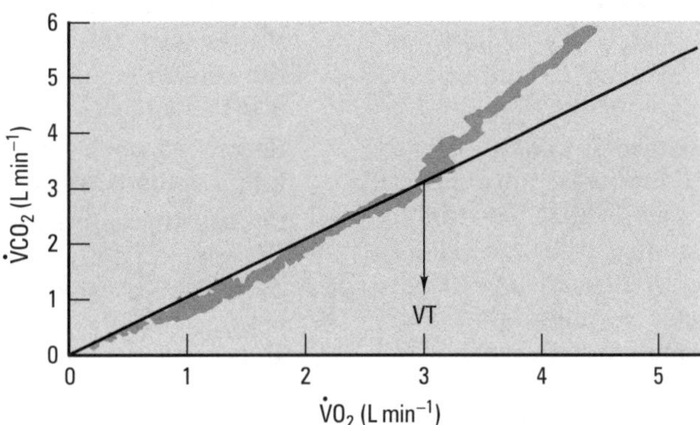

Fig. 43.3 An example of determining ventilatory threshold using the V-slope technique.

Measuring blood lactate thresholds

Understanding the difference between lactic acid and lactate – lactate is an important anion and is responsible for absorbing protons released during anaerobic energy production. It acts as a 'buffer' within the muscle to limit any decrease in pH by the conversion of negatively charged lactate molecules to un-ionised lactic acid molecules. Consequently, the concentration of lactate in the blood is an important physiological measure of a person's aerobic energy metabolism.

The increasing contribution of anaerobic energy metabolism during increasingly hard exercise can also be examined by the measurement of lactate in the blood (see margin note). Across continued high intensity exercise, lactic acid can accumulate and lower the pH of the muscle and blood owing to the release of protons, disrupting the ability of muscles to function and decreasing performance. During increasingly intense exercise, there is a balance between the production of lactic acid and its conversion to harmless metabolites (CO_2 and H_2O). The training of athletes specifically attempts to adapt muscle to tolerate higher production of lactic acid during anaerobic exercise and to improve the ability to resist and tolerate acidification (decreases in pH) and clear lactate from the circulation. Therefore, to quantify the characteristics of lactic acid production and tolerance, a number of physiological thresholds are determined by the analysis of blood lactate levels. These

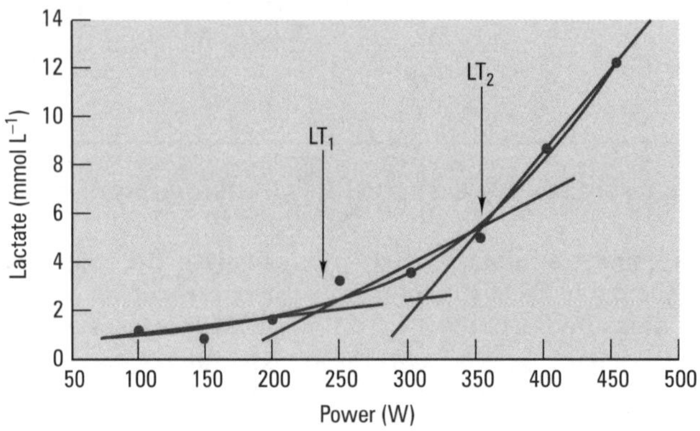

Fig. 43.4 A lactate–power curve identifying the LT_1 and LT_2 of a well-trained endurance cyclist.

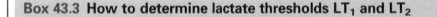

Box 43.3 How to determine lactate thresholds LT_1 and LT_2

1. **Determine the testing protocol to be used.** To determine LT_1 and LT_2, it is necessary to perform an incremental test on the subject, as detailed in Box 36.1.
2. **Complete the testing protocol, taking blood samples at appropriate time intervals.** Note that it is necessary that a steady state is reached during each stage of the test. You should draw a capillary sample of blood during the last 30 seconds of each stage (Chapter 36). It is also required that you record physiological measurements such as expired gas data, heart rate and rate of perceived exertion. However, it is not always practical to analyse blood lactate during training sessions.
3. **Continue the test at the prescribed work intensity stages until the criteria for VO_2max is reached or the subject cannot continue.** Ensure that you check that the subject is feeling fine after the test.
4. **Record all physiological measures and enter them into a spreadsheet** program for analysis.
5. **Choose the appropriate method to determine both LT_1 and LT_2.** Two principal methods have been developed to determine blood lactate thresholds (see below), namely fixed blood lactate concentrations and individualised lactate thresholds. The methods applied to assess blood lactate thresholds should be consistent across test–retest and be best suited to each subject.

thresholds help to provide information on work intensities that reflect important physiological events in terms of the shift in energy metabolism. Importantly, they all appear sensitive to change with training and are strongly related to performance. These include:

- **lactate threshold 1 (LT_1)** – first work intensity at which blood lactate appears to increase over resting values. LT_1 typically falls around 2.0 mmol L^{-1} (Fig. 43.4);
- **lactate threshold 2 (LT_2)** – the highest work intensity at which the production and clearance can be maintained. Increases in work intensity beyond this point produce an exponential rise in lactic acid in the blood and muscle owing to its increased production. LT_2 normally falls between 4 and 6 mmol L^{-1} (Fig. 43.4).

The testing methods and protocols used to determine LT_1 and LT_2 need to be consistent, to ensure that any changes observed are real and not

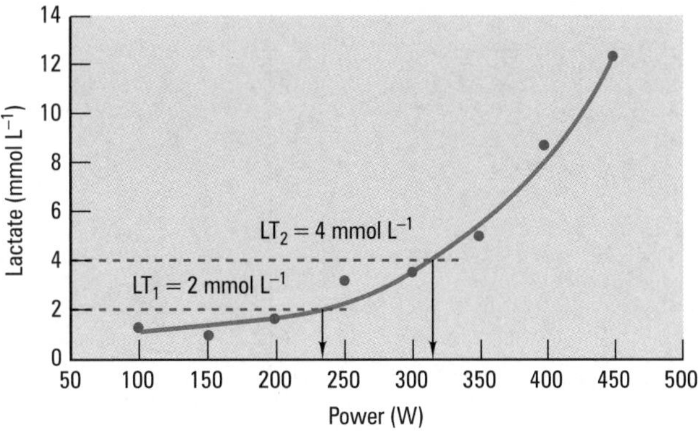

Fig. 43.5 An example of determining LT_1 and LT_2 using fixed blood lactate concentrations.

caused by testing errors (see Chapter 19). The exercise testing required to measure blood lactate thresholds requires incremental step tests (Chapter 36) and longer test stages (~5 minutes) to allow the subject to reach a physiological steady state. The exercise test must also be completed under appropriate laboratory conditions (Chapter 24), following appropriate pre-test preparation (Chapter 26). Box 43.3 describes the exercise testing and post-test analysis required to quantify LT_1 and LT_2.

Fixed blood lactate concentrations

This method is a simple way of identifying lactate thresholds. Typically, blood lactate concentrations of 2 mmol L^{-1} and 4 mmol L^{-1} are used to define LT_1 and LT_2, respectively. The measurement of LT_1 and LT_2 is simply performed by determining the power output at the set blood lactate concentrations (Fig. 43.5). Using fixed blood lactate concentrations helps to minimise biological variation in terms of where the inflection points are perceived to be in the blood lactate curve. However, this method is affected by an athlete's training state, nutritional status and other factors. This method may also demonstrate large intersubject variability.

Individual blood lactate thresholds

A variety of mathematical and visual interpretation skills are used to determine the blood lactate thresholds. Some of the most commonly used methods are detailed below.

LT_1: Adapt method

This method simply quantifies the LT_1 as the last workload completed before a rise greater than 0.4 mmol L^{-1} is recorded (Fig. 43.6a).

LT_1: Coyle method

This method uses a similar method to determine LT_1 as the Adapt method; however, LT_1 is recorded as the highest workload completed before a rise of >1.0 mmol L^{-1} is observed (Fig. 43.6b).

LT_2: D_{max} method

This is a common method used to assess LT_2. To identify LT_2, simply draw a straight line between the first and last data point on the blood

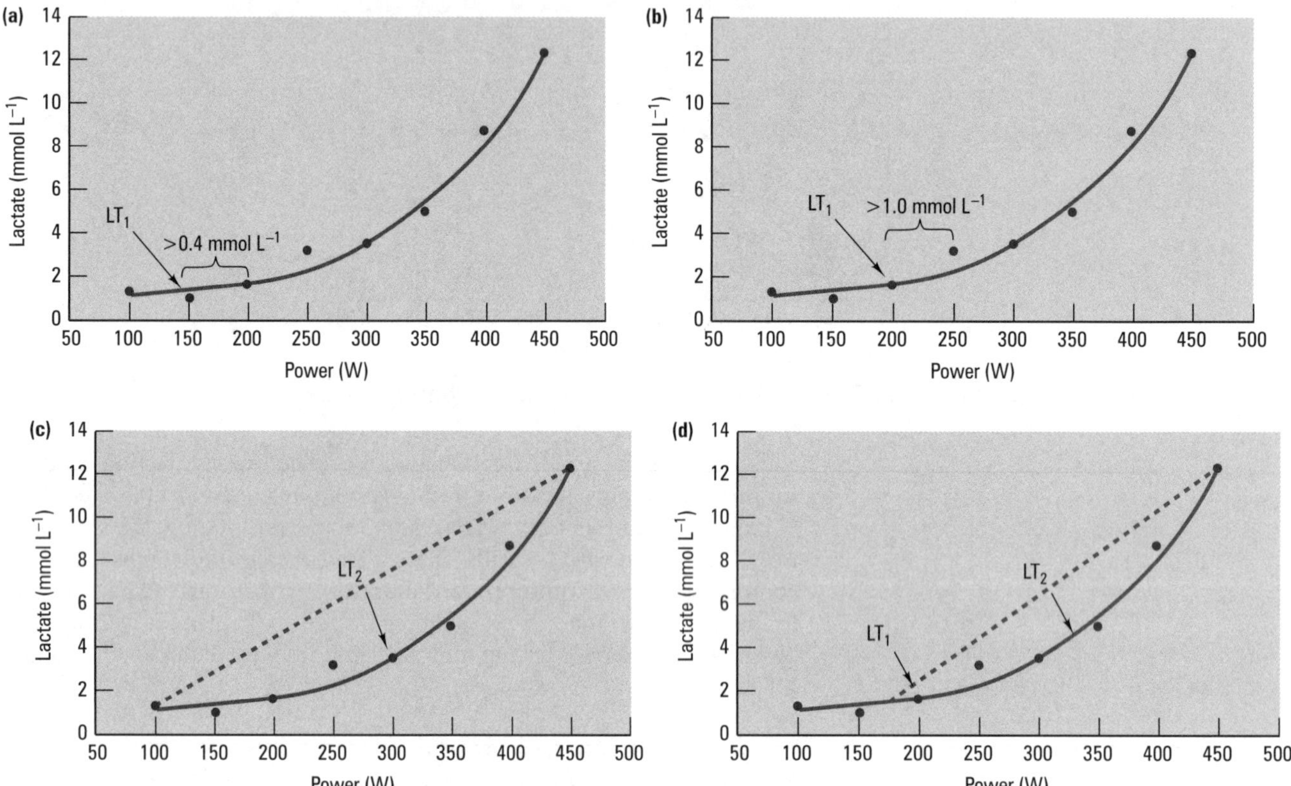

Fig. 43.6 Demonstration of the commonly used methods to determine both LT_1 and LT_2. (**a**) = Adapt method for LT_1; (**b**) = Coyle method for LT_1; (**c**) = D_{max} method for LT_2; (**d**) = modified D_{max} for LT_2.

lactate curve. LT_2 is recorded at the work intensity that is the most distant from the linear line (Fig. 43.6c).

LT_2: Modified D_{max}

This method is similar to the D_{max} method with the exception that the straight line is drawn between the LT_1 (as identified using the Adapt method) and the highest lactate on the curve. LT_2 is recorded as the work intensity that is the most distant from the linear line (Fig. 43.6d).

Interpreting shifts in blood lactate thresholds

While the ability to determine blood lactate thresholds is an important skill for a sport and exercise scientist, so is the ability to interpret changes in them over time. The changes in the blood lactate thresholds are valid measures of changes in an athlete's ability to perform, given that the testing and assessment is consistent to the individual. Assessing changes in blood lactate thresholds can easily be performed by graphically overlaying the data (Fig. 43.7).

The changes in the blood lactate thresholds can easily be assessed by the direction in which the curve moves. Adaptations occur with positive training, and then the blood lactate curve moves downwards and to the right, as seen in Fig. 43.7a). This indicates that the athlete demonstrates a lower blood lactate for the same intensity, i.e. that the athlete can exercise at a higher work intensity for the same blood lactate concentration. If a negative change occurs in the physiological profile, then the blood lactate curve moves upwards and to the left. This suggests that the athlete produces more blood lactate when working at the same intensity as before, i.e. that the athlete can work at a lighter intensity for the same blood lactate concentration. Changes in blood lactate thresholds can be interpreted using the above principles.

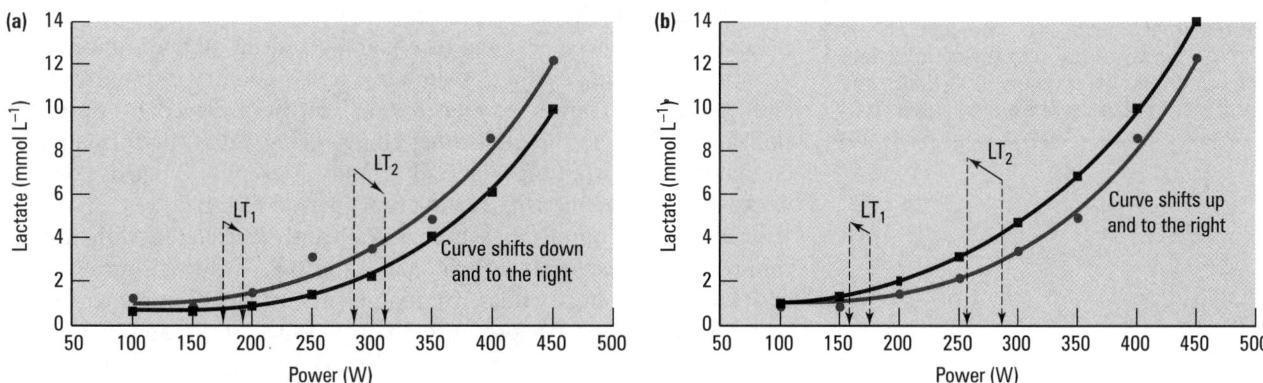

Fig. 43.7 Graphs demonstrating both positive (**a**) and negative (**b**) training adaptations in a blood lactate curve.

Sources for further study

Bourdon, P. (2000) Blood lactate transition thresholds: concepts and controversies. In: C. Gore (ed.) *Physiological Tests for Elite Athletes*. Human Kinetics, Champaign, IL.

Wilmore, J.H., Costill, D. L. and Kenney, W.L. (2008) *Physiology of Sports and Exercise*. Human Kinetics, Champaign, IL.

Weltman, A. (1995) The blood lactate response to exercise. *Current Issues in Exercise Science Series*. Human Kinetics, Champaign, IL.

44 Measuring economy of exercise

Definition

Economy – the relative oxygen cost (per unit of body weight) at a given submaximal pace or velocity. It is determined by measuring the steady state consumption of oxygen ($\dot{V}O_2$) at any particular submaximal exercise intensity.

Endurance performance is determined mainly by factors such as $\dot{V}O_2$max, the fractional utilisation of maximal aerobic capacity at race pace, and the anaerobic threshold. However, the economy of exercise has also been shown to account for a small amount of the variance in endurance performance of athletes.

Economy of energy expenditure is important in all endurance events, including running, cycling, swimming, cross-country skiing, kayaking and rowing. If a lower oxygen uptake can be achieved by optimising skill and technique then, all other things being equal, performance can be maintained for a longer period at a given exercise intensity, or at an increased exercise intensity for the same period of time.

In runners, economy has been significantly correlated with distance running performance. In a homogenous group of elite distance runners with similar $\dot{V}O_2$max values, running economy has been shown to be a better predictor of performance than $\dot{V}O_2$max itself and to vary by about 10%. Moreover, in a heterogeneous (recreational, club and elite) group of runners, elite runners have been shown to have significantly lower $\dot{V}O_2$ at any running speed than recreational or club runners.

In cycling, an elite cyclist wants to use a lower percentage of their $\dot{V}O_2$max at a given cycling speed. If two cyclists have similar $\dot{V}O_2$max profiles, the most economical cyclist will win most races. Even if a cyclist has a relatively low $\dot{V}O_2$max, they can often defeat other cyclists, because they may ride at a lower percentage of their $\dot{V}O_2$max at any given speed. If two cyclists are riding at the same speed, the more economical cyclist uses less oxygen to ride at this speed. An uneconomical cyclist may need to use 5–10% more energy (or oxygen) than an economical cyclist to cycle at a given pace. The uneconomical cyclist will be working closer to their maximal capacity than an economical cyclist. Since the physiological strain felt by the body is directly related to $\dot{V}O_2$max, the economical cyclist will have an advantage.

Protocols for measuring economy

The classic definition of economy demands the measurement of oxygen consumption ($\dot{V}O_2$) at a range of submaximal exercise intensities. Box 44.1 summarises a typical exercise protocol for measuring running economy. This treadmill running protocol and associated procedures can be adjusted to other sports and ergometers.

KEY POINT Treadmill gradients are sometimes set at 1% in laboratory tests where results are applied to field measures. This gradient may better reflect the cost of outdoor running where wind resistance and greater work by the hip extensors both add to increased energy cost.

Box 44.1 Protocol for measuring running economy

1. **Conduct a $\dot{V}O_2$max test on a treadmill** (Chapter 36).
2. **From the $\dot{V}O_2$max results, develop a regression equation relating VO_2 (ml kg^{-1} min^{-1}) to running speed (m s^{-1}).**
3. **Determine the running speeds that elicit 60, 70, 80 and 90% of $\dot{V}O_2$max.** For example, the British Association of Sport and Exercise Sciences developed the following regression equations for male (n = 58) and female (n = 44) physical education students:

   Males: $Y = 11.6\,X + 0.72$ (44.1)

   Females: $Y = 10.7\,X + 3.30$ (44.2)

   where $Y = \dot{V}O_2$ (ml kg^{-1} min^{-1}) and X = running speed (m s^{-1}).

   The training status of the athlete must be considered, since only well conditioned endurance athletes can cope with exercise intensities at 90% $\dot{V}O_2$max.
4. **Warm up on the treadmill at low intensity, building to the first exercise intensity (treadmill speed) of 60% $\dot{V}O_2$max.** Participants should be familiarised with treadmill running before the test.
5. **Run the participant on a level treadmill at the first running speed for four minutes, measuring the mean $\dot{V}O_2$ in the last minute.**
6. **Increase the running speed every four minutes until the speed that elicited 90% $\dot{V}O_2$max is reached and measure $\dot{V}O_2$ in the final minute of each four-minute stage.** For children under 15 years, a three-minute interval is suggested as they reach steady state more quickly than adults. Heart rates, rating of perceived exertion (RPE) and blood lactate values can also be measured at the end of each exercise stage (for more detail see Chapter 43).
7. **Plot oxygen uptake (ml kg^{-1} min^{-1}) on the *y* axis and running speed (m s^{-1}) on the *x* axis.** Linear regression equations (p. 397) can be developed for each subject, and group data can be compared using statistical techniques such as ANOVA (Box 50.3) or *t*-tests (Box 50.1). Heart rate–running speed, RPE–running speed and blood lactate—running speed graphs can also be drawn.

Once the protocol in Box 44.1 has been completed, a graph similar to Fig. 44.1 can be drawn. This example shows the effect of changes in economy over a 12-month period in the same runner.

Running economy is traditionally measured using treadmill running in a controlled laboratory environment. While treadmill running is not the same as running on a track or road, it gives a good indication of how economical a runner is and how running economy changes over

Monitoring economy between or within groups – it is crucial to account for differences or changes in body mass. As $\dot{V}O_2$ during submaximal exercise does not, in general, increase linearly with increases in body mass, reporting economy with respect to the 0.75 power of body mass is recommended, e.g., when comparing the oxygen cost to running speed relationships between well trained boys and men such as in Fig. 44.2.

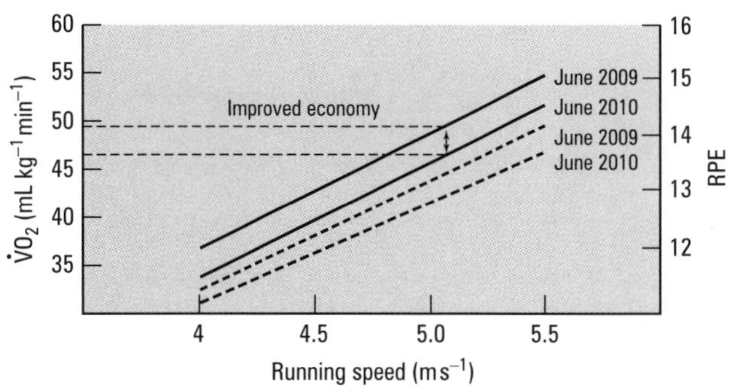

Fig. 44.1 Oxygen cost and RPE to running speed relationship for a runner, showing changes in economy over 12 months of run training.

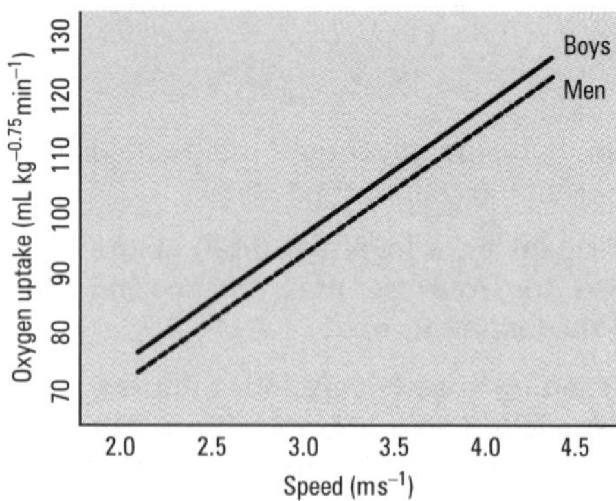

Fig. 42.2 Oxygen cost (ml kg$^{-0.75}$ min^{-1}) to running speed relationships for two groups (boys versus men) of well-trained male runners.

time. As with all laboratory tests, it is crucial that the following are standardised to ensure valid comparisons over time:

- protocol;
- footwear;
- clothing;
- time of day;
- nutritional and hydration status;
- body mass.

Over recent years, a number of lightweight, portable telemetry systems have been developed to measure oxygen uptake in the field and have been shown to give valid results when compared to laboratory-based gas analysis systems. For example, the *K4 Cosmed* analyser (Cosmed, Rome, Italy) has been used to measure running economy accurately, although it is difficult to control environmental conditions on different testing days (e.g. wind direction and speed).

Factors affecting economy

A number of studies and reviews have identified both physiological and biomechanical factors that can influence, for example, running economy in highly trained and elite runners. These are shown in Fig. 44.3.

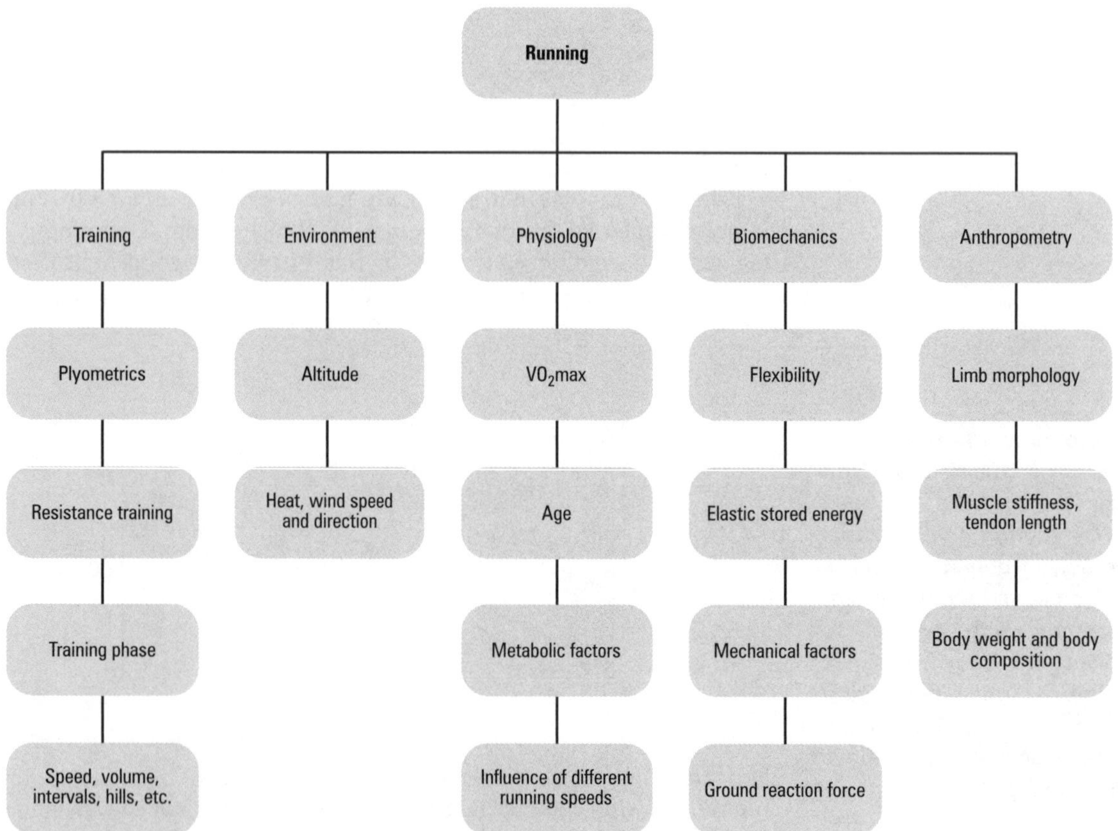

Fig. 44.3 Factors affecting running economy (Saunders *et al.*, 2004).

Efficiency

In engineering terms, efficiency is defined as:

$$\% \text{ efficiency} = (\text{work done/energy input}) \times 100 \quad (44.3)$$

In sport and exercise science, efficiency is rarely measured, but the equation to measure it is:

$$\% \text{ efficiency} = (\text{work accomplished/energy expended above rest}) \times 100$$
$$= (W/[E - e]) \times 100 \quad (44.4)$$

where W = mechanical work done (kJ), E = energy expenditure (kJ), e = resting energy expenditure (kJ).

W (work done in kilojoules) is measured using ergometry instrumentation (Chapter 37). Energy expended is calculated from the steady state VO_2 at each workload or speed. One litre of oxygen consumed is assumed to be equivalent to an energy expenditure of 20.9 kJ min^{-1}. Resting (basal) energy expenditure (BEE) can be measured directly or estimated from the following equations (Harris and Benedict, 1919) and then divided by 1440 (24 h × 60 min) to give the resting energy expenditure per minute:

$$\text{Males: BEE (kcal/day)} = 66.47 + 13.75\,(\text{weight}) + 5.0\,(\text{height}) - 6.76\,(\text{age}) \quad (44.5)$$

$$\text{Females: BEE (kcal/day)} = 655.1 + 9.56\,(\text{weight}) + 1.85\,(\text{height}) - 4.68\,(\text{age}) \quad (44.6)$$

Weight (body mass) is measured in kilograms, height in centimetres and age in years.

The World Health Organization has more recently developed equations for estimating daily resting energy expenditure based on age, gender and weight (Table 44.1).

Table 44.1 The World Health Organization equations for estimating daily resting energy expenditure (kcal day^{-1}) based on age, gender and weight. Data from National Research Council (1989).
wt = weight in kilograms.

Age range	Equation (males)	Equation (females)
0–3	(60.9 × wt) − 54	(61.0 × wt) − 51
3–10	(22.7 × wt) + 495	(22.5 × wt) + 499
10–18	(17.5 × wt) + 651	(12.2 × wt) + 746
18–30	(15.3 × wt) + 679	(14.7 × wt) + 496
30–60	(11.6 × wt) + 879	(8.7 × wt) + 829
>60	(13.5 × wt) + 487	(10.5 × wt) + 596

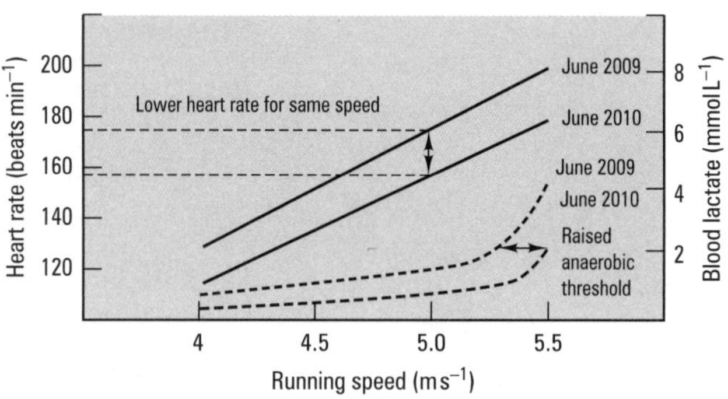

Fig. 44.4 Heart rate and blood lactate to running speed relationship for a runner, suggesting changes in economy over 12 months of run training.
——— heart rate
- - - - - - - blood lactate

Indirect measures of economy

Sport and exercise scientists can also indirectly measure economy via methods such as:

1. Plotting exercise velocity against RPE, blood lactate or heart rate (Figs. 44.1 and 44.4).
2. Measuring the number of strides (running) or strokes (swimming or rowing) taken to complete a known distance in a known time. For example, counting the number of strokes completed over 50 m (distance per stroke) in a swimming pool or the number of strides taken over 400 m (distance per stride) on a running track can give the coach an estimate of swim and running economy, respectively.

Text references

Harris, J.A. and Benedict, F.G. (1919) *A Biometric Study of Basal Metabolism in Man.* Lippincott, Philadelphia.

National Research Council (1989) *Recommended Dietary Allowances*, 10th edn, National Academy Press, Washington D.C.

Saunders, P.U., Pyne, D.B., Telford, R.D. and Hawley, J.A. (2004) Factors affecting running economy in trained distance runners. *Sports Medicine*, **34**(7), 465–85.

Source for further study

Kearney, J.T. and Van Handel, P.J. (1989) Economy: a physiologic perspective. *Advances in Sports Medicine and Fitness*, **2**, 57–90.

45 Monitoring training load

Definitions

Training load – measure used to describe training using an interaction of volume and intensity.

Training volume – measurement of how much work is completed by a person. Can be physical distances or training duration.

Training intensity – measurement of how hard an exercise session is.

TRIMPS – Training Impulse; a method used to quantify training load using duration and heart rate.

Adjusted TRIMPS – a method used to measure training load using duration and scaled heart rate zones.

Session RPE – a method used to measure training load using duration and perceived exertion.

Training monotony – a measurement of training variation using session-RPE loading data.

Training strain – the combined effect of training load and training monotony.

The ability to quantify the amount of exercise completed during a testing session is an important skill for a sport and exercise scientist. Without this skill, it is extremely difficult to programme exercise accurately and track changes that are related to training practices. To apply correct training principles such as overload correctly and to avoid reversibility, it is necessary for a sport and exercise scientist to be able to monitor both the volume (how much) and intensity (how hard) of a session. Typically, these two measurements can be integrated to provide a measure of the overall *training load.* Training load is the product of training volume and intensity, and a variety of measures can be used to quantify these parameters. Therefore, a number of methods have been developed to quantify the intensity, volume and overall load of an exercise session.

KEY POINT There is a distinct difference between training volume, intensity and load. Training volume does not incorporate training intensity over the session, and therefore does not provide a valid measure of training load. On the opposite side, while training intensity helps to describe how hard a session was, it does not provide any guide as to how long the session was. Therefore, the product of the two variables is equivalent to the 'load' of the training session.

It is important that you can easily track training load and be able to differentiate between different methods. This chapter provides information on typical measures that can be used to track training volume and intensity as well as several validated methods to monitor training load.

Training volume

The amount of physical training that is completed can be defined as training volume. Training volume can also be used to reflect training duration. Monitoring training volume is limited as it does not incorporate training intensity, and therefore is purely descriptive on how much was performed in training. Table 45.1 demonstrates some of the measures that can be used to monitor volume in athletes of different activities and sports. Plotting training volume with time is useful in predicting overreaching and overtraining that may lead to overuse injuries or illness. It can also be helpful in accurately planning training to ensure that programmes are sound and training progresses at a safe level.

Training intensity

Measuring how hard exercise is vital in assessing the training load that an exercise session can place on an individual. Training intensity is useful to help describe the physiological requirements of an exercise session that is useful in detailing the physical load placed on a subject. While many methods of monitoring training intensity (Chapters 31 and 43) have been discussed, there are different ways to monitor intensity

Table 45.1 Typical measures of training volume

Exercise mode/activity	Training volume measure
Typical exercises (i.e. running, cycling, rowing, swimming)	Distance (m or km)
	Time (min or h)
Weight training	Total weight lifted
Team sports	Total number of repetitions
	Distance covered (km)
	Time played (min)
Cricket	Number of physical involvements
	Distance covered (km)
	Time at crease
Racket sports	Balls bowled/faced
	Time (min)
	Number of points/games

Table 45.2 Typical measures of training intensity

Exercise mode/activity	Training volume measure
Typical exercises (i.e. running, cycling, rowing; swimming)	Velocity (min km^{-1}, m min^{-1}; km h^{-1})
	Incline (% gradient)
	Heart rate (b min^{-1}; %HRmax)
	% Heart rate reserve (%)
	VO_2 (mL kg min^{-1}, L min^{-1})
	% VO_2 reserve (%)
	Power (W; % maximum power)
	Rating of perceived exertion (RPE)
	Metabolic equivalents (METs)
	Physical observations
	Blood lactate (mmol L^{-1})
Weight training	% Repetition maximum (% RM)
	Movement speed (°s^{-1})
	Lifts per minute
Team sports (in addition to those from endurance sports)	Number of high intensity activities
	Average recovery time between sprints

across sports activities. In addition to those presented in Chapter 29, intensity can also be measured with respect to physical terms (i.e. speed, incline) or with reference to a physical limit (% RM). These measures are useful in helping to prescribe and monitor intensity during activities outside those of an endurance nature. Table 45.2 details some typical measures of exercise intensity that can be used for different activities.

Training load

The measurement of training load is an integral skill of a sport and exercise scientist to allow correct and safe programming of exercise. Training load is the product of both training volume and intensity and is directly influenced by changes to either variable. This allows a more valid approach to monitoring training, and a number of methods have been developed to allow the quantification of training load simply.

Measuring training load – the units are simply arbitrary units (AU). This overcomes the difficulty in using different units to measure training volumes and intensity across different activities.

Training impulse (TRIMPS) loading

As heart rate is the most commonly used measure of physiological intensity, it is no surprise that it can be a key tool in monitoring training loads. A simple method to calculate training load is the average heart rate across the session multiplied by its duration. This method has been defined as Training Impulse, or TRIMPS. The method of monitoring TRIMPS was originally developed to use heart rate responses to develop a single numerical value to gauge the intensity of a session. Monitoring training loads using TRIMPS requires that all subjects have their heart rate recorded across the session to provide a measure of physiological intensity. The purpose of TRIMPS is to provide a quantitative measure of load using the heart rate responses observed during the session. One of the benefits of TRIMPS is that it relies on very little post-session analysis of heart rate and is therefore faster than other methods. However, TRIMPS is only suited to endurance exercise with limited heart rate variation. TRIMPS does provide a simple and objective measure of training load from a session.

Some handy steps to make sure that TRIMPS is performed correctly include:

- **Make sure that the heart rate monitor is properly fitted before the session starts.** It may be difficult to adjust it during a session and any lost heart rate data will reduce the training load as measured by TRIMPS.
- **Try to record the heart rate across the session.** To do this properly, you will need to use a recordable heart rate monitor. This can be put on before the session and the recording started just before the warm-up and stopped immediately after the cool-down. This will provide you with the most accurate load for the session. Also, try to keep the recording times consistent across training sessions.
- **Record the duration of the session from the formal start of the session until its conclusion.** It is important to try to measure the total session duration accurately and best to run a stopwatch continuously over the session. During a team session, take note of any athlete who completes the session earlier or who continues training after the organised session.
- **Perform the calculations to calculate the TRIMPS loading.** Box 45.1 provides an example of a simple TRIMPS calculation.

Formula to calculate TRIMPS load:

$$\text{Duration (min)} \times HR_{av}\ (\text{b min}^{-1}) \qquad (45.1)$$

where duration = length of session (min), HR_{av} = average heart rate over the session.

Adjusted TRIMPS Loading

While TRIMPS provides a global measure of training load, the method can be adapted to ensure that the training load measure is more specific to an individual. This is done by calculating the heart rate as a relative percentage of the maximum heart rate (HR_{max}). The adjusted TRIMPS method than determines how much time was spent in a range of predetermined heart rate zones (as a relative percentage, e.g. 65–75 % HR_{max}). The time spent in each heart rate zone is then weighted with an incremental factor (see Box 45.2, p. 354) to represent the increasingly

Box 45.1 Example of a TRIMPS calculation

The data in Fig. 45.1 were obtained for a female runner in a training session during a specific preparation phase. The heart rate trace is shown and the TRIMPS calculations are shown underneath.

Heart rate information
Duration = 50 min
HRav = 153 $b\,min^{-1}$

TRIMPS load
= 50 × 153
= 7650 AU

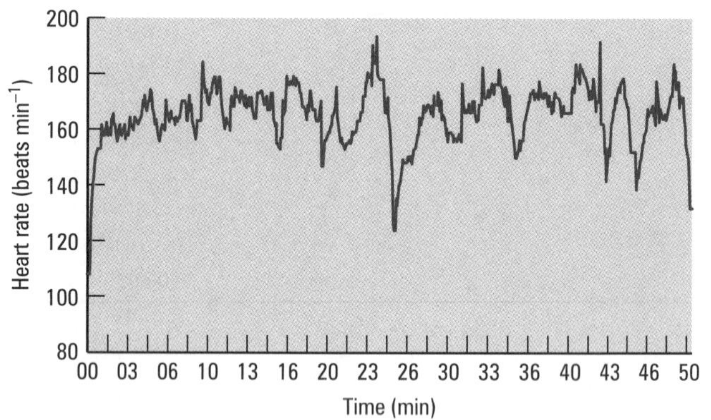

Fig. 45.1 Heart rate trace for a female runner.

difficult intensity. The weighted duration spent in each heart rate zone is summed to provide a measure of training volume. Once this is complete, the time spent in each heart rate zone and loading is summed, and this provides a quantitative measure of training load. While this method does provide an objective measure of training load, it is also limited by several factors. To provide an accurate indication of training load it requires an accurate measure of HR_{max}. However, this method can be particularly time-expensive to perform the calculation of time spent in heart rate zones, particularly if working with a team. Also of interest is the arbitrary loading of each zone with a sequential mathematical loading considered appropriate although potentially not validly representing the difference in physiological intensity across heart rate zones.

Some handy steps to make sure that the adjusted TRIMPS method is performed correctly include:

Using heart rate zones – these are commonly used to demonstrate the duration spent working at particular intensities. They are also frequently used to prescribe exercise intensity in training programmes.

- **Make sure that the heart rate monitor is properly fitted before the session starts.** It may be difficult to adjust it during a session and any lost heart rate data will reduce the training load as measured by TRIMPS.
- **Try to record the heart rate across the session.** To do this properly, you will need to use a recordable heart rate monitor. This can be put on before the session and the recording started just before the warm-up and stopped immediately after the cool-down. This will provide you with the most accurate load for the session.
- **Actually record the subject's maximum heart rate.** It is best to record the HR_{max} of each subject during maximal intensity exercise. This may be performed across a multistage fitness test (Box 41.7) or a laboratory

test of $\dot{V}O_2max$ (Chapter 36). If required, you may estimate HRmax using the formula for age-predicted HR_{max} (220– age), although this may reduce the accuracy of your results.

- **Record the duration of the session from the formal start of the session until its conclusion.** It is important to try to measure the total session duration accurately and best to run a stopwatch continuously over the session. During a team session make note of any athlete who completes the session earlier or who continues training after the organised session.
- **Use commercially available software to help calculate time spent in each heart rate zone.** Some heart rate monitors are purchased with analysis software, e.g. Polar, Suunto. From this, individual heart rate zones can be set and the time spent in each heart rate zone can be automatically calculated and then simply added into the equation below. If this is not available, then post-processing can be performed in software packages such as Microsoft Excel.
- **Perform the calculations to calculate the adjusted TRIMPS loading.**

Box 45.2 Example of an adjusted TRIMPS calculation

The data in Fig. 45.2 were obtained for a cyclist across a 50 km ride during a general preparation phase. Their HR_{max} is 200 b min^{-1}. The heart rate trace is shown, the time spent in each heart rate zone is calculated and then the adjusted TRIMPS calculations are shown.

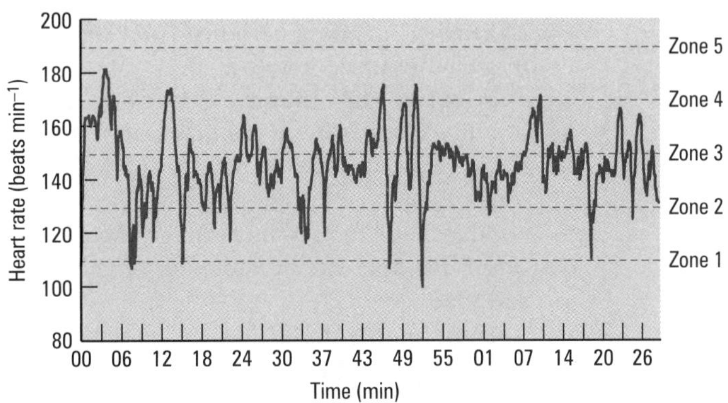

Fig. 45.2 Heart rate trace for a cyclist during a preparation phase.

Time spent in heart rate zones

Zone 1: 3 min	(100–119 b min^{-1})
Zone 2: 19 min	(120–139 b min^{-1})
Zone 3: 55 min	(140–159 b min^{-1})
Zone 4: 12 min	(160–179 b min^{-1})
Zone 5: 0.5 min	(180–200 b min^{-1})

Adjusted TRIMPS Load

(3 × 1) +	(3)
(19 × 2) +	(38)
(55 × 3) +	(165)
(12 × 4) +	(48)
(0.5 × 5)	(2.5)
	= 256.5 AU

Box 45.2 provides an example of the adjusted TRIMPS calculation.

Formula to calculate adjusted TRIMPS load:

$$(\text{Duration (min) spent in zone } 1 \times 1) + (\text{Duration (min) spent in zone } 2 \times 2) + (\text{Duration (min) spent in zone } 3 \times 3) + (\text{Duration (min) spent in zone } 4 \times 4) + (\text{Duration (min) spent in zone } 5 \times 5) \quad (45.2)$$

where Zone 1 = 50–60 % HR_{max}; Zone 2 = 60–70 % HR_{max}; Zone 3 = 70–80 % HR_{max}; Zone 4 = 80–90 % HR_{max}; Zone 5 = 90–100 % HR_{max}.

Using the session-RPE method – this can also help to educate coaches on the loading of particular training sessions or practices. It can be worth taking a 'desired' perceived intensity from the coach to plot against the loading of the athlete.

Session-rating of perceived exertion method

The majority of methods used to calculate training load use physiological data. This can be difficult, expensive and time-consuming to collect and analyse, in particular for teams. The session-RPE method of monitoring training load was originally devised to provide a subjective measure of training intensity that can be performed quickly on a large group following a training session. The method simply relies on the length of a session to provide a measure of training volume and uses a 1–10 scale (CR—10 scale – Table 31.3) for each athlete to gauge the intensity of the session. The session-RPE method is favoured as it can be used for all exercise modes, is non-invasive, provides an internal measure of training intensity, and is not influenced by compounding factors as are heart rate responses. However, it is limited by the fact that the intensity rating is subjective and is open to influence by a number of factors, such as time after session, mood state, nutritional status and nature of the session.

Further, the data gathered from the session-RPE method can be used to generate a score of training monotony and strain to provide further information on training practices. Training monotony (eqn. 45.4) provides a measure of training variability over a week, whereas training strain (eqn. 45.5) is the product of training load and monotony and is a measure of risk of illness or injury. The session-RPE method is a popular tool that is increasingly being used within sport owing to its simplicity and validity to physiological measures of training intensity and load.

Some simple steps to using the session-RPE method follow.

- **All athletes should be asked their perception of the session intensity around 30 minutes after the session finishes.** The validity of the method appears compromised if more time is taken to gauge the session and this reduces any bias that the intensity of the latter stages may have on the perception of intensity. All athletes should give their responses individually to reduce any group bias or consensus.
- **Ask the athlete to describe the session intensity.** Simply, they should be answering the question 'How hard was your workout?' in the hope that they provide a short and easy answer. The athlete's answer is then translated into a numerical score if possible using Table 45.4.
- **Ask the subject to rate how hard their session was between 1 and 10** if you are unsure of interpreting the athlete's response into a numerical value or you have communication issues.

- **Record the duration of the session from the formal start of the session until its conclusion.** It is important to try to measure the total session duration accurately and best to run a stopwatch continuously over the session. During a team session make note of any athlete that may complete the session earlier or who continues training after the organised session.
- **Have a spreadsheet to record all the data into immediately after the session.** It is important to be organised to make this as easy as possible following the session. In particular, if working with a team, collecting the intensity scores can be a confusing and difficult task. A spreadsheet with the names of all players and columns for the intensity and duration of each day's sessions is an easy method to simplify the task.

Box 45.3 Example of session-RPE loading calculations

Table 45.3 and Fig. 45.3 demonstrate the procedure involved in calculating and representing session-RPE.

Table 45.3 Representative data for session-RPE calculations, obtained for a swimmer preparing for the national swimming titles before the Bejing Olympics in 2008, taken across one week of heavy training before tapering for the competition.

Day	Mode	RPE	Duration	Session load	Daily load
	Swim	3	130	390	
1	Gym	5	60	300	690
	Swim	6	120	720	
2	Swim	5	155	775	1495
	Swim	3	120	360	
3	Swim	5	150	750	1110
4	Swim	5	65	325	325
	Gym	3	65	195	
5	Swim	5	130	650	845
	Swim	4	175	700	
	Gym	3	120	360	
6	Swim	5	55	275	1335
	Swim	5	155	775	
7	Gym	5	100	500	1275

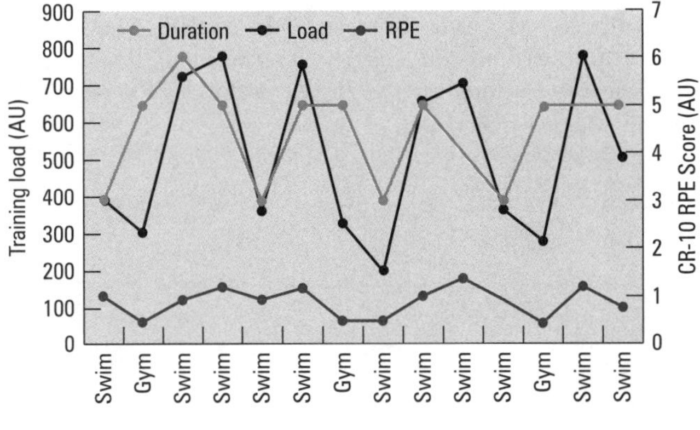

Fig. 45.3 Representative data for session-RPE calculations.

Measures of training load:

Average daily load = 1011 AU
Standard deviation of daily load = 412 AU
Training monotony = 2.45 AU
Weekly training load = 7075 AU
Training strain = 17 343 AU

Understanding training setbacks – illnesses or injuries are predated by large increases in training load (84%) and monotony (77%). However, training strain seemed the best measure of predicting training setbacks, at around 90% of the time.

Table 45.4 CR-10 scale for session – rating of perceived exertion

0	Rest
1	Really easy
2	Easy
3	Moderate
4	Sort of hard
5	Hard
6	
7	Really hard
8	
9	Really, really hard
10	Just like my hardest race

- **Perform the calculation to calculate the session-RPE loading.** Box 45.3 provides an example of how to apply the calculations listed below. Note that graphing the data is very useful in visually assessing patterns in the session-RPE parameters and load.

Understanding training monotony – values above 2.0 often indicate that the training may be excessive and performance may be being hindered. This suggests that training is not varied enough and that the athlete may not be able to recover sufficiently.

Formulae to calculate session-RPE load:

$$\text{Training load} = \text{duration (min)} \times \text{session} - \text{RPE} \quad (45.3)$$

where: session-RPE = subjective rating taken from the CR-10; RPE scale (Table 45.3).

$$\text{Training monotony} = \text{average daily load/standard deviation} \quad (45.4)$$

where: average daily load = average training load across the week; standard deviation = standard deviation of training load across the week.

$$\text{Training strain} = \text{training load} \times \text{training monotony} \quad (45.5)$$

Sources for further study

Ballister, E.W. (1991) Modelling elite athletic performance. In: J.D. MacDougall, H.A. Wenger and H.J. Green (eds) *Physiological Testing of the High-Performance Athlete*. Human Kinetics, Champaign, IL: pp. 403–27.

Foster, C., Florhaug, J.A., Franklin, J. *et al.* (2001) A new approach to monitoring exercise training. *Journal of Strength and Conditioning Research*, **15** (1), 109–15.

Lambert, M. and Borresen, J. (2010) Measuring training loads in sports. *International Journal of Sports Physiology and Performance*, **5**, 406–411.

Analysis and presentation of data

46. Manipulating and transforming raw data 359

47. Graphs 363

48. Presenting data in tables 374

49. Descriptive statistics 378

50. Choosing and using statistical tests 389

51. Statistics for sport and exercise science 401

46 Manipulating and transforming raw data

The process of discovering the meaning within your results can be fascinating. There are two main elements to this process:

- **Exploratory data manipulation** – this is used to investigate the nature of your results and suggest possible patterns and relationships within the dataset. The aim is to generate hypotheses for further investigation. Exploratory techniques allow you to visualise the form of your data. They are ideal for examining results from pilot 'studies', but should be used throughout your investigations.
- **Confirmatory analysis** – this is used to test the hypotheses generated during the exploratory phase. The techniques required are generally statistical in nature and are dealt with in Chapter 50.

KEY POINT Spreadsheets (Chapter 11) are invaluable tools for data manipulation and transformation: complex mathematical procedures can be carried out rapidly and the results visualised almost immediately using the inbuilt graphing functions. Spreadsheets also facilitate the statistical analysis of data (see Chapters 49–51).

Summarising your results – original, unsummarised data belong only in your primary record, either in laboratory books or as computer records. You should produce summary tables to organise and condense original data.

Organising numbers

To organise, manipulate and summarise data, you should do as follows:

- Simplify the numbers, e.g. by rounding or taking means. This avoids the detail becoming overwhelming.
- Rearrange your data in as many ways as possible for comparison.
- Display in graphical form; this provides an immediate visual summary that is relatively easy to interpret.
- Look for an overall pattern in the data – avoid getting lost in the details at this stage.
- Look for any striking exceptions to that pattern (outliers) – they often point to special cases of particular interest or to errors in the data produced through mistakes during the acquisition, recording or copying of data.
- Move from graphical interpretations to well-chosen numerical summaries and/or verbal descriptions, including, where applicable, an explanatory hypothesis.
- Use a tally chart (Fig 46.1) – a simple approach to summarise a dataset.

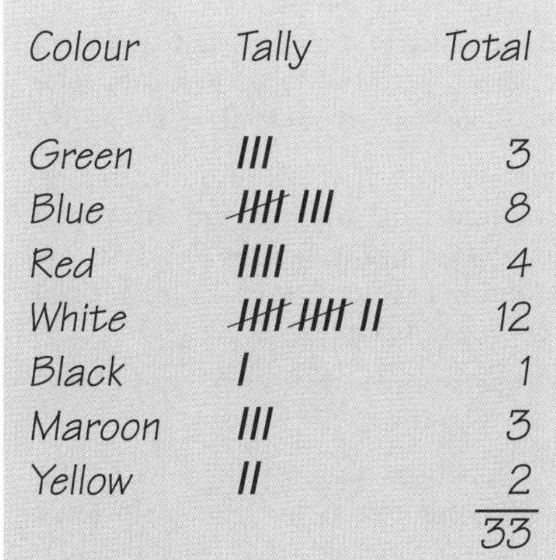

Colour	Tally	Total
Green	III	3
Blue	~~IIII~~ III	8
Red	IIII	4
White	~~IIII~~ ~~IIII~~ II	12
Black	I	1
Maroon	III	3
Yellow	II	2
		33

Fig. 46.1 An example of a tally chart.

Producing a histogram – a neatly constructed tally chart will double as a rough histogram.

Convert the data to a formal table when complete (e.g. Table 46.1). Because proportions are easier to compare than class totals, the table may contain a column to show the relative frequency of each class. Relative frequency can be expressed in decimal form (as a proportion of 1) or as a percentage (as a proportion of 100).

Table 46.1 An example of a frequency table

Size class	Frequency	Relative frequency (%)
0–4.9	7	2.6
5–9.9	23	8.6
10–14.9	56	20.9
15–19.9	98	36.7
20–24.9	50	18.7
25–29.9	30	11.2
30–34.9	3	1.1
Total	267	99.8*

* $\neq$ 100 owing to rounding error.

Definition

Histogram – a representation of a frequency distribution by means of rectangles whose widths represent category intervals and whose areas are proportional to the corresponding frequencies.

stem	leaves
7	23
7	55
7	6
7	9
8	000
8	233
8	45555
8	77
8	888899
9	0000111111
9	2333333
9	44555555555
9	66677777
9	88888999
10	00

Fig. 46.2 A simple 'stem and leaf' plot of a dataset. The 'stem' shows the common component of each number, while the 'leaves' show the individual components, e.g. the top line in this example represents the numbers 72 and 73.

Graphing data

Graphs are an effective way to investigate trends in data and can reveal features that are difficult to detect from a table, e.g. skewness of a frequency distribution. The construction and use of graphs is described in detail in Chapter 47. When investigating the nature of your data, the main points are as follows:

- **Make the values stand out clearly** – attention should focus on the actual data, not the labels, scale markings, etc. (in contrast with the requirements for constructing a graph for data presentation, see Box 47.2).
- **Avoid clutter in the graph** – leave out grid lines and try to use the simplest graph possible for your purpose.

KEY POINT Use a computer spreadsheet with graphics options whenever possible: the speed and flexibility of these powerful tools should allow you to explore every aspect of your data rapidly and with relatively little effort (Chapters 11 and 47).

Displaying distributions

A visual display of a distribution of values is often useful for variables measured on an interval or ratio scale (Table 18.1). The distribution of a variable can be displayed by a frequency table for each value or, if the possible values are numerous, groups (classes) of values of the variable. Graphically, there are two main ways of viewing such data:

- histograms are generally used for large samples;
- stem and leaf plots (Fig. 46.2), often used for samples of less than 100: these retain the actual values and are faster to draw by hand. The main drawback is the limitation imposed by the choice of stem values since these class boundaries may obscure some features of the distribution.

These displays allow you to look at the overall shape of a distribution and to observe any significant deviations from the idealised theoretical ones. Where necessary, you can use data transformations to investigate any departures from standard distribution patterns such as the normal distribution or the Poisson distribution (see Chapter 50).

Transforming data

Transformations are mathematical functions applied to data values. They are particularly valuable where your results are related to areas and volumes (e.g. frontal surface area, body mass).

The most common use of transformations is to prepare datasets so that specific statistical tests may be applied. For instance, if you find that your data distribution is unimodal but not symmetrical (Fig. 46.4), it is often useful to apply a transformation that will redistribute the data values to form a symmetrical distribution. The object of this exercise is often to find the function that most closely changes the data into a standard normal distribution, allowing you to apply a wide range

Using transformations – note that if you wish to conserve the *order* of your data, you will need to take negative values when using a reciprocal function (i.e. $-1/n^n$). This is essential when using a box plot to compare the effects of transformations graphically on the five-number summary of a dataset.

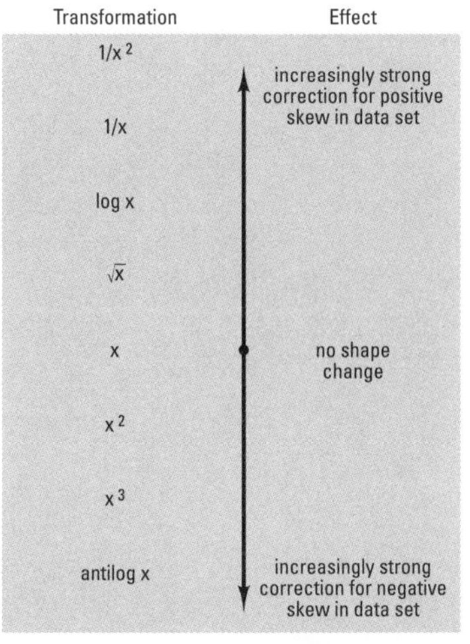

Fig. 46.3 Ladder of transformations.
Source: Jones, A., Reed, R. and Weyers, J. (2007) p. 385, afer J. W. Turkey.

of parametric hypothesis-testing statistics (Chapter 50). A frequently used transformation is to take logarithms of one or more sets of values: if the data then approximate to a normal distribution, the relationship is termed 'log-normal'.

Some general points about transformations are:

- They should be made on the raw data, not on derived data values: this is simpler, mathematically valid, and more easily interpreted.
- The transformed data can be analysed like any other numbers.
- Transformed data can be examined for outliers, which may be more important if they remain after transformation.

Fig. 46.3 presents a ladder of transformations that will help you to decide which transformations to try (see also Table 46.1). Note that percentage and proportion data are usually arc-sine transformed, which is a more complex procedure; consult Sokal and Rohlf (1994) for details.

Fig. 46.4 illustrates the following 'quick-and-easy' way to choose a transformation.

1. Calculate the 'five-number summary' for the untransformed data (p. 383).
2. Present the summary graphically as a 'box-and-whisker' plot.
3. Decide whether you need to correct for positive or negative skew (p. 386).
4. Apply one of the 'mild' transformations in Fig. 46.3 *on the five-number summary values only*.
5. Draw a new box-and-whisker plot and see whether the skewness has been corrected.
6. If the skewness has been undercorrected, try again with a stronger transformation. If it has been overcorrected, try a milder one.
7. When the distribution appears to be acceptable, transform the full dataset and recalculate the summary statistics. If necessary use a

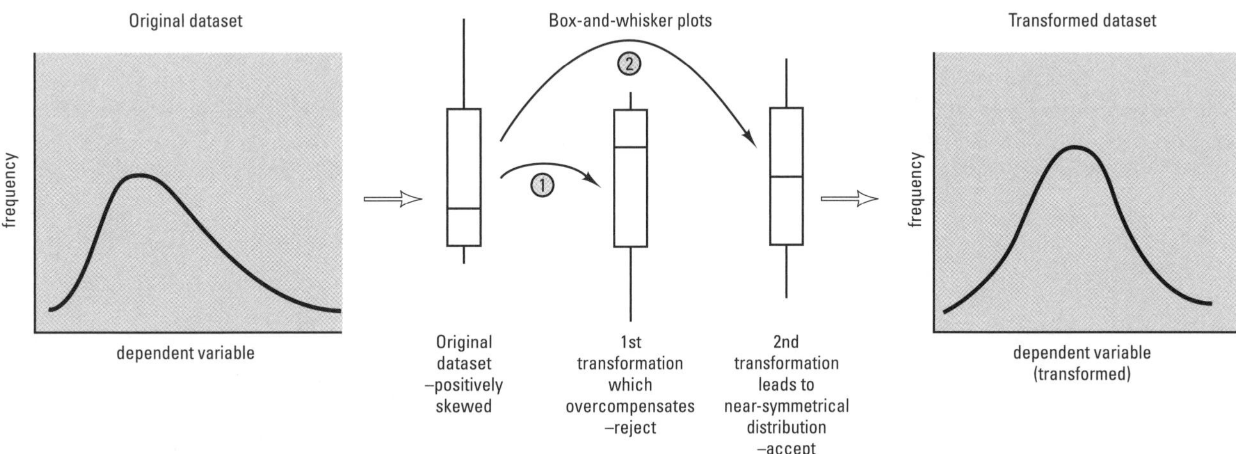

Fig. 46.4 Illustration of the processes of transforming a dataset.
Source: Jones, A., Reed, R. and Weyers, J. (2007) p. 385.

statistical test to confirm that the transformed data are normally distributed (p. 392).

8. If no simple transformation works well, you may need to use non-parametric statistics when comparing datasets.

Sources for further study

Fallowfield, J.L., Hale, B.J. and Wilkinson, D.M. (2005) *Using Statistics in Sport and Exercise Science Research.* Lotus Publishing Chichester.

Thomas, J.R., Nelson, J.K. and Silverman, S.J. (2005) *Research Methods for Physical Activity,* 5th edn, Human Kinetics, Champaign, IL.

Vincent, W.J. (2005) *Statistics for Kinesiology*, 3rd edn, Human Kinetics, Champaign, IL.

47 Graphs

Deciding whether to use a table or a graph – ask yourself the question 'Does the reader need the actual numbers or is a picture of the results more useful?' In general, if you have a choice, choose the graph as *one picture is worth ten thousand words.*

Graphs (figures) are pictorial presentations used to present data and reveal patterns or differences between two or more sets of data. In sport and exercise science, graphs are the most widely used form of communication. While tables are a way of presenting data as numbers, graphs are a better way of expressing trends (e.g. heart rate increasing linearly with an increase in exercise intensity) or comparing groups (e.g. athletes' versus non-athletes' skinfold totals). Graphs can be used to display the maximum amount of information in the minimum amount of space.

To decide whether you need a graph or not, consider whether it:

- adds to, rather than duplicates text or other figures
- contains important information
- is not visually distracting
- is easy to read and understand
- is the best way of representing both the location (e.g. mean) and the variability (e.g. standard deviation) of the data.

Graphs are most useful when presenting relationships and interactions between variables, and for data points for variables that change over time (e.g. with increasing age), before and after an intervention or between groups (e.g. sedentary versus active). Graphs convey such information more quickly and easily than a table. Moreover, a graph shows information more clearly and memorably than a table.

Illustrations such as photographs, figures and line drawings are rarely used in sport and exercise science. Illustrations should only be used if the experimental equipment or procedures are of a standard make or arrangement. As with tables, figures and illustrations are mostly used in the results section of a thesis, report or paper. However, there are some exceptions to this principle. These include the following:

- Put important summary tables, figures and illustrations in the text and all other material in the appendices.
- Do not clutter results with too many tables, graphs or illustrations.
- Do not put summary tables for ANOVA or MANOVA (Chapters 50–51) in the results. Use summary statements or tables in the text and include the output tables in the appendices.

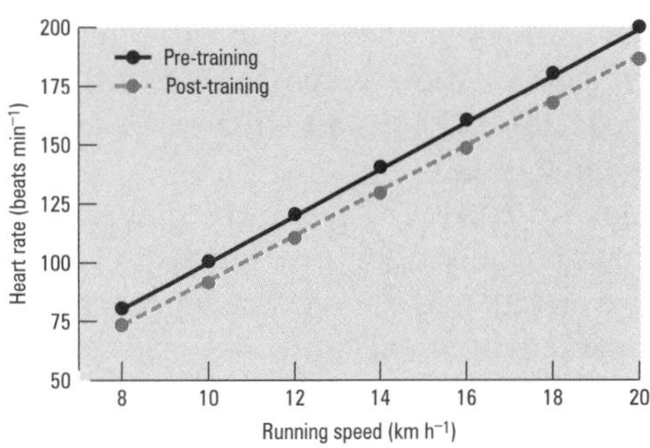

Fig. 47.1 Line graph showing the relationship between heart rate as function of running speed after endurance training.

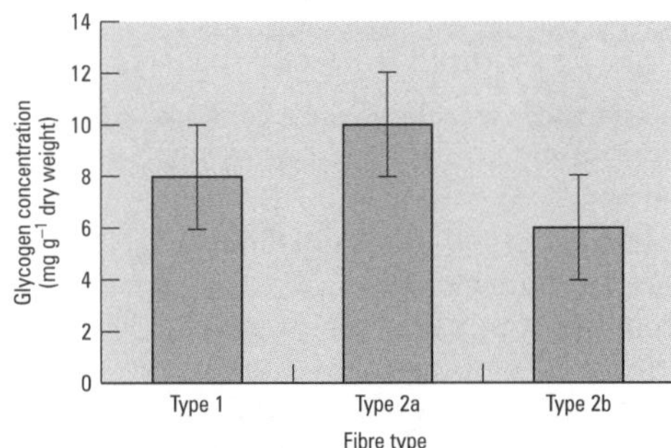

Fig. 47.2 Bar graph showing the glycogen concentrations of type 1, type 2a and type 2b fibre types in speletal muscle.

Types of graphs

The most common graphs used in sport and exercise science are:

1. **Line graphs** – used for data where the relationship between two variables can be represented as a continuum (Fig. 47.1).
2. **Bar graphs** – used to represent values of discrete qualitative or quantitative variables where the x axis is not a continuum (Fig. 47.2).
3. **Scatter graphs** (scatterplot; X–Y chart in Excel) – used to visualise the functional relationship between individual data values for two

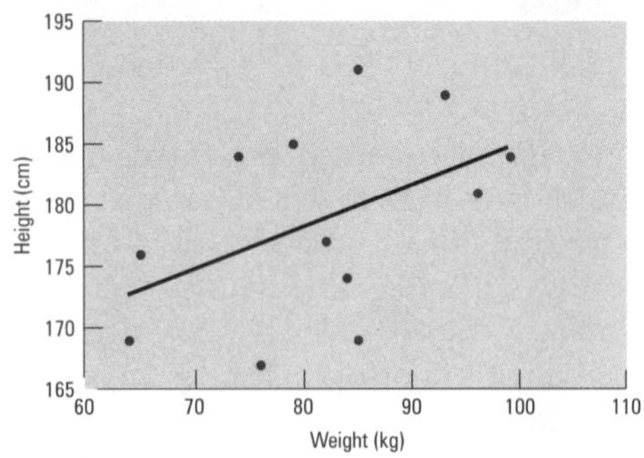

Fig. 47.3 Scatterplot or X–Y chart: the relationship between height and weight (body mass).

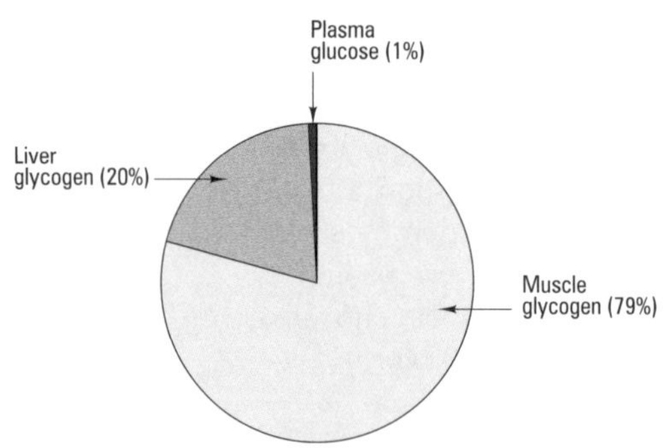

Fig. 47.4 Pie graph or pie chart showing distribution of carbohydrate energy stores in an average 80-kg person.

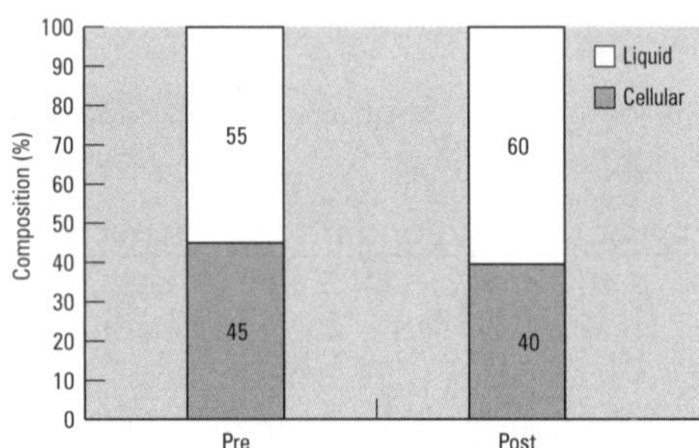

Fig. 47.5 Bar graphs with data included: normal cellular and liquid components of blood before and after heat acclimatisation in an endurance athlete.

interdependent variables (Fig. 47.3), often as a preliminary part of a regression analysis (p. 397).

4. **Pie graphs** – used to illustrate portions of a whole (100%) (Fig. 47.4).
5. **Graph with numerical values** – used when it is necessary to emphasise the exact data values (Fig. 47.5).

Line graphs

Line graphs are best for showing change over time, with time (independent variable) on the horizontal axis and the quantity (dependent variable) on the vertical axis. Line graphs also allow more than one curve to be compared (Fig. 47.1). Use different line and marker symbols to distinguish each dataset.

The data points and lines move the eye of the viewer naturally to simplify and clarify large amounts of data. Each axis must show units of measurement. Typically, the vertical axis should be approximately two-thirds to three-quarters of the length of the horizontal axis. If you

Box 47.1 Checklist for the stages in drawing a graph

The following sequence can be used whenever you need to construct a plotted curve: it will need to be modified for other types of graph.

1. **Collect all of the data values and statistical values** (in tabular form, where appropriate).
2. **Decide on the most suitable form of presentation**: this may include transformation (pp. 361–362) to convert data to linear form.
3. **Choose a concise descriptive title**, together with a reference (figure) number and date, where necessary.
4. **Determine which variable is to be plotted on the *x* axis and which on the *y* axis.**
5. **Select appropriate scales for both axes** and make sure that the numbers and their location (scale marks) are clearly shown, together with any scale breaks.
6. **Decide on appropriate descriptive labels for both axes**, with SI units of measurement, where appropriate.
7. **Choose the symbols for each set of data points** and decide on the best means of representation for statistical values.
8. **Plot the points** to show the coordinates of each value with appropriate symbols.
9. **Draw a trend line for each set of points**. Use a transparent ruler, so you can draw the line to have an equal number of points on either side of it.
10. **Write a figure legend**, to include a key that identifies all symbols and statistical values and any descriptive footnotes.

are using different symbols on the graph, you must provide a key to the symbols in the graph legend or on the graph.

Bar graphs

The simplest bar graph compares one or more sets of data against a single axis. Horizontally arranged bar graphs are often seen in business, rather than in science. Vertically arranged bar graphs are commonly used in sport and exercise science, as 'up' and 'down' are the usual representations for increases and decreases, respectively. Moreover, bar graphs are excellent for showing data measured at different times such as in intervention studies where data 'before' and 'after' an intervention are often displayed.

Shading should be used to distinguish between bars. Bars should be equal in width and spaced evenly. A key must be provided when using different symbols on the graph. The vertical axis should start at zero or have a scale break included.

Computer program charting options in Excel or Word may call the vertical arrangement a 'column graph' and the horizontal arrangement a 'bar graph'.

Scatter graphs

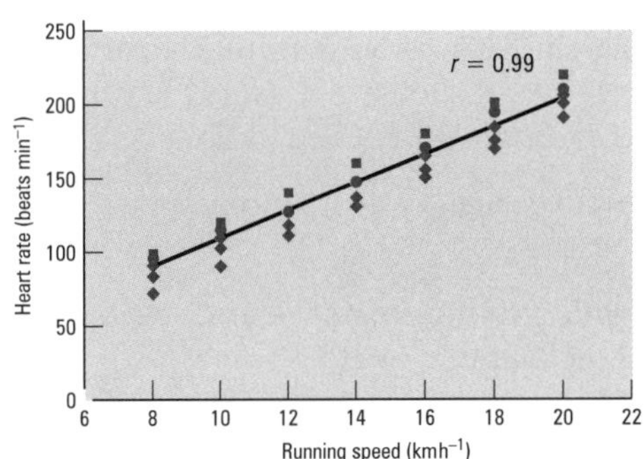

Fig. 47.6 Line graph showing the relationship between heart rate as a function of running speed with a trend line and *r* value shown.

Scatter graphs or X–Y plots show data values or individual scores, with each point representing a score on both the vertical and horizontal axis. These graphs highlight the relationship of one variable with another. Points that are grouped together suggest a strong correlation, as in Fig. 47.6. Indeed, by adding a simple line fit, the relationship between the two variables becomes clearer to the viewer. A computer program such as Excel can be used to calculate the correlation coefficient (Chapters 11 and 50). In contrast, points that are widely spread suggest a weak relationship, as in Fig. 47.3.

As with line graphs, each axis scale interval must be equal in length to designate equal amounts of the variable, and the vertical axis should be approximately two-thirds to three-quarters of the length of the horizontal axis. If you are using different symbols on the graph, you must provide a key to the symbols. In contrast to bar graphs, the scale of the vertical axis does not have to start at zero, as in Fig. 47.3.

Pie graphs

The circle or pie graph with its wedge-shaped pieces is easily understood by the viewer. It shows the whole with its parts. To be effective, the number of divisions should be limited to a maximum of six segments. Too many labelled pieces make it difficult to show smaller divisions or percentages effectively. Order the segments from large to small starting at 12 o'clock. The labels for each piece should be succinct; shadings should be used, with the smallest segment the darkest shade (Fig. 47.4).

Practical aspects

When preparing graphs for project reports, presentations or for a professional publication, they must be drawn to the specifications required by the department, university or publisher. The following points relate to each of the key components of an effective graph, highlighting common problems.

The title

It is a common fault to use titles that are grammatically incorrect – a widely applicable format is to state the relationship between the dependent and independent variables within the title, e.g. 'The relationship between enzyme activity and pH'.

- The title always should appear *below* a graph or figure. In contrast, table titles should appear *above* the table.
- The title needs to be succinct and should describe exactly what the figure is communicating.

The axes

- An axis is the scale that establishes regular intervals for presenting data. The *x* axis (horizontal axis or abscissa) runs from left to right. The *y* axis (vertical axis or ordinate) runs from bottom to top. One way of remembering which is which is to recall that 'x' is 'a cross' and that the *x* axis runs 'across' the page, while 'y' is the first letter of the word 'yacht', with a large vertical mast (vertical axis).
- The dependent variable is placed on the vertical axis and the independent variable or category on the horizontal axis.
- In general, the vertical axis should be two-thirds to three-quarters of the length of the horizontal axis. Axes should not extend beyond the last data point except to end the axis with a labelled 'tick mark'.
- Each axis must have a descriptive label, with the appropriate units separated from the label by brackets.
- Each axis must have a scale with reference marks ('ticks') on the axis to show clearly the location of the numbers used.
- Bar graphs such as those in Fig. 47.2 and 47.5 should not have a scale for the horizontal axis.
- Tick marks symbolise abbreviated gridlines and, as such, should appear *inside* the axis lines. Showing a whole grid in the area of the graph is not desirable as it obscures curves and makes the graph appear cluttered. The number of tick marks and their labels should be as equal as possible for both axes, so as not to draw attention to any one axis. The maximum number of major tick marks should be restricted to five.
- The reader should be able to see the major and minor scale increments easily, with labels only placed on the major increments. Eliminate unnecessary zeros on units to reduce clutter.
- Duplicate axes repeated at the top or right side of a graph are usually not recommended unless it is important to be able to make measurements across the graph. If this is the case, it may be that a table is a better way to communicate the data. Another option is to include gridlines (ensure they are light and unobtrusive).

Labels

- A label for each axis must be complete and succinct, and should include units where appropriate.
- Avoid long labels and use abbreviations if they are universally understood (e.g. $\sum$ skinfolds or $\dot{V}O_2max$).
- Label size should be in proportion to the size of the graph and should not dominate the graph. Axis numbers should be smaller than the axis label size. Label style should be in lower case.
- Axis labels may be positioned horizontally or vertically and are always centred on the axis. For slides in presentations or on posters, horizontal labels on the vertical axis make it easier to read. However, in written publications such as books or journals, vertical axis labels (Fig. 47.1) save space and are more commonly accepted.
- Legend or curve labels (Fig. 47.1) explain the symbols used in the graph. They should be succinct, unbolded and smaller in font size than the axis labels. They can be grouped as a legend after the title, or can be positioned within the graph area, e.g. beside each curve/line. They can be italicised to set them apart from other labels. Putting a box around the legend is not recommended as it again adds lines and clutter to the graph.

Symbols and lines

- These features identify and distinguish the different variables used in figures.
- When choosing graphical symbols, plotted curves are usually drawn using circles, squares and triangles, with circles and triangles more distinct than circles and squares.
- Open and closed symbols also show greater distinction more clearly – by convention, paired symbols (closed and open) are often used to represent 'plus' (treatment) and 'minus' (control) data. Thus, a combination of different symbols and fillings highlight differences between variables, as in Fig. 47.1.
- Symbol size should be in proportion to graph size and is generally automatically determined in graphing software such as Excel.
- Lines of different thicknesses and styles (dotted, dashed, coloured) can be used to reflect priorities. Solid lines are the most emphatic, dotted lines the least emphatic.

Texture and shading

- Stipple (small dots), shading (greyscale levels), hatching (lines that run vertically, horizontally or diagonally) and cross-hatching are useful ways of distinguishing between areas of a graph, especially a bar graph or a stacked bar chart. Black versus white gives the best contrast, as in Fig. 47.5. Too many textures, hatchings or stippling may confuse and distract from the clarity of the message.
- The greatest contrast is between black and white.

Box 47.2 How to create and amend graphs within a Microsoft Excel 2007 spreadsheet for use in reports and dissertations

Microsoft Excel can be used to create graphs of reasonable quality, as long as you know how to amend the default settings so that your graph meets the formal standards required for practical and project reports. As with a hand-drawn graph, the basic stages in graph drawing (Box 47.1) still apply. The following instructions explain how to produce an X–Y graph (plotted curve, p. 365), bar graph (p. 365) and pie graph using Excel 2007, where all types of graphs are termed 'charts'. Earlier versions use broadly similar commands, although not always in the same locations within the software.

Producing an X–Y graph ('scatter' chart in Excel)

1. **Create the appropriate type of graph (chart) for your data.** Enter the numeric values for your X variable data in the cells of a single column and the equivalent values for the Y variable in the adjacent cells of the next column to the right. Then select the whole data array (highlight the appropriate cells by clicking and holding down the left mouse button and dragging the cursor across the cells so that all values are included). Then select the *Insert* ribbon (tab) at the top of the sheet, and select (left-click) the *Scatter* chart from the options provided in the upper ribbon. Note that you should never use the *Line* chart option, as it is based on an *x* axis that is not quantitative, so all X values will appear as equally spaced categories, rather than having a true scale). Select the first option from the *Scatter* menu (*Scatter with only Markers*). Once selected, this will produce an embedded scatter chart of the type show in Fig. 47.7a. The line is then added later, as described below.

2. **Change the default settings to improve the appearance of your graph.** Consider each element of the image in turn, including the overall size, height and width of the graph (resize by clicking and dragging one of the 'sizing handles' around the edge of the chart). The graph shown in Fig. 47.7b was produced by altering the default settings, typically by moving the cursor over the feature and then clicking the right mouse button to reveal an additional menu of editing and formatting options. (Note that the example given below is for illustrative purposes only, and should not necessarily be regarded as prescriptive.)

Example for an X–Y graph (compare Fig. 47.7a with Fig. 47.7b):

- Unnecessary legend box on right-hand side can be removed using the (right-click) *Delete* option.
- Border to chart can be removed using *Format Chart Area* function.

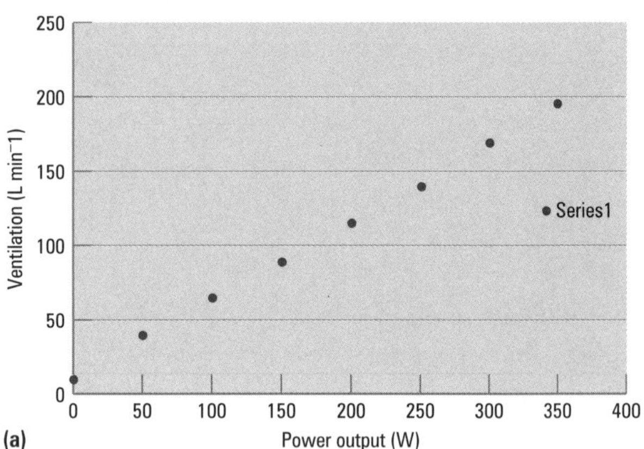

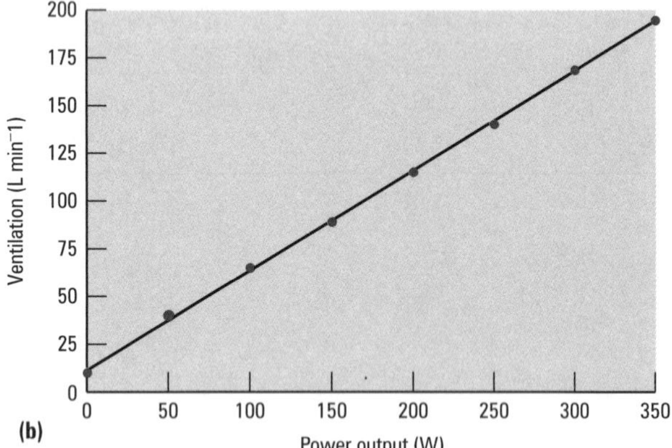

Fig. 1 The relationship between ventilation and power output during cycle ergometer exercise.

Fig. 47.7 Examples of an X–Y graph produced using Microsoft Excel 2007 using (**a**) default settings and (**b**) modified (improved) settings.

- Horizontal gridlines can be removed using the *Delete* function.
- *x* and *y* axes can be reformatted by selecting each in turn, and using the *Format Axis* menu options to select appropriate scales for major and minor units, style of tick marks, etc. Remember that it is better to use a figure legend in Word, than the *Chart Title* option within Excel.
- *x and y* axis labels can be added by selecting the *Layout* ribbon (tab), then *Axis Titles*, then *Primary Horizontal Axis Title* and *Primary Vertical Axis Title* options, which will produce a text box beside each axis into which can be typed the axis label and any corresponding units. This can then be changed from the default font using the *Home* ribbon (tab) options.

(*continued*)

Box 47.2 Continued

- Data point style can be changed by selecting (right-clicking) any data point and following the *Format Data Series* options to choose appropriate styles, colours and fill of the data markers.
- A straight line of best fit can be added by selecting any data point and using the *Add Trendline* options to choose a *Linear* line type with appropriate colour and style (explore other options within the *Format, Layout* and *Design* ribbon (tabs) at the top of the worksheet).

Producing a bar graph ('column' chart in Excel)

1. **Create the appropriate type of graph for your data.** Enter the category names (for *x* axis) in one column and the numeric values (for y axis) in the next column. Select (highlight) the data array, then select the *Insert* ribbon (tab), and choose the *Column* chart from the options provided. For a standard bar graph, select the first option from the *Column* menu (*Clustered Column*). Once selected, this will produce an embedded bar graph of the type shown in Fig. 47.8a.
2. **Change the default settings to improve the appearance of your graph.** The bar graph shown in Fig. 47.8b was produced by selecting each feature and altering the default settings, as detailed below (illustrative example).

Example for a bar graph (compare Fig. 47.8a with Fig. 47.8b):

- Unnecessary legend box on right-hand side can be removed using the *Delete* option.
- Border to chart can be removed using *Format Chart Area* function.
- Gridlines can either be removed using the *Delete* function or changed by selecting the gridlines and using the *Format Gridlines* option to alter the *Colour* and *Style.*
- *y* axis can be reformatted by selecting the axis, then using the *Format Axis* menu options to select appropriate scales, tick marks, etc. Note that the *x* axis should already contain category labels from the spreadsheet cells (modify original cells to update spreadsheet, if necessary).
- *x* and *y* axis labels can be added by selecting the *Layout* ribbon (tab), then *Axis Titles*, then *Primary Horizontal Axis Title* and *Primary Vertical Axis Title* options, as detailed for the plotted curve.
- Bar colour can be modified using the *Format Data Series* menu, selecting appropriate *Fill* and *Border* colours, e.g. white and black, respectively, in Fig. 47.8b.
- Individual Y data values can be shown using the *Add Data Labels* option (other options and adjustments can be made using the *Format, Layout* and *Design* ribbons (tabs) at the top of the worksheet).

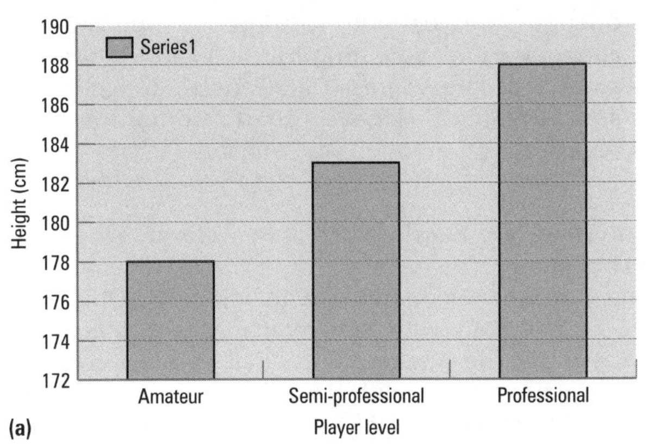

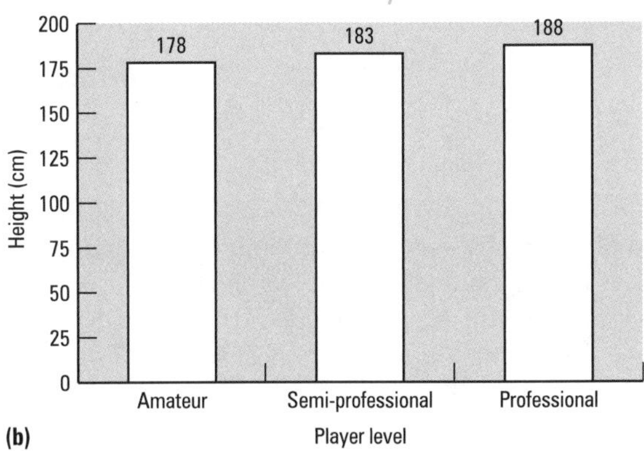

Fig. 2 Bar graph showing mean heights of amateur, semi-professional and professional basketball players.

Fig. 47.8 Examples of a bar graph produced using Microsoft Excel 2007 using **(a)** default settings and **(b)** modified (improved) settings.

Producing a pie graph ('pie' chart in Excel)

1. **Create the appropriate type of graph for your data.** Enter the category names for each part of the pie chart in one column, and the corresponding numbers (counts, fractions or percentages) in the next column. Select (highlight) the data array, then select (left-click) the *Insert* ribbon (tab), and choose the *Pie* chart from the options provided. For a standard pie graph, select the first option from the menu (*Pie*). Once selected, this will produce an embedded pie graph.

(continued)

Box 47.2 Continued

2. **Change the default settings to improve the appearance of your graph.** For example, you can show the data values (*Data labels*), adjust colours and shading, remove chart border, etc., as required.

Importing an Excel 2007 chart into a Word 2007 document

One problem encountered with Microsoft Office 2007 products (but not with earlier versions, e.g. Office 1997–2003) is that the standard *Cut > Paste* procedure gives a poor quality figure, with grainy appearance and fuzzy lines/text; similar problems occur using the *Insert* ribbon (tab) in Word 2007. The simplest approach is to follow the step-wise procedure below:

1. Select your Excel 2007 chart: right-click outside the chart itself, near to the edge, then choose the *Copy* option from the drop-down menu.
2. Open your Word 2007 file, go to the *Home* ribbon/tab and select *Paste special > Microsoft Office Word Document Object* from the *Clipboard* options (left-hand side of ribbon).
3. This should give a graph with the same crisp axis/line/text formatting as the original chart in Excel 2007.

The alternative approach is to use Excel 2007 to print the entire graph (chart) as a single sheet, and then add this to the print-out from your word-processed document. However, the disadvantage with this approach is that you cannot produce a professional looking figure legend below your graph.

Interpreting graphs

The process of analysing a graph can be split into five phases:

Examining graphs – do not be tempted to look at the data displayed within a graph before you have considered its context, read the legend and decided the scale of each axis.

1. **Consider the context.** Look at the graph in relation to the aims of the study in which it was reported. Why were the observations made? What hypothesis was the experiment set up to test? This information can usually be found in the Introduction or Results section of a report. Also relevant are the general methods used to obtain the results. This might be obvious from the figure title and legend, or from the Materials and Methods section.
2. **Recognise the graph form and examine the axes.** First, what kind of graph is presented (e.g. histogram, plotted curve)? You should be able to recognise the main types summarised on pp. 363–365 and their uses. Next, what do the axes measure? You should check what quantity has been measured in each case and what units are used.
3. **Look closely at the scale of each axis.** What is the starting point and what is the highest value measured? For the x axis, this will let you know the scope of the treatments or observations (e.g. whether they lasted for five minutes or 20 years; whether a concentration span was two-fold or fifty-fold). For each axis, it is especially important to note whether the values start at zero; if not, then the differences between any treatments shown may be magnified by the scale chosen (Box 47.3).
4. **Examine the symbols and curves.** Information will be provided in the key or legend to allow you to determine what these refer to. If you have made your own photocopy of the figure, it may be appropriate to note this directly on it. You can now assess what appears to have happened. If, say, two conditions have been observed while a variable is altered, when exactly do they differ from each other; by how much; and for how long?

Box 47.3 How graphs can misrepresent and mislead

1. **The 'volume' or 'area' deception** – this is mainly found in histogram or bar chart presentations where the size of a symbol is used to represent the measured variable. For example, the increase in muscle buffering capacity after sprint training might be represented on a chart by different sizes of a drum, with the *y* axis (height of drum) representing the change in buffering capacity. However, if the symbol retains its *shape* for all heights, as in Fig. 47.9a), its *volume* will increase as a cubic function of the height, rather than in direct proportion. To the casual observer, a two-fold increase may look like an eight-fold rise, and so on. Strictly, the *height* of the symbol should be the measure used to represent the variable, with no change in symbol width, as in Fig. 47.9b).
2. **Effects of a non-zero axis** – a non-zero axis acts to emphasise the differences between measures by reducing the range of values covered by the axis. For example, in Fig. 47.10a, it looks as if there are large differences in mass between males and females; however, if the scale is adjusted to run from zero, then it can be seen that the differences are not large as a proportion of the overall mass. Always scrutinise the scale values carefully when interpreting any graph.
3. **Use of a relative rather than absolute scale** – this is similar to the above, in that data compared using relative scales (e.g. percentage or ratio) can give the wrong impression if the denominator is not the same in all cases. In Fig. 47.11a, two treatments are shown as equal in *relative* effect, both resulting in 50% relative response compared (say) to the respective controls. However, if treatment A is 50% of a control value of 200 and treatment B is 50% of a control value of 500, then the actual difference in *absolute* response would have been masked, as shown by Fig. 47.11b.
4. **Effects of a non-linear scale** – when interpreting graphs with non-linear (e.g. logarithmic) scales, you may interpret any changes on an imagined linear scale. For example, the pH scale is logarithmic, and linear changes on this scale mean less in terms of absolute H^+ concentra-tion at high (alkaline) pH than they do at low (acidic) pH. In Fig. 47.12a, the cell density in two media is compared on a logarithmic scale, while in Fig. 47.12b, the same data are graphed on a linear scale. Note, also, that the log *y* axis scale in Fig. 47.12a cannot be shown to zero, because there is no logarithm for 0.

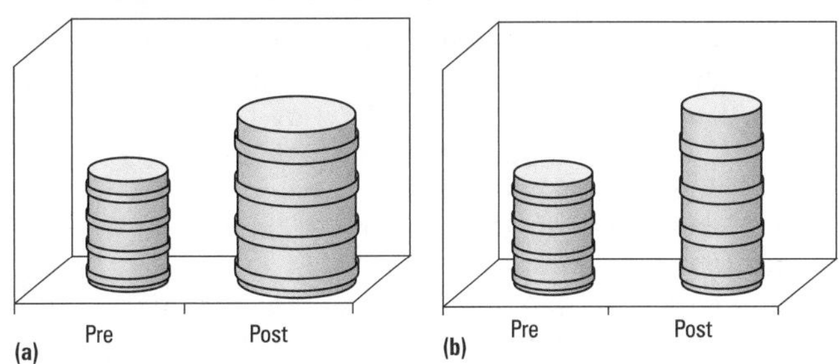

Fig. 47.9 Increase in muscle buffering capacity after sprint training.

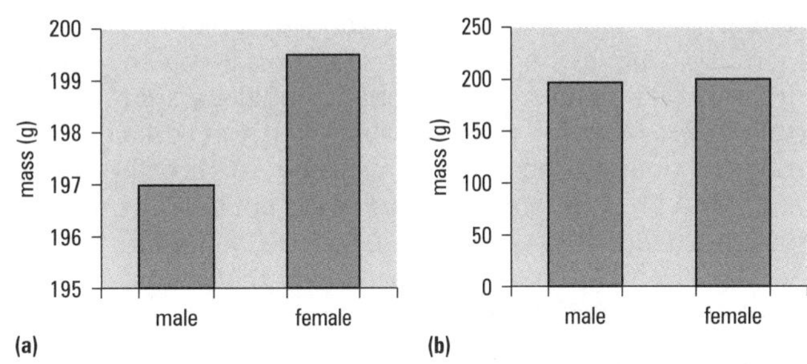

Fig. 47.10 Average mass of males and female rats in test group.

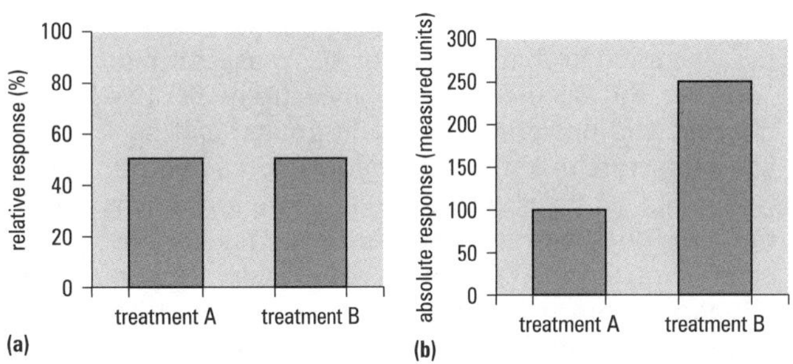

Fig. 47.11 Responses to treatments A and B.

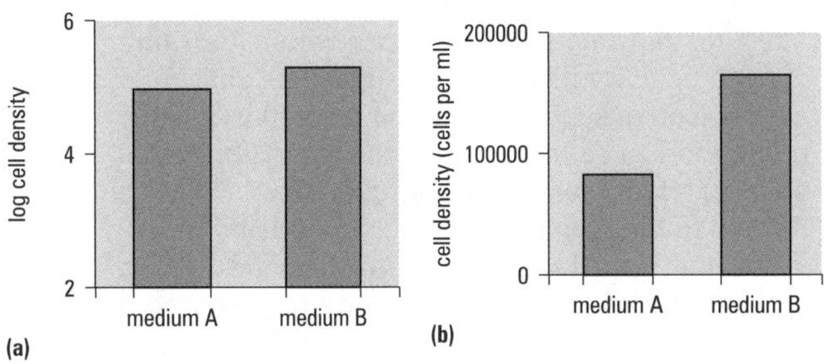

Fig. 47.12 Effect of different media on cell density.

(continued)

Box 47.3 Continued

5. **Unwarranted extrapolation** – a graph may be extrapolated to indicate what would happen if a trend continued, as in Fig. 47.13a. However, this can only be done under certain assumptions (e.g. that certain factors will remain constant or that relationships will hold under new conditions). There may be no guarantee that this will actually be the case. Fig. 47.13b illustrates other possible outcomes if the experiment were to be repeated with higher values for the *x* axis.
6. **Failure to account for data point error** – this misrepresentation involves curves that are overly complex in relation to the scatter in the underlying data. When interpreting graphs with complex curves, consider the errors involved in the data values. It is probably unlikely that the curve would pass through all the data points unless the errors were very small. Fig. 47.14a illustrates a curve that appears to assume zero error and is thus overly complex, while Fig. 47.14b shows a curve that takes possible errors of the points into account.
7. **Failure to reject outlying points** – this is a special case of the previous example. There may be many reasons for outlying data, from genuine mistakes to statistical 'freaks'. If a curve is drawn through such points on a graph, it indicates that the point carries equal weight with the other points, when in fact, it should probably be ignored. To assess this, consider the accuracy of the measurement, the number and position of adjacent points, and any special factors that might be involved on a one-off basis. Fig. 47.15a shows a curve where an outlier (arrowed) has perhaps been given undue weight when showing the presumed relationship. If there is good reason to think that the point should be ignored, then the curve shown in Fig. 47.15b would probably be more valid.
8. **Inappropriate fitted line** – here, the mathema-tical function chosen to represent a trend in the data might be inappropriate. A straight line might be fitted to the data, when a curve would be more correct, or vice versa. These cases can be difficult to assess. You need to consider the theoretical validity of the model used to generate the curve (this is not always stated clearly). For example, if a straight line is fitted to the points, the implicit underlying model states that one factor varies in direct relation to another, when the true situation may be more complex. In Fig. 47.16a, the relationship has been shown as a linear relationship, whereas an exponential relationship, as shown in Fig. 47.16b, could be more correct.

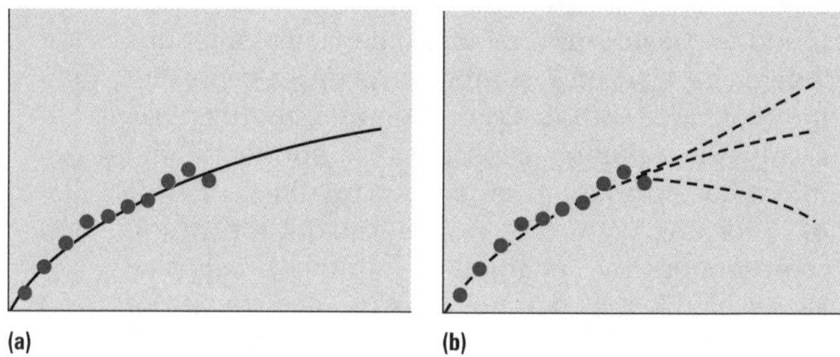

Fig. 47.13 Extrapolation of data under different assumptions.

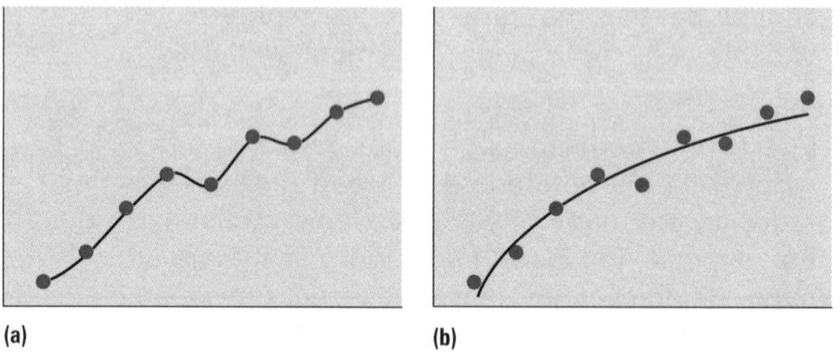

Fig. 47.14 Fitted curves under different assumptions of data error.

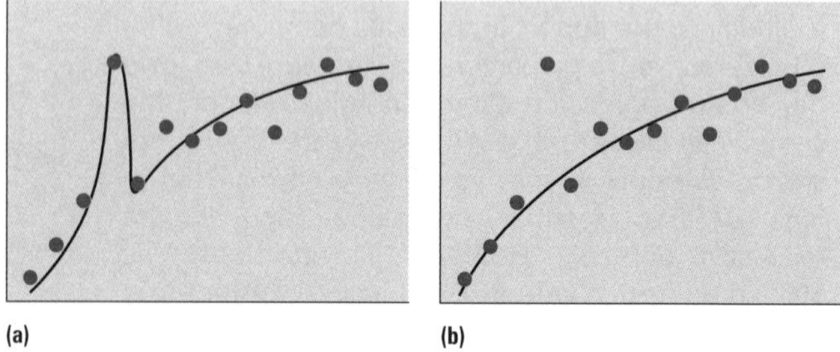

Fig. 47.15 Curves with and without outlier taken into account.

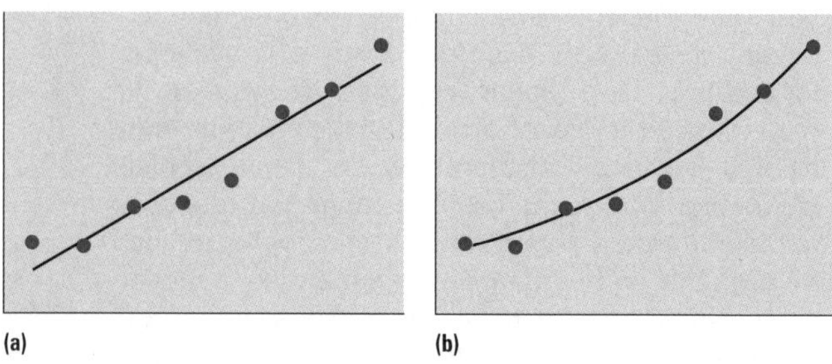

Fig. 47.16 Different mathematical model used to represent trends in data.

Understanding graphs within scientific papers – the legend should be a succinct summary of the key information required to interpret the figure without further reference to the main text. This is a useful approach when 'skimming' a paper for relevant information.

5. **Evaluate errors and statistics.** It is important to take account of variability in the data. For example, if mean values are presented, the underlying errors may be large, meaning that any difference between two treatments or observations at a given x value could simply have arisen by chance. Thinking about the descriptive statistics used (Chapter 49) will allow you to determine whether apparent differences could be significant in both statistical and practical senses.

Sometimes graphs are used to mislead. This may be unwitting, as in an unconscious favouring of a 'pet' hypothesis of the author. Graphs may be used to 'sell' a product in the field of advertising or to favour a viewpoint as, perhaps, in politics. Experience in drawing and interpreting graphs will help you spot these flawed presentations, and understanding how graphs can be erroneously presented (Box 47.3) will help you to avoid the same pitfalls.

Sources for further study

Briscoe, M.H. (1996) *Preparing Scientific Illustrations: a Guide to Better Posters, Presentations and Publications*. Springer-Verlag, New York.

Day, R.A. and Gastel, B. (2006) *How to Write and Publish a Scientific Paper*, 6th edn, Cambridge University Press, Cambridge.

Robbins, N.B. (2005) *Creating More Effective Graphs*. Wiley, New York.

48 Presenting data in tables

A table is often the most appropriate way to present numerical data in a concise, accurate and structured form. Assignments and project reports should contain tables that have been designed to condense and display results in a meaningful way and to aid numerical comparison.

Decide whether you need a table, or whether a graph is more appropriate. Histograms and plotted curves can be used to give a visual impression of the relationships within your data (pp. 363–365). On the other hand, a table gives you the opportunity to make detailed numerical comparisons.

KEY POINT Always remember that the primary purpose of your table is to communicate information and allow appropriate comparison, not simply to put down the results on paper.

Preparation of tables

Title

Constructing titles – take care over titles as it is a common mistake in student practical reports to present tables without titles, or to misconstruct the title.

Every table must have a brief descriptive title. If several tables are used, number them consecutively so they can be quoted in your text. The titles within a report should be compared with one another, making sure they are logical and consistent and that they describe accurately the numerical data contained within them.

Structure

Saving space in tables – you may be able to omit a column of control data if your results can be expressed as percentages of the corresponding control values.

Display the components of each table in a way that will help the reader to understand your data and grasp the significance of your results. Organise the columns so that each category of like numbers or attributes is listed vertically, while each horizontal row shows a different experimental treatment or variable, etc. (as in Table 48.1). Where appropriate, put control values near the beginning of the table. Columns that need to be compared should be set out alongside each other. Use rulings to subdivide your table appropriately, but avoid cluttering it with too many lines.

Headings and subheadings

These should identify each set of data and show the units of measurement, where necessary. Make sure that each column is wide enough for the headings and for the longest data value. Order the rows naturally. For instance, by time (past to present) or by size (biggest to smallest).

Table 48.1 Anthropometric and $\dot{V}O_2$max (mL kg^{-1} min^{-1}) characteristics (mean ± standard deviation) of amateur, semi-professional and professional rugby league forwards and backs

	Amateur (n = 62)		Semi-professional (n = 50)		Professional (n = 43)	
	Forwards	Backs	Forwards	Backs	Forwards	Backs
Height (cm)	178.4 ± 8.7	178.0 ± 5.2	178.2 ± 7.2	176.0 ± 5.9	184.0 ± 7.0	178.0 ± 7.0
Body mass (kg)	90.8 ± 10.2	79.7 ± 10.1	90.3 ± 14.0	80.7 ± 10.4	92.1 ± 10.4	79.8 ± 8.0
Sum of four skinfolds (mm)*	52.4 ± 14.7	46.1 ± 18.6	47.3 ± 17.9	38.8 ± 13.9	NR	NR
Estimated body fat (%)	19.9 ± 3.7	17.5 ± 5.0	17.6 ± 4.4	15.2 ± 4.1	15.2 ± 3.4	12.6 ± 3.2
$\dot{V}O_2$max (ml kg^{-1} min^{-1})[†]	38.1 ± 2.6	40.0 ± 2.7	45.8 ± 4.4	48.0 ± 3.6	56.4 ± 3.7**	55.4 ± 3.2**

*Sum of four skinfold sites (biceps, triceps, subscapular, suprailiac); [†]estimated from repeated 20 m shuttle run test.
**Significantly greater than both amateur and semi-professional ($p < 0.05$).
NR = Not reported.

Example If you measured the area of a type 1 (slow twitch) muscle fibre to the nearest square micrometre (μm^2), you would express it as 4190 μm^2 rather than 0.000000004190 m^2 or 4.19×10^{-9} m^2.

Numerical data

Within the table, do not quote values to more significant figures than necessary, as this will imply spurious accuracy. By careful choice of appropriate units for each column you should aim to present numerical data within the range 0 to 1000. As with graphs, it is less ambiguous to use derived SI units, with the appropriate prefixes, in the headings of columns and rows, rather than quoting multiplying factors as powers of 10. Alternatively, include exponents in the main body of the table to avoid any possible confusion regarding the use of negative powers of 10. Round off decimal places – usually one or two decimal places are enough. For example, a $\dot{V}O_2max$ value has no meaning rounded off to three or even two decimal places.

Saving further space in tables – in some instances a footnote can be used to replace a whole column of repetitive data.

Other notations

Avoid using dashes in numerical tables, as their meaning is unclear; enter a zero reading as '0' and use 'NT' not tested, NR = not reported or 'ND' if no data value was obtained, with a footnote to explain each abbreviation. Other footnotes, identified by asterisks, superscripts or other symbols in the table, may be used to provide relevant experimental detail (if not given in the text) and an explanation of column headings and individual results, where appropriate. Footnotes should be as condensed as possible. Table 48.1 provides examples.

Statistics

In tables where the dispersion of each dataset is shown by an appropriate statistical parameter, you must state whether this is the (sample) standard deviation, the standard error (of the mean) or the 95 % confidence limits and you must give the value of n (the number of replicates). Other descriptive statistics should be quoted with similar detail, and hypothesis-testing statistics should be quoted along with the value of P (the probability). Details of any test used should be given in the legend, or in a footnote.

Using spreadsheets and word processing packages – these can be used to prepare high-quality versions of tables for project work (Box 48.2).

Text

Sometimes a table can be a useful way of presenting textual information in a condensed form.

When you have finished compiling your tabulated data, carefully doublecheck each numerical entry against the original information, to ensure that the final version of your table is free from transcriptional errors. Box 48.1 gives a checklist for the major elements of constructing a table.

Box 48.1 Checklist for preparing a table

Every table should have the following components:

1. **A title**, plus a reference number and date where necessary.
2. **Headings for each column and row**, with appropriate units of measurement, usually in brackets.
3. **Data values**, quoted to the nearest significant figure and with statistical parameters, according to your requirements.
4. **Footnotes** to explain abbreviations, modifications and individual details.
5. **Rulings to emphasise groupings** and distinguish items from each other.

Box 48.2 How to use a word processor (Microsoft Word 2007) or a spreadsheet (Microsoft Excel 2007) to create a table for use in coursework reports and dissertations

Creating tables with Microsoft Word 2007

Word-processed tables are suitable for text-intensive or number-intensive tables, although in the second case entering data can be laborious. When working in this way, the natural way to proceed is to create the 'shell' of the table, add the data, then carry out final formatting on the table.

1. **Move the cursor to the desired position in your document.** This is where you expect the top left corner of your table to appear. Go to the ***insert*** ribbon (tab), then choose *Table*.
2. **Select the appropriate number of columns and rows.** Don't forget to add rows and columns for headings. As default, a full-width table will appear, with single rulings for all cell boundaries, with all columns of equal width and all rows of equal height.

   Example of a 4 × 3 table:

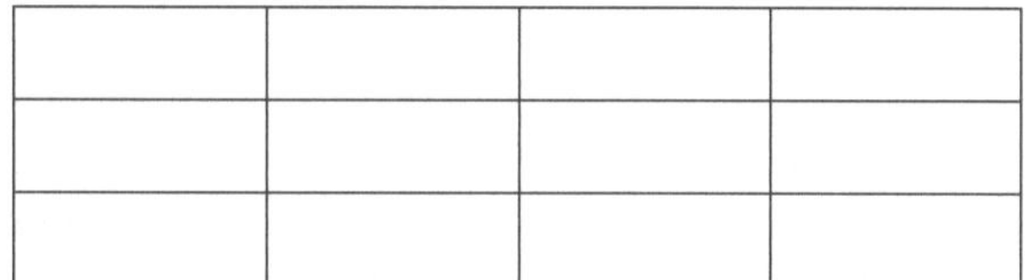

3. **Customise the columns.** By placing the cursor over the vertical rulings then 'dragging', you can adjust their width to suit your heading text entries, which should now be added.

Heading 1	Heading 2	Heading 3	Heading 4

4. **Work through the table adding the data.** Entries can be numbers or text.

Heading 1	Heading 2	Heading 3	Heading 4
xx	xx	xx	xx
xx	xx	xx	

5. **Make further adjustments to column and row widths to suit.** For example, if text fills several rows within a cell, consider increasing the column width, and if a column contains only single or double digit numbers, consider shrinking its width. To combine cells, first highlight them, then use *Merge Cells* from the menu available using the right-hand mouse button.

Heading 1	Heading 2	Heading 3	Heading 4
xx	xx	xx	xx
	xx	xx	xx

6. **Finally, remove selected borders to cells.** One way to do this is using the ***Borders*** options accessed from the ***Design*** ribbon (tab) on the toolbar, so that your table looks like the examples shown in this chapter.
7. **Add a table title.** This should be positioned *above* the table (*cf.* a figure title and legend p. 364).

   Final version of the table:

Table xx. A table of some data

Heading 1	Heading 2[a]	Heading 3	Heading 4
Aaa	xx	xx	xx
	xx	xx	xx

[a]An example of a footnote.

Creating tables with Microsoft Excel

Tables derived from spreadsheets are effective when you have lots of numerical data, especially when these are stored or created using the spreadsheet itself. When working in this way, you can design the table as part of an output or summary section of the spreadsheet, add explanatory headings, format, then possibly export to a word processor when complete.

1. **Design the output or summary section.** Plan this as if it were a table, including adding text headings within cells.

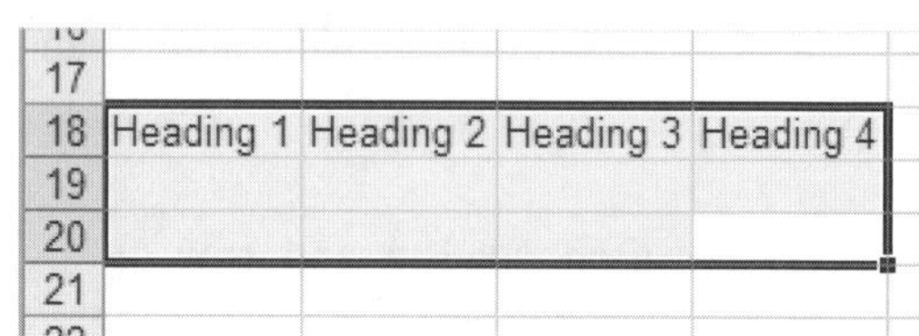

(continued)

Box 48.2 Continued

2. **Insert appropriate formulae within cells to produce data.** If necessary, formulae should draw on the other parts of the spreadsheet.

17				
18	Heading 1	Heading 2	Heading 3	Heading 4
19	Aaa	=A1	=C3*5	=SDEV(A1:A12)
20	Bbb	=A2	=F45/G12	=SDEV(B1:B12)
21				
22				

3. **Format the cells.** This is important to control the number of decimal places presented.
4. **Adjust column width to suit.** You can do this via the column headings, by placing the cursor over the rulings between columns then 'dragging'.

17				
18	Heading 1	Heading 2	Heading 3	Heading 4
19	Aaa	=A1	=C3*5	=SDEV(A1:A12)
20	Bbb	=A2	=F45/G12	=SDEV(B1:B12)
21				
22				

5. **Add rulings as appropriate**. Use the borders menu on the toolbar as described above.

17				
18	Heading 1	Heading 2	Heading 3	Heading 4
19	Aaa	=A1	=C3*5	=SDEV(A1:A12)
20	Bbb	=A2	=F45/G12	=SDEV(B1:B12)
21				

6. **Add 'real' data values to the spreadsheet.** This should result in the summary values within the table being filled. Check that these are presented with the appropriate number of significant figures.
7. **The table can now be copied and pasted to a Word document**. When you want to create a dynamic link between the content of your Word document and the content in an Excel workbook, insert the content as an object (*Insert* tab > *Object*). If you insert the cells into the document as an Excel object, Microsoft Office Word runs Excel when you double-click the cells, and you can use Excel commands to work with the worksheet content.

Sources for further study

Briscoe, M.H. (1996) *Preparing Scientific Illustrations: a Guide to Better Posters, Presentations and Publications.* Springer-Verlag, New York.

Day, R.A. and Gastel, B. (2006) *How to Write and Publish a Scientific Paper.* Cambridge University Press, Cambridge.

49 Descriptive statistics

Definition

Descriptive statistics – a way of organising and summarising data into numerical values that describe the characteristics of a group, event or condition. In sport and exercise science, the commonly used descriptive statistics are measures of central tendency (mean, median, mode) and variability/dispersion (range, variance, standard deviation).

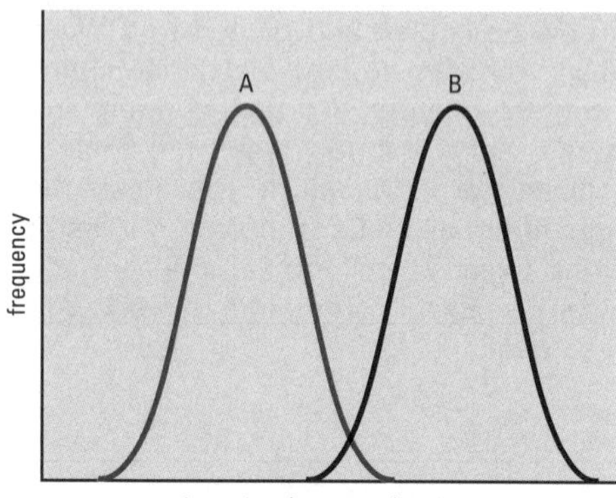

Fig. 49.1 Two distributions with different locations but the same dispersion. The dataset labelled B could have been obtained by adding a constant to each datum in the dataset labelled A.

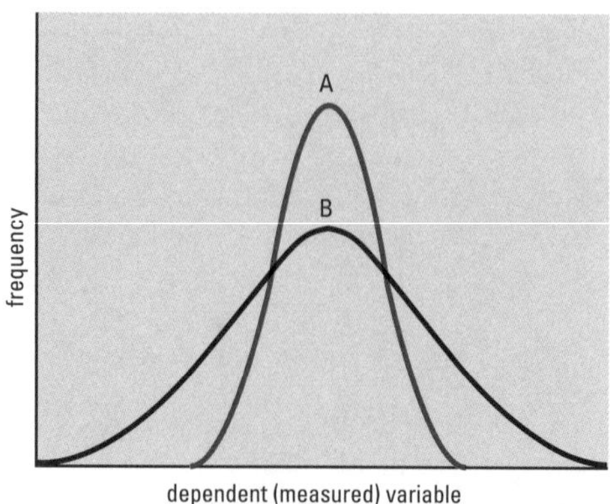

Fig. 49.2 Two distributions with different dispersions but the same location. The dataset labelled A covers a relatively narrow range of values of the dependent (measured) variable, while that labelled B covers a wider range.

Whether obtained from observation or experimentation, most data in sport and exercise science exhibit variability. This can be displayed as a frequency distribution (Fig. 49.1). Descriptive (or summary) statistics quantify aspects of the frequency distribution of a sample. You can use them to:

- condense a large dataset for presentation in figures or tables;
- provide estimates of parameters of the frequency distribution of the population being sampled (p. 390).

KEY POINT The choice of appropriate descriptive statistics depends on both the type of data, i.e. quantitative, ranked or qualitative, and the nature of the underlying population frequency distribution.

If you have no clear theoretical grounds for assuming what the underlying frequency distribution is like, graph one or more sample frequency distributions, ideally with a sample size >100.

The methods used to calculate descriptive statistics depend on whether data have been grouped into classes. You should use the original dataset if it is still available, because grouping into classes loses information and accuracy. However, large datasets may make calculations unwieldy, and are best handled using computer programs.

Three important features of a frequency distribution that can be summarised by descriptive statistics are:

- the sample's location, i.e. its position along a given dimension representing the dependent (measured) variable (Fig. 49.1);
- the dispersion of the data, i.e. how spread out the values are (Fig. 49.2);
- the shape of the distribution, i.e. whether symmetrical, skewed, U-shaped, etc. (Fig. 49.3).

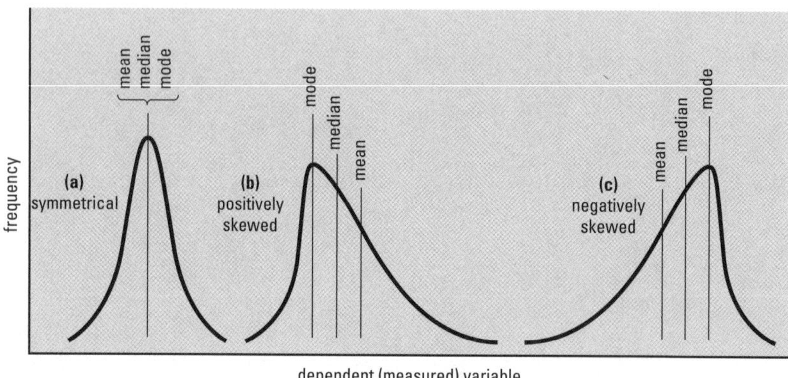

Fig. 49.3 Symmetrical and skewed frequency distributions, showing relative positions of mean, median and mode.
Source: Jones, A., Reed, R. and Weyers, J. (2007) p. 415.

Example Box 49.1 shows a set of data and the calculated values of the measures of location, dispersion and shape for which methods of calculation are outlined here. Check your understanding by calculating the statistics yourself and confirming that you arrive at the same answers.

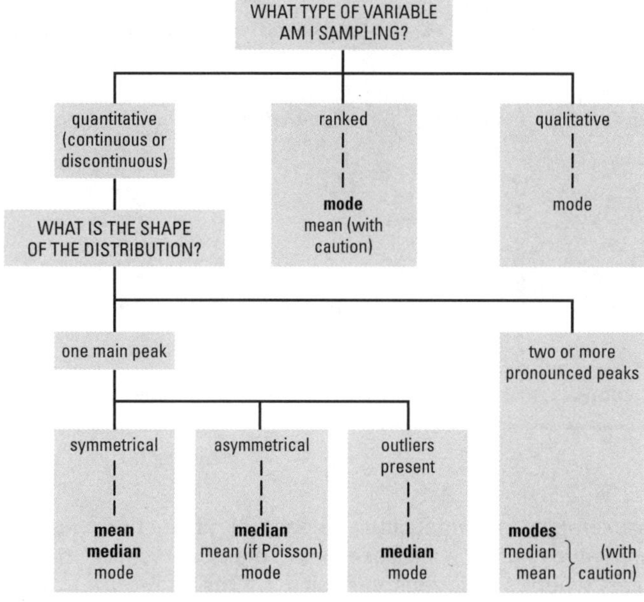

Fig. 49.4 Choosing a statistic to characterise a distribution's location. Statistics written in bold are the preferred option(s).
Source: Jones, A., Reed, R. and Weyers, J. (2007) p. 416.

Use of symbols – Y is used in Chapters 50 and 51 to signify the dependent variable in statistical calculations (following the example of Sokal and Rohlf, 1994). Note, however, that some authors use X or x in analogous formulae and many calculators refer to e.g. $\bar{x}$, $\sum x^2$, etc., for their statistical functions.

Definition

Rank – the position of a data value when all the data are placed in order of ascending magnitude. If ties occur, an average rank of the tied variates is used. Thus, the rank of the datum 6 in the sequence 1, 3, 5, 6, 8, 8, 10 is 4; the rank of each datum with value 8 is 5.5.

Definition

An outlier – any datum that has a value much smaller or bigger than most of the data. In general, an outlier will be ± 2 standard deviations (p. 383) from the mean.

Measuring location (central tendency)

Here, the objective is to pinpoint the 'centre' of the frequency distribution, i.e. the value about which most of the data are grouped. The chief measures of location are the mean, median and mode. Fig. 49.4 shows how to choose among these for a given dataset.

Mean

The mean (denoted $\bar{Y}$ and also referred to as the arithmetic mean) is the average value of the data. It is obtained from the sum of all the data values divided by the number of observations (in symbolic terms, $\Sigma Y/n$). The mean is a good measure of the centre of symmetrical frequency distributions. It uses all of the numerical values of the sample and therefore incorporates all of the information content of the data. However, the value of a mean is greatly affected by the presence of outliers (extreme values). The arithmetic mean is a widely used statistic in sport and exercise science, but there are situations in which you should be careful about using it (see Box 49.2 for examples).

Median

The median is the midpoint of the observations when ranked in increasing order. For odd-sized samples, the median is the middle observation; for even-sized samples it is the mean of the middle pair of observations. Where data are grouped into classes, the median can only be estimated. This is most simply done from a graph of the cumulative frequency distribution, but can also be worked out by assuming the data to be evenly spread within the class. The median may represent the location of the main body of data better than the mean when the distribution is asymmetric or when there are outliers in the sample.

Box 49.1 Descriptive statistics for an illustrative sample of data

Value (Y)	Frequency (f)	Cumulative frequency	fY	fY^2
1	0	0	0	0
2	1	1	2	4
3	2	3	6	18
4	3	6	12	48
5	8	14	40	200
6	5	19	30	180
7	2	21	14	98
8	0	21	0	0
Totals	$21 = \Sigma f\,(=n)$		$104 = \Sigma fY$	$548 = \Sigma fY^2$

In this example, for simplicity and ease of calculation, integer values of Y are used. In many practical exercises, where continuous variables are measured to several significant figures and where the number of data values is small, giving frequencies of 1 for most of the values of Y, it may be simpler to omit the column dealing with frequency and list all the individual values of Y and Y^2 in the appropriate columns. To gauge the underlying frequency distribution of such datasets, you would need to group individual data into broader classes (e.g. all values between 1.0 and 1.9, all values between 2.0 and 2.9, etc.) and then draw a histogram. Calculation of certain statistics for datasets that have been grouped in this way (e.g. median, quartiles, extremes) can be tricky, and a statistical text should be consulted.

Statistic	Value*	How calculated
Mean	4.95	$\Sigma fY/n$, i.e. 104/21
Median	5	Value of the $(n+1)/2$ variate, i.e. the value ranked $(21+1)/2 = 11$th (obtained from the cumulative frequency column)
Mode	5	The most common value (Y value with highest frequency)
Upper quartile	6	The upper quartile is between the 16th and 17th values, i.e. the value exceeded by 25% of the data values
Lower quartile	4	The lower quartile is between the 5th and 6th values, i.e. the value exceeded by 75% of the data values
Semi-interquartile range	1.0	Half the difference between the upper and lower quartiles, i.e. $(6-4)/2$
Upper extreme	7	Highest Y value in dataset
Lower extreme	2	Lowest Y value in dataset
Range	5	Difference between upper and lower extremes
Variance (s^2)	1.65	$s^2 = \dfrac{\Sigma fY^2 - (\Sigma fY)^2/n}{n-1} = \dfrac{548 - (104)^2/21}{20}$
Standard deviation (s)	1.28	$\sqrt{s^2}$
Standard error (SE)	0.280	$s/\sqrt{n}$
95% confidence limits	4.36 – 5.54	$\bar{Y} \pm t_{0.05}[20] \times \text{SE}$ (where $t_{0.05}[20] = 2.09$)
Coefficient of variation (CoV)	25.9%	$100s/\bar{Y}$

*Rounded to three significant figures, except when it is an exact number.

Box 49.2 Three examples where simple arithmetic means are inappropriate

Mean	n
6	4
7	7
8	1

1. **If means of samples are themselves meaned, an error can arise if the samples are of different size.** For example, the arithmetic mean of the means in the table shown on the left is 7, but this does not take account of the different 'reliabilities' of each mean owing to their sample sizes. The correct weighted mean is obtained by multiplying each mean by its sample size (n) (a 'weight') and dividing the sum of these values by the total number of observations, i.e. in the case shown, $(24 + 49 + 8)/12 = 6.75$.
2. **When making a mean of ratios (e.g. percentages) for several groups of different sizes, the ratio for the combined total of all the groups is not the mean of the proportions for the individual groups.** For example, if 20 athletes from a sample of 50 are male, this implies 40% are male. If 60 athletes from a sample of 120 are male, this implies 50% are male. The mean percentage of males $(50 + 40)/2 = 45\%$ is *not* the percentage of males in the two groups combined, because there are $20 + 60 = 80$ males in a total of 170 athletes = 47.1% approx.
3. **If the measurement scale is not linear, arithmetic means may give a false value.** For example, if three solutions had pH values 6, 7 and 8, the appropriate mean pH is not 7 because the pH scale is logarithmic. The definition of pH is $-\log_{10}[H^+]$, where $[H^+]$ is expressed in mol l^{-1} ('molar'); therefore, to obtain the true mean, convert data into $[H^+]$ values (i.e. put them on a linear scale) by calculating $10^{(-\text{pH value})}$ as shown. Now calculate the mean of these values and convert the answer back into pH units. Thus, the appropriate answer is pH 6.43 rather than 7. Note that a similar procedure is necessary when calculating statistics of dispersion in such cases, so you will find these almost certainly asymmetric about the mean.

pH value	$[H^+]$ (mol L^{-1})
6	1×10^{-6}
7	1×10^{-7}
8	1×10^{-8}
mean	3.7×10^{-7}
$-\log_{10}$ mean	6.43

Mean values of log-transformed data are often called geometric means. While rarely used in sport and exercise science, log-transformed data can be used when trying to reduce the effects of outliers or for skewed data, e.g. with an asymmetrical distribution but only one peak (see. Fig. 49.3). Log-transformation often changes the skewed distribution to make a 'normal' shape, since logarithms 'shrink' the spread of data.

Describing the location of qualitative data – the mode is the only statistic that is suitable for this task. For example, 'the modal (most frequent) eye colour was crimson'.

Mode

The mode is the most common value in the sample. The mode is easily found from a tabulated frequency distribution as the most frequent value. If data have been grouped into classes, then the term modal class is used for the class containing most values. The mode provides a rapidly and easily found estimate of sample location and is unaffected by outliers. However, the mode is affected by chance variation in the shape of a sample's distribution and it may lie distant from the obvious centre of the distribution.

The mean, median and mode have the same units as the variable under discussion. However, whether these statistics of location have the same or similar values for a given frequency distribution depends on the

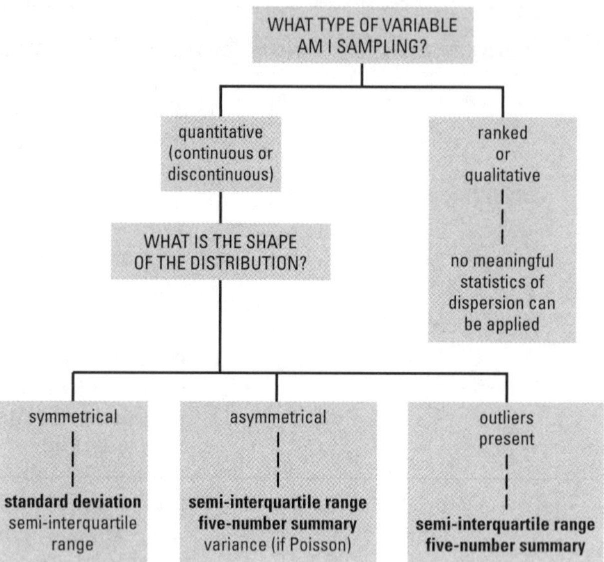

Fig. 49.5 Choosing a statistic for characterising a distribution's dispersion. Statistics written in bold are the preferred option(s). Note that you should match statistics describing dispersion with those you have used to describe location, i.e. standard deviation with mean, semi-interquartile range with median.
Source: Jones, A., Reed, R. and Weyers, J. (2007) p. 418.

symmetry and shape of the distribution. If it is near-symmetrical with a single peak, all three will be very similar; if it is skewed or has more than one peak, their values will differ to a greater degree (see Fig. 49.3).

Measuring dispersion (variability)

Here, the objective is to quantify the spread of the data about the centre of the distribution. Fig. 49.5 indicates how to decide which measure of dispersion to use.

Example In a sample of data with values 3, 7, 15, 8, 5, 10 and 4, the range is 12 (i.e. the difference between the highest value, 15, and the lowest value, 3).

Range

The range is the difference between the largest and smallest data values in the sample (the extremes) and has the same units as the measured variable. The range is easy to determine, but is greatly affected by outliers. Its value may also depend on sample size: in general, the larger this is, the greater will be the range. These features make the range a poor measure of dispersion for many practical purposes.

Semi-interquartile range

The semi-interquartile range is an appropriate measure of dispersion when a median is the appropriate statistic to describe location. For this, you need to determine the first and third quartiles, i.e. the medians for those data values ranked below and above the median of the whole dataset (Fig. 49.6). To calculate a semi-interquartile range for a dataset:

1. Rank the observations in ascending order.
2. Find the values of the first and third quartiles.

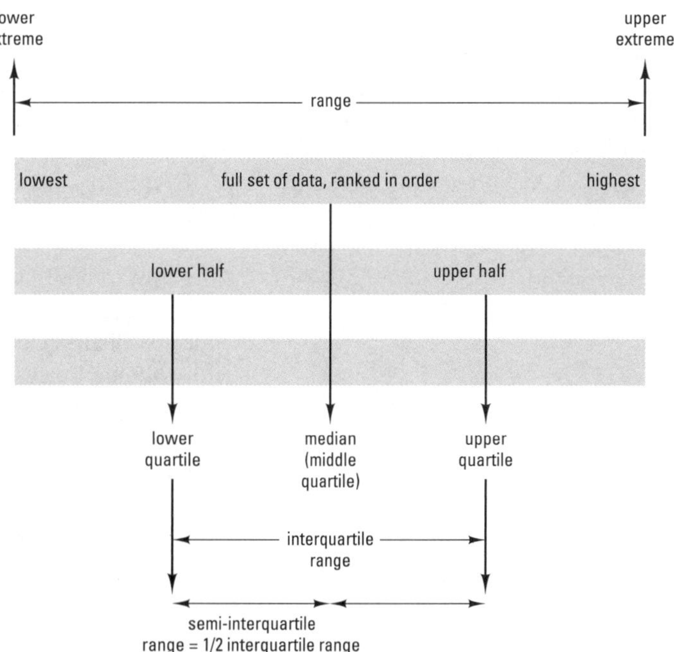

Fig. 49.6 Illustration of median, quartiles, range and semi-interquartile range.

Source: Jones, A., Reed, R. and Weyers, J. (2007) p. 419.

3. Subtract the value of the first quartile from the value of the third.
4. Halve this number.

For data grouped in classes, the semi-interquartile range can only be estimated. Another disadvantage is that it takes no account of the shape of the distribution at its edges. This objection can be countered by using the so-called 'five-number summary' of a dataset, which consists of the three quartiles and the two extreme values; this can be presented on graphs as a box-and-whisker plot (Fig. 49.7) and is particularly useful for summarising skewed frequency distributions. The corresponding 'six- number summary' includes the sample's size.

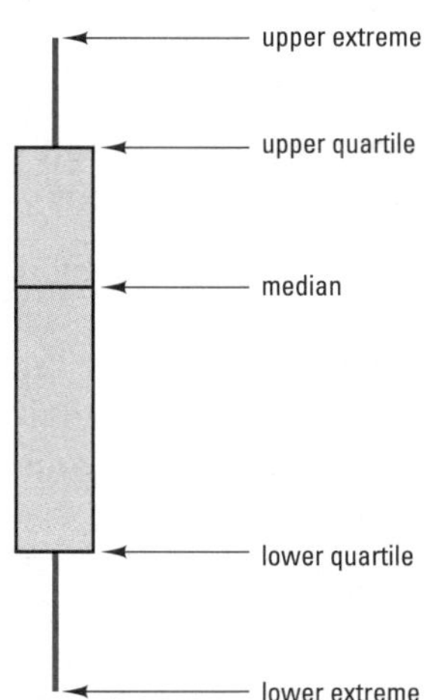

Fig. 49.7 A box-and-whisker plot, showing the 'five-number summary' of a sample as it might be used on a graph.

Source: Jones, A., Reed, R. and Weyers, J. (2007) p. 419.

Variance and standard deviation

For symmetrical frequency distributions, an ideal measure of dispersion would take into account each value's deviation from the mean and provide a measure of the average deviation from the mean. Two such statistics are the sample variance, which is the sum of squares ($\Sigma(Y - \bar{Y})^2$) divided by $n - 1$ (where n is the sample size), and the sample standard deviation, which is the positive square root of the sample variance.

The variance (s^2) has units that are the square of the original units, while the standard deviation (s, or SD) is expressed in the original units, one reason s is often preferred as a measure of dispersion. Calculating s or s^2 longhand is a tedious job and is best done with the help of a calculator or computer. If you don't have a calculator that calculates s for you, an alternative formula that simplifies calculations is:

$$s = +\sqrt{\frac{\Sigma Y^2 - (\Sigma Y)^2/n}{n - 1}} \qquad (49.1)$$

Using a calculator for statistics – make sure you understand how to enter individual data values and which keys will give the sample mean (usually shown as $\overline{X}$ or $\overline{x}$) and sample standard deviation (often shown as σ_{n-1}). In general, you should not use the population standard deviation (usually shown as σ_n).

To calculate s using a calculator:

1. Obtain ΣY, square it, divide by n and store in memory.
2. Square Y values, obtain ΣY^2, subtract memory value from this.
3. Divide this answer by $n - 1$.
4. Take the positive square root of this value.

Take care to retain significant figures, or errors in the final value of s will result. If continuous data have been grouped into classes, the class mid-values or their squares must be multiplied by the appropriate frequencies before summation (see example in Box 49.1). When data values are large, longhand calculations can be simplified by coding the data, e.g. by subtracting a constant from each datum, and decoding when the simplified calculations are complete (see Sokal and Rohlf, 1994).

Coefficient of variation

The coefficient of variation (CoV) is a dimensionless measure of variability relative to location that expresses the sample standard deviation, usually as a percentage of the sample mean, i.e.

$$\text{CoV} = 100s/\bar{Y}\,(\%) \qquad (49.2)$$

This statistic is useful when comparing the relative dispersion of datasets with widely differing means or where different units have been used for the same or similar quantities.

A useful application of the CoV is to compare different analytical methods or procedures, so that you can decide which involves the least proportional error – create a standard stock solution, then base your comparison on the results from several subsamples analysed by each method. You may find it useful to use the CoV to compare the precision of your own results with those of a manufacturer, e.g. for a blood lactate analyser. The smaller the CoV, the more precise (repeatable) is the apparatus or technique (*NOTE*: this does not mean that it is necessarily more *accurate*; see p. 123).

Example Consider two different testers measuring the sum of seven skinfold measures in a team of 15 female football players. Tester A has a mean skinfold total of 80 mm and a standard deviation of 8 mm, while Tester B obtains a mean of 115 mm and a standard deviation of 10 mm. Which tester gives the more reproducible results? The answer can be found by calculating the CoV values, which are 10.0% and 8.7%, respectively. Thus, Tester B is more precise, even though their standard deviation is greater.

Measuring the precision of the sample mean as an estimate of the true value using the standard error

Most practical exercises are based on a limited number of individual data values (a sample) that are used to make inferences about the population from which they were drawn. For example, the haemoglobin content might be measured in blood samples from 100 adult females and used as an estimate of the adult female haemoglobin content, with the sample mean ($\bar{Y}$) and sample standard deviation (s) providing estimates of the true values of the underlying population mean (μ) and the population standard deviation (σ). The reliability of the sample mean as an estimate of the true (population) mean can be assessed by calculating a statistic termed the standard error of the sample mean (often abbreviated to standard error or SE), from:

$$\text{SE} = s/\sqrt{n} \qquad (49.3)$$

Strictly, the standard error is an estimate of the dispersion of repeated sample means around the true (population) value: if several samples were

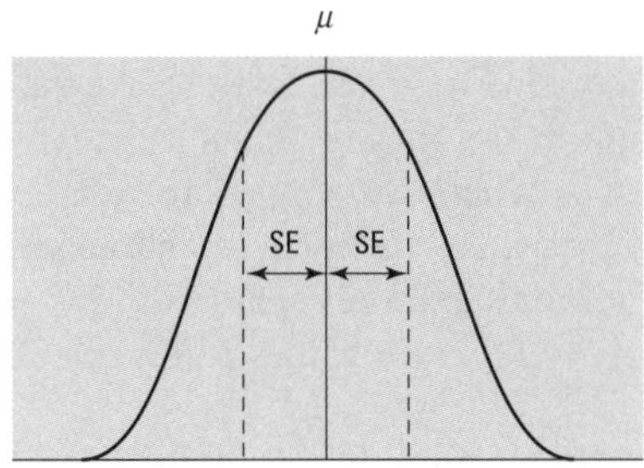

Fig. 49.8 Frequency distribution of sample means around the population mean (μ). Note that SE is equivalent to the standard deviation of the sample means, for sample size = n.

Source: Jones, A., Reed, R. and Weyers, J. (2007) p. 421.

taken, each with the same number of data values (n), then their means would cluster around the population mean (μ) with a standard deviation equal to SE, as shown in Fig. 49.8. Therefore, the *smaller* the SE, the more reliable the sample mean is likely to be as an estimate of the true value, since the underlying frequency distribution would be more tightly clustered around μ. At a practical level, equation 49.3 shows that SE is directly affected by the dispersion of individual data values within the sample, as represented by the sample standard deviation (s). Perhaps more importantly, SE is inversely related to the *square root* of the number of data values (n). Therefore, if you wanted to increase the precision of a sample mean by a factor of 2 (i.e. to reduce SE by half), you would have to increase n by a factor of 2^2 (i.e. four-fold).

Summary descriptive statistics for the sample mean are often quoted as $\bar{Y} \pm \text{SE}\,(n)$, with the SE being given to one significant figure more than the mean. For example, summary statistics for the sample mean and standard error for the data shown in Box 49.1 would be quoted as 4.95 ± 0.280 ($n = 21$).You can use such information to carry out a t-test between two sample means (Box 50.1); the SE is also useful because it allows calculation of confidence limits for the sample mean.

Definition

Confidence limits – the range within which the true value will fall. A 95% confidence limit (interval) suggests the true value will most likely fall in this range 95% of the time.

Describing the 'shape' of frequency distributions

Frequency distributions may differ in the following characteristics:

- number of peaks;
- skewness or asymmetry;
- kurtosis or pointedness.

The shape of a frequency distribution of a small sample is affected by chance variation and may not be a fair reflection of the underlying population frequency distribution: check this by comparing repeated samples from the same population or by increasing the sample size. If the original shape were due to random events, it should not appear consistently in repeated samples and should become less obvious as sample size increases.

Genuinely bimodal (two peaks) or polymodal (three or more peaks) distributions may result from the combination of two or more unimodal distributions, indicating that more than one underlying population is being sampled (Fig. 49.9). An example of a bimodal distribution is the height of adult humans (females and males combined).

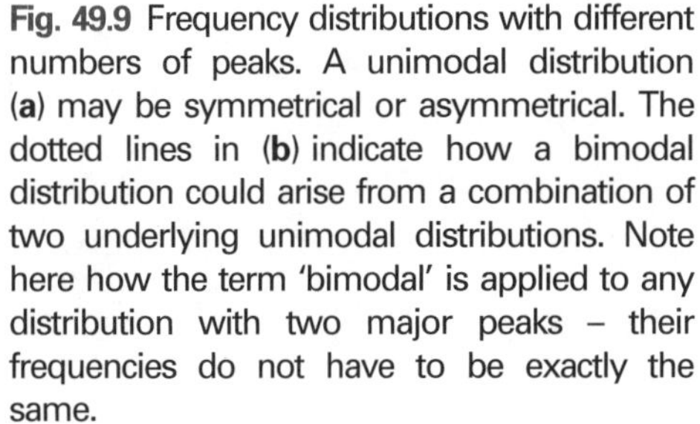

Fig. 49.9 Frequency distributions with different numbers of peaks. A unimodal distribution (**a**) may be symmetrical or asymmetrical. The dotted lines in (**b**) indicate how a bimodal distribution could arise from a combination of two underlying unimodal distributions. Note here how the term 'bimodal' is applied to any distribution with two major peaks – their frequencies do not have to be exactly the same.

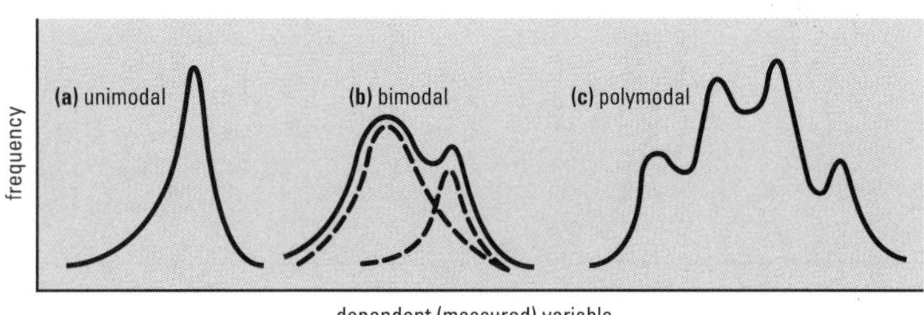

Source: Jones, A., Reed, R. and Weyers, J. (2007) p. 421.

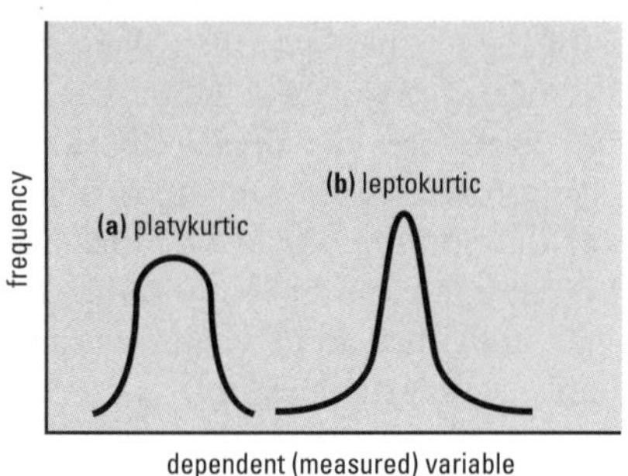

Fig. 49.10 Examples of the two types of kurtosis.

Source: Jones, A., Reed, R. and Weyers, J. (2007) p. 422.

A distribution is skewed if it is not symmetrical, a symptom being that the mean, median and mode are not equal (Fig. 49.3). Positive skewness is where the longer 'tail' of the distribution occurs for higher values of the measured variable; negative skewness is where the longer tail occurs for lower values. Some sport and exercise science examples of characteristics distributed in a skewed fashion are volumes expired air in $\dot{V}O_2max$ tests, insulin levels in human plasma and blood lactate values following sprint run tests.

Kurtosis is the name given to the 'pointedness' of a frequency distribution. A platykurtic frequency distribution is one with a flattened peak, while a leptokurtic frequency distribution is one with a pointed peak (Fig. 49.10). While descriptive terms can be used, based on visual observation of the shape and direction of skew, the degree of skewness and kurtosis can be quantified, and statistical tests exist to test the 'significance' of observed values (see Sokal and Rohlf, 1994), but the calculations required are complex and best done with the aid of a computer.

Using computers to calculate descriptive statistics

There are many specialist statistical packages (e.g. SPSS) that can be used to simplify the process of calculation of statistics. Note that correct interpretation of the output requires an understanding of the terminology used and the underlying process of calculation, and this may best be obtained by working through one or more examples by hand before using these tools. Spreadsheets offer increasingly sophisticated statistical analysis functions, some examples of which are provided in Box 49.3 for Microsoft Excel 2007.

The following functions could be used to extract descriptive statistics from this dataset:

Box 49.3 How to use a spreadsheet (Microsoft Excel 2007) to calculate descriptive statistics

Method 1: Using spreadsheet functions to generate the required statistics

Suppose you had obtained the following set of data, stored within an array (block of columns and rows) of cells (A2:L6) within a spreadsheet:

	A	B	C	D	E	F	G	H	I	J	K	L
1	**My data set**											
2	4	4	3	3	5	4	3	7	7	3	5	3
3	6	2	9	7	3	4	5	6	6	9	4	8
4	5	3	2	5	4	5	7	2	8	3	6	3
5	11	3	5	2	4	3	7	8	4	4	4	3
6	3	6	8	5	6	4	3	4	3	6	10	5

(continued)

Box 49.3 Continued

Descriptive statistic	Example of use of function[a,b]	Result for the above data set
Sample size n	=COUNT(A2:L6)	60
Mean	=AVERAGE(A2:L6)[c]	4.9
Median	=MEDIAN(A2:L6)	4.0
Mode	=MODE(A2:L6)	3
Upper quartile	=QUARTILE(A2:L6,3)[d]	6.0
Lower quartile	=QUARTILE(A2:L6,1)	3.0
Semi-interquartile range	=QUARTILE(A2:L6,3) – QUARTILE(A2:L6,1)	3.0
Upper extreme	=QUARTILE(A2:L6,4) *or* =MAX(A2:L6)	11
Lower extreme	=QUARTILE(A2:L6,0) *or* =MIN(A2:L6)	2
Range	=MAX(A2:L6) – MIN(A2:L6)[e]	9.0
Variance	=VAR(A2:L6)	4.464
Standard deviation	=STDEV(A2:L6)	2.113
Standard error	=STDEV(A2:L6)/(SQRT(COUNT(A2:L6)))[f]	0.273
Coefficient of variation	=100*STDEV(A2:L6)/AVERAGE(A2:L6)	43.12%

[a] Typically, in an appropriate cell, you would select the *Formulas* ribbon (tab) then > *Insert Function* > *COUNT*, then select the input range and press the return key.
[b] Other descriptive statistics can be calculated – these mirror those shown in Box 49.1, but for this specific dataset.
[c] There is no 'MEAN' function in Microsoft Excel.
[d] The first argument within the brackets relates to the array of data, the second relates to the quartile required (consult the *Help* feature for further information).
[e] There is no direct 'RANGE' function in Microsoft Excel.
[f] There is no direct individual 'STANDARD ERROR' function in Microsoft Excel. The SQRT function returns a square root and the COUNT function determines the number of filled data cells in the array.

Method 2: Using the *Data Analysis* option This can automatically generate a table of descriptive statistics for the data array selected, although the data must be presented as a single row or column. This option might need to be installed for your network or personal computer before it is available to you – consult the ***Help*** feature and search for ***Load the Analysis ToolPak*** to download the ***Data Analysis*** add-in that will then be found under the *Data* ribbon (tab). Having entered or rearranged your data into a row or column, the steps involved are as follows:

1. Select **Data** ribbon (tab) > *Data Analysis.*
2. From the *Data Analysis box,* select *Descriptive Statistics.*
3. Input your data location into the *Input Range* (left-click and hold down to highlight the column of data).
4. From the menu options, select *Summary Statistics* and *Confidence Level for Mean: 95%.*
5. When you click *OK* you should get a new worksheet, with descriptive statistics and confidence limits shown.

Table 49.1 Descriptive statistics for a dataset.

Column1[a,b]	
Mean	4.9
Standard error	0.27
Median	4.0
Mode	3
Standard deviation	2.113
Sample variance	4.464
Kurtosis	0.22
Skewness	0.86
Range	9.00
Minimum	2.0
Maximum	11.0
Sum	294
Count	60
Confidence level (95.0%)	0.55

[a] These descriptive statistics are specified (and are automatically presented in this order) – any others required can be generated using method 1.
[b] A more descriptive heading can be added if desired – this is the default.

(*continued*)

Box 49.3 Continued

Alternatively, at step 4, you can select an area of your current worksheet as a data output range (select an area away from any existing content as these cells would otherwise be overwritten by the descriptive statistics output table).

6. Change the format of the cells to show each number to an appropriate number of decimal places. You may also wish to make the columns wider so you can read their content.
7. For the dataset shown above, the final output table should look as shown in Table 49.1. (adjust column width so that you can read text).

Text references and sources for further study

Hopkins, W. (2008) *A New View of Statistics*. Available: http://www.sportsci.org/resource/stats/index.html
Last accessed: 23/12/10.

[Without a doubt the best website for sport and exercise science information, including common statistical tests used in sport and exercise science.]

Schmuller, J. (2005) *Statistical Analysis with Excel for Dummies*. Wiley, Hoboken, New Jersey.

Sokal, R.R. and Rohlf, F.J. (1994) *Biometry: The Principles and Practice of Statistics in Biological Research*. W.H. Freeman, San Francisco.

Vincent, W.J. (2005) *Statistics in Kinesiology*. Human Kinetics, Champaign, IL.

50 Choosing and using statistical tests

This chapter outlines the philosophy of hypothesis-testing statistics, indicates the steps to be taken when choosing a test, and discusses features and assumptions of some important tests. For details of the mechanics of tests, consult appropriate texts (e.g. Vincent, 2005; Schmuller, 2005). Most tests are now available in statistical packages for computers (see Chapters 11 and 12) and many in spreadsheets (Chapter 11).

To carry out a statistical test:

1. **Decide what it is you wish to test** (create a null hypothesis and its alternative).
2. **Determine whether your data fit a standard distribution pattern.**
3. **Select a test and apply it to your data.**

Setting up a null hypothesis

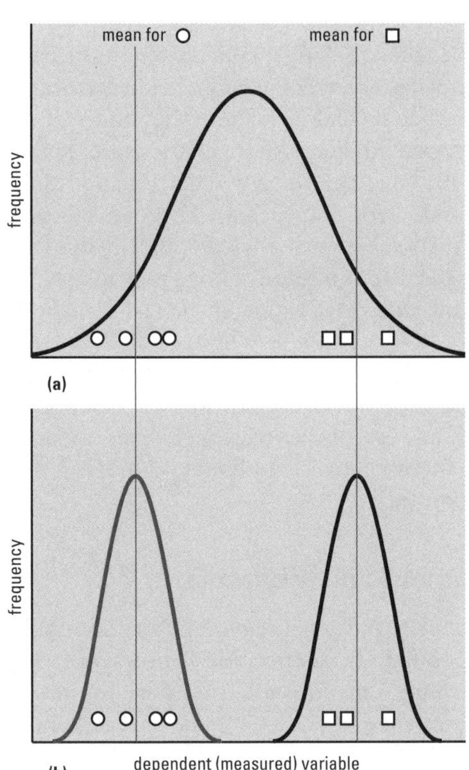

Fig. 50.1 Two explanations for the difference between two means. In case (**a**) the two samples happen by chance to have come from opposite ends of the same frequency distribution, i.e. there is no true difference between the samples. In case (**b**) the two samples come from different frequency distributions, i.e. there is a true difference between the samples. In both cases, the means of the two samples are the same.

Hypothesis-testing statistics are used to compare the properties of groups, either with other groups or with some theory about them or with respect to an intervention. For instance, you may be interested in whether measurements of the same variable in two different groups can be regarded as having different means, whether the outcomes of two training programmes are different or whether the relationship between two physical capacities is linear.

> **KEY POINT** You can't use statistics to *prove* any hypothesis, but they can be used to assess *how likely* it is to be wrong.

Statistical testing operates in what at first seems a rather perverse manner. Suppose you think a treatment has an effect. The theory you actually test is that it has no effect; the test tells you how improbable your data would be if this theory were true. This 'no effect' theory is the null hypothesis (NH). If your data are very improbable under the NH, then you may suppose it to be wrong, and this would support your original idea (the 'alternative hypothesis'). The concept can be illustrated by an example. Suppose two groups of subjects were treated in different ways, and you observed a difference in the mean value of the measured variable for the two groups. Can this be regarded as a 'true' difference? As Fig. 50.1 shows, it could have arisen in two ways:

- because of the way the subjects were allocated to treatments, i.e. all the subjects liable to have high values might, by chance, have been assigned to one group and those with low values to the other (Fig. 50.1a);
- because of a genuine effect of the treatments, i.e. each group came from a distinct frequency distribution (Fig. 50.1b).

A statistical test will indicate the probabilities of these options. The NH states that the two groups come from the same population (i.e. the treatment effects are negligible in the context of random variation). To test this, you calculate a test statistic from the data, and compare it with tabulated critical values giving the probability of obtaining the observed

Understanding 'degrees of freedom' – this depends on the number of values in the dataset analysed, and the method of calculation depends on the statistical test being used. It relates to the number of observations that are free to vary before the remaining quantities for a dataset can be determined.

Definition

Modulus – the absolute value of a number, e.g. modulus −3.385 = 3.385.

Quoting significance – the convention for quoting significance levels in text, tables and figures is as follows:

$P > 0.05$ = 'not significant' (or NS)
$P \leqslant 0.05$ = 'significant' (or *)
$P \leqslant 0.01$ = 'highly significant' (or **)
$P \leqslant 0.001$ = 'very highly significant' (or ***).

Thus, you might refer to a difference in means as being 'highly significant ($P \leqslant 0.01$)'. For this reason, the word 'significant' in its everyday meaning of 'important' or 'notable' should be used with care in scientific writing.

Choosing between parametric and non-parametric tests – always plot your data graphically when determining whether they are suitable for parametric tests as this may save a lot of unnecessary effort later.

or a more extreme result by chance (see Boxes 50.1 and 50.2). This probability is sometimes called the significance of the test.

Note that you must take into account the degrees of freedom (d.f.) when looking up critical values of most test statistics. The d.f. are related to the size(s) of the samples studied; formulae for calculating d.f. depend on the test being used. Sport and exercise scientists normally use two-tailed tests, i.e. we have no expectation beforehand that the treatment will have a positive or negative effect compared with the control (in a one-tailed test we expect one particular treatment to have a bigger effect than the other). Be sure to use critical values for the correct type of test.

By convention, the critical probability for rejecting the NH is 5 % (i.e. $P = 0.05$). This means we reject the NH if the observed result would have come up by chance a maximum of one time in twenty. If the modulus of the test statistic is less than or equal to the tabulated critical value for $P = 0.05$, then we accept the NH and the result is said to be 'not significant' (NS for short). If the modulus of the test statistic is greater than the tabulated value for $P = 0.05$, then we reject the NH in favour of the alternative hypothesis that the treatments had different effects and the result is 'statistically significant'.

Two types of error are possible when making a conclusion on the basis of a statistical test. The first occurs if you reject the NH when it is true and the second if you accept the NH when it is false. To limit the chance of the first type of error, choose a lower probability, e.g. $P = 0.01$, but note that the critical value of the test statistic increases when you do this and results in the probability of the second error increasing. The conventional significance levels given in statistical tables (usually 0.05, 0.01, 0.001) are arbitrary. Increasing use of statistical computer programs now allows the actual probability of obtaining the calculated value of the test statistic to be quoted (e.g. $P = 0.037$).

Note that if the NH is rejected, this does not tell you which of many alternative explanations is true. Also, it is important to distinguish between statistical significance and scientific relevance: identifying a statistically significant difference between two samples does not mean that this will carry any scientific importance.

Comparing data with parametric distributions

A parametric test is one that makes particular assumptions about the mathematical nature of the population distribution from which the samples were taken. If these assumptions are not true, then the test is obviously invalid, even though it might give the answer we expect. A non-parametric test does not assume that the data fit a particular pattern, but it may assume some things about the distributions. Used in appropriate circumstances, parametric tests are better able to distinguish between true but marginal differences between samples than their non-parametric equivalents (i.e. they have greater 'power').

The distribution pattern of a set of data values may be scientifically relevant, but it is also of practical importance because it defines the type of statistical tests that can be used. The properties of the main distribution types found in sport and exercise science are given below with both rules of thumb and more rigorous tests for deciding whether data fit these distributions.

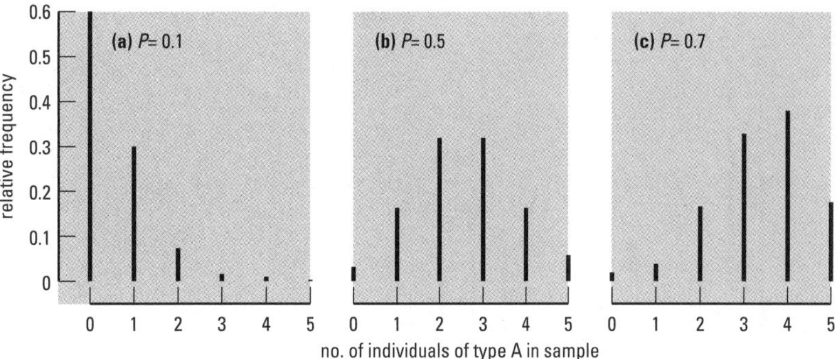

Fig. 50.2 Examples of binomial frequency distributions with different probabilities. The distributions show the expected frequency of obtaining *n* individuals of type A in a sample of 5. Here *P* is the probability of an individual being type A rather than type B.

Binomial distributions

These apply to samples of any size from populations in which data values occur independently in only two mutually exclusive classes (e.g. type I or II). They describe the probability of finding the different possible combinations of the attribute for a specified sample size k (e.g. out of 100 muscle fibres, 60 are type I). If p is the probability of the attribute being type I and q the probability of it being type II, then the expected mean sample number of type A is kp and the standard deviation is $\sqrt{kpq}$. Expected frequencies can be calculated using mathematical expressions (see Chapter 49). Examples of the shapes of some binomial distributions are shown in Fig. 50.2. Note that they are symmetrical in shape for the special case $p = q = 0.5$, and that the greater the disparity between p and q, the more skewed the distribution.

Some exercise science examples of data likely to be distributed in binomial fashion are: muscle fibre distribution (e.g. type I or II); whether an athlete is male or female or; whether a team has won or lost. To establish whether a set of data is distributed in binomial fashion, calculate expected frequencies from probability values obtained from theory or observation, then test against observed frequencies using a χ^2 test or a *G*-test.

Tendency towards the normal distribution – under certain conditions, binomial and Poisson distributions can be treated as normally distributed:

- where samples from a binomial distribution are large (i.e. > 15) and p and q are close to 0.5;
- for Poisson distributions, if the number of counts recorded in each outcome is greater than about 15.

Poisson distributions

These apply to discrete characteristics that can assume low whole-number values, such as the number of goals in a football match, time or the number exercise repetitions in a specified time. The events should be 'rare' in that the mean number observed should be a small proportion of the total that could possibly be found. The shape of a Poisson distribution is described by only one parameter, the mean number of events observed, and has the special characteristic that the variance is equal to the mean. The shape has a pronounced positive skewness at low mean counts, but becomes more and more symmetrical as the mean number of counts increases (Fig. 50.3).

To decide whether data follow a Poisson distribution:

- use the rule of thumb that if the coefficient of dispersion is ≈ 1, the distribution is likely to be Poisson;
- calculate 'expected' frequencies from the equation for the Poisson distribution and compare with actual values using a X^2 test or a *G*-test.

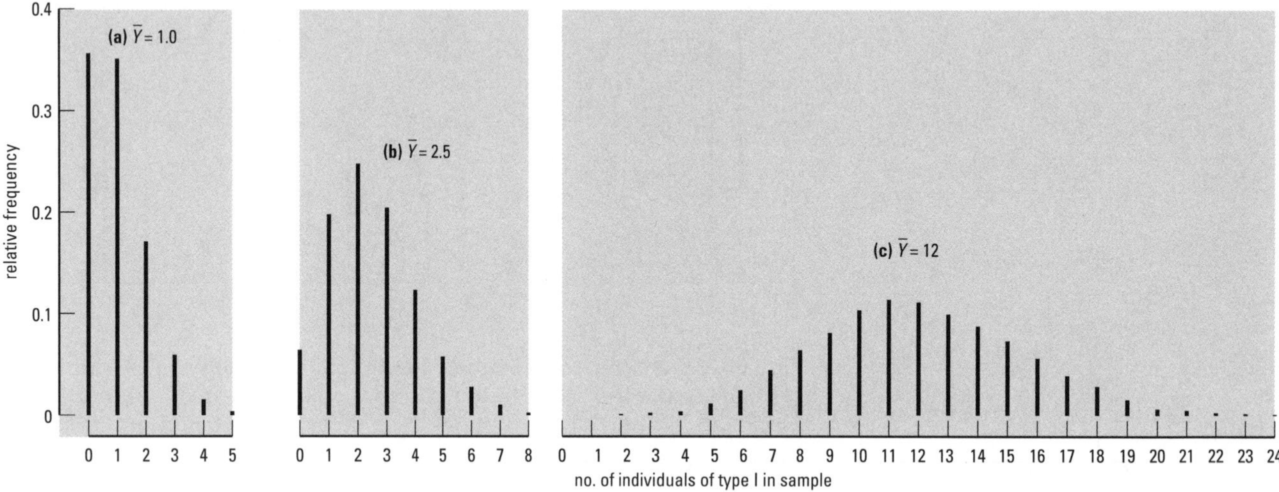

Fig. 50.3 Examples of Poisson frequency distributions differing in mean. The distributions are shown as line charts because the independent variable (events per sample) is discrete.
Source: Jones, A., Reed, R. and Weyers, J. (2007) p. 429.

Definition

Coefficient of dispersion $= s^2/\bar{Y}$. This is an alternative measure of dispersion to the coefficient of variation (p. 384).

It is sometimes of interest to show that data are *not* distributed in a Poisson fashion, e.g. the distribution of age in team selection. If $s^2/\overline{Y} > 1$, the data are 'clumped' and occur together more than would be expected by chance; if $s^2/\overline{Y} < 1$, the data are 'repulsed' and occur together less frequently than would be expected by chance.

Normal distributions (Gaussian distributions)

These occur when random events act to produce variability in a continuous characteristic (quantitative variable). This situation occurs frequently in exercise science, so normal distributions are very useful and much used. The bell-like shape of normal distributions is specified by the population mean and standard deviation (Fig. 50.4): it is symmetrical and configured so that 68.27% of the data will lie within ±1 standard deviation of the mean, 95.45% within ±2 standard deviations of the mean, and 99.73% within ±3 standard deviations of the mean

Some exercise science examples of data likely to be distributed in a normal fashion include: body mass, physiological characteristics (i.e. $\dot{V}O_2$max, peak power) and physical performance (i.e. sprint speed, vertical jump). To check whether data are normally distributed, you can:

- Use the rule of thumb that the distribution should be symmetrical and that nearly all the data should fall within $\pm 3s$ of the mean and about two-thirds within $\pm 1s$ of the mean.
- Plot the distribution on normal probability graph paper. If the distribution is normal, the data will tend to follow a straight line (Fig. 50.5). Deviations from linearity reveal skewness and/or kurtosis (p. 386), the significance of which can be tested statistically (pp. 386–388).
- Use a suitable statistical computer program to generate predicted normal curves from the $\overline{Y}$ and s values of your sample(s). These can be compared visually with the actual distribution of data and can be used to give 'expected' values for a χ^2 test or a G-test.

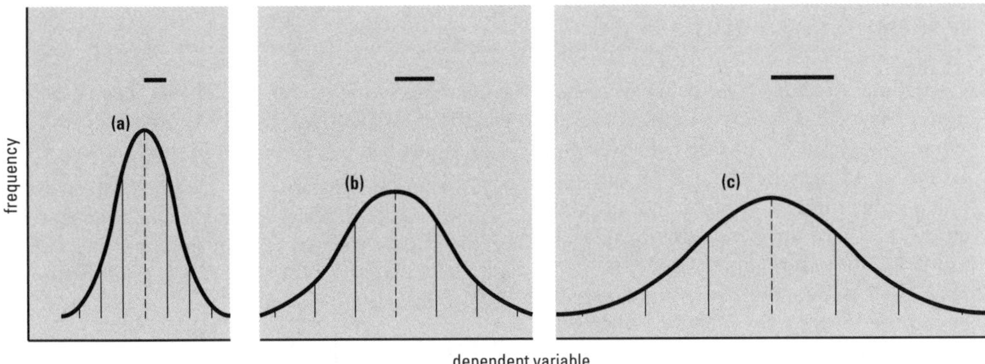

Fig. 50.4 Examples of normal frequency distributions differing in mean and standard deviation. The horizontal bars represent population standard deviations for the curves, increasing from (**a**) to (**c**). Vertical dashed lines are population means, while vertical solid lines show positions of values ±1, 2 and 3 standard deviations from the means.

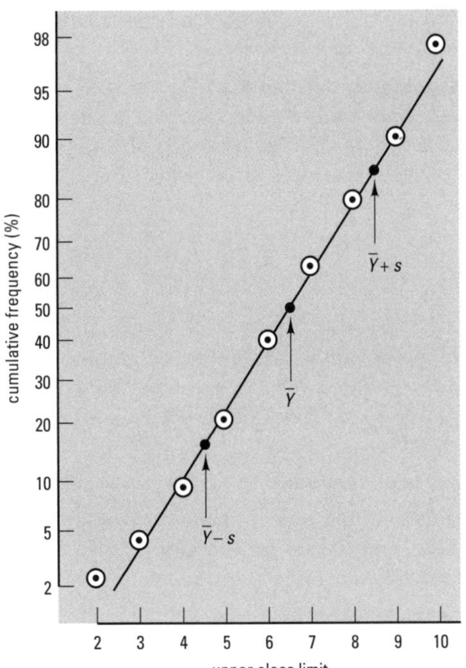

Fig. 50.5 Example of a normal probability plot. The plotted points are from a small dataset where the mean $\overline{Y} = 6.93$ and the standard deviation $s = 1.895$. Note that values corresponding to 0 % and 100 % cumulative frequency cannot be used. The straight line is that predicted for a normal distribution with $\overline{Y} = 6.93$ and $s = 1.895$. This is plotted by calculating the expected positions of points for $\overline{Y} \pm s$. Since 68.3% of the distribution falls within these bounds, the relevant points on the cumulative frequency scale are 50 ± 34.15 %; thus this line was drawn using the points (4.495, 15.85) and (8.285, 84.15) as indicated on the plot.

The wide availability of tests based on the normal distribution and their relative simplicity means that you may wish to transform your data to make them more like a normal distribution. Table 50.1 provides transformations that can be applied. The transformed data should be tested for normality as described above before proceeding – don not forget that you may need to check that transformed variances are homogenous for certain tests (see below). A very important theorem in statistics, the central limit theorem, states that as sample size increases, the distribution of a series of means from a frequency distribution will become normally distributed. This fact can be used to devise an experiment or sampling strategy that ensures data are normally distributed, i.e. using means of samples as if they were primary data.

Choosing a suitable statistical test

Comparing location (e.g. means)

If you can assume that your data are normally distributed, the main test for comparing two means from independent samples is Student's *t*-test (see Boxes 50.1 and 50.2, and Table 50.2). This assumes that the variances of the data sets are homogeneous. Tests based on the *t* distribution are also available for comparing means of paired data or for comparing a sample mean with a chosen value.

Table 50.1 Suggested transformations altering different types of frequency distributions to the normal type. To use, modify data by the formula shown; then examine effects with the tests described on pp. 394–95.

Type of data; distribution suspected	Suggested transformation(s)
Proportions (including percentages); binomial	arcsine $\sqrt{x}$ (also called the angular transformation)
Scores; Poisson	$\sqrt{x}$ or $\sqrt{(x + 1/2)}$ if zero values present
Measurements; negatively skewed	x^2, x^3, x^4, etc. (in order of increasing strength)
Measurements; positively skewed	$1/\sqrt{x}$, $\sqrt{x}$, ln x, $1/x$ (in order of increasing strength)

Box 50.1 How to carry out a *t*-test

The *t*-test was devised by a statistician who used the pen name 'Student', so you may see it referred to as Student's *t*-test. It is used when you wish to decide whether two samples come from the same population or from different ones (Fig. 50.1). The samples might have been obtained by selective observation or by applying two different treatments to an originally homogeneous population.

The null hypothesis (NH) is that the two groups can be represented as samples from the same overlying population (Fig. 50.1a). If, as a result of the test, you accept this hypothesis, you can say that there is no significant difference between the group means.

The alternative hypothesis is that the two groups come from different populations (Fig. 50.1b). By rejecting the NH as a result of the test, you can accept the alternative hypothesis and say that there is a significant difference between the sample means, or, if an experiment were carried out, that the two treatments affected the samples differently.

How can you decide between these two hypotheses? On the basis of certain assumptions (see below), and some relatively simple calculations, you can work out the probability that the samples came from the same population. If this probability is very low, then you can reasonably reject the NH in favour of the alternative hypothesis, and if it is high, you will accept the NH.

To find out the probability that the observed difference between sample means arose by chance, you must first calculate a '*t* value' for the two samples in question. Some computer programs (e.g. Minitab) provide this probability as part of the output, otherwise you can look up statistical tables (e.g. Table 50.2). These tables show 'critical values' – the borders between probability levels. If your value of *t* equals or exceeds the critical value for probability *P*, you can reject the NH at this probability ('level of significance').

Note that:

- for a given difference in the means of the two samples, the value of *t* will become larger as the scatter within each dataset becomes smaller;
- for a given scatter of the data, the value of *t* will become larger as the difference between the means becomes greater.

So, at what probability should you reject the NH? Normally, the threshold is arbitrarily set at 5 % – you quite often see descriptions like 'the sample means were significantly different ($P < 0.05$)'. At this 'significance level' there is still up to a 5 % chance of the *t* value arising by chance, so about one in twenty times, on average, the conclusion will be wrong. If *P* turns out to be lower, then this kind of error is much less likely.

Tabulated probability levels are generally given for 5, 1 and 0.1 % significance levels (Table 50.2). Note that this table is designed for 'two-tailed' tests, i.e. where the treatment or sampling strategy could have resulted in either an increase or a decrease in the measured values. These are the most likely situations you will deal with in sport and exercise science.

Examine Table 50.2 and note the following:

- The larger the size of the samples (i.e. the greater the 'degrees of freedom'), the smaller *t* needs to be to exceed the critical value at a given significance level.
- The lower the probability, the greater *t* needs to be to exceed the critical value.

The mechanics of the test

A calculator that can work out means and standard deviations is helpful.

1. **Work out the sample means $\overline{Y}_1$ and $\overline{Y}_2$ and calculate the difference between them.**
2. **Work out the sample standard deviations s_1 and s_2.** (NOTE if your calculator offers a choice, choose the '$n - 1$' option for calculating *s* – see p. 384).
3. **Work out the sample standard errors $SE_1 = s_1/\sqrt{n_1}$ and $SE_2 = s_2/\sqrt{n_2}$; now square each, add the squares together, then take the positive square root of this** (n_1 and n_2 are the respective sample sizes, which may, or may not, be equal).
4. **Calculate *t*** from the formula:
$$t = \frac{\overline{Y}_1 - \overline{Y}_2}{\sqrt{((SE_1)^2) + ((SE_2)^2)}} \qquad (50.1)$$
The value of *t* can be negative or positive, depending on the values of the means; this does not matter and you should compare the modulus (absolute value) of *t* with the values in tables.
5. **Work out the degrees of freedom** $= (n_1 - 1) + (n_2 - 1)$.
6. **Compare the *t* value with the appropriate critical value (see e.g. Table 50.2) and decide on the significance of your findings (see p. 395).**

Box 50.2 provides a worked example – use this to check that you understand the above procedures.

Assumptions that must be met before using the test

The most important assumptions are:

- The two samples are independent and randomly drawn (or, if not, drawn in a way that does not create bias). The test assumes that the samples are quite large.
- The underlying distribution of each sample is normal. This can be tested with a special statistical test, but a rule of thumb is that a frequency distribution of the data should be (a) symmetrical about the mean and (b) nearly all of the data should be within 3 standard deviations of the mean and about two-thirds within 1 standard deviation of the mean (see p. 383).
- The two samples should have uniform variances. This again can be tested (by an *F*-test), but may be obvious from inspection of the two standard deviations.

Box 50.2 Worked example of a *t*-test

Suppose the following data were obtained in an experiment (the units are not relevant):

Control: 6.6, 5.5, 6.8, 5.8, 6.1, 5.9
Treatment: 6.3, 7.2, 6.5, 7.1, 7.5, 7.3

Using the steps outlined in Box 50.1, the following values are obtained (denoting control with subscript 1, treatment with subscript 2):

1. $\bar{Y}_1 = 6.1167$; $\bar{Y}_2 = 6.9833$: difference between means $= \bar{Y}_1 - \bar{Y}_2 = -0.8666$
2. $s_1 = 0.49565$; $s_2 = 0.47504$
3. $SE_1 = 0.49565/2.44949 = 0.202348$

   $SE_2 = 0.47504/2.44949 = 0.193934$
4. $t = \dfrac{-0.8666}{\sqrt{(0.202348^2 + 0.193934^2)}} = \dfrac{-0.8666}{0.280277} = -3.09$
5. d.f. $= (5 + 5) = 10$
6. Looking at Table 50.2, we see that the modulus of this t value exceeds the tabulated value for $P = 0.05$ at 10 degrees of freedom ($= 2.23$). We therefore reject the NH, and conclude that the means are different at the 5 % level of significance. If the modulus of t had been $\leqslant 2.23$, we would have accepted the NH. If the modulus of t had been > 3.17, we could have concluded that the means are different at the 1 % level of significance.

Definition

Homogeneous variance – uniform (but not necessarily identical) variance of the dependent variable across the range of the independent variable. The term homoscedastic is also used in this sense. The opposite of homogeneous is heterogeneous (= heteroscedastic).

When comparing means of two or more samples, analysis of variance (ANOVA) is a very useful technique. This method also assumes that data are normally distributed and that the variances of the samples are homogeneous. The samples must also be independent (e.g. not subsamples). The test statistic calculated is denoted F and has two different degrees of freedom related to the number of means tested and the pooled number of replicates per mean. The nested types of ANOVA are useful to let you know the relative importance of different sources of variability in your data. Two-way and multi-way ANOVAs are useful for studying interactions between treatments.

Table 50.2 Critical values of Student's t statistic (for two-tailed tests). Reject the null hypothesis at probability P if your calculated t value equals or exceeds the value shown for the appropriate degrees of freedom $= (n_1 - 1) + (n_2 - 1)$.

Degrees of freedom	Critical values for $P = 0.05$	Critical values for $P = 0.01$	Critical values for $P = 0.001$
1	12.71	63.66	636.62
2	4.30	9.92	31.60
3	3.18	5.84	12.94
4	2.78	4.60	8.61
5	2.57	4.03	6.86
6	2.45	3.71	5.96
7	2.36	3.50	5.40
8	2.31	3.36	5.04
9	2.26	3.25	4.78
10	2.23	3.17	4.59
12	2.18	3.06	4.32
14	2.14	2.98	4.14
16	2.12	2.92	4.02
20	2.09	2.85	3.85
25	2.06	2.79	3.72
30	2.04	2.75	3.65
40	2.02	2.70	3.55
60	2.00	2.66	3.46
120	1.98	2.62	3.37
∞	1.96	2.58	3.29

For data satisfying the ANOVA requirements, the least significant difference (LSD) is useful for making planned comparisons among several means. Any two means that differ by more than the LSD will be significantly different. The LSD is useful for showing on graphs.

The chief non-parametric tests for comparing the locations of two samples are the Mann–Whitney *U*-test and the Kolmogorov–Smirnov test. The former assumes that the frequency distributions of the samples are similar, whereas the latter makes no such assumption. In both cases the sample's size must be $\geqslant 4$ and for the Kolmogorov–Smirnov test the samples must have equal sizes. In the Kolmogorov–Smirnov test, significant differences found with the test could be caused by differences in location or shape of the distribution, or both.

Checking the assumptions of a test – always acquaint yourself with the assumptions of a test. If necessary, test them before using the test.

Suitable non-parametric comparisons of location for paired data (sample size $\geqslant 6$) include Wilcoxon's signed rank test, which is used for quantitative data and assumes that the distributions have similar shape. Dixon and Mood's sign test can be used for paired data scores where one variable is recorded as 'greater than' or 'better than' the other.

Non-parametric comparisons of location for three or more samples include the Kruskal–Wallis *H*-test. Here, the number of samples is without limit and they can be unequal in size, but again the underlying distributions are assumed to be similar. The Friedman *S*-test operates with a maximum of five samples and data must conform to a randomised block design. The underlying distributions of the samples are assumed to be similar.

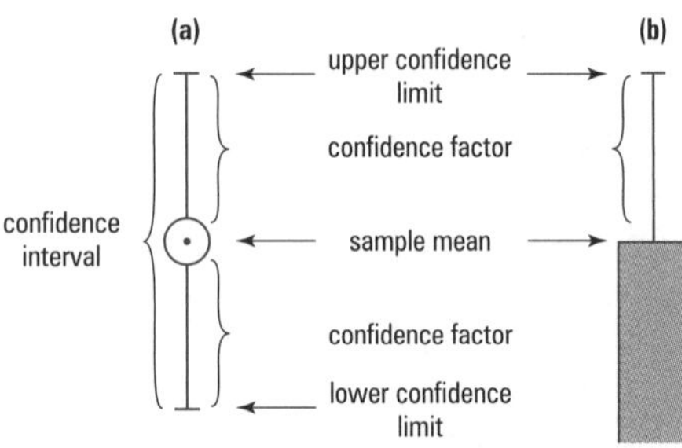

Fig. 50.6 Graphical representation of confidence limits as 'error bars' for (**a**) a sample mean in a plotted curve, where both upper and lower limits are shown; and (**b**) a sample mean in a histogram, where, by convention, only the upper value is shown. For data that are assumed to be symmetrically distributed, such representations are often used in preference to the 'box-and-whisker' plot shown on p. 383. Note that SE is an alternative way of representing sample imprecision/error (e.g. Fig. 49.8).

Comparing dispersions (e.g. variances)

If you wish to compare the variances of two sets of data that are normally distributed, use the *F*-test. For comparing more than two samples, it may be sufficient to use the F_{max}-test, on the highest and lowest variances. The Scheffé–Box (log-anova) test is recommended for testing the significance of differences between several variances. Non-parametric tests exist but are not widely available: you may need to transform the data and use a test based on the normal distribution.

Determining whether frequency observations fit theoretical expectation

The χ^2 test is useful for tests of 'goodness of fit', e.g. comparing expected and observed progeny frequencies in genetics experiments or comparing observed frequency distributions with some theoretical function. One limitation is that simple formulae for calculating χ^2 assume that no expected number is less than 5. The *G*-test (2*I*-test) is used in similar circumstances.

Comparing proportion data

When comparing proportions between two small groups (e.g. whether 3/10 is significantly different from 5/10), you can use probability tables such as those of Finney *et al.* (1963) or calculate probabilities from formulae; however, this can be tedious for large sample sizes. Certain proportions can be transformed so that their distribution becomes normal.

Confidence limits for statistics other than the mean – consult an advanced statistical text if you wish to indicate the reliability of estimates of, for example, population variances.

Placing confidence limits on an estimate of a population parameter

On many occasions, a sample statistic is used to provide an estimate of a population parameter, and it is often useful to indicate the reliability of

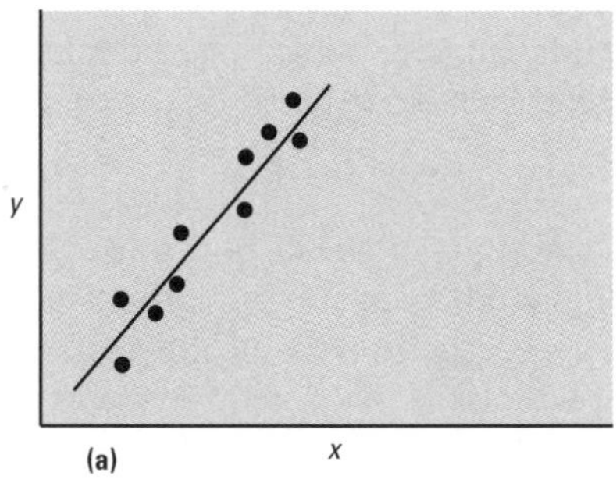

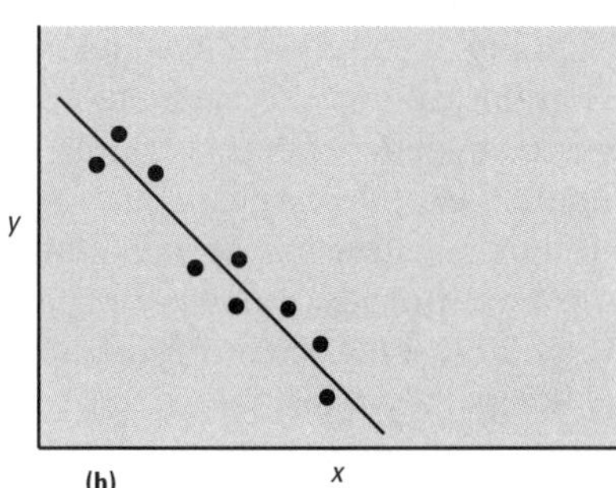

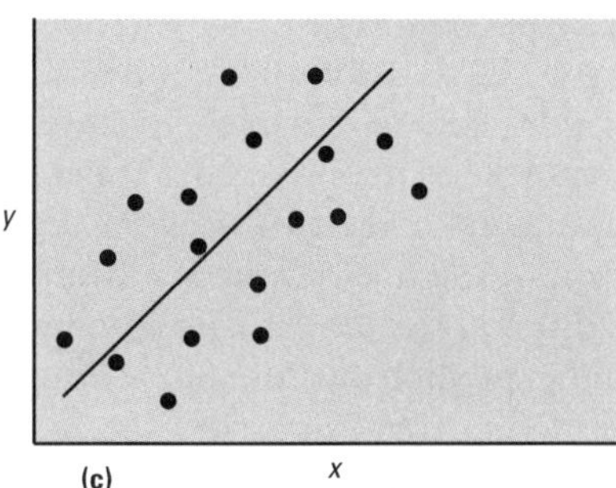

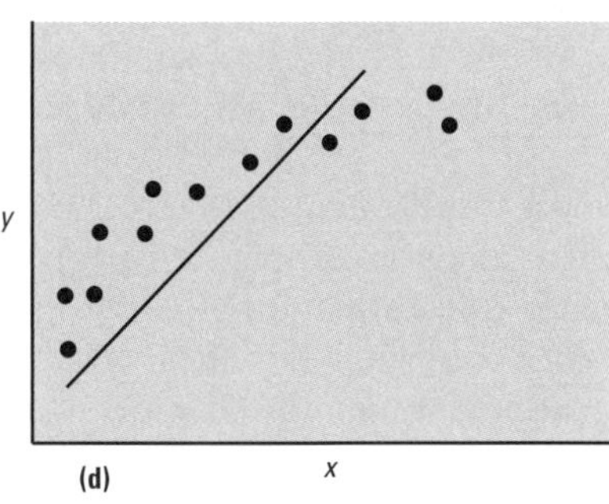

Fig. 50.7 Examples of correlation. The linear regression line is shown. In (**a**) and (**b**), the correlation between x and y is good: for (**a**) there is a positive correlation and the correlation coefficient, r, would be close to 1; for (**b**) there is a negative correlation and the correlation coefficient would be close to −1. In (**c**) there is a weak positive correlation and r would be close to 0. In (**d**) the correlation coefficient may be quite large, but the choice of linear regression is clearly inappropriate.

such an estimate. This can be done by putting confidence limits on the sample statistic, i.e. by specifying an interval around the statistic within which you are confident that the true value (the population parameter) is likely to fall, at a specified level of probability. The most common application is to place confidence limits on the mean of a sample taken from a population of normally distributed data values. In practice, you determine a confidence factor for a particular level of probability that is added to and subtracted from the sample mean ($\bar{Y}$) to give the upper confidence limit and lower confidence limit respectively. These are calculated as:

$$\begin{aligned} &\bar{Y} + (t_{P[n-1]} \times \text{SE}) \text{ for the upper limit and} \\ &\bar{Y} - (t_{P[n-1]} \times \text{SE}) \text{ for the lower limit} \end{aligned} \qquad (50.2)$$

where $t_{P[n-1]}$ is the tabulated critical value of Student's t statistic for a two-tailed test with $n - 1$ degrees of freedom at a specified probability level (P) and SE is the standard error of the sample mean (p. 384). The 95 % confidence limits (i.e. $P = 0.05$) tells you that, on average, 95 times out of 100 the interval between the upper and lower limits will contain the true (population) value. Confidence limits are often shown as 'error bars' for individual sample means plotted in graphical form. Fig. 50.6 illustrates how this is applied to plotted curves and histograms (note that this can be carried out for data series within a Microsoft Excel graph (chart) using the *Format data series* and *Y error bars* commands).

Correlation and regression

These methods are used when testing the relationship between data values for two variables. Correlation is used to measure the extent to which changes in the two sets of data values occur together in a linear manner. If one variable can be assumed to be dependent upon the other (i.e. a change in X causes a particular change in Y), then regression techniques can be used to provide a mathematical description of the underlying relationship between the variables, e.g. to find a line of best fit for a data series. If there is no a priori reason to assume dependency, then correlation methods alone are appropriate.

A correlation coefficient measures the strength of the linear relationship between two variables, but does not describe the relationship. The coefficient is expressed as a number between −1 and +1: a positive coefficient indicates a direct relationship, where the two variables change in the same direction, while a negative coefficient indicates an inverse relationship, where one variable decreases as the other increases (Fig. 50.7). The nearer the coefficient is to −1 or +1, the stronger the linear relationship between the variables, i.e. the less 'scatter' there would be about a straight line of best fit (note that this does *not* imply that one variable is dependent upon the other). A coefficient of 0 implies that the two variables show no linear association and therefore the closer the correlation coefficient is to zero, the weaker the linear relationship. The importance of graphing data is shown by the case illustrated in Fig. 50.7d.

Pearson's product moment correlation coefficient (r) is the most commonly used statistic for testing correlations. The test is valid only if both variables are normally distributed. Statistical tests can be used to decide whether the correlation is significant (e.g. using a one-sample t-test to see whether r is significantly different from zero, based on the equation:

$$t = r \div \sqrt{[(1 - r^2) \div (n - 2)]} \text{ at } n - 2 \text{ degrees of freedom,} \qquad (50.3)$$

where n is the number of paired observations. If one or both variables are not normally distributed, then you should calculate an alternative non-parametric coeffcient, e.g. Spearman's coefficient of rank correlation (r_s) or Kendall's coefficient of rank correlation (τ). These require the two sets of data to be ranked separately, and the calculation can be complex if there are tied (equal) ranks. Spearman's coefficient is said to be better if there is any uncertainty about the reliability of closely ranked data values.

If underlying theory or empirical graphical analysis indicate a linear relationship between a dependent and an independent variable, then linear regression can be used to estimate the mathematical equation that links the two variables. Model I linear regression is the standard approach, and is available within general purpose software programs such as Microsoft Excel (Box 50.3), and on some scientific calculators. It is suitable for experiments where a dependent variable Y varies with an *error-free* independent variable X in accordance with the relationship $Y = a + bX + e_Y$, where e_Y represents the residual (error) variability in the Y variable. For example, this relationship might apply in a laboratory procedure where you have carefully controlled the independent variable and the X values can be assumed to have zero error (e.g. in a time course experiment where measurements are made at exact time points). The regression analysis gives estimates for a and b (equivalent to the slope and intercept of the line of best fit): computer-based programs usually provide additional features, e.g. residual values for Y (e_Y), estimated errors for a and b, predicted values of Y along with graphical plots of the line of best fit (the trend line) and the residual values. In order for the model to be valid, the residual (error) values should be normally distributed around the trend line and their variance should be uniform (homogeneous), i.e. there should be a similar scatter of data points around the trend line along the x axis (independent variable).

Using more advanced types of regression – these include:

- model II linear regression, which applies to situations where a dependent variable Y varies with an independent variable X, and where both variables may have error terms associated with them:
- multiple regression, which applies when there is a relationship between a dependent variable and two or more independent variables;
- non-linear regression, which extends the principles of linear regression to a wide range of functions. Technically, this method is more appropriate than transforming data to allow linear regression.

Advanced statistics books should be consulted for details of these methods, which may be offered by some statistical computer programs.

If the relationship is not linear, try a transformation (see p. 393). For example, this is commonly done in analysis of physiological data. However, you should be aware that the transformation of data to give a straight line can lead to errors when carrying out linear regression analysis: take care to ensure that (a) the assumptions listed in the previous paragraph are valid for the transformed dataset and (b) the data points are evenly distributed throughout the range of the independent variable. If these criteria cannot be met, non-linear regression may be a better approach, but for this you will require a suitable computer program, e.g. GraphPad Prism.

The strength of the relationship between Y and X in Model I linear regression is best estimated by the coefficient of determination (r^2 or R^2), which is equivalent to the square of the Pearson correlation coefficient. The coefficient of determination varies between 0 and +1 and provides a measure of the goodness of fit of the Y data to the regression line: the closer the value is to 1, the better the fit. In effect, r^2 represents the fraction of the variance in Y that can be accounted for by the regression equation. Conversely, if you subtract this value from 1, you will obtain the residual (error) component, i.e. the fraction of the variance in Y that cannot be

Example If a regression analysis gives a value for r^2 of 0.75 (i.e. $r = 0.84$), then 75 % of the variance in Y can be explained by the trend line, with $1 - r^2 = 0.25$ (25 %) remaining as unexplained (residual) variation.

Box 50.3 Using a spreadsheet (Microsoft Excel 2007) to calculate hypothesis-testing statistics

Presented below are three examples of the use of Microsoft Excel to investigate hypotheses about specific datasets. In each case, there is a brief description of the problem, a table showing the data analysed and an outline of the Microsoft Excel commands used to carry out the analysis and an annotated table of results from the spreadsheet.

Example 1: a *t*-test

As part of a project, a student examined the effects of caffeine loading on sprint performance in eight semi-professional football players. Each subject performed a 20 m sprint both in placebo and caffeine conditions on separate occasions. The student reported the following data:

20 m sprint speed (s)

Group	1	2	3	4	5	6	7	8	Mean	Variance
Placebo	3.46	3.49	3.63	4.04	3.48	3.66	3.72	3.50	3.62	0.04
Caffeine	3.34	3.25	3.52	3.94	3.40	3.60	3.60	3.45	3.51	0.04

The student proposed the null hypothesis that there was no difference between the two means and tested this using a *t*-test, as she had evidence from other studies. She had also established that the assumption that the populations had homogenous variances was likely to be valid. Using the *Data* ribbon (tab), then selecting *Data Analysis* > *t-Test:Two-Sample Assuming Equal Variance* option with *Hypothesized Mean Difference* = 0 and *Alpha* (=*P*) = 0.05, the following table was obtained:

t-test: two-sample assuming equal variances

	Variable 1	Variable 2
Mean	3.6225	3.5125
Variance	0.037793	0.044764
Observations	8	8
Pooled variance	0.041279	
Hypothesised mean difference	0	
d.f.	14	
t stat	1.08283	
P(T <= t) one-tail	0.148591	
t Critical one-tail	1.76131	
P(T <= t) two-tail	0.297182	
t Critical two-tail	2.144787	

The value of *t* obtained was −1.08283 (row 7, 't stat') and the probability of obtaining this value for the two-tailed test (row 10) was 0.297 (or 29.7%), so the student was able to accept the null hypothesis and conclude that caffeine loading has no effect on sprint performance in this group.

Example 2: an ANOVA test

An exercise scientist measured the blood glucose concentrations in six athletes after consuming four different sports drinks, and obtained the following data:

Blood glucose concentrations (mmol L^{-1})

	Athlete							
Sports drink	1	2	3	4	5	6	Mean	Variance
A	6.8	6.7	6.8	6.1	6.7	5.9	6.5	0.16
B	6.5	6.9	6.6	6.5	6.4	6.7	6.6	0.03
C	7	7.2	7.2	6.9	7	6.9	7.0	0.02
D	6.6	6.4	5.3	6.5	6.3	7.1	6.4	0.35

The exercise scientist wanted to know whether the observed differences were statistically significant, so he carried out an ANOVA test, assuming that the variances across speeds were not homogenous. Using the *Data* ribbon (tab) > *Data Analysis* > *ANOVA Single Factor,* with *Alpha* (=*P*) = 0.05, the following table was obtained:

ANOVA: single factor

SUMMARY

Groups	Count	Sum	Average	Variance
Row 1	6	39	6.5	0.156
Row 2	6	39.6	6.6	0.032
Row 3	6	42.2	7.033333	0.018667
Row 4	6	38.2	6.366667	0.350667

ANOVA

Source of Variation	SS	d.f.	MS	*F*	*P value*	F_{crit}
Between groups	1.498333	3	0.499444	3.58453	0.031947	3.098391
Within groups	2.786667	20	0.139333			
Total	4.285	23				

The *F* value calculated was 3.58453. This comfortably exceeds the stated critical value (F_{crit}) of 3.098391, and the probability of obtaining this result by chance (*P* value) was calculated as 0.031947 (3.20 %, to three significant figures); hence the scientist was able to reject the null hypothesis and conclude that there was a significant difference in average blood glucose concentration between the group who consumed the four sports drinks, since $P < 0.05$. Such a finding might lead on to an investigation into why there was a difference in blood glucose responses, e.g. was this due to the different sugars contained in each sports drink?

(continued)

Box 50.3 Continued

Example 3: testing the significance of a correlation

A researcher wanted to know whether the heart rate responses of a cyclist were related to their power output across a range of intensities. She collected the following data:

Observation	Power output (W)	Heart rate (b min^{-1})
1	50	98
2	75	110
3	100	125
4	125	139
5	150	153
6	175	166
8	200	177
9	225	189
10	250	202

The exercise scientist used the Microsoft Excel function *PEARSON(array1,array2)* to obtain a value of +0.999233 for Pearson's product moment correlation coefficient *r*, specifying the heart rate as array1 and power output as array2. She then used a spreadsheet to calculate the *t* statistic (p. 399) for this *r* value, using equation 50.1. The value of *t* was 204.14, with 8 degrees of freedom. The critical value from tables (e.g. Table 50.2) at $P = 0.001$ is 5.04, so she concluded that there was a very highly significant positive correlation between the two datasets.

explained by the line of best fit. Multiplying the values by 100 allows you to express these fractions in percentage terms.

Using computers to calculate hypothesis-testing statistics

As with the calculation of descriptive statistics (Chapter 49), specialist statistical packages such as SPSS can be used to simplify the calculation of hypothesis-testing statistics. The correct use of the software and interpretation of the output requires an understanding of relevant terminology and of the fundamental principles governing the test, which is probably best obtained by working through one or more examples by hand before using these tools (e.g. Box 50.2). Spreadsheets offer increasingly sophisticated statistical analysis functions, three examples of which are provided in Box 50.3.

Text reference

Finney, D.J., Latscha, R., Bennet, B.M. and Hsu, P. (1963) *Tables for Testing Significance in a 2 × 2 Table*. Cambridge University Press, Cambridge.

Sources for further study

Schmuller, J. (2005) *Statistical Analysis with Excel for Dummies*. Wiley, Hoboken, New Jersey.

Vincent, W.J. (2005) *Statistics in Kinesiology*. Human Kinetics, Champaign, IL.

Using statistical software packages – these do not suit all needs for sport and exercise scientists – Microsoft Excel is an excellent program to analyse data with several prepared spreadsheets also available for download from websites such as www.sportsci.org.

Sport and exercise science has traditionally taken the approach of using statistical significance ($P > 0.05$) to define an actual change or improvement in a measure (Chapter 50). However, the domain of sport and exercise science typically does not attract the large samples of participants needed to elicit statistical significance as a meaningful difference. Therefore, research within sport and exercise science can be prone to type II errors by accepting the null hypothesis when it is false. For research examining elite sports performance, this is even more likely, given the smaller variability in performance measures and lower participant numbers, making statistical significance difficult to achieve. However, this does not mean that meaningful changes are not being observed.

As a sport and exercise science student, it is important that you can interpret the results of research and determine whether the intervention will produce a meaningful change in performance or health, despite no statistical significance being observed. The section below summarises some of the more recent methods used within sport and exercise science that will allow you to determine whether a meaningful change or difference exists between variables or groups.

Effect size formulae

T-test

$$\text{ES } \eta^2 = \frac{\overline{X}_1 - \overline{X}_2}{SD_{control}} \tag{51.1}$$

ANOVA

$$R^2 = \frac{SS_B}{SS_W} \tag{51.2}$$

Where $\overline{X}_1$ and $\overline{X}_2$ are the respective means of the two groups; $SD_{control}$ is the standard deviation of the control condition; SS_B is the sum of squares of the deviations of each score from the mean between the groups, and SS_W is the sum of squares of the deviations of each score from the mean within the group.

Effect size

An effect size (ES or η^2 - eta squared) is a useful method to quantify the strength of an effect, especially if the relationship is approaching statistical significance. The effect size helps to provide a measure of practical significance and can be used in conjunction with the determination of statistical significance. Simply, the effect size helps to present some information on the size of the mean difference. In an ANOVA, a large sample size and a low standard error of the mean might return a significant F value despite it not being of any practical value in terms of a meaningful change. The effect size is calculated for the t-test (equation 51.1) and an ANOVA (equation 51.2), as in the margin note.

Each formula allows the difference between means to be made relevant to the standard deviation of the control group. The variance within the control group is typically used to correct the difference in means given that it has not been influenced by any intervention. The size of the effect size determines the strength of the effect, with 0.2 representing a small difference, 0.5 being a moderate effect, and >0.8 being a large effect. In summary, the use of effect sizes helps to provide a quantitative measure of the strength of the relationship, regardless of whether the difference is statistically significant or not.

Smallest worthwhile change

For a new sport and exercise science student, the concept of the smallest worthwhile change can be somewhat confusing, as traditionally emphasis is placed on determining whether statistical significance is observed or not. However, when implementing a new intervention in athletes, it might be apparent that, while there is an effect of the intervention, it does not have the statistical strength to become significant at the $P < 0.05$ level. However, just because the intervention is not significant does not mean that it would not benefit the athlete's performance to some degree, which, when working with elite level sports people, is still extremely important. The smallest worthwhile change is defined as the smallest outcome magnitude that is deemed to be clinically or practically important to the athlete or scientist. However, for sports performance the smallest worthwhile change can simply be calculated as:

$$\text{Smallest worthwhile change} = 0.5 \times \text{within-subject variability} \quad (51.3)$$

The formula to estimate the smallest worthwhile change is based upon the smallest differences that would have resulted in a chance of winning and/or medal outcomes in track and field. However, a sport and exercise science student may feel obliged to make an informed decision for their sport depending upon what they feel makes a difference. Changes in performance that are less than the smallest worthwhile change may be taken as trivial, even if they fall outside of the 90–95 % confidence limits for the measure. In this case, the change may be identified as a 'real' change, yet it can also be defined as 'trivial' as it does not substantially alter the performance of the athlete or cohort. The interpretation of the smallest worthwhile change can also be used to quantify the magnitude of the inference that the intervention was beneficial, neutral or harmful (see below). In summary, calculation and interpretation of the smallest worthwhile change is an important skill in sport and exercise science, as it may be used to define the magnitude or likelihood of an intervention changing performance, despite statistical significance not being reported.

Magnitude-based inferences

The use of the smallest worthwhile change in performance to gauge the effect of an intervention is important, as it helps to highlight that the magnitude of the intervention can be interpreted in three ways. That is, it can be harmful, trivial or beneficial. A more traditional statistical approach would suggest that the intervention has a significant impact or not, rather than demonstrate the likelihood of it benefiting, harming or being benign in its impact as magnitude-based inferences do. With magnitude-based information, the approach uses the value of the outcome statistic and its 95% confidence interval to determine the magnitude of its effect (see Fig. 51.1).

This statistical approach is relatively new to sport and exercise science and, while somewhat complex, provides an approach to determine the practical significance of the effect of an intervention. A simple spreadsheet can be downloaded (www.sportsci.org) to complete the calculations required to infer the magnitude of the effect of an intervention. This spreadsheet is useful in determining the probability of the magnitude being beneficial, trivial or harmful. The likelihood for each outcome is estimated using the same assumptions around the effect statistic (i.e. t or F value) as when estimating a P value or calculating confidence intervals. To provide a more probabilistic statement rather than statistical conclusion that is open to either type I or II error, the percentage probability for each effect (i.e. harmful, trivial or beneficial, see margin text) is listed and described using a qualitative descriptor. These

Qualitative descriptors for likelihood:

- <1% – almost certainly not
- 1–5% – very unlikely
- 5–25% – unlikely or probably not
- 25–75% – possibly or maybe
- 75–95% – likely or probably
- 95–99% – very likely
- >99% – almost certain.

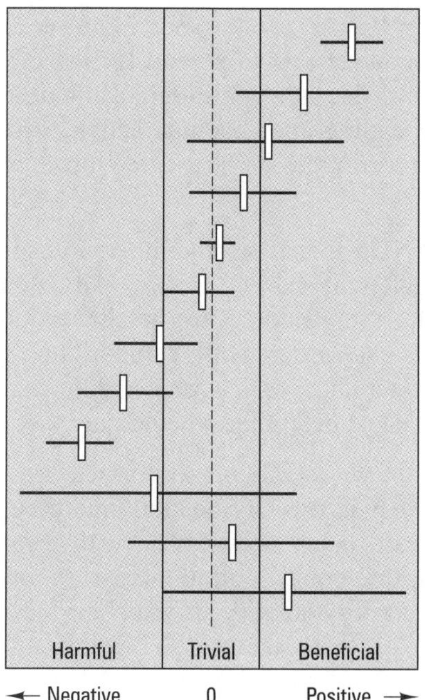

Fig. 51.1 An example of how magnitude-based inferences can be used to describe the usefulness of an intervention (adapted from Batterham and Hopkins, 2005).

qualitative descriptors help to translate the numerical likelihood of the outcome into simple and easy to understand language.

Overall, the use of magnitude-based inferences provides sport and exercise scientists with a new approach to determine the strength of the effect, rather than simply defining statistical significance. As a sport and exercise student, it is important that you are familiar with such new methods that may be favourable to exercise science research and that help to quantify and describe the impact of an intervention.

Determining differences in multiple groups

Analysis of variance with repeated measures

As discussed in Chapter 50, an analysis of variance (ANOVA) is used to compare the difference in means between three or more groups. The simple ANOVA assumes that the means are taken from independent groups that have no relationship to each other (similar to an independent sample t-test). As such, the total variability relies upon the interindividual variation, intraindividual variation, group variability and the error. The same cannot be said for the same group measured more than twice, given that subsequent datasets are dependent upon each other. Therefore, the variability of the scores is now not influenced by interindividual variation as the test is using a single sample. This allows subjects to serve as their own control, and strengthens that any significant differences are the result of either the treatment, intraindividual variation or error. As such, an ANOVA with repeated measures is used to identify any significant mean differences within the data.

An ANOVA with repeated measures relies upon the same assumptions that a simple ANOVA does. An ANOVA with repeated measures also demands that the data shows sphericity and homogeneity of covariance. Sphericity requires the repeated measures to demonstrate homogeneity of variance (equal variance across each dataset). The homogeneity of covariance is the assumption that all correlations based on the dependent variable for all groups are equal. If the ANOVA with repeated measures does not allow the assumption of sphericity, the likelihood of a type I error is increased. To overcome this violation of the assumption of sphericity, you can adjust the sphericity using the Greenhouse–Geisser or the Huynh–Feldt adjustment. Similar to a simple ANOVA, if a significant effect is flagged by the ANOVA with repeated measures, post hoc tests can be applied to determine where the significant difference lies. The mathematical equations to perform an ANOVA with repeated measures are well outside the scope of this text; however, it can be simply performed using a common computer statistical program such as Predictive Analytics Software or Statistical Package for Social Science (SPSS).

Assumptions of an ANOVA – there are several statistical assumptions on which an ANOVA is based. Simply, these include:

- The populations from which the samples are drawn are normally distributed.
- Each sample has homogeneity of variance.
- All groups are independent.
- Data are based on a parametric scale.

Factorial analysis of variance

Common research practice in sport and exercise science relies upon being able to determine the effect of separate factors on measures. Both a simple ANOVA and ANOVA with repeated measures only allow the effect of one factor to be examined. However, this is not conducive to being able to determine the effect of one condition on an indicator over time. A simple flowchart is shown in Fig. 51.2 to help decide which

Definitions

Intraindividual variation – the amount of variability in measurements caused by the natural variation in performance of a single subject.

Interindividual variation – the amount of variability in measurements caused by the dierences between subjects.

ANOVA to use. A factorial ANOVA allows sport and exercise scientists to quantify the simultaneous effects of several factors on the dependent variable at once. However, several different models of factorial ANOVA are possible depending upon the interaction between the independent and depending variables. There are three main variations of a factorial ANOVA:

1. **A between–between factorial ANOVA** analyses the differences in the dependent variable between different subject groups. An example would be determining the effect of gender (two levels) and four different diets (four levels) on changes in body composition. This analysis would determine whether there was a gender difference in the response to each diet, as well as determine whether any diet was significantly better.

2. **A within–within factorial ANOVA** is used where the same group is tested repeatedly across separate interventions. The within–within design would be used when the power output across a rowing ergometer sprint was compared with and without visual feedback in the same group of subjects. In this example, the within-subject differences within each condition are of interest.

3. **A between–within factorial ANOVA** is a common design in sport and exercise science. An example of a between–within design would be if three groups of athletes completing different training routines (three levels – between) are tested for repeat–sprint ability, four times across a season (four levels – within). This analysis would determine whether there was an effect of the different training routines on repeat sprint ability across the season.

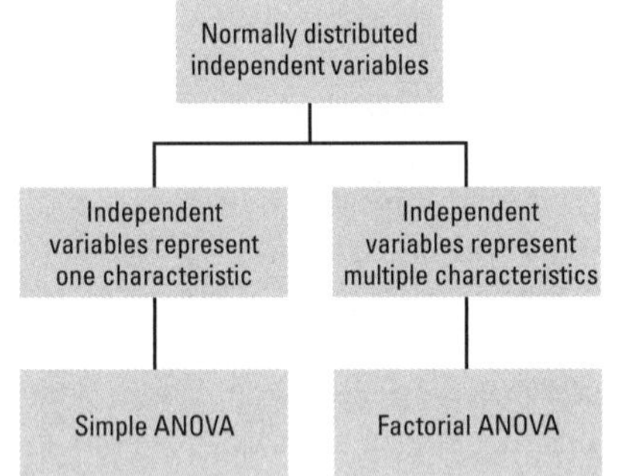

Fig. 51.2 Flowchart of decision-making for an ANOVA (adapted from Vincent, 2005).

A factorial ANOVA provides an F value to each factor as well as an effect statistic (F value) for the interaction of the two values. This second value may indicate whether there was a significant interaction in the study. That is, there is a combined effect of the factors on the dependent variable. More simply, an interaction occurs when the mean values of one factor depend strongly on another factor. A simple method to identify an interaction is to graph the data (Chapter 47); if the lines for each condition are parallel or the slopes of the lines are not significantly different, then there is no significant interaction. If the slopes of the lines are significantly different, then a significant interaction is present. Again, the equations required to perform a factorial ANOVA are complex, and such a statistical test can easily be performed using a computer statistical package.

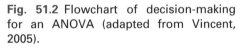

Text References

Batterham, A. and Hopkins, W. (2005) Making meaningful inferences about magnitudes. *Sportscience*, **9,** 6–13.

Vincent, W.J. (2005) *Statistics in Kinesiology*. Human Kinetics, Champaign, IL.

Sources for further study

Sportscience (2010) *Research Resources*. Available: http://www.sportssci.org Last accessed: 23/12/10.

Thomas, J., Nelson, J. and Silverman, S. (2005) *Research Methods in Physical Activity*. Human Kinetics, Champaign, IL.

Index

Note: Boxes, Figures and Tables are indicated in index by *italic page numbers*

abbreviations
  for journals/periodicals 52
  in lecture notes 17, 19
  in project report *148*
abdominal skinfold 245
abdominal strength test (multistage) *312–13*
absolute muscle strength 304, 307
absolute TEM 126
abstracts (of papers) 51
acceleration tests 322, *323*
accelerometers 288, *291*, *292*
accuracy of measurements 123
acromiale landmark 243
Actiheart® device 288
activity records and logs 289
Adapt method for blood lactate threshold determination 341, *342*
adjusted TrImps (training impulse) loading 351–4
  example of calculation *353*
Adobe Acrobat reader 68
Adobe Photoshop 85
aerobic–anaerobic transition 337
aerobic fitness testing
  field tests 274–6
    1.5 mile (2.4 km) run test 275
    12-minute walk–run test 275, *276*
    advantages 274
    disadvantages 275
    Rockport 1-mile walk test 276
  risk stratification for participants *183*, *184*, 274
  submaximal VO_2max tests 276–80
agility tests 323
  5-0-5 test 323, *324*
  cricket-specific agility tests 330
  'run-a-three' test 330, *332*, *334*
  tennis agility test 329, *331*, *332*
air displacement plethysmography 257–8
alactic cycling test 296–7
  data analysis for *298*
  normative data *298*
alactic energy production 294
altitude tests 320
ambient temperature and pressure saturated (ATPS) conditions *212*, 267
  conversion to BTPS conditions *212*
  conversion to STPD conditions 267
American College of Sports Medicine (ACSM)
  guidelines
    on exercise ECG test *206*
    on fitness tests 176
    on pre-exercise screening 181
  on SI units 138
  website 71
American Heart Association (AHA), on cardiovascular screening 183–4, *185*
anaerobic capacity 294
anaerobic capacity tests 297–303
  modified MAOD test 301–3
  Wingate cycling test 297–301
anaerobic energy production 294
anaerobic power 294
anaerobic power tests 294–7
  alactic cycling test 296–7, *298*
  vertical jump test 294–6
anaerobic threshold 337
analysis of information *25*, 55
analysis of variance (ANOVA) 395–6, 401
  assumptions on which based 395, 403
  Excel example *399–400*
  factorial ANOVA 403–4
  with repeated measures 403
analytical writing *98*
angular velocity, units *133*, *135*, 137
anthropometric profiles 242
  full profile measures 242
  restricted profile measures 242
anthropometry *see* kinanthropometry
anxiety (in exams) 38–9
application of knowledge *25*
Archimedes' principle 256
area, units *133*, *135*
arithmetic mean *see* mean of data
arm-flexed circumference *248*
arm-relaxed circumference *248*
arrhythmia 197, 198, 208
assessed coursework 26–7, 31–2
assessments, role in learning process 24–6
assignment work 27
ATPS conditions *see* ambient temperature and pressure saturated conditions
attributes 121
'aural' learning style *23*
Australian Association for Exercise and Sports Science (AAESS), health screening procedure 181, 183
authorship 57–8
autonomy *154*
axilla temperature 233–4

back squat test *311*
  normative data *312*
back strength test *305*
  normative data *306*
bar graphs 363, *364*, 365, 366
  in Excel *369–70*
  misrepresentations *371*
barometric pressure, units 138
basal energy expenditure (BEE) 347
basal metabolic rate (BMR)
  energy expenditure of activities as multiples *287*
  measurement of *286*
'beep test' 125, 324
behavioural observation 289, *291*
bell-shaped distributions 392, *393*
bench press test *308*
  normative data *309*
  YMCA bench press test *315–16*
beneficence *154*
between–between factorial ANOVA 404
between–within factorial ANOVA 404
bias in measurement 123
bibliographic database software 52, 104
bibliography 51, *148*
biceps skinfold 245
biepicondylar femur breadth *248*, 251
biepicondylar humerus breadth *248*, 251
bimodal frequency distributions 385
binomial distributions 391
  examples 391
bioelectrical impedance analysis
  fat-free mass determined by 258–9
  total body water determined by *228*, 232, 258
biohazard 165
  warning symbol for *162*, *167*
'blind' study 141
blood analytes 190
  normal ranges *192*
blood lactate concentration, as exercise intensity measure 227
blood lactate curves 337, *340*, *341*, *342*, *343*
blood lactate–running economy relationship *348*
blood lactate thresholds 339–43
  determination of
    Adapt method 341, *342*
    Coyle method 341, *342*
    D_{max} method 341–2, *342*
    by fixed blood lactate concentrations 341
    modified D_{max} method 342, *342*
  interpretation of shifts in 342–3
blood sampling 189–92
  adverse reactions 190
  lancet for *171*, 189, *191*
bloodborne pathogen 165
BMI *see* body mass index
body composition
  determination of
    by bioelectrical impedance analysis 258–9
    by computerised tomography 261
    dual-energy X-ray absorptiometry 260–1
    by isotopic dilution method 260
    by magnetic resonance imaging 261–2
  models 253–4
  prediction equations 254–6
body density
  measurement of
    by air displacement plethysmography 257–8
    by hydrodensitometry 256, *257*
  prediction equations 254–5
body fat percentage
  determination of 258, 261
  prediction equations *253*, 255–6, *255*
  variability between test methods 254
body fluids 165–72
  disposal of 170, 196
  ethical aspects 169
  management of spills and accidents 170–1
  safety precautions *168*
  spill containment plan 165, 170
  standard precautions 165, 168
  transport of 169–70
  and vaccination 168–9

Index

body mass 122, 136
  body fat as percentage 254
  diurnal variation 249
  hydration status assessed by *228*, 232, *233*
  measurement of 248–9
body mass index (BMI) 122, 249–50
  calculation of 250
  range scale *250*
body temperature
  measurement of 233–5
  pill telemetry system 235
  variations 233
body temperature and pressure saturated (BTPS) conditions *212*
bone breadth measurement 251
  callipers 251
  location of bones *248*
  technique 251
bookmarks (Internet browser) 67, 71
books, notes from 20
Borg scales 223–4, 225
box-and-whisker plots 361, *383*
brackets in spreadsheets 75
brainstorming 12, 15, 94
British Association of Sport and Exercise Science (BASES)
  Code of Conduct 161
  website 71
browsers (internet) 63, 66–7

calculators 155–6
  use for statistics 384
calf circumference *248*
Calorie (kilocalorie) 347
calorimetry 281
  direct 281, *282*
  indirect 265, 281–4, *291*, *292*
capillary 189
capillary action 189, 191
capillary blood sampling 190–2
capillary puncture 189, *191*
capillary tube, blood collection in 189, 191, *192*
carbon dioxide (CO_2) clearance 337
cardiac function
  measuring 197–210
  see also ECG test; heart rate monitor
cardiovascular disease, diagnostic measurements 210, 247
cardiovascular fitness test 177
cardiovascular screening of athletes 183–4, *185*
case study 141
CDs *64*
Celsius scale 122, 137
central limit theorem 393
central tendency, measuring 379–82
chemical hazards warning symbols *162*
chi^2 (χ^2) test 391, 392, 396
chin-up test *307–8*
  normative data *308*
citations 51–3, *56*, 58
  in bibliography 52–3
  Harvard system 51–2
  in literature review 106
  Vancouver/numerical system 52
  of websites 53
closed-circuit spirometry 282–3
coefficient of dispersion 392
coefficient of variation (CoV) *128*, 129, *380*, 384
  spreadsheet function for *387*
cold conditions, field tests in 319–20
collaboration 12–13
column charts (Excel) *369*
  see also bar graphs
communication skills *4*, 12
comparative writing *98*
comprehension *25*
computerised tomography (CT) 261
computers, guidelines for using *64*
concentration units *133*
Concept II rowing ergometer *333*
confidence interval (CI) 92, 127
confidence limits *380*, 385, 396–7
  graphical representation *396*, 397
confidentiality 89
confirmatory analysis 359
confounding variables 124, 142
consent 155, 161, 169, 184
consistency in measurement 123
construct validity 125
constructive criticism 12
content validity 125
continuous variables 121
control group in study 141
conversion factors for units *135*, *137*, 138
Cooper 12-minute walk–run test 275, *276*
copyright law 51, *56*
core body temperature, measurements of 234, 235
correlation 397
  Excel example *400*
correlation coefficients 397–8
coursework 31–2
Coyle method for blood lactate threshold determination 341, *342*
criterion validity 125
critical thinking 60–1
cross-over study 142
cross-referencing 58
cross-sectional study 141
current awareness databases 50
curriculum options 31
curriculum vitae (CV) 40–5
  adjusting/'fine-tuning' 45
  covering letter 42, 44
  development of 41–2
  presentation and structure 42–4
  skills and personal qualities in 40–1
cycle ergometers
  in anaerobic tests 296, 299
  in submaximal tests 136, 277–9
cycling, VO_2max test protocols *271*

D_{max} method for blood lactate threshold determination 341–2, *342*
  modified method 342, *342*
data
  interpretation of 61, 90–2
  organising 359
  presentation in graphical format 360, 363–73
  presentation in tabular format 374–7
  transformations 360–2
data points in plotted curves *372*
databases 49, 50, 71, 83–4
  spreadsheet functions 76, 84
degrees of freedom 390
  calculation of *394*, *395*
dehydration 228
  clinical signs *228*, 233
delegation/sharing of tasks 12
density
  meaning of term 256
  of water *256*
  see also body density
deontology *154*
dependent variables 121, 140
depolarisation 197, 199, 200
dermal puncture 189
descriptive statistics 378–88
  computers used to calculate 386–8
  examples *380*
descriptive writing *98*
Dewey Decimal system 49
DEXA *see* dual-energy X-ray absorptiometry
diagrams
  in essays 103
  in exams *34*
  in lecture notes *18*
  on posters 109
diary-based system (for time management) 8
dictionaries 50, *99*
direct calorimetry 281, *282*
directories (web resources) 71
discontinuous variables 121
discrete variables 121
disinfection 165
  of equipment 168, 198, *270*
  of laboratory space 171
dispersion of data (variability) 378
  comparing 396
  dimensionless measures 384, 392
  measuring 382–4
dissertations 147
distributions
  displaying 360
  see also frequency distributions
Dixon and Mood's sign test 396
DOI (digital object identifier) 53
doubly labelled water technique, energy expenditure measured by *282*, 284–5
Douglas bas methods 284
dual-energy X-ray absorptiometry (DEXA) 254, 259, 260–1
duty of care 157, 161
dynamic strength tests 304, 307–13
  normative data *308*, *309*, *310*, *312*, *313*
dynamometers 304, *305*, *306*

earlobe blood sampling 189, *190*
e-books 50, 71
ECG test
  3-lead 200
  12-lead 200
  chest leads 200, 202–3
  electrode *204*
  electrode placement sites 202–4
  exercise ECG
    electrode placement sites 202–3, 204
    indications for stopping *206*
    performing 205–7

female patients 201
information obtained from 198, 208–10
limb leads 200, 203–4
removal of electrodes 207–8
resting ECG
electrode placement sites 202–3
performing 204–5
signal noise in 197, 205, *207*
site preparation for electrodes 200–1
standardised ECG paper 205
ECG trace
ectopic beats 209
manual interpretation 208–10
P–Q interval 200
P–R interval 199, 209
Q–T interval 210
QRS complex 200, 210
R–R interval 209
signal direction 208
ST segment 200, 210
T wave 200, 210
economy of exercise
factors affecting 346
indirect measures 348
measurement of 344–6
ectomorphy 242, 243
editing text (word processing) 81
effect size 401
efficiency 347
Einthoven's triangle in ECG 197, 200, *201*
e-journals 50, 71
e-learning *65*, 66
electrocardiography 198–210
see also ECG test
email etiquette 65–6
email updates 51, *69*
employability 5, 6
endomorphy 242, 243
endurance capacity 314
see also VO_2max test
endurance exercise intensity
measuring 221–7
see also exercise intensity
endurance training thresholds
measuring 337–43
see also blood lactate thresholds; ventilatory threshold
energy, units *133*, *135*, 136–7
energy expenditure 281
basal 347
measurement of 137, 281–7
by direct calorimetry 281, *282*
by doubly labelled water technique *282*, 284–5, *291*
by indirect calorimetry 137, 281–4, *291*
by non-calorimetric methods 284–7
metabolic calculations *286*
per litre oxygen consumed 137, 282, 347
prediction equations for *282*, 285–6
resting 347
energy expenditure of activity 281
measurement of 287
as multiples of BMR *287*
for various activities *287*
English Institute of Sport, website 71
ergometers
cycle ergometers 136, 277–9, 296, 299
rowing ergometers *333*
error bars *396*, 397
errors
of measurement 125–6
minimising 126
see also technical error of measurement
essay questions 34
instructions used in *102*
reasons for poor answers *35*
essay writing 101–3
golden rules *102*
information sources used 49
planning 101–2
reviewing 103
time allocation 101
ethical approval 145
ethics *154*
euhydration 228
evaluation of facts/ideas/information *25*, 55–62
exam papers, use in revision *28*
examinations 32–9
action list for 37
anxiety before and during 38–9
essay questions 34
final preparations 29
multiple-choice questions 34–6
oral exams 37
practical and information-processing 36
preparing for 26, 32
question-spotting in 29
reasons for poor essay answers *35*
short-answer questions 34–5, 36
time management in 33, 34
Excel *see* Microsoft Excel
exercise ECG test
electrode placement sites 202–3, 204
indications for stopping *206*
performing 205–7
exercise intensity
classifications *181*, *222*, *225*, *226*, *227*
factors affecting 221
measuring 197, 221–7
by blood lactate concentration 227
by HRR method 222–3
by METs 226–7
by MHR-based method 221–2
by RPE method 223–6
by VO_2-based methods 223
exercise prescription
fitness tests for 175
risk stratification for *183*, *184*
exercise science institutions, web resources 71, 72
exercise testing, interpretation of results 90–2
exhalation 211
experimental design 140–4
constraints on 142–3
randomisation of treatments 141
experiments
checklist for *143*
interaction of treatments 143
multifactorial 143–4
terminology for 140–2
expiratory reserve volume (ERV) 211, *213*, 219
measurement of 216, 219
normative values *217*
exploratory data manipulation 359
exponents 375
extrapolation of graphs *372*
extremes (statistical) *380*, *383*
spreadsheet functions for *387*

F-test 396
factorial analysis of variance 403–4
variations 404
Fahrenheit scale *122*, 137
FAQ, meaning of term 63
fat mass 254
determination of 258–9
fat-free mass 254
determination of 258–9
fatigue index
in anaerobic tests *298*, *300*
in phosphate recovery test *325*
FEV_1 *see* forced expiratory volume
Fick equation 265
field tests 317–34
for aerobic fitness testing 274–6
agility tests 323, *324*
in cold conditions 319–20
cricket-specific agility tests 330, *332*, *334*
equipment preparation and transport for 318
general principles 317–19
generic tests 317–27
in hot conditions 320
multistage fitness test (MSFT) 324, *326–7*
one-repetition maximum (1RM) test 322
1RM strength tests 322
order of testing 318–19
phosphate recovery test 323–4, *325*
preparation and planning for 318
rowing ergometer test 330, *333*, *334*
scheduling of 317–18
seated medicine ball throw test 321, *322*
speed tests 322–3
sports-specific tests 328–34
tennis agility test 329, *331*, *332*
time management of 317
vertical jump test 320–1
waste disposal for 319
in wet conditions 319
YOYO intermittent recovery test 328, *329*
fieldwork, safety rules for 163
figures *see* diagrams
file management
computer files *64*
lecture notes 26
literature references 51
final power, in anaerobic tests *298*, *300*
finger blood sampling 189, *190*
fitness tests
clothing and footwear 176
examples *130*
factors affecting results 130, 175
familiarisation 177–8
interpretation of results 90–2
order of testing 177
planning 176–8
pre-test instructions 175–6
pre-test logistics 175
pre-test screening procedures 179–85
preparing for 175–8
specificity 176–7

fitness tests (*continued*)
  time of day 177
  warm-up for 177
fitting of data in plotted curves *372*
fitting of line graphs *372*
'five-number summary' 361, 383
flexibility 236
  measurement equipment 236, *237*
  measuring 236–41
  shoulder flexibility test 239, *240*
  sit-and-reach test 236–8
  straight leg raise test 238, *240*
  Thomas test 238, *239*
flexometer 236, *237*
food, thermic effect of 281, 286–7
force, units *133*, *135*, 136
forced expiratory volume in 1 second (FEV_1) 212, 214, 218
forced vital capacity (FVC) 211, 217
  mathematical estimation of 214
  test 215
    pulmonary functions obtained from 217–18
formative assessments 26
Frankfort plane 249
FRC *see* functional residual capacity
frequency distributions 378
  characteristics 385–6
frequency tables 359, *360*
Friedman *S*-test 396
front thigh skinfold 245
FTP, meaning of term 63
functional residual capacity (FRC) 212, *213*, *217*
functions in spreadsheets 75–6
FVC *see* forced vital capacity

G-test 391, 392, 396
gas analysis systems 266, 283–4
Gaussian (normal) distributions 392–3
  examples 392
  tendency towards 391
geometric mean *381*
girth measurements 247
  locations *248*
  technique for 247
  see also hip circumference; waist circumference
glossary 104
gluteal circumference *248*
glycosuria 193
goal setting 7
goniometer 236, *237*
goodness-of-fit tests 396
Google Earth *69*
Google Scholar *69*
Google searches 55, *69*
'graduateness' attribute 6
grammar check 83, 100
graphics
  in documents 82
  packages 84–5
  in spreadsheets 77, 359, 360
graphs 360, 363–73
  axes 366
  bar graphs 363, *364*, 365, 366
  checklist for drawing *364*
  Excel examples *368–70*
  interpreting 61, 370–3
  labels 367
  line graphs 363, 364–5
  line styles 367
  misrepresentations *371–2*
  non-linear scale *371*
  non-zero axis *371*
  pie charts/graphs 364, 365
  on posters 109
  practical aspects 365–7
  relative vs absolute scale *371*
  scatter graphs 363–4, 365, *368–9*
  in scientific papers 373
  symbols 367, *371*
  texture and shading 367
  titles 366
  types 363–4
grip strength test *305*
  normative data *306*
group discussions 14
groups, working in 11–16

Haldane transformation 267–8
hamstrings, flexibility assessment of 236, 239
handgrip strength test *305*
handwashing 166–7
Harris–Benedict equations 347
Harvard system for citations 51–2
hazards 157
  examples *158*, *160*
  identifying 158
  warning symbols for *162*
health and safety 157–64
health screening procedures 179–85
  for low- and moderate-intensity exercise 179, *180*
  for vigorous exercise 179, 181–3
heart
  atrium *199*
    signal conduction through *198*, 199, 209
  AV node 199, 209
  depolarisation in 199, 200
  electrical activity of *198*, 199–200
  repolarisation in 200
  SA node 199
  ventricles *199*
    signal conduction across *198*, 199–200, 209–10
heart rate
  calculation from ECG trace 209
  effect of medications *222*
  maximal 221–2
  as measure of exercise intensity 197, 221, 350
  resting 221
  training zones 222, 223, 353
heart rate monitoring, physical activity measured by 287–8, *291*, *292*
heart rate monitors 197–8, 222, 288
heart rate reserve (HRR) method 222–3
  exercise intensity classification using *181*, *222*, *225*
heart rate–running economy relationship *348*
height measurement 249
helix of ear 189, *190*
HERON service 50
hip circumference *248*, 250
hip flexor flexibility, assessment of 238, *239*
histograms 359, 360
  Excel examples *369*
  misrepresentations *371*
homogeneity of covariance 403
homogeneous variance 395
hot conditions, field tests in 320
hydration assessment techniques 228–33
  body mass *228*, 232
  clinical signs *228*, 233
  plasma osmolality *228*, 229
  plasma sodium concentration *228*, 232
  plasma volume changes *228*, 232
  saliva osmolality *228*, 233
  total body water determination *228*, 229
  urine concentration *228*, 229–31
hydration status
  measuring 228–33
  self-monitoring of 233
hydrodensitometry, body density measured by 256, *257*
hyperhydration 228
hypothesis 139
  development of 139–40
hypothesis testing 60, 127, 389–90
  computer calculations 400

iliac crest skinfold 245
iliocristale landmark 243
iliospinale landmark 243–4
image storage and manipulation 85
incline leg press test *309–10*
  normative data *310*
independent variables 121, 140
indexing of literature references 51, 104
indirect calorimetry 265, 281–4, *291*, *292*
indirect measurement of aerobic capacity 274–80
  factors influencing choice of test 274, 275
  indirect tests 274–6
  submaximal laboratory tests 276–80
indirect open circuit calorimetry 265
information
  citations for 51–2
  evaluation of 55–62, *70*
  indexing 51
  organising 51
  sources 49–50, 57–8, 71–2, 145
information-processing exams 36
informed consent 155, 161, 169, 184–5
inhalation 211
initiative and enterprise skills *4*
inspiratory reserve volume (IRV) 212, *213*, 219
  measurement of 216, 219
  normative values *217*
instrument error 125
intercostal space 197, 202
inter-individual variation 404
International Physical Activity Questionnaire (IPAQ) 289, *290*
International Society for the Advancement of Kinanthropometry (ISAK) 242
  accreditation scheme 242
  profile measures 242

internet 63
  browsers 66–7
  directories 71
  downloading from 68, 71
  Google searches *69*
  as information source 71–2, 145
  as resource 71–2
  search engines 67–8
  tools 66–71
interpersonal skills 12
interval scale 122
intraclass correlation coefficient (ICC) 128–9
intra-individual variation 404
investigator error 125–6
ISAK *see* International Society for the Advancement of Kinanthropometry
ischaemia 197, 198, 210
isokinetic muscle contraction 304
isometric strength tests 304, *305–6*
  normative data *306*
isotope dilution method
  energy expenditure measured by 284–5
  total body water determined by *228*, 229, 260
IT skills *4*, 63

journals/periodicals
  abbreviations for 52
  taking notes from 20
junk mail 65
justice *154*

K4 Cosmed analyser 346
Karvonen method 222–3
Kelvin scale 122, 137
Kendall's coefficient of rank correlation 398
ketone bodies 193
key words
  in CV or résumé *44*
  in internet search 67, *68*, 145
  in scientific paper or project report 147, *148*
kilopond (unit of force) *135*, 136
kinaesthetic learning style *24*
kinanthropometry 242–52
  body composition monitored using 253, 254, *255*, 256
  body mass index 249–50
  bone breadths 251
  girth measurements 246–8
  landmarks 242–4
  skinfold measurement 244–6
  stature (height) 249
  waist circumference 250
  waist-to-hip ratio 250–1
knowledge (knowing facts) *25*
Kolmogorov–Smirnov test 396
Kruskal–Wallis *H*-test 396
kurtosis 386

laboratory work
  project work 146
  safety rules 162–3
lactate 337
  see also blood lactate. . .
lactate–power curves *340*, *341*, *342*, *343*
lactate thresholds
  LT_1 340
  LT_2 340
lactic acid *19*, 337
  production of 337, 339
lancet for blood sampling *171*, 189, *191*
landmarks, anatomical 242–4
learning
  assessment and feedback in 24–6
  collaboration for 12–13
  from examples 60
  objectives 26, 27
  problem-based *32*
  skills *4*
  styles 22–4
least significant difference (LSD) 396
lecture notes 17–20
  organising 26–7
leg press test *308*, *310*
  normative data *310*
leg strength test *306*
  normative data *306*
length, units *132*, *133*, *135*, 136
leptokurtic frequency distribution 386
Library of Congress system 49
library resources 49–50
line graphs 363, 364–5
  misrepresentations *372*
linear regression 398
listening skills 12
literature reviews and surveys 103–6
  information sources used 49–50, 104
  structure and content 105–6
  time allocation *103*
  topic for 104
lobule of ear 189, *190*
local muscular endurance 314
location (central tendency of distribution) 378
  comparing 393–6
  measuring 379–82
Lode cycle ergometer *296*
log-normal distribution 361
log-transformation of data *381*
Loughborough Intermittent Shuttle test 125
lower back flexibility, assessment of 236
lower body power, tests for 294–5, 320–1
lower body strength, tests for *311*, 322
lower extreme *380*, *383*
  spreadsheet function for *387*
lower quartile *380*, *383*
  spreadsheet function for *387*
lung function *see* pulmonary function

macros in spreadsheets and word processors 73, 82
magnetic resonance imaging (MRI), body fat determination using 261–2
magnitude-based inferences 402–3
Mann–Whitney *U*-test 396
MAOD test
  example of data from *303*
  modified MAOD protocol 297, 301–3
  procedure 301–2
mass units *132*, *133*, 136
mathematical functions in spreadsheets 75
mathematical model 140
mathematical operators 75
maximal accumulated oxygen deficit 294, 301
  see also MAOD test
maximal aerobic capacity 265
  measuring 265–73
  see also VO_2max
maximal heart rate (MHR)
  direct measurement of 222
  estimation of 221–2
  exercise intensity classified using *181*, *222*, *225*
maximal oxygen uptake
  indirect measurements 274–80
  see also VO_2max
maximal tests 276
  ECG monitoring in 205
maximal voluntary ventilation (MVV) 211, 216
  mathematical estimation of 214
  test 216–17
mean *378*, 379, *380*
  comparing 393–6
  geometric mean *381*
  inappropriate use *381*
  measuring of precision 384–5
  spreadsheet function for *387*
mean power in Wingate test *300*
measurement
  accuracy 123
  bias 123
  consistency 123
  errors 123–4
  principles 121–4
  scales 122
  SI units 132–8
  variables 121
medial calf skinfold 245
median *378*, 379, *380*, *383*
  spreadsheet function for *387*
medications, heart rate affected by *222*
medicine ball throw test (seated) 321, *322*
mesomorphy 242, 243
metabolic cart for VO_2max test 265, *266*
METs (metabolic equivalents)
  calculations *226*
  as exercise intensity measure 226–7
Microsoft Excel *74*, 75, 76
  graphs *368–70*
  hypothesis-testing statistics calculations *399–400*
  linear regression 398
  statistical analysis functions *386–8*
  tables *376–7*
  see also spreadsheets
Microsoft PowerPoint 19, 84, 109, *110*, *113*
  for posters 84, 109, *110*
  in presentations 17, 19, 84, *113–14*
Microsoft Word 79, 82
  Excel chart imported into *370*
  tables *376*
mid-acromiale–radiale 243
mind maps *18*, 28, 29, *34*, 94
Minitab statistical package 84, *394*, 400
MMEF (mid-maximal expiratory flow rate) 218
mobile phones 153
mode *378*, *380*, 381
  spreadsheet function for *387*
modules in course 31

Index

modulus of number 390
Monark cycle ergometer 136, *277*
monographs 50
motion sensors *291*, *292*
multifactorial experiments 143–4
multimodal learning style *24*
multiple-choice questions (MCQs) 34–6
multiple regression 398
multistage abdominal strength test *312–13*
  normative data *313*
multistage fitness test (MSFT) 324
  procedure *326*
  VO_2max calculations *327*
MultiStix reagent strips 230, *231*
muscular endurance 304
muscular endurance tests 314–16
  push-up test *314*
  YMCA bench press test *315*
muscular fitness tests 177
muscular strength 304
  normative data *306*, *308*, *309*, *310*, *312*, *313*
muscular strength tests 304–13
  back squat test *311*
  back strength test *305*
  bench press test *308*
  chin-up test *307–8*
  dynamic strength measures 304, 307–13
  grip strength test *305*
  incline leg press test *309–10*
  isometric strength measures 304, *305–6*
  leg strength test *306*
  multistage abdominal strength test *312–13*
MVV *see* maximal voluntary ventilation

needlestick injury 171
negative results 147
negative skewness of dist *378*, 386
networked computers, rules for using *64*
newsgroups 66
nominal scale 122
non-linear regression 398
non-linear scale in graph *371*
non-malificence *154*
non-parametric statistical tests 390, 396
non-zero axis in graph *371*
normal (Gaussian) distributions 392–3
  examples 392
  tendency towards 391
note-taking
  in lectures 17–20
  practical work 155
  in project work 146
null hypothesis 389–90
numbers, organising 359
numerical data
  interpreting 61
  recording 155

obese people
  BMI *250*, *251*
  MHR equation 221
objectivism *154*
obstructive diseases 211, 216
  diagnosis of 217, 218, 219
oesophageal temperature 234–5
office suite (programs) 73, 79
OMNI scale 225
one-repetition maximum (1RM) tests 307, *309*, *310*, *312*, 322
online communications 64–6
online journals 50, 71
online resources 49, 50, 63–72
  citation of 53
open-circuit spirometry 265, 266, 283–4
  computerised gas analysis systems 284
  Douglas bas methods 284
  portable gas analysis systems 283–4
oral exams 37
oral presentations 112–17
  see also presentations
oral temperature 233
  measurement of *234*
orbitale landmark 243, *249*
ordinal scale 122
organising work 8–10
outliers 359, *372*, 379
overhead transparencies 156
overweight
  BMI *250*, *251*
  disease risks due to 253
  effects in sport 253
oxygen consumption
  and energy expenditure 137, 282, 347
  maximal 265, 274
  relationship to running speed *345*, *346*
  see also VO_2

palpation 197
  for ECG electrodes 201, 202, 203, 204
papers (scientific/research), citations 51–2
paradigm 139
parameter 121
parametric distributions 390–3
  binomial distributions 391
  Gaussian distributions 392–3
  normal distributions 392–3
  Poisson distributions 391–2
parametric tests 390
paraphrasing 20
patellare 244
pathogen infection 165
pattern diagrams *18*, 29
.pdf files 68
peak aerobic capacity 265, *272*
peak power, in anaerobic tests *298*, *300*
Pearson's correlation coefficient 128, 397–8
pedometers 287, *288*, *291*, *292*
peer assessment 11
peer review 57, 149
PEFR (peak expiratory flow rate) *218*
  meter 214–15, 217
performance testing, factors affecting 125–31
personal communications, citation of 53
personal development planning (PDP) 3, 5, 40
personal injury claims 161–2
personal protective equipment (PPE) 160, 165–6
personal qualities in CV *41*
phishing 65
phosphate recovery test 323–4
  procedure *325*
physical activity 281
  measuring 287–8
  self-reporting of 288–9
physical activity measurement tools, choosing 289, 291–3
Physical Activity Readiness Questionnaire (PAR-Q) 179, *180*
pie charts/graphs 364, 365
  examples *103*, *115*, *364*
  in Excel *370*
piezoelectric devices 288
plagiarism 12, 31, 55
  avoiding *56*, 71
planning (of work) 8–10, 32
planning and organising skills *4*
plasma osmolality 228, 229, *233*
platykurtic frequency distribution 386
plotted curves *372*, 374
Poisson distributions 391–2
  examples 391
polymodal frequency distributions 385
positive skewness of dist *378*, 386
poster displays 107–11
  colour 109
  content 109, 111
  design 107–9
  handouts 111
  poster session 111
  PowerPoint used 84, 109, *110*
power, units *133*, *135*, 136
PowerPoint *see* Microsoft PowerPoint
practical exams 36
practical skills 153
practical work 153–6
  calculators 155–6
  ethical and legal issues 153–5
  preparation for 153
  presentation of results 155, 156
  recording results 146, 155
pre-exercise screening procedures 179–85
  high-risk clients screening 181, *182*
precautionary principle *154*
precision 123
prefixes for SI units *133*, 135, 375
presentations 112–17
  audience for 112, 114
  audiovisual aids for 114
  content 114–15
  hints on speaking *116*
  PowerPoint used 84, *113–14*
  preparation for 112
  time allocation *115*
pressure, units *135*, 138
primary sources of information 49, 50, 57
printing of documents and posters 78, 83, *110*
probability graph paper 392, *393*
problem-based learning (PBL) *32*
problem-solving skill *4*
proceedings of scientific meetings 51
professional indemnity insurance 162
project work 145–9
  experimental design 141–4, 146
  laboratory work 146
  planning 145–6
  topic for 145
  writing up 147
proportion data, comparing 396
proportions 359
proteinuria 193
provenance (of sources) 57–8

public liability insurance 162
public speaking *116*
pulmonary function measures
 correction for environmental factors *212*
 ERV 211, *213*, 216, 219
 FEV_1 212, 214, 218
 $FEV_1\%$ 212, 214, 218
 FVC 211, 214, 217
 IRV 211, *213*, 216, 219
 mathematical estimates 214
 MMEF 218
 MVV 211, 216
 normative data listed *213*, *217*
 PEFR 212, *218*
 RV 211, *213*
 SVC 211, 219
 TLC 211, *213*
 TV 211, *213*, 216, 219
 VC 211, *213*
pulmonary function testing 211–20
 interpretation of 217–19
 terms used 211–12, *213*
 see also spirometry testing
push-up test *314*
 normative data *315*

qualitative variables 121
quantitative variables 121
quartiles *380*, *383*
 spreadsheet functions for *387*
Queen's College step test *280*
question-spotting strategy (in revision) 29

radiale landmark 243
ramp test
 in ventilatory threshold determination *338*
 in VO_2max determination 265, 268, *271*, *272*
randomisation 141
range *380*, 382, *383*
rank 379
rank correlation, coefficients of 398
ranked variables 121
rating of perceived exertion (RPE) method 223–6
 advantages 225
 Borg scales 223–4, 225
 category ratio (CR-10) scale used *225*, *356*
 exercise intensity classified using *181*, *225*, 354–6
 factors affecting 226
 limitations 225–6
 RPE–running speed graph *345*
 session-RPE method of monitoring training load 354–6
ratio scale 122
rationality *154*
'read–write' learning style *23*
reagent strips, urine testing by 193–4, *195*, 230, *231*
'real decline' 92
'real improvement' 92
recovery heart rate 274, *276*
rectal temperature 234
references *see* literature references
refractometer 193, 194
 urine specific gravity determination 194–5, *196*
regression analysis 398
relative frequency 359
relative humidity 138
relative mean power in Wingate test *300*
relative peak power, in anaerobic tests *298*, *300*
relative strength 304
 normative data *306*, *309*, *310*, *312*
relative TEM 126–7
relative work capacity in Wingate test *300*
reliability analysis statistics *128*
reliability of measurement 127–9
repetition 304
repetition maximum (RM) 304
repolarisation 197, 200
research papers
 obtaining and organising 50–1
 storage of 51
residual volume (RV) 211, *213*, *217*
 determination of *257*
respect *154*, 155
respiratory exchange ratio (RER), in VO_2max test 268
respiratory quotient (RQ) 284
resting ECG test
 electrode placement sites 202–3
 performing test 204–5
resting energy expenditure 347
 estimation of 347, *347*
resting heart rate (RHR) 221
resting metabolic rate (RMR)
 calculations *285*
 measurement of *286*, 287
restrictive diseases 211, 216
 diagnosis of 219
résumé 40
 see also curriculum vitae
review articles 50, 57
revision 27–9
 lecture notes used in 26–7
 past exam papers used in *28*
 preparing for 26, 27–8
 and question spotting 29
 time management for 27
risk 157
 control measures for 159–60
risk assessment 157–61
risk factors, in health screening *183*
risk management 157
Rockport 1-mile walk test 276
rounding of numbers 359, 375
rowing, VO_2max test protocols *271*
rowing ergometer test 330
 normative data *334*
 procedure *333*
RPE *see* ratings of perceived exertion
RSS feeds 51
run tests for aerobic fitness testing 275
'run-a-three' agility test 330
 normative data *334*
 procedure *332*
running economy
 factors affecting *346*
 indirect measures 348
 measurement of 344–6

safety measures/notes 160
 in blood sampling 190
 in fitness testing 178
 flexibility testing 237
 in spirometry testing 215
 thermometers 233
 in urine testing *194*, 232
 VO_2max test 268
saliva osmolality *228*, 233
scanning of texts 19
scatter graphs 363–4, 365, *397*
 in Excel *368–9*
Scheffé–Box test 396
Science Citation Index (SCI) 50
scientific law 139
scientific method 139–44
scientific papers/reports
 citations 51–2
 graphs in 373
 steps in producing *150*
 structure *148*
scientific writing 94–100
 information, organising 94–5
 personal reference library used *99*
 style 95, *97–8*
 time management for 94
search engines 67–8
 tips for using *68*
seated medicine ball throw test 321
 procedure *322*
secondary sources of information 57
self-management skills *4*
self-report questionnaires for activity recording 289, *290*, *291*, *292*
semi-interquartile range *380*, 382–3
 spreadsheet function for *387*
sensitivity of measurement 129–30
session-RPE method of monitoring training load 354–6
 category ratio (CR-10) scale used *356*
 example of calculations *355*
'sharps' 163
 disposal of 167
short-answer questions (SAQs) 34–5, 36
shoulder flexibility
 assessment of 239, *240*
 rating scale *241*
SI units 132–8
 base units 132
 conversion factors *135*, 138
 derived units 132, *133*
 prefixes *133*, 135, 375
 style 133–5
 supplementary units 132
significance levels 390
sit-and-reach test 236–8
 normative data *238*
skewed distributions *378*, 386
skewness 386
skimming through texts 20
 SQ3R technique *20*
skin temperature 234
skinfold measurement 243–6
 callipers 246
 factors affecting accuracy 246
 location of sites 245
 normal values for athletes *246*
 sum of seven skinfolds 246, *246*
 technique 243

slow vital capacity (SVC) 211, 219
  test 216
    pulmonary functions provided from 219
smallest worthwhile change 401–2
SMART approach to goal setting 7
somatotyping 242
sources of information 49–50
  internet as 71–2
  notes from 20
  primary 49, 50, 57
  provenance of sources 57–8
  secondary 57
spam 65
Spearman's coefficient of rank correlation 398
specific gravity 193
  determination of by refractometer 194–5
  see also urine specific gravity
speed
  tests 322–3
  units *133*, *135*, 137
spellcheck facility 82, 100
sphericity of data 403
spider diagrams *34*, 94, *95*
spill containment plan 165, 170
spirometry testing 211
  equipment 211–12
  flow rate–volume curve 212, *218*
  flow-sensing spirometers 212
  PEFR (peak expiratory flow rate) meter 214–15
  safety in 215
  volume-displacement spirometers 211, *212*
  volume–time curve 212, *218*
spoken presentations 112–17
  see also presentations
Sports Medicine Australia (SMA), health screening procedure 181–3
spreadsheets 73–8
  advantages 73
  cell formatting options *74*
  copying 76
  data entry for 73, 75
  database functions 76, 84
  graphics facilities 77, 359, 360
  mathematical functions 75
  naming blocks in 76–7
  parts *74*, 75
  printing of 78
  statistical analysis functions 76, 84, 359, *386–8*, *399–400*, 400
  tables in *376–7*
  templates in 73, 77
  see also Microsoft Excel
sprint speed tests *323*
SPSS statistical package 84, 386, 400, 403
spurious accuracy 123, 375
SQ3R technique (for skimming texts) 20, *21*
'stable' measure in test results 92
standard atmospheric pressure 138
standard deviation (SD) *380*, 383–4
  spreadsheet function for *387*
standard error (SE) 127, *380*, 384–5
  spreadsheet function for *387*
standard precautions with body fluids 165, 168
standard temperature and pressure dry (STPD) conditions 267
statistical analysis packages 84, 386, 401
statistical calculations 383–4
  in spreadsheets *386–8*
statistical functions in spreadsheets 76, *387*
statistical measures
  dispersion (variability) 382–4
  location (central tendency) 379–82
statistical tests 389–400
  choosing 393–400
stature measurement 249
stem-and-leaf plots 360
step test in VO_2max determination 265, 268, *271*, *272*
sterilisation 165
stimulated rowing performance test 330, *333*, *334*
straight leg raise test 238, *240*
strength tests *see* muscular strength tests
Student's *t*-test 393
  critical values of *t* statistic *395*
  Excel example *399*
  procedure *394*
  worked example *395*
'study buddying' 12
submaximal tests 276
  cycle ergometer tests 277–9
    Astrand–Rhyming protocol 279
    calculations *278*
    procedure 277–8
    YMCA protocol *277*, 279
  ECG monitoring in 205
  step tests 279–80
  treadmill tests 279
  VO_2max estimated using 276–80
subscapular landmark 244
subscapular skinfold 245
sum of seven skinfolds 246
  typical data for athletes *247*
summary statistics 378
  see also descriptive statistics
summative assessments 26
summative exams 32–3
supraspinale skinfold 245
SVC *see* slow vital capacity
symbols
  in graphs 367
  in statistics 379
symmetrical distributions *378*
synthesis (thinking process) *25*
systematic variation 142

t statistic
  calculation of *394*
  critical values *395*
t-test
  assumptions to be met *394*
  effect size calculated using 401
  Excel example *399*
  procedure *394*
  worked example *395*
  see also Student's *t*-test
tables 61, 359
  checklist for *375*
  preparation of 374–5
  saving space in 374, 375
  in spreadsheets *376–7*
  word-processed 82, *376*
tally chart *359*
task organising 8–9
team members, contributions to team success 15–16
team role(s) *13*
  meaning of term 11
teamwork 11–16
  advantages 11
  dynamics 13–14
  negative feelings towards 11
  skills *4*, 12
technical error of measurement (TEM) 92, 126–7, 131
  absolute 126
  interpreting *92*, 127
  relative 126–7
technology skills *4*
temperature
  body temperature 233–5
  measurement scales 122, 137
  units *132*, 137
temperature pill telemetry system 235
templates in spreadsheets 73, 77
tennis agility test 329
  normative data *332*
  procedure *331*
test results
  interpreting 90–2
  reporting 89, *90*, *91*
theory, meaning of term 139
thermic effect of food 281, 286–7
thermometers 233, *234*
thesaurus *99*
theses 145, 147
thinking processes 24, *25*
thirst, as hydration status measure *228*, 233
Thomas test 238, *239*
three-repetition maximum (3RM) tests 307, *309*, *310*, *312*
tidal breath 211, 213
tidal volume (TV) 211, *213*, 219
  measurement of 216, 219
  normative values *217*
time log 7–8
time management 7–10
  essays 101
  in exams 33, 34
  of field tests 317
  literature surveys 103
  presentations *115*
  for revision 27
  scientific writing 94
  tips for planning and working 10
time units *132*, *133*
time-wasting activities 8
TLC *see* total lung capacity
torque, units *133*, 137
total body water (TBW)
  bioelectrical impedance analysis *228*, 232, 258
  as hydration status measure *228*, 229, *233*
  isotope dilution method *228*, 229, 260
total energy expenditure (TEE)
  components
    basal metabolic rate 281, 286
    energy expenditure of activity 281, 287
    thermic effect of food 281, 286–7

total lung capacity (TLC) 211, *213*, *217*
tragion 249
training impulse (TrImps) loading 350–1
  adjusted method 351–4
  example of calculation *352*
training intensity 349–50
  measures used 197, 221–7, *350*
training load 349
  measurement of 350–6
    by adjusted TRIMPS method 351–4
    by session-RPE method 354–6
    by TRIMPS method 350–1, *352*
  monitoring of 349–56
training monotony 349, 356
training strain 349, 356
training volume 349
  measures used *350*
transcript 31
transferable skills 3–6
  employer's interests 5–6
  examples *4*, 79
  range 3–4
  transferability 4–5
transformations 360–2, 393, 398
treadmill
  metabolic calculations to determine speed *224*
  running economy measurement 345–6
  submaximal tests 279
  VO_2max test protocols *271*
triceps skinfold 245
TV *see* tidal volume
two-compartment body composition model 253, 254
tympanic membrane temperature 234

underwater weighing, body density measured by 256, *257*
unimodal frequency distributions *385*
units
  conversion factors *135*, *137*, 138
  SI system 132–8
upper body power, tests for 321–2
upper body strength, tests for *308*, 322
upper extreme *380*, *383*
  spreadsheet function for *387*
upper quartile *380*, *383*
  spreadsheet function for *387*
urine
  disposal of 170, 196
  reference ranges of analytes *196*
  specific gravity determination 194–5, 230, *231*
  testing using reagent strips 193–4, *195*, 230, *231*
urine colour, as hydration status measure 229, *230*, *233*
urine concentration, as hydration status measure *228*, 229–31
urine osmolality 229, *233*
urine sampling 193, *194*
  timing 193, 230
urine specific gravity (USG) 228
  determination of
    by reagent strips 193, 230, *231*
    by refractometer 194–5
  as hydration status measure 229, *230*, *233*

URLs 63, 67, 71
  in citations 53
USB drives *64*
Usenet Newsgroup service 66
utilitarianism *154*

V-slope technique, ventilatory threshold determined by 337, 338, *339*
vaccination 168–9
validity of measurement 125–6
Vancouver system for citations 52, 53
variability of data *see* dispersion of data
variables 121
  confounding 124, 142
  continuous/discontinuous 121
  control of in experiments 142
  dependent/independent 121
  meaning of term 121
  qualitative 121
  quantitative 121
  ranked 121
variance (s^2) *380*, 383
  spreadsheet function for *387*
VARK learning styles scheme 22, *23–4*
VC *see* vital capacity
velocity, units *133*, *135*, 137
ventilation 211, 337
ventilatory equivalents 337
  ventilatory threshold measured by 337–8, *338*
ventilatory threshold (VT) 337
  determination of 337–9
    by V-slope technique 337, 338, *339*
    by ventilatory equivalents 337–8, *338*
ventilometer 266
Vertec device 294–5, *320*, *321*
vertex 243, *249*
vertical jump explosive power 295
vertical jump height 295
  normative data *296*, *321*
vertical jump test 294–5, 320–1
  procedure 294–5, *321*
virtue theory *154*
'visual' learning style *23*
vital capacity (VC) 211, *213*, *217*
  see also forced vital capacity; slow vital capacity
vivas (oral exams) 37
VO_2, measurement at submaximal exercise intensity 344
VO_2/running speed relationships *345*, *346*
VO_2max 265
  calculations 267–8
  estimation using multistage fitness test data *327*
  factors affecting 265–6
  indirect measures 274–80
  measurement equipment for 266
  normative data *272*, *279*
  units 266
VO_2max percentage, as exercise intensity measure 223
VO_2max reserve 223
VO_2max reserve percentage
  as exercise intensity measure 223
    calculation 223, *224*
    classification *181*, *225*

VO_2max test
  exercise protocols for 268, 270, *271*
  expired gas analysis *271–2*
  hand signals for communication *270*
  identifying VO_2max *273*
  procedure *269–70*
  types of exercise tests 268
VO_2peak 265, *272*
volitional exhaustion 265, *273*
volume units *133*, *135*, 137

waist circumference *248*, 250
  effect on disease risk 251
  recommended values 250
waist-to-hip ratio 251
  normal values *251*
warm-up procedures 177
  in cycle ergometer tests 277, 297, 299
  for VO_2max test *269*
waste disposal 167
  for field tests 319
water
  density at various temperatures *256*
  partial pressure in atmosphere 267
web resources 50, 63–72
websites 63, 71
  on brainstorming 13
  changes 57, 70
  citations for 53
  evaluation of *59*, *70*
weight *see* mass
wet conditions, field tests in 319
Wikipedia 70
Wilcoxon's signed rank test 396
Wingate cycling test 294, 297–301
  data analysis for *300*
  normative data *301*
  procedure 299
within–within factorial ANOVA 404
word processing 79–83
  adding text 80
  advantages 79
  disadvantages 79
  editing 81
  fonts 81
  formatting 80
  graphics and special characters 82
  line spacing 81–2
  tables in 82, *376*
  tools 82–3
  see also Microsoft Word
work, units *133*, *135*, 136
work capacity in Wingate test *300*
workplace health and safety regulations 157
workstation, disinfection of 168
World Health Organization, resting energy expenditure equations *347*
world wide web (www) 49, 63
  evaluating information on *70*
  search tools 67–8
  see also internet
'writer's block' 96
writing
  errors in 100
  essays 34, *35*, 101–3
    golden rules *102*
    planning 101–2

writing (*continued*)
reviewing 103
time management for 101
in exams *34*
literature reviews and surveys 103–6
information sources used 49–50, 104
structure and content 105–6
time allocation for *103*
topic for 104
project report 147
revising and reviewing text 100, 103
scientific 94–100
information, organising 94–5
personal reference library used *99*
style 95, *97–8*
time management for 94

X–Y charts (Excel) 77, 363–4, 365, *368–9*
see also scatter graphs

YMCA bench press test *315*
normative data *316*
YMCA protocol for cycle ergometer test *277*
YOYO intermittent recovery test 328
procedure *329*